WITHDRAWN

TD 794.5 .P68 1992

Powelson, David R.

The recycler's manual for business, government, and

BRADNER LIBRARY
SCHOOLCRAFT COLLEGE
LIVONIA, MICHIGAN 48152

The Recycler's Manual for Business, Government, and the Environmental Community

To Louise,
Truest of friends

Contents

Chapter 17 Wood Pallets 161

Chapter 18 Other Metals 166

Part IV Effective Recycling Programs 221

Acknowledgment

We are grateful to many of our friends, family, and business associates for assisting with the preparation of this manuscript. We are especially thankful to Louise Powelson who worked tirelessly on the Appendix and to Kim Abraham and Valerie Backlund for their thoughtful reading of the manuscript. We also owe a debt of gratitude to Paul Sundstrom for his creative illustrations.

We also wish to acknowledge the support we received from true friends, such as Jack and Sally Alexander, Linda, Chuck, and Stephanie Burton, Megan Benton, Judy and Jack Cozzens, Bill Chrismer, Marilyn and Stan Collins, Sue Davies, Janet and Keith Farrell, Moses George, Brad Heinrich, Nancy and Jim Hester, Gloria and Dennis Martin, Robbie and Henry Nieto, Cliff Rowe, Laura and Mary Jane Scott, Patsy Sims, Julie Sisneros, Sergie Thomas, Shirleen and Scott Tucker, and David Singer. While our normal life was on hold during the writing of this book, we were happy for their attitude of good cheer and active help.

Certainly in this aspect we were lucky to be a part of a family who helped preserve a normal lifestyle while the book consumed a greater and greater share of every waking moment. Andrea Powelson spent her college vacation time doing research and making changes to the manuscript. Jennifer made certain that the household ran smoothly.

We would also like to thank the people at TRI-R Systems, Joe Scherman of Specialty Fibres, Wayne DeCastri of Pioneer Fibers, James Russell and others from the Colorado Bureau of Mines, Andy Mckeon from the Complete the Cycle Center, and the researchers at the National Appropriate Technology Assistance Service, and so many others for being valued sounding boards and contributors of the information. Finally, we would like to thank Steve Zollo at VNR for his constant encouragement and support, and Pete Grogran, R. W. Beck and Associates, for his thorough review.

A note about this book

For over 18 years in the recycling business I have been steadily learning about recycling through experience and by reading everything I could get my hands on. In retrospect my education has at times been very expensive. One of the most troubling aspects of recycling is that it changes rapidly. Recycling has never been a field with hard and fast answers. In fact it is the very nature of recycling to change. Just when you think you have a commodity or market all figured out, something happens that is completely unexpected. Recycling is a field with its own unique "entertainment" value and is an utterly fascinating subject.

This book has been written with the many new people entering the recycling field in mind. It seems unlikely that an investment in this book will not be returned many times over. In fact, because recycling is rapidly changing, this book contains valuable insights to many who have spent a lifetime in the business. At least this is my hope.

Over the years I have listened to the questions of a few thousand people about recycling, and the answers to the most frequently asked questions are in the book. What happens to "X" after it is collected? How many times can paper be recycled? How can we make our recycling program more effective? How does the landfill crisis impact recycling? An so on.

Then when my daughter offered to co-author the book, this manuscript became a reality. Together we set out to provide a comprehensive reference source about recycling for all types of recyclable materials and for today's popular recycling programs.

Our introduction begins by discussing recycling—what recycling is and its scope. After introducing recycling, we included an introductory chapter on solid waste because solid waste issues are the major driving force impacting recycling today. Also, in the introductory section we felt it was important to discuss the history of recycling in the United States, to place today's recycling dilemmas in a historical context.

The next section of the book deals with commodities, from aluminum to zinc. Our purpose in explaining different materials is that this body of knowledge is critical to locating and identifying recyclable materials in an unstructured environment. It is also critical knowledge for processing and marketing recyclable materials. Further, commodity knowledge helps in understanding how recyclable materials compete with virgin materials. Lastly, without specific commodity knowledge, it is difficult to see how recycling rates can effectively be increased.

A section about recycling influences follows. One chapter deals with unsettled issues, and because recycling is a "new" priority in the United States there are many unresolved subject matters and differing perspectives. A second chapter deals with the issue of recoverability. There are many different points of view concerning the economic costs of collecting recyclable materials. For example, does recycling make sense regardless of its costs? Further, there's uncertainty about what percentage of material consumption can be recovered as recyclable materials, even if cost was not considered as a factor. The third chapter deals with legislation. Because the regulation of solid waste is largely a local matter, there is a proliferation of regulations seeking to drive recycling activities to new heights. A combination of factors produces an amazing variety of regulatory approaches, and a highly complex structure is emerging.

The concentration of the next major section is effective recycling programs. Our goal was to offer practical help and to suggest shortcuts to effective programs, but for those readers who want a detailed step-by-step approach, the information is included. Some chapters deal with the common elements of effective programs and differentiate recycling programs for government and business interests. Some areas of mutual concern exist between government and business, such as office recycling programs and cardboard recycling programs. There are specific chapters for these subjects. Some businesses are specialized, and recycling programs are described for a number of these businesses. The marketing of recyclable materials is dealt with in this section, and an appendix identifies many of the buyers for recyclable materials. The marketing section has been placed in the program section, since it makes little sense to collect recyclable materials until skills are developed to sell the products that will be collected through a recycling program.

Throughout the book we refer to the need for consumers to purchase recycled products. Our last chapter, "Complete the Cycle," provides additional information on how this accomplished.

Finally, the bibliography and appendix incorporate many potential sources of additional information. One of the highlights of the appendix is information about buyers of each commodity. The section is organized by state and, within state, by city. It is believed that this will help in locating the nearest markets to each reader.

We sincerely hope this book will be informative and that it will help people understand more of the details about recycling so that recycling can become more of a way of life.

Introduction

In the next years the recycling movement will face great challenges. The future of recycling and the credibility and momentum of the United States environmental movement hang in the balance. It is increasingly obvious that the Environmental Protection Agency's (EPA) new landfill standards might force up to 70 percent of the nation's existing landfills to close. Also clear is that state and local governments, who are responsible for municipal waste, are launching an unprecedented number of recycling programs to collect the vast amount of potentially recyclable materials in order to head off the waste disposal crisis that has been brewing since the late 1970s or early 1980s.

In 1984 Congress ordered the EPA to develop new landfill standards because of groundwater contamination problems. Seven years later, in September 1991, these standards became operational. Most of the nation's landfills cannot meet these new stringent standards in the period mandated by the EPA, so by law they must close within the next two years. To further complicate the issue, strikingly few landfills have been built in the past seven years while these changing standards were being discussed and finalized. In that time the media has exposed to the public that landfills are environmental time bombs. The landfill permitting process alone, assuming a politician has the courage to recommend a landfill for his or her community, now takes an interminable number of years to complete.

With landfill space shrinking and solid waste radically increasing on a per capita basis, recycling is the main solution proposed for waste disposal problems. Nearly everyone agrees that recycling is a major answer to America's garbage problem. The public is inundated by recycling propaganda from industries such as aluminum and steel, which boast a recycling rate of close to 60 percent, and even from the plastics industry, which recycles less than 1 percent of its products. Industries throughout the United States are beating the drums about recycling to everyone who will listen: "Recycling is the solution. Recycling is the solution." Entire states have joined the effort by establishing goals to recycle 50 percent of solid waste in just a few years. Two short years ago a mere 13 percent of solid waste was recycled. The state of Wisconsin has been even more vigorous in its mandates—nearly 100 percent of recyclable materials will be banned from the landfills by 1995.

Despite warning after warning that markets must exist to complete the recycling process, local politics is such that the warnings are ignored. "If we collect it (recyclables), they (markets) will come" seems to be the predominant belief. Collection programs continue to expand, despite the fact that 1990-91 markets are largely saturated with goods. Governments and environmentalists insist on collection, but ignore the danger of a system unbalanced by collection overload. Unless action is taken to develop markets and balance the process, the recycling momentum will come to an abrupt halt. Curbside programs costing millions of dollars cannot be sustained with no return, unless the public is willing to pay for recycling services in the same manner as it pays for trash service or highway maintenance.

Industry is beginning to recognize that it needs to adapt manufacturing processes to incorporate recycled materials. If businesses do not adapt voluntarily, recycling content legislation will force them to. A rash of state and local laws—like one in Minneapolis, Minnesota that bans plastic packaging from grocery store shelves—will mandate the changes. Products with wasteful designs will be banned in stores, prohibited at landfills, and "taxed" to death with advance disposal fees, deposits, and disposal fee increases.

Historically, recycling as an American way of life has been up to bat twice before, and struck out both times. During World War II, everybody recycled and the movement enjoyed a golden age. But when the war was over the nation went right back to using virgin resources. More recently, recycling resurfaced in the 1970s when energy costs were soaring; recycling saved energy and conserved valuable resources. Although a few changes resulted from the energy crisis, recycling again failed to become a permanent way of life. Secondary materials can take precedence over primary materials, only if the interest groups involved—consumers, governments, industries, and environmentalists—work together.

Without doubt, consumers, government, industry, and environmentalists make strange teammates. But if they cannot work together to balance the recycling process between them, history shows that the country will once again return to using virgin resources, without having solved the solid waste crisis. Environmentalists and the government must listen to industry's concerns. Many of the industries that must use recyclable materials have genuine problems that cannot be resolved before the deadline for landfill closures.

Some of industry's problems are economic, while others are technical. The current recession discourages expanding capacity. Another difficulty is that some industries do not have the production capacity that even begins to approach the volume of materials that can be collected for recycling. Still other companies lack the ability to write off their $100 million investments in virgin resources and their plant capacity to process virgin materials, and then turn around and invest further millions in new production capacity to handle recyclable materials.

On the other hand, industry must develop an understanding of the solid waste dilemma and natural resource concerns that face the government. Reducing materials, reusing recyclable materials, and implementing recycling programs can all make economic sense. Industry should not resist recycling legislation, without carefully considering the long-term effect manufacturing has on the earth.

Clearly, business and government must develop greater cooperation. But ultimately, recycling cannot become a way of life until consumers are brought into the solution. Industry will not give up using virgin materials without the support of customers. It would be cutting its own throat. Consumers often demand products made from virgin materials—like snowy white stationary and brand new tires. In some industries there are no quality differences between using virgin or recycled materials; in other industries, such as paper, plastics, and glass, the quality differences are noticeable to customers or create added problems in manufacturing. Industry cannot afford to give up its traditional use of virgin materials until consumers vote in favor of it by spending their dollars for recycled products in the marketplace.

By Paul Sundstrom

Environmentalists and the government seem to agree that recycling's time has come, and they are warming up to be serious this time around. Without a new four-way partnership, involving customers and industry, social change of the necessary magnitude cannot take place. To some degree, however, this change is taking place solely due to legislation. Industry must become the satisfied customer for raw materials that will be supplied by government-sponsored collection programs. This new partnership must be forged on an industry-by-industry basis, and the sooner this is understood, the sooner the United States can get on with the business of solving the 180 million-ton annual solid waste disposal crisis.

I

Overview of Recycling

1

Recycling Overview

At first glance recycling seems to be an easy solution to a variety of complex environmental problems. The message promulgated by the media and by educators is that recycling consists of simply collecting newspaper, aluminum cans, glass, plastic, and other familiar recyclable materials. Slogans such as "Save the Earth" and "Recycling is the solution to our garbage problem" abound. This simple view of recycling has been oversold. Recycling is a far more complex process than most people realize. Because 70 percent of the nation's landfills are projected to close within the next two years (based on recent EPA regulations), Americans are caught up in a frenzy to collect all recyclable materials currently being disposed of as trash.

Therefore, it is vital for the general American consumer, manufacturer, and business person to achieve a greater understanding of recycling and its importance in the cycle of raw materials, consumer goods production, and disposal. Until then, the country faces surpluses from a new supply of recyclable materials that industry does not have the capacity to convert to products and that industry cannot sell in the form of products made from recyclable materials. Until consumer buying practices change, the material now being collected through existing recycling programs will begin to back up, causing the costs of existing programs to skyrocket. If these programs are dismantled due to high cost, they would be difficult to restart when it becomes crucial to conserve our natural resources. Environmentalists have a great deal at stake because they have been identified as the grass roots force behind the recycling movement. If recycling fails to achieve its promise, the environmental movement as a whole will lose credibility.

These problems can only be avoided through a realistic understanding of the recycling process. Fortunately, industry is adding new production capacity to utilize more recycled materials, but these investments must be rewarded or the growth in recycling will come to a screeching halt. Reliable suppliers must be developed to provide the correct quality of raw materials to feed this new capacity, and consumers must be developed to support a marketplace that favors an ever-increasing amount of products made from recycled materials.

Our objective in writing this book is to facilitate the development of recycling by providing critical new information about the process, especially about finding markets for new collection programs. We also hope to link together the people charged with the responsibility for managing the solid waste crisis, the people running recycling programs, and the industries that have a vital interest in responding to this rapidly changing scene. Finally, recycling professionals—in every aspect of the industry—need to be aware of the symbolic impact of their field. Recycling has the potential to literally change the way people think about and deal with their environment in a very positive and long-lasting manner.

WHY RECYCLE?

Recycling is a simple process that can help resolve many of the problems created by our modern way of life. Nonrenewable resources are clearly saved when recyclable materials are supplemented in the manufacturing process. Renewable resources, such as trees, are also saved in the short run, but it's naive to imagine that recycling will result in large tracks of untouched forest. Eventually, fewer renewable resources will be planted, cultivated, and harvested. Producing recyclable materials consumes less energy. When this energy reduction is in the form of fossil fuels, there is less acid rain produced, and a decreased greenhouse effect.

Another recycling benefit is that it extends the life of landfills. The United States' waste stream is the biggest in the world. In 1988, only 13 percent of the waste stream was diverted into the recycling stream. The recycling potential for most commodities is a diversion rate of more than 50 percent. Table 1-1 summarizes the amount of recycling activity in the United States.

On the financial frontier, recycling could potentially create a net increase in jobs. Waste material sources are fragmented, and materials are not concentrated in areas such as mines and forests. Compared to virgin materials, recyclable materials must be collected, sorted, and processed in smaller quantities. This would require a large work force. In addition to creating income for employees, the recycling of high-grade materials generates revenue. Recycled materials are often a very inexpensive raw material for industry, and many consumers prefer some products that have a recycled content. Recycling can also reduce trash hauling costs by as much as 70 percent, by saving the hauling fees to the landfill and the landfill dumping fee.

In short, recycling makes sense. It's important for every individual, business, government, and industry to make a commitment to recycling. Every day people make purchasing decisions that could potentially help balance the recycling process, and every day they dispose of materials that have outlived their usefulness in one form, but still may have a second life if used for recycling. Each person has

TABLE 1-1. **Amount of Material Recycled and Recovery Rate**

Commodity	Apparent Consumption	Industrial Scrap	Old Scrap	Total Recycled	% Recovery
		(1990, Short Tons)			
Top Five					
Steel	95,900,000	22,137,000	35,363,000	57,500,000	60.0
Paper	86,756,500	N/A	N/A	28,926,900	33.3
Aluminum	5,291,000	1,102,000	1,102,000	2,204,000	41.7
Glass[1]	11,300,000	N/A	1,500,000	1,500,000	13.3
Copper	2,425,000	837,700	584,200	1,421,900	58.6
Subtotal	201,672,500	N/A	N/A	91,552,800	45.4
Other					
Antimony	45,500	0	16,500	16,500	36.3
Cadmium	4,080	0	Nil	Nil	Nil
Chromium	466,300	0	97,900	97,900	21.0
Cobalt	8,650	0	1,270	1,270	14.6
Gold	253	73	48	121	47.8
Lead	1,344,800	0	782,600	782,600	58.1
Magnesium	163,100	0	29,800	29,800	18.3
Mercury	1,320	0	239	239	18.1
Nickel	170,000	Nil	25,000	25,000	14.7
Pallets	N/A	N/A	N/A	N/A	N/A
Plastic	30,740,000	N/A	266,500	266,500	0.8
Platinum	109	69	6	75	68.8
Silver	4,740	1,320	550	1,870	39.5
Textiles	N/A	N/A	1,000,000	1,000,000	N/A
Tin	53,900	4,400	12,100	16,500	30.6
Tires	3,360,000	N/A	604,800	604,800	18.0
Titanium	1,018,500	22,600	330	22,930	2.3
Tungsten	9,370	N/A	N/A	2,204	23.5
Zinc	1,400,000	253,500	132,300	385,800	27.6
Subtotal				3,254,109*	
Total				94,806,909*	

*In subtotal and total, when data was not available (N/A) or identified as nil, it was assumed to be zero.

[1]Glass consumption and recycling data is for 1988, and the source is from The National Municipal Solid Waste Association data used in Table 2-2. The Glass Packaging Institute estimates the 1990 recycling volume to be 2,000,000 tons, but data on 1990 consumption was not available.

Other data was derived from *Mineral Commodity Summaries 1991,* U.S Department of the Interior, Bureau of Mines; *1990 Annual Statistical Summary, Waste Paper Utilization,* American Paper Institute, June 1991; and various industry sources.

the opportunity and the responsibility to incorporate recycling into both their business community and their own lifestyle. The alternative is simply more waste.

THE DEVELOPING SOLID WASTE CRISIS

On September 11, 1991, the EPA implemented new landfill standards. While it has taken the EPA seven years to develop these standards, state and local governments have been given two years to implement them. The essence of the new standards changes the way in which landfills are constructed, so that leachate is controlled. Landfills that do not comply must be closed within two years. Since the new standards require a clay base and two liners to be installed, as well as a collection system for leachate, it is clear that most landfills that existed only seven years ago will not meet the requirements. Old landfills cannot be effectively modernized because old trash cannot simply be hydraulically lifted while a clay bottom and liners are installed.

In addition, during the past seven years, few new landfills were built while the new standards were being negotiated. Because landfills are environmental time bombs, the process of having new landfills approved has become extremely difficult. All the political red tape involved in getting a permit for a landfill virtually guarantees that few landfills not currently approved will be built within the next several years.

Part of our solid waste disposal problem has been "manufactured" by a federal government that can consume seven years determining new landfill standards. Obviously, standard setters and those who must comply are not from the same organization. Complaining about this inequity will not eradicate the fact that local governments—cities and counties—will continue to generate trash and have no place to put it. States, cities, and towns that manage to retain landfill capacity that meets the new standards may find themselves the dumping ground for neighboring regions not so lucky or farsighted. Trash from New York may travel to Iowa to be buried. In this situation, recycling is considered one of the only practical courses of action because it can radically reduce the tonnage of solid waste destined for disposal.

THE NEW DYNAMIC FORCES IN RECYCLING

This new pressure on recycling as a solution to solid waste management has led to legislation requiring mandatory recycling (meaning the collection of recyclable materials) and to legislation prohibiting certain materials from going into landfills. These are two of the most popular solutions being sought to relieve the solid waste crisis. Neither solution, however, deals with recycling on realistic terms.

At first glance, the mandatory diversion of recyclable materials from landfills seems reasonable: in fact, diverting materials is only one-third of the recycling process. The materials must also be used and accepted by both manufacturers and consumers, to complete the cycle. In most cases, the industries initially expected to handle these vast quantities of waste materials are not prepared to convert recycled material into new products. Stated another way, there are no existing markets for many of these recyclable materials. Despite the obvious wisdom of not collecting something guaranteed not to sell, many collection programs throughout the country continue to develop because of the pressure associated with disappearing landfills. Mandatory recycling is gaining momentum as a regulatory solution, despite the fact that it is only a partial solution.

Many people believe that the solution to developing the necessary markets is simple—namely, substitute recyclable materials for the raw materials made from resources such as trees, iron ore, silica sand, petroleum products, or bauxite. Most of the basic industries involved are capital intensive, so the major projects that would allow them to utilize more recyclables require lead times of several years.

Projects of major size require a great deal of diligence. Major projects are supported by market studies and detailed economic analysis. They are designed by engineers, and preliminary cost estimates are verified. Financing is arranged to support major expenditures. Land is acquired, which in turn involves the site selection process, environmental assessments, zoning approvals, and special arrangements for utilities. Then, after extensive preparation, equipment can be ordered and construction can begin. Facilities may be under construction for an entire year or possibly two years. Most boards of directors must approve most major projects, and, due to financing requirements, negotiations with investment bankers and others in the financial community can become protracted.

New projects that will provide markets for recyclable materials within the next several years are already beyond the planning stage and are in the implementation stage. Projects in the implementation phase are now identifiable. Even with the projected output of these new facilities, industry may be unable to handle the potential wave of new materials. Yet this manufacturing capacity is only a part of the problem facing industry. Markets for the finished goods must also be ready to accept the products made from these recyclable materials. Significant new production capacity added to existing industry capacity produces excess capacity rather quickly and results in competitive pressures, which generally produces declining prices. This reduces the rate of return on investment and tends to discourage the development of new capacity. This fact is not lost on primary producers who, in order to discourage new investment, have "put the word out" to the investment community that the wholesale conversion of pulp mills to secondary fiber mills is possible.

In all cases, these products must compete with other products already on the shelf and, coincidentally, produced from a different source of raw material. No one knows with any reasonable degree of certainty whether markets will be available for recycled goods. In any event, the dynamics suggest that the wave of new recyclable materials will arrive. Figuratively and literally, the industry that uses secondary materials is about to be dumped on.

Not surprisingly, an infrastructure of scrap dealers and processors, as well as a network of brokers, already exists to serve the needs of the manufacturers who use secondary materials. Their financial strength and even their very existence is now threatened because they rely on economic factors to stay in business. They depend on receiving a certain price for the materials they collect, but, with the wave of new materials unbalancing market demand, prices will initially weaken. Whether this situation remains depends on the rate at which new manufacturing comes on line. At a minimum, the new wave of raw materials will create chaos, and many existing private sector collectors will become financially distressed in the ensuing surge of new recyclable materials. If this occurs on a massive scale, the manufacturers who use recyclable materials must educate a new set of suppliers while simultaneously maintaining record-breaking production rates. The situation could look like Figure 1-1.

Recycling can be a powerful tool for solving solid waste disposal problems, but as a tool recycling must be understood in all of its complexity in order to achieve its potential. It can't "Save the Earth," but it can make a substantial contribution. Recycling can diminish the impact of closing 70 percent of the nation's landfills

FIGURE 1-1. By Paul Sundstrom

over the next few years. Collecting recyclables cannot be justified if programs run at significant losses over long periods of time, but responsible collection programs should proceed if reasonable markets, user fees, or tax subsidies can support the cost. The supply of recyclable materials must be approximately in balance with new manufacturing capacity and markets. And in the long run, only widespread market development can absorb the quickening pace of collection efforts.

WHAT IS RECYCLING?

Surely the popularity of recycling suggests that there is widespread agreement about what recycling is. However, nothing could be further from the truth. Recycling has many different meanings. Some groups claim recycling is any process for using material again and again. This definition is so broad that it is possible to consider the evaporation of water and the formation of rain to be a "recycling" process. To others, even the "ashes to ashes, dust to dust" scenario represents recycling. Philosophically speaking, we may all have to meet The Great Recycler someday. This definition is so broad that composting solid waste, reusing kitchen utensils, and making new aluminum out of old aluminum cans all fall under the recycling umbrella. While a broad definition has a useful purpose in freeing our thought processes, a narrower definition has more utility for purposes of measuring the amount of material that is recycled.

For the general public, recycling is synonymous with collecting recyclable materials. The enormous increase of curbside recycling programs throughout the nation is one outward example of the public's willingness to demonstrate its commitment. But as curbside and other recycling programs continue to gain momentum, it is becoming increasingly clear that collection is just the beginning of the recycling process.

Another definition is that recycling is the conversion of materials otherwise destined for disposal into useful materials or products. This definition is custom tailored to solve the waste disposal crisis, but it completely ignores all the material that has been used again and again as part of ordinary commerce. It leads quickly to a conclusion, for example, that recycling steel from automobiles is not recycling because cars are not disposed of as trash. It makes paper recycled out of the municipal waste stream "better" than paper recycled from printer's waste, which has been made into tissue products for decades. Also, if the recycling of waste products becomes part of ordinary commerce, then it won't be recycling any more because like automobiles, they won't be "destined for disposal."

A more precise definition of recycling could include any process where waste materials are collected, manufactured into new material, and used or sold again in the form of new products or raw materials. When measurement is important, such as establishing a database and tracking progress, this definition can be useful in monitoring the amount of recycling activity in the United States, but it too needs refinement.

THE RECYCLING PROCESS

To determine a comprehensive definition of recycling, it helps to understand the three major activities involved in the recycling process.

1. *Collection*—As part of the collection activity, similar types of material are consolidated and contamination is removed (usually by a sorting process) and packaged for shipment.
2. *Manufacturing*—Waste materials must be used as raw materials or to make new products. For example, old aluminum products can be made into new aluminum sheet or new cast aluminum parts.
3. *Consumption*—Waste materials must be consumed. Individual buyers must purchase products that have a high percentage of recycled waste materials in it. Without a consumer demand, the recycling process stops.

For recycling to function in an orderly manner, these three activities must operate more or less in harmony. Realistically, however, collection, manufacturing, and consumption will not always grow at the same rate. Also, in any specific geographical area, the supply of collected material, the capacity to manufacture raw materials or products, and society's consumption patterns may be out of balance. These factors will inevitably make the recycling field a challenging occupation for thousands of individuals because the idea of a totally "balanced" system is not realistic.

ESTABLISHING PRIORITIES

Most people who learn about the nation's solid waste crisis would like to see today's waste materials being used as a primary source for new products. They reason that this would both save our natural resources and stimulate recycling markets. This might, in fact, be the ultimate evolution of recycling. However, in a capitalistic system, products made from recycled materials *must* be able to compete with products made from renewable and nonrenewable resources. This is true even in the unlikely event of legislation giving waste materials an upper hand. Competition among different raw materials is not new, but many environmentalists want a "level playing field," arguing that mining, petroleum, and forestry currently receive favorable tax treatment to the detriment of secondary materials. The solid waste crisis may bring about an atmosphere where this level playing field may occur, but seasoned politicians provide little hope.

For products to be made mostly from recycled materials would require a major reorientation of industry and a major change in the spending habits of consumers. The toughest decisions would have to be made by consumers. Buyers would consciously have to choose to purchase goods that are made with recycled contents—even if it means paying a few cents more for paper towels or buying writing paper that is a little less bright.

If it were not for the current environmental climate, industry leaders would probably not use waste materials for manufacturing—that is, unless it made economic sense. The aluminum, steel, and paper industries have been using large quantities of recycled goods for years. Plastic production plants have not. But, since the public is now demanding recycled content in many items, consumer industries are compelled to increase the recycled content in their products.

This does not mean, however, that industries are prepared to lose money. Some products made from recycled materials command a premium price. For example, this has been true for some tissue products and writing papers that are packaged for the green consumer. In other cases, the prices charged must be very competitive and the industry must benefit with a lower raw material or processing cost.

Consumers are successfully adjusting to accept "inferior" products simply because the product is made from recycled material. Envelopes never had to be pure white and as bright as possible. Toilet paper does not have to be 80-percent bright or better. If the recycled product is adequate for the purpose, consumers are beginning to accept slightly lower quality in order to feel like they are making a difference. With more education there's the prospect that consumers will change the way products are made from the grass roots level.

RECYCLING OBSTACLES

While recycling has obvious benefits, there are also some major roadblocks to overcome. The industry faces many social, legislative, and economic barriers in the coming years. Because the recycling process must exist in three-part harmony—collection, manufacturing, and consumption—leaders need to face these issues head on.

The greatest challenge for people who wish to make the recycling process work is that of educating the public. People lack a true understanding of what is happening to the planet, especially where natural resources are concerned. Few people realize, as David Morris of the Washington-based Institute for Local Self-Reliance, that each year "a city the size of San Francisco disposes of more aluminum than is produced by a small bauxite mine, more copper than a medium copper mine, and more paper than a good sized timber stand" (*Worldwatch Paper 76,* 1987).

Even if Americans do realize that we are exhausting finite materials, the recycling industry faces the challenge of dispelling the myth that recycled products as a whole are inherently inferior. It would be impossible to discern the difference between an aluminum can made from new aluminum and one made from recycled materials. The paper industry, on the other hand, faces a different problem. Some people are unwilling to buy recycled products, such as toilet paper, because they don't understand that it is not made from toilet paper screened out at the sewage plant. In reality, recycled toilet paper is made largely from office papers. Consumers judge a recycled product's quality based on how it looks because in general the public does not understand how they are made.

Social problems related to recycling will not, however, be solved by education alone. Societies as a whole are resistant to change. The traditional purchase-consume-dispose cycle will be difficult to break. Recycling at home or at work requires an effort to wash and separate materials. It is simply more convenient to maintain our throw-away habits. This is especially true if people do not know what to do with their recyclables when no recycling program is in place.

Legislative Obstacles

Finding the time and money to educate the public becomes more difficult because there is no real national commitment to recycling. While the EPA has suggested a nationwide 25-percent recycling goal, legislation, funding, and enforcement is left up to individual states. Federal tax laws are currently structured in favor of virgin industries, by allowing these companies to deduct depreciation and depletion of resources as a business expense. Through this accounting treatment, income is sheltered and the virgin material producers receive a benefit for consuming these resources. As a result of the federal tax code, companies who use recyclable materials operate at a disadvantage from those who use virgin materials.

At the state level, making recycling a priority becomes a challenge because of the legislative process itself. The key players in recycling are government and industry, two traditionally opposed entities. High-powered lobbyists appear when a mandate threatens industries' practices and, as a result, the legislative process, not known for its efficiency, is drawn out further. Also as a part of many regulations, a requirement is included requiring that facilities handling solid waste be permitted. This permitting process can be onerous and may become a barrier to entry, especially by small businesses.

Technological Obstacles

Some of the barriers to recycling are technological. Many of the products that line store shelves are not designed to be recycled. Computer equipment, televisions, and toys are just a few examples of products that are not designed with recycling in mind. Manufacturers of grocery packaging, on the other hand, are taking strides to ensure that their designs can easily be recycled.

Other technological problems include the high quality standards mandated by some industries. Glass plants must have a nearly pure post-consumer product to produce new glass without any flaws. Plastic plants require post-consumer plastic to be sorted by individual resins, because resins are generally incompatible with each other. If collection programs cannot meet these standards within economic boundaries, subsidies are required or the recyclable materials cannot be used until technology provides a solution.

Economic Obstacles

The biggest obstacle currently facing recycling is economics. Recycling is expensive. Collection programs can cost governments and businesses a great deal of money, especially compared to garbage disposal costs, which continue to be relatively cheap in many parts of the country. However, the end of cheap disposal costs are in sight. Compared to the expense of proper disposal procedures, recycling may come to be looked at as far less costly. Frequently, the value of a commodity is lower than the cost of transportation and where this occurs recycling may become impractical. Industry faces the economic decision of why to buy secondary materials when virgin materials are available at competitive prices. Finally, there can be a lack of financial resources to sustain government recycling programs or, on the part of businesses, to invest new capital into recycling equipment.

WHO IS INVOLVED IN RECYCLING?

Just about everyone is involved in recycling. Everyone from children to senior citizens, from dumpster divers to Fortune 500 corporate executives, and from bureaucrats to entrepreneurs throws materials in the trash. Everyone makes consumer decisions. And everyone can make better decisions with recycling in mind.

Some entities that can play a major role in establishing the recycling movement include federal, state, and local governments. Other groups that will impact recycling include manufacturers, solid waste companies, professional managers, business leaders, and media professionals. To help spread the news about recycling to the general population, teachers and leaders of civic and charitable groups can both take part. Purchasing agents for businesses and individuals, both as collectors and consumers, can help make environmentally sensitive purchasing decisions.

WHY STUDY RECYCLING?

The enthusiasm that most people have for recycling is one of the most exciting phenomenons of our time. Rarely do people have an opportunity to embrace an activity that has so many positive implications for the planet. People who care about the environment appear to have an insatiable curiosity about recycling, and they are incredibly action-oriented—at least for the time being. It will take knowledgeable, committed people to make a lasting impact.

Recycling reached an all-time high in the United States during World War II, but when the war and rationing ended, recycling activity declined. Approximately 25 percent of solid waste was recycled in WWII; in the 1980s the United States recycled only 13 percent. Almost 50 years ago recycling activity peaked because the nation's survival was at stake. Now there has been a resurgence of interest because, according to many, America is being threatened by more subtle faces; like Pogo said, "We have found the enemy, and it is us." What we do with our waste materials will determine our future.

As a body of knowledge, recycling is relatively new, and the millions of people who care about the environment need to know more. Some people are challenged by a body of knowledge that changes rapidly and that is governed by few fixed rules. Yet this has always been true in recycling. An example from the area of paper recycling will illustrate how quickly recycling knowledge changes. Years ago, paper mills developed a system of how to convert the scrap from computer tab cards to make paper. (A tab card is a punch card with 96 columns that reveals information to an electronic sensor in areas where the paper has been removed by a precise rectangular shaped punchout.) Soon thereafter, the computer industry began storing data magnetically on tapes and discs, making tab cards obsolete. At the same time the paper mills' supply of scrap tab cards began to dwindle, business people started to read computer printouts to keep up with the volumes of new information available. Paper mills adapted. They learned to make new paper out of discarded computer printout paper, instead of being dependent on old tab cards as a raw material.

As demand for computer printout paper increased, different grades of printout paper were made available to the computer industry, such as NCR paper (carbonless paper), groundwood printout paper, and bond quality printout paper. Some of these new grades were not as good for making end products, such as tissue paper. Paper mills and scrap processors had to learn to differentiate each type of paper. To further complicate the issue, printing technology from computers also changed. Initially, impact printing was the only method for putting ink on paper, but then laser printing started to take a bigger share of market. This created problems for paper mills because laser printing did not bleach the same way that impact printing did.

Everyone involved in the recycling process had to adapt as technology changed. This is but one small example of how technological advances create changes in recycling. It illustrates how manufacturers of recyclable materials and collectors adapt, as well as why it is important to be flexible.

Uncertainty is also part of recycling. Markets for waste commodities change, and prices fluctuate according to supply and demand. Primary markets also change, and for most industries the prices of primary and waste materials have an impact on each other. Recessions come and go, and this has an impact on consumption, overall demand, and prices. Predicting future prices is difficult because there are so many variables involved. Experienced people use their best judgment about the future and know they have only two chances—lucky or wrong.

Price fluctuation discourages, to some degree, both the collection and use of recycled materials. Manufacturers like predictable prices. This accounts for why many manufacturers of paper and metals are vertically integrated; that is, these companies operate mines and manage forests, as well as producing products from these materials and selling them to consumers. One clear effect of vertical integration is that costs become more predictable. Using recyclable materials has been regarded as a guarantee of price *in*stability.

MEASURING RECYCLING ACTIVITIES

An issue as critical to the environment as recycling must be measured accurately. Understandably, when numbers have such significance it is often easier to become "creative" with numbers, in order to have the data support a "desired" conclusion, than it is to create accurate data. Unfortunately, the "desired" conclusion depends on the self-interest of the issuer. Much inconsistent data exists at this stage of development in recycling. To complicate matters, definitions concerning recycling are not widely accepted, and a certain "license" exists to be creative with definitions. It is therefore important to examine carefully the definitions being used as well as the data.

Before measuring the amount of recycling, here are some of the definitions we used:

Recycling—Any process in which waste materials are collected and sold to manufacturers, manufactured into new material, and used or sold again in the form of new products or raw materials. (The reason "reuse" is excluded is that it can't be measured. For example, cleaning the dishes in your home is a "reuse" application for plates, cups, and kitchen utensils, but the value can't be measured.)

Recycling industry—Since recycling includes collection, manufacturing, and the distribution and sale of products, it is important to recognize what can and what cannot be measured. The value of collected materials can be approximated. The "value added" from manufacturing is also part of the industry, but is far harder to measure, since waste materials are often blended with primary materials. The "value added" from distributing and selling recyclable materials is also part of the industry, but is even more difficult to calculate than manufacturing, since the recycled part of the product might reflect only recycled packaging, while the soap, or whatever the container holds, may have nothing whatsoever to do with recycling.

Recovery rate—This term describes the amount of waste material recovered as a percentage of the amount of the raw material that is apparently consumed in the nation.

$$\frac{\text{Tons of Waste Material Recovered*}}{\text{Apparent Consumption of Raw Material (Tons)}} = \text{Recovery } \textit{Rate } \%$$

*Preconsumer Scrap + Postconsumer Scrap = Waste Material Recovered
No home scrap or mill broke is included.

One inherent problem in this measurement is that it appears to imply that a single ton in the numerator is equivalent to a single ton in the denominator. In reality, there is usually some loss of material involved in processing secondary materials. The term used to describe this loss is shrinkage, which can be 10 percent or more of the actual recyclable material consumed.

A better and more accurate recovery rate would include a factor for shrinkage. The method we are using will tend to portray a recovery rate higher than it actually is, but we do not have accurate data on shrinkage at this time. Since shrinkage is not considered, a 110 percent recovery rate would be possible, but it would imply that no primary raw materials were required if shrinkage was 10 percent.

Apparent consumption—This represents the total materials produced in the United States plus the amount of material imported minus the amount of material exported. The assumption regarding inventory is that beginning and ending inventory are the same. In other words, inventory changes are not considered when calculating apparent consumption.

Home scrap (run-around scrap)—Waste material generated during the manufacturing process of creating new raw material or products from either primary or secondary materials. Home scrap is waste material that is internally recovered and reintroduced to the manufacturing process to create new raw material. The waste material is considered part of the manufacturing process and is not sold to others. For example, in the steel-making process not all the steel produced meets the requirements of customers. In this case the steel is remelted and produced again into an acceptable product. We do not consider home scrap to be "recycled material" and thus eliminate it from the recovery rate if we can identify the amount.

Preconsumer scrap, industrial scrap, new scrap—This waste material is generated during a manufacturing process, or in converting raw materials to a product, such as by the printing industry or by stamping aluminum cans from sheets of aluminum. Since the waste material cannot be reprocessed by the generator of the waste, it must be sold to another party to be recycled. This is what makes pre-consumer scrap different from home scrap. It is part of the material recovered through recycling.

Postconsumer scrap, old scrap—This waste material is generated after the product is consumed and presumably after its life as a product has expired. Used aluminum cans, used computer printout, old aluminum lawn chairs, and obsolete automobiles are examples of post-consumer scrap. It is part of the material recovered through recycling. Generally, post-consumer scrap grades are not as clean as pre-consumer scrap. As a result, pre-consumer scrap frequently commands a higher selling price.

Primary materials—Primary materials are those being used for the first time. These materials are made from renewable and nonrenewable resources. Primary materials are also known as virgin materials.

Secondary materials—Waste materials that can be used in competition with primary materials.

Short ton—In the United States, the avoirdupois system of weights is commonly used for commodities. There are 16 ounces to the pound and 2,000 pounds to the short ton. One short ton is the equivalent of .90718 metric tons. Every effort has been made to show the data in this book in short tons and to convert other published information to this unit of measurement.

Troy weight—This system of weights is commonly used for precious stones and for precious metals, such as gold and silver. It is based on a troy pound weighing 5,760 grains. A troy pound consists of 12 ounces and weighs .82286 avoirdupois pounds.

$$24 \text{ grains} = 1 \text{ pennyweight} = 1.5552 \text{ grams}$$

$$20 \text{ pennyweights} = 1 \text{ troy ounce}$$

$$3.086 \text{ grains} = 1 \text{ caret} = 200 \text{ milligrams}$$

$$480 \text{ grains} = 12 \text{ ounces} = 373.24 \text{ grams}$$

Metric ton—This system of weights and measures is commonly used by the scientific community worldwide. There are 1,000 grams in a kilogram and 1,000 kilograms in a metric ton. A gram is equivalent to .035274 ounces avoirdupois. A kilogram weighs 2.2046 pounds, avoirdupois. A metric ton is equivalent to 2,204.6 pounds, avoirdupois. A metric ton is equivalent to 32,150.7 troy ounces.

Subsequent chapters provide details about each of the recyclable materials in Table 1-1. Also, the following chapter will describe the amount of recycling of solid waste as 23.5 million tons in 1988, according to EPA data. The EPA data is based on a narrower definition of recycling than the one we use to define recycling. Actual recycling is almost four times greater at 95 million tons in 1990.

2

Solid Waste

As a resource-rich, highly industrialized society, the United States historically has not paid much attention to solid waste management. A major reason for this has been ignorance. If you visit historical Jamestown, Virginia, the site of the first permanent English colony in America in 1607, you'll learn that drinking water was obtained from wells located alongside of the community's outhouses. The early Jamestown community had a great deal of trouble with disease in their swampy surroundings, partly as a result. In Old Jamestown people were ignorant of the importance of keeping their wells free from contamination, and they probably would have been surprised that their practices were a formula for disaster.

It is amazing, but it appears that over 375 years later new knowledge surfaced in the 1970s and early 1980s that showed that the leachate that oozes from virtually all landfills is gradually contaminating the nation's groundwater supply. This "new" knowledge is creating a whole new way of looking at solid waste and the problems created by its disposal. Gradually, as awareness has spread, the problems of solid waste disposal have been identified, and in some regions of the country the problem has reached critical dimensions. Little by little, the problem will affect every community. Landfills, which have historically been the least expensive way of disposing of solid waste, are forecasted to become the most expensive method.

The solid waste problem has been creeping up on communities from several directions. First, the amount of waste generated by our lifestyles has been growing, so that landfills are reaching capacity. Second, since 1984 very few new landfills were built and the permitting of new landfills also became a time-consuming, very expensive, and uncertain process. NIMBY ("Not in my backyard") and NIMTOO ("Not in my term of office") attitudes made, and still make, siting new landfills politically very difficult. The scarcity of new landfills causes existing landfills to fill up and trash disposal costs to rise out of sight.

According to Eugene J. Wingerter, executive director and CEO for the National Solid Wastes Management Association, industry revenue in 1970 was "estimated at less than $1 billion dollars." Twenty years later he estimated "annual revenue in both solid and hazardous waste to be about $25 billion." In April 1990, Wingerter predicted in an article in *Waste Age* that the waste industry "is on its way to $50 billion in annual sales by the mid-Nineties" (*Waste Age,* April 1990).

The rapidly increasing revenue of the waste industry, in addition to the nation's landfill problems, comes from the very fact that per capita volume of municipal solid waste (MSW) is increasing. Add an increasing degree of regulation and an increasing demand for new services, such as separate systems for collecting recyclables, and the outlook for the industry is extraordinary. One only needs to follow these rising sales to know that they represent somebody else's cost of disposal. Disposal costs will increase in the range of 25 percent to 40 percent annually. Unless plans are made to control these costs by eliminating the cause—solid waste—they will gradually grow to hamper the operations of any business and usurp a greater part of local government budgets for those communities that provide trash disposal services.

THE NUMBER ONE SOLUTION TO THE ABSENCE OF LANDFILL CAPACITY

When government officials sit down to discuss solid waste disposal options, the choice with the least headaches is clear:

- Site and build a new landfill.
- Install a fully integrated solid waste program.
- Send the garbage out of town.

The number one expedient solution is "Send the garbage out of town." Not only did the outrageous "garbage barge incident" of 1987 raise awareness about the solid waste issue, but it also revealed that many communities would prefer to pay the high cost of transportation in order to make the landfill issue disappear—at least locally for them.

To transport solid waste over great distances requires that garbage be baled. In bales weighing approximately 2,000 pounds, solid waste can then be loaded onto trucks, piggyback trailers, or railcars and transported to landfills, where the bales are unloaded and buried. Transportation costs of $.05 to $.10 per mile per ton are typical. It costs $25 to $50 per ton to ship solid waste 500 miles. Some landfills across the country charge disposal fees of $15 to $20 per ton, while other landfills have disposal fees more than $100 per ton. It doesn't take a mathematical whiz to calculate that for many communities sending the garbage out of town is economically correct, as well as politically expedient.

For some landfills that face closure, a situation exists where a two-year window of opportunity exists to acquire as much lucrative income as possible. There could be a rush to acquire more business, and there's plenty of out-of-town solid waste available. Advertisements appear in solid waste journals for this very purpose. For communities that adopt this strategy, recycling solutions can be delayed. As long as it is cheaper to landfill solid waste than to recycle it, it is unrealistic to expect less.

Garbage will become an increasingly important interstate commodity, receiving widespread political scrutiny and attention. Populous states will be characterized as taking advantage of recipient states, and emotional fires will be fanned to a frenzy. Yet part of managing solid wastes will be to adopt regional approaches to landfills that follow the hub-and-spoke concept from the transportation industry.

WAYS TO CREATE LESS GARBAGE

Reducing solid waste is quite simple, or at least the concept is. Unfortunately, there is little recognition or glamor in executing the many tasks and details required to achieve a meaningful reduction in solid waste generation. The basic approaches to managing solid waste are reducing or eliminating solid waste, composting, reusing and recycling materials, converting waste to energy, and landfilling the remainder. Regarding these strategies as a hierarchy is logical, and is one of the few generally accepted concepts in managing solid waste.

REDUCING OR ELIMINATING SOLID WASTE

Reducing or eliminating solid waste through product design represents the first strategy in facing the landfill crisis. It requires a multifaceted approach from industry and will have to be spurred on by consumer interest. For decades, U.S. industry has developed methods to persuade the American consumer to buy its products, which often involve expensive or extravagant gimmicks designed to make items attractive and competitive. Industry will not want to change these established advertising practices in the name of eliminating solid waste; alterations will have to make economical sense, but without the risk of losing market share. Manufacturers can help reduce solid waste with careful product design if they keep the following criteria in mind.

Reduce Packaging

Manufacturers can produce goods that are surrounded by less packaging, but they need to be persuaded by consumers to do so. Traditional marketing techniques fall into the "bigger is better" category, and as a result consumers buy a lot of air. In some cases the cardboard packaging is twice as large as the item it covers. Whenever possible, manufacturers should avoid individually wrapping items and then further packaging the whole product in third and fourth layers of plastic and cardboard. One simple way to reduce packaging is to reuse shipping boxes while they are still in good condition. Another is to market refillable detergent bottles.

Design Products To Last Longer

Manufacturers should be encouraged to create long-life products, that create less waste. When items break down because of poor quality design, they create excess waste. Manufacturers should market durable products that have long warranties. In the long run these items save money and landfill space.

Design Products To Use Less Material

When aluminum cans first appeared there were 10 cans to the pound. Now there are 29 cans to the pound, and if cans get much thinner the bubbles will be visible. Products can be made smaller. For example, small cars create less waste than large cars. Concentrated juice, laundry soap, and other cleaners reduce garbage and save money.

Products Should Be Easy To Repair Instead of Disposable

Manufacturers should market products that are designed to be repairable, rather than thrown away when breakdowns occur. This is particularly true with household appliances because of the problems they create in landfills.

Design Products To Be Rechargeable

Products such as household batteries and automobile batteries should be designed to be rechargeable. This is because the internal fluids are often toxic and contaminate groundwater when they ooze out at landfills. Manufacturing rechargeable batteries would eliminate one solid waste concern. One way to encourage industry to produce more rechargeable goods would be to make them responsible for disposing of the batteries that have only one lifetime. Some activists already mail spent batteries back to the manufacturer.

Design Products To Use Recyclable Materials

Manufacturing products out of recyclable materials is a big step toward reducing solid waste. Of course, there are technological limitations to how much material industry can incorporate because of quality considerations. If industry could adapt its practices to use even 25-percent recycled materials, it would help reduce the nation's waste crisis.

Design Products To Be Recyclable When No Longer Useful

Initially soft drink manufacturers began making plastic bottles out of two different plastic resins. A transparent container was supported by a hard plastic base cup. To make recycling easier, the next generation of bottles had an indented base and the entire bottle was made of one resin rather than two. This product became more recyclable at the end of its life.

Obviously, creating a recyclable product helps to reduce solid waste. In Germany and France the most highly publicized use of this concept is by automobile producers. BMW and Peugot have both created their new car models to be easily recycled. Each part—from door handles to engine casing—is labeled with the kind of material it contains. A numbering system is used to identify each material. The real success of BMW's and Peugot's recycling will be demonstrated when special factories actually dismantle these new car models along "dis-assembly" lines.

PRECYCLING

Precycling, one of the most logical ways to reduce solid waste, means purchasing products that do not contribute excessively to the solid waste problem. Precycling means considering the alternatives. Precycling means reducing waste before making a purchase. Is it necessary to purchase a product packaged in a non-recyclable, mixed media container, when a simple recyclable container would do? If a local collection program handles glass, plastic, and aluminum, buyers should consider purchasing products in these containers instead of non-recyclable ones.

Buyers make choices with each trip to the store. Consumers who precycle consciously decide to buy products that have fewer solid waste implications than competing brands. Rather than buy items that are packaged excessively, for example, the precycler would purchase refillable containers. Why not use a ceramic mug instead of a Styrofoam cup? Or a pen with a refillable cartridge? The basic relationship between a manufacturer and a consumer is an economic one. Ideas such as reducing waste gain more substance when consumers vote with their dollars.

While precycling is a relatively new philosophy, it is beginning to have an impact on the manufacturing community. Large companies such as Proctor and Gamble have already changed some product designs that should appeal to the environmentally conscious consumer. Even wrapping disposable diapers in plastic, instead of using a box wrapped in plastic is a step in the right direction. If the precycling mentality prevails and consumers in fact adapt these conscientious buying practices, manufacturers will inevitably change the way products are shipped to the consumer.

While there are hundreds of examples of how people can precycle, some of the most practical strategies are also the most simple.

Buy Products Sold in Bulk Quantities

When consumers purchase goods in bulk quantity, they reduce the amount of packaging manufacturers use when they sell each item individually. Goods such as paper towels and toilet paper commonly come in bulk packages. A precycler recognizes that buying these items in bulk quantities reduces the amount of shrink-wrap and cardboard that will go to the landfill.

Buy Products with Returnable Containers

Many states have mandatory deposit laws to encourage the recycling of glass, plastic, and aluminum containers. In California, for example, collection sites pay up to 10 cents per aluminum can and 5 cents per plastic milk jug.

Other systems also operate under a voluntary deposit system. Beer, soft drink cans, and glass bottles are often returnable at local grocery stores. In some countries, glass beverage products are merely sterilized and reused as the typical method for distributing products.

Buy Products with Refillable Containers

People who purchase and use refillable containers also reduce solid waste. Products on the market that have refillable containers include liquid hand soap and window cleaner.

Buy Products that Last Longer

Product guides such as *Consumer Reports* can help individuals find brands and models of products that require less repair and are more reliable. This is especially true for high-priced items, such as automobiles and appliances. Buying tires with higher mileage ratings is also a way to reduce waste. These choices will become increasingly critical as more materials are banned from landfills.

Buy Products that Are Reusable

Many of the products we purchase can be reused. For example, the marketplace offers rechargeable batteries. These require an additional investment for first-time buyers, but they reduce waste and could ultimately save money. Other reusables include cloth napkins in place of paper ones, razors with replaceable blades rather than disposables ones, and cloth bags for sacking groceries instead of the traditional paper and plastic varieties. In Europe, as well as some parts of the United States, customers are charged for grocery bags if they do not bring their own. The fact that

United States consumers expect disposable bags for "free" is just another wasteful practice that has become "normal."

Other ways of reusing items that are traditionally disposed include donating items like excess paint to a neighbor, school, theater group, or community organization. Many elementary school teachers have creative ways to reuse household items, such as old milk jugs, egg cartons, candle and soap stubs, loose nails, and large cardboard shipping boxes.

Avoid Buying Over-packaged Items

In the era of microwaveable food the food industry has gone crazy with excess packaging. Beyond the outer paper-board box, many meals are packaged on polystyrene platters and further surrounded by a plastic seal. Other overpackaged items include compact discs, which are sold with 6 × 12 -inch paperboard boxes, double the size of the CD. Shrink-wrap seals the disc in the paperboard box. All of this packaging is in addition to the plastic box used to hold the disc itself.

Many corporations are becoming aware of overpackaging and are taking steps to reduce waste. The most largely publicized effort is probably the McDonald's fast-food chain. With advice from the Environmental Defense Fund, McDonald's abandoned its polystyrene clamshell burger container for a paper wrapper.

Avoid Disposable Products

Purchasing disposable products only serves to further the use–consume–dispose mentality that is largely responsible for the solid waste crisis. Consumers who buy reusable food storage containers, rather than disposable aluminum foil and plastic food wrap, can individually help the amount of waste that goes to landfills.

One of the biggest controversies in disposable products is the disposable diaper debate. Obviously, they add to landfill problems, but the debate rages on. The main factors in the controversy include convenience, healthiness for the baby, and the energy and water usage associated with cleaning cloth diapers.

Buy Products Made of Recycled Materials

An obvious, but often overlooked, way of precycling is purchasing products made of recycled materials. Recycled paper products are encompassing a greater share of the market and are making their way into mainstream stores. Purchasing belts made out of recycled rubber, glass jewelry made out of recycled glass, and floor mats made from recycled plastic are all environmentally responsible decisions.

Give Unwanted Possessions Away

Even if you no longer have use for materials, someone else probably does: community centers, church and civic organizations, day care facilities, as well as friends and neighbors. Give-aways can range from books to outdated furniture to broken but repairable appliances. Children's clothing and toys can be handed down to families with younger children or other organizations, such as Goodwill and the Salvation Army.

Other Strategies

Other strategies aimed at reducing or eliminating solid waste occur on a legislative level. These include banning certain materials from use. For example, in Washington state legislation has been proposed to ban Styrofoam products, including coffee cups, take-out containers, and containers used to sell fishing bait.

Many areas base trash disposal costs on how much volume business and industrial plants generate. They rationalize that managers will reduce the amount of trash they produce if the company is charged enough money to dispose of it. This concept has been transferred to the household level in new systems that charge households for trash disposal according to the number of containers they generate. From all indications, these systems do change how households look at solid waste issues. When these systems are started, consumers are personally affected by the previously abstract concept of solid waste disposal. The issue becomes real and personal, to the extent that the conversations at unlikely places like dinner parties turn to "how did you get your garbage down to one trash can?"

COMPOSTING

Composting is the second most desirable strategy for keeping solid waste from going to the landfill. In composting, organic matter, such as grass clippings, weeds, leaves, coffee grounds, and vegetable and fruit scraps, are put into a pile. Over time, the material decomposes into a soil supplement rich in nutrients. Meat waste can create odor and a number of health problems, so it is typically buried in landfills. Composting can be done in residential backyards or through a large-scale community effort.

A backyard compost pile modelled on the popular aerated static method requires a structure to contain the yard and vegetable waste. The structure may be made from wood slats, chicken wire, snow fencing, or concrete blocks that are staggered to let in air. The three-bin method permits different batches of organic material to be composted at the same time. New material is put into bin number one, in addition to some moisture. When it has decomposed to a large degree, it is transferred to bin two for curing. Transferring the compost between bins allows the pile to be aerated. Later, it is transferred to bin three, for further aeration, and it is allowed to sit until it is ready for use. By moving the material around, it allows moisture and air to speed the decomposition process. The pile should be approximately 4 feet by 4 feet and the sides should either be designed with holes to let air in or be made from wire mesh. There are a number of details required to maintain an environment in the compost pile that keeps the tiny microorganisms, which break down the material, active.

The second largest component of MSW is yard waste, which comprises 18 percent of the total tonnage. Some communities have banned yard waste from landfills as a result. Some are using pay-by-the-bag programs that cost households money for a special pickup service. (In the pay-by-the-bag approach, anticipate a problem if leaves from a neighbor's tree spill into the adjacent yard, which has only evergreen trees.) Although the lowest cost alternative for most communities is to require households to compost their own yard waste, large-scale composting is becoming a viable option for local governments.

In King County, Washington, 16,000 compost bins were distributed to households at a cost of $8.75 each, with an objective of diverting 90 percent of the yard waste from the waste stream. (*Resource Recycling,* February 1990, pg. 18.) Another strategy is to offer a pickup service at the end of autumn for leaves and another in January for Christmas trees. An educational program outlining the benefits of using live versus artificial Christmas trees might encourage some families to switch to the safer, more economical, and more environmentally sound choice.

With pressure building for neighborhood composting, mulching lawn mower sales are on the rise, supported by studies that now show leaving grass clippings where they lay saves mowing time and is actually healthier for your lawn. (Isn't capitalism amazing?) Shredder and chipper sales are also increasing as environmentally concerned households join in reducing solid waste and in using natural fertilizer to enrich the soil.

REUSING MATERIALS

Reusing products and material is the third most important strategy in reducing solid waste. There are a number of reuse strategies that can cut down substantially on the amount of solid waste.

Single-use Items

People should try not to purchase single-use items, but instead invest in long-term devices. Using cloth towels instead of paper towels is one easy solution. Using grocery sacks twice or using a canvas sack as an alternative to using a new sack is another. And using handkerchiefs instead of tissues is yet another example.

Using Products Again

Instead of buying new products each time something breaks down, people should try to use the item again in a different capacity. For example, rather than tossing out old tire casings, it is possible to have the tire retreaded. This can easily give you another 40,000 miles at a fraction of the cost. Another example is using scrap paper as note pads or using the reverse side of paper for a draft copy. Yet another example is to reuse envelopes. A rubber stamp can be designed to mark out the old address with the word "recycled," and stamp the current address in unused space.

Buying Reused Items

While selling used items, giving old appliances to Goodwill Industries, donating to the Salvation Army, and having garage sales are familiar ways to reduce solid waste, purchasing reusable items is another, less familiar strategy. Items such as cardboard boxes can be purchased used. Also, paper products, shredded paper, appliances, bicycles, and other items can be purchased used. Check the newspaper classified advertisements before buying a new product. Even building products, aggregate, and steel can be purchased used.

RECYCLING MATERIALS

Despite the fact that recycling is listed as waste reduction strategy number four, it conceivably has more potential in managing the solid waste problem than any other strategy. Recycling involves using waste materials in the manufacturing of new raw materials and products. Collecting more recyclable material represents the most popular approach to reducing solid waste. Historically, the nation's scrap industry has played the biggest role in collecting material and represents a community's best existing resource. The scrap industry is highly fragmented, and the way to get assistance with a collection program is to look up "recycling," "scrap," and "waste materials" in the local Yellow Pages.

Collection

Both individually and collectively, the scrap industry has raised concerns about "overcollecting" because an abundance of material drives prices down. But, despite the fact that no one wants to hear negative information about the marketplace, local scrap dealers/processors usually know more about the market potential for collected material than anyone else. Although the scrap dealer/processor represents the more traditional methods of collecting material, there are also new, quite successful methods. Curbside recycling programs now exist in over 3,000 communities nationwide, and many communities are developing Municipal Recovery Facilities (MRFs) of their own to collect even more material.

Another area of change is building design. All buildings are designed to have space for a trash disposal system. It used to be rare to find an office building with room for a recycling system, but as times change they will become standard because this arrangement permits more efficient collection.

Manufacturing

Manufacturing capacity is increasing to absorb more collected material, and investments are being made based on forecasts for increased demand of recycled products. Manufacturers and end users for recyclable materials are listed in the appendix. Where known, the appendix lists facilities that are on-line or proposed.

Consumption

Rapid changes are taking place in the consumption aspect of recycling. Government at all levels and many businesses are giving preference to recycled materials in their purchasing decisions. Consumers are beginning to realize that they are not truly recycling unless they purchase recycled products.

Recycling content legislation requires that a certain percentage of a product's makeup be from recycled materials. It takes effort to assure that a demand will exist for material being removed from the waste stream. Recycling content legislation was first enacted in response to the problem of collecting more old newspapers than paper mills could handle. Some excess newspaper collected for recycling had no place to go other than the landfill, while other newspaper was exported or put into storage. When legislators in Connecticut began to understand that recycling was not just collection, they sought to stimulate demand. They passed the first legislation of this type, and it has been successful in producing a better balance between supply and demand. The general idea is that newspaper publishers are required to buy a specific percentage of recycled material and to escalate the percentage over future years.

Another sign that recycling consumption practices are changing is the increase in catalogs specializing in recycled goods. Supermarkets are also beginning to feature environmental aisles. Green tags that show environmentally "friendly" items are designed to help conscientious shoppers make their purchasing decisions. Recycling symbols are also appearing on packaging. Since consumers are beginning to rely on these symbols to make choices, use of the symbols is subject to abuse. Regulation of what these symbols represent and how they can be used is just around the corner.

Consumer education is also on the rise. In Denver, the first Complete the Cycle Center was started in 1989. More than 300 products made from recycled materials are on display at this non-profit organization. The purpose of The Complete the Cycle Center is to raise awareness and inform people about where to purchase recycled products.

CONVERTING WASTE TO ENERGY

The incineration of solid waste is the fifth strategy recommended for solid waste management. It reduces the volume of solid waste by 90 percent and has the added benefit of creating energy in the process. Regrettably, incineration is a controversial issue. Opponents of this strategy play on the public's fear of air pollution to stop discussion before it starts by asking loaded questions. These questions include the following:

1. Why do people call incinerators "airfills" ?
2. Can dioxins and other toxic chemicals be controlled both in airborne discharges and ash waste?
3. Is it true that there is no nationwide standard for waste-to-energy plants?
4. Why aren't there standard models for incinerators for cities and towns of different sizes?
5. How are hazardous wastes kept out of the material going into the incinerator?
6. Where can we dispose of the fly ash and bottom ash reliably?

The future direction of incineration will be determined by an objective evaluation of the risks of landfills balanced against the risks of incineration.

LANDFILLING THE REMAINDER

The last strategy in the hierarchy for dealing with solid waste is to landfill the material. There is a vast difference between the concept of the hierarchy and practice, with respect to landfilling. Generally, landfilling remains the cheapest and easiest solution and will continue to be, until landfills actually close in substantial numbers in response to Subtitle D. Regulation D will dramatically increase the cost of disposal, and the end of cheap, but environmentally unsound disposal, is in sight.

COMPOSITION OF MSW

The major components of MSW, according to the EPA, are ranked as shown in Table 2-1. The composition of solid waste varies with individual communities. Various recycling and regulatory strategies relate differently to each component of solid waste. The following brief review suggests how these matters are interconnected.

TABLE 2-1. Major Components of Municipal Solid Waste

Product	Short Tons Generated (millions)	Percent of MSW Stream	Total Tons (millions) Recycled	Total Tons (millions) Landfilled
Yard waste	31.6	17.6	0.5	31.1
Corrugated boxes	23.1	12.9	10.5	12.6
Newspaper	13.3	7.4	4.4	8.9
Food waste	13.2	7.4	0.0	13.2
Glass jars and beverage bottles	11.3	6.3	1.5	9.8
Subtotal (top five)	92.5	51.6	16.9	75.6
Consumer electronics	10.6	5.9	0.1	10.5
Furniture	7.5	4.2	0.0	7.5
Office paper	7.3	4.1	1.6	5.7
Books and magazines	5.3	3.0	0.7	4.6
Paper toys and games	5.2	3.0	0.0	5.2
Folding cartons	4.4	2.4	0.3	4.1
Junk mail	4.1	2.3	0.6	3.5
Clothing and shoes	4.0	2.3	0.0	4.0
Large appliances	3.0	1.7	0.2	2.8
Subtotal (top 80%)	143.9	80.5	20.4	123.5
Paper tissue and towels	3.0	1.7	0.0	3.0
Paper bags	2.9	1.6	0.2	2.7
Disposable diapers	2.7	1.5	0.0	2.7
Rocks and dirt	2.7	1.5	0.0	2.7
Steel food cans	2.5	1.4	0.4	2.1
Rubber tires	2.2	1.2	0.1	2.1
Wood crates and pallets	2.1	1.2	0.0	2.1
Misc. plastic products	1.7	1.0	0.0	1.7
Lead acid batteries	1.6	0.9	1.5	0.1
Aluminum cans	1.4	0.8	0.8	0.6
Plastic wrap	1.1	0.6	0.0	1.1
Plastic bags	0.8	0.4	0.0	0.8
Paper plates and cups	0.7	0.4	0.0	0.7
Paper milk cartons	0.5	0.3	0.0	0.5
Plastic soft drink bottles	0.4	0.2	0.1	0.3
Plastic milk bottles	0.4	0.2	0.0	0.4
Other	9.0	4.6	0.0	9.0
Total	179.6	100.0	23.5	156.1

Source: National Municipal Solid Waste Association and the EPA, Characterization of Municipal Solid Waste. Based on 1988 generation rates by weight before recycling.

Yard Waste 31.6 million tons. Composting, even in backyards, can reduce yard waste 50 to 90 percent, or 16 to 28 million tons. Some states have banned yard waste from landfills.

Corrugated Boxes 23.1 million tons. Recycling of corrugated was estimated to be 13 million tons in 1990. Currently, new production capacity is under construction and, when completed, the American Paper Institute expects a 66-percent recovery rate by 1995. This will be a substantial improvement from the 52-percent recovery rate in 1988. The 14-percent improvement in recovery, assuming no growth in corrugated consumption, would amount to 3 million tons of additional waste being diverted from landfills. Business and government are expected to provide the major share of the added corrugated for recycling.

Newspaper 13.3 million tons. Recycling of newspaper was estimated to be 5.8 million tons in 1990. Currently, new production capacity is expected and, when completed, a 52-percent recovery rate is expected by 1995. This will be a substantial improvement from the 35-percent recovery rate in 1988. The 17-percent improvement in recovery, assuming no growth in newspaper consumption, would amount to 2 million tons of additional waste being diverted from landfills. Community based recycling programs in the form of curbside and drop-off programs are expected to provide the major share of added newspaper for recycling. Recycling content legislation and voluntary guidelines established by the newspaper industry are expected to increase the market for recycled newsprint.

Food Waste 13.2 million tons. Food waste cannot be recycled. It does make good compost, but it will take large-scale composting to achieve a meaningful reduction. Data regarding large-scale composting projects does not appear to exist at this time, and no forecast for improvement is possible at this time.

Glass 11.3 million tons. Recycling of glass was estimated to be 1 million tons in 1990 by the Glass Packaging Institute. New methods of adding cullet are expected to provide the industry with a capacity to produce more recycled glass. Two-and-one-half-million tons of glass is expected to be recovered by 1991 because of community-based recycling. This would be an improvement of approximately 1 million tons over the 1.5 million tons that the EPA study shows were recycled in 1988.

Consumer electronics 10.6 million tons. No specific recycling program targets this material. Therefore, no improvement is forecast.

Furniture 7.5 million tons. No specific recycling program targets this material. Therefore, no improvement is forecast.

Office Paper 7.3 million tons. The American Paper Institute projects that the recovery rate of deinking grades of paper will grow from 37 percent in 1988 to 50 percent in 1995. Office paper recycling programs are being implemented in record numbers and will contribute a major share of the projected 2 million tons of increased recovery expected for printing and writing paper.

Books and Magazines 5.3 million tons. New uses for magazines in making recycled newspaper have been developed, but it is difficult to find many significant recycling programs focused in this area. However, curbside programs collect magazines in areas where there is a market. This is expected to increase in upcoming years.

Paper Toys and Games 5.2 million tons. No specific recycling program targets this material. No improvement is forecast.

Folding Cartons 4.4 million tons. No specific recycling program targets this material. No improvement is forecast. However, an improved market for mixed paper may absorb a small percentage of this material.

Junk Mail 4.1 million tons. Junk mail (advertising mail) is currently recycled as mixed paper. As environmental groups continue to ask the public to take their names off mailing lists, the percentage of MSW should decrease. Direct mail organizations are considering adopting voluntary recycled content guidelines, and some small amount of junk mail can be marketed as mixed paper.

Clothing and Shoes 4.0 million tons. On a net basis, 1 million tons of used clothing and textiles are currently recycled. About 25 percent of the waste collected for recycling is ultimately landfilled because it has lost its ability to be recovered.

Large Appliances 3.0 million tons. White goods are also being banned from landfills in some states. Often, these appliances contain freon, which can damage the ozone layer, and some older appliances contain PCBs. The steel in white goods can be recycled, but, since these appliances also contain plastic, insulation, and other components, some parts must ultimately be landfilled.

Paper Tissue and Towels 3.0 million tons. Paper tissue and towels are not recycled.

Paper Bags 2.9 million tons. No specific recycling program targets this material.

No improvement is forecast. The use of reusable shopping bags has been recommended, but at this time the practice is not widespread.

Disposable Diapers 2.7 million tons. Not recycled.

Rocks and Dirt 2.7 million tons. Not recycled.

Steel Food Cans 2.5 million tons. The Steel Can Recycling Institute has announced a 24.6-percent recovery rate for steel cans in 1990, largely as a result of curbside recycling programs. The industry's goal is to achieve a 66-percent recovery rate by 1995. If achieved, this will result in a savings of 1 million tons annually.

Rubber Tires 2.2 million tons. Tires for the most part are being banned from landfills. Industry trends indicate that a majority of tires will be shredded for use in either waste-to-energy facilities or as an additive for asphalt. Until these uses materialize, tires will be stockpiled in locations other than landfills. A reduction of 2.2 million tons in MSW could result.

Wood Crates and Pallets 2.1 million tons. Wood crates and pallets can be chipped for use as mulch, but no evidence exists that this is a major trend. They are also consumed as fuel.

Miscellaneous Plastic Products 1.7 million tons. While most plastic products are technically recoverable, there are not facilities that recycle mixed plastics in most areas of the country.

Lead Acid Batteries 1.6 million tons. Lead acid batteries are being banned from landfills and can be recycled. A 1.6 million-ton reduction in MSW could result.

Aluminum Cans 1.4 million tons. Approximately 65 percent of aluminum cans were recycled in 1991, and the recovery rate is expected to grow to 75 percent by the year 2000, according to the Can Manufacturers Institute.

Plastic Wrap 1.1 million tons. Not recycled in significant quantities, except that stretch wrap from businesses is recycled at approximately a 5-percent rate.

Plastic Bags 0.8 million tons. Post-consumer plastic bags are not recycled in significant quantities.

Paper Plates and Cups 0.7 million tons. Not recycled.

Paper Milk Cartons 0.5 million tons. Not recycled.

Plastic Beverage Bottles 0.4 million tons. Approximately 30 percent of PET soft drink bottles are recycled, primarily through states with mandatory deposit legislation.

Plastic Milk Bottles 0.4 million tons. Plastic milk bottles are recycled in many community-based collection programs and in some buy-back programs at a recycling rate of approximately 5 percent.

Other 9.0 million tons.

Of the 180 million tons of MSW, 23 million tons are now recycled, according to the EPA. With a combination of composting, landfill bans, and industry recycling, over 30 million additional tons can be diverted from the landfill, lending credence to the EPA's goal of a 25-percent recovery rate by 1995. However, in the analysis shown above, the single largest contribution to solving the problem is using backyard composting to remove yard waste.

As discussed in Chapter 1, "Overview to Recycling," 95 million tons of material are actually recycled, and, in an effort to reconcile the difference in point of view, we could go on to indicate that 23 million of the tons were from MSW. An additional discussion of this debate over definitions is included in Chapter 20, "Unsettled Issues."

MSW is defined by the EPA as including "wastes such as durable goods, nondurable goods, containers and packaging, food wastes, yard wastes, and miscellaneous inorganic wastes from residential, commercial, institutional, and industrial sources. Examples of waste from these categories include appliances, newspapers, clothing, food scraps boxes, disposable tableware, office and classroom paper, wood pallets, and cafeteria wastes. MSW does not include wastes from other sources, such as municipal sludges, combustion ash, and industrial nonhazardous process wastes that might also be disposed of in municipal waste landfills or incinerators."

Figure 2-1 illustrates the MSW stream and the recycling stream. One hundred percent of the hazardous waste stream and part of the recycling stream are not included as part of the MSW stream. A second recycling stream separates from the MSW stream.

Widespread agreement exists that the recycling stream should be made as large as possible and that the MSW stream should be minimized. While this book is about the subject of making the recycling stream as wide as possible, the accurate measurement of the tons of material that are being deposited in landfills should be a national and local priority.

With fewer landfills to monitor in the future, this measurement task is manageable and a standard reporting system needs to be developed. Then, and only then,

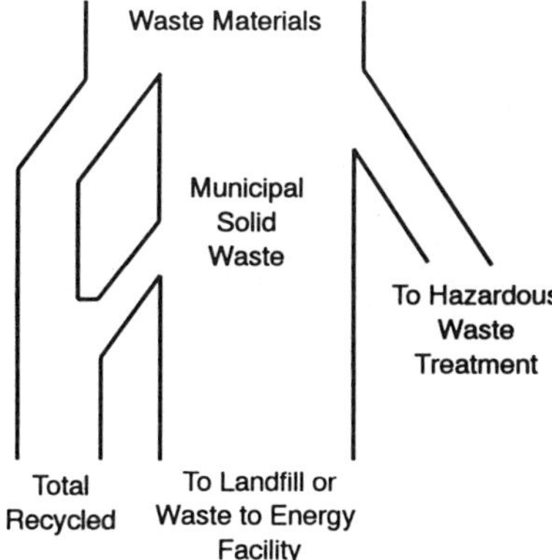

FIGURE 2-1. Municipal Solid Waste and Recycling

will the nation discover if it is making progress with reducing the 157 million tons that are presently discarded or if the trend is moving in the wrong direction. The nation needs to know its trash report card by region, by state, and for the country as a whole. It needs to determine if the average citizen really accounts for 1,300 pounds of trash annually.

3

History of Recycling

The study of history tends to focus on wars, exploration, momentous events, and great personalities. Recycling meets none of the requirements. When viewed in the historical context of the United States, recycling is obviously a modern phenomenon. In fact, recycling did not even exist as a word until after both the EPA and Earth Day were founded, in 1970. Widespread awareness of recycling did not occur until media attention was riveted on the garbage barge incident of 1987 and again on the twentieth anniversary of Earth Day in 1990.

But looking back over history it is clear that solid waste management is not a new topic. In Athens in 500 B.C., solid waste evidently got out of control and an ordinance was passed prohibiting the disposal of trash in the streets. Instead it required that trash be taken at least one mile outside the city limits. In Greece, travelers could probably tell by smell when they were getting close to a city. Today, hovering pollution foreshadows to travelers that they are nearing modern city limits. In medieval Paris, the practice of throwing trash out of open windows was eventually prohibited, probably for no more noble reason than that the neighborhood pigs were finally unable to keep up. The point is that solid waste problems certainly are not new.

COLONIAL TIMES IN THE UNITED STATES

Recycling's roots can be traced to the use of scrap textiles and metals in pre-revolutionary war times. In 1690 America's first paper mill was built in Philadelphia and rags were used to make new paper. In the 1770s Paul Revere bought scrap copper and brass for use in his metalworking business. Also during colonial times scrap metal was used in making pewter buttons. In 1793 Eli Whitney invented the cotton gin, signaling the beginning of the industrial revolution in the United States. The industrial revolution brought with it the end of an agrarian economy and the beginning of an urban-oriented economy. With urban areas, population density increased and higher volumes of recyclable materials were brought together, thereby making large-scale recycling feasible.

Significant events in the colonial United States:

1607—Settlement in Jamestown, Virginia.
1620—Pilgrims land in Plymouth, Massachusetts.
1775—1783—American Revolution.
1793—Eli Whitney's cotton gin was invented while George Washington was president.

THE NINETEENTH CENTURY

When the American Revolution ended, the nation went through a period of getting organized. Then, just as original states had been colonized by European cultures, America set out to colonize the rest of the continent. During its first 100 years as an expanding nation, the United States absorbed immense chunks of land—a tradition that lasted from 1803 with the Louisiana Purchase until 1867 with the acquisition of Alaska. A number of wars mingled with expansionism—a second conflict with Great Britain during the war of 1812, a third conflict over the Northwest Territories, a war with Mexico ending in 1848, and a civil war (1861-1865). During this time, Native Americans were pushed into remote regions.

The words of Chief Speckled Snake of the Creeks in 1829 proved prophetic. After having listened to President Andrew Jackson, the chief summarized his sense about what the president was saying as "Get a little further, you are too near me, I have spoken." The Homestead Act of 1862 and the Mining Laws of 1867 and 1872 were designed to entice people to populate the new lands and to exploit its richness. Indians continued to retreat to remote regions, and as expansion continued these remote regions became less and less able to support their communities.

It was a happy coincidence for the new nation that the Industrial Revolution of the 1800s required a huge supply of natural resources and that a huge reservoir of resources came as part of these new lands. The only missing ingredient to industrialization was people. Settlers were attracted to the West by laws giving them acres of land in exchange for their willingness to become citizens. Wave after wave of immigrants came from all over the world to populate this new promised land and to take part in exploiting its resources. Mining claims were established with just a few dollars. Grazing on public land was freely permitted. The conservation movement developed as a force only after 100 years of exploration and exploitation. Yellowstone Park, later the first national park, was founded in 1872. The park was to be free from unbridled development and set aside to preserve its natural state.

In 1891 Congress authorized the President to set aside some land for a reserve, but, while oil and agricultural development were restricted, mineral development was allowed, a clear indication of Congress's priorities. In the next 16 years, 195 million acres were set aside. By 1907, Congress had had enough and withdrew the President's authorization. In almost all cases, pressures for development outweighed pressures for conservation.

Significant events in the nineteenth century:

1803—Louisiana Purchase made by Thomas Jefferson. 827,987 square miles were bought for $15,000,000.
1812-1814—Second war with Great Britain, settled by Treaty of Ghent while James Madison was president.
1845—Republic of Texas.
1846—Oregon Compromise with Great Britain settled the northwestern boundary, forming the present states of Washington, Oregon, Idaho, and parts of Montana and Wyoming.
1848—Treaty of Guadalupe Hidalo. Territory that is now California, Nevada, Utah, most of New Mexico and Arizona, and parts of Colorado and Wyoming was acquired for $15 million, and the Mexican War (1846-1848) was officially ended.
1848—Discovery of gold in California.
1853—Gadsden Purchase. Present day southern Arizona purchased from Mexico for $10 million for a southern transcontinental railroad route.
1861-1865—Civil War. Abraham Lincoln, president 1861-1965.
1862—First Homestead Act allowed citizens over 21 and people who wanted to become citizens to acquire 160 acres.
1867—Mining laws of 1867 and 1872 encouraged miners to explore for and extract minerals on public land.
1867—Alaska acquired. "Seward's folly" was acquired for $7 million—2 cents per acre.
1869—First transcontinental railroads linked up at Promontory Point, Utah.
1872—Yellowstone Park was set aside to preserve its natural resources. Ulysses S. Grant, president.
1881—Bureau of Forestry created as part of the Department of Agriculture. Initially, their job was to protect the forest against disease, insects and fire.
1891—General Revision Act authorized the President to establish forest reserves. This authority was withdrawn in 1907 by Congress after 195 million acres set aside.

THE EARLY TWENTIETH CENTURY

As the 1800s gave way to the 1900s, industrialization continued and lifestyles continued to improve. Automobiles were mass produced from abundant sources of steel and became affordable to the average family. Textile mills wove miles of fabric to clothe a more style-conscious population. Packaging and advertising were in the infancy of their existence. Early industrialists as well as the average person on the street seemed unaware of the toll these and other activities would eventually take on the earth. Not only were they draining the earth of its natural resources, they were piling solid wastes into work dumps, symbolizing progress with smoke-stacks billowing plumes of smoke, and pouring liquid wastes into local rivers and streams, without regard to the downstream consequences.

For most of the second hundred years, the record shows that conflict appeared between development and conservation. The land previously freely available for mining interests became harder to develop when, in 1920, the Mining Leasing Act was passed. The Taylor Grazing Act, passed in 1934, restricted the previously unregulated grazing rights of western ranchers.

During World War I, cutting down clothes to fit younger family members was a natural thing to do. Every home had a ball of twine saved from one package to use later for the next package. Worn oilcloth table covers became book covers or shelf lining. Old sheets were cut into handkerchiefs and pillowslips. In retrospect, people seemed frugal, but perceiving their activities as frugal is only possible in today's throw-away society. Reusing material was as second nature then as tossing an unmatched sock into the trash can is today.

During World War II, the nation's resources were stretched to their limits and rationing became a way of life. Saving tin cans, newspapers, textiles, and grease drippings was a familiar routine for most households. Volunteer organizations went door to door to collect paper and other recyclables as part of a nationwide effort. But immediately after the war was won, using used tin cans to make products became socially undesirable. Toys made from scrap were frowned upon. When rationing disappeared, recycling also faded. It has taken generations for the recycling ethic to become fashionable again.

Significant events in the early twentieth century:

1910—Pickett Act allowed the President to remove public lands from development for oil and agricultural use, but not for mining use.

1913—The National Association of Waste Dealers was formed in 1913. It was a predecessor to the Institute of Scrap and Recycling Industries (ISRI).

1914-1918—World War I.

1916—Stockraising Homestead Act allowed graising on public lands.

1918—WWI ended, and war surplus materials were auctioned off for scrap and reuse.

1920—Mineral Leasing Act returned control of public lands for mining development to the federal government.

1934—Taylor Grazing Act—revoked the right of grazing on public lands and began a public policy of retaining public lands and managing them.

1939–1945—World War II. Rubber shortage at the beginning of the war made recycling tires, boots, and inner tubes critical. Newspapers, tin cans, and textiles were collected at the curb and at drop-off sites.

1946—Bureau of Land Management became the federal caretaker for public lands. Modern day balancing act between utilitarianism and conservation begins.

1950–1953—Korean War.

THE BEGINNING OF A NEW ERA

The accumulated damage from the industrialization of the United States did not reach the pain threshold until the 1950s. In 1955 the Clean Air Act was passed, followed by the Water Pollution Act of 1956. When the Solid Waste Act of 1965 became law, the package was complete. Because pollution of every kind was out of control, it would take a highly regulated approach to get the environment back in balance. Industry, which had improved the quality of life for generations, had finally created enough negative by-products that the industries and products were becoming a severe health risk. Quality of life was perceived to be headed in the wrong direction.

The public appeared willing to support legislation that regulated smokestack emission because they could see the sky change color, or smell odors, or have trouble breathing. Water pollution also could be measured on the basis of "personal experiences." When Congress passed the first federal law requiring safeguards and encouraging environmentally sound methods for disposing of waste, it has been more difficult to understand. Landfills are not accessible and groundwater contamination can't be seen. The pollution is just as real, yet industries that create solid waste think they are somehow different than, for example, the automotive industry, which creates the cars that pollute air. Just as the products of the auto industry are heavily regulated today, the products causing today's solid waste problems are entering a period of heavy-duty changes designed to reduce or remedy their polluting impact on the land.

In the 1970s the United States experienced an energy crisis. Cars lined up for gasoline in queues that were 20 cars long. The nation flirted with conservation, but the crisis ended even before all the gas guzzlers were traded in. A few years later and it was business as usual.

In 1988 the EPA established a national goal of recycling 25 percent of solid waste, a substantial improvement from the 11 percent of solid waste that was recovered at that time. The twentieth anniversary of Earth Day in 1990 revitalized the perspective for a whole new generation.

In the context of the much higher rates of other countries, a 25-percent recycling goal for the United States appears to be easily attainable. But the countries that currently recycle 50 percent of their solid waste have never been rich in natural resources, and have learned over decades to recycle their solid waste as an alternative. The countries, especially around the Asian Pacific Rim, do not have the vast natural resources to compete with recyclable materials. For the United States, our traditions and habits are different, and tremendous credit must go to the educators who are making recycling a part of an elementary and high school education.

Significant events in the new era:

1955—Clean Air Act. First passed in 1955, the act addressed cleaning up air pollution. Dwight D. Eisenhower, president. Later, the Clean Air Act was replaced by the Air Quality Act of 1967.

1956—Federal Water Pollution Control Act of 1956 became the first substantial legislation regulating water quality. Amended many times since.

1963—First aluminum can appeared in marketplace.

1964—U.S. Wilderness Act set aside lands for preservation.

1964-1973—Vietnam War.

1965—Solid Waste Disposal Act. This act was the first major legislation dealing with land pollution. Later it became the Resource Recovery and Conservation Act (RCRA) of 1976.

1968—Reynolds Aluminum started recycling aluminum cans in Los Angeles, California.

1970—Environmental Protection Agency founded.

1970—Earth Day founded.

1971—General Services Agency sets initial standards for purchases of recycled paper products.

1971—Oregon passed first deposit law.

1974—The EPA presented a resource recovery report to Congress stating that "the use of recycled materials appears to result in a reduction in atmospheric emissions, generated waste, and energy consumption levels, when compared with virgin materials utilization." (Stauffer, 1989).

1976—The Federal Land Policy and Management Act of 1976 made the sale of public lands possible under very restrictive conditions.

1977—Maryland adopts a recycled paper procurement policy. Richard Keller was named procurement director and was an early and persistent advocate of purchasing recycled materials.

1978—First two-liter plastic bottle introduced.

1981—National Recycling Coalition founded.

1986—Mandatory recycling legislation passed in Rhode Island. New Jersey, Connecticut, Maryland, Pennsylvania, and Florida passed similar legislation up to 1988.

1987—Garbage barge incident. A barge with 3,000 tons of garbage travels over 6,000 miles in search of a dump site. It finally returns from the cruise with the contents still aboard and was a media event from start to finish. It created an indelible impression that solid waste was a problem. Shortly thereafter, medical waste washed up on the beaches of New York, and the national media's attention has been riveted to the problem since.

1988—11 percent of solid waste recycled and composted.

1989—The EPA sets a 25-percent recycling goal for the nation.

1990—Twentieth anniversary of Earth Day, which has become a focal point for environmental causes.

1991—Persian Gulf War.

1993-95—More than 70 percent of the existing landfills may be closed.

CONCLUSION

The United States is blessed with an abundance of resources, and, when history is reviewed, it is clear that the unrestrained development of these resources forms a long tradition in which the recycling movement is only a footnote. The United States faces a unique challenge, since in the future, industry will be asked to use recycled materials despite the fact that neither a war nor a shortage of resources makes it necessary.

The nation is adjusting to a new era—perhaps best called The Environmental Revolution. Part of the new era is a reaction to the quality of life issues created by the Industrial Revolution, and part is a new awareness of the earth. The challenge is to have a growing economy that is also is "earth friendly."

If we are indeed in an environmental revolution, it is difficult to see the beginning or the end; we are too close to the events. Examining colonial history, it is clear where we have come from and it is clear that conservation has been becoming a more prominent force for some time. Those people who are aware that the American public throws perfectly usable secondary resources into landfills by the millions of tons annually are growing less tolerant about industry using virgin resources. The closure of many landfills over the next few years guarantees that the solid waste issue will never be viewed in the same light again.

II

Understanding Commodities

4

Understanding Commodities—Overview

One of the most basic yet essential steps toward understanding the recycling industry is learning about the individual commodities that comprise the waste stream. It is impossible to fully comprehend the dynamics of recycling, without having a basic knowledge of what recyclable materials are, how they are identified, and ways they can be reprocessed into new materials. There are no effective shortcuts to learning about these commodities, which include far more than newspaper, plastic, and aluminum. By definition, recycling deals with materials.

Probably the best reason for learning about recyclable materials is the fierce competition among collectors for limited recycling markets. To successfully compete, collectors must understand how to take recyclable materials from the waste stream and transform them into a high-quality product for end users. When recycling professionals and managers do not understand quality, they are unable to communicate adequately with workers, and are unable to give quality assurances to end users or others in the marketplace.

THE WASTE STREAM

There is a good reason why the waste stream is called what it is and not the commodities stream or the raw materials stream. The waste stream is a composite of materials that are not marketable in their existing form. Waste is unstructured. If waste material is to be recycled it must be organized and classified and must conform to quality standards that are required in production—waste materials in particular are not immune to specific quality standards. At first, paper is paper, plastic is plastic, steel is steel, and copper is copper. In reality, there are dozens of grades of recyclable materials for each of these commodities.

The distinction of these different grades relates to the purity of the recyclable materials and the composition of the original material. For example, pure copper wire, which is free from insulation and is shiny and bright, constitutes a very high grade of copper, but a copper pipe that is green from oxidation and has soldered joints possesses foreign matter and belongs to a lower grade of material. Grades sell for different prices as a result of the variations of purity.

Even newspaper—the daily or weekly publication delivered by carriers and purchased at newsstands—has a different meaning when it comes to using it as a recycled material. There are several commonly sold grades of recycled newspaper. Some grades may be in high demand close to paper mills. Other grades of newspaper may be impossible to recycle. It is important to realize that different grades exist for a purpose, usually because of quality standards for the finished product or because of production economies.

Manufacturers using recyclable materials need raw materials that meet their specifications. These manufacturers are accustomed to selecting their materials according to the various grades of scrap. It is fundamental to know these grades of scrap and to be able to identify them, for how can a seller and a buyer of recyclable material communicate without sharing the confidence that both parties know what grade of material they are discussing. The grade of material defines the basic parameters of what the recyclable material will be like.

However, even experienced individuals need to visit the manufacturing plant to bring home exactly what type of material is required. If this is not practical, a small physical sample will confirm to both parties that they are seeing the material though the same eyes. Many potentially good business relationships are destroyed because the seller and the buyer share different views of quality.

Since scrap by its very nature is imperfect, it takes many transactions between buyer and seller before a solid relationship is developed. In any new relationship, it makes sense to describe the product, send samples, and then send a test load. It also makes sense to start slow, gradually increasing shipments so that a trustworthy relationship can be built based on a number of high-quality loads. A manufacturing environment emphasizes efficiency, and substandard material creates problems that cost many times the value of the raw material.

There is another reason to learn details about each grade of material. Different grades sell for different prices. The recycling industry is sometimes mistakenly thought to be one in which the lowest processing cost per ton is desired. Plants attain the lowest cost per ton by producing the lowest grade of material. This minimizes sorting costs, but produces a low-quality product that may be difficult to market because it will have a correspondingly low price.

The real economic objective is to add value to waste materials. When the price of different grades is understood, value can be maximized. When cost per ton is the driving factor, sorting costs are eliminated and high grades of materials are comingled with low grades. The value of the high-grade material is lost because the grade of scrap is generally determined by the lowest grade present, not the highest grade nor the average grade. When the value added per labor hour is maximized, economic performance is at its highest level.

THE PROCESS FOR UNDERSTANDING EACH COMMODITY

Each commodity has different recycling characteristics and different recycling potential. To understand each commodity, follow a six-step process.

First, know the physical characteristics of each commodity. For example, recognizing that aluminum is a metal that is silvery makes it easier to find in the environment. Galvanized steel can also be "silvery." Both materials are recyclable. Both also can be painted, but the point is that silvery as a physical characteristic can become a basis for separating materials from the waste stream, since most "silvery" materials can be sold at a profit.

Second, know how materials are used. To continue using aluminum as an example, understand that aluminum is used to make wire, foil, TV dinner trays, disposable baking pans, light poles, ski poles, baseball bats, lawn chairs, window frames, ducts for clothes dryers, license plates, and so on. Obviously, aluminum does not have an exclusive use in making many of the products that are described, but knowing how a material is used is just one of the clues to identifying it in the waste stream. Also, recognizing how a material is used provides useful information for finding markets.

Third, know how to identify each item and be able to discriminate between a number of materials that, on a physical basis, have a similar appearance. A simple magnet can detect the difference between galvanized steel and aluminum. Chemical tests are described where appropriate. For example, a chemical test easily differentiates groundwood papers from other grades of papers. However, in this book we have stopped short of highly technical methods. Spark tests, spectrographic methods, metallurgy and chemistry extend beyond the scope of this book.

Fourth, know how materials must be collected and processed. Different materials require different collection methods. Processing generally involves grading, sorting, and packaging materials for shipment, but it varies with each commodity.

Fifth, understand that marketing recyclable materials varies with commodity and grade. End users rarely consume more than one commodity and generally use only a few grades of scrap materials. Each recyclable material represents a unique marketing challenge. Geographical factors also influence the potential for each commodity, but the marketing process starts with a detailed understanding of recyclable materials. The basis for a good business relationship depends on communicating clearly and providing the correct quality for the market. This process cannot be efficient without product knowledge and without some empathy for the problems of end users.

Sixth, learn that recycling can't become a solution unless consumers purchase products made from recycled material. Gleaning specific knowledge about each commodity is the key to becoming a purchaser of raw materials and products that are recycled.

5

Aluminum

Overview: *Apparent consumption:* 5,291,000 short tons
Amount recycled: 2,204,000 short tons
Recovery: 41.7%

Benefits: *Energy use reduction:* 95%, 119,000 Btus/lb
Air pollution reduction: 95%
Resources saved: Bauxite ore
Miscellaneous: 97% water pollution reduction

Outlook: Excellent. Aluminum recycling will continue to grow because of the economic incentive to recover the metal. The aluminum can represents the biggest single success story in recycling for a specific product, as well as in source reduction.

INTRODUCTION

Aluminum is one of the most important and versatile alloyed materials in use today. It is a metal found in almost every household and business, in hundreds of different forms. While aluminum is abundant, it is very expensive to produce because it is not found naturally in the earth. Various compounds of aluminum make up more than 8 percent of the earth's crust. Traditionally, aluminum is recovered from bauxite ore, which is removed from open pit mines. Unlocking aluminum from bauxite requires chemicals and a great deal of electricity, which explains why aluminum plants are often located near hydroelectric plants. It takes approximately four tons of bauxite ore to produce one ton of aluminum.

Aluminum is distinguished by its silver-white color. The metal is soft, very light, strong, and durable. Aluminum will not rust, it conducts electricity, and it is nonmagnetic. The metal can be rolled into sheets, drawn into bars and rods, forced through dies, and made into tubes and other complex shapes for items such as door and window sections and structural parts. It can be pulled to make wire or cast into molds to form items such as cast aluminum barbecue housings. Aluminum can also be hammered into shapes.

Because of aluminium's characteristics and malleability, it is one of today's most useful and important materials. According to the Bureau of Mines, the consumption of aluminum in the United States was 4,800,000 tons in 1990, with a market value of more than $8 billion. The Bureau reports that aluminum was consumed in the areas oulined in Table 5-1.

Investors, recyclers, and other interested parties stay acutely aware of aluminum's value. Primary aluminum prices are quoted continuously on the Commodity Exchange (COMEX) and London Metal Exchange (LME). Most major daily newspapers report the spot price for aluminum ingots in their financial section. Aluminum can also be purchased in the future through these commodity exchanges. On June 8, 1991, for example, aluminum could be purchased for $.625 and guaranteed at that price through March 1992.

Analysts can compare current and future market prices for aluminum and make judgments about the strength or weakness of the market from their findings. For example, the June 1991 price of $.625 and the price in March 1992, nine months in the future, is the same. If aluminum was inventoried at today's prices for nine months, the time value of money would normally make aluminum nine months out in time to be more expensive. If, for example, the current rate of interest was 12 percent annually, the price nine months later would be 9 percent higher. Since the commodities market is quoting the same price, it could be concluded that the market is very weak.

However, forecasting the future direction of the market is much more complex. The factors affecting supply and demand around the world are many, and the interplay of these forces is even harder to calculate. The futures market provides a method to reduce risk of investment through a practice called "hedging," which is demonstrated below, and also provides a method of speculating by taking a position in the market.

The futures market allows for the purchase or sale of contracts at a fixed price for future delivery. For example, if a contract for future delivery was sold by an

TABLE 5-1. Aluminum Consumption

(1990)	
Packaging	31%
Transportation	22%
Building	19%
Electrical	10%
Consumer durables	8%
Other	10%

Source: U.S. Bureau of Mines

aluminum producer for delivery in March 1992 at $.625 per pound, the producer could "hedge" against a price decline in the market. In this hypothetical example the aluminum producer would find this option attractive, if the price dropping below $.625 would destroy the company's profit. The aluminum producer, in buying the futures contract, could lock in a profit. In March 1992, if the market is below $.625, the company would lose money on the sale of the aluminum it delivers, but would make a profit buying low-priced aluminum at the spot price to fulfill the futures contract. However, if the price for aluminum is more than $.625 in March 1992, the aluminum producer would make more money by selling the product it delivers, but would lose potential profit on the futures contract. In effect, the aluminum producer avoids a risk of losing money, but it also has to forego the prospect of additional gain.

In other words, the chance for economic gain is diminished by hedging, but so is the chance for loss. Certainty replaces speculation. However, to complicate matters, actual speculators in addition to recyclers enter the futures market, and some of the risk is effectively passed on to them. Knowing spot prices and future prices is important because in recycling aluminum there is both a buying market and a selling market for scrap. Both markets relate to, and affect the prices for primary aluminum.

RECYCLING ALUMINUM

In 1990 2.2 million tons of aluminum scrap were recovered in the United States, at a recycling rate of 41.7 percent. This recycling rate includes aluminum beverage cans, which have a recycling rate of 65 percent. If an award could go to a single product for recycling success, it would undoubtedly go to the aluminum beverage can. Used beverage cans are widely recycled on a voluntary basis. In states that charge deposits on each container, consumers redeem cans for their deposit and cans are then recycled. In years past, steel cans were often used for beverage containers. Aluminum's high conductivity for cold (or heat), its recyclability, and its high value per pound has made it the metal of choice for consumers when they purchase their favorite beverage. In addition, aluminium cans took over the beverage market because of mass media promotions that emphasized its recyclability—a strategy now emulated by others in the container business.

Additional aluminum is recovered by its producers in the form of scrap. This is called "run-a-round" scrap and, because it never enters the world of consumption, its recovery is not considered to be true recycling.

FINDING RECYCLABLE ALUMINUM AROUND THE HOUSE

Aluminum goods are especially prevalent in households. This source is often overlooked in locating aluminum. Items commonly made of aluminum include:

Cookware and kitchen supplies
- foil for cooking, freezing
- drip pans for stove heating coils
- TV dinner trays
- pie plates
- cookie sheets and baking pans
- disposable baking pans

Light household goods
- venetian blinds
- levelers
- screens

Miscellaneous items made from clean sheet
- lawn chairs
- ladders
- poles (e.g., picnic table umbrella poles, tent poles)
- tent stakes
- base for picnic table umbrella
- aluminum sheet and panels
- roofing on sheds
- pots and pans
- trays
- automobile wheel covers
- automobile grills and trim
- beer kegs
- truck bumpers
- fishing net frames
- ramps for move-it-yourself trucks
- picture frames
- TV antennas
- screen protectors
- light poles
- boat paddles
- baseball bats
- ice cube trays
- rulers
- car and house keys

Painted items
- siding
- gutters and down spouts
- license plates
- pickup truck covers
- canoes and boats

ski poles
Extrusions
window frames
door frames
thresholds
I-beams, over 1/4-inch thick
Radiators
radiators for heating
Cans
beverage cans
food cans
Wire
steel reinforced wire
insulated wire
Cast items
pistons
certain engines
lawn mower housing
barbecue grill housing

This is an important list. If consumers want to be able to divert aluminum from going into landfills, they must cultivate the ability to find and recognize aluminum. By starting with consumer products, it becomes easier to trace the aluminum back to the companies that manufacture aluminum products. This knowledge will help identify end users for aluminum scrap. Learning to identify aluminum is similar to being a mining engineer—the difference is developing the skills to find aluminum in an urban setting, rather than within the earth's crust.

FINDING RECYCLABLE ALUMINUM OUTSIDE THE HOUSE

Aluminum outside the home is not only plentiful, but valuable too. People occasionally resort to stealing products made of aluminum to make extra money. Most states and cities have laws requiring scrap dealers to record the materials they purchase. Ethical scrap dealers, supported by vigilant police departments, are constantly on the lookout for certain forms of aluminum. They know that street signs, bleacher seats, irrigation pipes, street light poles, guard rails, manhole covers, and handrails are among recycled aluminum items that have probably been stolen. When they see these items, they often notify the police.

The best single resource for finding aluminum outside the home is the Yellow Pages. Roofing companies, aluminum siding companies, window replacement companies, automobile and boat repair shops, lawn mower repair shops, printers who use aluminum lithoplates, electricians, plumbers, picture framing shops, heating contractors, home improvement companies, and farms all use or process aluminum.

Other sources of aluminum scrap outside the household include aircraft companies, automobile manufacturers, semitrailer repair facilities, the local electric power utility, machine shops, car shredding operations and auto dismantling yards, aluminum warehouses, and highway departments.

IDENTIFYING ALUMINUM

Learning to differentiate aluminum from other materials is a critical skill, one that is largely developed by learning to identify aluminum's physical characteristics. There are a number of approaches used to identify aluminum. One method alone is not necessarily foolproof.

One set of clues resides in knowing how aluminum is used. The rustproof characteristics of aluminum are desired for lawn furniture, siding materials for houses, and door and window frames. In other applications, aluminum's light weight causes it to be the material of choice. For camping equipment such as tent poles and stakes, engine blocks, truck bumpers, canoe paddles, and baseball bats, aluminum's light weight is a significant advantage.

Because aluminum is able to conduct electricity, it has traditionally been used for wiring many homes and for television antennas. However, aluminum is not currently installed in new homes because under some conditions it may cause fires. Aluminum's ability to conduct heat and cold makes its use ideal in beverage cans or ice cube trays. However, understanding its applications is not the only way to prove that a metal is actually aluminum.

Aluminum's silver-white color provides another clue to its identity. Unfortunately, aluminum is frequently painted or anodized. In these cases, the softness of the metal will often provide an indication. A dull knife or a metal file will scratch the surface and reveal the telltale, silver-white color.

A pocket magnet is one of the best tools for detecting aluminum because aluminum is nonmagnetic. Steel, for example, often looks silver-white and can have many of the same applications as aluminum, particularly when it is galvanized (coated with zinc) to prevent rust. But a magnet won't be fooled. It will be attracted to steel and not to aluminum.

Sometimes chemical substances can provide an answer. Steel is not the only imposter. Magnesium and zinc have many of the same properties as aluminum. Aluminum is far softer than magnesium, which is also lightweight, rustproof, and, like aluminum, can be used as lawn mower housings or exotic wheel rims for automobiles. Zinc is also silver-white, but it is a much more dense metal than aluminum or magnesium. It, too, is nonmagnetic. Applying a drop of nitric acid to the unknown material will solve the mystery. If it is aluminum, there will be no effect. If the material is magnesium, a tan color will appear. If it is zinc, a brown puff of smoke will result.

Hydrochloric acid can also be used to distinguish between aluminum and similar metals. It is relatively easy to tell the difference between stainless steel and aluminum because stainless steel is much harder. But, because some types of stainless steel are nonmagnetic or only slightly magnetic, there may be some question. A drop of hydrochloric acid, very carefully applied, will quickly offer the answer. If the material is stainless steel, there will be no reaction. But if it is aluminum, there will be very vigorous bubbling.

Note: When using acid, consumers should use extreme caution and pay strict attention to the warning labels, avoiding contact with clothing, skin, or eyes.

COLLECTING ALUMINUM

Collecting aluminum can be challenging. It is light and bulky, comes in awkward shapes, and often has sharp edges. It is usually transported in this condition. To make the collection of aluminum economical, recyclers should accumulate it in an organized manner.

Aluminum can recycling starts in the home. Most aluminum is collected by individual families. Disposing cans in a plastic bag or curbside collection container represents the most popular method. Even at picnics and yard parties, a container for aluminum cans can be set up so that valuable cans don't get thrown into the trash.

Another area where it is easy to collect aluminum is at any soda vending machine. A trash can marked "aluminum cans only" with a round hole slightly larger than the diameter of an aluminum can works very well. A plastic bag insert helps to make handling the cans easier. The bag of cans may be sold at a recycling center, scrap yard, or reverse vending machine. In deposit law states, the cans are usually redeemed where they are purchased.

When aluminum cans are flattened, they take up one-third of their original space. To reduce cans, there are wall-mounted can flatteners and mechanical can flatteners for high-volume areas, as well as the old standby—feet stomping on the can.

Businesses often appreciate someone willing to provide containers for aluminum can recycling, provided that some revenue is given to a favorite charity of the company or the company's party fund. The best container for this purpose is a trash can with a small hole for aluminum cans cut out of the top.

Many people combine the need for fresh air and exercise with the need for a little extra money, and collect cans that have been discarded along the sides of the roads. Most people walk, but some use a bicycle and basket. Can collectors have learned that almost anywhere people congregate, thousands of aluminum cans are found. Parks, especially on weekends, and parking lots after a professional athletic event are usually littered with cans.

COLLECTING OTHER ALUMINUM

It would be extremely rare to find a large-scale producer of scrap aluminum who does not understand aluminum recycling and its economics. These companies are generally serviced by a scrap company that provides large bins for collecting the scrap. These bins are usually picked up by specialized trucks. Small scrap producers, however, are frequently happy to have someone set up barrels for scrap and will often share their revenues with a recycler.

Collecting aluminum in any form requires effort. Some collectors are only concerned that the material they collect is recycled. Others are more interested in financial gain and want the maximum revenue for the material they collect. For either type of collector, it is important to know how to prepare the material in order to achieve these goals.

Simply stated, the cleaner and purer the aluminum is, the more it is worth and the easier it is to recycle. To maximize the value of aluminum scrap, it must be free of dirt, grease, and other metals. The removal of steel screws, for example, can increase the value of the item from a few cents per pound to more than 40 cents per pound, depending on the current market.

GRADES OF ALUMINUM

It is the job of the scrap yard or recycling company to sort and clean the material according to the specifications of end users, and then to package the material so that it can be shipped economically. The value of aluminum depends on several variables. First is the aluminum content. End users need to know whether the aluminum is pure or if it is mixed with other alloys. Secondly, if an alloy is used, it is important to be able to identify what type. Some grades are more versatile because they can be used for almost any aluminum product. Other grades are more limiting. For example, cast aluminum can only be used as cast aluminum, but extrusions can be used for many purposes. The third factor in determining the value is recoverability. The ease and rate of recovery affects value. Some grades, such as light aluminum, have low recovery rates and are therefore worth more. The fourth factor is contamination. Some grades are contaminated with steel, dirt, or paint.

Specific Grades

Grades of aluminum vary to some degree from company to company and in different geographical areas, but usually comply with the following descriptions:

Aluminum cans—Aluminum cans consist of clean, old or new aluminum cans, decorated or clear, free of iron, dirt, liquid or other foreign contamination. Standard soft drink cans fall in this category.

Aluminum castings—Castings consist of clean aluminum casting and no ingots. Free of iron, brass, oil, grease, and other foreign materials. Cast aluminum is made by pouring melted aluminum into a mold. Pistons and lawn mower housings are often cast aluminum.

Cast aluminum is sometimes confused with pot metal, a mixture of copper and lead used in the manufacture of large pots and faucets. When placed on pot metal, nitric acid will bubble. *Caution:* Use extreme care when handling acid.

Aluminum foil—Foil consists of clean, old, or new foil, free from anodized foil, paper, plastics, food, or foreign materials. Reynolds Wrap and aluminum pie plates belong in this grade.

Clean aluminum (old sheet aluminum)—Sheet consists of clean, old, or new sheet aluminum. This sheet must be free of foil, venetian blinds, casting, screen wire, food or beverage containers, pie plates, dirt, oil and grease, plastic, and other foreign substances. Aluminum sheet, lawn chairs without steel screws or other steel parts, and most unpainted aluminum belongs in this grade.

Painted aluminum—Painted aluminum is similar to clean aluminum sheet, except it has been painted or it possesses some type of coating. It can also include painted extrusions.

Lithoplate—Lithoplate consists of thin gauge aluminum, with a photosensitive coating. It is used exclusively in the printing industry to transfer ink to paper.

Light aluminum—Light-gauge consists of venetian blinds, hair wire, screen, or other similar material. It may be painted or unpainted.

Extrusions—Extrusions are formed when aluminum is forced or pressed through a mold and expelled, usually as a complex shape. Extrusions are usually window and door frames.

Aluminum radiators (aluminum copper radiators)—Radiators consist of clean aluminum and copper radiators, and/or aluminum tins on copper tubing, iron, and other contamination.

Aluminum wire (old pure aluminum wire and cable)—Wire consists of unalloyed aluminum wire or cable, free from hair wire, wire screen, iron, insulations, and any other foreign substance.

Mixed aluminum—Mixed aluminum consists of pure aluminum, which may include painted, cast, clean aluminum, wire, and clean or painted extrusions. The aluminum must be separated by hand into grades or sold at a substantial discount.

Dirty and iron aluminum—Dirty aluminum consists of aluminum with steel screws or fittings, such as assembled screen and storm doors or windows, lawn chairs with webbing, casting with steel bolts, lawn mower housings with wheels, and insulated aluminum wire.

Other grades—A large number of specialty grades also exist. Some include mixed low copper clips, steel reinforced aluminum wire, EC wire, insulated aluminum wire, new aluminum castings, aluminum pistons, aluminum transmission casings, aluminum borings, aircraft aluminum, and aluminum dross. Other grades also exist.

Anyone who separates aluminum into grades is considered a serious collector. Top serious collectors all compare scrap processors to find the best price. Often, scrap processors specialize in a few items and provide the top price for selected material. Sometimes, as a result of good service convenience, a serious collector will sell all the material to a "favorite" processor. It is not unusual for a small collector to keep an eye on the aluminum market, to time transactions in order to make a profit.

ROLE OF THE SCRAP PROCESSOR

Aluminum comes to scrap processors in almost every form and quantity imaginable. The scrap processor must organize the material based on how it can command the best price. The processor will identify the material when it is received, weigh the material accurately, and direct it to a specific location. The material may be cleaned and sorted further, or it may be sold in the same condition that it was received.

In general, the processor's purpose is to ship the aluminum based on its specific alloy. Aluminum is identified by alloy and has its own complex nomenclature. Some aluminum is pure, but most contains copper, zinc, magnesium, or silicon. It requires dedication to detail and genuine skill for a scrap processor to sort by alloy and to be a reliable supplier to an end user. When large quantities of similar materials are involved, the scrap processor might even perform a spectrographic analysis to pinpoint the specific alloy. Just as primary aluminum is a worldwide commodity, so is scrap.

The scrap processor uses shears to cut material, furnaces to remove contamination or create ingots, shredders to chop the material into pieces, magnetic separators to remove steel, screens to separate material by size, and hand tools to disassemble extrusions. The finished product is usually baled to create high-density packages for shipment. However, shredded material can be blown into railcars or trailers, and material can be boxed, strapped onto pallets, or shipped loose.

Scrap processing plants come in all sizes. Some are large enterprises and ship all of their output to end users, possibly all over the world. Others are small and ship to wholesale processors. And others are in the middle, shipping some material directly to end users, some to scrap brokers, and some to bigger processors.

WHAT HAPPENS TO ALUMINUM AFTER IT LEAVES THE SCRAP YARD

Most aluminum smelters use scrap material in refining aluminum, and some smelters also use bauxite ore. Using scrap aluminum saves 95 percent of the energy used in making aluminum out of bauxite ore, and the capital cost of output per ton is far lower for scrap materials than for bauxite ore.

When scrap aluminum is received by a smelter, it is carefully inspected. If iron is present, the aluminum will probably have to be crushed or shredded so that the iron can be magnetically removed. Materials are inventoried by grade and, based on the type of aluminum being manufactured, are scheduled into a furnace.

The scrap usually is batched and added to a furnace, to produce a type of aluminum that is chemically similar to the original material. Contaminants, such as unwanted metals, or coatings, such as paint, are removed, either by skimming or by drawing the aluminum off the bottom of the molten material. The aluminum beverage can sold today could have been scrap just a few months or weeks ago.

COMPLETING THE CYCLE

Because the economics of making aluminum is tilted heavily in favor of using scrap, the problem is not in having an insufficient demand for recycled aluminum; indeed, the demand for scrap aluminum is practically unlimited. Therefore, the obstacle lies in the supply side of the equation—in collecting enough material.

With municipalities beginning curbside collection programs that include aluminum cans, secondary smelters should begin to see an increase in scrap aluminum. Recycling programs must publicize the true extent of aluminum recycling possibilities in order for this commodity to extend its marketshare.

6

Automobiles

Overview: *Apparent consumption:* N/A
Amount Recycled: Approximately 7 million
Recovery: 100%

Benefits *Energy use reduction:* Approximately 80 million barrels of oil
Air pollution reduction: N/A
Resources saved: Steel, aluminum, platinum, lead, copper, auto parts

Outlook: In recent years, automotive recycling has evolved into a highly sophisticated, technology-driven industry. Virtually 100 percent of automobiles at the end of their product life are recycled, making automobiles the greatest single source of recycled materials.

INTRODUCTION

Most people are surprised to learn that the largest single segment of the recycling industry is in automobiles. In fact, automotive recycling is the sixteenth largest industry in the United States. With more than $5 billion in sales annually, automotive dismantlers have transformed the junkyard of the 1960s into a highly technical business.

In the past 30 years, the automotive recycling industry has advanced light years in the technological processes it uses. Observers must look beyond the traditional view of this industry to understand its magnitude and degree of organization. Automobiles that were once simply towed to a junkyard, only to be slowly taken apart by customers who wander the yard in search of a rear view mirror or carburetor, are now dismantled in an organized manner.

Although the automotive recycling industry has evolved into a sophisticated business where satellite communications and computer-driven inventory systems govern its success, the main ingredients have not changed. Auto recyclers must still purchase the vehicles that are towed to their lot for as little as possible, and the customers who buy the recycled parts shop with the same idea in mind—to buy a dependable part for a bargain price.

RECYCLING

The U.S. automotive industry recycles approximately 7 million automobiles each year, in addition to buses, trucks, and motorcycles. According to the Automotive Dismantlers and Recyclers Association (ADRA), a trade group that represents more than 1,500 national auto recycling businesses, the industry recycles 15 million tons of cast iron and steel, one-half million pounds of aluminum, and up to 200,000 troy ounces of platinum, from cars alone. This represents about 26 percent of the ferrous scrap recycled in the United States.

While recovering natural resources is the most obvious benefit of recycling these vehicles, the industry also helps to save energy. The ADRA reports that one university study estimates that automotive recycling saves the equivalent of 80 million barrels of oil annually, all of which would normally be used in the manufacture of new parts.

Automotive recycling also helps keep insurance costs down. More than half the vehicles dismantled by recyclers are purchased from insurance companies for thousands of dollars. This helps lower insurance companies' premiums for customers because it reduces the companies' losses. No automobiles wind up in the nation's landfills. Wrecked and abandoned vehicles disappear quicker from highways than aluminum cans.

Presently, about 75 percent of an average car can be recycled using existing technology. The remaining quarter, which is made up of plastics, foams, fluids, textiles, glass, and wood, is generally shredded and disposed into landfills. In Germany, auto manufacturers are striving to meet a recycling quota of 100 percent for their vehicles. This is largely in response to legislation that will require auto manufacturers to reclaim their goods. The potential for legal changes like this makes everyone nervous. Additionally, the German government is considering classifying the lightweight automotive refuse as a "special waste," which would cause the disposal costs to soar.

To avoid this possibility, in 1990 BMW commissioned an 18-month pilot dismantling operation in Landshut, Bavaria. The project tested ways to recycle more automobile parts. The project—the first of its kind—used new and proven recycling technologies to examine dismantled parts for recyclability potential. Its goals included developing cost-effective ways to collect recyclable materials from scrapped cars, finding environmentally favorable uses for these materials, and reducing the amount of waste to be disposed of in landfills. The practice may evolve into auto manufacturers using secondary materials to make automobile parts.

Another development to impact automotive recycling is the evolution of car construction. During the gas crunch of the 1970s, Congress passed legislation that required automobile manufacturers to increase the mileage per gallon of cars. The Corporate Average Fuel Economy legislation unexpectedly forced manufacturers to create structural changes in automobile design. These design changes made cars less recyclable. Unibody construction, just one of the implemented changes, incorporates the use of less steel to save weight. Using less steel and more plastic to make cars, according to industry sources, results in more severe damage to the automobile and reduces the availability of recyclable parts and the repairability of the car. This results in less market demand for the parts that can be salvaged.

COLLECTING AUTOMOBILES

Because automobiles are not yet at the stage where they can be easily dismantled, a typical automotive recycling operation has its work cut out for it. Recovering battery cables, distributors, fuel pumps, starters, catalytic convertors, and radiators from the vehicle hulk is labor intensive. Rather than merely crushing wrecked, abandoned, and disabled motor vehicles, today's automotive recyclers have operational schemes that maximize the vehicle's true market value. Automobiles, buses, and farming equipment that no longer function are first brought into an automotive recycler's facility to be properly drained of both hazardous and recyclable fluids. If the vehicles are not too old, undamaged parts of these vehicles are then dismantled, cleaned, tested, and inventoried. Warehouses provide storage space for the parts that still function until they are sold. The remaining shell is then prepared for shredding. At a minimum this preparation includes removing the gas tank.

In a typical recycling operation, the vehicle is fed into a giant shredder that literally pulverizes the inside and turns the body into fragmentized scrap. The material that emerges is essentially a mix of steel, plastic, dirt, and other metals. Steel and iron are magnetically separated from the rest of the pile to be either baled, bundled, or loaded into a railcar. The remaining shredded material can be hand sorted, to recover zinc, chromium, copper, and other recyclable materials.

Generally, the dirt, plastic, and foam are shipped to landfills because it is difficult to produce a high-quality product from the refuse. Shredding efficiently processes a high volume of cars and produces steel scrap acceptable for use in electric furnaces.

Automobile shredding operations are capital-intensive businesses. Low-cost operations can only exist with a constant supply of automobiles. For this reason, finding an automotive recycler in a large urban area is as easy as looking in the Yellow Pages.

Other methods of recycling automobiles include incineration, hand dismantling, and cryogenics. With incineration and hand dismantling, automobile scrap processors strip each car of its radiator, battery, tires, and engine before putting it into a smokeless burning chamber. Once the car is incinerated, it is stripped to remove nonferrous metals, such as copper, aluminum, and zinc-based die castings. The excess heat makes these metals brittle, and helps create a purer product. Incineration results in a clean and marketable steel that can be easily baled for shipping. Compared with shredding operations, a baler-type operation requires significantly less capital and less capacity. The disadvantage of incineration is the difficulty in meeting amendments to the Clean Air Act.

Using cryogenics for automotive dismantling produces much the same result as using incineration. Many materials become brittle at both extremely high and low temperatures. Research from the U.S. Bureau of Mines indicates that cryogenic processing could have numerous applications in both ferrous and nonferrous scrap handlings if the costs were not prohibitive (Dean et al., 1983). Products that have undergone the cryogenic process are cleaner and denser than those produced from incineration and other conventional processing methods. One advantage of freezing metal rather than burning it is the reduction of air pollution.

The U.S. Bureau of Mines focused its research on nonferrous metal concentrates from automobile shredders. These concentrates were obtained from the nonmagnetic residue from the shredder. The material was either dipped into a liquid nitrogen bath or sprayed with liquid nitrogen gas. Once the material was chilled, a hammer mill crushed it into components and the auto scrap was separated by simple screening. While the prospect of using cryogenics to create a higher-quality scrap for automobile recycling is great, costs are prohibitive for this option.

Automobile shredding operations now dominate the auto recycling industry in metropolitan areas. In rural communities, auto bodies are usually compressed in hydraulic presses that make it possible to load a number of auto bodies on a flatbed trailer.

GRADES OF AUTOMOBILES

Grading automobile scrap is challenging because many different types of recyclable materials can be recovered. Automobile scrap includes a variety of metals and plastic, rubber tires, and glass. Steel from the outer shell is the predominant material recovered. It is generally classified as No. 2 bundles, when relatively free of zinc, aluminum, and copper contaminants.

Aluminum, copper, lead, zinc, and stainless steel are other metals that can be recovered from automobiles. When these metals are contaminant free, they can be graded into normal scrap classifications. For further description of these metals, please see their individual chapters in the "Understanding Commodities" section.

Plastic is also a major component of automobile scrap, particularly in newer model cars. Unfortunately, the plastics used in even one automobile contain as many as 60 different resins. This effectively discourages most recycling. Interest probably won't be generated until either a market develops for comingled plastics, or fewer types of resins are used, or these materials can be coded with a universal code common to all automobile manufacturers. Some of the plastic resins in automobiles include acrylic, bakelite, nylon, polyethylene, polypropylene, polyurethane foam, and vinyl.

Scrap tires also find their way into automotive recycling operations. While these tires are not specifically graded, they are clearly recyclable. In fact, some parts of the country only use recycling or incineration as the way to dispose of tires. Many landfills ban them because of the public health and fire hazards they create. Fortunately, there are many recycling options available. These are discussed in Chapter 16, "Tires."

Finally, automobile recycling consists of salvaging and reconditioning replacement parts. These parts include car batteries, brake drums and cylinders, bumpers and trim, carburetors, distributors, electric motors, engines, flywheel housing, fuel pumps, generators, alternators, heater cores, horn and relays, mirrors and light covers, radiators, radios, starters, steering gear boxes, thermostats, transmissions, tubings, voltage regulators, wheel covers and wheels, and window frames.

There are basically four recycling alternatives for these replacement parts. They can become factory authorized parts, after market parts, rebuilt parts, and used parts. Used parts are by far the least expensive to buy. However, the only way to get a real bargain is to know the prices of the new parts that are comparable. Often times, used parts can save from 60 to 80 percent of the cost, and many are even cleaned and tested before they are sold.

ROLE OF THE SCRAP DEALER/PROCESSOR

Automotive recyclers play a major role in conserving and reusing the functionable parts of abandoned vehicles. A typical recycling business uses computer-driven parts information that connects through a network of similar businesses using a satellite communications system. Recyclers can assess their inventories in seconds or locate parts at other recycling operations across the continent by simply entering appropriate data into their computer systems. This allows recyclers to maximize their inventory turnover while providing quick and efficient service to customers.

These inventories often include the history of the part, meaning how many miles are on it and whether it has been cleaned and tested. With electrical parts, the scrap dealer/processor usually tests and warrants the item.

While it appears that automotive scrap dealers contend primarily with technological improvements, they must also deal with legislative regulations. These include requirements that they recycle all fluids from vehicles. Used oil can be burned as fuel or re-refined, but, as it might soon be classified as a hazardous waste, oil presents some hazards to the operation. Antifreeze can be recycled, and gas is burned in company vehicles after filtering.

COMPLETING THE CYCLE

After cars are dismantled and shredded, the scrap is shipped to various end users to complete the cycle. Steel is remelted. Aluminum, zinc, and lead are also reprocessed into new materials. Old tires have a myriad of recycling possibilities. They can be retreaded, used for tire-derived fuel, or shredded for use in rubberized asphalt. Reusable parts go on to extend the service life of other vehicles.

7

Building Materials

Overview: *Apparent consumption:* N/A
Amount recycled: N/A
Recovery: N/A

Benefits: *Energy use reduction:* N/A
Air pollution reduction: N/A
Resources saved: Wood, concrete, plastics, and assorted metals
Miscellaneous: Saves landfill space

Outlook: Good. Building materials recycling should become more common because of the current pressure to transport fewer materials to landfills. Many of the bulky items found in demolition waste are fully recyclable.

INTRODUCTION

Each year, demolition companies tear down thousands of buildings across the country. Until recently, trucks dumped the rubble into local landfills. But when demolition companies were faced with exorbitant landfill tipping fees in the late 1980s, they began searching for ways to recycle the waste.

Most buildings are composed of a varicty of materials, including brick, concrete, wood, plastic, glass, and metal. On their own, each of these materials is technically recyclable: concrete can be reduced to an aggregate, wood can be chipped into mulch, and plastic can be remanufactured. Unfortunately for recyclers, demolition projects don't stack these recyclables into neat, homogeneous piles. Instead, indiscriminate wrecking balls and dynamite blasts reduce buildings to mountains of dirt, wood, and concrete. To further complicate matters, carpet, insulation, sheet rock, and hundreds of other contaminants litter the mounds.

This creates a multitude of problems for companies who wish to recycle building materials. Cost-effective separation of materials is one of recycling's greatest challenges.

RECYCLING

It's virtually impossible to accurately predict what kind of building materials can and cannot be recycled, without examining the specific site. When a structure is torn down, everything—from the cement foundation, to lead piping, to roofing material—is a possible candidate for recycling. What determines a material's recyclability is how it is processed.

The first step in recycling building materials begins long before a crew is brought in for demolition. The most valuable scrap is found in electronic wiring along walls, ceilings, and floors. Copper and lead plumbing and heating pipes follow electronic wiring in value. To reduce contamination of these materials, it is best if they are removed while the building is still intact. This extra care of the materials will inevitably increase their value; local scrap dealers/processors are usually eager to purchase these goods.

Further increasing the scrap value of these metals usually involves only a minimal investment in time. Insulated copper wire, for example, should be stripped from the insulation whenever possible. The value of copper and lead pipes increases when the scrap arrives free of dirt and stone contaminants. Instructions for preparing metals for recycling appear in the "Understanding Commodities" section of this book. Before demolition, buildings are also scrutinized for brass railings, ornate fixtures, brass door knobs, old bricks, hand-carved woodworking, usable door and window frames, and salable lighting fixtures.

After these metals and other valuables are removed, the building is ready for demolition. While many techniques are employed to level buildings, the end result is the same for recyclers—a giant mass of building materials and dirt. In some states, landfills ban construction debris entirely.

At this point many demolition companies pay a specialized recycling facility to sort through the huge quantities of concrete, plastics, wood, and other debris. Some of these facilities charge a tipping fee and require the material to be brought to them. Others bring equipment on-site and sort through the material immediately.

PROCESSING

With either process, the most efficient way to begin sorting is by gathering large pieces of steel, wood, cardboard, and sheet rock, and separating them each into clearly marked roll-off containers. A giant magnet helps separate ferrous metals (iron and steel) from other waste.

A second separation of dirt occurs when the debris is placed through a giant sieve. Small particles make their way through the screen, resulting in a dirt that is suitable for use in landscaping and as fill for construction projects. If the recycling facility has the proper equipment, materials on top of the screen can be further sorted into metals, plastic, and wood through different flotation processes. More frequently, facilities employ workers to hand-sort the waste. While this is labor intensive, it greatly improves the end product.

With manual separation, many operations use a conveyer system, in which the material is slowly transported through a series of sorting stations. One station may be responsible for separating paper goods, such as paper and cardboard, while another sorts out wood. When these commodities are spotted, they are merely tossed down a chute for further processing. Using human labor rather than machinery helps reduce contamination levels.

The unrecyclable materials—insulation, sheet rock, and other debris—that remain on the conveyer are then disposed of at local landfills or specialized construction material landfills.

HOW TO MARKET BUILDING MATERIALS

There are many avenues to pursue with regard to marketing building materials. These include finding buyers for bulk items, such as brick and concrete, wood, and re-refined dirt, along with locating specific scrap dealers who purchase specialty metals. In all cases, the place to begin is the Yellow Pages.

When first discussing a purchasing agreement, recyclers must be honest with the processor/end user. Recyclables recovered from demolition sites do not often yield high-quality material. The levels of contamination will greatly limit how the material can be used.

Another big consideration will be transportation costs. Proximity may be more important than price paid for materials, and this must be taken into consideration during negotiations.

COMPLETING THE CYCLE

With the possible exception of metals, the quality of materials recovered from demolished building is low. Dirt and debris contaminate most of the recyclables, limiting their recoverability. Pieces of wood have often outlived their usefulness as building materials. They are thus reduced to mulch and chunkcrete. Bricks that are broken must be ground into aggregates for asphalt. However, if the materials are processed and free of contaminants, the potential for true recycling is much greater.

Wood

Although most applications for recycled wood are still being developed, it is clear that wood slats have great potential for reuse. One valuable method is chipping the slats for mulch. Another use is cutting up the wood for use in fireplaces. While this is not recycling, it does not contribute to the landfill crisis.

Another recycling option is to produce particleboard from wood chips. This alternative is a bit more expensive, but it does meet the requirements of recycling. Composites are a combination of wood flour or chips mixed with recycled plastic granules that are heated to form a solid panel or board. Spaceboard is another possibility, where natural wood adhesives bind a fiber slurry together to make a sheet. The waffled sheet could be glued together with another sheet to form furniture cores.

Concrete and Bricks

Concrete can be crushed and used as aggregate in new concrete or asphalt. Other building projects can reuse whole bricks.

Plastic

Because plastic recovered from building materials is full of multiple resins, its recoverability is limited. A study produced by the Center for Plastics Recycling suggests that mixed plastics could be used in horse fencing, farm pens, roadside posts, and pallets.

Scrap Metal

If it is pure enough, scrap metal can be recycled into new products. Scrap dealers/processors should grade steel reinforcements and ship them to a steel foundry. Copper wiring can be recovered into new copper products, as can aluminum, iron, and lead.

Dirt

Once the dirt is separated from other large contaminants, it can be used for landscaping and other outdoor applications.

Gravel and Aggregate

Material that has be shredded and sized can be sold as gravel and aggregate for use in road building, parking lots, and construction projects.

8

Copper and Brass

Overview: *Apparent consumption:* 2,425,000 short tons
Amount recycled: 1,421,900 short tons
Recovery: 58.6%

Benefits: *Energy use reduction:* N/A
Air pollution reduction: N/A
Resources saved: Copper ore

Outlook: Copper recycling has a strong economic advantage over mined copper. Although copper recycling has declined since the 1940s, the recycling rate is beginning to steadily rise again.

INTRODUCTION

Copper, the shiny metal found in U.S. pennies, has been used since at least 5,000 B.C., when ancient civilizations employed it to make tools, weapons, and ornaments. Today, copper finds its chief use in the form of electrical wire. Pure copper is easy to shape. It does not crack when hammered, stamped, forged, die-pressed, or spun. Copper can be shaped either hot or cold and, like many other metals, is extremely recyclable.

In the mid-1800s, people discovered that copper conducts electricity. In terms of conductivity, copper is second to silver, which is too expensive for common use. Copper's low cost and efficiency pushed world copper mines to produce an estimated 50,000 tons in 1850. Demand for copper wire increased as electric appliances became more popular. By the turn of the century, world production had increased tenfold, reaching an estimated 500,000 tons per year. By 1912, production had doubled again, and close to 1 million tons of copper were mined worldwide. Since that time, copper production has continued to grow. In 1989 it reached nearly 9 million tons.

Today, 60 countries mine copper. The top 13 countries account for 85 percent of production. The United States and Chile are the leading producers, each bringing in about 17 percent. Thirteen states across the United States produce copper, with more than half the domestic supply coming from Arizona. Electrical applications, and the construction, machinery, and transportation industries each use copper as a primary metal. Table 8-1 shows the copper consumption for end-user categories. The U.S. Bureau of Mines forecasts that demand for copper will grow about 1.9 percent annually in the United States between now and the year 2000. This indicates that there will be a strong market for copper for years to come.

Copper as an Alloy

When copper is combined with other metals, it forms such alloys as brass and bronze. More than 2,000 years ago, zinc was added to copper to produce brass. Brass is the most easily recognized alloy of copper. The amount of copper used to make brass ranges from 55 to 95 percent. The color and properties of brass vary with its composition; when the alloy contains about 70-percent copper, it has a golden yellow color and is called yellow brass. When it contains 80-percent copper, it has a reddish color and is called red brass. Brass is a metal used for modern piping, faucets, and automotive parts.

Another common alloy of copper is bronze. Bronze is a combination of copper and tin. Its hardest and strongest alloy contains a high percentage of tin and a small amount of lead. Statues and ornamental pieces generally are made of bronze.

Copper and its alloys can be made into thousands of useful and ornamental articles, most of which are recyclable. Table 8-2 lists how much copper is reclaimed from different alloy bases. Chemical compounds of copper help improve soil and destroy harmful insects. Copper compounds protect materials against corrosion. Also, copper in small amounts is vital to all plant and animal life.

TABLE 8-1. Apparent Consumption of Copper, By End-use Sector

Thousand Metric Tons of Copper and Percent of Consumption

Year	Electrical Quantity	%	Construction Quantity	%	Machinery Quantity	%	Trans-portation Quantity	%	Ordance Quantity	%	Other Uses Quantity	%	Total Con-sumption
1986	1,410	66	384	18	150	7	107	5	21	1	64	3	2,136
1987	1,494	68	395	18	132	6	88	4	22	1	66	3	2,197
1988	1,592	72	332	15	133	6	66	3	22	1	66	3	2,211
1989	1,571	72	327	15	131	6	65	3	22	1	65	3	2,182

Source: U.S. Bureau of Mines

TABLE 8-2. Copper Recovered from Scrap Processed in the United States, By Type of Scrap and Form of Recovery

	Metric tons			
	1986	1987	1988	1989
Type of Scrap				
New scrap:				
Copper-base	635,495	689,999	764,490	731,629
Aluminum-base	22,891	25,871	24,104	23,761
Nickel-base	221	240	118	47
Zinc-base	27	12	—	—
Subtotal	635,677	716,122	788,712	755,437
Old scrap:				
Copper-base	461,490	481,460	498,797	526,534
Aluminum-base	15,859	16,401	19,271	16,957
Nickel-base	84	70	86	78
Zinc-base	36	6	25	27
Subtotal	477,469	497,937	518,179	543,596
Total	1,136,103	1,214,059	1,306,891	1,299,033
Form of Recovery				
As unalloyed copper:				
At electrolytic plants	292,686	311,312	347,442	376,595
At other plants	121,760	112,445	109,036	110,385
Subtotal	414,446	423,757	456,478	486,980
In brass and bronze	671,184	736,725	800,221	767,951
In alloy iron and steel	1,366	973	763	546
In aluminum alloys	45,781	47,932	45,662	41,356
In other alloys	359	506	327	252
In chemical compounds	2,967	4,166	3,470	1,948
Subtotal	721,657	790,302	850,413	812,053
Total	1,136,103	1,214,059	1,306,891	1,299,033

Source: U.S. Bureau of Mines

RECYCLING

Unlike the recovery of metals such as aluminum and steel, the solid waste crunch did not stimulate copper recycling. Copper is, and always has been, recycled because it makes economic sense. High grades of scrap copper generally are worth more than $1 per pound—making it one of the most profitable and stable metals. Recycled copper comprises about one-third of the copper used for industrial manufacturing in the United States. This is primarily because of the increasing availability of scrap generated from industrial use and scrap metal dealers. Curbside programs rarely, if ever, collect copper. Private recycling companies and scrap dealers dominate the market.

Copper's long life and essential uses, however, limit the rate of its recovery. Because more than 60 percent of it is used for electrical utilities, the only time the material can be recovered is when the wiring is replaced or the building is torn down. However, Table 8-3 shows that the largest segment of post-consumer scrap copper comes from the secondary grade of copper wire.

Because copper is the best low-cost conductor of electricity, its use is generally easy to track. Scrap copper is recovered from the wire used for homes, factories, and offices. Large amounts of copper wire are recovered from telephone and telegraph systems, as well as from television sets, electric motors, generators, other kinds of electrical equipment, and machinery.

The Process

A scrap dealer interested in recycling copper and brass should be knowledgeable about different grades of copper and its alloys. Generally, copper and brass scraps come into the plant in a wide variety of shapes and forms, making the process of identifying and sorting copper and copper-based alloys a complex one. It can be broadly classified into the following categories:

1. No. 1 copper
2. No. 2 copper and light copper
3. Refinery brass
4. Copper-bearing material

Once these materials are identified, the first step is to group similar grades together because each grade may be handled differently. Large pieces of copper may be sheared and baled or briquetted. Wire might go to a chopping line, where the wire will be chopped into pieces 1/16 of an inch in length. Insulation is separated from the wire as the small pieces travel along the conveyer, shaker tables, and air separating system. At the end of the line, small pure pieces of copper are put into multi-wall gaylord boxes. An alternative preparation of insulated copper wire is to bale the wire.

In some facilities and at end user, No. 1 copper can be remelted in a furnace and eventually cast and refined into copper shapes. It does not go through electrolysis, a process of removing all impurities. Because the possibility of contamination exists, No. 1 copper must be made exclusively from scrap from unalloyed copper. It must appear to be clean and free of all contaminants, and it must not be more than 1/16 of an inch thick.

No. 2 copper is first melted in a furnace and then passed through the electrolysis process. This process will remove more impurities.

TABLE 8-3 Consumption of Purchased Copper Scrap in the United States in 1989, By Class of Consumer and Type of Scrap

Class of Consumer/ Type of Scrap	*Metric Tons, Gross Weight*		
	New Scrap	Old Scrap	Total
Secondary Smelters/Refiners			
No.1 wire, heavy	87,370	34,810	122,180
No. 2 wire, mixed heavy/light	41,155	301,751	342,906
Composition or soft red brass	6,166	32,657	38,823
Railroad-car boxes		523	523
Yellow brass	38,098	27,252	65,350
Cartridge cases	—	508	508
Automobile radiators	—	94,444	94,444
Bronze	2,594	12,808	15,402
Nickel, silver and cupronickel	837	3,304	4,141
Low brass	385	2,214	2,599
Aluminum bronze	17	194	211
Refinery brass	1,716	38,589	40,305
Low-grade scrap and residues	56,493	45,854	102,347
Subtotal	234,831	594,908	829,739
Brass and Wire-rod Mills			
No.1 wire, heavy	245,751	19,287	265,038
No.2 wire, mixed heavy/light	35,584	10,723	46,316
Yellow brass	239,954	7,581	247,535
Cartridge cases and brass	125,235	434	125,669
Bronze	4,613	—	4,613
Nickel, silver and cupronickel	18,927	272	19,199
Low brass	17,085	77	17,162
Aluminum bronze	9	—	0
Subtotal	687,158	38,383	725,541
Foundries, Chemical Plants, and Other Manufacturers			
No. 1 wire, heavy	8,748	19,220	27,968
No. 2 wire, mixed heavy/light	941	2,485	3,426
Composition or soft red brass	5,510	8,254	13,764
Railroad-car boxes	1	2,663	2,664
Yellow brass	1,718	3,786	5,504
Cartridge cases	—	46	46
Automobile radiators	629	1,322	1,951
Bronze	40	857	897
Nickel, silver and cupronickel	94	127	221
Low brass	2,374	57	2,431
Aluminum bronze	1,393	1,083	2,476
Low-grade scrap and residues	64	67	131
Subtotal	21,512	39,967	61,479
Total	943,501	673,258	1,616,759

Source: U.S. Bureau of Mines

IDENTIFYING COPPER

Color alone identifies copper. Using a magnet will help determine if the copper is pure because pure copper is nonmagnetic. If doubts remain, try spark testing. There should be no spark. The metal is very ductile, meaning that it can be hammered very thin without breaking.

Copper-clad iron-based material is a common copper contaminant, and it should be avoided. Using a magnet can help avoid this problem. Frequently, steel is coated with copper in items such as grounding rods, and using a magnet will help to prevent mistaking steel for copper. Other metals can also coat copper wire. Scraping the coating will reveal its copper base. This coating makes the copper material belong in the No. 2 copper grade.

GRADES OF SCRAP COPPER

The Institute of Scrap and Recycling Industries (ISRI) recognizes more than 50 grades of scrap copper and copper alloys. To improve the value of the metal, processing plants should sort copper into the highest grade. It is important to properly identify each grade to ship the material correctly and maintain a good relationship with the end user. Grades for copper include the following:

Shiny and bright copper—Similar to No. 1 copper, except that the material has a brand new appearance and is "shiny and bright."

No. 1 copper—This grade consists of clean, unalloyed, uncoated copper clippings, punchings, bus bars, and commutator segments. It also includes copper tubing and wire not less than 1/16 of an inch thick. The tubing and wire must be free of burnt wire, which is brittle. It is 99.5-percent pure.

No. 2 copper—No. 2 copper consists of miscellaneous unalloyed copper having a 96-percent copper content. It should be free from excessive lead, tin, solder, oil, and, in the case of copper tubing, sediment. This grade must also be free of burnt wire.

Sheet copper—Sheet copper is generally used in roofing and guttering materials, copper boilers and kettles, and burnt copper wire. Its purity ranges between 90 and 92 percent.

Insulated copper wire No. 1—This grade of copper wire is 1/8-inch in diameter or greater and is insulated with material that does not weigh more than 10 percent of the total weight.

Insulated copper wire No. 2—This grade of copper wire is less than 1/8 of an inch thick. Or it has an insulated covering that does not exceed 10 percent of the total weight. It is usually sold on a recovery basis.

Automobile radiators, clean—This grade of clean radiators consists of automobile radiators free of aluminum radiators and iron finned radiators. All radiators are subject to a deduction of actual iron, but exterior iron must be removed to qualify for this grade.

Radiators, dirty—Dirty radiators include radiators that still have steel parts attached. The radiator is subject to a deduction of the estimated weight of actual steel. The market price of the remaining weight is lower than clean radiators, to compensate for the labor involved in removing the steel.

Light copper—This grade of copper consists of miscellaneous unalloyed copper scrap that has a 92-percent copper content. It is found in sheet copper, gutters, downspouts, kettles, copper wire from burning, fire extinguishers, and excessively leaded, tinned, and soldered scrap. This grade does not include copper grindings.

Other grades—There are several other grades, including copper bearings scrap, which is known to the industry as drove; No. 1 copper wire nodules, No. 2 copper wire nodules, and copper wire nodules. These grades are considerably less common.

BRASS

While pure copper attracts some of the highest prices of all recycled scrap, most copper is not pure. In fact, more often than not, copper is used as an alloy, either in zinc, lead, nickel, or tin. Combining copper with other metals reduces its recovery value, but these other metals often draw significant markets.

When copper and zinc are used as an alloy, the mixture is called brass. There exist thousands of brass alloys, but many scrap dealers only purchase two major grades—yellow brass and red brass. Most often, these items are judged only by their color. Often, the item itself helps to indicate the type of brass. For example, an old piece of mining equipment would suggest red brass.

Yellow brass—Yellow brass is used in brass castings, rolled brass, rod brass, and tubing. Typically, yellow brass includes chandeliers, brass bedposts, furniture hardware, ship trimmings, sprinklerheads, radiator fittings, and light fixtures. Yellow brass must be free of manganese bronze (e.g., ship propellers), aluminum bronze (gears and acid-resisting pumps and valves), unseated radiators, and radiator parts. It may be sorted into yellow brass scrap castings, old rolled brass, new brass clippings, and brass pipe.

Other grades of yellow brass:

Brass shell cases without primers
Brass shell cases with primers
Brass small arms and rifle shells, clean fired—or free of bullets
Brass small arms and rifle shells, clean muffled (popped)
Yellow brass primer
Machinery or hard brass solids

Machinery or hard brass borings
Cocks and faucets
Mixed brass screens
Refinery brass
Yellow brass rod turnings
New yellow brass rod ends
Yellow brass turnings
Brass pipe
Admiralty brass condenser tubes
Aluminum brass condenser tubes
Plated rolled brass

Red brass—Red brass is made up of 85-percent copper, and 5 percent each of tin, lead, and zinc. It is found in low-pressure valves, machinery bearings, fire extinguisher fittings, pumps and pump bodies, pipe fittings, small gears, and markers and plaques. Red brass is always cast.

Red brass is fairly easy to identify. When nicked with a file, the color is reddish grey.

Other grades of red brass

Red brass composition turnings
Genuine babbit-lined brass bushings
Unlined and lined standard red car boxes
Railroad boxes and car journal bearings

MARKETS

Scrap copper and brass is sold to smelters and refineries (51 percent), brass and wire rod mills (45 percent), and to foundries, chemical plants, and other markets (4 percent). By taking the grades of material and referring to Table 8-3, the logical type of end user for each grade is easily discernable. If truckloads of material are available, these may be good prospects. If several thousand pounds of multiple grades are on hand, a large scrap dealer/processor is a logical outlet. If more than several thousand pounds are on hand, a scrap broker may also be a good alternative to investigate.

TRANSPORTATION

Railcars and trucks can transport both copper and brass to copper refineries. The material is usually shipped in one-ton boxes or crates, or baled. When shipping, make sure the grade of material is evident. If there is not enough metal to constitute shipping a special grade of brass or copper, combining it with other grades is an acceptable practice.

9

Glass

Overview: *Apparent consumption:* 11,300,000 short tons
Amount recycled: 1,500,000 short tons
Recovery: 13.3%

Benefits: *Energy use reduction:* 25%
Air pollution reduction: 20%
Mining waste reduction: 80%
Water use savings: 50%
Resources saved: Sand, soda ash, and limestone

Outlook: Most glass company recycling directors expect glass recycling to increase in the coming years. Technology in glass plants continues to improve, which will allow them to add larger amounts of post-consumer cullet to the new glass batches.

INTRODUCTION

Each year, America tosses out nearly 10 million tons of glass in the garbage. Most of this is from clear, amber, and green bottles and jars—some of the most recyclable of all packaging products. In addition to its recyclability, glass is probably the most inert item in landfills. For this reason, discovering ways to recover container glass—either through reuse or recycling—should be a priority.

Glass was one of the world's earliest manufactured products, first produced by the Phoenicians nearly 3,500 years ago. Today, glass claims to be the most preferred of all packaging materials, primarily because its inert nature and purity connotes quality. Once melted, glass is easily formed into any shape or size. Because it is inert, glass is not susceptible to attack by chemicals. Finally, glass is versatile. It can be either transparent or opaque, and colored or uncolored, giving it much flexibility in the eyes of packagers. These qualities have led to its widespread use as a packaging material.

HOW GLASS IS MADE

Glass is produced from some of the most abundant raw materials in the earth's crust—silica (sand), soda ash, and limestone. Of the three, silica is the most important, and its supply is virtually limitless. Soda ash can be chemically produced using salt, and it can be found as a naturally occurring mineral. Supplies of limestone are also plentiful.

The raw materials used to make glass are blended in a bin or silo and then melted in huge furnaces that reach temperatures of at least 2,600 degrees Fahrenheit. The molten glass is then cooled to 2,000 degrees Farenheit, and, depending on the type of product desired, is later shaped by blowing, pressing, or drawing it. The shaped pieces are put into an annealing oven, where they are strengthened by being reheated and cooled.

Heat provides the energy required to produce glass containers. One way that glass makers conserve energy is by using reclaimed bottles and jars. Broken glass material, called cullet, can then be recycled in the melting furnaces with other raw materials. As more reclaimed bottles are added to the furnace, less heat is needed. This is because recycled glass melts at lower temperatures than sand, soda ash, and limestone. When 100-percent cullet is used, the energy savings are 25 percent.

RECYCLING

Large-scale glass recycling is being pressured by many different causes. Collecting glass will help extend the life of landfills, preserve natural resources, and reduce waste disposal costs. The glass industry has responded to this push by establishing recycling programs throughout the United States, setting an overall goal of 50-percent cullet usage by the mid-1990s.

The question arises, however, of why the glass industry is so willing to establish a market for recycled glass. It already has an abundant supply of raw materials that are not prohibitively expensive. While there are many answers to this question, the primary reason is that scrap glass is an economic one. From the standpoint of the glass manufacturer, using cullet lowers manufacturing costs. The glass industry estimates that each ton of recycled glass saves the equivalent of nine gallons of fuel oil. This means that for each 1-percent increase in reclaimed glass, the average glass furnace saves 2,400 cubic feet of gas.

However, while these savings are significant for manufacturers, large-scale glass collection programs are not self-supporting on an economic basis. Collection activities require a subsidy. To encourage glass recycling, a subsidy must come from one of the following sources.

Government

Government can help support glass recycling in a number of ways. It can make glass collection mandatory, forcing the collection costs to be paid in some manner. If a local government is in control of disposal service, it can absorb the cost of collecting glass. Or the government can support a collection program through an outright grant, such as San Francisco did in supporting their Bar and Restaurant Glass Recycling Program. Restaurant workers sort glass, and the bar or restaurant is paid for its effort.

Glass Producers

To encourage greater glass recycling, producers could pay $80 per ton for scrap, instead of the $40 to $50 per ton it is evidently worth. This would definitely provide an economic incentive to collectors, but would be a strain on the industry itself.

Consumers

Through deposit laws and redemption systems, the consumer could be forced to pay the cost of glass recycling. A per-container charge would help fund collection programs and offset the low scrap value of the material. Deposit and redemption systems could also help ensure a high quality of material. These systems could refuse redemption to dirty or contaminated bottles. Consumers would be forced to take further action in recycling.

Scrap Dealers/Processors

Although selling prices for cullet do not cover the cost of collection activity, some scrap dealers/processors handle glass regardless. The objective for these organizations in handling glass is that by providing a needed service the volume of other recyclable materials that are profitable will increase.

Beverage Industry

Retailers may subsidize glass containers through beverage industry recycling programs. The industry helps establish the collection program, and then provides a market outlet for the cullet.

It appears that most large U.S. glass container manufacturers support the buy-back center concept. These programs cost them less money and generally provide high-quality, recyclable glass. Consumers, on the other hand, seem to prefer to recycle glass through curbside collection programs.

COLLECTING GLASS

With or without subsidies, glass recycling faces obstacles beyond economics. Its fragile composition makes it one of the most difficult commodities to handle because it breaks easily during the collection process. This is particularly annoying when the breakage occurs along streets, sidewalks, and playgrounds, or when broken glass must be sorted by hand from other materials collected in curbside programs.

Household Preparation of Glass

No matter what type of collection program is used, the initial preparation for recycling glass is the same. First, if there are any solids remaining in the bottles, empty the contents and rinse the container. Second, remove all metal caps and rings. Paper labels may remain. Finally, separate the glass by color—clear, amber, and green.

Quality

The preparation required for glass recycling may take time, but it is absolutely essential. End users need to be assured of color separation because of the problems brought about by an impure product. It is critical for manufacturers to maintain the high quality in products made of recycled glass. Even the tiniest amount of green or amber in a batch of flint glass will render the resulting containers cloudy, instead of clear. Flawed material would cause the glass industry to lose its crucial reputation—that glass is a product that connotes purity.

Mixed-color cullet may also cause chemical composition problems. Amber and green glass can cause a "foaming" reaction in melting furnaces because the reducing and oxidizing agents are incompatible. These problems multiply when they occur in large quantities. An even greater contamination worry lies with the problems that metal caps and lids, ceramics, and dirt create. These items do not melt at the 2,600-degree Fahrenheit temperature required for glassmaking. Rather, these contaminants remain whole and damage the furnace or appear in new glass products.

Many of the packaging companies expect extremely high quality as well. In one instance, a major baby food company requires its manufacturer to have less than two breaks per million bottles.

COST

In many areas, the cost of recovering glass from residential and industrial waste mixes has risen to the point where cullet recovery has become unprofitable. Glass must be chemically acceptable, ground into fine pieces, cleaned of contaminants (such as metal) with 99-percent accuracy, and sorted by color with 98-percent accuracy, except for clear glass, which requires perfect accuracy.

Separating glass from other municipal solid waste and then sorting the waste glass by color substantially adds to the cost of glass recovery. The best way to retrieve glass is to separately dispose of it at the household level. But most people don't take the time. Studies on glass recycling programs indicate that many people consider separating glass from their household wastes too much trouble. The financial incentive for an individual household to do so is insufficient. If people do make an effort to recycle glass, it helps to provide them with one or more of the following collection programs.

Curbside

The most convenient way for people to participate in glass recycling is through curbside collection programs. In a comingled, multi-material curbside program, families simply separate recyclables from their household trash. Comingled curbside collection programs require little effort from household members, resulting in high participation rates—and more recycled goods.

The glass produced from curbside programs usually must be color-sorted after collection. If mixed glass remains, it generally cannot be used by glass plants, and must go to glasphalt or other alternatives. In Europe, glass is collected separately from other items because of the breakage and contamination problems.

Buy-back Center

Buy-back centers pay consumers on the basis of weight or volume of glass delivered to a centrally located spot. This type of collection works well for glass because the quality of material can be closely monitored. If the glass comes into the center reasonably clean, the collector does not need to prepare the material much more before it is shipped to end users.

Drop-off Centers

Consumers bring glass to drop-off centers that are centrally located, but they are not paid for it. Collection at a drop-off center requires more consumer effort, and generally results in a lower participation rate. It is, however, an effective option in communities where curbside collection is not yet underway. Drop-off centers have the highest contamination rate of any collection program because they are usually unsupervised.

Deposit Legislation

Deposit legislation for glass containers is used to collect glass in many areas around the country. Consumers initially pay a higher deposit for certain bottled items at the grocery store, and the deposit is refunded when the container is returned. In Iowa, where the per-container deposit is 5 cents, the legislation is particularly successful, keeping 92 percent of bottles out of landfills. Cullet from deposit legislation programs often contains metal caps and foil contaminants.

TRANSPORTATION

Freight costs have always concerned the glass industry. Regulated rates and specialized equipment have had a negative affect on glass recovery. However, this is changing. Some glass recyclers use bulk boxes, basically large cardboard containers on regular pallets, to store cullet. The box holds a ton of crushed glass. A standard 45-foot trailer can hold 22 boxes or 22 tons. This can enable the operator to take advantage of back-haul opportunities from the glass plant.

Another factor that affects transportation cost is the location of end users. Of the 89 glass plants in the United States, most are located in the Midwest. The transportation cost for states such as Florida, which produces a greater amount of post-consumer cullet than local glass plants can handle, is prohibitively expensive.

ROLE OF THE SCRAP DEALER/PROCESSOR

Most scrap dealers/processors buy glass from the public, bottling plants, or materials recovery facilities, and then sort the bottles. Because the only way to make money collecting glass is to provide manufacturers with a contaminant-free product, a scrap collector must invest time and money into a sorting system—unless the collector has one of the few available markets for mixed glass.

Once glass is purchased, the processor can put the glass bottles into a chain-flail crusher and store the densified cullet for shipment. Many processors choose not to crush the glass and to save the capital investment in additional machinery. If the glass is shipped in bulk, crushing is usually unnecessary.

SORTING

To cope with post-consumer cullet, glass manufacturers use a different cullet sorting process, sometimes referred to as benefication, to create a product suitable for use. Waste glass can be color separated through the use of an optical-electronic sorter, which operates by measuring the optical properties of particles. Waste particles are first passed through a transparency detecting device to remove stones, residual metals, and ceramic pieces. The transparency of the glass particles is measured and electronically processed. The sorter matches the color of particles with a background for flint, amber, and green glass. Air jets then deflect the particles into the appropriate bins. This method works well and improves the quality of the recovered glass, but the device requires frequent calibration. Organic residuals sometimes cloud the reading, and the machine cannot read pieces smaller than 3⁄16 of an inch.

A significant problem is that glass manufacturers cannot risk contaminating a batch of new glass with the foreign matters so often found in post-consumer glass. Glass containers that have been discarded in household garbage and contaminated with household wastes are virtually unacceptable for reuse. Even glass that has been separated by the resident is rarely color-sorted and nearly always contains caps, labels, and neck rings. In some cases, scrap ceramic materials, metals, plastics, heat resistant glass, lead-based glass (such as crystal or television tubes), and paper are returned with this post-consumer cullet. This practice is nearly impossible to govern and represents one of the greatest commercial risks to the glass container manufacturer.

Mechanical Separation

Some mechanical methods have been developed to separate glass from municipal solid waste. Two techniques used most often are the float-sink method and the froth flotation method.

The float-sink method involves placing a stream of trash into a tank filled with a dense liquid medium. The lighter material will remain afloat, while heavier materials will sink. This process is accomplished in stages, using liquid of different densities. Eventually, when the glass is fully separated from the waste stream, it is ready for further processing.

The froth flotation method is more efficient than the float-sink process, producing a glass purity of more than 95 percent, although it costs more. This method separates solids by surface characteristics, using an organic medium that clings to the surface of glass.

These methods work well, but the single largest problem facing glass recycling today is the separation of different colored glass wastes.

GRADES OF GLASS

There are essentially four grades and colors of post-consumer cullet: flint, amber, green, and mixed. The most lucrative of these to recycle is flint because of the dominance that clear glass has in the packaging market. But while it commands the most money, flint also requires the most care.

Individual glass plants set their own specifications for cullet. These vary, but most often glass processors cannot tolerate aluminum neck rings and caps, light bulbs, ceramic dishes, laminated plate glass, and window glass. These contaminants can create aesthetic and structural defects in the glass product. Some plants can tolerate a small degree of color contamination. The ranges are generally as follows:

Flint: 95–100% flint; 0–5% amber; 0–1% green; and 0–5% other colors.
Amber: 90–100% amber; 0–5% flint; 0–10% green; 0–5% other colors.
Green: 80–100% green; 0–15% amber; 0–10% flint and other colors.

Post-consumer cullet that reaches these minimum standards (and only requires crushing) must meet other minimum quality criteria. In a ton of glass, an end user may specify no refractory materials greater than 1 millimeter; no metals greater than 10 grams in weight, with no more than 20 grams per ton of cullet; and no paper, plastic, wood, or other organic contamination greater than 10 centimeters. Processors should have the majority of their cullet reach standards above these guidelines, to ensure a problem-free operation.

Green Glass Dilemma

While flint glass claims the highest price for color-separated material, green glass claims the lowest. This is because the United States has an imbalance among the colors. Amber and clear glass are needed, but green glass is often identified with imported beverages. Green glass containers have a lower demand than the available supply. As a result, in 1991, over 50,000 tons of green glass has accumulated as surplus inventory at processor locations. This situation may be better or worse at printing time. Most manufacturers simply don't want the material, however, some glass plants are exporting green glass to Puerto Rico and other countries.

Mixed Glass

Crushed glass that has not been sorted by color has the least value of all, often much less than $40 per ton because it has fewer potential uses. Typically, it is used to manufacture products other than bottles, including ceiling tiles, roofing, and glass fibers. A supply of some mixed glass results at all processors, due to the inability to sort glass that arrives broken. The recycling industry requires additional applications for mixed-color cullet, as well as for cullet that has been contaminated by small debris. One possible application is as a substitute for gravel in road bases, but for most glass operations this residue must be landfilled.

MARKETS

While there are many end users for post-consumer container glass, the most logical ones are the glass plants in which they were made. Nearly all glass plants purchase cullet from the general public. If a collection center is not near a glass plant, a scrap broker might help make the transaction economically viable. In rural areas, recycling cooperatives are beginning to serve the same function.

When looking for an end user, the first step is to contact local plants or brokers to learn prices paid and any particular specifications that would make the transaction attractive or unattractive. If the quantity for sale is large enough, the purchasing agent for the glass plant will probably make arrangements for purchase. Most plants and brokers have a formal procedure for purchasing glass.

The Procedure

Formal procedures usually explain the plant's exact specifications for cullet. When collectors try to sell material that does not meet these specifications, the end user generally reserves the option not to purchase the cullet. If the material is not up to par, the end user can either charge for cleaning the material or bill for the cost of disposing of the rejected material to a landfill.

The procedure also defines when and how delivery is made to glass plants. In the early stages of a relationship, the plant may insist on an inspection of the cullet before purchase. The delivery procedure also outlines how the material is weighed and recorded. Finally, the procedure explains how the seller is paid, including the time period for payment and who pays for transportation costs.

Prices

Glass prices are more stable than most recyclable commodities because glass is not traded on the world commodity market. Aluminum, steel, and paper all fluctuate with currency rates and international demand. Glass prices, on the other hand, reflect the avoided cost of raw materials and energy savings.

LEGISLATION

Two types of laws affecting glass bottle recycling are generally passed by states. The most common is the bottle deposit law, which requires that customers pay a deposit that they get back when they return the bottles to a recycling center. Reaction to this type of bill has been mixed. The glass bottle industry opposes such bills. More productive is the second type of bill, which requires a higher content of cullet in new bottles. These so-called market development bills stimulate the recycling market by requiring bottle manufacturers to purchase cullet. California passed a bill in 1990 requiring all glass bottles to contain at least 15-percent recycled materials by 1992, and 65-percent by 2005. This will sharply stimulate glass recycling.

NEW USES FOR GLASS

Recycled glass has very few uses beyond making new glass. Researchers have used it in place of gravel as a base for new roadways, and some have used it as a component of asphalt, but neither of these applications presently consumes a significant amount of material. It is particularly important to find new applications for cullet that has not been separated before being crushed, and thus has little value for making new glass.

Some of the uses for glass other than new glass containers include use in roadbeds—"glasphalt"—and in manufacturing glass wool insulation. Owens Corning uses varying amounts of post-consumer glass in its process. Some is used in brick and terrazzo manufacturing (clay costs $2 to $6 per ton, but feldspar fluxing agent costs from $15 to $35 per ton). When glass is ground to −200 mesh, it reduces the firing temperature for brick as much as 500 degrees Fahrenheit from a normal temperature of 2,150 degrees Fahrenheit when used as 50 percent of the brick mix. The mixed cullet can be used as a filler in plastic resins (where it replaces resins costing $.30 to $.60 per pound). Mixed glass can also be used in sandblasting, where its abrasive qualities compete with sand or steel shot. Clean flint glass has a use in manufacturing glass beads or micro-spheres, which are primarily used as reflective road signs.

10

Gold and Silver

INTRODUCTION

Gold and silver have more romance than any other recyclable materials. Typical recycling programs do not ordinarily encounter either of these metals. Due to the high value of these metals, specialized recovery programs exist in locations where these commodities are used.

Due to market prices that range from $300 to $500 per troy ounce, gold recycling far exceeds the intensity of silver recycling, which achieves market prices between $5 to $10 per troy ounce. Identifying either metal is complicated by the fact that their high value provides an incentive for deception. In addition, the collection of gold and silver requires strict security measures and financial controls.

GOLD

Overview: *Apparent consumption:* 253 short tons
Amount recycled: 121 short tons
Recovery: 47.8%

Benefits: *Energy use reduction:* N/A
Air pollution reduction: N/A
Resources saved: Gold ore
Miscellaneous: Recycling gold from electronic scrap keeps other metals such as lead and solder from entering landfills.

Outlook: Because of its high intrinsic value, gold has always been recycled. The percentage of gold recovered is not expected to increase dramatically because of its current high recovery percentage.

Gold captures human emotions in a profound way. Merely mentioning the word creates a response different from all of the other recycling markets. On the global front, one of the things that most cultures seem to have in common, even as far back as ancient times, is that gold is highly valued. As a way of explaining that gold has been recycled throughout the ages, a Bureau of Mines report suggested that "a modern article of jewelry containing recycled gold could conceivably contain atoms of gold from a gold earring worn by Helen of Troy." Table 10-1 outlines the major uses of gold in the United States.

The uses of gold in jewelry and dentistry are self-evident. The industrial uses for gold are in printed circuit boards, contacts, and solder joints in applications that require chemical and metallurgical stability for the life of the electronic equipment. Military equipment and equipment used in the space program typically utilize gold in these applications. Gold also is used in the form of coins that are minted at the U.S. mint and by other countries for comparative and investment purposes, but this use has declined.

Initially, gold is mined or recovered from placer deposits in gravels and sands. Seventy-five percent of gold is recovered by 25 companies. Various commodity exchanges trade gold contracts.

TABLE 10-1. Gold Usage

Jewelry	51%
Dental	8%
Industrial uses	40%
Coinage/Investments	1%
Total	100%

Source: U.S. Bureau of Mines

Recycling Gold

Gold is recovered by gold and silver retail stores that purchase gold and silver coins, gold and silver jewelry, silverware, and even gold fillings. Laws exist for these types of buyers as well as pawn shops that require the holding of material for a period of time to aid in the detection of crimes. Due to the value of these metals, it is obvious that products made from them are targets for criminals.

Gold is also recovered from electronic scrap (see Chapter 19 "Miscellaneous Items"). Wherever products made from gold are manufactured, the scrap gold is generally returned to its supplier and credit is received against new gold that is shipped.

SILVER

Overview: *Apparent consumption:* 4,740 short tons
Amount recycled: 1870 short tons
Recovery: 39.5%

Benefits: *Energy use reduction:* N/A
Air pollution reduction: N/A
Resources saved: Silver ore
Miscellaneous: Recycling silver from negatives keeps the chemical coatings out of landfills.

Outlook: Silver is at historically low prices, and its recovery has been diminished because many applications that justified recovery at higher prices are not economically feasible. Its recycling outlook is stable.

Silver has been regarded as a store of value since its discovery. Its use as a standard in coinage can be traced back to the Roman Empire, but in modern times in the United States the escalating value of silver resulted in its removal from coins in 1965. For a period in the early 1960s the value of silver used in coinage made the coins worth more for their silver content than for their monetary worth as coins. This was resolved by the U.S. Treasury Department by first reducing the silver in coins and then later by removing silver completely.

Today the main use for silver is for photographic processing. It is used in the manufacture of film, photographic paper, photocopying paper, X-ray film, and photo-offset printing plates. Technological improvements have vastly lessened the amount of silver used in each negative. For example, new X-ray film contains twice the silver per pound of X-ray negatives used in the 1960s. Silver is also used in the manufacture of jewelry, in dentistry, silverware, silver plating, in mirrors, and in chemicals used in medicines and as catalysts for chemical processes. Table 10-2 outlines the uses for silver.

Recycling Silver

Retail stores and pawn shops purchase silver jewelry, coins, and silver ware. Film negatives are purchased by the pound and on a recovery basis to silver refiners. Silver is recovered from photographic fixer solution by small recovery units that use an electrolytic process to remove the silver and deposit it on electrodes in the form of flakes. Refiners recover the silver and purify it.

TABLE 10-2. Uses of Silver

Photography	45%
Electrical	22%
Sterlingware/jewelry	11%
Brazing alloys/solder	5%
Other	17%
Total	100%

Source: U.S. Bureau of Mines

In recycling silver, it is important to keep in mind facts such as German silver and Nickel silver contain no silver. They are an alloy containing nickel, copper, and zinc. In dealing with film negatives, the blacker the negative, the more silver it contains. Old X-ray negatives are very dark and contain only a small area where the silver compounds have been washed away. Litho-negatives used in the printing contain the next highest amount of silver. 35mm black and white negatives contain very little silver at all. Naturally, any negative that is clear, regardless of type, contains no silver.

11

Lead

Overview: *Apparent consumption:* 1,344,800 short tons
Amount recycled: 782,600 short tons
Recovery: 58.1%

Benefits: *Energy use reduction:* N/A
Air pollution reduction: N/A
Resources saved: Lead
Miscellaneous: When lead is recycled, it does not have to be dumped into a hazardous waste landfill.

Outlook: Good. For the second year in a row, the domestic secondary sector operated at 90 percent of capacity and set new production records for old scrap. As a result, reliance on lead imports dropped to the lowest level since before World War II. However, as plastics begin to replace lead as a material used for piping, lead will become a less-dominant metal.

INTRODUCTION

Lead, a very soft, bluish-white metal, has been used since the beginning of civilization. As the fifth most important metal in the world (on a tonnage basis), lead has many applications. The most important of these is use in lead-acid storage batteries that power most automobiles. Lead is also used in ammunition, pigments, as a chemical additive, and as a material in construction and plumbing. It can also serve as a noise dampener and a radiation shield for X-rays and nuclear reactors.

The physical characteristics that make lead attractive as a building material include its high malleability and its resistance to corrosion. These make it ideal for holding sulfuric acid and other liquids. Lead can also be used as an additive to gasoline to help engines run more smoothly. But because leaded gasoline adds significantly to air pollution, its use has declined steadily over the past 15 years. Since 1975, the amount of tetreathyl lead used in gasoline has gone from 250,000 metric tons per year to 30,000 metric tons in 1989.

Lead is also a metal that forms alloys easily. An alloy of lead and tin make solder, a substance that is heated to join metal surfaces to make electrical connections. Printers use an alloy of antimony, lead, and tin to mold type used for printing. Manufacturers of heavy machinery use babbit metal, a lead alloy, to reduce friction in bearings that hold moving parts. Bullets and shotgun pellets contain lead alloyed with antimony or arsenic.

It is lead's physical characteristics, however, that also limit its use. While lead itself is not poisonous, people who swallow or inhale lead compounds may become sick or even die from lead poisoning. Because the body eliminates lead very slowly, the federal government requires lead smelters and refineries to limit the amount of fumes and dust breathed by workers. If large amounts accumulate in the body, the worker is likely to become severely ill.

HOW LEAD IS MADE

Lead is mined in many areas throughout the world, chiefly in Australia, Canada, Mexico, Peru, Russia, and the United States. It is found in many different ores, the most common of which is lead sulfide, commonly called galena. To obtain pure lead, the lead ore is mined, smelted, and finally refined for purification.

Lead smelting begins by separating the lead ore from the dirt and other substances. The process is called concentration. Most smelters concentrate lead ore by a process known as flotation. Workers mix finely crushed ore with frothing agents, such as soap or oil, in a separation tank. The mixing forms bubbles that cling to the lead ore and lift it to the surface. Particles of dirt and rock remain on the bottom of the tank. Workers then skim off the concentrated ore.

Smelters roast the concentrated galena in the air to remove sulfur. The sulfur combines with oxygen in the air and escapes as sulfur dioxide gas. During the roasting process, lead in the galena changes to particles of lead oxide. Additional heat applied to the lead oxide causes it to sinter, or join into hard lumps. Workers mix the sintered lead oxide with lumps of coke and feed it into the top of a blast furnace. Inside the furnace, the burning coke reacts with the lead oxide to produce liquid lead. The metal flows from the bottom of the furnace along with slag that can be easily separated.

The crude lead that comes from the blast furnace contains many other metals. These impurities include copper, gold, and silver. To remove the copper, refiners skim off the crude lead, where most of the copper collects. Refiners also remove gold and silver.

RECYCLING LEAD

Lead is recovered from a wide range of scrap materials. Recycled lead is generated from industrial production, the automotive industry, batteries, and the demolition of buildings. Secondary lead smelting and refining plants then consume these materials, in some of the oldest recycling operations in the United States. As with most metals, lead recycling is driven by economic incentives rather than municipal solid waste issues. Presently, 58 percent of all lead consumed by U.S. industry is recycled.

Lead recycling in this country is important to manufacturers who use the metal. This is because secondary lead accounts for more than half the total domestic production. Industry specialists speculate that the recovery percentage would be even higher if government regulations pertaining to lead recycling were not so strict. As it stands, only very specialized collection operations can afford to deal in lead.

INSTITUTIONAL DETERRENTS

Collectors who handle lead face many regulatory challenges. Tough legislation regarding the recycling of spent lead-acid batteries continues to proliferate; 37 states have legislation to prevent them from reaching landfills. Six other states are contemplating the formation of state lead-acid battery laws, which would require businesses to pay more attention in handling the material.

In 1985 the EPA opted to bypass state legislation and nationally categorize automobile batteries as a hazardous waste. This means that people who collect them have to spend a lot of money to meet the EPA's requirements or must stop their collection operations altogether.

Another deterrent to lead recycling is economics. While secondary lead is probably the most promising sector of the lead industry, domestic demand for lead has been steadily declining for a number of years. This is because its use is slowly being replaced by other commodities, such as plastic, aluminum, tin, and iron.

Imports present another obstacle. Countries such as Australia and Chile could potentially ship lead to the United States and sell it for far less than a U.S. producer of primary or secondary lead.

Finally, the health hazard of handling lead must be addressed. Unless battery acid spills can be handled without risk to the environment or conflict with the EPA, many scrap dealers/processors will choose not to recycle lead.

IDENTIFYING LEAD

Lead is one of the easiest primary metals to identify because of its physical characteristics. Lead is a very dense, soft, dark gray metal. Because of its composition, lead melts at a low temperature and is very malleable. There are two types of lead commonly brought in for recycling. First is soft lead, which consists of sheet lead, water and waste pipes, power cable strippings, and caulking lead. A simple test will distinguish this type of lead: it cuts very easily with a knife and will bend back and forth many times before breaking.

Hard lead, the other type, is found in battery lugs, wheel weights, telephone cable strippings, lamp bases, and lead castings. When cut with a knife, hard lead will break off right away.

GRADES OF LEAD

Lead can be separated into many different grades, most of which are easily determined by visual means. These grades include sheet lead and pipe, lead cables, and lead batteries. Grades that are harder to distinguish often are contaminated by alloyed metals, plastics, and insulation. All of these grades are divided into soft and hard types of lead, and are separated by their contaminants.

Grades of Lead

Following are the different grades of lead:

Scrap lead, soft
Scrap lead, mixed hard/soft
Battery plates
Drained whole batteries
Battery lugs
Lead covered copper cable
Lead dross
Lead weights

The Institute of Scrap and Recycling Industries (ISRI) has a complete listing of lead specifications. Material should be graded according to the specifications from local buyers to achieve the best price.

ROLE OF THE SCRAP DEALER/PROCESSOR

Because lead is not collected in most curbside or drop-off collection programs, the role falls to the traditional scrap dealer/processor. But as the EPA and the U.S. Department of Transportation regulations for lead continue to evolve, many scrap dealers will bow out of the process as well—at least for automotive batteries. This leaves the door open for specialty collectors who are willing to tackle the economic and legislative challenges.

Dealers who opt to collect lead need to be aware of all aspects of recycling in order to run profitable operations. They should understand the grades of lead, local markets, and how the consumer will use the material. A lead collector also needs to stay abreast of changing legislative requirements. If a collector understands only part of the process, it will be difficult to adequately prepare a product for consumers or, even more critical, to stay in business.

Finding a Buyer

Most lead smelters and foundries employ a purchasing agent who is on the lookout for scrap. These buyers may wish to acquire a large tonnage of lead for delivery each month and negotiate a contract over a period of time. Contracts of this nature generally include exact specifications about weight and quality requirements, and often guarantee a price to the supplier. Some consumers may wish to purchase scrap on a future price basis related to COMEX or the London Metal Exchange market, to be priced at the consumer's option within a specific time.

If the collection center is not located near a lead smelter or foundry, regional brokers help fill the gap. Since brokers are paid on commission, they usually spend their time searching for the best markets possible, and secure for the dealer the highest return. Brokers arrange all facets of the transaction, including freight, packing, and payment terms.

Negotiating

When negotiating with a purchasing agent or broker, be sure that the quantity, packaging, and shipment period is clearly specified, and that the material quality specifications are fully described in a purchase order. Based on meeting the expectations, the buyer and the seller can strive for a long-term relationship and perhaps then negotiate for an above-average market price.

Quality

Like every other commodity in recycling, lead requires some attention to quality. Buyers and sellers must make sure that lead pipes are not filled with contaminating fluids, that batteries are drained of sulfuric acid, if required, and that contaminating alloys are separated from pure products.

Rejection

Secondary smelters and foundries reject lead if it is contaminated with materials not specified in the order. It could have mixed alloys in what was supposed to be a pure product. Another common reason for load rejection is improper packaging.

When the material arrives at the consumer's door, it should be easy to unload. If the material is loose, not packaged, some consumers ship the lead back to the processor—at the processor's cost.

TRANSPORTATION

Transporting lead, especially spent automotive batteries, factors greatly in its recovery cost. The U.S. Department of Transportation (DOT) has established a specific procedure for the packaging of this waste. This procedure hopes to eliminate hazardous waste spills between the collection site and the secondary smelter. Contact the local DOT office to obtain the latest requirements. Lead is generally shipped either by semitrailer truckload or rail. Baling of shredded material is the most common way to ship non-battery lead.

WHAT HAPPENS TO LEAD AFTER IT LEAVES THE COLLECTION CENTER

Once collected, lead is generally shipped to secondary lead smelters. These operations face the severe challenge of complying with new environmental regulations that try to protect smelter workers, the public, and the environment from the dangers of this toxic metal. Another obstacle that secondary smelters must face involves becoming an EPA-approved hazardous waste disposal facility. This entails finding funds for liability insurance, installing groundwater monitoring systems, and setting up a cleanup trust fund. To compensate for these risks, secondary lead must achieve a market price close to that of virgin material.

Most secondary lead smelters sell their material to battery manufacturing companies. In fact, more than 80 percent of the lead used to make batteries comes from this source. Secondary lead plants generally accept shipments of whole batteries from their suppliers. To prepare the lead for refining, the plants separate the batteries into plastic cases, sulfuric acid, and lead. Smelters store the plastic (polypropylene) cases, recycle them back into new cases, neutralize the sulfuric acid, and prepare the lead-bearing material for melting.

Once in the furnace, chemicals are added to help remove impurities from the lead. When the refining process is complete, about 71 percent of the lead is reclaimed. The remaining 29 percent is placed into a blast furnace for further processing. This percentage is again reduced until the waste has 3 to 5 percent of the original lead remaining. When given the toxicity test, the waste usually exceeds the EPA's standards for hazardous waste, and must be disposed of in a special facility—yet another big cost for the secondary smelter.

Despite these challenges, secondary smelters in the United States are thriving and are responsible for about 65 percent of the lead produced in the United States.

COMPLETING THE CYCLE

Most of the lead recovered in this country is converted back to automotive batteries. Table 11-1 shows the applications for the remaining amount of recovered lead. Examining the trends from 1988 to 1989 demonstrates that, while the automotive battery showed a 1-percent increase per year, other uses for lead declined. As more and more plastics are used for piping and construction purposes, the use for soft lead will continue to decrease.

TABLE 11-1. Consumption of New and Old Lead Scrap in the United States, by Type of Scrap

	Metric tons, gross weight		
Type of Scrap	New Scrap	Old Scrap	Total
1988			
Soft lead		28,721	28,721
Hard lead		6,093	6,093
Cable lead		3,668	3,668
Battery plate		819,470	819,470
Mixed babbit		1,833	1,833
Solder lead		20,425	20,425
Type metals		1,877	1,877
Drosses	60,559		60,559
Total	60,559	882,087	942,646
1989			
Soft lead		31,914	31,914
Hard lead		8,585	8,585
Cable lead		9,381	9,381
Battery plate		922,651	922,651
Mixed babbit		1,990	1,990
Solder lead		20,057	20,057
Type metals		1,725	1,725
Drosses	67,934		67,934
Total	67,934	996,303	1,064,237

Source: U.S. Bureau of Mines

12

Motor Oil

Overview: *Apparent consumption:* 1.4 billion gallons per year
Amount recycled: 800 million gallons
Recovery: 57%

Benefits: *Energy use reduction:* One gallon of used oil contains 140,000 Btus
Air pollution reduction: N/A
Resources saved: Petroleum
Miscellaneous: If used oil is recycled, it will help reduce surface and groundwater contamination.

Outlook: Mediocre. Because of the strict regulatory climate that surrounds used oil, there is not likely to be a tremendous increase in re-refining and reprocessing operations. If the EPA decides to classify waste oil as a hazardous waste, the number of collection programs will probably decrease as well.

INTRODUCTION

One of the more serious, but little-recognized environmental problem the United States faces is how to dispose of the 1.4 billion gallons of used motor oil that American cars and trucks generate each year. When consumers take their vehicles to mechanics to change their oil, the waste is most likely collected and processed through a managed system for recycling. However, only about half of America's oil is disposed of in this way. The remaining 600 million gallons is changed by individuals called "do-it-yourselfers," or DIYs, who choose to save money and do the work themselves. Most DIYs are not aware of used oil recycling programs and dispose of the waste themselves.

According to a recent EPA study, all automotive oils can be recycled safely and productively. This practice avoids environmental pollution and helps save natural resources and energy. Unfortunately, millions of gallons of oil are not recycled and are disposed of improperly. Many people who change their own oil dump the waste into sewers, which clogs up pipelines and disrupts sewage treatment plants. Worse, the waste could go directly into waterways.

Other DIYs dump their waste oil directly onto the ground to kill weeds or to suppress dust on dirt roads. This practice allows the oil to seep into groundwater sources, which lie as little as seven feet under ground. Still other DIYs toss their dirty oil into the trash. This is how millions of gallons of waste oil end up in the landfill—and potentially seep into groundwater as well. EPA estimates show that only 10 percent of DIY motor oil is properly collected and sent off for recycling.

RECYCLING

There are two major sources of used oil—passenger and truck crankcase lubricating oil, and industrial oils, such as hydraulic oil and grease. About 90 percent of this oil is potentially recyclable and can be used again as lubricating oil or for heating fuel oil in industrial furnaces (Becker, 1982). Other uses include indirect application to roads when mixed with asphalt or diesel fuel.

There are very few technical problems concerning waste oil recycling. Local reprocessors or regional re-refiners handle the process. Virgin crude oil refiners stay clear of recycling because the metallic contaminants present in waste oil can damage the refining equipment; when lubricating an engine, oil becomes very dirty. It picks up traces of lead, arsenic, cadmium, chromium, barium, and zinc.

The primary method of recycling used oil is to reprocess it into fuel oil. Most areas have at least one oil reprocessor who collects waste oil. These operations clean the oil enough for it to burn efficiently in asphalt plants or cement kilns. Reprocessed oil can also be used as a fuel additive to diesel trucks. Reprocessing oil allows it to be utilized rather than disposed, but the waste oil is not necessarily being used to its full potential.

A more efficient, but less common method of oil recycling is re-refining waste oil into lubricating oil. This process strips the oil of most of its contaminants and allows it to be resold for its original purpose. Re-refined oil is close to the same quality as virgin stocks, but, because of the expense involved in its recovery, it costs about the same. Largely for this reason, the use of re-refined oil is not widespread throughout the country.

Institutional Deterrents

Both reprocessors and re-refiners have competing legislative interests with regard to used oil collection. Re-refiners would like to see used oil classified as a hazardous waste by the EPA. They claim that the mismanagement of used oil has caused significant environmental damage and threatened human health. This argument is well supported by the fact that more than half the Superfund clean-up sites were established to correct damage from the mismangement of used oil.

Reprocessors, on the other hand, would like to see waste oil exempted from a hazardous waste classification, which would likely drive many out of business because of the costs associated with operating a hazardous waste facility. They argue that it would be cost-prohibitive to recycle oil. With the reduction of oil recycling operations, the waste would most likely be disposed of improperly.

Reprocessors were therefore pleased when in 1986 the EPA made its decision not to classify used oil as a hazardous waste, but instead to issue recycled oil management standards. The EPA determined that such a classification would discourage recycling of used oil, and "ultimately be environmentally counterproductive because used oil left unrecycled would be disposed of in manners posing greater risks than recycling." (*Federal Register,* Vol. 51, No. 233). This left the door open for reprocessing businesses and for larger scale collection than most other alternatives.

However, in September 1991, the EPA placed a notice in the *Federal Register* that requested comments on the latest data regarding whether to add used oil to the list of wastes determined to be hazardous. As of publication date, the issue remains unresolved.

REPROCESSING

There are hundreds of companies throughout the country that collect used oil for reprocessing. These tend to be local businesses that collect small quantities from quick-lube and automobile service stations, and sell an upgraded product for use as burner fuel. Oil reprocessors also collect waste from the drop-off centers where DIYs deposit oil. About 80 percent of the used oil collected from community programs is blended with virgin stock to make industrial heating fuel.

In reprocessing, waste oil is first put into a receiving tank where it is left to settle. Large contaminants such as leaves and other miscellaneous solids are separated through a screening process. The remaining mixture is filtered into a heating tank. In this tank the oil is further distilled from water and contaminants. When enough water has been extracted, the oil is processed into a centrifuge, where it is agitated again. The material is filtered a third time, which helps produce a finished fuel oil with a water content of less than 2 percent.

Advantages

Oil reprocessors provide an easy way to recover used oil because of their proximity. Transportation costs are minimal for both supplier and consumer, and, as a result, the reprocessed fuel can be sold at a price significantly lower than virgin stock. Another advantage to local reprocessors is that they often pick up low quantities of oil that do not attract large buyers. This probably saves the waste from being disposed of improperly.

Obstacles

Oil reprocessors face many risks in collecting waste oil. These include the possibilities of oil spills and fires, which cost thousands of dollars to clean up. A more common risk is collecting oil that is contaminated. Frequently, washer solvents, carburetor cleaners, and fluid from radiators are deposited in oil collection tanks. When this happens, the entire barrel becomes hazardous waste and must be disposed of at a hazardous waste dumping facility. This adds a great deal of cost to the reprocessing operation.

Another obstacle to reprocessors is that they must classify their product as either specification fuel or unspecification fuel. The first grade is acceptable for burning in most facilities. Unspecification fuel, on the other hand, is subject to many more restrictions. For example, marketers must keep the EPA aware of most of their activities, including detailed records for each shipment.

RE-REFINING

Re-refiners recycle used oil into lubricating oil for motor vehicles. This process restores used oil to its former state, and yields a high market value when oil is in short supply. Re-refineries enjoyed great success in the 1960s, when more than 150 were servicing the country's needs. Today, only ten companies re-refine waste oil in North America. Because they are spread out across the continent, transportation costs severely limit the effectiveness of large-scale recycling.

While there are many highly technical processes that have been developed for re-refining oil, this chapter will briefly discuss the acid/clay and distillation/hydrofinishing processes.

Acid/Clay

With acid/clay re-refining, the oil is first filtered and heated, to remove water. The dehydrated oil is then pumped to an acid treating unit where it is agitated with air and mixed with acid for one to two days. This process forms an acid sludge. This sludge is generally classified as hazardous waste and must be disposed of properly.

The treated oil is then transferred to a clay treatment tank where it is stripped with steam to remove light fuel fractions. The hot oil and clay are then filtered. The re-refined oil is mixed with additives, and the resulting blended oil is the lube oil product. The spent clay should be disposed of in a hazardous waste facility. Because of this added cost, most re-refiners have adapted distillation re-refining.

Distillation Re-refining

During distillation the used oil is first put through a settling system designed to eliminate free water in the used oil feedstock and to normalize contamination and temperature. Next, the oil is dehydrated by heating it to 425 degrees Fahrenheit, which vaporizes the water and fuels. The water and light-end fraction is then condensed and separated with gravity, which produces a by-product that is marketed as a low-grade fuel.

The waste oil is then heated a second time, up to 625 degrees Fahrenheit. Again, the light-end fraction is gravity separated and sold as a base blending oil. The process is repeated, with temperatures increasing at each increment. Finally, the remaining liquid is vaporized.

This lube oil is then condensed, polished, and marketed as high-quality, base blending oil. The resultant bottom fraction, containing the remaining lube oil percentage, can then be marketed directly into the asphalt industry without further processing.

One disadvantage of the distillation process is that metallic sludge remains in the bottom of the furnace. This must be disposed of in a hazardous waste landfill.

Advantages

The most clear advantage to re-refining is that it upgrades waste oil to its original use, fulfilling the objectives of pure recycling. Because the end product is relatively pure, it meets EPA specification standards for use in any application.

Obstacles

Re-refiners face many of the same risks that reprocessors do: fire, oil spills, and contamination. In addition, these operations also have problems with odor and proper disposal of the residues, wastes, and other by-products of their activities. The acid/clay mixture associated with older re-refineries, as well as the sludge that comes as a result of distillation, are both expensive to dispose of. These factors escalate the cost of doing business.

Further, because reprocessed oil must compete with virgin stock, worldwide oil price fluctuation creates yet another dimension of economic instability. When oil prices are low, re-refining may not be profitable.

DIESEL FUEL

One of the most cost-effective ways to recycle waste crankcase oil is to use it as fuel for diesel engines. This requires only minimal processing—filtering the oil to remove the large contaminants that could block fuel injectors. The oil is then mixed with virgin diesel fuel at a ratio of 9 to 1. This process reduces fuel costs and removes the problem of disposing of used oil.

Fleet operators must each determine their satisfaction with the quality of fuel derived from oil, and consult with engine suppliers for advice on its effectiveness. One potential problem with using waste oil in this manner is that it may affect the warranty on the engine. Operators should also be aware of this.

COLLECTING

Deciding to collect used oil on a community-wide basis involves a great deal of planning. The first step is to find out how much used oil the community generates. Local retail stores who sell motor oil can help by providing information on how many gallons are sold on a monthly basis. Retailers also might be able to pinpoint the months when most people purchase oil. This information can shape the early stages of what kind and what size of a program will be needed to collect the waste.

Another tactic includes finding out if there is used oil collection available in the area. The Yellow Pages should help locate which private used oil haulers are currently doing business. These companies should be consulted before designing a program. A sample survey of the neighborhood will show if haulers perform the service adequately. If so, perhaps the community's used oil collection program can piggyback on the service and help with additional publicity.

If the hauler's service is inadequate, the recycling manager should conduct a mini-survey to learn where convenient points for collecting used oil should be added. The community could install oil barrels and drums at clearly marked drop-off locations at relatively low cost.

One final alternative is linking the used oil collection to a community-supported hazardous waste or recycling program.

Curbside

Used oil can be collected at the curb with regular trash pick up service or with other recyclables. The used oil program must work with collectors so they can integrate used oil into their operations. Trash collection trucks or vehicles designed for collecting recyclables can be retrofitted with a used oil collection tank or rack for storing containers of used oil. The used oil will need to be transferred from the truck to a holding tank until it is picked up by a used oil hauler.

Educational materials about used oil recycling must accompany curbside programs. If residents place other liquid contaminants out for collection, the entire load runs the risk of being labeled "hazardous waste."

Special Collection

Periodic special curbside collections of used oil are an economical alternative to routine curbside collection. In a Market Facts survey, 70 percent of all respondents said they would always save their oil if it were picked up at home. Periodic collection requires a lot of publicity and coordination with sanitation departments or trash/recyclable collectors, unless the program can arrange alternative trucks and personnel to make the pickups. Oil collected at the curb is generally transferred to a centrally located tank until pickup.

The best time for special curbside collection for DIYs is during the peak oil change seasons—late fall and early spring. A program combining special collections during the oil change seasons with central collection points might be convenient for DIYs as regular curbside collection in selected neighborhoods. At the same time, the program might do a mini-survey to define homeowner's preferences for used oil collection.

Drop-off Program

A permanent central drop-off center is another option for collecting used oil. This center should be well marked to ensure that it is used for uncontaminated lubricating oil only. The barrel or tank should be regularly serviced by a hauler to make sure that there is always room to receive more oil. It should also be periodically checked for leakage.

One drawback to unsupervised drop-off centers is that the end product is often contaminated. Citizens not properly educated about the collection program will often place spent antifreeze and other hazardous wastes into the barrel, thus rendering the oil unsuitable for use.

Some operations, such as auto garages, by their nature have used oil on the premises. Some states encourage these sites to be used for depositing waste oil through legislation.

ROLE OF THE OIL COLLECTOR

Used oil, whether obtained from a central collection program or at the curb, must be picked up expediently by authorized used oil haulers and sent to recyclers. Haulers and collectors can be found easily in the Yellow Pages, under "Used Oil," "Recycling," or "Petroleum."

It is important for a community program to make sure haulers have a valid license from the EPA and operate in an environmentally responsible manner. The operation should look neat and clean, with no evidence of spills. The hauler should also be able to document where oil is coming from and going to, and have reports that indicate whether the oil it is receiving is acceptable for processing. Haulers should also provide evidence of having an insurance policy to cover the cost of oil spills and fires.

For the community, the program manager should maintain regular records of quantities collected, delivered, and handled. The manager should also make sure the used oil is delivered to a proper management facility.

ENVIRONMENTAL RISKS FOR THE COLLECTOR/GENERATOR

Under the current Resource Conservation Recovery Act (RCRA), which governs used oil collections, there are substantial environmental risks for both collectors and generators of used oil. More than half of the EPA Superfund clean-up sites are used oil recycling operations. Most of these facilities allowed waste oil containing polychlorinated biphenyls (PCBs) to seep into the ground to potentially contaminant groundwater. Other common citations relate to the risk of fire.

The Comprehensive Environmental Response, Compensation and Liability Act (CERCLA) of 1980 states that all generators are partially responsible for sites that have been contaminated with hazardous substances. Under CERCLA's strict liability standard, exercising due care in arranging for disposal or ensuring that the disposal facility complies with all applicable environmental and safety requirements are not defendable arguments (National Oil Recyclers Association, 1989) The only three exceptions are if the contamination was caused solely by an act of war, an act of God, or an act of a third party who is not involved in a contractual relationship with the defendant.

For this reason alone, it is absolutely essential for generators—such as communities—to make sure that the oil hauler or recycler is taking proper care to reprocess or re-refine the material properly.

FINDING MARKETS

Markets for used oil are directly linked to virgin oil prices. If there is an oversupply of oil in the nation, oil reprocessors and re-refiners will probably charge for picking up the material. Because there are very few remaining disposal options, most auto repair shops and quick-lube stations feel it is worth the price. When oil is in seemingly short supply—as it was during the Persian Gulf War—these operations may pay 20 to 30 cents for a gallon of oil. Obviously, this makes oil collection a profitable disposal alternative.

COMPLETING THE CYCLE

Once used oil is reprocessed or re-refined, it can be used in many applications, including fuel for asphalt plants, cement kilns, and other utilities. It can also be used again as lubricating oil for motor vehicles and machinery.

Despite liability risks connected to it, investing in a used oil recycling program makes sense. The potential benefits of preventing oil from seeping into groundwater are worth working toward. The risks associated with oil spills and fires can be controlled by haulers who keep their operation within federally approved oil management standards.

13

Paper

Overview: *Apparent consumption:* 86,756,500 short tons
Amount recycled: 28,926,900 short tons
Recovery: 33.3%

Benefits: *Energy use reduction:* 24–54%, 3,000–12,000 Btus/lb.
printing paper: 33%
newsprint: 34%
tissue: 54%
OCC: 24%
Air pollution reduction: 74% less
Water Pollution: 35% less
Resources saved: 7,000 gallons of water per ton
Miscellaneous: Each ton of paper recycled may save 17 small trees.

Outlook: Paper recycling will undoubtedly increase because significant new production capacity is committed to recycling. Paper makes up 40 percent of municipal solid waste, the number one component by far. As a result, the paper industry will be under intense pressure. Consumer response to recycled paper products will be a significant factor in how the paper industry responds.

INTRODUCTION

Paper is the most abundant commodity in the waste stream. More than 71 million tons or 40 percent of waste is paper. Even yard refuse, which is the next most abundant component of solid waste, tallies a distant second at 31.6 tons or 18 percent of total waste. Paper's prominence in the waste stream is what gives it top billing as a recycling priority.

Americans use large quantities of paper, both in the workplace and at home. Newspaper, computer paper, white ledger, and colored paper are just a few of the

7,000 kinds of paper abundant in daily life. U.S. residents consume approximately 700 pounds of paper per person each year. This compares to 127 pounds per capita for Europe.

Currently two-thirds of new paper and paper products manufactured in the United States are made from trees and one-third is made from recycled paper, known as secondary fiber. Experts faced with solving the nation's solid waste problem hope the scales will tip in favor of using vastly more recycled paper so that less paper clogs the nation's landfills. From existing paper industry expansion plans it is clear that paper recycling will grow substantially to a 40-percent recovery rate by 1995. But sadly this will hardly make a dent in the solid waste problem.

HOW PAPER IS MADE

The paper industry derives its raw materials from two sources—trees and waste paper. Paper made from trees is composed of virgin fiber. Paper made from waste paper is composed of secondary fiber. Some paper is made from blending virgin and secondary fibers.

Virgin fibers are cellulose fibers from trees that are extracted by a pulping process and then matted and bound together. Lignin is a chemical substance that binds together the fibers found in trees and other types of woody plants. The pulping process separates the cellulose fiber from the lignin.

The paper industry uses various types of pulping processes. Mechanical pulping forces wood chips or entire logs against rapidly revolving grindstones. Mechanically processed virgin fibers are generally called groundwood pulp. This process is destructive to the length and strength of the fiber, and most lignin remains with the cellulose fibers. Consequently, the paper that is produced from the groundwood pulp has little strength and does not maintain brightness over time. Newspaper and phonebooks are examples of papers with high groundwood content. Mass-produced magazines are also made from groundwood pulp, but a clay coating is added to make the paper glossy and to improve its printability.

Several chemical pulping processes exist as well. These include kraft, sulphate, and alkaline processes. To briefly take one example, an alkaline cooking solution is combined with wood chips at high temperatures and high pressures in a closed digester. After the cooking is completed, the digester charge (steam) is blown through a pipe into a separator, allowing the steam to dissipate and the fiber to be cleaned. The fibers may be further cleaned and bleached to attain whiteness. Thereafter, a paper machine cleans the fibers. The machine is made up of dozens of synchronized components operating in a continuous flow. The components process the fibers together, and then press, dry, and finish the paper.

The completed roll of paper may weigh three tons and usually will be sent to a paper convertor where products familiar to consumers are made. Paper products, such as boxes, tissues, paper bags, and office supplies, are often produced from this type of fiber. It is generally not possible to differentiate paper made from virgin fiber and secondary fiber by a simple physical inspection.

PAPER RECYCLING

Recycled waste paper comprises the remaining 33 percent of the paper consumed in the United States. The secondary fiber industry recognizes approximately 50 different grades of waste paper that may be used either individually, blended with other grades, or blended with virgin fibers to make new paper. The Paper Stock Institute, a division of the Institute of Scrap Recycling Industries (ISRI), develops these standards, and reviews and updates them when required—usually on an annual basis. Different grades of waste paper make different grades of new paper. For example, waste newspaper may make new newspaper; corrugated boxes may make new boxes; mixed paper may make roofing shingles, tar paper, or the facing on gypsum board; and computer printouts may make tissue products or paper towels.

After scrap paper is collected from various sources such as supermarkets, curbside recycling programs, printers, data processing installations, and large industrial firms, it is sorted and cleaned. A knowledgeable scrap dealer/processor sorts and grades these recyclable papers, mindful that some grades are more valuable than others and that the requirements are different for each end user. The paper is then baled into blocks weighing more than 1,000 pounds each. Since freight is an important economic consideration for the paper mill, significant effort is made to reach the greatest legal weight in each shipping container.

Once the scrap materials arrive at the paper mill, they are unloaded and inspected. Ultimately, a paper mill is responsible to its customers for shipping a high-quality product. One of the best ways for a paper mill to achieve its high-quality goals is to start with the correct quality of incoming materials. Paper that fails to meet the standard is "downgraded" or "rejected," while paper of the proper quality is either inventoried for use at a later time or conveyered to a hydrapulper.

A hydrapulper resembles a giant blender. The hydrapulper is approximately 12 feet across and is full of hot water and chemicals moving like a giant whirlpool. When a bale of paper is thrown into this environment, it is reduced to a slurry within minutes. Similar to a spitball, the paper loses its form and becomes a mass of fibers.

The next step in making paper is to pipe this slurry, which is close to 200 parts water to 1 part fiber, onto a conveyer, that in reality is a very fine screen. In effect, this screen is 8 feet wide and runs at 60 miles per hour through a papermaking machine as long as a city block.

The slurry is piped onto the screen and the fibers are trapped on top of it. The water immediately begins flowing through the screen, and then rollers squeeze additional water from the fiber. The water that flows through the screen carries with it fillers, clay coatings, and fines. Fines are paper fibers too small to be carried by the screen mesh. This is a major cause of shrinkage. It takes more than one ton of waste paper to make a ton of finished product.

The next step is for the wire conveyer to "ribbon" itself over and under a section of the papermaking machine that has a number of steam dryers. Finally, when the paper is dry, it will leave the conveyer belt to be wound onto a roll, which when completed will weigh about three tons. The conveyer belt continues the trip over and over. Because this is a continuous process that happens at blinding speed, some allowances must be made for this oversimplified explanation.

In the actual process, contaminants, including some inks, are removed, bleach is frequently added, and tolerances of thickness must be maintained. The amount of electronic controls and lights on a papermaking machine looks like it would belong to nuclear power plant instead of a papermaking machine. There's no doubt that a modern paper mill is a machinery-intensive, quality-oriented, high-production environment that has more than its share of humidity and relatively few people. The paper mill operates in a highly competitive business climate and to be successful must deliver a high-quality product.

The secondary fiber mill, despite that its raw material is practically by definition imperfect, must produce a final paper product that can compete in the marketplace with paper made from virgin fiber. It takes hands-on training and skill to create the quality required from recyclable paper.

PAPER RECYCLING CONSTRAINTS

A number of factors influence the potential growth for paper recycling. One constraint is the ability to recover *usable* waste paper. Usable waste paper implies that what is recovered must meet the quality and quantity standards that exist for those companies who manufacture waste paper into end products. For example, wet newspaper and newspaper that has been bleached by the sun have fiber that is weak and brittle. If newspaper of poor quality was used to make new newspaper, the latter would also have weak and brittle fiber and might break in the high-speed web presses used to print the daily paper.

A second constraint for paper recycling growth relates to the cost of recovering usable waste paper. As recovery programs progress from superficial recycling to efficient, no-waste recycling, the cost of recovery grows exponentially. For example, a drop-off location for newspaper will result in some recovery, but a pickup service would generate more volume. Yet costs rise dramatically for the incremental volume generated by the pickup service, even though the price that will be paid for the collected newspaper has nothing to do with the cost of collection. Supply and demand influences price. There are many programs that cost $200 per ton to collect paper and can only sell it for $10 per ton.

A third economic factor that constrains the further development of paper recycling is geography. Primarily distance, but also modes of transportation, affect the cost of delivering a commodity to the location of end users. An individual paper mill will use only specific grades of waste paper, but at the same time it is concerned with obtaining quality fiber at the lowest delivered cost. This fact puts an outer limit on how far a mill can transport material to supply its needs. For instance, if freight where a mill is located costs $10 per ton and all of its needs can be met by the local supply, the mill will be reluctant to use more distant sources where the freight cost might rise to $20 or even $50 per ton. It is rational to expect mills to satisfy their needs for material using the minimum freight cost. This is why recycling mills are generally located in large population centers. Sometimes, metropolitan areas are called the "urban forest." Pulp mills are located near forests.

The exception to distance as a guideline for freight costs is when the mode of transportation available is very inexpensive per ton. This is certainly true for costal locations, which have easy access to ports for water transportation. The United States is the largest exporter in the world of fiber to other countries.

A fourth constraint to growth of paper recycling is quality. Magazines and newspapers, large consumers of paper, are influenced primarily by advertisers. These advertisers want their ads to look good and to be as appealing as possible. This usually means that the paper should be very glossy and very bright. Often, recycled papers, because their quality is lower, do not produce the high-quality images that advertisers want. This limits, to some degree, what publishers are willing to do in terms of using recycled paper.

In completing any specific analysis of the potential to recover waste paper, the focus must be on individual grades of paper. Each grade has a specific commodity value. A grade that has delivered value of $20 per ton has a different potential than one selling for $50 or $200 per ton. It's obvious that the cost of freight has a bigger impact in measuring how far the low-value material can be transported. Demand for each grade varies, and the true potential to recycle varies for each grade, based on quality, quantity, the cost of recovery, and transportation costs.

Historically, the trend of paper recycling also reflects another critical variable—attitude. Table 13-1 shows the recycling rate from 1944 to the present.

During this 50-year period, attitudes of consumers have greatly influenced the recycling rate. In 1944, during World War II, curbside recycling and conservation programs for the war effort produced the highest recycling rates this country has seen—until very recently. After the war, it appears that U.S. citizens went back to throwing it all away.

Conservation of natural resources rested on the back burner for 40 years, until

TABLE 13-1. **Paper Recycling Rate**

Year	API Recycling Rate	Census Bureau Recycling Rate
1944	N/A	35.3
1945	N/A	34.6
1946	N/A	32.3
1947	N/A	32.4
1948	N/A	29.1
1949	N/A	26.7
1950	N/A	27.4
1951	N/A	29.7
1952	N/A	27.2
1953	N/A	27.2
1954	N/A	25.0
1955	N/A	26.0
1956	N/A	24.2
1957	N/A	24.1
1958	N/A	24.7
1959	N/A	24.3
1960	N/A	23.1
1961	N/A	22.4
1962	N/A	21.5
1963	N/A	22.0
1964	N/A	21.2
1965	N/A	20.8
1966	N/A	20.1
1967	N/A	19.0
1968	N/A	18.4
1969	N/A	18.6
1970	22.4	18.3
1971	22.5	18.5
1972	22.1	18.2
1973	23.4	18.4
1974	24.8	N/A
1975	24.2	N/A
1976	24.9	N/A
1977	25.4	N/A
1978	24.8	N/A
1979	25.7	N/A
1980	26.7	N/A
1981	26.1	N/A
1982	26.4	N/A
1983	26.3	N/A
1984	26.7	N/A
1985	26.8	N/A
1986	28.2	N/A
1987	28.8	N/A
1988	30.6	N/A
1989	31.8	N/A
1990	33.3	N/A

Source: 1990 Annual Statistical Summary Waste Paper Utilization, API June 1991, and U.S. Bureau of Census.

two conditions arose in the 1990s: landfills were filling up, and new landfills were becoming increasingly difficult to site. The grass roots strength of the Environmental Movement of the 1980s and its caring approach to "spaceship earth" combined with the practical themes of landfill issues, and the United States once again has a socially motivated agenda for recycling.

If historical data teaches anything, it is that paper recycling rates cannot be taken for granted. This is because the forces that promote recycling are fragmented and the basic resource-oriented industries are more concentrated and focused. While recycling did not exist as a word in 1944, the recycling habit was lost because recycling was not supported by tax policies, legislation, educational programs, and mass media efforts, including advertising. Interest in recycling waned with time, and it can happen again. One need only remember the 1970s when lines at gas stations were thought to create an unstoppable trend toward energy conservation to realize that it will take more than a landfill crisis to create an unstoppable trend toward more recycling.

THE CATEGORIES OF RECYCLED PAPER

There are four broad categories of waste paper. Three of these categories are often called low-grade paper. These include newspaper, corrugated, and mixed paper. The fourth category is called high-grade paper. High-grade paper is often broken into two subcategories called pulp substitute grades and deinking grades.

Newspaper is a groundwood paper used in mass publications. Newspapers main use as a recycled product is to be made back into unprinted newsblank. The ink is floated off and the fiber is bleached at the papermill so that it can be sold to a local newspaper company again for a new edition. Old newspaper is also used for boxboard, chip board, the backing for note pads, cellulose insulation, and animal bedding.

Corrugated paper is often referred to as cardboard. Made with a fluted medium that is sandwiched between two layers of brown kraft paper, corrugated boxes are used for shipping almost every conceivable product. Industry experts believe that charting the volume of corrugated boxes sold is a good measure of economic activity. There is approximately 500 pounds of corrugated paper associated with a sale of a single automobile and more than 1,800 pounds associated with the building of an average house. Frequently, people refer to boxes that food such as cereal is packaged in as cardboard, but this is incorrect. This material is properly called boxboard or chipboard, not cardboard or corrugated paper. Sometimes, corrugated paper is referred to as OCC, or "old corrugated containers."

Mixed paper includes almost any paper imaginable and is the lowest grade of paper. Mixed paper may contain newspaper, corrugated paper, high-grade paper, boxboard, and other varieties. There are not too many products that can be made from mixed paper, especially in relationship to the potential supply. Some mixed paper is made into boxboard products, the facing on gypsum board, and the medium for a corrugated box.

High-grade paper is sub-divided into two groups: pulp substitute grades and deinking grades. Paper is categorized as a pulp substitute if it is of such brightness and fiber strength that it can be used as a substitute for wood pulp. Unprinted paper used in making white envelopes is one of the specialty grades belonging to this subcategory. Deinking grades usually have printing inks or other coatings, and the ink must be removed or bleached to get the brightness desired by a paper mill. These types of scrap papers make items such as tissue products and writing paper.

IDENTIFYING WASTE PAPER

For the recycler, learning to identify different grades of paper is a major accomplishment. Nearly everyone unfamiliar with the process is surprised that there is more than one type of paper, but only through learning the subtle and not so subtle differences can successful recycling take place. Unfortunately, the process of identifying and labeling paper is not simple. There are five major observations in identifying paper:

1. Visual characteristics
2. Groundwood quality
3. Bleachability
4. Water solvability
5. Chemical makeup

VISUAL IDENTIFICATION

Visual identification is a reasonably accurate method for determining if paper belongs in one of the major classifications:

Corrugated containers—Corrugated containers are commonly called cardboard—specifically, a box made from brown kraft linerboard with a wavy medium and then sandwiched and glued between two layers of linerboard to make a rigid box.

Newspaper—A cheap thin paper made from groundwood pulp, used in the publication of daily and weekly publications.

Mixed paper—A conglomeration of papers mixed together, including cardboard, magazines, newspapers, and high-grade papers.

High-grade paper—Usually white writing papers, computer printouts, forms, printed materials, and publications other than magazines and newspapers. There are two subcategories—deinking grades and pulp substitutes. Deinking grades require the removal and/or bleaching of inks to acquire brightness, and pulp substitutes are extremely clean and bright and are appropriate as a substitute for pulp.

IDENTIFYING GROUNDWOOD GRADES

It is important to distinguish between groundwood paper, which contains lignin, and higher-grade papers (sulphate or sulphite), which do not contain lignin. To some degree this can be done visually, but a chemical test using phloroglucinol is far more accurate.

After applying one drop of phloroglucinol, groundwood papers turn a deep purple. When papers are coated it may take as long as a minute for the chemical to show a result, but if the paper is ripped and the chemical is applied to the ripped end, time can be saved by examining the exposed fibers.

Some paper is a blend of groundwood papers and other papers. When exposed to phloroglucinol, this paper may turn only light purple and may take as long as two minutes to change color. This paper should be sorted into the groundwood paper group.

Caution: Consumers must use care with phloroglucinol acid to avoid contact with eyes, skin, and clothing. Another chemical product, anniline sulphate, will also detect lignin, but in the presence of lignin will turn yellow.

DETERMINING BLEACHABILITY

Another basic characteristic of paper is bleachability. The ability of paper to be treated chemically to improve its whiteness (brightness) is critical in making end products such as tissue paper and fine writing paper. Most unbleachable paper can be identified visually. Extremely bright colors such as fluorescent orange or green, and extremely dense black colors will not bleach. Deep or bright red, green, and blue papers are also unbleachable because often their color dye is added to the fiber before the fiber is made into paper (beater dyed). If the paper is ripped and the color does not appear throughout, the paper may be bleachable. But if the blue, green, or red color penetrates all fibers, the paper is probably not bleachable.

Gold- and silver-colored paper is also not bleachable. The glittery, metallic particles used in producing these colors do not bleach. Likewise, goldenrod papers and brown kraft papers are unbleachable. Carbon paper is not bleachable because the wax and particles will not lighten, and heavily inked papers, such as newspapers, are often questionable in terms of bleachability.

If in doubt, a chemical test using household bleach will help determine if paper is bleachable. Simply put a strip of paper into Clorox bleach, available at a supermarket, and after an hour there should be significant amount of whitening if the fibers are bleachable.

WATER SOLVABILITY

Most papermaking processes involve disintegrating paper into fibers in hot water. Certain factors impede this process, and it is important to know these factors because they affect the uses of paper. These factors include:

Coatings—Clay coatings are water solvable. Lacquer, plastic, chromecoat, and vinyl are not water solvable. New coatings are continuously developed and must be scrutinized.
Glue—Some glue is water solvable, but glues such as the hot melt glues used by most binderies are not water solvable.
Wax—Wax is clearly not water solvable, and it is used in making certain boxes to give them the ability to remain strong in a moist atmosphere.
Laminated plastics—Paper and plastic can be laminated together to make products such as sturdy envelopes or even computer printouts.
Wet strength—Wet strength can be added chemically to corrugated paper, such as in boxes for the meat packing industry and in papers used to produce maps that will hold up under heavy use. Wet strength is easy to test. Simply put a sample in hot water for a few minutes and then rub the paper between two fingers. If it dissolves easily, wet strength has not been added.

There is also a chemical test for wet strength papers. To test for wet strength, put two drops of Solution Number 1 on the paper to be tested, followed by two drops of Solution Number 2. If the mixture turns pink, wet strength is present.

CHEMICALLY TREATED PAPERS

These papers are identifiable because they are designed for special purposes:

1. NCR (no carbon required) transfers writing from one page to another based on pressure and is widely used in forms.
2. Brownstain is a specialized paper used on checks to detect forgery. If the forger uses bleach to eradicate numbers or words written in ink, the paper will turn brown. At the paper mill, bleach is added to improve the brightness, but, on brownstain, instead of getting brighter, the paper may turn darker.
3. Blueprint papers are a method of chemical reproduction used mostly by engineers and designers.
4. Ozalid paper is another chemical reproduction process using photosensitive paper.
5. Copy paper can sometimes be chemically treated, and it usually has a distinctive feel and sheen.
6. Fax paper and EKG paper are usually chemically treated.

Categorizing paper by specific grade needs to be done by touching, feeling, seeing, and sometimes chewing and tasting. Tasting paper is not as unusual as it first sounds, but it takes considerable experience to understand that this approach can help identify paper when other distinctions are hard to discern.

Fitting each grade into broad categories can help expedite the process. One area where distinctions are becoming increasingly important is with pre-consumer grades and post-consumer grades. A pre-consumer grade often carries a premium price because it has less contamination, but some people do not consider this "true" recycling. As a result, some products specify the amount of post-consumer products used.

BROWN AND KRAFT PAPER GRADES

These papers are recognizable by their brown color and coarsely grained appearance. The different types of brown and kraft paper grades are as follows:

Corrugated containers—Post-consumer. Consists of cardboard boxes often called OCC for old corrugated containers. These are brown boxes with a squiggly waffle in the middle. The center material is called the medium. The outside walls are generally made from kraft liner board.

Corrugated containers are usually found in large volumes at retail stores that receive goods in cardboard boxes and at manufacturing firms that receive raw material in cardboard boxes. One major problem with cardboard boxes is their very low density. Unbroken cardboard boxes take up space and weigh as little as 50 pounds per yard, making them expensive to transport. Breaking down boxes and laying them flat takes considerable time, but makes it possible to dramatically improve the density. Balers and compactors can improve the density of cardboard up to 1,000 pounds per cubic yard, thus improving the efficiency of transporting them. Some tape is unavoidable in this grade, but Styrofoam and the molded purple fruit containers create problems for many paper mills.

Boxes are also made from chipboard—the type of material used to make most cereal boxes and the backing material on a notepad of paper. This material is not categorized as corrugated. Another problem with cardboard boxes occurs when rice paper is encountered. Rice paper is typically associated with imported goods. The fiber is not as strong, and many paper mills that use OCC have a low tolerance for this material.

New double-lined kraft—Pre-consumer. Consists of corrugated cuttings made with unbleached kraft linerboard. The material is generated by convertors who make corrugated boxes. The medium section must be laminated with a water soluble glue. Nonsoluble adhesives, butt rolls, tape, and dark medium are not acceptable in this grade.

Used brown kraft—Post-consumer. Consists of brown kraft bags free of objectionable liners or contents.

New kraft—Pre-consumer. Consists of new bags or kraft cuttings free of sewed and stitched paper.

Carrier stock—Pre-consumer. Consists of new kraft cuttings and sheets that are wet strength treated. Six-pack carriers for beer and soft drinks are typically made of this material. However, when carrier/board is heavily printed or is printed in gold, silver, or black, it should be sampled to prospective end users.

Mill wrappers—Post-consumer. Consists of wrappers for rolls, bundles, or skids of finished paper.

Boxes sold for reuse—Pre- or post-consumer. Consists of boxes that can be sold for reuse. Normally, these boxes are new, but they can be used again if they are in good condition. The boxes must be available in large quantities and be of uniform size. One size that sells consistently is the size for storing books, especially for people who are moving their belongings. Another size that sells in most markets is "gaylord boxes." These boxes have very thick walls, are approximately the size of a 4-foot × 4-foot wood pallet, and are 32 inches high.

Bags sold for reuse—Pre-consumer. Consists of bags with and without liners. These bags must be available in large quantities and have a uniform size. Plastic bags are also marketable.

Other brown kraft grades—Pre-consumer. Boxboard cuttings (polycoated, waxed, foil), mixed kraft cuttings, new colored kraft, grocery bag waste, kraft multi-wall bag waste, corrugated cuttings (wet strength, asphalt laminated, and waxed), beer carton waste, and brown wet strength waste are some of the more specialized grades.

COMPUTER PRINTOUT GRADES

These grades are designed to operate in printers that are connected to computers and word processing machines. The different types of computer printout grades are as follows:

Computer printout (laser free)—Post-consumer. Composed of sulphite or sulphate paper (bond or offset quality paper) for use in data processing equipment, with pastel green bars, blue bars, or pink bars on the paper. Printing can be done with an impact printer. Sometimes this is referred to as "bond" quality printout. It is free of groundwood papers and cannot include any carbon paper or NCR paper.

Computer printout (laser)—Post-consumer. Can be similar to the above pastel bar type paper or may consist of 8½ × 11-inch white paper; however, the printer must be a laser printer. To test for laser printing, use a drop of tolulene. It causes laser printing to smear, but has no effect on impact printing.

White manifold ledger—Pre-consumer. Consists of white, continuous forms used in data processing machines that are unprinted, like the forms used for word processing and high-speed printers. Also printed as custom forms for invoices, purchase orders, statements, and so on.

Colored manifold ledger—Pre-consumer. Same as white manifold ledger, only printed on colored paper or with colored inks. This grade may require bleaching at the mill, and, as a result, the colors require a grade different than white.

Groundwood computer printout—Post-consumer. Consists of any green bar, blue bar, or pink bar computer printout that reveals the presence of lignin when tested with phloroglucinol. Material that is a blend of materials falls into this category. The paper is like newsprint. Sometimes people erroneously refer to this as "recycled" printout, in an effort to explain the difference between this and "bond" quality printout.

Unprinted computer printout—Pre-consumer. Produced only by forms manufacturers that produce bond quality computer printout. Since there is no printing, the grade often sells for a premium over laser-free computer printout.

ENVELOPE GRADES

Envelope manufacturing companies almost exclusively produce these grades. On rare occasions, a large company may change stationery and produce a large volume on a one-time basis. The different types of envelope grades are as follows:

Hard white envelope cuttings—Pre-consumer. Consists of new white envelope cuttings and sheets of untreated papers completely free of printing and groundwood. This is a premium pulp substitute grade.

Manila envelope cuttings—Pre-consumer. Consists of new manila-(cream) colored envelope cuttings and sheets of untreated papers completely free of printing and groundwood.

Brown kraft envelope cuttings—Pre-consumer. Consists of new kraft envelope cuttings and sheets of untreated papers completely free of printing and groundwood.

Colored envelope cuttings—Pre-consumer. Consists of new bleachable colored envelope cuttings and sheets of untreated paper completely free of printing and groundwood.

Plastic window envelopes—Pre- and post-consumer. Consists of new envelopes with plastic windows of normal size. These must be free of groundwood and kraft paper. They can be colored or white. Some end users will accept post-consumer quantities, but without pressure sensitive labels.

MIXED PAPER GRADES

The type of mixed paper grade is as follows:

Mixed paper—Post-consumer. Consists of a mixture of various qualities of paper containing less then 10-percent groundwood. Mixed paper is very plentiful and has a very low economic value and a limited market. The backs of notepads, chipboard boxes, and the facing on gypsum wall/board are a few of the major sources of mixed paper.

GROUNDWOOD GRADES

These grades are found mostly in high-volume publications that have a shelf life of one year or less. Newspapers, phonebooks, most magazines, and paperback books are made from groundwood papers. All groundwood papers turn purple when exposed to phloroglucinol. The different types of groundwood grades are as follows:

Deinking news—Post-consumer. Consists of newspaper that is fresh, dry, clean, and free from wet, or sun-bleached newspaper, with only normal percentage of rotogravure sections. Paper bags, plastic bags, or magazines cannot be mixed in.

Number 1 news—Post-consumer. Similar to deinking news, except that quality standards are lower. This means that some old newspaper or sun-bleached newspaper, grocery sacks or other papers may be included.

Over-issue news—Pre-consumer. Overruns or paper that is not sold in publishing. The grade can sell at a premium price because the paper is free from all contamination.

Magazines—Post-consumer. Consists of a groundwood-type paper sometimes found in small quantities in mixed paper and sold as a separate grade to some paper mills. These mills usually are interested in the clay coating because it helps in the flotation of inks that need to be separated from fiber, such as in newsprint.

Telephone books—Post-consumer. Consists of a groundwood paper, which like mixed paper is available in large quantities. Usually, the availability is seasonal in any given locale due to the distribution of new phonebooks. There are limited markets.

Mixed groundwood shavings—Pre-consumer. Trim of magazines, catalogs, and other coated groundwood papers. This may include *coated and uncoated groundwood paper* and small amounts of other paper grades from the cover and from inserts. This is a grade found in the printing industry.

Flyleaf shavings—Pre-consumer. Consists of trim of uncoated groundwood paper free from glue, coated groundwood paper, and other paper grades. This is a grade found in the printing industry.

White news blank—Pre-consumer. Consists of *unprinted* cuttings and sheets of white newsprint paper (uncoated groundwood) or other papers of groundwood quality, free of coated stock. Newspapers, printer shops, and other places in the printing industry contain white news blank.

Publication blank—Pre-consumer. Consists of *unprinted* sheets of white *coated groundwood* paper. This is a grade found in the printing industry.

Coated groundwood sections—Pre-consumer. Consists of new printed or unprinted coated groundwood papers in sheets or trim (shavings). Free of insoluble glues. Another grade found in the printing industry.

COMMON OFFICE GRADES

Other than computer printout grades, most offices carry at least some of the following paper grades:

White ledger—Post-consumer. Consists of copy paper, typing paper, and other printed and unprinted white sulphate or sulphite papers. This also includes bond paper, uncoated copy paper, or offset style paper. White ledger must be free of coatings, and the printing must be black or, if inks are colored, it must have very little printing and be free of non-water soluble glue and pressure-sensitive adhesives.

Colored ledger—Post-consumer. Consists of white or colored sulphate or sulphite papers with colored inks. Typically, accounting forms, business forms, and many of the papers found in files and records are colored ledger.

One way to determine the difference between colored ledger and white ledger is to put the sample into a blender. If the resulting slurry is colored, the type of ledger is colored and the paper will likely require more bleaching at a paper mill. It must be free of coated stock and pressure-sensitive adhesives.

Files and records, file stock—Post-consumer. Comparable to a poor grade of colored ledger. The name implies that it consists of any group of files and records—definitely not a correct assumption. The files must be bleachable, which means that bright colored, brown kraft, and red rope file folders and carbon paper do not qualify. Also, the grade can contain only a very small amount of non-water soluble glues, which eliminates most files with self-adhesive labels. Also, chemically treated papers must exist only in trace amounts. This eliminates files that contain photographs, fax paper, and EKG paper. Marketing this grade successfully requires a clear meeting of the minds between buyer and seller with regard to what can and cannot be included.

Obsolete forms—Pre-consumer. Includes modified forms, overprinted catalogs, financial reports, direct mail literature, or advertising literature. This is usually a good source of recyclable paper, but the specific grade depends on the paper and printing.

Tab cards—Post-consumer. Consists of computer cards that are uncoated and made from card stock to store information by punching out holes with key punch machines. They can be colored or manila.

COATED GRADES

Coated grades that have groundwood paper fibers are listed under groundwood. If phloroglucinol does not change color but the material is clearly coated, the grades can probably be found among the following:

Coated book (coated sulphite)—Pre- or post-consumer. These are sulphate and sulphite papers that are coated with water soluble coatings. The paper may be unprinted or printed, but is usually heavily printed. This grade is normally encountered in the printing industry or in companies in the form of surplus advertising literature or obsolete annual reports.

IGS-coated (insoluble glue sulphite–coated)—Pre- or post-consumer. Otherwise categorized as coated book, except that a non-water soluble glue is found in binding the paper to make a book or booklet.

Soft white—Pre- or post-consumer. Consists of white, coated sulphite paper free of any printing. No groundwood papers are acceptable.

Label stock—Pre- or post-consumer. Consists of sulphite paper with coating on one side. It may be printed. Contains only water soluble glue.

Greeting card stock—Pre-consumer. Made from a "lighter-than-board" material and used for greeting cards. It is free from foil, high gloss finishes, heavy printing, and non-water soluble glue.

COMMON GRADES FROM BOXMAKERS

Boxes are usually made in local markets by convertors. These convertors take rolls of paper and make items such as corrugated boxes from linerboard and medium (the fluted middle section of a cardboard box). Convertors also make boxes for manufacturers and other packagers, or boxes for gifts. The different types of common grades from boxmakers are as follows:

New double-lined kraft cuttings (DLK)—Pre-consumer. Described under brown kraft paper grades.

Boxboard cuttings—Pre-consumer. In manufacturing boxes such as cereal and food boxes, gift boxes, and chipboard boxes, waste is generated. Trimmings of this material are known as boxboard cuttings.

Unprinted bleached sulphate (UBS)—Pre- or post-consumer. Consists of sulphate board that is free of insoluble glue, polycoatings, and TMP (thermal mechanical pulp). TMP appears as a cream-colored (not white) center.

Lightly printed bleached sulphate (LPBS)—Pre- or post-consumer. Includes bleached sulphate board with less than 15-percent ink coverage. This ink normally appears on the edges of trim and on only one side.

Heavily printed bleached sulphate (HPBS)—Pre-or post-consumer. Similar to LPBS, except the ink coverage is considerably heavier than 15 percent.

IGS board—Pre- or post-consumer. Consists of printed sulphate board stock with an insoluble glue.

Printed polycoated board—Pre- or post-consumer. Made from bleached kraft board laminated with a thin layer of plastic on one side for use as food containers. It can be printed.

Unprinted polycoated board—Includes unprinted kraft board laminated with a thin layer of plastic on one side.

Chipboard—Material commonly found on the backs of tablets of paper.

PRINTER GRADES

The different types of printer grades are as follows:

Colored manifold ledger—Described above.

White manifold ledger—Described above.

Coated book—Described above.

IGS coated or uncoated—Coated IGS is described above. Uncoated IGS is similar, except that the paper is not coated.

Hard white—Pre-consumer. Consists of uncoated, white, sulphite paper, completely free of printing. Often located near paper shears, where large sizes of paper are cut into smaller sizes.

Butt rolls—Pre-consumer. Roll fed printing presses usually are unable to utilize the last inch or less of paper that each roll contains. The rolls with these remnants of paper are known as butt rolls. Butt rolls are further identified by the grade of paper on the roll (e.g., a "hard white butt roll").

Groundwood shavings—Described above.

Flyleaf shavings—Described above.

Publication blanks—Described above.

Coated groundwood sections—Described above.

CONTAMINANTS

A contaminant is a type of material that is an impurity in a specific grade of scrap. This is a difficult concept to grasp, without an understanding of the basic grades of paper. Even when paper grades are understood, it continues to be a difficult concept.

For example, a cardboard box is a contaminant in white ledger, but it is perfectly acceptable in old corrugated containers. White ledger that contains printing is a contaminant in hard white, but is perfectly acceptable in colored ledger, since white ledger is a higher grade than colored ledger. Two terms exist to describe contaminants: outthrows and prohibited materials.

TABLE 13-2. Contamination of Paper

Contaminant	Description	Reason
Carbon paper	Commonly a problem in white and colored ledger, printout, and file stock. Permitted only in trace amounts in mixed paper.	Not bleachable, creates black flecks in paper.
Pressure-sensitive adhesives	Found in white and colored ledger and file stock.	Won't disperse, clogs cleaning equipment.
Gold and silver ink, glitter, foil	Found in printers grades, school papers, and white and colored ledger or coated sulphate.	Not bleachable, metal flecks in paper.
Beater dyed and construction paper	Found in printers grades and in schools.	Not bleachable.
Tyvek envelopes, synthetic paper	Found in office recycling programs.	Not paper.
Blueprint paper	Found in office recycling programs.	Chemically treated.
Waxed cardboard	Found in cardboard from food stores and the meat packing industry.	Wax does not disperse.
Onion skin paper, parchment	Found in office recycling programs.	No fiber.
Flourescent inks, goldenrod yellow, gift wrapping	Found in printer waste, office files, advertisements, and gift wrap.	Not bleachable.
Roll cores	Found in printer waste.	Too much glue.
Fax paper, coated copier papers, EKG paper	Found in office recycling programs.	Chemically treated.
Ultra violet inks	Printers, box plants.	Not bleachable.
Wax, varnish, chromecoat, and plastic coatings	Found in printers, advertising materials, annual reports.	Coatings don't dissolve.
Brown kraft envelopes	Found in recycling.	Not bleachable.
Binders	Found in recycling.	Not paper.
Wet strength papers	Used for maps, certificates.	Very slow to pulp.
Magnetic ink	Found on checks, accounting systems.	Not bleachable.

An outthrow is a contaminant that is allowed in a small percentage. For example, a small amount of white ledger could exist in cardboard.

A prohibited material is a contaminant that cannot be contained to any degree in a specific grade. For example, carbon paper is a prohibited material in computer printout because it will not bleach.

It is helpful to learn how to identify common contaminants. In dealing with buyers of material, it is also important to ask them about the contaminants that are common or that create problems in their production process. Table 13-2 is one example of a contamination guide. Technology creates new contaminants and resolves problems with existing ones. Manufacturing technology varies with specific paper mills.

14

Plastics

Overview:	*Apparent consumption:* 30,740,000 short tons *Amount recycled:* 266,500 short tons *Recovery:* 0.8%
Benefits:	*Energy use reduction:* 88% *Air pollution reduction:* N/A *Resources saved:* Petroleum *Miscellaneous:* Saves landfill space
Outlook:	Plastic recycling faces many economic and technological obstacles before it can become widespread. However, the industry may be faced with taking the responsibility for some of the waste it contributes to municipal solid waste. For this reason, it is likely that plastic recycling will soon advance to new levels of prevalence and efficiency.

INTRODUCTION

Learning about plastics recycling is like taking a lesson in chemical engineering. Each year, the highly technical plastics industry produces more than 150 types of the resins known as plastic. Each resin contains a unique chemical equation and different set of recycling obstacles. The diverse physical and chemical properties of these individual resins make recycling very difficult because these characteristics do not often mesh with each other. Mixing two plastic resins—such as polyethylene and polystyrene—together is comparable to combining steel and wood. But, with a product that makes up an estimated 8 percent of municipal solid waste (MSW), the plastics industry is quickly becoming motivated to examine the disposal issue and help further the cause of plastic recycling.

Plastics are found everywhere in an average household. From grocery bags to computers, children's toys to egg cartons, plastics made of hundreds of shapes and colors abound. They can be hard or soft, opaque or transparent, rigid or flexible, and solid or liquid. To make matters even more complicated, different types of plastic resins can be used for the same application. It is almost tempting to say that plastic is plastic.

Truthfully, though, there's nothing simple about plastic. The chemistry involved in connecting the chains of molecules that produce various resins cannot easily be explained to a non-chemist. The tongue-twisting names associated with everyday plastics would create panic in any spelling bee. Take, for example, the transparent plastic in the liter bottle that contains soft drinks: polyethylene terephthalate. For most people, that's PET.

Various estimates show that on a per capita basis each American contributes 115 pounds of plastic to the waste stream annually making up 8 percent of MSW. However, while the amount of MSW in the United States grew from 112.8 million tons in 1975 to 126.5 million in 1984—an increase of 12 percent—the percentage of plastics waste almost doubled during the same period. In the past 20 years plastic bottles and containers have surpassed breakable glass bottles. To begin to understand plastics recycling, the complexities of this industry must be faced squarely.

Controversial Commodity

Plastics are one of the more controversial commodities in recycling. Disposal of plastics has been blamed as a principal cause of dwindling landfill capacity and dioxin emissions from MSW incinerators. Local governments and states, as well as Congress, have considered restrictions on plastic products, including requiring that some be degradable. To respond to public concern regarding plastic wastes and to highlight the best means of handling these wastes, Congress asked the EPA to investigate the role that plastics plays in the solid waste stream, as well as the management methods available for disposing of these wastes.

The EPA's Role

Despite technical uncertainties, the EPA reports that recycling appears to be a promising alternative to landfilling plastic waste. In its study "Methods to Manage and Control Plastic Wastes," the EPA concludes that if plastics recycling is implemented with the collection of other MSW recyclables, it can develop into a major option for managing plastic wastes. The EPA is providing technical assistance on plastics recycling and other MSW management issues through peer match programs and a national MSW information clearinghouse. Peer match programs strive to link up municipalities starting a recycling program with others that have programs in place. The EPA is also encouraging additional industry involvement to demonstrate the potential of plastic recycling technologies and to foster the inception of local and regional recycling programs.

HOW PLASTIC IS MADE

Plastics are molded from synthetic resins. These resins consist of billions of molecules, made up of carbon, hydrogen, oxygen, and nitrogen. The molecules are then linked in a chain called a polymer. Resin manufacturers build polymers by combining chemical compounds in a complicated process called polymerization. This process chemically changes the molecules into synthetic resins.

There are two classifications of plastics made from these resins: thermoplastics and thermosets. Both of these consist of long chains of molecules; the practical distinction is that thermoplastics can be remelted and reformed and thermosets cannot.

With thermoplastics, the polymers are not connected to each other. Therefore, when the material is heated, the polymers can "flow" easily, without damaging the resin's chemical or physical properties. Thermoplastic waste can theoretically be recycled because the material can be melted and cooled to reassume the molecular structure of a rigid shape.

Thermoset plastics, on the other hand, have long molecules that are bonded together, or cross-linked. When they are heated, the molecules are restricted and cannot move about freely. One common thermoset plastic is epoxy. If it is heated to progressively higher temperatures, the molecules will be destroyed before the polymers will "flow." Therefore, once the molecular structures of thermoset plastic is formed, it cannot be reheated and reshaped into new products. Because of this, the recycling options are obviously fewer.

TYPES OF PLASTIC

It is plastic's versatility that accounts for its growth as a material. It can be made as strong as steel, and used to contain two liters of soda with only a few ounces of plastic and withstand a shock that would break most glass bottles. It can also be made into a resilient, brightly colored paint, or into a strong adhesive. Table 14-1 summarizes the major resins.

PLASTIC MARKETS

During the past two decades plastics have been developed and modified to be both stronger and more capable of being shaped than in the past. As a result, plastics are capturing a larger share of many markets. Since 1970 the use of plastics has more than doubled in building and construction materials, transportation, and furniture. This is especially true in the automobile industry, where plastic parts are being manufactured to take the place of steel. Automobile designers are increasingly trying to build energy efficient transportation. Replacing steel with industrial

TABLE 14-1. Summary of Plastic Resins Sold in the United States

		Short Tons	
Type Of Resin Sold	1989 (Tons)	1990 (Tons)	% Increase (Decrease)
ABS	618,500	606,000	(2.0)
Acrylic	369,500	375,500	1.6
Alkyd	162,500	160,000	(1.5)
Cellulosics	45,500	40,000	(12.1)
Epoxy	241,500	232,000	(3.9)
Nylon	290,000	285,000	(1.7)
Phenolic	1,413,000	1,413,500	—
Polyacetal	71,500	71,500	—
Polycarbonate	312,000	310,000	(0.6)
Polyester (PBC, PCT, PET)	1,048,500	1,168,500	11.1
Polyester, Unsaturated	659,500	613,500	(6.9)
Polyethylene, High-density	4,086,500	4,252,500	4.1
Polyethylene, Low-density	5,401,500	5,938,000	9.9
Polyphenylene-based Alloys	98,000	99,500	1.5
Polypropylene and Copolymers	3,651,500	4,066,000	11.1
Polystyrene	2,565,500	2,568,500	0.1
Other Styrenics	590,000	558,000	(5.4)
Polyurethane	1,612,000	1,632,500	1.3
Polyvinyl Chloride and Copolymers	4,268,000	4,648,500	8.9
Other Vinyls	450,000	457,500	1.6
Styrene Acrylonitrile (SAN)	54,000	67,000	24.1
Thermoplastic Elastomers	271,000	292,000	7.7
Urea and Melamine	690,500	719,500	4.2
Others	155,000	165,000	6.4
Total	29,126,000	30,740,000	5.5

Source: *Modern Plastics*. January 1991

strength plastics helps to reduce the weight of the vehicle and increase its miles-per-gallon rating.

Plastics used for packaging has also increased tremendously. It has come to symbolize a consumer society sold on disposability and convenience. Microwave food products are probably the best example of items that appeal to this mentality. For the next decade the packaging market is expected to be the biggest segment of the plastics industry. Because most people maintain the purchase–consume–dispose mentality, additional plastic packaging means more waste.

In a recent major breakthrough, the Food and Drug Administration has allowed recycled plastic to be used in making food containers. This opens an entire new market for recycled PET and HDPE.

Table 14-2 summarizes the major uses for plastic resins.

TABLE 14-2. Uses for Plastic Resins in 1990

Major Market Area	Short Tons: Tons	%
Appliances	623,000	2.0
Building/Construction	5,942,500	19.3
Electrical/Elecrtonics	1,156,000	3.8
Transportation	1,167,500	3.8
Packaging	7,410,500	24.1
Housewares	738,000	2.4
Furniture	591,500	1.9
Toys	380,000	1.2
Other	12,731,000	41.5
Total	30,740,000	100.0

Source: *Plastics World*. January 1991.

PLASTIC RECYCLING TECHNOLOGY

The technology used to make plastic involves starting with a known polymer and then adding chemicals to obtain desired physical characteristics. To recycle plastic, it would be desirable to put various types of plastic into a "black box" and reverse the process. The only problem? The black box does not exist. Plastic is one of the few materials that begins with a pure ingredient. Next, the pure ingredient is contaminated with additives. Most industries with high recycling rates, such as steel, begin with a crude ore and refine the ore into a pure product. Steel scrap, which may be contaminated, enters a refining process similar to the one that made the steel from the ore. No corresponding flow of material exists for plastic.

At the present time the burden is on collection activities to provide reasonably pure products made from the same resin to the manufacturers. Manufacturers clean the material and remelt it. Limited applications exist for mixed plastics.

PLASTIC RECYCLING PROCESS

One way to handle this expected increase in waste is through recycling. But before recycling becomes viable for plastics on a large scale, a number of technical and economic issues must be resolved. Unlike recycling practices for paper, glass, and metal, plastic recycling is in its infancy. While scientists have determined that it is technically feasible to recycle most discarded plastics, to date plastics recyclers have focused on only a few post-consumer products—mainly plastic milk jugs and pop bottles.

Plastic containers have been targeted for recycling because they are the easiest to separate from the waste stream. Households need only be aware of their recyclability and have access to local programs to keep the containers from going to landfills. Plastic containers constitute approximately 30 percent of all plastic waste, or about 2 percent of MSW.

Of plastic containers, the two types of resins usually collected are HDPE, used in making milk bottles, and PET, used in making plastic beverage bottles. In 1990, approximately 1,102,000 tons of HDPE were used to make milk bottles and containers. Manufacturers produced 544,000 tons of PET in this same year. In total, these resins make up 5.3 percent of total plastics sold in the United States.

The remaining post-consumer plastic waste is a greater challenge. Unlike plastic packaging, these items were not designed for easy disposability, but nevertheless make their way into the waste stream. Most children's toys, computer housing, car fenders, lawn furniture, and automotive plastics are theoretically recoverable, but most areas in the country do not have access to an end user. This is not to say that end users do not exist; somewhere in the country exists a company that recycles worn-out dolls or lawn chairs. The problem figuring out what resin was used, locating an end user, and figuring a way to ship the item without excess cost.

One type of plastic recycling that does take place on a regular basis is in-house recycling. For years, plastic companies have incorporated their own waste into the manufacturing process. Industrial plastic is generally clean and composed of one known resin, so it is relatively easy to blend it back into the process.

Another type of pre-consumer plastic recycling relates to plastic bag waste, which can be recovered from business and industry, plastic parts, which can be recovered from manufacturers, and plastic slip sheets and pallets, which can be recovered from distributors. These products can be processed through grinders and remelted to use as new plastic.

The Code System

One distinguishing factor with regard to plastics recycling is the plastic container code system. Legislation requiring an imprinted code has been passed in at least 27 states. Outlined in Table 14-3, the code offers uniformity to bottle manufacturers and recyclers alike. However, while many bottle and product manufacturers have adopted this system, plenty of containers on the market remain mysterious.

While this nomenclature is a good start, there's a chemical difference between plastic that is blow molded, extruded, and injection molded, even for the same basic resin. Now that more material is being recycled, it will be interesting to see how or if plastic recycling will change its coding system. Table 14-3 summarizes the current system.

TABLE 14-3. The Plastics Code System

Code	Material	% of Bottles	Reclaimed For
1 PETE	Poly-ethylene-terephthalate (PET)	20-30%	Carpet, paint containers, non-food packaging, fiberfill, fibers, insulation, auto parts, recreational/household items, and engineering plastics
2 HDPE	High-density polyethylene	50-60%	Drainage pipes, toys, drums, traffic cones, plastic lumber, docks, recycling bins, and combs
3 V	Vinyl/ chloride	5-10%	Pipes, building products, hoses, mud flaps, and tile
4 LDPE	Low-density polyethylene	5-10%	Mixed with HDPE to produce plastic pallets and cases, recycling bins, and garbage bags
5 PP	Polypropylene	5-10%	Household and janitorial products
6 PS	Polystyrene	5-10%	Insulation, food trays, fence posts, and desk accessories
7 Other	All other resins and layered multi-material	5-10%	Recycling and other storage containers, lumber, and animal pen floors

COLLECTING PLASTIC CONTAINERS

The critical first step in plastic container recycling is to segregate it from the waste stream. The most logical place to start is in the home, because this is where most plastic containers are found. Collecting these containers can be a bit challenging because they are light, bulky, and made in awkward shapes and sizes. Most people keep collected plastics in a bag or recycling bin. When plastic bottles are flattened—as by stepping on them—they take up significantly less space.

Preparation in the Household

Preparing plastic containers for recycling is a simple three-step process. First, look at the bottom of the container to see if it has a number stamped upon it. If it does and the number is a 1 or 2, the local collection program will usually accept the container. If the number is higher, call to see if that variety of plastic is acceptable. When the program requires it, separate the plastic types.

Second, empty all remaining contents and rinse the container to remove any remaining solids. Third, remove all metal or plastic caps and rings. The paper labels may remain.

Curbside Methods

Curbside collection of plastics is probably the most effective way to divert a large proportion of MSW from landfills and incineration. Curbside recycling, however, faces some significant barriers with regard to plastics. While most programs only want to collect PET and HDPE resins, they often receive plastics of all varieties. This makes sorting the materials at an intermediate processing center more difficult. One way for recyclers to handle this contamination is to leave the undesirable plastics at the curb, with a note explaining why the material was not accepted.

Many curbside programs do not take time to sort between different grades of plastic because of the expense. These programs instead market their materials as mixed plastic.

Deposit Legislation

Some states have adopted container deposit legislation to reduce litter and to promote materials recovery for recycling. This legislation has proven very successful in capturing a large percentage of targeted items—as much as 90 percent of designated glass, metal, and plastic beverage containers. To date, deposit legislation has only targeted polyethylene terephthalate (PET) soft drink bottles, which constitute just a small percentage of all plastics discarded.

Some recycling authorities fear that deposit legislation will have a negative impact on curbside recycling, primarily because the plastic that is easiest to characterize and economically most valuable will not be collected at the curb. When evaluating collection methods, local and state officials should consider the relationship between these options before selecting an approach.

The grade of plastic collected through deposit legislation is considerably higher than that of curbside and drop-off programs; HDPE and PET containers can be easily sorted before the deposit is paid to the consumer.

Buy-back Centers

Buy-back centers provide one way to collect a wider variety of plastic while keeping it separated. Individuals bring in items made from HDPE, PET, and other resins, and the buy-back center chooses whether to purchase the material. Buy-back centers generally collect a wider range of plastic than most programs, but usually do not pay for materials that are not cost-effective to recycle.

Drop-off Centers

Drop-off centers, like buy-back programs, offer recycling to communities that do not have curbside programs. They are generally located in a centralized area, with bins labeled for glass, paper, and plastic. If the center is unsupervised, the biggest problem with this type of program is contamination. Glass, paper, and metal are often comingled with plastic containers, producing a sorter's nightmare.

Automobile Shredders

Post-consumer plastics also are produced as by-products from recycling other materials. When automobiles are shredded to recover steel and other valuable metals, about 25 percent of the remaining waste is plastics. Recycling for this type of plastic is not widespread because of the extreme technological difficulties it brings. However, as landfill space diminishes, it seems inevitable that the material will have to be reclaimed in some form or other.

SORTING

Because mixed plastic waste in MSW encompasses a variety of plastic polymers and resins, its recycling uses are limited to big, bulky products, such as fence posts and picnic tables. But these markets, while large, are not infinite. Collection programs could greatly increase the marketability of plastics by separating the resins. Post-consumer plastic separated to obtain a homogeneous single resin typically has higher economic value. Putting the results of automated sorting of mixed MSW plastics into homogeneous resins, however, faces significant technical hurdles. Some hand sorting of mixed plastics is currently performed, but it is an expensive, labor-intensive process.

A number of automated sorting technologies are under development, including infrared sorting, laser reading of an encoded label, chemical marking of different resins, and density separations. Of these, only density separation has proven commercially effective, but it cannot efficiently separate the large number of resins found in the MSW stream. Nevertheless, industry analysts hope that one or more of these technologies will prove realistic in the next few years, and that separation problems will not remain a barrier to plastics recycling.

Quality Requirements

While preparing plastic for recycling may seem like a hassle, it is important. End users need to be assured that their product is pure and free from the risks of contamination. Even a small amount of polystyrene or nylon in a batch of polyethylene could result in products of poor quality. Contaminating an entire batch of plastic resins is costly to the manufacturer.

An even greater contamination worry lies with the problems that metal caps and lids, dirt, and stones create because they do not melt at the same temperature as most plastic resins. Instead, they remain in one piece and can do significant damage to the equipment used to manufacture plastics.

TRANSPORTATION

Transportation is another major consideration in plastics recycling. Some have likened transporting plastic to carting feathers; the material is lightweight but bulky. Economically speaking, this is not a good combination. Collection trucks can be outfitted with densification equipment, so the compartments do not fill up with air. For long distance shipments by truck or railcar, the cost of transportation can be prohibitive because it is difficult to load plastic to take advantage of the maximum weight limits. When the weight shipped falls far short of the maximum allowable weight, it is as if there is a high charge for shipping air.

HOW PLASTIC IS RECYCLED

Despite the complexity of the plastics industry, the actual process of recycling is relatively simple. Incoming plastic containers are inspected for contaminants, such as metal caps, glass containers, and other types of material, that cannot be incorporated into the plastic making process. Some plants go as far as separating different types of plastic resins, while others accommodate a mix.

After inspection, the containers are washed and chopped in a high-speed grinder. Some materials are washed with hot water and detergent, while others are merely sprayed with cold water. Environmentally sensitive manufacturers filter and reuse the water. If mixed plastics are being processed, they are separated in a flotation tank where some types of plastics sink and others float.

From the washing/grinding machine, a high-speed blower dries the materials. Damp plastics can grow mold, resulting in an inferior product. Once the material (flake) is dried, it is fed into an extruder where heat and pressure melt it. Each type of plastic has a different melting point. The hot, or molten, plastic is forced though a fine screen to remove any contaminants that slipped through the washing process, and then it is forced through a die. The plastic comes out of the die in spaghetti-like strands. The strands are collected in water and then chopped into pellets, which are stored in standard sized boxes.

COST

Another obstacle that plastic recycling must overcome is the competition with virgin material. While processing technology is probably sufficient to produce plastic that is near-virgin quality, the industry still harbors some skepticism. In the normal course of a free market economy, manufacturers insist on receiving a discounted price for using recycled plastics, even though the production cost of creating the recycled product is high.

The public could overcome this problem by deciding to purchase recycled material rather than products made from virgin materials. This would not only put post-consumer plastics on an equal playing field, it might even give it a boost.

With present technology, the main plastics that are economically attractive to reclaim are PET and HDPE. The costs to reclaim other plastics are generally higher than their market value. One exception to this rule is when a large supply of plastic material from the same resin is available. Converting plastics to ethylene or fuel is not economically attractive. Some new technologies are being developed to help bring the cost down. These include altering the manufacturing equipment to prevent it from being damaged by non-plastic materials in the waste stream; altering the chemical properties of manufacturing to compensate for the incompatibility of different resins in mixtures; combining post-consumer plastics with virgin material to improve the quality of the material; and grinding the waste plastics as fillers in mixtures with virgin resins.

GRADES OF PLASTIC

There are as many grades of plastic as there are plastic resins. While most plastics are potentially recyclable, collectors should establish that there is a market before they recover a large quantity. Most recycling programs accept PET and HDPE, the plastics with 1s and 2s stamped onto the container.

Acrylonirile Butadiene Styrene (ABS)—This is strong plastic capable of withstanding significant impact. It is commonly used in telephone casings or automobile parts, such as grills.

Acrylic—This plastic resists weather and chemicals. It is typically used in paint, floor wax, signs, and taillight covers for automobiles.

High-density polyethylene (HDPE)—Plastic made from this type of resin is rigid and stiff. It is used to make milk bottles, detergent bottles, molded seats, garbage cans, barrels, and some shopping bags (which tend to crinkle and are noticeably different from those made of low-density polyethylene). HDPE containers are never clear, but colored or opaque, with a dull finish. HDPE floats in water.

Low-density polyethylene (LDPE)—LDPE is characterized by its flexibility. It finds its primary use in traditional plastic garbage and grocery store bags. Other items made from this resin are cling wrap, squeeze bottles, and toys.

Nylon—Nylon is tough plastic that resists abrasion. It is commonly used for parts such as gears and bushings, and is also used in bristles for brushes, fabric, and fishing line.

Phenolic—Phenolic is a plastic that is easily shaped and is heat resistant. Automotive parts and some household appliances use phenolic plastic.

Polyacetate—This resin is used to make vinyl. Its uses include paints, coatings, and adhesives. Polyacetate is resistant to water and abrasives.

Polycarbonate—This plastic resists heat and weather, and has high-impact strength. Toys, machine parts, and electrical connectors use polycarbonate plastic.

Polyester—Polyester is another strong plastic used in place of some metals. It is often made into furniture and fender extensions. Sometimes it is utilized in the packaging process.

Polyethylene—There are two types of polyethylene—high-density and low-density. Both types are tough and are impermeable to moisture. According to Franklin Associates, 47 percent of all plastic in municipal solid wastes is polyethylene.

Polyethylene terephthalate (PET)—This material is lightweight and tough and it resists penetration of water and carbon dioxide. It's mainly used in making beverage bottles and clear bottles, such as for cooking oils. Its advantages over glass are considerable—it is lightweight, difficult to break, and can be blow molded relatively inexpensively. According to Franklin Associates, 5 percent of plastic found in MSW belongs in this group of plastic.

Polypropylene—This plastic is lightweight, flexible, and resists chemicals and heat. Its main applications include automotive battery cases, rope, appliance housings and parts, and screw-on tops. It can also be used to mold furniture frames. According to Franklin Associates, 16 percent of the plastic found in MSW belongs in this group of plastic.

Polyvinyl acetate (PVA)—This plastic is abrasion resistant and can be dissolved in water. It is typically used in adhesives, paint, packaging, and phonograph records.

Polyvinyl chloride (PVC)—PVC is used in making pipes and mud flaps. It resists chemicals, water, and abrasion.

MARKETING POST-CONSUMER PLASTICS

While markets exist for most collected plastics, they often do not cover the costs of collection and transportation. For this reason, it's difficult to call them markets. Most analysts agree, however, that the markets for homogeneous recycled plastics will be limited only by their availability.

Mixed plastics, on the other hand, are almost exclusively made into lower-value commodities, comparable to items produced from metal, lumber, and cement. Unless processing costs are reduced, many of these recycled products face economic barriers in expanding their markets. The key to marketing plastics is to provide a product that is sorted. As more cost-effective collection and processing techniques develop, the dynamics of post-consumer plastics will change and the product will be worth more money.

When looking for an end user, first contact local plastic manufacturers or brokers to learn who accepts post-consumer plastic. The plastic 800 number at 1-800-2 HELP 90 is a good place to start. Once an end user is found locally, place a call to find more information. In initial conversations, find out what prices the manufacturer pays for post-consumer plastics and the specifications that the end user desires. Like many other recyclable commodities, having access to a large quantity of a desired grade puts the seller in a position to negotiate a special price.

COMPLETING THE CYCLE

The opportunity for using post-consumer plastics in manufacturing is astounding. Recycled PET bottles can be transformed into high-quality carpeting, paint brushes, fence posts, fiberfill, and fuel pellets. Surfboards, sailboat hulls, and skis also use PET. Now with Food and Drug Administration approval, PET will reappear as PET bottles. As technology improves, scrap PET is likely to show up in many other products as well.

There are also many uses for post-consumer HDPE. Large quantities can be utilized in agricultural arenas. Drain pipes and pig and calf pens are three of the more common applications. Post-consumer HDPE can also be manufactured into pallets, trash cans, flower pots, traffic cones, and building products.

Most of the recovered post-consumer plastics will be mixed material. Its manufacturing potential is in making parking lot stops, speed bumps, plastic lumber, and fencing. Like everything else in recycling, once the technology improves, the prospects for completing the cycle become much brighter.

15

Steel

Overview: *Apparent consumption:* 95.9 million short tons
Amount recycled: 57.5 million short tons
Recovery: 60%

Benefits: *Energy use reduction:* 47–74%
Air pollution reduction: 85%
Water pollution reduction: 76%
Mining wastes reduction: 97%
Water use reduction: 40%
Resources saved: Iron ore, coal, limestone

Outlook: Steel has the highest recycling rate of any major commodity and, with new emphasis on steel cans, recycling is likely to maintain its position.

INTRODUCTION

Steel has the highest recycling rate of any major commodity. More than 50 percent of all steel is recycled and has been since the conservation efforts of World War II. Because of a public relations push in the early 1980s, steel recycling remains a rapidly growing industry, despite its low economic return. This success is largely due to steel's magnetic properties.

Ferrous scrap (iron and steel scrap) is used by almost all manufacturers of both steel and cast iron. Fully 50 percent of U.S. steel is made from scrap iron and steel, with 35 percent coming from post-consumer sources. Every process for making steel has the capacity to use ferrous scrap, and each one of them does so to some degree or another. Steel can be recycled endlessly and has been since the times when swords were formed into plowshares.

Each year, Americans dispose of urban refuse containing 12 million tons of ferrous materials. About 10 percent of this amount, or 1.2 million tons, comes from incinerator residue. The remainder of the ferrous material, or almost 11 million tons, is unburned. The U.S. Bureau of Mines found that steel cans comprise about 47 percent of the ferrous scraps in the total municipal waste stream. Fortunately, the magnetic properties of these metals makes it easy to separate steel from the raw refuse of incinerator residue.

For years, steel recycling mainly came from industry scrap, railroad rails, and automobiles. In 1988, however, the Steel Can Recycling Institute (SCRI) initiated a public relations campaign aimed at recycling the steel cans that line most kitchen shelves. In 1989, 17.9 percent of all steel beverage cans were recycled. In the first half of 1990, that percentage grew to 30.1. This is a 39.3 percent increase over 1989, according to the SCRI.

For each ton of steel recycled, the SCRI estimates that 2,500 pounds of iron ore, 1,000 pounds of coal, and 40 pounds of limestone are saved. For every pound of steel cans that is recycled, 5,450 British thermal units (Btus) of energy are conserved—enough to light a 60-watt light bulb for more than 26 hours. For these reasons, the availability of steel scrap results in a competitive advantage for U.S. steel producers over most countries.

INSTITUTIONAL DETERRENTS

One deterrent that hinders the recycling of ferrous materials is the need for both a steady supply of scrap by the purchaser and a steady market by the seller. Unfortunately, both the supply of and demand for the ferrous fraction of urban refuse are subject to fluctuations that are largely beyond the control of both the buyer and the seller. For example, during economic recessions, the demand for iron and steel will diminish. The effect on the seller is twofold: first, the seller receives a lower price for the scrap sold; second, the seller is unable to sell all the scrap.

A second factor inhibiting recycling is the difficulty in financing a prototype refuse separation plant. This difficulty is caused by the reluctance of communities to break new ground in a technological sense, the high capital cost of these facilities, and the need for long-term financing.

HOW STEEL IS MADE

Steel is made in three types of furnaces: the open hearth furnace, the electric arc furnace, and the basic oxygen furnace. This equipment currently accounts for 26, 18, and 56 percent of domestic production, respectively. Both the open hearth and the basic oxygen furnaces are charged with a combination of hot metal and ferrous scrap. The open hearth furnace can process these materials in any proportion, although the usual ratio is 40-percent scrap and 60-percent hot metal. The hot metal is obtained from a blast furnace.

The electric furnace is similar to the open hearth furnace. It, too, is capable of accepting a charge ranging from 100 percent hot metal to 100 percent scrap. However, in most cases, it is charged with 100 percent scrap.

RECYCLING

There are two methods of processing for recycled steel. One uses remelting and the other uses chemicals. In chemical reprocessing, tin, copper, and other types of metals are recovered. In remelting, these same metals become contaminants that must be minimized or eliminated. Each type of processing requires steel scrap of different specifications. In general, specifications include yield, metallurgical properties, and physical characteristics.

The yield with regard to recycled steel is a particularly critical variable. For example, if the yield is lower than expected, the scrap dealer/processor is penalized for the tonnage that was lost for the value of the scrap and freight, to the extent of the shortfall in yield. The steel mill is also penalized because of increased charge time, slagging problems, and probably excessive air pollution. For a guaranteed, continuous market, the quality must be consistent.

Another specification that affects steel recycling is metallurgical properties. Metallurgy refers to other metals that are plated, physically attached, or alloyed with ferrous product. The most critical metals are tin, lead, aluminum, and copper. Each end user has unique metal specifications.

Physical characteristics in steel recycling refer to the density and/or size and shape of individual fragment of ferrous metal. These properties are largely determined by how the scrap steel is processed.

Shredding and baling are two processes that increase density. But while shredding and baling cost money, they produce significant freight savings. The delivery cycle for raw materials is typically short and, in order to be considered a reliable supplier, the scrap dealer/processor normally stores raw material in anticipation of future need. In buying or selling steel, prices customarily are quoted on a gross ton basis (2,240 pounds).

Remelting

Post-consumer products such as automobiles and large appliances are usually remelted in a variety of furnace types (electric, basic oxygen, open hearth, and blast furnaces). Blast furnaces offer a slightly broader tolerance for metallurgical impurities than the other types of furnaces.

The presence of tin, carbon, and copper is a critical concern of those using steel for remelt. Aluminum generally slags in processing and is therefore less critical. Generally, a minimum density of 70 pounds per cubic foot is required for remelting. Some end users insist on bales or bundles, and maximum size varies with each plant. Some end users prefer a nuggetized or briquetted product.

Iron foundries represent a large potential market for post-consumer steel scrap. The products of foundries include gray iron, a term indicating low-grade cast iron, and products such as manhole covers, pipes, and grates. Foundries normally purchase premium grades of scrap metal. With recent changes in technology, some foundries accept lower-grade raw materials. There are approximately 5,000 foundries in the United States.

Chemical reprocessing

Detinning, recovering the tin from tin-plated steel cans, is an alkaline chemical process in which scrap is treated with hot caustic soda in the presence of an oxidizing agent, such as sodium nitrate. The tin is then dissolved as sodium stannate and recovered as metal through electrolysis. There are about 7½ pounds of tin in one ton of scrap cans.

One possible future development is that the steel industry may subsidize a recycling program for steel cans because of the perceived threat of aluminum entering the steel food can market. In steel mills, tin is a contaminant, and therefore large-scale detinning would have to be supported by can manufacturers, not the steel scrap industry, as it is now structured.

Ferro-alloy producers use scrap iron with carefully controlled amounts of other elements, such as silicon and manganese. Ferro-silicon, for example, is made in this manner. The total market is relatively small. Copper precipitation uses thin sheet metal scrap, especially reclaimed cans, to leach copper from low-grade copper ore. In this process, a 5- to 10-percent solution of sulfuric acid is percolated through low-grade ore. The resulting product is copper sulfate, which is collected in concrete vats (launders) full of steel cans. Iron sulfate is formed and the copper deposits are then smelted. An estimated 15 percent of copper in the United States is produced using this process.

Minimills

There are more than 50 minimills in the United States that use steel scrap as their primary raw material. For this reason the minimill concept is of vital importance to recyclers. Three sources of ferrous scrap feed minimills: obsolete scrap, home scrap, and process scrap. The most important of these is obsolete scrap, which comprises about 55 percent of the supply. Obsolete or post-consumer steel consists of discarded or worn-out products, such as automobiles. Obsolete scrap is usually plentiful, but often contains a high percentage of contaminants. Home scrap, which comprises 45 percent of the minimill supply, is scrap generated by the steel industry. Industrial scrap, which equals less than 5 percent of the scrap supply, is generated by steel-consuming manufacturers who cannot reprocess the scrap themselves.

In the past 25 years these mills have captured 20 percent of the steel market. The "minimill" concept has substantially changed the economics of steel-making. Companies such as Nucor Steel, (headquartered in Charlotte, North Carolina), Birmingham Steel, Chapparal, Florida Steel, and Northstar Steel are leaders in the minimill business.

Italy developed the first minimills during World War II. Small steel producers saw the opportunity to use electric furnaces to convert scrap war material into new steel. This concept made its way to the United States by the late 1950s, when technological advances in electric furnaces improved to the point where small companies could readily accept scrap steel.

Because their primary raw feedstock is ferrous scrap, minimills don't handle iron ore pelletizing, coking operations, or blast furnace operations. Thus, minimills save on the capital and costs associated with an integrated steel producer's up-front processes. Some minimills, however, do maintain scrap processing facilities as part of their operations.

Today many minimills process their steel through compact strip production, a process in which molten metal is fed into a funnel-shaped mold to produce a long, thick slab. When the slab comes out of the mold, it is sheared and moved through a soaking furnace, a descaler, and then directly into a finishing mill. The finishing mill flattens the mold. After rolling, the sheet passes through a cooling unit and is coiled. The minimill process eliminates slab handling, reheating furnaces, and the breakdown mills found in conventional plants.

STEEL CANS

Although steel is recycled more than all other materials combined, the percentage of food and beverage cans recovered is relatively small. Steel cans are an ideal scrap source because of their makeup. The steel used in cans is low in carbon, manganese, and phosphorous. This means that it is very clean steel.

Another advantage to recycling steel cans is that steel's magnetic properties make it easy to separate from solid waste. Some food cans are made from both steel and aluminum. Beer and soft drinks often use bi-metal cans. It is easy to magnetically separate these cans from all-aluminum ones at recycling centers. It is not necessary to separate the aluminum tops from the steel can bodies.

At least six steel makers, including Bethlehem and USS, a division of USX Corporation, actively purchase steel can scrap from recycling subsidiaries of major can companies, independent recyclers, detinners, resource recovery operations, and municipalities. Unfortunately, steel can scrap is not as accessible as it could be. The missing link in many areas is a network for getting the containers from consumers to the mills. SCRI is working in this area to convince scrap dealers/processors and recycling center operators to add steel cans to their mix of recyclables. To this end, SCRI has identified 40 industrial end users for steel can scrap.

STEEL CAN COLLECTION

There are at least four easy ways for communities to institute steel can recycling: Curbside collection, resource recovery plants, and drop-off or buy-back centers. Each of the collection systems has been tested—and is currently used—in communities throughout the country.

Curbside Collection

The easiest way for individual households to participate in steel can recycling is through a curbside collection program. In a comingled, multi-material curbside program, families simply separate recyclables from their household trash. Comingled curbside collection programs require little effort from household members, resulting in high participation rates—and more recycled goods.

Resource Recovery Plants

No household trash separation is required when all of a community's trash is collected by garbage trucks and taken to a resource recovery plant. There, steel cans and other post-consumer steel products can be magnetically separated from the solid waste. The remaining trash is then burned in a process that creates energy and reduces the volume of solid waste prior to landfilling.

Drop-off and Buy-back Centers

Voluntary drop-off and buy-back centers are usually found in communities where curbside programs have not yet been instituted or are impractical because of small populations. These centers are beginning to accept more of recyclable products, and increasingly are accepting steel food and beverage cans.

Preparation

Preparing steel food and beverage cans for any of these collection systems is simple because the cans do not have to be flattened or have their ends removed, and labels can be left on. The only preparation necessary is to rinse them before collection. Some recycling programs ask customers to remove can labels and crush the container. These processes require an extra effort for the consumer, and tend to reduce the overall participation rate of the program. The extra steps do not affect the quality of steel can scrap. During the remelting process labels burn off easily.

Paint and aerosol steel cans are also recyclable. They do, however, require extra preparation. Paint cans must be emptied before collection. There should not be a liquid layer of paint on the bottom of the cans. A thin skin of paint on the bottom is permissible, but it must be dry. In this condition, paint cans can be included in most collection programs. Steel aerosol cans that hold products such as hairspray, deodorant, whipped cream, and shaving cream are also recyclable. When the can is empty, it can be included in collection programs.

Many non-steel containers use lids and closures made of steel. These, too, are recyclable. Testing whether a cap, lid, or crown is made from steel is simple. Touch the item with a household magnet, if it sticks, the material is steel. Consumers should include these items in local collection programs because they blend into the process for post-consumer steel containers.

ROLE OF THE SCRAP DEALER/PROCESSOR

Scrap metal dealers and brokers purchase all types of recovered scrap and sell different grades of steel scrap to various end users. The scrap metal dealer might process the metal by baling, shredding, shearing, briquetting, breaking, burning, or nuggetizing. Or the dealer might simply sort and store the material for resale. Normally, it takes several million dollars worth of equipment to handle large volumes of steel. A scrap dealer/processor has ready-made markets for many items, along with the sorting and grading skills that are needed.

Businesses generally find scrap processors easy to deal with because the industry is competitive and the dealers are always looking for new customers. Many of these dealers have been less than aggressive in helping resource recovery plants find markets because they see government as an interference and as unfair competition. The reality is that in any community they are a knowledgeable resource and, if dealers wish to make a profit, they should be eager to sign up a resource recovery plant as a customer, just as they would be with any other business.

Quality

Scrap dealers/processors have participated in developing metal standards that describe the products they process and sell. These specifications include descriptive language that has evolved over many years of buying and selling scrap products. The Institute of Scrap and Recycling Industries (ISRI) maintains a listing of current standards that are revised and updated periodically. In reality it is not possible to sell "scrap steel" to an end user. The type of scrap steel must be sorted into one of the following grades.

PURCHASING GRADES

The different types of purchasing grades are as follows:

No. 1 heavy melting steel—Consists of steel scrap and wrought iron at least 1/4 inch in thickness and with individual pieces not over 60 × 40 inches.

No. 2 heavy melting steel—Consists of steel scrap and wrought iron at least 1/8 inch in thickness of charging box size.

No. 2 light—Consists of old sheet steel compressed to charging box size, weighing more than 75 pounds per cubic foot and being less than 1/8 inch thick.

Plate and structural steel, five feet and under—Consists of cut structural and plate scrap, five feet and under not less than 1/4 inch thick.

Cupula cast—Consists of clean cast iron scrap, such as columns, pipes, plates, and castings of a miscellaneous nature, including automobile blocks and cast iron parts of agriculture and other machinery. May include all grades of cast iron, except burnt iron, brake shoes, or stove plate. Dimensions not over 24 × 30 inches and nothing over 150 pounds.

Other grades of steel—There are five broad categories and approximately 90 to 100 published grades of steel. The grades are categorized according to thickness, size of material, packaging, and coatings. Most of these grades are rare. Another distinguishing factor between grades is how the steel will be reprocessed by the end users.

Basic hearth and basic oxygen grades:

No. 1 Heavy melting steel
No. 1 Heavy melting steel 3 feet × 18 feet
No. 1 Heavy melting steel 5 feet × 18 feet
No. 2 Heavy melting steel
No. 2 Heavy melting steel 3 feet × 18 inches
No. 2 Heavy melting steel 5 feet × 18 inches
No. 1 Busheling not exceeding 12 inches in any direction. Might include old body and fender stock.
New black sheet clippings
No. 1 Bundles
No. 2 Bundles
No. 3 Bundles
No. 2 Light
Shredded scrap
Shredded clippings
Shredded tin cans for remelting
Incinerator bundles
Terne plate bundles—Terne plate is steel late coated with an alloy of tin and lead used for roofing and lining packing cases.
Bundled No. 1 steel

Bundled No. 2 steel
Machine shop turnings
Machine shop turnings and iron borings
Shoveling turnings
Shoveling turnings and iron borings
Iron borings
Auto slabs
Briquetted iron borings
Briquetted steel turnings
Mill scale—ferro-magnet iron oxide

Electric furnace casting and foundry grades:
Billet, bloom, and forge crops
Bar crops and plate scrap
Plate and structural steel, five feet and under
Caste steel
Punchings and plate scrap
Electric furnace bundles
Cut structural and plate scrap
Silicon busheling
Silicon clippings
Chargeable ingots and ingot butts
Foundry steel
Springs and crankshafts
Alloy-free turnings
Alloy-free short shoveling steel turnings
Alloy-free machine shop turnings
Hard steel cut, 30 inches and under
Chargeable slab crops
Silicon bundles
Heavy turnings

Cast iron grades:
Cupola cast
Charging box cast
Heavy breakable cast
Hammer block or bases
Burnt iron—stove parts, grate bars, etc.
Mixed cast
Stove plate, clean cast iron stove
Clean auto cast
Unstripped motor blocks
Drop broken machinery cast
Clean auto cast, broken, not degreased

Clean auto cast, degreased
Malleable
Broken ingot molds and stools
Unbroken ingot molds and stools

Special boring grades:

No. 1 Chemical borings
Briquetted cast iron borings, hot process
Briquetted cast iron borings, cold process
Malleable borings
No. 2 Chemical borings

Special grades for railroad industry—Approximately 20 grades exist for axles, spikes, tie plates, brake shoes, springs, wheels, switches, rail, and the structural components of railroad cars.

MARKETING

The marketing of steel is generally of a regional nature. Most often, the buyers in the closest geographic area will purchase scrap steel. Large, national detinning companies are the exception to this rule. They have their own transportation networks, and work to establish regional buying networks for steel.

The negotiating power for selling scrap steel will greatly increase with volume. Marketing options for any specific collection center will vary, depending on the volume of material collected and the geographic region of the center. Generally, collected steel will be sold to detinning companies, steel mills, iron and steel foundries, minimills, or local ferrous scrap processors. Contacting the SCRI (800-876-SCRI) or the American Iron and Steel Institute at (202-452-7277) may help with initial market development.

STAINLESS STEEL

Stainless steel is often used in American industry. Kitchens are usually equipped with stainless steel silverware because the metal does not rust or leave a bad taste in the mouth. Stainless steel is also heavily used in automobile manufacturing as the shiny trim that adds decorative qualities. For the scrap collector, identifying stainless steel presents one of the most difficult and highly technical tasks in grading scrap. The process involves a series of chemical tests.

The first step in identifying stainless steel is to apply nitric acid to it. There should be no reaction. Second, add hydrochloric acid. The reaction should be strong and produce a yellowish-green color. The third test uses potassium ferricyanide (10 percent). If the spot turns dark blue, the material is stainless steel.

There are four basic types of stainless steel. The first is the 400 series, which consists of basic chrome and iron. It is highly magnetic and has a very light and diffused spark. The chemical test for the 400 series is one drop of nitric acid and one drop of water. The spot will remain clear on stainless, but will turn brown or rusty if the material is iron.

The second type of stainless steel is the 300 series, which is commonly called 18/8. The number indicates the alloy contains 18-percent chrome and 8-percent nickel. It is the most plentiful type of stainless steel.

The 200 series of stainless steel was developed in 1957 and 1958. It contains 15–20 percent chrome, 3–6 percent nickel, and 5–10 percent manganese. This material is highly magnetic and has a very light and diffused spark, making it indistinguishable from the 400 series.

Finally, nickel-chrome alloys of stainless steel contain at least 20-percent nickel. Series 309, 310, and 330 belong to this category.

Other grades of stainless steel include:

200 Series stainless steel scrap solids
Stainless steel turnings
11–14-percent chrome stainless steel scrap
14–18-percent stainless scrap

COMPLETING THE CYCLE

Once collected, scrap steel has the capacity to become the raw material for any other steel product. Today's cans may become a new car. Recycled steel from automobiles may become an appliance, and recycled steel from appliances may become the basis for a steel-belted tire.

16

Tires

Overview: *Apparent consumption:* 240 million tires per year
Amount recycled: 43.2 million tires
Recovery percent: 18%

Benefits: *Energy savings:* 12,000 to 16,000 Btus per pound
Resources saved: Oil, rubber, steel, and textiles
Miscellaneous: Used tires create serious problems when they are stockpiled in landfills. By recycling them, these environmental hazards are removed.

Outlook: *Good.* State and local governments are highly interested in eliminating hazardous stockpiles of used tires. Therefore, considerable attention will focus on tire recycling.

INTRODUCTION

One of the biggest challenges in solving the nation's solid waste problem is finding a way to reuse, recycle, or safely dispose of the more than 2 billion waste tires currently stockpiled throughout the country. These stockpiles pose a serious environmental and public health threat. When disposed of in landfills, whole tires create air pockets where noxious gases develop. When gases build under pressure, the tires can reportedly explode several feet into the air. This is not only a danger to potential passersby, but also to the integrity of a carefully balanced landfill.

When tires are disposed in stockpiles separate from other waste, the hazards become even more pronounced. Whole tires stacked on top of each other trap enough oxygen to start a fire. This, combined with the fact that the average passenger tire has a petrochemical content equal to about two and a half gallons of oil, is a potentially lethal combination. Once on fire, tire stockpiles are notorious for burning for months on end, leaving toxic oils to ooze into the ground and potentially contaminate groundwater. Additionally, tire piles provide an ideal breeding ground for disease-carrying mosquitoes and rodents.

In recent years, the media has publicized the problems associated with stockpiling and landfilling tires. National broadcasts kept viewers updated on the progress of an eight-month tire fire in Winchester, Virginia, which cost the federal government nearly $1.2 million to extinguish. This attention has helped make the safe management of tires a legislative priority. As state and local lawmakers continue to develop regulations concerning waste tire disposal, industry organizations that represent tire manufacturers—such as the Scrap Tire Management Council and the Tire Retread Information Bureau—are scrambling to develop uses for the waste.

Disposal Alternatives

Each year, Americans generate about one scrap tire each, totalling about 240 million tires (Hershey, 1987). These tires present unique disposal problems because of their size, shape, weight (an average of 28 pounds), and composition. The materials used to make tires are exceptionally strong, designed to endure thousands of miles of abrasive contact with asphalt roads. Even when the tread on a tire is worn, its individual components remain bonded together. Technically, all the rubber, steel, and fabric can be recovered from tires through recycling, even after the tires no longer function.

Despite public awareness of the hazards associated with the improper management of used tires, only a fraction of tires are recycled. About 80 percent of used tires are still disposed of in landfills and stockpiles.

Retreading operations account for approximately 15 percent of used tire disposal, while shredding tires for use in rubber products or incineration account for less than 5 percent. This low percentage is largely due to the high cost of tire recycling operations, and the lack of substantial markets for used rubber products. However, if the current trend to ban tires from landfills and stockpiles continues, tire recycling will be an issue with which all state and local governments will be forced to contend.

RECYCLING

There are many ways to recycle tires. These include everything from recapping the worn casings to shredding the tires into rubber, steel, and textiles. Ideally, waste tire management would follow a hierarchy, first recycling the tires in their original application, and lastly converting the waste to energy. But because the nation's tire problem is so enormous, most communities are placing their first priority with reducing tire piles, rather than recycling them. Most often, this is accomplished through incineration.

Collection

Before recycling can become a method of managing waste tires, the materials must be collected in a system suitable for reprocessing. This can be approached in a number of ways. The responsibility can rest on the tire dealer's shoulder, as it does in Minnesota, where dealers are required to accept as many used tires from buyers as they sell. Washington state, on the other hand, requires generators to properly dispose of the waste at legal recycling or disposal facilities. Other states have collection systems that assign responsibility to manufacturers. Regardless of the collection system, most tires will either end up in a tire recycling or stockpiling facility, or a tire-derived fuel plant.

Semi-trucks haul tons of tires collected from residential, commercial, and industrial sources to both of these facilities. The tires are immediately examined to determine if they can be reused, retreaded, or if the tires need to be reprocessed into another application. This initial work is generally done manually, making tire recovery a labor-intensive operation. Once the tires are divided, they are resold to retreaders or resalers, or are processed through machinery that will break them into pieces.

Shredding/granulating equipment is a substantial investment for these facilities. The machinery requires frequent upgrading as recycling technologies continue to improve. Because tire material is made up of steel and abrasive rubber, the shredding process is tough on equipment. Blades need to be changed every two to three months. Additional expenses include vector control to keep out obnoxious mosquitoes and rodents, and fire safeguards to contain sudden combustion.

Many local governments provide subsidies to tire collection centers, to help make the operations economically viable.

Bringing Shredding Equipment to Landfills/Stockpiles

One alternative to transporting tires is to bring mobile shredders to stockpile locations. The shredder could be kept very close to the tire stockpile, shifting locations when the nearest supply is depleted. Semi-trucks could haul the shredded chips to the plants that use crumb rubber.

Various areas throughout the country have tested the concept of mobile shredders. The biggest problem that operators find is contamination by dirt and mud, because, often, tires have been piled for years. Contamination jams the shredder and makes the end product less pure.

REUSE

Many tires are tossed out well before their treads are worn. These can be sorted from tire dumps and resold on the used tire market. Sorting used, resalable tires is a fairly well established enterprise that is already reducing the number of tires going to landfills by 5 to 10 percent.

Other simple ways of reusing tires include making playground swings and ship dock bumpers.

Off-shore Fishing Reefs

Using whole tires for shoreline protection and dock building is already in practice in some parts of the United States. This is another one-time application for tires that at this point has limited growth, largely because there is not much known about the long-term impact of leachate that might be generated from tires sitting under water for decades. Also, the tire reefs, which are supposed to provide good fish habitat, tend to collapse over time as a result of tidal and storm action, turning the underwater site into a virtual dump.

Michelin Mansion

One of the most widely publicized uses of whole waste tires is the "Michelin Mansion," which was built by Dennis Weaver. Weaver used whole tires as the basis for the walls of his house, filled them with dirt, and plastered adobe on the exposed treads. The project used 3,000 waste tires.

RETREADING

The EPA promotes tire retreading as the highest and best use for a worn tire. Retreaded tires are subject to the same safety and performance standards as new tires. In fact, many school and municipal bus systems, federal and military vehicles, and race cars and emergency vehicles use retreads. Retreaded passenger car tires are manufactured according to Federal Safety Standards developed by the Department of Transportation.

More than 50 percent of the annual market demand for medium trucks is met by used tires. For passenger cars the percentage is much smaller, although this was not always the case. In the mid-1970s the passenger car retreading industry reclaimed 30 percent of the used tire market (Kozier, 1989). The percentage slipped to less than 6 percent in 1991.

Probably the biggest problem facing the retread industry is in overcoming a poor image. By and large, the public associates tire retreads with the overwhelming amount of rubber tire casings that line highways, and choose not to buy them.

According to the Tire Retread Information Bureau and industry specialists, the improper use of the tire by the user causes most rubber on the road. Almost exclusively, they say, the rubber on the road comes from truck tires; overloading, underinflation, and mismatching of dual axle truck tires are the real culprits responsible for tire failure that result in rubber on the road, whether the tire is new or retreaded. Faulty manufacturing is another very small contributor to tire failure, whether the tire is new or retreaded.

There is much evidence that retreads are as safe as new tires, according the Tire Retread Information Bureau. School buses, city buses, emergency vehicles, airlines, taxis, trucks, and passenger cars have safely used retreaded tires for many years, the Bureau says.

When to Buy a Retread

Consumers should replace tires when a tire tread is down to the wear bars—one-sixteenth of an inch for passenger cars, and one-eighth of an inch for truck tires. Federal regulations require that tires have tread wear bars.

Retread Benefits

Retreading tires has many benefits aside from taking less landfill space. It conserves the oil used to produce new tires and provides economic benefits for the manufacturer and buyer. Retreaded tires cost up to 50-percent less than their virgin counterparts, while offering the same mileage as comparable new tires. Finally, if used casings are retreaded, it helps eliminate the risk of tirepile fires.

How to Get Retread Tires

Retreading services can be purchased in a number of ways. Typically, a buyer asks a retreading salesperson/contractor for the type of tread desired. The contractor may also be asked to guarantee the tread for a specified mileage, with provisions included for refunding a percentage of the retreading cost, depending on the amount of tread remaining, when and if the tire fails.

Retread tires are available from several sources. For example, Sears sells retreads through its catalog. These tires carry the same warranty used with virgin tires. Many retreaders operate wholesale or retail outlets where retread tires can be purchased.

TIRE-DERIVED PRODUCTS

While retreading is the most environmentally sound way to deal with a used tire, it can only postpone the time when a tire is ready for the scrap pile. Eventually, the tire must be disposed of in a properly managed system. One alternative is to shred the tire, and further process it into crumb rubber.

According to the Scrap Tire Management Council, there are about 15 companies that manufacture crumb rubber. The most common way that this is achieved is through a series of shredding machines. Shredding systems allow processors to choose the size of granule for a specified purpose. Some buyers will accept the industry's standard two-inch chips, while others require much smaller granules. The key to a processor's success is being able to supply a specific sized chip and a consistent end product. In order for crumb rubber operations to remain competitive, processors must provide a wide range of options.

Tire shreds and chips are used to provide material for sports mats, industrial process filters, and fuel for boilers. Shredding also can be the first stage of preparing a whole used tire for grinding or granulating. Fuel additives or other similar applications consume most of the chips.

Cryogenics

Cryogenics is a second, less common way to disintegrate used tires. With cryogenics, the shredded tires are frozen using liquid nitrogen. A hammermill then smashes the brittle pieces, breaking up the rubber, textiles, and steel in the tire. The process produces very fine crumb rubber with relatively smooth surfaces that can be used to make some of the best value-added products.

Cryogenics is not actively practiced in most parts of the country because it is more energy-intensive and expensive than grinding and granulating.

Rubber Asphalt Paving

One of the more optimistic prospects for using waste tires is using a small percentage of tire rubber in asphalt. When this technology was developed in the late 1960s, rubber was added to asphalt mixes because it improved the road's flexibility and durability. While improving roads remains the central purpose for asphalt rubber applications, agencies in charge of reducing stockpiles can't help estimating how many waste tires could be used in the process. Having a potential market for crumb rubber is appealing to everyone involved in solving the tire problem.

Scrap tire rubber can be used in asphalt paving in two ways: either as part of the asphalt binding material or seal coat, or as an aggregate to replace concrete. Crumb rubber must be finely ground for use in the first application, while regulation-sized tire chips are used in the second. A study by the Scrap Tire Management Council indicates that both of these asphalt rubber uses approximately double the service life of pavings.

The major barrier to asphalt rubber cited in several recent studies is the lack of asphalt rubber product information specifications, application procedures, and the proof that the higher installation costs are recovered through longer life and other benefits claimed by the asphalt manufacturers. The use has been plagued by slow growth, primarily because the economic gains are unclear.

Nevertheless, the industry is optimistic about this use. Studies estimate that 16,000 tires can be recycled per mile in a two-lane highway overlaid with three inches of rubber modified asphalt concrete pavement. This goes a long way in solving the nation's tire problems.

Public and industrial acceptance of asphalt rubber is not perceived as a barrier to its greater use. The public will accept virtually any paving that provides a smooth ride and is not frequently out of service for maintenance. Industry will accept the product if it meets all performance standards and is economical in relation to competing materials.

Reclaimed Rubber

When the granules for crumb rubber are small enough, they can be used in place of virgin materials in floor mats, waste baskets, rubber ties, mower deflectors, and sandals with tire tread soles. The use of granules has great potential for growth, especially as consumers begin to demand products with a recycled content.

Playground Matting

Crumb rubber can be used to replace gravel in playground matting. This is a safer substitute for children because it is less abrasive. Playground matting is most likely a one-time application for shredded tires, which therefore limits the markets.

TIRE DERIVED FUEL

Tire derived fuel (TDF) is yet another use for scrap tires because of their high petrochemical content. Some facilities with incinerators can burn whole tires or two-inch tire chips in place of the coal they traditionally use. This requires an initial investment to retrofit the incinerator, something a facility should not invest in until there is a guaranteed long-term supply of tires.

The economics of using TDF depends greatly on how refined the tires must be before they are tossed into the incinerator. Facilities that are able to burn tires whole are in a better economic position than facilities that require the tires to be chipped because they can charge more for the tires or, if they must pay, they will pay less. Still another economic distinction is whether the incinerator can accept tires with the steel wire or whether the wire must be removed.

For tire shredding operations, the trend is to create a smaller, more uniformly sized TDF that has been screened and separated to remove most of the wire and cord. This is to incorporate an even greater share of the market. As the fuel market grows, shredded tire processors will be required to develop quality control. Standard specifications for the fuel product will include size, gradation, and surface structure.

While converting tires into fuel is probably the best way to address the overwhelming over-supply of tires, some people argue that this use should not be employed at a large scale. They say that TDF is the lowest value because the tire is only used once and the product's value will be limited by the competitive price of fuels. Secondly, incinerating tires can generate toxic emissions, such as lead, cadmium, and dioxins, if it is done improperly. This could potentially contribute to global warming.

Tire-to-Energy Plants

The Oxford Energy plant in Modesto, California, is probably the best known incinerator of whole tires. The plant is located next to one of the largest tire piles in the world. This guaranteed supply of tires warranted the capital investment of $100 million to build the waste-to-energy facility, which supplies the surrounding area with electricity. Most areas throughout the country do not have a supply of tires that can feed a plant of Oxford's size, however. Furthermore, the low cost of electricity in certain areas may not justify the investment.

Cement Kilns

Cement plants in Europe, Japan, Canada, and parts of the United States have a successful record of using whole and shredded scrap tires as a fuel substitute. This is because the temperature required for making cement—2,600 degrees Fahrenheit—will completely combust used tires. Cement kilns are also ideal for using tires because of their geographic locations: both kilns and tire piles are close to major population centers.

In the United States, the Genstar Cement Co. in Redding, California, has been using TDF for about eight years. The Genstar kiln gets 10 percent of its Btu input from TDF. The tire pieces are fed into the lower end of the kiln, replacing its former fuel, coal. The remaining 90 percent of the fuel is natural gas. Genstar has found that burning tires instead of coal has helped cut operating costs (Kearney, 1990). With coal, the company had to add iron to the mixture. But, because most tires contain steel belts, they no longer require an iron additive.

The economics of using TDF in cement kilns depends greatly on the comparative cost of other fuels. Only this substitution cost will justify a cement producers installing a tire fuel handling adjustment system.

Electric Utilities

Electric utilities, as well as cement kilns, are being looked to as a possibility to use waste tires. Many of the utility plants that now use coal for fuel could be retrofitted to accept a percentage of TDF. The problem is that utilities are typically conservative facilities, and there is no real incentive to bring on possible air quality problems.

PYROLYSIS

Pyrolysis is still another method of deriving fuel from tires. Technically, pyrolysis is the process of breaking organic chemical bonds by heating. With regard to tires, this means breaking the tires down into carbon black, gas, steel, and oil by melting them.

Different quantities of each by-product is determined by the process used for pyrolysis and the temperature for melting. When temperatures increase, more gas is generated. When the temperature decreases, oil is the primary fuel recovered. For pyrolysis to function, the tires must be heated between 500 degrees Fahrenheit and 1100 degrees F (Kearney, 1990).

According to the Scrap Tire Management Council, an average tire produces one gallon of oil, seven pounds of carbon black, three pounds of gas, and two pounds of steel and ash. The oil and gas are then sold as low-quality fuels, suitable for boilers and other facilities. Secondary smelters and foundries recycle the steel.

Two companies convert tires to fuel through pyrolysis. Lack of widespread use is due to major economic barriers relating to product marketability, product quality, and prices.

LANDFILLING

Since most tires in the United States are still disposed of in landfills, it seems prudent to mention that these tires should, at a minimum, be split in half before disposal. This would help solve some of the fire hazards and mosquito breeding problems associated with landfills. Disposing of tires in this way does, however, waste a valuable natural resource, and does not help eliminate landfill capacity problems. To discourage this practice, landfills should charge a higher tipping fee for used tires.

LEGISLATION

Most states are well aware of the problems associated with waste tires and are working toward developing legislation to handle their disposal. When the state of Minnesota implemented its waste tire management program in 1985, it set the tone for legislation throughout the country. Minnesota first conducted a study to learn where the biggest tire piles were located; second, it attached a fee to the purchase of used tires; third, it ended the illegal dumping of these tires. More than 30 states have implemented this legislation in modified terms. California, for example, has initiated a 25 cent tire disposal fee. It is currently looking into TDF for cement kilns. Florida imposed a $1 tax on the retail sale of tires, and bans the disposal of whole tires; they must be shredded before landfilling. In Maryland, tire dealers, recyclers, and other tire collectors cannot store used tires unless they prove within 90 days that they have a market for them, either by showing contracts for materials or otherwise documenting efforts to secure markets.

Federal Legislation

While tire disposal legislation has been proposed on a federal level, it has yet to be seriously considered. Like most other commodities related to recycling, the issue will have to be addressed at the state and local level.

COMPLETE THE CYCLE

The most obvious way to complete the cycle with regard to waste tires is to purchase retreaded tires instead of buying new ones. But, eventually, all tires wear out. When this happens, the rubber can be used for products such as dock bumpers, carpet undercushion, entrance mats, floor tile, wheel chocks, and containers for curbside programs. In addition, tires can be used for playground surfaces.

Manufacturing Improvements

If it were not for manufacturing improvements, America's current tire problem would be much worse. When the tire industry switched from bias ply to radial tires 20 years ago, the per capita consumption of tires decreased dramatically. In turn, so did the amount of tires being disposed of in landfills. The switch also increased the longevity of tires 300 percent—from 15,000 miles to 45,000 miles.

Today, the industry continues to provide tires of greater quality. The average passenger tire is designed to stay in service between 80,000 and 100,000 miles.

Life Cycle of a Tire

Despite the fact that tires are supposed to last 80,000 to 100,000 miles. Most passenger tires have a life span of 40,000 miles. This is because most drivers do not take proper care of their tires. Tires need to be checked frequently for proper inflation. An underinflated tire creates drag or rolling resistance, which leads to uneven wear. Underinflation is also less energy efficient, and wastes fuel unnecessarily. Tires should be rotated and balanced every 6,000 to 8,000 miles.

If a tire has a small leak caused by a nail puncture, its life can be extended by a tire repair. The repair does not give the tire new life, but extends its current one.

17

Wood Pallets

Overview: *Apparent consumption:* N/A
Amount recycled: N/A
Recovery: N/A
Benefits: *Energy use reduction:* N/A
Air pollution reduction: N/A
Resources saved: Trees
Miscellaneous: Saves landfill space
Outlook: Wood pallet recycling will become more and more prevalent as disposal costs continue to escalate.

INTRODUCTION

Wood pallet recycling is a relatively young industry. As such, hundreds of unexplored opportunities exist for enterprising individuals. Pallets are generally wood platforms used as supporting material that allow a forklift to efficiently load, unload, and move a great deal of stacked material at one time. Cardboard boxes filled with everything from food stuffs to stereos are stacked on pallets. Moving one pallet is equivalent to moving all the stacked boxes individually.

Pallets come in a variety of sizes. Many are customized for the material being transported and others come in standard sizes. Two common sizes are 4 feet by 4 feet and 4 feet by 3 feet. These sizes usually are also four-way pallets, which means that there are openings on each side so that forklift tines can access them from any direction. Pallets are made from a variety of materials, including plastic, oak, ash, and pine. The thickness of the materials can vary because pallets are used in large quantities and are required to have the strength to handle specific loads. Also, pallets are designed to carry different weights of material.

The price of pallets differs, depending on quality. Flimsy pine pallets cost a few dollars each, and heavy oak pallets can sell for $20 a piece. Some pallets are disposable. Others are returnable, and a fee is charged at the time goods are delivered. The money is refunded only if the pallet is returned.

Pallets are often used to ship material long distances. When the goods reach their destination, their purpose has been served. Although some pallets are made from hardwoods, such as oak, and can be returned economically for a limited distance, most are designed for one-way trips and become waste materials at their destination. Local markets exist for expensive pallets, but those made from soft woods are usually disposable because they also are not sturdy and are the type of pallet most likely to be damaged through use.

RECYCLING

As an industry, wood pallet recycling is in its infancy. Pallets were innovations that followed the development of forklifts in order to minimize material handling costs. In the past, throwing them into landfills was both convenient and economical. Some small companies chipped up wood pallets for garden fertilizer or turned the waste into mulch, but this was minimal.

Now, however, wood pallets, like many other items in the solid waste stream, are too expensive to throw away. In 1990 alone, 500 million pallets were made, generating 10–12 million tons of wood waste, of which 40 percent was landfilled, according to the National Wooden Pallet and Container Association (NWPCA). Rising landfill costs have forced people who use pallets to explore other ways to use them.

According to the NWPCA in Arlington, Virginia, pallets find final resting places in the ways outlined in Table 17-1.

LIMITED RECYCLING OPPORTUNITIES

Unfortunately, opportunities for recycling pallets are presently limited. Use of pallets in making wood chips will grow as disposal costs escalate because the wood chips are less expensive to make than the cost of disposal. Most of the businesses involved in recycling pallets also build and manufacture them. The biggest

TABLE 17-1. How Wood Pallets Are Disposed Of

40–70%	Landfilled
10–20%	Used as boiler fuel
5–15%	Composted
10%	Mulched
5–10%	Incinerated
5%	Use as animal bedding

Source: National Wooden Pallet and Container Association.

challenge for those in pallet recycling is transportation costs. When pallets are shipped across the country, there is not always a recycling facility near their final destination.

The standard-sized pallets (4 feet by 42 inches and 4 feet by 3 feet) are generally reusable. A pallet repair yard will pay $1.00 to $1.50 for a pallet in good condition (no broken slats), while end users will pay $4–$6. The price really depends on how competitive the market is.

INCINERATION

Some companies have found that the most effective way to use broken wood pallets is to convert them to fuel. Throughout history, wood has been a source of heat, and pallets can be used on a large scale by fuel boilers. This possibility is threatening to other commodities in the solid fuel industry, particularly those that use coal to fuel their boilers. It is unlikely that wood pallets could compete with boilers that use oil for fuel because boilers are too costly to convert.

Retrofitting solid fuel burners from coal to wood, however, only involves making hopper adjustments. This is an economically viable adjustment to make. In 1991 coal sold for about $ 2.56 per million Btus, while wood was priced at $2.50–$3.00 per million Btus. Coal generates more energy than wood, but wood burns cleaner.

Another advantage that wood has over coal is that in burning it produces one-sixth the sulfur. Wood also produces substantially less ash. One hundred pounds of wood yields one-half pound of ash, while 100 pounds of coal yields 18 to 20 pounds of ash. The ash from wood can be spread over gardens, experts say, while that from coal is generally landfilled.

Despite all the advantages that wood burning has, the fuel markets for wood are advancing quite slowly. However, new landfill restrictions might accelerate wood burning under environmentally acceptable conditions. Another thing that could be detrimental to wood pallet incineration efforts is the Clean Air Act Amendments. The new Act would affect wood-fired facilities with regard to smog and toxic air. Title I of the new Clean Air Act, for example, cracks down on urban smog and ozone depletion. Cities such as Denver and Los Angeles, which have consistently failed to meet standards set in 1977 and 1987, will likely exclude new wood combustion systems.

The biggest challenge that this exclusion presents to the wood-to-energy industry may be in locating and operating new wood and wood waste combustion facilities. Already, many large regions may be exempt from consideration due to high failure to meet other Clean Air regulations. The entire coastal corridor from Philadelphia to Boston is an example of one such area. However, many rural and semi-rural areas remain possibilities for sitings.

COLLECTING WOOD PALLETS

Wood pallets are not collected by most municipalities or scrap dealers. Instead, they are processed by wood chipping operations. To find out where the nearest location is, simply look in the Yellow Pages under "wood" or "wood chippers." Most companies find it more economical to pay a company to pick up the used pallets than to pay the landfill tipping fee. Other chipping operations require the pallets to be delivered directly to them. If this is the case, store the broken wood until there is enough of a stack to justify transportation.

COMPLETING THE CYCLE

Most of the uses for wood pallets are still being developed. The exception is wood chippers, who were in business long before it became fashionable to recycle. The chips are primarily used as mulch to spread across gardens and under trees, to help retain the soil's nutrients. Mulch is often applied about 2 to 3 inches thick and helps keep in water, reducing evaporation. It also decays and enriches the soil and keeps down the number of weeds that would otherwise group and compete with plant crops. Wood chippers sell mulch to gardeners and landscaping companies. The different uses for pallets are as follows:

Rebuilding Pallets—Some companies also rebuild pallets to resell at a discounted price. This is a labor-intensive process, but it probably yields a higher profit per pallet than mulch. To rebuild pallets, the broken pieces are torn off and replaced with new slats. Destroyed pallets are simply tossed into the chipper.

Firewood—Cutting up wood pallets to use as firewood is one way to utilize wood pallets. Pallets made of oak burn for a long time and provide a great deal of heat for a normal fireplace. On a small scale, this helps cut down on waste.

Fuel—Some wood can be processed by wood-fired boilers. The boilers can be easily retrofitted to accept wood pallets, but, before this conversion takes place, managers should make sure that there is a constant supply of wood to keep operations running and that compliance with air pollution regulations is not a problem.

Sludge—Wood chips can be mixed with sewage sludge to accelerate the composting process. The wood chips provide carbon fuel for microorganisms and after approximately 20 days the compost is stabilized and ready for sale or use.

Particleboard—Another recycling option is producing particleboard from old pallets. This is an expensive alternative because the pallet must be ground to specific fiber sizes and quality. Grinding it requires at least $500,000 in equipment. However, material capable of making good quality particleboard can earn $35-50 per ton on the market.

Chunkcrete—The U.S. Forestry Service is just beginning to develop chunkcrete, a hard substance designed to replace the gravel aggregate in concrete. Although experimental, limited testing has shown that, when concrete breaks, chunkcrete bends and continues to hold up the weight.

Composite Board—Composites are a combination of wood flour or chips mixed with recycled plastic granules that are heated to form a solid panel or board.

Spaceboard—Spaceboard is another possibility for used wood pallets. Natural wood adhesives bind a fiber slurry together to make a waffle sheet that can be glued together with another sheet to form furniture cores.

There are many options for wood pallet recycling. The potential for this market is likely to increase as landfill tipping fees skyrocket and communities ban wood waste from disposal.

18

Other Metals

ANTIMONY

Overview: *Apparent consumption:* 45,500 short tons
Amount recycled: 16,500 short tons
Recovery: 36.3%

Benefits: *Energy use reduction:* N/A
Air pollution reduction: N/A
Resources saved: Antimony

Outlook: Poor. Analysts do not predict a big increase in the recycling of antimony because of the decreased use of antimony-lead batteries. Antimony is virtually impossible to recover from flame retardants, which consume more than 65 percent of the metal.

Introduction

Antimony, a brittle, bluish-white metal, is used to harden and strengthen lead. Its commercial uses include electric cable coverings, ammunition, and antimony-lead batteries. Antimony oxide, the most sought after form of the metal, is used to make fire retardants. Antimony is most commonly found combined with sulfur in the mineral stibnite.

Antimony can exist in four forms. Metallic antimony is the most common, followed by yellow antimony, a yellow, transparent solid; black antimony, a black powder; and explosive antimony, a black solid much like graphite. Explosive antimony explodes and changes to metallic antimony when heated.

The world's most productive antimony areas include South Africa, Mexico, Bolivia, Peru, China, Yugoslavia, Algeria, Hungary, Czechoslovakia, Italy, and Japan. In 1988, U.S. domestic reserves of antimony were estimated to be 90,000 short tons, and world resources were 5.6 million tons. Both levels were essentially unchanged from the year before.

Seven U.S. companies produce antimony oxide and metal. These are Amspec Chemical Corp. New Jersey; Anzon America Inc, New Jersey; Asarco Inc., New York; Laurel Industries Inc., Ohio; M & T Chemicals Inc., Rahway, New Jersey; Sunshine Mining Co., Idaho; and U.S. Antimony Corp., Montana.

Table 18-1 illustrates the way antimony was utilized in 1991.

Recycling

Antimony recycling constitutes an important part of the antimony supply. Until fairly recently, about half of the U.S. supply of antimony was delivered from scrap. The proportion has fallen with reduced requirements for antimony in lead for batteries. Most scrap is antimonial lead recovered from used batteries. When it is recycled it is recovered as antimonial lead. Smaller amounts of antimony-lead are recovered as lead alloys from type metal, cable sheathings, drosses, and bearings. A tiny amount of tin base scrap is recycled.

In the past 20 years, however, the demand for antimony metal has declined. This is largely because of the increased use of maintenance-free batteries, which requires a metal other than antimony. Despite the decrease in its use, the United States still could not meet the domestic demand for antimony. In 1988, for example, the United States output a supply of antimony that decreased to less than one-half of the estimated domestic demand. Total imports of antimony materials increased 20 percent from those of 1989.

With the decreased demand for antimony, the rate of recycling for the metal has also declined. Other uses for antimony include bearing metals, solder, type metal, ammunition, cable coverings, and other minor uses. In these applications antimony is added to lead and lead alloys to impart hardness. With the exception of ammunition, the demand for antimony has declined in recent years because of the use of new materials and technology.

TABLE 18-1. Antimony Consumption

Flame retardants	70%
Batteries	10%
Chemicals	10%
Ceramics/glass	4%
Other	6%

Source: U.S. Bureau of Mines.

CADMIUM

Overview: *Apparent consumption:* 4,080 short tons
Amount recycled: Nil
Recovery: Nil

Benefits: *Energy use reduction:* N/A
Air pollution reduction: N/A
Resources saved: N/A
Miscellaneous: Cadmium

Outlook: Cadmium recycling has been practical only for nickel-cadmium batteries and some alloys and industrial wastes.

Introduction

Cadmium is a soft, silvery-white metallic element used for alloys and plating. The German chemist Freidrich Stromeyer discovered it in 1817. Concentrations of cadmium do not occur in nature. The metal is found only with zinc minerals and is mostly obtained as a by-product of electrolytic zinc and lead refining.

The largest industrial application for cadmium is its use in nickel-cadmium storage batteries. Another common use is substituting cadmium for zinc in galvanizing iron and steel. It provides poorer long-term protection than zinc, but it keeps a brighter color for longer periods. Nuclear reactors use cadmium rods to control nuclear reactions. Alloys of cadmium make high-speed bearings and are used as a protective coating for other metals. Table 18-2 shows cadmium's estimated consumption pattern.

Like many other minor metals, cadmium markets are faced with competition from substitute materials. Coatings of zinc or vapor-deposited aluminum can be substituted for cadmium plating applications. Tin may be used in place of cadmium compounds for plastic stabilizers. Zinc and iron pigments can be used in place of cadmium pigments, but often at the risk of reduced performance.

Another challenge cadmium faces is that it is a poisonous metal. Some people have become seriously ill or have died soon after breathing dust or fumes of cadmium oxide. As people have become seriously concerned about environmental pollution, they have feared that hazardous amounts of cadmium were reaching the

TABLE 18-2. Cadmium Usage

Batteries	40%
Coating and plating	25%
Pigments	13%
Plastics/synthetics	12%
Other	10%

Source: U.S. Bureau of Mines

environment from widespread industrial use of the metal. Despite this environmental concern, however, three companies in Illinois, Oklahoma, and Tennessee recovered cadmium as a by-product of smelting domestic and imported zinc concentrates. A fourth company in Colorado recovered cadmium from other sources, such as lead smelter baghouse dust. Based on the average New York dealer price, the output of primary metal in 1990 was valued at $13.5 million.

Recycling

With the exception of its application in batteries, cadmium usage is largely dissipative. Recycling has been practical only for nickel-cadmium batteries and some alloys and industrial wastes.

An acid test identifies cadmium. One drop of nitric acid will turn the metal yellow. The spot will clear up in about 15 seconds. Often, cadmium is confused with zinc. To differentiate the two, place one drop of cadmium chloride on both metals. Cadmium will be unaffected, while zinc will turn black.

CHROMIUM

Overview: *Apparent consumption:* 466,300 short tons
Amount recycled: 97,900 short tons
Recovery: 21 %

Benefits: *Energy use reduction:* N/A
Air pollution reduction: N/A
Resources saved: Chromite and chromium ferroalloys, metal and chemicals

Outlook: Since chromite mining on a regular basis stopped in 1961, the recovery of secondary chromium from stainless steel is becoming increasingly important.

Introduction

Chromium is a hard, brittle, steel-gray metal that derives its name from the Greek word for color—chroma. When combined with other elements, chromium forms compounds of brilliant colors. Chromium does not occur in nature as an uncombined metal. It is usually found combined with iron and oxygen in a mineral called chromite. Chromite is mined chiefly in Cuba, New Caledonia, the Philippians, Rhodesia, Russia, South Africa, and Turkey.

Many chromium compounds are important in industry. Potassium di-chromate is used in tanning leather. Lead chromate is a paint pigment called chrome yellow. Chromium compounds are used in the textile industry as a substance that fixes dyes permanently to fabrics, and it is used in the aircraft industry to coat aluminum.

Chromium resists corrosion and becomes bright and shiny when polished. For these reasons, chromium is widely used to plate other metals, giving them a durable, shiny finish. Chromium is used to plate automobile bumpers, door handles, and trim. It also hardens steel. Chromium-steel alloys are used to make armor plate for ships and tanks, safes, ball bearings, and the cutting edges of high-speed machine tools. Alloys that contain more than 10 percent of chromium are called stainless steels. Stainless steel does not rust easily. It is commonly used to make eating utensils and kitchen equipment. Table 18-3 illustrates chromium's usage.

Between 60 to 70 percent of the world's chromium is consumed in the metallurgical industry. Most often, it is consumed in the form of ferro-chrome, which is used to make stainless steel. By far the most important outlet is in the manufacture of stainless steel.

Recycling

Chromium is chiefly recycled from stainless steel products. In 1990, the Bureau of Mines reported that chromium contained in purchased stainless steel scrap accounted for 21 percent of chromium demand. In recent years the supply of high carbon ferro-chrome, the major chromium product, has been in demand because of the increased use of stainless steel. For this reason, the outlook for increased recycling of chromium looks good.

Chromium can also be recycled from chemicals. While this practice is not yet widespread, chemical waste plants are introducing the technology to recycle more. This could save up to 50 percent of the chemicals used in plating plants. The impact of this will not be large, however, since in the United States chemicals account for about 18 percent of chromite consumption. Thus, the maximum effect that the widespread introduction of this recovery system would have would be to reduce overall chromite consumption by less than 3 percent.

TABLE 18-3. Chromium Usage

Stainless steel	78%
Full-alloy steel	9%
Low-alloy steel	3%
Other	7%

Source: U.S. Bureau of Mines.

COBALT

Overview: *Apparent consumption:* 8,650 short tons
Amount recycled: 1,279 short tons
Recovery: 14.6%

Benefits: *Energy use reduction:* N/A
Air pollution reduction: N/A
Resources saved: Cobalt

Outlook: Most secondary cobalt is derived from recycled superalloy or cemented carbide scrap from spent catalysts. About 13 recyclers accounted for nearly all the cobalt recycled in superalloy scrap.

Introduction

Cobalt is a tough, silver-white metallic element that was discovered by George Brandt of Sweden in 1737. The name cobalt is derived from the German word, Kobald, meaning underground spirit. Cobalt resembles nickel and iron in hardness, but it is stronger than both. It also does not rust or tarnish. Cobalt occurs in compounds with arsenic, oxygen, and sulfur, and in ores that bear nickel, iron, copper, lead, and zinc.

Large deposits of silver-nickel-cobalt ores are found in the Sudbury District of Ontario, Canada. Deposits also have been found in Zaire, Zambia, and Morocco. There is little cobalt mined in the United States. Pennsylvania, Missouri, and Idaho have small deposits of cobalt that occur mostly in pyrites.

Cobalt is chiefly used in alloys, especially in alnico and stellite. Alnico contains nickel and aluminum, and makes powerful permanent magnets for use in radio, television, and other electronic devices. Stellite contains chromium and tungsten. It is used to make drilling bits and cutting tools that stand considerable wear. Cobalt also goes into alloys used for jet engines and gas turbines, because it remains hard even at temperatures up to 1800 degrees Fahrenheit.

Cobalt compounds, such as cobalt blue, ceruleum, new blue, smalt, cobalt yellow, and cobalt green, are used as pigments by artists and interior decorators and in ceramics. The ceramics industry also uses large amounts of cobalt oxide for tinting glass and enamel.

Cobalt is classified as a strategic and critical metal because of its many industrial and defense-related uses. The United States is heavily dependent on imports for its supply. Cobalt is used primarily in the superalloys and cemented carbide industry. Table 18-4 illustrates the way cobalt is used.

Recycling

In 1990 the Bureau of Mines reported that about 1,150 tons of cobalt was recycled for purchased scrap in 1990. This represented about 16 percent of estimated reported consumption for the year. Since cobalt metal production in the United States stopped at the end of 1971, recycling cobalt is becoming increasingly important. Most secondary cobalt is derived from recycled superalloy or cemented

TABLE 18-4. Cobalt consumption

(1991)	
Superalloys	40%
Magnetic alloys	12%
Catalysts	12%
Paint driers	10%
Wear-resistant metals	9%
Other	17%

Source: U.S. Bureau of Mines.

carbide scrap and from spent catalysts. About 13 recyclers accounted for nearly all the cobalt recycled in superalloy scrap.

A chemical spot test can help to identify cobalt. Apply one drop of nitric acid to the metal; if the sample is pure cobalt, it will turn a deep shade of red. A second test includes applying one drop of hydrochloric acid. If a turquoise blue color results, cobalt is present in an alloyed metal.

MAGNESIUM

Overview: *Apparent consumption:* 163,100 short tons
Amount recycled: 29,800 short tons
Recovery: 18.3%

Benefits: *Energy use reduction:* N/A
Air pollution reduction: N/A
Resources saved: Magnesium
Miscellaneous: N/A

Outlook: Resources from which magnesium metal may be recovered range from large to virtually unlimited and are globally widespread.

Introduction

Magnesium is the lightest metal that people use to build things. This brilliant, silvery metal weighs one and a half times less than aluminum, and ranks as the third most abundant structural metal in the earth. Only aluminum and iron are more plentiful. An even greater source of magnesium is the sea, where the element naturally occurs with underground brine and dolmite. At the present time, it seems as if sources of magnesium are inexhautible.

Pure magnesium does not have enough strength for general structural uses. However, alloys of magnesium and other metals have been developed to meet specific needs. Magnesium alloys are made by adding small amounts of aluminum, lithium, manganese, silver, thorium, zinc, zirconium, and the rare earth metals.

Manufacturers use magnesium alloys to build airplanes and guided missiles, electronic equipment, trucks, portable tools, furniture, ladders, and other equipment where light weight is important.

Magnesium is also widely used in baseball catcher's masks, snowshoes, skis, boats, horseshoes, and in the wheels and bodies of racing cars. Other uses of magnesium alloys include automobile parts, cameras, hospital equipment, and motion picture and television equipment. Magnesium's dampening capacity (the ability to absorb vibration) has opened many new uses for the metal.

Magnesium has many nonstructural uses. For example, it is alloyed with aluminum to produce most of the usable forms of aluminum. Magnesium plays an important part in the chemical reactions used to produce important metals such as titanium, beryllium, uranium, and zirconium. Magnesium is also used to protect pipelines, underground storage tanks, and the hulls of ships from corrosion. In the home, the ability of magnesium to protect other metals keeps rust and corrosion from water heaters and oil tanks. Magnesium also finds a place in home medicine chests in such compounds as milk of magnesia and Epsom salts. Table 18-5 illustrates magnesium's usage.

Because magnesium is so plentiful in seawater, it is available to most of the countries in the world. Even nations that do not border on the oceans can produce magnesium because the metal is so common in the earth's crust. It usually occurs in combination with other elements in such mineral rocks as dolmite, magnesite, and olivine. These rocks are available in many places.

Recycling

In 1990 the Bureau of Mines reported that about 29,800 tons of magnesium were recovered from secondary scrap. Magnesium can be recovered economically if it comes to the refinery relatively free of moisture, excessive oil, or excessive contamination.

Magnesium is identifiable by its color, but aluminum and magnesium look so

TABLE 18-5. Magnesium consumption

(1991)	
Aluminum industry	49%
Castings	19%
Dulsufurization	10%
Reducing agent	10%
Cathodic protection	6%
Other	6%

Source: U.S. Bureau of Mines.

much alike that merely looking at the metals may be inadequate. The characteristic that separates the two is that magnesium is highly flammable and aluminum is not.

MERCURY

Overview: *Apparent consumption:* 1,320 short tons
Amount recycled: 239 short tons
Recovery: 18.1%
Benefits: *Energy use reduction:* N/A
Air pollution reduction: N/A
Resources saved: Mercury

Introduction

Mercury is a silver-colored metal that turns to liquid at room temperature. It is most often refined from an ore called cinnabar. To obtain pure mercury, refiners heat cinnabar in a flow of air. Oxygen in the air combines with sulfur in the ore, forming sulfur dioxide gas and leaving mercury behind.

Mercury was produced as the primary product at one mine in Nevada and as a by-product from nine gold mining operations in Nevada, California, and Utah. About 200 companies, universities, and government facilities located east of the Mississippi River accounted for most of the nation's mercury consumption.

Mercury has many properties that make it useful. For example, mercury expands when it is heated, and contracts when it is cooled. It also remains a liquid over a wide range of temperatures. Mercury thermometers use these properties to indicate temperature. It also conducts electricity. Industrial chemical manufacturers use mercury to change substances with electricity. Mercury vapor, used in fluorescent lamps, gives off light when electricity passes through it.

In 1991 it was estimated that approximately 33 percent of the mercury consumed domestically was used in electrical and electronic applications, an additional 33 percent was consumed in the manufacturing of chlorine and caustic soda, and the remaining 34 percent was used for applications such as measuring and control instruments, dental equipment, and paint.

Mercury, like lead, is a hazardous metal. It causes a poisonous compound in plants and animals, which can result in serious illness and possibly death. It is said that a few teaspoonsful of mercury can poison an average-sized lake for hundreds of years. Government and industry are working to keep mercury from entering the environment. In 1970 the EPA banned mercury from sanitary landfills, requiring it to be disposed of in hazardous waste facilities.

Recycling

The Bureau of Mines reports that about 14 percent of mercury used each year is recycled. Mercury was recovered from dental almalgams, batteries, fluorescent light bulbs, and instruments. It was also recovered at chlorine and caustic soda plants and from U.S. Department of Energy stocks of secondary mercury.

Because mercury is classified by the EPA as a hazardous waste, it makes economic sense to try and recycle it. Whatever material mercury comes into contact with—glass, steel, copper, or aluminum—becomes tainted by mercury's association. Separating the waste vastly reduces disposal costs and allows the truly toxic portions to be handled more efficiently.

In California two companies have received state grants to develop recycling technology for fluorescent lamps. The process developed by Lighting Resources Inc. involves dissembling the lamp and mechanically separating the materials. The other company, Mercury Technologies, first crushes the glass tubes and then uses mechanical and chemical means to isolate the substances.

Once separated, the materials go their own way. End caps are combined with other aluminum in the aluminum manufacturing process. Phosphor can be used to enhance fertilizer. Glass can be used for glasphalt, a filler for concrete. Mercury could be collected and reused, but a poor market makes it difficult to close the loop.

NICKEL

Overview: *Apparent consumption:* 170,000 short tons
Amount recycled: 25,000 short tons
Recovery: 14.7 %

Benefits: *Energy use reduction:* N/A
Air pollution reduction: N/A
Resources saved: Nickel

Introduction

Nickel is a highly magnetic, light-gray metal that finds its primary use in making stainless steel. Nickel does not tarnish easily, or rust. It can be drawn into wires, which facilitates its use in electroplating work. Nickel is also used as a catalyst in a process called hydrogenation. This causes some organic compounds to combine with hydrogen to produce new compounds.

Nickel finds its best use as an alloy, particularly when it is combined with steel and iron. It improves these substances by making them more ductile and increases their resistance to corrosion. Nickel also makes steel more resistant to impact. For this reason manufacturers frequently use steel alloyed with nickel to make armor and machine parts.

One of the large domestic consumers of nickel is the aerospace industry. When this industry is stable, so is the price of nickel; when aerospace production is low, so is that of nickel. High-nickel alloys are also used in the pollution control industry. Because of the new Clean Air Act standards, this market is growing. Nickel is also used in construction, electrical equipment, machinery, and household appliances. Table 18-6 illustrates nickel's usage.

There are many factors that affect the prices of primary and secondary nickel. These include foreign competition, foreign imports, government regulation, and substitution. Nickel is one metal that does not have too much to fear in the way of substitution because the change would result in an increased cost or some sacrifices in performance.

Recycling

The Bureau of Mines estimates that about 25,000 tons of nickel were recovered from scrap in 1990. Secondary nickel was recovered from stainless and alloy steel scrap, nickel-base alloy scrap, and copper scrap. One firm converted particulate wastes from stainless steel plants and spent catalysts into nickel-bearing ingots for making stainless steel.

Most often, scrap dealers encounter nickel as an alloy. Any metal that contains more than 20-percent nickel is considered an alloy. The most common alloys are nickel-chrome, nickel-cadmium, and nickel-copper. The identification and segregation of these alloys is crucial to their recycling, since secondary smelters and foundries have rigid specification for remelting.

Since nickel itself is magnetic, this only serves as an initial classification. Nickel can be identified by its color and by the fact that it develops a very short red spark on the grinding wheel.

TABLE 18-6. Nickel Consumption

(1991)	
Stainless steel	49%
Nonferrous alloys	34%
Electroplating	17%

Source: U.S. Bureau of Mines.

TITANIUM

Overview: *Apparent consumption:* 1,018,500 short tons
Amount recycled: 22,930 short tons
Recovery: 2.3 %

Benefits: *Energy use reduction:* N/A
Air pollution reduction: N/A
Resources saved: Titanium

Outlook: Because titanium is expensive to produce, manufacturers are looking into ways to increase the recovery percentage from scrap. At the present time there is no substitute for titanium in aircraft and space, without some sacrifice of performance. For these reasons the prospect for increased recycling looks good.

Introduction

Titanium is a lightweight, silver-grey metal that ranks as the ninth most plentiful element in the world. It is an extremely ductile metal that can be drawn into thin wire, but has a higher strength-weight ratio than steel. This combination makes it ideal for use in the construction industry, where high strength and high structural efficiency are required. Titanium is never found in a pure state. It usually occurs in ilmenite or rutil. It may also be found in titaniferous magnetite, titanite, and iron.

The leading titanium-producing countries are Brazil, Canada, Finland, Malaysia, Norway, and the United States. Russia also has large titanium deposits, but production figures are not available. Florida, Idaho, New Jersey, New York, and Virginia are the chief titanium-producing states. Quebec is the only Canadian province that produces the metal.

Titanium was discovered by William Gregor of England in 1791. It took nearly 40 years until a refining method adaptable into large-scale production was developed. In the United States the Du Pont Company first produced the metal commercially in 1948. Titanium dioxide is also used in the manufacture of linoleum, rubber, textiles, paper, porcelain enamels, and welding rods. Compounds of barium and titanium can be used in place of crystals in television and radar sets, microphones, and phonographs. Presently, production of titanium remains low because it is difficult and expensive to separate from other ores.

Titanium metal serves as an important alloying element because it unites with nearly every material except copper and aluminum. It is used principally as an alloy in iron. The armed forces use large amounts of titanium in aircraft and jet engines, because it is strong but light. It also withstands operating temperatures up to about 427 degrees C, which makes it useful in many types of machinery. Because of its superior qualities, titanium has a number of potential uses, such as armor plate and propeller blades for ships' steam-turbine blades, surgical instruments, and tools. The transportation industry would use large amounts of titanium in buses, railroad trains, trucks, and automobiles, if the price of titanium could be lowered enough to compete with the price of stainless steel. Table 18-7 shows how titanium was consumed in 1990.

TABLE 18-7. Titanium Consumption

(1991)	
Airline industry	80%
Chemical processing	20%

Source: U.S. Bureau of Mines.

Recycling

Titanium is predominantly recovered from scrap generated by the airlines industry. The Bureau of Mines reports that 22,930 short tons of the metal was recovered, at a rate of less than 3 percent. This is because its applications are meant to last a long time.

Titanium is identifiable by its light gray color, its nonmagnetic qualities, and the fact that it will produce a brilliant white spark when it is touched to a grinding wheel. Rarely, if ever, will a scrap processor/dealer come in contact with pure titanium. More often, titanium alloys, such as aluminum and vanadium, or aluminum and manganese, will be collected. Since scrap price is largely determined by the purity of the metal, it makes sense to separate the various titanium alloys. The Institute of Scrap and Recycling Industries has a complete listing of the current grades.

TUNGSTEN

Overview: *Apparent consumption:* 9,370 short tons
Amount recycled: 2,204 short tons
Recovery: 23.5 %
Benefits: *Energy use reduction:* N/A
Air pollution reduction: N/A
Resources saved: Tungsten

Introduction

Tungsten is a hard, silver-white metal that has many uses. It has the highest melting point for all metals, and it retains its strength at very high temperatures. For these reasons it is used in equipment that must withstand high temperatures. Tungsten is added to steel to make steel harder, stronger, and more elastic. Tungsten and carbon form tungsten carbide, an extremely hard substance used in the tips of high-speed cutting tools and in mining and petroleum drills.

Tungsten is widely used in the electronics industry. It is made into heating filaments for vacuum tubes, used in radios, television sets, and other electronic equipment. It is also used to make filaments for electric lights and contact points for the ignition systems of automobiles. Compounds of tungsten with either calcium or magnesium are phosphors, which are used in fluorescent lamps. Table 18-8 shows how tungsten was consumed in 1990.

Tungsten occurs in nature in the minerals scheelite and wolframite. Russia and China are the leading tungsten-mining countries. In the United States, California and Colorado lead in mining tungsten. Tungsten is prepared from the minerals by first adding sodium hydroxide to convert the insoluble tungsten compounds into a solution of sodium tungsten state. Acid is then added to make tungsten trioxides heated with hydrogen to form the pure metal.

Recycling

The Bureau of Mines reported that about 2,204 short tons of tungsten were recovered from scrap. This is mostly achieved by recycling high-speed steel and carbide cutting tools. Scrap is also produced in the form of wire, clips, plate, and bar. Most often, tungsten scrap is pure, but it is sometimes alloyed with molybdenum.

Tungsten can be identified by its silver-white color and slightly magnetic properties. When spark-testing the metal on a grinding wheel, it produces a short yellow-white spark. Tungsten does not react to nitric acid.

Since more than 90 percent of the world's tungsten resources are located outside of the United States recycling may soon become a greater priority.

TABLE 18-8. Tungsten Consumption

(1991)	
Construction equipment	67%
Lamps and lighting	12%
Electronic machinery	10%
Chemicals	6%
Other	5%

Source: U.S. Bureau of Mines.

ZINC

Overview: *Apparent consumption:* 1,400,000 short tons
Amount recycled: 385,800 short tons
Recovery: 27.6 %

Benefits: *Energy use reduction:* N/A
Air pollution reduction: N/A
Resources saved: Zinc

Outlook: Because the United States is heavily reliant on imports of zinc to meet its industrial need of the metal, recycling will continue to grow in importance.

Introduction

Zinc is a shiny, bluish-white metal that can be found everywhere, from automobile door handles to the lining of ships. When zinc is oxidized, it can even be found adorning your lifeguard's nose. Zinc is an important and versatile metal used in many industries. About 40 percent of the zinc consumed in the United States is used in a process called galvanization, which coats metals such as iron or steel, to prevent them from rusting. Brass and oxides each accounted for about 10 percent of zinc's usage, and 11 percent of America's zinc is used in paints, non-oxide chemicals, and rubber products. This means that more than 60 percent of the zinc consumed goes into products from which it is difficult, if not impossible, to recover for further use.

Recycling

Zinc scrap is classified as post-consumer or pre-consumer, depending on its source. Pre-consumer scrap consists primarily of zinc-base and copper-base alloys from metal processing operations, and drosses from galvanizing and diecasting operations. Depending on who generates the zinc, it may be sold to smelters or reprocessed as "run-around" scrap by the same company. The major sources of old scrap include diecastings, engraver's plates, brass, and bronze.

Recovering zinc from scrapped automobiles is highly efficient and is a major source of scrap. But because of new automobile regulations that require the vehicles to be of a lighter weight, zinc diecasting is being replaced with lighter materials.

Scrap zinc is the source material for most of the domestic output of zinc dust and chemicals and about one-half of the zinc oxide production. One problem with zinc's image as a recyclable material is that many of its uses are dissipative, or non-recoverable. Zinc used as galvanizing, in paints or in rubber products, has at best, only limited recoverability.

Post-consumer zinc can be made into a full range of products if it is carefully collected, sorted, and reprocessed. If the scrap is prepared properly, it is virtually indistinguishable from primary zinc made into these products. Zinc diecasting from automobiles is the principal source of old scrap. About 25 percent of the zinc consumed goes into diecasting alloys, and recovery from scrap diecastings is a fairly efficient process. Unfortunately, this is not a growing market. Due to downsizing and weight reductions of vehicles, the zinc content per vehicle has been falling. The problem is made even more acute by the use of thin-walled diecastings,

TABLE 18-9. Zinc Consumption

(1991)	
Construction material	46%
Transportation	21%
Machinery	12%
Electrical	10%
Other	11%

Source: U.S. Bureau of Mines.

as well as the increasing use of substitute materials from zinc. Table 18-9 shows how zinc was used in 1991.

Aluminum, magnesium, and plastic are the main competitive materials for zinc. In diecastings, where temperature tolerances weight limitations and surface finishes are important, aluminum and magnesium are competitive. So far, there is no suitable substitute for zinc in galvanizing high-volume iron and steel products.

19

Miscellaneous Items

CHEMICALS

Overview: *Apparent consumption:* N/A
Amount recycled: 400 million gallons
Recovery: N/A

Benefits: *Energy use reduction:* 30,000 Btus per pound
Air pollution reduction: reduces emissions into environment
Resources saved: Various chemical compounds
Miscellaneous: Utilizing recycled solvents conserves natural resources, and spares the hydrocarbon material needed to manufacture solvents, as well as the energy that would have been expended to manufacture virgin solvents.

Introduction

Most companies that use solvents in their business recognize the risks associated with disposing of waste chemicals. Each year the EPA and Congress add more restrictions to transportation and disposal of these wastes. In 1986, for example, Congress banned the disposal of chemical solvents from landfills. Since that time the list of chemicals that have been classified as hazardous wastes has grown considerably.

Companies who generate chemical waste are faced with huge hazardous waste dumping bills. Recycling these wastes costs a fraction of the cost of incinerating them. It saves natural resources in the process. For these reasons and more, recycling solvents has become a sensible, economic solution to the hazardous waste disposal problem.

The Process

Chemical recyclers usually collect used chemicals from a wide variety of large-and-small quantity generators of chemical waste. These generators use chemicals, usually solvents, for degreasing heavy machinery, cleaning circuit boards, processing pharmaceutical products, treating leather, and a host of other purposes.

The recycler tests the incoming material to be certain of its chemical properties and then processes it through distillation to separate the clean chemical from its contaminants—dirt, grease, water, and paint residues—called still bottoms. The remaining bottoms are blended into fuel because of their high Btu content.

The fuel is used in cement kilns. These rotating kilns are up to 700 feet long with temperatures as high as 3,000 degrees. To maintain these temperatures, which are needed to create the chemical reaction that produces cement, the kilns require tremendous quantities of fuel. They use waste-derived fuels as an economical supplement to coal. These high temperatures safely destroy any hazardous components in the fuel while incorporating any residues into the cement product.

Thus, the combination of distillation and fuel blending enables chemical recyclers to utilize 100 percent of the waste they take in. Recycling chemicals helps to minimize the amount of materials being dumped in hazardous waste facilities, in addition to saving natural resources.

Collection

Many companies sell equipment for on-site recycling of chemical solvents. These range from a small pot that recycles about five gallons of solvents to a continuous-run system that handles a tank load. On-site recycling has many advantages. These include a one-time capital investment in equipment, which gives the facility control over waste management. This investment eliminates the need to transport hazardous waste, and helps reduce the number of reports filled out on the waste.

The second option for recycling solvents is to hire a chemical recycling company. If the business utilizes small quantities of solvents, the advantages of off-site recycling are economic. Chemical recyclers handle the waste disposal process from the moment they pick up the material.

Because of the cradle-to-grave liability of hazardous waste generators outlined in RCRA, selecting a solvent recycler is extremely important. The recycler should be registered with the EPA to handle hazardous waste. It is wise to ask to see the registration, and also to conduct an on-site inspection of the recycling facility. Checking references is also a smart practice.

ELECTRONIC SCRAP

Overview: *Apparent consumption:* N/A
Amount recycled: N/A
Recovery %: N/A
Benefits: *Energy use reduction:* N/A
Air pollution reduction: N/A
Resources saved: N/A
Outlook: Specialty shops exist to recover electronic scrap in every metropolitan area. In an era where computers are technologically obsolete before they are marketed, a steady supply of parts appears certain.

Electronic scrap includes everything from an old black and white TV set with electron glass tubes to a modern computer that fell off a delivery truck traveling 40 miles per hour. The people who operate the specialty shops that handle electronic scrap, not surprisingly, act and talk like electrical engineers and electronic repair-persons. When you have electronic scrap to sell, it pays to be prepared with specific information about exactly what equipment is for sale.

Essentially one line of questioning attempts to discover if the equipment is too obsolete for any of the parts to be saleable. If the equipment is too obsolete, the next questions relate to finding precious metal. If the item in question is an old cash register, unless it is an antique, interest is quickly lost. Old cash registers have no gold contacts or silver wire. If the obsolete electronic item is military in origin or an old computer, it just might be "recyclable." The next step will be a physical inspection of the scrap material.

The problem with electronic scrap is that it can cover a wide array of products that have a small recyclable potential. Electronic scrap may have a steel frame, aluminum chassis, thin gauge insulated wire, obsolete transistors, plastic knobs, capacitors and resistors, rubber insulators, ceramic parts, and other plastic and metal parts. Altogether, this can be virtually worthless without consideration of the labor cost involved in dismantling the equipment. In high-valued old equipment, the electronic contacts can be pure gold and the wire can be pure silver. In newer equipment the contacts may be coated with gold so thinly that it can't be measured without sophisticated tools.

The treasure in electronic scrap can be in silicon chips and parts that are reusable. Beyond the specialized knowledge required, electronic scrap intrinsically is difficult to recycle. Small quantities of aluminum, steel, precious metal contacts, steel, and nickel are present. After valuable components are removed, shredding offers just about the only economical method for recovery. After shredding, magnetic separation of the fragmented parts, air removal of paper components, and hand sorting of aluminum, copper, and other valuable components follow.

It is normal to look at electronic scrap as very low valued material. Yet it makes good recycling sense to determine if electronic scrap can be useful to scrap dealers/processors or to specialized buyers of electronic scrap before considering disposal.

TEXTILES

Overview: *Apparent consumption:* N/A
Amount recycled: 1 million tons
Recovery: N/A

Benefits: *Energy use reduction:* N/A
Air pollution reduction: N/A
Resources saved: Fiber

Outlook: Good. With the prospect of shipping used clothing to the Third World, textile recyclers are looking to increase their markets. For this reason, the future for textile recycling looks promising.

Introduction

Textile recycling, or the "rag" trade, is a well-established but little-known industry. For as long as people have been making clothing, textile recyclers have purchased the fabric cuttings from mills to save the valuable fibers. Today, the business also includes processing used clothing in a variety of ways. The main ways that textiles are recycled include being sold as reused clothing, in this country and overseas; being manufactured into wiping rags; and being shredded into fibers.

Businesses that process textiles are located in most cities throughout the country. They are typically labor-intensive organizations that spend much of their time sorting the material into specific grades. The clothing/material is then baled and shipped off to end users. Table 19-1 illustrates the end uses for textiles.

Pre-consumer

Factory clippings get sorted into various grades, mostly determined by the fiber content. If the clippings are large enough, the used remnants are sold in sewing and craft stores for a discounted price. Smaller scraps are cut up into the wiping cloths

TABLE 19-1. Where Textiles End Up

	Domestic	Exports	Total
Used clothing	—	35%	35%
Fiber for reprocessing	7%	26%	33%
Wipers	25%	—	25%
Landfill	7%	—	7%
Total	39%	61%	100%

Source: International Association of Wiping Cloth Manufacturers.

that gas station attendants, manufacturers, and printers use to clean their machinery. The smallest pieces are shredded into fibers.

At one point in time the fiber from these scraps of material was worth a lot of money. If a piece of fabric was pure wool, for example, the fibers were cleaned and sold at a price competitive with virgin fibers. Other fibers were added to fine-quality paper. But with the proliferation of synthetic fibers today, fabric fibers do not hold the same value. Rayon, nylon, acrylic, and polyester fibers are used to make soundproof materials and roofing products or are sent to the landfill.

Post-consumer

When people donate clothing to charity organizations such as Good Will Industries, St. Vincent DePaul, and the Salvation Army, they are beginning the first stages of textile recycling. These clothes are taken to a processing facility where workers sort the material into clothes that can be resold in thrift shops, and those that cannot. The clothing is separated into hundreds of categories: men's pants, shirts, and shorts; women's blouses, dresses, and skirts; and so on.

Clothing that is not selected for resale in the United States is sorted a second time for possible shipment to Third World countries. Here, the grading becomes even more specific, ranging from broad categories such as women's shirts, to specific sizes, styles, and fabric content. In recent years this sector has become the largest part of textile recycling. Once graded, the clothes are baled and transported to countries throughout the world.

Finally, clothing that is not fit for reuse in the United States or the Third World is cut into wiping cloths. First, the buttons, zippers, and snaps must all be removed. Next, the material is cut into pieces about the size of napkins. These scraps are dyed black or red, and sold to gas stations, automotive factories, trucking companies, and manufacturers, for use as wiping cloths.

WHITE GOODS

Overview: *Apparent consumption:* N/A
Amount recycled: N/A
Recovery: 30–50%
Benefits: *Energy use reduction:* N/A
Air pollution reduction: N/A
Resources saved: N/A

Introduction

White goods are the bulky appliances found in most American homes. These include refrigerators, freezers, stoves, washers, driers, air conditioning units, microwave ovens, dishwashers, trash compactors, and hot water heaters. Americans take about 35 million of these appliances to landfills each year (Shepard, 1990). With the nation's recent focus on saving landfill space, many communities have begun to look into recycling these appliances as a possible alternative to permanent disposal.

Until fairly recently, scrap dealers/processors removed appliances from landfills to recover the steel. Higher-grade metals, such as aluminum and copper, can also be stripped from the steel to generate higher revenues. But when the EPA discovered that many of the older appliances contained hazardous wastes, many collectors stopped accepting the goods. Appliances such as air conditioners, refrigerators, and washers contain capacitors filled with an excessive amount of dielectric fluid that contains polychlorinated biphenyls (PCBs). This fluid is toxic and a known carcinogen.

Refrigerators and air conditioners also contain chlorofluorocarbons, CFCs, which should also be withdrawn before recycling. CFCs are known to cause the reduction of ozone in the atmosphere. In most of these old appliances, this gas is released into the atmosphere in the course of their disposal.

Scrap collectors who choose to accept white goods must remove these capacitors and fluids by disassembling the appliance to some degree. Collectors usually charge a fee to take white goods because of the expense this creates. In addition to the labor costs of removing the hazardous materials, these fluids must be transported to a hazardous waste dumping facility.

This does not negate that fact that white goods still contain valuable metals. Once white goods are free of PCBs and CFCs, the appliances are usually shredded in machines that are designed for shredding automobiles, to recover the steel.

One thing that can be done to make the recycling of white goods easier is for the appliance industry to make appliances easier to take apart. Motors are a problem, but they could be installed in units so that they could be easily removed. The appliance industry could also give consideration to reducing the number of different materials that go into any appliance.

III

Recycling Influences

20

Unsettled Issues

The recycling movement is filled with controversies and unsettled issues. This chapter will attempt to advance some of the arguments on the major issues that divide industry and government. The fact that these issues are unsettled is just another confirmation that recycling is undergoing a metamorphosis from an economically driven activity to an activity driven by environmental factors.

THE WAR OVER DEFINITIONS

People, and even government agencies, cannot agree about the definition of recycling. The EPA defines recycling as the diversion of materials that would otherwise be garbage. The EPA approach is clearly focused on using "recycling" in a narrow sense so that the word can be connected to solving the immense municipal solid waste (MSW) problem.

The U.S. Bureau of Mines (Department of Interior) has a different sense of the definition for recycling. In *The New Materials Society,* recycling is:

> The diversion of materials from the solid waste stream by means of collection, separation, and processing: (1) for use as raw materials or feedstocks in substitution for, or in addition to, virgin materials in the manufacture of goods sold or distributed in commerce; or (2) for reuse of such materials as substitutes for goods made from virgin materials, e.g. washed and reused bottles. Ideally, these diversions are more than one-time, dead-end events. However, in a less restrictive sense, the burning of waste in waste-to-energy incinerators to recover inherent energy values and reduce waste volume, popularly called resource recovery, is also considered recycling. Various other labels apply such as quaternary recycling under ASTM's plastics recycling definitions and "thermal recycling" in Germany (U.S. Bureau of Mines, 1990).

The difference in these meanings is substantial. We used a broad definition for recycling in Chapter 1, and documented 95 million tons of material that is currently being recycled. In Chapter 2, recycling was defined as 23.5 million tons because the narrower definition was used. The difficulty in having the definition unsettled is that it creates additional confusion for the terms "recycled" and "recyclable."

Taking these words one at a time, "recycled" used as an adjective, as in "recycled material," means that material has undergone the recycling process of collection, processing, and distribution. Yet under the EPA definition the conversion of automobiles to steel and industrial scrap do not create "recycled materials," since neither automobiles nor industrial scrap are garbage. Under the Bureau of Mines definition, automobiles and industrial scrap can create "recycled materials."

One of the problems with a narrow definition of recycling is that it requires a line to be drawn around when reusing material is recycling and when it is not. To take cardboard as an example, according to the EPA's definition, the collection of cardboard is recycling because cardboard can become garbage. The cardboard recovered from retail food stores is regarded as recycling. Yet the cardboard scraps from a box plant is not recycling. The reason for this apparent contradiction rises from the objective to have a definition for recycling that is focused on MSW.

Pre-consumer Versus Post-consumer Scrap

Clarifying the distinction between cardboard boxes in retail stores and factory scrap leads directly to two other terms considered important: pre-consumer and post-consumer scrap. Pre-consumer scrap means what it says—scrap generated in the production or fabrication process prior to the product's distribution to the consumer. Post-consumer scrap is used to describe waste materials that have been generated after the consumer receives the product. When packaging, for example, is discarded after the product has been purchased, it is post-consumer scrap. Likewise, the product itself is post-consumer scrap when it reaches the end of its product life.

Tying pre- and post-consumer scrap back to the EPA's definition of recycling is easy. When pre-consumer scrap is used to make a product, it is not true recycling because the practice of using this material to make products has existed for years and because the waste materials have not been a part of the garbage stream. A product made from post-consumer scrap is a recycled product. Products made from 100-percent pre-consumer scrap are not recycled. Or are they?

In the past the definition for a recycled product was important, but somewhat of an academic issue. Now that consumers are making decisions about which product to buy based on a label indicating "recycled," the issue is also about economics. When the labeling issue is resolved, an entire new meaning will be imparted to the term "recycled." Support seems to be growing for the concept that the "recycled" label should require that the labeled product contain a specified minimum percentage of post-consumer scrap. But the issue is still unsettled.

Recyclable

This controversy over the word "recycled" is equalled over the term "recyclable." "Recyclable" does not imply that the product has been recycled, but means that if the "recyclable" product is collected, processed, and distributed, it can be turned into a "recycled" product. It is possible for a product to carry both labels. To use cardboard as an example, a cardboard box can be made from post-consumer cardboard, making the product "recycled," and the box can be used again to make cardboard, making it "recyclable" as well.

Where the term "recyclable" becomes an issue is when it is used to label items such as aseptic packaging and paper diapers. There is no doubt that the impression created by the label "recyclable" is that "this is a wholesome, earth-friendly product." The controversy results because, although these products are theoretically recyclable, there is no infrastructure to collect and sort these materials and because only prototype facilities for the conversion of these materials to a recycled product exist at present. Support seems to be growing for the concept that "recyclable" claims must be backed up by an accessible infrastructure. But the issue is unsettled. Should we expected anything less from a word that was not even in the dictionary until the 1970s?

THE FUROR OVER TREES

The statement that "recycling saves trees" represents a substantial controversy. To someone in the forestry profession or timber industry, the statement is clearly false. Trees designated for the paper industry are grown and harvested just like corn. It is puzzling to the entire timber industry that their industry has been singled out for attack by people concerned about the environment. Why aren't people saying, "When you eat eggs for breakfast, you're not eating corn flakes and this saves corn." Both statements have a similar logic. Recycling will not save trees in the same way that not eating corn will save corn. If corn is not consumed, it won't be planted in the next planting cycle.

One difference between corn and trees is that trees are harvested from forests, not tree farms. Corn is clearly grown on a farm, a controlled setting. A forest looks natural and wild, yet 72 percent of timberlands are on private land. Most people intuitively understand that a farmer cares for and nurtures a plot of ground because self-interest requires that the farmer live on the farm and be looking ahead to the next planting and harvesting cycle. No one is shocked to see a cornfield standing bare in the winter, but many are outraged at sections of cut forests. Some people have intuitive problems trusting corporations to plan for the long-term benefit of the planet. While timber companies actually do plan in 20- and 30-year cycles, it is simply difficult for people outside of the industry to grasp that fact.

Another obvious difference is that corn has a life cycle of several months, whereas trees take a decade or two or three to grow. The renewable character of corn is much easier for people to see and to relate to. When a forest is harvested, especially by the clear cutting method, people who do not think in terms of 20- to 30-year planting and harvesting cycles only know that the forest will not be same for the rest of their lives. The switch from trees 30-feet high to seedlings only a few inches in height appears to be a bad deal. This is a difference in perception between harvesting corn and harvesting trees that is hard to rationalize. However, the basis for this perception difference is the life cycle of the crop.

Unfortunately for the timber industry, their business has other major differences from farming. The timber industry relies on both public and private lands. Since recent history shows the United States to be less concerned about development and more concerned about conservation, the use of public lands for the timber industry is becoming increasingly difficult. Public pressure to stop subsidizing the timber industry through the sale of cheap cutting rights is increasing. Public pressure is also mounting to set aside more land so that trees will not be cut down in the future. Public pressure also exists on the government agencies that regulate the timber industry to be a lot less cozy and a lot more adversarial. However, because 72 percent of all timberlands are owned by the private sector, the timber industry has room to adjust to these pressures on public lands. Nonetheless, some communities will be totally disrupted if these changes occur.

There is nothing the timber industry can do to greater accentuate the differences between the farming industry and the timber industry than leveling an old-growth or ancient forest. Why does the industry do it? It makes just about everybody think that something has gone awry. It brings into question the idea that the industry harvested only seeds that were sown years ago. And these events make people question if recycling more would save trees.

With further analysis it seems apparent that clear-cutting is an environmental issue, not one about recycling. If paper recycling rates did, in fact, reach 60 percent, the privately owned land could still be altered. Instead of new forests every 30 years, the land would most likely be sold to developers to recover the capital investment.

Another subject related to the tree furor is the often repeated, "Recycling one ton of paper saves 17 trees." Reality does not support this statement unless the statement refers to small trees. The image this statement conjures in most peoples mind is a 40-foot tree or a giant Douglas fir tree. The statement is misleading unless the word "small" is inserted before the word "tree."

A MAJOR CONFLICT BETWEEN THE EPA AND THE DEPARTMENT OF AGRICULTURE OVER THE SUBJECT OF RECYCLING

"The Forest and Rangeland Renewable Resources Planning Act" (RPA) of 1974, as amended by the National Forest Management Act of 1976, directs the Secretary of Agriculture to prepare a Renewable Resource Assessment. Unfortunately for the nation and forestry industry, which uses this study, the EPA's recycling goals are not integrated into *An Analysis of the Timber Situation in the U.S.: 1989–2040.* The study mentions but does not incorporate the impact of the paper industry's goal of 40-percent recycling by 1995. The report also states that new technologies "may make a 50-percent (recycling) goal achievable."

The primary concern of this 268-page study is to discuss trends and project the supply and demand for timber. The study, which was published in December 1990, "assumes that the recycling of paper will increase from about 25 percent of consumption to 31 percent in 2040." Based on this assumption and others, the report "projects rising demand for timber products, as have previous assessments."

The report mentions three potential areas that relate to the supply side of timber. First, continued development of pine plantations in the south is projected but might change. Second, global warming might increase tree planting as a prevention measure, but if global warming effects the climate it may effect growth rates—in a positive way or negative way, depending on rainfall and other factors. Last, increased recycling of paper and paperboard could shift the outlook during the next decade.

The American Paper Institute, no stranger to the timber industry, reported a 25.2-percent consumption rate for recycled paper in 1988, a 25.8-percent consumption rate in 1989, and a preliminary 27.1-percent consumption rate in 1990. (1990 Annual Statistical Summary, Waste Paper Utilization, dated June 1991). Another API study projects that the consumption rate will be 30 percent by 1995.

Note: Consumption rate is the amount of waste paper used in domestic production measured in tons divided by the total tons of paper and paperboard produced domestically measured in tons.

Since the consumption rate of 30 percent, projected for 1995, already is approximately the same as the consumption rate of 31 percent that the timber study projects for 2040, it is obvious one or both studies is wrong. Since the API projections are based on plant expansions that have already been announced, it appears that the timber study is too optimistic for the timber interests. This optimism will lead to overharvesting to meet a projected growing demand, result in low prices for wood pulp, and make it more difficult for the secondary fiber industry to justify an investment in new capacity because the spread between secondary fiber and wood pulp prices will be low.

It would be helpful in the future if the Department of Agriculture gave some additional weight to the EPA's goals, which are soundly based on trying to provide direction in solving the landfill crisis. To outsiders it looks as if the problems are not simply virgin fiber competing with secondary fiber. It looks like government is not coordinated within itself.

HOW THE PAPER INDUSTRY IS COPING WITH RECYCLING

That the paper industry is committed to recycling is a fact. Approximately 18 million tons of waste paper was utilized in 1986, and nearly 30 million tons is forecasted to be utilized by 1995. This is a 67-percent increase over nine years—a stellar performance for an industry with a slow growth rate. One look at some of the data reveals that there is a great deal remaining to be done. Table 20-1 reveals that the U.S. paper industry forecasts will result in more trash in 1995 than in 1986. The industry will also utilize more fiber from trees than was consumed in 1986.

While clearly an oversimplification due to the fact that some paper is permanently removed from circulation, the domestic industry placed 54 million net tons of trash into the environment in 1986, 59 million net tons in 1990, and is planning on 62 million net tons in 1995. This is because, in the growing paper industry, waste paper utilization was historically a small part of the fiber supply. Recycling has not grown fast enough to catch up to, much less overtake, the industry's total growth rate.

Export demand for secondary fiber is increasing at a faster growth rate than domestic demand (see Table 20-2). It is expected to rise from 3 million tons in 1986 to 9 million tons in 1995. These markets are expected to triple in size from 1986 when compared to a 1995 forecast. If these export amounts are achieved, the volume of paper products seeking a place at the landfill will be approximately the same in 1995 as it was in 1986. At least landfill problems will not be growing.

Paper accounts for 40 percent of MSW, and it appears that the industry's recycling efforts will not compensate for the loss in landfill facilities that is expected.

RESPONSIBILITY FOR WASTE AND RECYCLING

Who is responsible for creating waste, solving the problem of disposal, and developing recycling alternatives? Consumers, manufacturers or distributors, and government should all share in finding the solution. But, at present, the main problem-solving role rests with government—state and local government, in particular.

TABLE 20-1. U.S. Production of Paper and Utilization of Fiber*

	(*short tons*)		
Year	Production of Paper	Waste Paper Utilized	Paper Fiber Derived from Trees
1986	72,505,400	17,934,200	54,571,200
1990E	80,402,400	21,791,500	58,610,900
1995F	100,000,000	29,935,000	62,065,000

Data for this table was derived from *1990 Annual Statistical Summary Waste Paper Utilization* and *Paper Recycling: The View to 1995.*

**Note:* Not every ton of waste paper used equates to a ton of finished product due to shrinkage. By subtracting the amount of waste paper used from the total tonnage produced, the implication is that shrinkage is zero. The approach used understates the tons of fiber required from trees to the extent of the waste paper shrinkage.

TABLE 20-2 Domestic and Export Consumption of Waste Paper

	(*Short Tons*)		
Grade of Paper	Actual 1986	Forecast 1995	Change Incr/(Decr)
Domestic Consumption			
Newspaper	3,518,000	5,335,000	1,817,000
Corrugated	8,634,000	15,000,000	6,366,000
Mixed paper	2,725,000	4,100,000	1,375,000
Pulp substitutes	2,762,000	3,150,000	388,000
Deinking grades	1,570,000	2,350,000	780,000
Subtotal	19,209,000	29,935,000	10,726,000
Net Exports/(Imports)			
Newspaper	770,000	2,665,000	1,895,000
Corrugated	1,731,000	3,800,000	2,069,000
Mixed paper	(43,000)	0	43,000
Pulp substitutes	387,000	850,000	463,000
Deinking grades	466,000	2,000,000	1,534,000
Subtotal	3,311,000	9,315,000	6,004,000
Total Capacity and Recovery	22,520,000	39,250,000	16,730,000

The Resource Conservation and Recovery Act (RCRA) assigns responsibility with the force of federal law to the states to develop solid waste management plans that, at a minimum, comply with federal guidelines. Regulation D, which is part of RCRA, imposes new standards on landfills. Since landfills are regulated by state and local governments, and in some cases are actually operated by government directly, it is clear who is left holding the bag. Solving the problem of solid waste belongs to state and local government.

The concept of a "product life cycle" suggests that all products go through a cradle-to-grave cycle, which is basically fixed after a product is designed. The product life cycle assigns responsibility for solid waste to manufacturers. Because of the wide range of products in the marketplace, legislation cannot encourage manufacturers to create products that last longer, to market repairable products, or to design products to be recycled at the end of their life cycle.

However, some types of legislation can be sharply focused. Recycling content legislation is one of them. It has been used effectively in getting newspaper publishers to purchase newsprint with a recycled fiber content. This type of legislation will likely be extended to other industries. Advance disposal fees target items such as tires, and these fees also are being extended to other items. Chapter 22 deals with legislation in further detail, but just like federal legislation was used to put the problem squarely at the state and local level, legislation at the state and local level will likely shift that responsibility to the products themselves and their manufacturers.

In many cases the process of assigning the burden of the landfill crisis will materialize as a public sector versus private sector conflict. Another obvious burden-carrying group will be waste generators. Businesses that generate trash already pay variable disposal costs. Variable rates have been tried with single-family homes, with excellent results. Rates for all generators will go up, to cover whatever cost is necessary.

Consumers clearly have the opportunity of accepting responsibility for recycling and solid waste through their purchasing decisions. It is not clear that they will, however.

HOW SHOULD COOPERATION BE ATTAINED TO INCREASE RECYCLING?

Problem solving among interests that are as diverse as environmentalists, businesses, government, and consumers represents a great challenge. How solutions should be forged is a great unsettled issue. Before long, the proliferation of state laws dealing with recycling and solid waste issues will bring interstate commerce to its knees—provided that all the product bans, landfill bans, recycling content laws, advance disposal fees, deposit laws, and so on, are enforced. These unsettled conflicts may well end up as the subject matter of litigation, and may get resolved ultimately in the judicial process. But for now, these state and local regulations are effectively creating an atmosphere for positive change.

All Commodities Are Not Created Equal

Problem solving should consider one commodity at a time. Steel has a 60-percent recycling rate. Plastic has less than a 1-percent recycling rate. Commodities are not created equal. Steel can be sorted magnetically, while plastic requires hand sorting, and beyond a few recognizable resins, plastic is very difficult to sort. If, for example, advance disposal fees are considered in legislation, steel should be exempt and plastic should pay a substantial penalty.

Deposit laws that treat aluminum cans (with a recycling rate of 65 percent) the same as glass containers (with a recycling rate of 30 percent) in the final analysis burden aluminum unfairly. Commodities compete in the marketplace. Now that solid waste and recycling factors are deemed important, a system of rewards and penalties reflecting this importance should be considered, one commodity at a time.

Rewards and Penalties Should Be Based on Results

Whether advance disposal fees of content legislation is directed towards a commodity should depend on results. On a commodity-by-commodity basis, it should take a specific recycling rate or a specific rate of improvement to avoid the burden of an advance disposal fee or other legislative requirement. This criteria, based on "results," will create a situation where the industry with a stake in the commodity focuses less on hype and more on performance.

Leadership

It will take leadership on a national scale to effect change. At the federal government level, the Department of Agriculture, the Department of Commerce, the Department of Energy, the Environmental Protection Agency, and the Department of Interior (Bureau of Mines) could create a task force that addresses these problems.

An alternative is to leave the leadership where it is—at the state level—and wait until 50 different solutions battle for position.

SHOULD RECYCLING BE A SERVICE OFFERED BY LOCAL GOVERNMENT?

In most communities the private sector offered the opportunity to recycle long before anybody even heard of a landfill crisis. Quite frequently the recycling services that exist in a community are not exactly the way government wants them, and the government has no control over the private sector scrap dealer/processor. This can lead to the community making a substantial investment in a recycling program. Then, when the individuals who run the community program want more control over recycling, the situation often leads to looking at the private sector as competition.

It is not surprising that private sector recycling operations fail in this milieu, and when they do, the public sector initiators "feel bad" at the outcome. Some community recycling programs compete with private sector recyclers for items such as aluminum cans on a price basis, while others compete for limited markets. In addition, most government-sponsored recycling offers services that cost a great deal more to operate than the revenue that they bring in. This contrasts with private sector recyclers, who must survive on the economic value of the items that they collect.

When a community decides to start its own recycling program, it should ask if their decision is effective, efficient, and equitable for all those in the community. If a private recycler is already in place and doing a decent job, he or she shouldn't be replaced by a city program without cost/benefit analysis. However, as an additional factor for consideration, local governments should consider that multinational waste hauling/recycling companies are also reducing the number of private scrap dealers/processors through acquisition and competition.

SHOULD LANDFILLS BE AVOIDED AT ALL COSTS?

Most people believe that economic considerations should govern solid waste and recycling decisions. Some argue that recycling programs are valuable to the environment and should be in place despite the costs. As we point out in Chapter 26, which deals with program costs, it is vital to add up all the costs of a recycling program. It is relevant if your specific program spends $500 per ton to collect plastic bottles that are sold for $20 per ton (approximately 11,000 one-liter bottles). No one can answer the environmental question "Is it worth it?" without having some concept of the costs involved in recycling.

Every community faces its own priorities and limitations. Education, health care, job training, the homeless, and other issues may compete with the dollars spent on recycling. Each community must answer the question "Is it worth it?" on the basis of their unique priorities.

If communities as a group subsidize recycling, the subsidy required may get larger and larger. Ultimately, subsidies create surpluses and surpluses create falling markets, which require greater subsidies, and so on. Each community would have to produce more to get less.

IS IT ETHICAL TO SHIP A COMMUNITY'S WASTE OUT OF TOWN?

Trash has a long and honorable tradition of being shipped out of town. Why stop now? The fact that 70 percent of the nation's landfills are forecasted to close within a few years changes the definition of "out of town." In some cases, out of town will not mean beyond the city limits, it will mean out of state. Frankly, few people stay up nights worrying about this ethical decision.

The incentive to deal with this ethical dilemma belongs to the communities with landfills that may become the local landfill to half the nation. They can choose to not accept out-of-state garbage and preserve their own dumping sites, or choose to earn money by charging substantial tipping fees. States that do not have enough EPA-approved landfill sites will also have to consider this dilemma. Tractor trailers loaded with trash could conceivably become garbage barges on wheels, searching from border to border looking for a place to unload.

Since the EPA estimates that the solid waste will grow from today's 180 million tons annually to 216 million tons annually by the year 2000, it is obvious that better solutions need to be developed.

THE PROBLEM OF DEFINITIONS, MEASUREMENT, AND COMPARISONS

There are different views about recycling—some agree with the EPA and say recycling relates only to material that would otherwise become solid waste. We take the position that recycling is any process in which waste materials are collected, manufactured into new material, and used or sold again in the form of new products or raw materials. With wide differences between definitions of recycling, it's a small wonder that people do not agree on how to measure the effectiveness of a solid waste program.

The term "recycling rate" can mean the amount of recycled solid waste compared to the amount of waste generated. Diversion rate can mean the same thing. As concepts, these are useful; as measurement tools, the implication is that you can measure: 1. waste generated, and 2. amount recycled. Theoretically, waste reduction is not measured. When yard waste is composted or grass is left to decompose on the lawn, how is this waste to be measured? Is the amount to be extrapolated and then counted as recycled material, or should it be removed from the waste stream altogether? Can automotive scrap be considered waste, since it was never headed for the garbage? Since it is not waste, can reused scrap be considered recycled? Is donating furniture to the Salvation Army really recycling, since the items were never part of the waste stream? When used clothing is put in the trash, it is considered waste, but can the same clothes hanging in a second hand store be recycled if they were never thrown out in the first place? Bypassing the waste stream may not be equivalent to recycling, which by most definitions involves converting or reusing items considered to be garbage. Clearly, yard waste can be measured before and after a community-wide composting facility is built and the recycling or diversion rate easily calculated. But under less ideal conditions, how can programs measure the impact of unknown numbers of mulching lawnmowers?

Cost comparisons, when they are reduced to cost per ton, are also difficult to trust. We have made an effort in Chapter 26 to include a complete list of costs. If the costs are compared on a line-by-line basis, some meaningful comparisons can be made, but so long as the money received from grants or the volume of material recycled is not treated in the same manner, the comparisons are meaningless.

Participation rates are used to indicate the success of a recycling program. As a concept it is meaningful: What percentage of the community supports the program? As a measurement, it can mean a variety of things because "community" and "participant" are elastic terms. If a high percentage is desired, the community definition can become very narrow, and a participant can be defined to include even the once-a-year recycler. However, if recordkeeping is thorough and done by a system such as a hand-held computer, the concept of participation can be used as a management tool to reward consistent participants and encourage nonparticipants and poor participants.

"Set-out rate" usually refers to curbside programs. The concept is used to define the frequency at which an average household puts its recycling container(s) out at the curb. The problem with the concept is twofold. First, the concept says nothing about the quantity set out. Second, a high set-out rate requires frequent stops, while a low set-out rate requires less stops and costs less. If containers are sized for a monthly accumulation of materials, a set-out rate of once per month of a full container would be preferable to a set-out rate of four times per month of a one-fourth full container. It is difficult to compare programs that don't have similar objectives and get an accurate and consistent measurement system.

The bottom line—it is time to define terms so that they have meaning and to make comparisons on a professional basis.

21

Theoretical vs. Economical Recoverability

The recovery of recyclable materials cannot begin to approach 100 percent of apparent consumption, due to four major constraints. The first constraint is physical. Many products are physically not available to be recycled because the materials have become a part of another product. The second constraint relates to production technology. Some materials, such as toilet paper, simply cannot be recycled, and other materials are lost in the production process. The third constraint relates to economic factors. In many cases, the recycling of materials is cost prohibitive. The fourth constraint is attitudinal. The United States for the most part does not embrace a conservation attitude. It takes a genuine mental commitment to push for new frontiers in recycling. Some people and industries have this commitment. Others do not.

For these reasons it is impossible to recycle as much as is consumed. Only 23.5 million tons were recycled out of 180 million tons of solid waste in 1990. While working on reducing solid waste, it should be possible for the United States at the same time to recycle at least 90 million tons—approximately a 50-percent recovery rate. However, exploring the various constraints will help in differentiating real obstacles from imagined constraints and can expedite the process of recycling more material.

PHYSICAL CONSTRAINTS

When materials are converted into products, these products may have a life of minutes or decades. Based on this characteristic, the product either becomes a prospect for waste and recycling shortly after it is sold or it can continue to function for years. Comparing an aluminum can to the Washington Monument's aluminum cap is a useful example. When the contents of an aluminum can are consumed, the useful life of the can is over. If the can is recycled, it may take three months to return to the consumer as an aluminum can. The aluminum atop the Washington Monument will never be recycled. A newspaper obviously has a short life, but the steel used in the construction of buildings and bridges will not be available for recycling for 50 to 100 years. Other durable goods may have product lives of 10 to 15 years.

Products may not be available for other physical reasons. For example, the apparent consumption of paper includes a quantity of paper bonded to gypsum, to make gypsum board. It can also be used for the backing of fiberglass insulation or made into tissue products. Paper used in any of these applications is physically impossible to recycle later. Numerous applications for plastic products, such as plastic lamination, are simply not recoverable. They will never be available for recycling.

In any growing industry, some primary materials would be required, even if it were theoretically possible to recycle 100 percent. Even if the growth rate was 2 percent annually, that 2 percent would by necessity have to come from primary sources.

TECHNOLOGICAL CONSTRAINTS

Shrinkage in the manufacturing process exists for every recyclable material. In every manufacturing process, one ton of recycled material at the front end of the process produces less than one ton of finished product. For example, when paper fibers are originally formed, they are in their best condition. These fibers shorten and weaken as they age, and the recycling process cannot restore or repair the condition of brittle, broken fiber. If no additional virgin fiber is introduced, recycled paper would consist of fibers that get shorter and shorter on each cycle, until eventually they are too short to make paper at all. Fibers that are too short will push through the fine mesh screen that supports the fiber in the paper-making process. This material, called "fines," becomes solid waste.

The percentage of fibers that becomes "fines" increases during each manufacturing cycle. A ton of collected paper material recycled without adding virgin fiber might make 1,800 pounds of recycled paper, but if this same paper were to be recycled again, it might yield only 1,600 pounds. The next cycle might yield only 1,400 pounds. How many times can the same paper be recycled? Approximately seven times. But that is not the whole story.

With each cycle, the quality deteriorates. If paper bags were made from short and brittle fibers, the bag would lack the necessary strength to contain any weight, and the contents would burst onto the ground. Newspapers would rip at the slightest stress. To maintain the physical properties that are valued in paper products, some virgin fiber must be introduced. If the secondary fiber usage was increased beyond the amount technically appropriate for the qualities needed in a type of paper, it would be impossible to have both the quality and the secondary fiber usage.

In processing metals, material is lost through oxidation and contaminants or through slag and dross, created in the formation of unwanted alloys. These by-products contain some valued material. Shrinkage is a factor in smelting and processing metal, and the shrinkage tends to go up with lower grades of recyclable materials.

ECONOMIC CONSTRAINTS

The economic constraints to recycling begin to erode the recycling potential after the physical and technological limits have already taken a toll. To complicate matters, there is no one way to look at economics. Each member of the cycle—end user, government, scrap dealer/processor, and waste generator—has a different perspective.

To an end user, recycling will make economic sense if a reliable supply of the correct quality materials is available at a price that is low in relation to the price of primary materials. There must be a profit incentive to use recyclable materials. In most applications the quality of recyclable materials may be lower than primary materials, and the cost difference must more than make up for the quality difference because the quality difference may show up in lower production rates, increases in rejected material, and shrinkage.

To a local government responsible for the community's trash bill, recycling will make economic sense if the revenue received for the collected product and the cost avoided at the landfill are less than the cost of collecting and processing the material. Viewed by people struggling with solid waste and environmental issues, recycling will make sense if it can be done less expensively than the lowest-cost disposal alternative.

To a scrap dealer/processor, recycling will make economic sense if a recyclable material can be sold for more than its acquisition and processing costs. To a waste generator, recycling will make economic sense if it can be done more cheaply than disposal. In this respect a waste generator has a great deal in common with a community that must pay its trash bill. Ordinary waste generators, however, usually have the simple task of analyzing a single monthly trash bill. It is usually a great deal more difficult for a community to know its cost of disposal.

Analyzing economic factors would be easy, except that the bottom line is not the same for different situations.

Impact of Changing Prices for Recyclable Materials

For end users the cost advantages of using recyclable materials are dynamic. As mentioned earlier, the decision to use recyclable materials is made because there is a differential between the cost of primary materials and the cost of recyclable materials. The costs for both primary and secondary materials are dynamic, making the differential also dynamic. To complicate matters, most plants are not designed to switch back and forth; therefore, decisions about which material to use are usually based on long-term projections of the differential.

For organizations collecting recyclable materials, the definition of "economically recoverable" is dynamic because it is a function of the price paid for the specific recyclable material. When prices rise, more material is economically recoverable. Additional sorting and additional transportation costs can be incurred because the higher revenue will offset the added costs. When prices fall, less material is economically recoverable due to the opposite effect on revenue.

For a scrap generator, fluctuating scrap prices reflect on the feasibility of recycling. Higher prices for recyclable materials tend to result in more material being recycled. Higher disposal fees have a similar effect. On any occasion, when the spread between disposal and recycling widens, more recycling results.

Even if quality was for some reason not a factor, simply recycling the material would ultimately become cost-prohibitive as shrinkage amounts climbed. The economic limits are determined by a number of key variables, such as the market price of the recyclable material, shrinkage experienced in processing, cost of disposal where the material is collected, cost of collection, cost of sorting, costs of grading and packaging the recyclable material for the end user, the transportation costs to the end user, and so on. Both theoretical and economic limits vary based on the commodity, but to approach a maximum recycling rate requires at the least a framework for dealing with all of the variables.

The effect of rising prices for recyclable materials helps to increase recycling for collectors and waste generators, but would not help end users unless the price of primary materials increased even more. Falling prices help end users, but break collectors. Rising disposal costs generally make recycling a more attractive alternative to disposal, and therefore in maximizing recycling they are a benefit. But obviously, any increase in the cost of doing business must be passed on to consumers.

Considerations in Evaluating Disposal Costs

Disposal costs impact recycling decisions for organizations that pay them. Waste generators and communities that pay disposal fees must use the cost of disposal in evaluating recycling decisions. One basic question that must be answered is whether current costs or expected future costs are used in analyzing alternatives. With disposal costs increasing 25 to 33 percent annually in some communities, the use of current costs would hardly be appropriate. In the time it takes to make a decision, using today's cost would understate the true costs. Also, time must be factored into any schedule for implementation. Future disposal costs might be very different from current costs by the time any sizable project gets launched.

Since future disposal costs impact the amount of material that can be recovered economically, a forward-looking approach to disposal costs may include getting answers to the following questions:

1. What is the expected life of the closest landfill? The next closest?
2. Will the landfills comply with Regulation D?
3. What is the distance to each landfill?
4. What are the dumping rates at each landfill? How often and how much do the rates increase?
5. Are there intermediate locations, such as transfer stations? What are the tipping fees?
6. What are the other alternatives? Incineration? Waste to energy? Baling trash and shipping by rail?

After disposal costs are reduced to their lowest cost and those costs are projected into the future, it makes economic sense to evaluate a recycling program and maximize the amount of material recovered within those financial limits. For example, if trash costs in the present are $50 per ton and they are expected to be $200 in five years, it may make economic sense to aggressively push recycling to its limits.

ATTITUDINAL CONSTRAINTS

To maximize recycling in the United States it will take a major change in attitude. The nation's history is weighted heavily toward exploiting resources. Convenience foods replete with packaging, disposable diapers, packaging that helps to sell merchandise, and furniture that is thrown away after its wear begins to show are just a few of the habits that are resistant to change. To maximize recycling will require a massive change in attitude.

Recycling can grow only to the extent that market demand exists for secondary materials. No amount of money spent on collecting can solve the problem. Collecting material for which there is no demand will merely assure that it will pile up in warehouses instead of in landfills. The demand for secondary materials can only be created when attitudes change.

Efforts to change the attitude of children in school show great promise. Legislation also changes behavior, although we are unsure about its effect on attitudes. When society is willing to recognize the hidden social costs of disposal, it will be a great step towards maximizing recycling.

CONCLUSIONS

Normally, as recyclable material is recovered at higher and higher levels, it costs more to retrieve it. With landfill and disposal costs rising, the economic stage is set for more recycling. With additional legislation on the way and with recycling being taught in schools, the social stage is set for more recycling. If attitudes and the demand for recycled products continues to improve, then products designed for recyclability will win the day.

Then we can push recycling to its outer limits.

22

Legislation

The conscience of the nation is reflected in its legislation. From the legislation being developed in countless state and local governments, it appears that Americans feel guilty about our consumer-driven economy and waste disposal practices. From a legislative perspective, we are ready to admit that the environment has taken the back seat long enough. Laws designed to avert permanent environmental damage are being enacted at an urgent rate.

Legislation relating to recycling exists at the federal, state, and local levels. At the federal level, the Resource Conservation and Recovery Act of 1984 (RCRA) will expire in 1993. The U.S. Congress is currently considering its reenactment. At the state level, more than 2,000 laws relating to solid waste and recycling are being presented to legislatures each year. At city and county levels, the detailed implementation of recycling programs requires even more regulation activity.

FEDERAL GOVERNMENT INVOLVEMENT WITH RECYCLING AND SOLID WASTE

At the federal level, Congress has been willing to recognize that a solid waste problem exists, but Congress has stopped short of providing comprehensive solid waste and recycling solutions. The executive branch has likewise been less than enthusiastic to provide a comprehensive direction. For example, in 1984 Congress asked the EPA to come up with new landfill standards by 1988. The assignment was completed in September 1991. The politicians in Washington recognize that trying to change the "No.1 throwaway society" is fraught with political and economic risks. The fact that solid waste problems are not visible like air and water pollution makes the subject easier to avoid. An industry that has a low recycling rate and leaves a high percentage of pollutants on the land is not looked at the same way as an industry that pollutes the air we breath. So they have done what astute politicians sometimes do—they pass the tough issues off to others.

Actually, even without being cynical it is easy to understand the reluctance of politicians to commit to solid waste and recycling legislation. Since the nation's wealth has always been based on its extensive raw materials, it would be a difficult decision to give secondary materials a leg-up legislatively. Mandating that the lumber industry be second priority to reclaiming waste paper and that the petroleum and plastics industry must stop manufacturing resins if the recycling rate is not up to 50 percent by the year 2000 would be a politician's nightmare. Getting solid waste under control by substituting secondary materials for primary materials implies massive change and massive industry resistance. This explains why the federal government defers most of the detailed decisions concerning solid waste issues and recycling to local and state government.

Local Consequences

The state and local government approach to recycling and solid waste issues has resulted in a highly fragmented patchwork of legislation. Yet because these issues are not being addressed comprehensively, leadership in any form is what is needed. However, the emerging legislative and local solutions are less efficient in solving the problem because they cannot confront the conflict between primary materials and secondary materials directly. To do so would interfere with interstate commerce.

What state and local regulations can do is treat the obvious results. It is analogous to a doctor treating the symptoms of an illness without dealing with the cause. In addressing the problem of limited landfill space, governments who ban materials that cannot be recycled from supermarket shelves or ban them from landfills will mitigate the landfill problem. But in the long run the state and local approach will interfere with commerce on a national scale because the regulations will be different for each state and community. A federal approach will be required to untangle the foreseeable mess. The conflict might well be resolved through the court system, based on conflicts between interstate commerce and local regulations.

Federal Legislation and Initiatives

The major piece of federal legislation dealing with recycling issues is the Resource Conservation and Recovery Act of 1976. RCRA evolved out of the Solid Waste Disposal Act, passed in 1965 to improve disposal methods. RCRA was revised in 1980 and again in 1984. The legislation is currently being reviewed by Congress and includes the following major sections.

Subtitle C Subtitle C deals with hazardous waste. This section regulates and defines hazardous wastes in terms of their generation, transportation, treatment, storage, and disposal. Hazardous wastes are legally excluded from Subtitle D facilities (landfills). This means that hazardous waste must be kept separate from municipal solid waste. Generators must provide for separate disposal.

Subtitle D This section establishes technical standards for the safe operation of landfill and solid waste disposal facilities, encourages states to develop their own solid waste management plans, and seeks to encourage recycling and resource conservation.

Another federal initiative under Subtitle D is the EPA's new landfill standards. These standards were announced on September 11, 1991, and impact approximately 6,000 municipal landfills. This regulation applies to landfills that receive waste 24 months after September 11, 1991. All other landfills must close and comply with the EPA's final cover. In a nutshell: comply with the new regulations or close by September 11, 1993.

If landfills wish to continue operation, they must meet with a majority of the following requirements:

Operating requirements—There are eight essential operating requirements that landfills must meet to comply with Regulation D. First, landfill operators must keep all regulated hazardous waste out of the landfill. Second, they must apply a daily cover and monitor methane gas. Landfill owners must also control disease vector (i.e., rats) population, restrict public access, control storm run-off, protect surface water from pollutants, and keep records of what is deposited.

A key feature of Regulation D is that landfills that do not meet these standards within two years must close. This is the provision that is creating the need for more recycling because there will not be sufficient landfill capacity left to handle today's volumes of waste.

Design standards—Landfills must also meet new design standards. Some states are fortunate enough to already have EPA-approved programs. These programs equal or exceed the EPA's basic requirements that ensure drinking water standards are kept in groundwater. States that do not have EPA-approved standards must add a two-foot clay liner covered by a composite liner made of synthetic material. Leachate must be collected through a kind of sewer system, and the leachate must be disposed of as toxic material.

Groundwater monitoring and corrective action—Landfills must have wells to monitor groundwater contamination. If tests reveal contamination, the landfill operator must clean up the landfill and meet the drinking water standards.

Closure and post-closure care—A protective cap must be placed on a closed landfill, and the groundwater and methane gas must be monitored for 30 years.

Financial assurance—Landfill owners and operators must produce surety bonds, letters of credit, insurance, guarantees, or other evidence that they have the financial resources for closure, post-closure care, monitoring, and corrective action if it is needed.

Exemptions exist for small communities that dispose of less than 20 tons of waste per day, do not cause groundwater contamination, and have either a very dry or very remote location.

A more detailed listing of landfill requirements can be found in the *Federal Register*, dated September 11, 1991. The financial ability of landfill operators to close and clean up the landfill must be proven by approximately March 11, 1994—30 months after the publication of the new standards. Groundwater monitoring and corrective action may take up to five years (September 11, 1996) to prove financial ability.

Subtitle F Subtitle F relates to government procurement practices. It is also known as Section 6002. This section requires the federal government, state and local governments, and contractors receiving federal funding to purchase items with the highest percentage of recovered materials practical, and to delete requirements that products be made from virgin materials.

Tax incentives Historically, the basis for much of America's wealth from colonial times to the present has been its resources. Although times have changed and environmentally concerned individuals would like to see the playing field between using primary materials and secondary materials leveled, getting the tax code changed is politically difficult. There is no doubt that the tax code favors the industries that built this nation.

As indirect evidence that the tax code distorts the real economics of using virgin resources, exports of scrap are growing at a faster rate than the domestic consumption of these same materials. Since the global economy is liberated from the United States tax code, genuine economics prevail. Foreign buyers purchase the least expensive raw material (secondary materials), transport the materials vast distances across half the world, add value to it, and then return these same materials to the United States in the form of new products. The identical ships then load up with additional secondary materials for the return trip. The tax code is actually causing the United States to waste its lowest-cost raw materials and deplete its reserves of nonrenewable resources.

STATE AND LOCAL REGULATIONS

The rate of change in rulemaking at state and local government levels is unprecedented and mirrors the urgency of displacing the waste stream with a recycling stream. With a majority of the landfills projected to close due to Regulation D, the seriousness of the problem is being resolved by changing the regulatory climate. The new regulations propose numerous solutions, but there is no uniformity on a state-by-state basis or even on a community-by-community basis. Because the rate of change is staggering, readers must become acquainted with the regulations for their own state, county, and town or city.

Focal points in legislative initiatives and regulations include the following:

1. Sale bans of specific products.
2. Disposal bans of specific products.
3. Advance disposal fees.
4. Deposit laws for beverage containers.
5. Recycling content legislation.
6. Taxing the sale of materials that are not being recycled.
7. Mandatory recycling.
8. Bid preferences for products made from recyclable materials.
9. Set asides: policies that require a percentage of purchases be set aside for recyclable materials.
10. Community materials recovery facilities.
11. Community composting programs.
12. Flow control legislation.
13. Mandatory recycling goals.
14. Taxation of trash to discourage disposal.
15. Raising landfill fees.
16. Grant or loan programs.
17. Anti-scavenging ordinances.
18. Zoning.
19. Licensing.
20. Tax incentives: sales tax exemptions and tax credit for recycling equipment.

Sales Bans

The outright ban of the sale of specific products is often based on a perception that a product is particularly offensive to the environment. The items that have been singled out by this regulatory remedy commonly include polystyrene drinking cups, beverage containers with detachable rings or tabs, and multi-material beverage containers (aseptic packaging).

Disposal Bans

A disposal ban prohibits various materials from being disposed of as trash. Three benefits of the strategy are the exclusion of material from landfills that are toxic, recyclable, or that represent a high volume of the material. The enforcement of disposal bans is often left to the trash service or to recycling police, with the first violation being a warning and other violations requiring fines. For banned items, the community should have an educational program in place, a sufficient number of collection alternatives, and be prepared for a substantial challenge in enforcement.

One of the boldest bans is represented by Wisconsin's regulation to ban all recyclable materials from landfills by 1995. Other items banned from disposal include yard waste, lead-acid batteries, oil, tires, white goods (large appliances), nickel-cadmium batteries, construction and demolition debris, nondegradable grocery bags, batteries containing mercuric oxide or silver oxide, sealed lead-acid batteries, aluminum, plastic, glass containers, polystyrene packaging, magazines, newspaper, and office paper.

Advance Disposal Fees

This concept makes disposal the problem of the industry creating the solid waste. Some states have waste disposal fees on tires, as much as $4 per tire sold at retail. In Florida, newspapers are given a tax credit based on so many cents per ton for each ton of recycled newsprint used.

Deposit Laws for Beverage Containers

Deposit legislation creates a redemption system in which a product, typically a beverage container, is assigned a deposit value. The deposit is collected from consumers at the point of sale and refunded when the empty container is redeemed. The beverage containers are then recycled.

As a state, California's bottle bill legislation has met with great success. After a two-year campaign, the governor signed a bill to increase refunds on soft drinks, beer and wine cooler bottles, and aluminum cans. These new rates are five cents for every two containers and a full nickel on large plastic bottles. If recycling rates do not reach 65 percent by the end of 1992, the refund goes to a full nickel for containers and a dime on plastic bottles. Table 22-1 demonstrates the effectiveness of the bottle legislation thus far.

Recycling Content Legislation

This type of legislation offers one of the few regulatory methods that works toward creating a demand for recyclable materials. The concept was first enacted into law in Connecticut, and the first law was directed towards newspaper publishers. The law grew out of the frustration that newspapers were collected for recycling, but were not used to make new newspapers because the demand for recycled newsprint

TABLE 22-1. California Recycling Rates

	(Percentage)		
	Pre-legislation	1989 Rates	1990 Rates
Aluminum	41%	64%	76%
Glass	14%	45%	50%
Plastic	1%	7%	15%

Source: Californians Against Waste

was insufficient to encourage paper mills to spend the hundreds of millions of dollars to construct new papermaking machinery.

The recycled content legislation specified that newspapers were to be required to use a percentage of recycled newspaper in the papers that were published. This percentage was designed to escalate over the years, and the amount of recycled newspaper that is used in Connecticut will grow at a predictable rate. After sweeping into the legislative agenda of state after state, newspapers and their industry trade associations have adopted voluntary guidelines, and the rate of passage of this specific type of legislation has slowed down. The concept of recycled content legislation has been extended to other products. It is one of the most promising types of legislation in its long-range impact in that it is thus far the only type of legislation proposed because of the impact it makes in the balance between primary and secondary materials.

Taxing the Sale of Items That Are Not Recycled

To reduce the amount of materials destined for disposal, some Florida counties tax items that do not exceed their targeted recycling rates. The tax is designed to escalate if the targeted recycling rates are not achieved by a certain deadline. Items included for the special sales tax include glass, metal, aluminum, and plastic beverage containers and plastic-coated paper. The tax is refundable if the material is recycled.

Mandatory Recycling (Collection)

Mandatory recycling is in reality mandatory collection of recyclable materials. At this stage it addresses only one of the three aspects of recycling. Notwithstanding, mandatory recycling is one of the most popular regulatory programs. The term "mandatory recycling" has misled millions to equate collection with recycling, creating a significant educational task to teach that curbside programs are only the first step in the recycling process. The mandatory aspect of collection is designed to assure manufacturers that the supply will be reliable. The evolution from voluntary recycling to mandatory recycling is reasonably predictable, given legislation requiring industry to use recycled material. To meet mandatory recycling requirements, communities generally must implement curbside recycling programs or drop-off centers for residential areas, and businesses are also often required to have source segregation programs of their own.

Another method used by some communities require that trash haulers offer a recycling alternative for their customers. This method indirectly forces the trash haulers to pass on to their customers the costs of collecting the recycling stream. Large haulers frequently wait a considerable period before passing on these costs because the smaller trash hauling companies often lack the staying power. It has become a conventional way to increase marketshare in that industry. Other communities franchise a single hauler for a neighborhood, to reduce the number of trash trucks traveling the local streets.

Bid Preferences for Recycled Products

A bid preference implies that if a product made from recyclable material is competitive or within 5 or 10 percent of the price of a similar product made from primary materials, it should be purchased. Laws stop short of indicating that the purchase is mandatory, but instead require that a certain percentage of recycled materials be considered as a first choice.

Community Materials Recovery Facilities

A number of communities attempt to meet recycling goals by investing in materials recovery facilities (MRFs). In these facilities trash or sorted recyclables are dumped onto conveyers and recyclable materials are sorted out in order to reduce the volume of trash going to landfills. MRFs are a capital- and labor-intensive alternative because they require government to purchase land and equipment, and to hire a staff to operate the facility. Frequently, the tipping fees virtually guarantee a "profit" on the facility, but to assure that this can be accomplished the legislation requiring the substantial investment in the materials recovery facility is almost always also combined with flow control legislation.

Community Composting Programs

Materials such as leaves and Christmas trees are often collected by the government for mass composting. Other communities require that the composting be done in backyards. Still others combine composting with MRFs and with sewage sludge to make a product that can be sold or used as fertilizer in parks and along highways.

Flow Control Legislation

Flow control legislation takes the position that trash belongs to the government and by law must go to where the government directs it to go. The government therefore controls the trash stream and makes it into a revenue stream that can generate income. Trash collection fees can be adjusted upward to cover the cost of the government's program. Normally, the flow is directed to a "captive" transfer station, MRF, or waste-to-energy plant.

States usually must give to local government the authority to control waste flow, so that the local government can obtain private financing and demonstrate that they have the ability to repay the loan. The legislation also typically exempts the local government from anti-trust laws, to eliminate an obvious legal objection.

One of the other issues that flow control legislation raises is whether recyclable materials are included in the definition of regulated materials. Generally, recyclable materials are not included within the definition, so that recycling is encouraged in every way possible.

Mandatory Recycling Goals

Many states have established mandatory recycling goals and have placed the burden on local government for meeting the standards. Mandatory goals frequently exceed the 25-percent goal established by the EPA. Most state recycling goals are in the range of 35 to 50 percent of solid waste. Local government is at a minimum, forced into initiating curbside collection programs, mandatory business recycling, and banning yard waste from landfills in order to comply with the goal. Cities and businesses can also be required to submit written plans to show how they are implementing their recycling plan.

Taxation of Trash

Since many communities have direct or indirect control of landfill facilities within their borders, fees can be charged either outright or as a tax to pay for the government's solid waste and recycling program. This type of regulation is very popular because it gives the community the capital to achieve its objectives. Since the community expects trash to cost more, there is often little resistance to taxation, and this makes the taxation of trash a genuinely popular idea.

Raising Landfill Fees

Raising tipping fees and dump fees is a common method of generating revenue.

Grant or Loan Programs

The most popular way to fund government recycling programs is to apply for grants from local, state, or federal agencies. The helps to defray the cost of collection. States such as Minnesota automatically fund the programs of communities. Other states rely on written requests and evaluate the grants based on an evaluation of the grant proposals. Before the money becomes available, however, it must be set aside in the state budget.

Tax Credits for Recycling Equipment

A number of states give 10-percent tax credits for investments in recycling equipment. California gives a 40-percent tax credit for the cost of equipment used to manufacture recycled products. Wisconsin provides up to $300,000 in direct credit for manufacturers using secondary materials. Other states have programs for specific items that are currently difficult to recycle, such as tires, lead batteries, or oil. Utah, for example, will pay $21 for each ton of tires incinerated or made into new products.

Anti-scavenging Ordinances

Curbside programs are susceptible to scavengers who beat the recycling truck to valuable items assembled at the curb. Typically, items such as aluminum cans are stolen by scavengers, and this increases the cost of the curbside program by depriving the program of revenue. To protect these programs and keep neighborhoods free from unwanted traffic, local government often passes anti-scavenging laws to prohibit this practice.

SUMMARY

Legislation effects social change. With effective federal legislation, the prospect exists to deal efficiently with the national solid waste problem, landfill issues, market demand for recycled materials, and an improvement in recovery rates. It is not clear that this will occur.

State and local solutions will take many different forms, but people who care about the environment have more influence in shaping direction locally. Unfortunately, state and local solutions cannot directly become involved in the competition among commodities and will approach these matters indirectly. At the state and local level, strategies will deal with extending the lives of scarce landfill space or will deal with rapidly escalating costs of disposal.

Regrettably, without legislation at the federal level, a conflict seems inevitable between local regulations and federal laws dealing with interstate commerce. It would be unfortunate to have to resolve solid waste and recycling issues in the court system, but this looms as a real possibility.

Part 4

Effective Recycling Programs

23

Elements of a Successful Recycling Program

Everyone who has organized a successful recycling program has found it to be a test of organizational and leadership skills. It is also one of the most exciting aspects of recycling, and it is a task that should be approached enthusiastically. The following approach results from the author's 17 years of experience helping people establish more than 1,000 recycling programs. The model works well and will result in programs that are customized for each situation. As attractive as a standard recycling program seems, successful recycling programs are like snowflakes—each is unique in some respect from the other. The "correct" recycling program for a particular area varies from business to business and from organization to organization. It also varies over time.

As an industry, recycling changes all the time. Even the best-planned program continues to evolve as the program matures and recycling opportunities change. The only way to develop the right recycling program is to go through a process that covers all the elements.

STEPS IN ORGANIZING A RECYCLING PROGRAM

Whether your interests are government- or business-related, whether you have a small town or major metropolitan perspective, or whether you are new to recycling or are an experienced professional, all successful programs evolve through the following steps:

1. Research the regulatory and legislative climate—learn about your legal obligations.
2. Determine the preliminary goals and objectives of the program. Answering a series of questions helps define a direction.

3. Survey the attitudes and perceptions of the people who need to support the program. Recycling is a team activity, and, ideally, it is an activity that everyone will support.
4. Explore existing solid waste practices and understand any existing recycling programs. Analyze the waste stream and recycling stream and determine how additional waste can be eliminated or recycled. Before setting a new direction it is fundamentally important to know all you can about the existing situation.
5. Find out what commodities are marketable for your area. Nothing undermines a program faster than people learning that elements of their recycling program are bogus. Put another way, people become furious if the materials they are trying to recycle go to the landfill or are incinerated, so that all of their efforts have been wasted.
6. Design the recycling program, and determine the method of collection. To accomplish this element you will need to become familiar with all collection options and choose the right ones for your program.
7. Assign responsibility for operation of the program. Designating an operational leader for the recycling program is a critical decision. A persuasive and effective recycling manager is difficult to recruit. By the time many programs get to this stage, the tendency is to simply give the job to anyone who wants it. Resist this tendency at all costs. The job of recycling manager is far too important for "wanting the job" to be the only or even the major criterion.
8. Establish measurable goals for your program. Just as your program is unique to your situation, the goals should reflect your specific objectives.
9. Obtain financial support for the program, if needed. Ongoing financial support can be just as important as having people supporting the program. It takes money to provide initial publicity and education. Some recycling programs do not cover their full cost, and often find it difficult to purchase the equipment they need.
10. Execute the startup phase, including publicity, education, and training. If facilities and equipment are involved, they should be put in place and be made operational.
11. Monitor progress, evaluate the program, and make adjustments to the program to improve its effectiveness. If you maintain high standards for the program, you will constantly discover opportunities for improvement.

RESEARCHING SOLID WASTE AND RECYCLING REGULATIONS

With more than 2,000 pieces of legislation being proposed annually in state legislatures, and countless thousands of other rules being proposed at the local government level, it is probably an understatement to say that the regulatory climate for recycling is dynamic. Frenzied is probably a more accurate word. As a practical matter, there is probably no one place to inquire about the legislation that impacts your specific interests.

You should begin looking up legislation at the local level and work upward. If your city and county have recycling ordinances, they may have been developed in concordance with a state law. There are presently no recycling mandates at the national level. Chapter 22, "Legislation," will help you to locate what kind of legislative situation you face.

DETERMINING PRELIMINARY GOALS AND OBJECTIVES

Even if you become the world's greatest authority on recycling and are able to size up the type of recycling program and goals that fit a specific situation, you would be wise be to wait to apply this information until after you have asked a great many questions and have listened to the answers. By asking questions, instead of supplying answers, you will learn information critical to designing a successful recycling program.

In fact, you will keep learning by using this method. Recycling programs are something like a kaleidoscope, where the same components are present, but the design is different each time. The reason for this is that recycling is dynamic: markets change, priorities change, waste streams change, collection methods change, attitudes change, technology in how recycled materials are used change, and so on.

Questions should begin with the person or group acting as the potential program's originator. The more questions asked, the better the resulting program. The important early questions should be similar to these:

1. What are you trying to achieve with your new recycling program?
2. What do you like about what you are doing now?
3. What don't you want to have happen? What would constitute disaster in your mind?

It is also extremely important to take notes and to record the answers to these questions. The benefits of taking notes are twofold: first, it will help you to remember the answers, and second, it will help build the relationship between you and the program's originator—whether individual or committee. You are effectively saying "what you say is important, important enough for me to write down." If you are dealing with a committee, drive for a consensus answer. If you can't arrive at an agreement, the subject will need to be raised later when more information has been gathered. The answers to these questions tell you a great deal of important information. You will learn about the depth of understanding and thought behind the proposed recycling project, and you'll learn about the important elements that must be a part of the plan. You'll also begin to build a relationship that is based on genuine mutual understanding. As you personally build knowledge and confidence, you'll want to add many more questions to these basic questions, such as:

1. Is it important to you to divert as much material as possible from the landfill?
2. Do you want to recycle items even if they don't make short-term economic sense?
3. Does your organization insist on a return on investment if/when any capital is committed?
4. What rate of return do you typically earn on projects considered successful?
5. What percentage of people do you think will actively participate in a recycling project?
6. Are some recycled materials more important to you than others? Why?
7. Do you have any existing recycling programs?
8. What do you like about them?
9. What do you dislike about them?
10. Are there any funds that can be used to start the program?
11. Are there funds to support the program if the revenue earned does not support the program?
12. Do you consider the avoided disposal costs to be important in calculating the economic success of the program?
13. What is more important in evaluating success—participation, the amount of material diverted from the landfill, economic return, complying with the law, or doing the right thing? What is least important?
14. How important is service to the program?
15. What constitutes good service? Bad service?
16. What would happen to your program if it gets started and then funding stops?
17. Are there alternative funding sources that can be developed?
18. Can the program be built in sections so that it can grow and shrink in a more or less orderly manner based on funding availability?
19. Are there markets for the material we are going to collect?
20. Can we obtain reliable contracts with scrap dealers/processors?
21. Other than price considerations, are some markets reliable and others not reliable?
22. What prices can we expect for the various materials?
23. Have you considered the following materials in your program? Presumably you would know which materials have been left out.
24. How do you expect to collect the materials?
25. Are more materials concentrated in one location than in others?
26. To what extent are you planning on processing the material to make sure it represents the quality that the market requires?

When you determine the answers to questions such as these, there will be little doubt as to the scope of the recycling project to be considered. Sometimes you will have 15 minutes to introduce, discuss, and conclude the subject. Other times, it may be 30 minutes, but rarely—unless there is a big organization involved—will there be substantial time to collect the preliminary data.

Priorities are rarely the same between communities or businesses, so a "cookie cutter" approach simply will not produce the best program. Specific options for various types of recycling programs are given in detail in subsequent chapters, but it is important at this point to get the process elements understood, because the process is similar in all cases.

Sometimes the expectations of the originating group are not realistic. For example, a rural community might want to achieve a curbside program, with no investment in equipment, at no extra cost to the community, and to generate revenue on what is collected to purchase land for a community park. If this is the case, your work begins at once. If realism prevails, the data you collect will help set up the next step, which is to determine the level of existing support.

SURVEY OF ATTITUDES

Beginning every program with an informal survey of attitudes about recycling is a fundamentally sound practice. It is extremely important to have a gauge to measure the amount of general support for recycling and to determine the type of program that will be supported. Since you presumably know what the originator wants, it is not difficult to design a questionnaire to discover if similar ideas are shared by the community at large and if a specific program will be supported.

It is commonplace for programs to be initiated by a small core of committed people, but recycling represents a type of activity requiring support from a large number of people and throughout most organizational levels. This is especially true for a small community. You need the support of the city or town council, the managers of the community, the activists in the community, the haulers of trash and/or recyclables, and the general population. If support is not broad-based and strong at all levels, the program is at risk. For example, it would be disastrous, when the next election brings about a change in city council, for this new council's agenda not to include recycling. The recycling program must be supported by the entire community and not be just the brainchild of the current local government.

This is also true for businesses. The program needs the support of top management, middle management, and front line management. It also needs support through the ranks from informal leaders to formal leaders. The larger the organization, the more people are empowered to defeat a new idea, and the harder it is to get an affirmative response. Recycling, however, requires the cooperation of everyone because it takes a significant effort to generate quality material. If the support is widespread, the first ingredient for a successful program is in place.

As a general rule, a 75-percent approval rating is a satisfactory starting place.

If for some reason your survey falls short, it indicates that a sales program is needed prior to beginning a new recycling effort, or it may indicate that a small-scale program is needed to demonstrate the feasibility of a large-scale one. Sometimes a negative result means that the timing is wrong to start any program at all.

Many of today's successful programs were started by a committed core of volunteers who persevered despite all odds. But the collection and handling of tons of newspapers, glass bottles, and aluminum cans has worn out the backs and tested the resolve of many, many people. It is therefore important to have broad support to rescue these volunteers before the point of exhaustion.

The maintenance of high quality is also an extremely important variable in collection programs. In a community recycling program, someone has to clean the peanut butter out of the jar before it is collected for recycling, and someone must remember to take the caps off the plastic bottles and glass containers. In business, the worker who throws the cardboard in the recycling bin must take care to throw wood pallets somewhere else. It is just not usual practice to be concerned about quality issues when throwing things away. Non-caring people can sabotage the best-intentioned recycling program, but uninformed people do the greatest damage. Without broad-based support, any program can run into trouble before it gets very far along. In particular, this is what makes recycling programs in large urban areas a unique challenge.

WHAT ATTITUDES SHOULD BE SURVEYED?

Leading questions, such as "You want to save the earth, don't you," which force an affirmative answer, are not really helpful. What you want to know is how committed people are to recycling and what types of programs they would support. This is important data to collect because you want a realistic idea about how many people are currently committed to recycling and how many would like to be. In determining these statistics, it is essential to ask questions in a responsible manner. Asking "Do you recycle?" will yield many positive responses because even a person who has recycled one aluminum can in the past five years is likely to answer yes. A sample survey is included in Chapter 26 on government programs.

COMPILING DATA

Historical data regarding waste disposal and recycling should be collected for at least a two-year period. Fluctuations in amounts may reflect seasonal factors, business cycles, or some other phenomenon that should be understood. If you live in a ski resort or a summer resort, you can make intelligent assumptions about the seasonality of trash generation, but there are few substitutes for hard facts. Ultimately, systems need to account for both peaks and valleys.

In addition, studying the flow will give you an idea about trends. Data should be collected on both volume and price of recyclables. If you are in a new and growing community, you should see these facts reflected in the steadily growing volume of trash; however, if business activity has been off in the past few years, the declining volume data should reflect that trend as well. Developing relationships between trash and population expressed as tons of trash per person can be a useful planning tool. Other relationships like those between number of employees and trash or between sales revenue and trash generation, might be meaningful. Collecting data on the escalating costs of disposing of a ton of trash will help in analyzing the past and projecting the future. Businesses, for example, will have to target price increases, to offset increasing trash bills, or become committed to a serious trash reduction and recycling program. Governments will be compelled to raise taxes or find new sources of revenue to offset increased costs.

It is a great deal harder to analyze the components of the waste stream than it is to document the volume or costs of disposal. The easiest method is visual inspection. By taking a look at what is in dumpsters you can get a general idea about the potential to recycle. One dumpster might be filled with old corrugated, another with tree limbs and branches, and another with something so awful smelling it denies a closer inspection. Although very little good data can be collected, it is still much better than no data at all. One of the frequent problems in determining waste components is in converting how much space something takes up to the percentage of total it comprises. For example, corrugated can look dominant, but it is very light per cubic foot and may represent only a small percentage of the waste stream's weight. Stones and dirt, on the other hand, are hard to see when looking in dumpsters because they work their way to the bottom, but they may make up most of the weight of the trash.

A better method, which avoids this problem, is sampling. In some sampling techniques all of the discarded material is weighed and categorized by type of material for a specified time period. This method requires having a scale at each sampling location and keeping accurate records. Sampling can produce very reliable data, especially if the total weight of the trash can also be obtained through a secondary method. If the sum of the parts adds up to the total weight generated, you can be very confident that the data has been accurately gathered.

Another sampling method that produces excellent data is sorting the waste by hand. However, this method can be expensive and time-consuming. Samples are selected from actual loads and separated by hand into various types of material. Then each type of material is weighed. Residential trash loads are typically very wet. Sorting this kind of waste is among the most unpleasant jobs imaginable, and you can imagine how intolerable the stench would become on a hot summer day.

A suggested alternative is to establish procedures so that during the sample period wet trash is collected separately from dry trash. Two trash trucks should be used—one to pick up wet trash and one for dry trash. Since wet trash includes restroom trash, food wastes, cafeteria wastes, and so forth, it will not be sorted, but its total weight should be recorded. The total weight of the trash is computed by subtracting the weight of the empty truck from the weight of the full truck. A physical inspection of the wet trash can be used to indicate if it justifies a large-scale composting facility. The dry component of trash can be first weighed and then dumped on the ground in a suitable area and manually separated by type of material. Each type of material should then be weighed. Loads or routes should be randomly selected. The data that is collected in this manner can produce very high confidence levels, even though only a small percentage of the total trash stream has been studied.

If a local study is not possible, it may be practical to use a similar-sized city's study and make the assumption that your waste stream is similar. The reference point might be a national study of municipal solid waste, an example of which is shown in Chapter 2, Table 2-3.

Analyzing the waste stream properly is an expensive and hardly prestigious task. But you really must get acquainted with the composition on a detailed basis to get accurate results. A proper assessment includes planning and designing the assessment, conducting physical inspections and on-site interviews, selecting samples properly, analyzing waste streams, analyzing and summarizing the data for the community or company as a whole, and, finally, presenting the data—all of which are activities that cost money.

For government the data can be used to determine who generates the trash and what types of programs are needed. For example, the data can help to determine the number and size of trucks if a curbside program is indicated, to determine the minimum size of any intermediate processing facility, or to determine the amount of material available for a waste-to-energy facility. For business, the data can determine what can be collected, the economic impact of recycling, and the amount and kinds of equipment needed. For both government and business the data can be used to determine the amount and kinds of materials that must be sold and to determine the scope of the marketing effort.

FINDING OUT WHAT IS MARKETABLE IN YOUR AREA

A waste material remains a waste material until it is sold as a recyclable material or used again. Every geographical area has a unique set of market alternatives—some items may be easy to market and others may be impossible to market on an economic basis. It takes a great deal of market research to determine not only if a market exists, but also where the best market exists. It makes good sense to look at market research as a continual process, since markets are dynamic.

Chapter 24 deals exclusively with the marketing process, and the Appendix has been set up to be as user-friendly as possible in assisting this research.

Once markets are discovered, material specifications and contamination are easier to define.

DESIGNING THE PROGRAM

After determining goals, surveying attitudes, analyzing the waste stream, and accessing markets, you have assembled most of the information you need. You will know what to recycle and who wants what kind of recycling program. Specialized programs are described in Chapters 25 through 31. Hereafter, you will have to choose the programs that fit your circumstances.

ASSIGNING RESPONSIBILITY FOR ACHIEVING THE GOALS

A single person should be designated as recycling manager and given the responsibility, budget, and authority for executing the recycling program. This person must have strong leadership skills. Running meetings, communicating in front of groups, and gaining a consensus for action among strong-willed competing interests will be a constant challenge. This manager must be able to establish goals, develop strategies, implement the details of the program, monitor performance, and enforce compliance with the goals and objectives of the program.

The recycling manager must also be capable of getting others to achieve the program's goals through effective recruiting, training, and, if necessary, must be willing to terminate employees for non-performance. It would help if the manager were a salesperson because the recycling programs must be sold to participants and the recyclable materials must also be sold to dealers. Other personal qualities, such as integrity, willingness to work hard, above-average intelligence, positive attitude, and pride in accomplishments, round out the ideal candidate.

ESTABLISHING MEASURABLE GOALS

The bottom lines for government and for business are different. Each organization, each program, and each recycling manager will have different ideas about what is important. In developing measurable goals, it is important that two criteria be met: The goals must be both achievable and acceptable. The goals must not only be realistic, but must also show improvement over the current situation or meet other criteria, such as a minimum return on investment.

A common objective is to reduce waste by a certain percentage. The amount of waste should be measured before a program starts and then periodically thereafter. Also, controlling cost to below X dollars per ton or Y dollars per person may be a typical objective. Whatever the goal, it should be a product of a spirited negotiation between the recycling manager and his or her employer. If the recycling manager is a volunteer, the board of directors or the recycling committee should be targeted for negotiation.

OBTAINING FINANCIAL SUPPORT

One of the biggest factors in determining the scope of your recycling program is funding. Obtaining secure financial support in the early stages of the program can help set the tone of how well it will be accepted. When you are looking for funding, it is important to put together a well-organized prospectus with clear, reasonable goals.

A written plan, including a capital budget as well as projections for revenues and costs, should be part of every recycling program. The plan should also emphasize that recycling costs can be offset by avoided waste disposal costs. Top level management should be consulted during the planning process, to determine if guidelines exist about how data should be presented and to learn how the review and decision process operates. If recycling is mandatory in your area, obtaining financial support for your plan will be made easier. If recycling programs are voluntary, selling the plan may be more difficult. Much will depend on the financial constraints of your organization.

START UP PHASE

Almost everyone in the United States has been trained to dispose of waste materials as trash. To change these ingrained habits will require a sustained educational program, utilizing repetition and diverse approaches. Public education can borrow the strategies of successful advertising, since the goal is in effect to sell a recycling program. And as in advertising, a lag time can be expected between appeals to recycle and consumer response. Meetings, posters, signs, color-coded containers, printed instructions, refrigerator magnets, advertisements, video tapes, and TV messages are all part of the educating process. This process must be continual because new people in the community and new employees must all be contacted or the program will gradually unravel.

Every program will benefit from a letter of support from the head of the appropriate organization—a mayor, the city council, a CEO, and so on. Recycling is still new to many, and, according to existing successful programs, strong leadership helps convince the wary.

CONTROL OF RECYCLABLE MATERIALS

Controlling the materials that leave your facility is very important. If you recycle with a scrap dealer/processor, a good procedure to follow is to have a designated contact person. Each pickup should involve a two-part prenumbered form with a space to describe what types of materials are being taken and the number of containers, boxes, or skids of each grade of material. When this pickup slip is signed by the authorized contact, a copy should be retained. Later, when paid, the prenumbered receipt should correspond to information contained on the check. In approximate terms, the weights and grades of material recorded on the original copy of the pickup ticket can be compared to the amounts that are paid. With proper controls there is reasonable assurance that proper payment has been made and that profit won't slip out the back door.

Another reason for checking the material being picked up is that occasionally it is possible that wrong material can be taken. For example, a pallet of new paper might have just been delivered and be located adjacent to pallets of scrap that are to be shipped. The representative from the scrap dealer might have no way to detect that the new material is not scrap.

CONTROLLING DISPOSAL COSTS

Controlling disposal costs is one major advantage of recycling programs because, through astute purchasing practices and an aggressive recycling program, it is possible to minimize trash tonnage. But even the most aggressive program will still result in a waste disposal fee. This is because disposal companies charge for the equipment (such as dumpsters) they provide, the rental rate of that equipment, the frequency of pickup, the fullness of the containers, and the cost of disposal. This last charge is usually the hauling rate plus a tipping fee or landfill disposal charge.

Normally, trash haulers provide a great deal of detail with their monthly invoice. Charges may be based on a monthly fee for disposal services, a fee for each pickup, a fee for volume hauled, or a fee for weight hauled. If the charges are based on volume, a method of compaction might be worth considering. Compaction equipment will cost more, but the volume can be reduced by a factor of three. Also, if compaction equipment is already used, it makes sense to check the pressure occasionally to assure that it is set properly.

QUALITY CONTROL

A quality control system must be a part of every recycling program if the program has any hope of being economically viable. The system should take into account the full implications of the recycling process and recognize that collection programs are only the beginning of the recycling cycle. The programs should cater to increasingly sophisticated end users who need a quality product on a regular basis. The system must also recognize rapidly changing technology and a growing complexity in grades of material. Quality control should also incorporate competition from other materials and for global markets and changing regulations. In short, a quality control system provides the flexibility to quickly, efficiently, and effectively respond to new developments in the recycling industry.

COMMUNICATING QUALITY STANDARDS

Quality standards for each commodity must be explained clearly to those involved in collection programs. Most scrap grades have some allowable contamination because it is virtually impossible for the end users to expect perfect material. However, if standards are explained clearly, experience indicates that sorters and graders will strive for perfection. To do less virtually assures quality problems and rejected material. In fact, if you do not concern yourself with quality, it would be less expensive to let the material end up in a landfill. Without strict quality standards, the material is headed there anyway.

Quality control must be built in throughout the process—in receiving material, sorting material, and in shipping material to an end user. First, standards have to be understood by management, and then they must be communicated in an effective manner to employees. Container glass can be used effectively as an example for both requirements.

First, management must understand the glass industry's requirements for high-quality cullet: Container glass must be separated by color into amber, green, and clear colors. The following items are not acceptable: metal or plastic tops, window glass, ceramic bottle caps, heat resistant ovenware, opaque glass, auto headlights, laboratory glass, light bulbs or fluorescent lamps, pottery, or drinking glasses.

Once management understands the quality specifications, it must explain them to employees. There are good and bad ways to explain to employees the importance of separating the material to provide a high-quality product. A bad way to explain the system is:

"Your job is to sort food and beverage glass into 3 colors—amber, green, and clear. Here's the list of what is not acceptable. Of course, you can't catch everything, so do the best job you can. Do you have questions?"

A more positive way to instruct a new employee:

"Your assignment is to prepare glass so that it can meet or exceed the quality required to be made into new glass at a glass plant. Your job is important in the process of making new glass from old glass food and beverage containers. The slightest imperfection in a batch of sorted glass bottles is not acceptable to the glass plant. That is why I am going to ask you to make certain that *only container glass* goes into the recyclable bin. Everything else, including bottle tops, goes in the trash container. If you are not sure, hold the material aside so you can ask me. Also, you must separate the material into three transparent colors—amber, green, and clear. If you can't see through the glass, that means it either contains something or is not transparent, so throw it in the trash. Labels disintegrate in the furnace where the glass is made, so they are not a problem, but all metals and other types of glass contaminate the new glass. Are there any questions?"

In teaching how to receive, sort, and ship material it is important to define success. After proper instruction, the list of contaminants can be built by the employee you instructed, after he or she has accumulated some experience. When he or she encounters an old stained glass Tiffany lamp, there will be no doubt it doesn't belong in the recycling bin. The same is true for an old Mason Jar with its built-in steel tightener for a glass cover. With proper instructions, even if your sorter is 18 years old and has never seen one of these items, it won't end up in the recycling bin. Another way to encourage employees is to let them develop their own judgement. Finally, always praise employees for doing a good job.

FOLLOWING UP

Reviewing the quality of sorted material requires five minutes of visual inspection a few times each day. Developing a keen eye for defects requires effort, but if everything looks perfect, you should check your eyeglass prescription, or if you don't have eyeglasses, you should consider them. Waste materials can't be handled without some problems. One of the best ways to develop a keen eye is to ask a seasoned buyer to review your quality. If he or she says your quality is good, you should be proud, and the praise should be passed on to your crew.

There is another opportunity to check quality when materials are shipped. You should train forklift drivers to set aside material if they are concerned about quality. Making quality everybody's job instead of just the sorter's will differentiate your program from others.

MONITORING PERFORMANCE

Plotting the financial impact of poor quality is one way to monitor performance. End users do not pay for below-standard material. Your accounting department should identify by supplier and by material each chargeback. Often, asking questions of end users is the only way you can obtain the information that will point you in the right direction.

Quality standards change in response to market conditions, to the financial condition of the end user, and to changes in technology. For example, if the market is flooded with glass, manufacturers can afford to hike the standards and accept only top-notch glass. Sometimes change occurs in your own organization. If the operation is downsized, this could potentially affect the quality of your end product. This may necessitate selling glass as "mixed," rather than striving for a sorted product.

THE PAYOFF

An organization committed to quality reaps dividends in a number of ways. End users are more likely to want the superior product that a well-organized business can provide. In marginal markets it is always the poor quality suppliers who see their orders cut. Providing good quality helps improve the financial condition of your organization and provides job security for all employees at all levels.

Attention to quality also results in fewer complaints, which reduces stress and generates pride. There is nothing worse than knowing you are not making the grade, and there is nothing better than knowing you are a valued supplier.

Finally, paying attention to quality improves efficiency. A superior product will not suffer backcharges for poor quality materials. The organization will also be confident that the material that is billed will actually represent the dollar amount collected later.

SUMMARY

In conclusion, there are many elements to a successful recycling program, which include obtaining a full understanding of the recycling process, designing a program that includes fully marketable materials, and implementing a quality control system that will result in a good product. In the following chapters, specific programs for business, industry, and government are outlined. It will be possible to take basic elements from any of these programs and apply them to the program in your area.

24

Markets

"If we collect it, they will come." With a smile at her parody on "The Field of Dreams," a Minnesota recycling manager referred to an all-too-common attitude about recycling markets. An incredible number of people start collecting recyclable materials without ever thinking about how to market the materials they intend to collect. This results in a common phenomenon of "My only problem is markets, markets, markets."

Anyone currently involved in recycling knows that marketing recyclable materials in the wake of the solid waste crisis is a challenge. Overwhelming amounts of paper, plastic, and glass have saturated many available markets and caused prices to plummet. Even marketing materials that are in high demand and generally sell for a good price requires skill. Given these market difficulties, how then do recyclers find markets for the materials they have generated through various collection programs? And further, how do they achieve a price that will keep their programs viable? In order to run an effective recycling program, the operation must be run as a retail business. This means that the people who buy collected materials are customers. Before collecting recyclables, the seller must first determine what it is that the customer requires.

The marketing problems that face most recycling programs are only solved *after* customers are found who need the specific collected materials the program has to sell. Further, who are satisfied with the quality and quantity of these recyclable materials. This implies that, in addition to finding out what potential customers wish to purchase, the recycling retailer must also inquire exactly what their quality requirements are. Then, and only then, is a successful business relationship established.

So where are potential customers? The answer is not the same for everyone. It is easier to market large volumes of material (even if they are relatively worthless) than it is to find a buyer for small volumes. It is also easier to sell high-priced materials, such as copper and brass, than it is to sell low-priced materials such as mixed plastics. This is because high-priced materials can be shipped greater distances economically.

Marketing recyclable materials is a process that involves moving the various grades of materials to an end user as efficiently as possible. The key word is "efficiently." Somewhere the idea has been developed that everyone who is a serious collector of recyclable materials must deal directly with the end users, namely the manufacturers. While this is certainly where the highest price can be obtained, it is not necessarily "efficient" or even possible for every program to deal directly with an end user. There is also a myth that dealing directly with an end user assures stability. While it is true that end users are generally large, financially responsible corporations, they more often than not have escape clauses in their contracts that effectively make the contract a mere letter of intent. This allows them to honor the contract only so long as it makes economic sense. Dealing with only one end user for each type of material may cause problems, such as when scheduled maintenances and work stoppages occur and the collected material has nowhere to go.

CHANNELS FOR SELLING RECYCLABLE MATERIALS

It may help to think of recycling as a "retail business in reverse." In a retail business, items are purchased from relatively few manufacturers and wholesalers, shipped to retailers, and sold to thousands of customers. With recycling, the opposite happens. Materials are collected from thousands of people, sorted and packaged in intermediate processing facilities, and sold to relatively few manufacturers. In marketing recyclable materials there are a small number of channels to the end user. It is possible to use all of the channels in selling recyclable materials, but each for a different grade of materials. The main channels include scrap dealers/processors, scrap brokers, marketing cooperatives, and end users.

SCRAP DEALER/PROCESSOR

Scrap dealers/processors are an efficient way to put materials into the recycling stream, particularly for materials sold on an "as collected" basis. The scrap dealer/processor collects recyclable materials, grades the incoming materials, sorts them to the specifications of end users, and packages the material for the end user, usually through baling or some other large-scale method, so that the transportation costs are minimized. A scrap dealer/processor sometimes is called a recycling company, but no actual recycling is performed on location. Recycling is done by manufacturers. The scrap dealer/processor operates a unique type of business because it is a business with two completely different sets of customers.

The first set of customers represents generators of recyclable materials. The scrap dealer/processor is often on the lookout for reliable suppliers of recyclable materials. These suppliers are typically scrap generators, and they are, in turn, the key to the scrap dealer/processor's second set of customers. This second set of customers are either end users for recyclable materials or brokers of recyclable materials who represent the interests of end users. It is important to evaluate the scrap dealers/processors, to best match the needs of the customer. One criterion for selecting a dealer/processor is the company's ability to handle material efficiently. Scrap dealers/processors handle many different kinds of material. Some handle a wide range of materials, while others handle only a few recyclables. Some have the ability to sort materials, while others have a limited ability to sort materials, and therefore the material can be handled only if they can be shipped in the condition in which they are received.

A second criterion for selection is the scrap dealer/processor's ability to provide required services. Some dealers/processors operate a fleet of trucks and take pride in providing reliable pickup service. Some will pick up material only if it is at a single convenient location. Others will pick up material throughout a building. Some will provide desktop containers and larger containers for the recyclable materials, like the bins at copy machines, as part of the package at a fee or included as part of the agreement. Others can respond quickly if you need emergency service.

One of the first things to determine when dealing with a scrap dealer/processor is whether pickup service should be regularly scheduled or on an "on call" basis. Scrap accumulation tends to be "lumpy," meaning that containers fill at random. A purge of files in an office area or a job that has a great deal of trim may run through a printer's shop, and, if it is on a scheduled basis, the resulting overflow of materials will at a minimum create a housekeeping problem. Some businesses generate scrap on a predictable, level basis. Every program will fit one scenario or the other, and a scrap dealer/processor should be selected based on their ability to fit the program's needs.

Finally, some dealers/processors must have their materials delivered. If the amount of collected material does not merit pickup service, the material will have to be delivered to their door.

A third criterion for choosing a scrap dealer/processor is the price paid per grade of material. The economics of the recycling program may vary with each dealer/processor. Price alone can be considered only when all the other services are comparable. The price paid for material or the charge for the services will vary among scrap dealers/processors. It is normal for prices to fluctuate with market conditions, and some dealers will relate price changes to published markets for recyclable materials. Some pay for materials, but have a pickup fee. The economics of any transaction depend on the local market, how competitive it is, and the program director's negotiating ability. Table 24-1 shows a list of the variables involved in choosing a scrap dealer/processor.

A fourth criterion to consider with scrap dealers/processors is the financial controls exercised over the materials. Some dealers/processors will provide a

TABLE 24-1. Negotiation Variables

Variable	Different Possibilities
Price for each grade	Fixed for a period of time Fluctuate with published markets Fluctuate with local markets
Program startup	Included as part of a package Charge based on flat fee Charge based on hourly rate
Containers	Included as part of a package Monthly fee Deposit may be required
Pickup service	Included as part of package Charge per pickup Charge per pickup if below a minimum quantity
Range of materials handled	May be narrow or wide ranging

prenumbered receipt for all material that is picked up, so all transactions can be traced to a monthly summary. The data may include information about the grades of material and number of containers so that an approximate control exists relative to weights and grades. Others will be far more casual about paperwork. Ultimately, price is meaningful only if the weights and grades are the same for the same material. It takes good financial controls to make certain that price alone is a way of determining the economic reality.

Other criteria include intangibles, such as a dealer/processor who is extremely knowledgeable and has the ability to help organize a recycling program for your company. Some are very willing to spend time to assure that their customers are satisfied because they are truly committed to their customer's successful program, while others have narrow interests, such as for one recyclable commodity. Proximity may also be a key factor. Dealers/processors that are close by may be able to respond inexpensively and quickly. If the operation is across town it will not be as convenient. A final criterion should be references. These should be available from the better dealers/processors.

The ideal dealer/processor will be very knowledgeable, help you design the best program for your needs, handle a wide range of materials, provide reliable service, have good control of paperwork, and give a good economic proposal for the specific program that you require.

SCRAP BROKER

A scrap broker may be an appropriate channel for recycling programs if processing equipment is in place and the program has a proven track record in making a quality product. A scrap broker markets materials without acquiring title to them by arranging a transaction or series of transactions between suppliers of recyclable materials and end users. The broker earns a fee in this process. Most scrap brokers are quite knowledgeable about the transportation of the materials that they market, and typically they will arrange for material to be picked up at the supplier's location and delivered directly to an end user. The scrap broker usually will not even see the material, but will only handle the paperwork, including payment to the supplier for the goods and billing and collecting funds from the end user.

Some brokers are experts in most phases of the recycling business, while others can be referred to as fair-weather marketeers. This latter type succeed when market demand is substantial, but they frequently lack the ability to move material when markets get tight. Brokers also vary in how they handle material when a quality problem occurs. Some brokers are scrupulous in watching out for the best interests of their suppliers; they investigate each low-quality claim, and send along samples so that corrective action can be taken. Others merely pass along any backcharges without the slightest investigation, which is a disservice to their suppliers.

Good brokers can be a very valuable asset to any collector. They keep up with the latest trends, anticipate when markets are changing, and pass along information that can enhance profitability. A scrap broker is practically essential for access to export markets. Their services, like extending credit and dealing with quality problems that come up from time to time in even the best of relationships, can take on an added dimension when the end user is up to 8,000 miles away. Brokers also negotiate language barriers when handling international transactions. Trade customs are different from country to country, and letters of credit add a degree of complexity that makes exporting recyclable materials a specialty.

HOW TO FIND A BROKER

How do you find a good broker? This question is not easy to answer. In a strong scrap market just about every broker can move material at a fair price. In a weak scrap market, however, it is rare to find a broker who will work to find markets for new customers. In a weak market a good scrap broker is usually found scouring the marketplace to protect old and established clients, while the mediocre brokers have gone on to another way of making a living. In a weak market a good broker can be anyone who has a door open to the material that is being offered.

One way to test the reliability of a broker is to see if phone calls are returned promptly. This tells a lot about the broker's organizational skills and attention to detail. Plus, if phone calls are not returned, it is often a clear signal that the broker has no better idea of how to move your material than you do. In the search for good brokers, it pays to remember that brokers are people and it is difficult to find the best in any profession.

Joe Scherman of Specialty Fibres in Walnut Creek, California says "You don't have to find a good broker, a good broker will find you." This is well stated, because a good broker is also aggressive and actively looking for opportunity. Many brokers develop great relationships with end users, acquire an adequate cliental, and sport good tans due to the time they spend on the golf course. In effect they are like doctors who have a sign out that says "Practice Closed." Some of these individuals are the best in the business, but it could well be irrelevant when it comes to satisfying your own needs.

Another way to locate brokers is by reputation. If there are businesses or agencies that collect similar commodities, they may be willing to share the name of a good broker. It is more likely that these organizations will protect this information in the same way people protect the location of their favorite fishing hole.

Finally, all trade publications feature advertisements. Calling regional brokers is one way to begin a relationship. This method is mostly trial and error. In the beginning it may cost the recycling program serious money, but over time it will lead to good channels to the market.

MARKETING COOPERATIVES

A marketing cooperative is a group of people or organizations with similar interests who join together to create a pool of recyclable materials in order to increase their leverage in the marketplace. It is appropriate and profitable to create a cooperative if there are a number of businesses and recycling programs who are of similar size and have similar operations in one area. In all markets there is definitely strength in numbers. Each small program, however, is totally subject to the quality of the controlling members. This is fine if they are concerned about end users' quality standards and are well motivated, but the opposite can also be true. A co-op's rules may be too rigidly binding in their decisions. It may be better to maintain flexibility as to where material is sold. Marketing cooperatives may have membership fees, may charge a percentage of the revenue for marketing services, or may limit access based on the ability to pay.

Some of the most successful marketing cooperatives exist in areas that have serious transportation problems. These generally exist in rural communities because they are so far from the industrial centers that purchase the recyclable materials. When the entities ban together, their bargaining position during negotiations increases dramatically.

END USERS

An end user is usually a manufacturing company that uses recyclable materials and converts them into new products or new raw materials. The person to contact about selling materials is the purchasing agent.

The purchasing agent for a paper mill or smelter is responsible for locating suppliers, negotiating prices, and placing orders for raw materials and other goods. The purchasing agent generally reports to the manager of operations, and since high-quality raw materials make the operations task easier, the purchasing agent frequently selects suppliers based on quality considerations. Prices are also determined by the purchasing agent, and the extent to which the purchasing agent can influence price depends on the grades of recyclable materials, the competition for the particular grade of material, and the quantity of available material. In a nutshell—unless a program develops a good business relationship with the purchasing agent, it will not go anywhere with that particular end user. Three ingredients must exist to consider dealing directly with end users:

1. There must be a large volume in order to deal with the end user directly. Different materials are ordered in different economic quantities. For example, a secondary fiber paper mill might use 300 to 500 tons per day (9,000 to 15,000 tons per month) of raw material, and the purchasing department might not find it efficient to deal directly with any supplier with less than 150 tons per month. The secondary fiber mill might not have a staff large enough to manage relationships with more than 75 to 100 suppliers. For aluminum cans, however, it is possible to ship to an end user in units of five tons of material because the suppliers are highly fragmented and the purchasing departments of most aluminum companies are set up to handle a great many suppliers.
2. When dealing directly with end users, it is important to know what the specific grades of material are that the program produces and also how it will be packaged and shipped to the consumer. To continue with the example of a paper mill, many mills will want the paper baled into 1,000-pound bales or greater to minimize their material handling costs.
3. The program must be a reliable supplier. If the purchasing agent wants 150 tons per month of high-quality material, then month after month the program should keep the standards high. A good relationship will develop for both parties if the program demonstrates reliability.

CONSTANT FACTORS IN MARKETING

It is not easy to establish a marketing program, but a disciplined approach improves a collector's chance of being successful. Many aspects of recycling change continuously, such as the prices for the various commodities; however, there are a number of critical factors that remain constant. Keeping these factors in focus will help guarantee success.

The first constant factor is based on the fact that marketing requires building and maintaining personal relationships. Since recycling changes rapidly, no single person can possess all the knowledge and connections that are required. Market research can produce a list of logical buyers for specific recyclable materials, but it takes numerous phone calls, letters, personal visits, and good timing to actually sell these materials. This is especially true because each quality supplier produces a virtually identical product. It takes something special to obtain an order for material. It takes building a relationship based on the principles of good business.

The second constant factor is that the seller and buyer must have a similar understanding of the grades of recyclable materials and the required quality standards. Visits to the end user are the single best way to understand raw materials for the specific customer. Questions such as What runs well here? What are the most frequent sources of quality problems? What do new suppliers typically screw up? can all be asked while touring the receiving area, so that the collector can see what is good and bad through the eyes of the buyer. Hopefully, the purchasing agent will "stop by" some day and see the operation, and look over the types of materials collected to see if there is further interest.

The third constant is negotiating skills. Asking as many questions as possible leads to learning about the end user's priorities. It is also important for the collector to have a clear grasp of his or her own priorities. Is a steady market more or less important than price? Can a special grade be created to earn a bonus price? Price is a major area of concern in negotiations. Where to find the published prices on various recyclable materials will appear later in this chapter.

The last constant factor is that recycling markets are dynamic: Very few tools can help to anticipate the dramatic changes, so trade publications as a whole tend to be optimistic. They are quick to forecast that times are getting better and nearsighted when it come to identifying a poor market. Perhaps this may be because journals need to be optimistic when it is unclear what the future has in store. A network of associates in the recycling business can help collectors to predict market changes. Attending recycling workshops and recycling conventions is yet another way to learn what is happening. But despite our human need to anticipate change, sometimes it would be easier to be an ostrich, only periodically checking market conditions and making the necessary adjustments.

Particularly in forecasting prices, getting a reliable set of indicators is difficult. It may help to take the advice about price from another field. Bernard Baruch, a financial wizard in the stock market, once said that price was simply a matter of supply and demand, and "everything else is hooey." Even the most seasoned professionals in the industry are caught by surprise.

THE MARKET SURVEY

The market survey begins by defining the grades of material that a program is collecting and defining the amount it will have to sell each month and on an annual basis.

Analysis of monthly volume should show that for some recyclable materials it is possible to ship to end users by the trailer load or by the rail car. High-volume materials are candidates for direct shipment to an end user or for shipment through a broker. Low-volume materials will of necessity be sold in mixed truckloads to wholesale scrap dealers/processors or in smaller lots to local scrap dealers/processors. Finding markets, especially good ones, is the most financially rewarding aspect of a recycling program. A wide range of prices exist for most commodities, and the key to making many programs viable is to find a price that is high enough to keep the program alive.

FINDING MARKETS: BEGIN LOCALLY—EXPLORE THE YELLOW PAGES

If a program manager knows or can forecast what materials he/she will offer for sale, the best place to begin looking for markets is with the local businesses and with the Yellow Pages. Transportation costs can be significant, and exploring local markets is a good place to begin. Headings such as recycling, scrap, waste paper, paper mills, plastic, copper, aluminum, glass plants, and so forth should be reviewed. Using the Appendix in this book may also provide some local leads.

FINDING MARKETS: EXPANDING THE SEARCH

While it is wise to begin a market search locally, a program may be financially able to expand its search to other parts of the country. A map with a length of string fastened to the program's location can help determine how far away markets are. An arc that is 50 miles in radius may take in some cities that merit the "Yellow Page" treatment. This is the chance to "be the center of the universe" and to explore market options in an ever-widening search. Sooner or later a market for each collected material will be found. Figuring out how many miles the program can afford to transport each recyclable material ahead of time will limit the scope of the search to affordable distances.

It is useful to develop rules of thumb about the cost of shipping a semitrailer per mile, or the cost of shipping a rail car per mile. The price at which collection programs are willing to sell a specific commodity is based on the maximum practical shipping distance for that commodity. However, in an area with high landfill costs, it makes economic sense to send materials over long distances, even if the net result produces a cost. If that cost is less than cost to landfill the material, it still is a better solution than disposal.

Trade Publications

Trade publications are an excellent source of potential markets for recycled materials. A collection program doesn't necessarily have to subscribe directly to these publications, but can refer to them in a library and discover the names of companies looking for materials, because they advertise their services in these publications on a regular basis.

State Recycling Agencies

State recycling agencies and solid waste departments often publish recycling directories, and, either through the directory or by asking directly for market information, a program may turn up some good leads to new markets.

Another approach to finding markets is to *reverse the process*. Often, companies can find out who sells or manufactures the type of materials for which they need markets. Thomas Register, for example, lists manufacturers and the products that they sell. A phone call may turn up new markets or new leads.

Originators of solid waste are another resource. For example, if there is no newspaper market, the general manager of the newspaper may have suggestions. If there is no glass market, the industry association for soft drinks or the industry association for the beer or liquor industry will probably be glad to help because they know that the goodwill of the community depends to some measure on the recyclability of their products.

CONTACTING POTENTIAL BUYERS

Purchasing agents, scrap processors, brokers, and marketing cooperatives are generally prospecting for new sources of material. They may be involved in upgrading their suppliers, or they may be interested in new materials, lower transportation costs, or simply more volume due to plant expansions or increased business. Persistence on the part of the collector is often rewarded because timing is important.

Phone calls are also an easy place to start. For the program just feeling its way in the recycling business, it is best to reveal this fact early in the conversation. Admission of small knowledge often results in the kind of information that is genuinely helpful. On both sides of the transaction there is a matching process of material that is needed to material that is available. The more efficiently each party can get the information they are looking for, the better.

Progress is usually made in developing a new relationship in small steps. For example, a trial shipment is a good way to begin because it allows both parties to learn from the transaction without a heavy investment on either part. Some buyers buy on only a month-to-month basis; others operate on a contractual basis.

Earning the opportunity to do business and to sell a product that is identical among quality suppliers usually takes more than a phone call. A beginning program needs to know what types of scrap are in demand. Once a buyer is found, it will be important to find out what specifications exist for the materials, specifically what grade specifications the company requires. Most companies will communicate what degree of contamination is unacceptable, what their minimum quantity requirements are, and how their prices are determined.

It is also important to ask what the current prices are and whether the prices include freight on board (FOB), or if the end user expects the collection program to pay for shipping at the quoted price. Finally, the collector needs to find out whether sales arrangements are made on a month-to-month basis or if long-term contracts are preferred. When both parties determine that the collected materials and the end user are a good match, contractual negotiations can begin.

COMPONENTS OF A CONTRACT

Signing a contract for the sale of recyclable materials is much like signing contracts for other aspects of business. A contract should reflect all important elements of an agreement, including the names of the two legal entities who are doing business and their addresses. It should also include what materials are to be purchased, specifying either the commonly recognized scrap grade or the quality required.

Quantity of material, defined in weight, specifying whether pounds, short tons, or metric tons are to be provided each month/week, should also be outlined on the contract in addition to the price to be paid for the material. Prices may be fixed or fluid, but either choice should be spelled out. Prices may be based on published prices, in which case the contract should reference the name of publication; the geographical market involved; the high price quoted, the low price quoted, or the average price; and the issue involved. The issue may be the issue on the date shipped, the second issue of the month, or whatever is agreed to. Prices may also be based on the current market price of the end user. Minimum prices, sometimes referred to as "floor" prices, may be specified. Maximum prices also may be specified. The price may be FOB shipping point, in which case the freight is to be paid by the buyer, or the price may be on a "delivered" basis, in which case the freight is paid by the person who ships the material. Quality is also a contractual consideration. Deciding who determines quality and weight should be negotiated. Normally, the buyer reserves the right to determine quality and weight of material based on his or her receiving records.

Contracts should also outline shipping requirements. This includes how the material is to be packaged for transportation. It may be shipped baled, on skids, in gaylord boxes, or by any number of other methods. Other transportation requirements should be spelled out in the contract. What types of containers, trailers, or piggyback trailers, railcars, or export containers are to be shipped? What are the minimum weights for each shipment? What adjustments are made if the minimum is not attained? Obviously, the net price is most important to the shipper, and in making any decision it is critical to look beyond the quoted price to the net price including transportation costs.

Payment terms are also a standard contractual item. Markets can pay immediately, within 24 hours, 30 days after shipment, or 45 days after receipt of the goods. It is important to find out what the terms of payment are. It is also good business to insist that the terms be lived up to.

A contract should outline the length of the agreement, usually specified in the number of years, with an expiration date. This generally includes the terms of renewal, whether it is negotiated prior to the end of the agreement, or whether renewal is automatically renewed unless it is cancelled.

Finally, rights to terminate agreement or penalties for noncompliance should be agreed upon. This includes deciding how disputes should be settled. Arbitration with the losing party paying for the arbitration is better than protracted legal conflict, especially since the continued relationship is frequently important to both parties. The state of jurisdiction is also important to note, so that legal disputes can be interpreted based on certain rules.

All contracts should be reviewed by the institution's attorney.

SELLING SKILLS

The marketing of waste materials requires different skills and a different mental attitude than the other aspects of recycling. It requires product knowledge, market research, persuasiveness, and negotiating skills to be effective. Sales ability is very important because there is likely to be a great deal of good quality material that needs to find its way to an end user, and the problem with a good quality product is that it is the same no matter where it comes from. The job of selling a commodity material, especially in an oversupplied market, should be assigned to the best salesperson in the organization, and to a person who is authoritative about the quality and reliability of the products.

Here are some guidelines for effective selling:

1. Create a good first impression. If in a letter, spell correctly. If on a personal visit. look neat and dress professionally.
2. Be enthusiastic, friendly, and open.
3. Have a well-thought-out message. Get to the point quickly, and respect that time is valuable.
4. Search for ways to create a win-win relationship.
5. If you do not know something, admit it. Then learn the answer and communicate the information when you are sure of yourself.
6. Keep personal difficulties private.
7. Never downgrade a competitor. It is best to avoid discussing the competition altogether. If anything, damn them with faint praise and move the conversation along to another subject.
8. Exhibit pride in the organization.

9. Show appreciation. Send letters of thanks even if the visit was unsuccessful.
10. Confirm any agreements in writing.

NEGOTIATING PRICE

One way to judge if a quoted price is fair is to compare it to the prices published in trade newspapers and magazines. Another indicator is price quoted by others in the marketplace. In the final analysis it is the price that is *paid* net of backcharges and transportation costs that is important.

Ultimately, the collector has a stake in transportation costs, even if the price quoted is FOB. Collectors should always examine the alternatives. This includes investigating transportation by truck, piggyback, railcar, and yak (if available). Often, the end users of recyclable materials have traffic departments and can negotiate far better rates for material as an individual company because they coordinate pickup service with the delivery of materials.

25

Government

As the nation's focus on the environment deepens, it seems clear that state and local government will be expected to take the lead with regard to recycling. Enthusiasm for this issue is at an all-time high. This, combined with the solid waste crisis and a need to conserve natural resources, creates a climate for exciting developments in the recycling movement. Government can set the pace for this movement by educating the public about the recycling process, creating collection programs that may become a way of life, and producing recyclable materials that will be readily accepted by industry.

National agencies are also pulling local government into the recycling movement. In 1991 the EPA decided that landfills must conform to new standards to protect the public welfare. Since more than half of the country's landfills cannot comply, cities and counties are going to have to find new places to landfill their waste. Recycling strategies will play a role in solid waste planning.

It is becoming increasingly clear that waste disposal is a poor solution for the solid waste problem. Instead, waste reduction and recycling are much higher priorities. Government can encourage these activities by enacting legislation that discourages the disposal of specific materials and by setting recycling goals. Government can help recycling through specific systems and programs that make recycling available for single-family residents, multi-family residents, rural areas, and businesses of all types. Finally, government can provide education about the solid waste crisis and show how recycling fits into the solution.

Clearly, government's role in recycling is immense. In this chapter we will limit the scope of discussion to the early stages of government's involvement: developing a recycling program.

ORGANIZING SOLID WASTE AND RECYCLING SOLUTIONS FOR COMMUNITIES

The first step toward making solid waste and recycling solutions real happens when government designs and implements a program or series of programs for a specific community. Three bodies of knowledge come together during this process: knowledge of recyclable materials, knowledge of specific programs, and knowledge about the process of moving a community to a consensus and through an action plan.

The perspective in this chapter is that the specific programs are "tools" of the solid waste professional and the process of building a consensus in a community will result in the "design" or "plan," with the correct programs being phased in, in a logical sequence.

GOVERNMENT'S PRIMARY CHALLENGE

Landfills have historically represented a low-cost solution for disposing of solid waste. Recycling has historically been a method of generating revenue from the sale of certain specific materials. During the late 1990s waste disposal costs could climb out of control and recycling markets could remain weak. At the same time the public is demanding that recycling services be integrated into the array of services that government offers the community it serves. The challenge for government, then, is to resolve the landfill crisis, install recycling programs, and remain financially viable and to do it all simultaneously.

Soon, the United States will be entering a new era in waste management, and choices on the front line will be difficult. Issues are boiling, and there is a great deal of controversy in communities about what government should do. This confusion added to the fact that the composition of solid waste is different for different communities and that market opportunities are also different, yields a kaleidoscope of possibilities. Fortunately, the process is reasonably straightforward, even if the answers are not the same for every community.

FULLY INTEGRATED APPROACH

Since the solid waste solutions for each community differ dramatically, we will discuss a fully integrated approach that can be easily adapted to each area. This process recognizes that there is no single solution to solid waste management. While recycling has many obvious benefits, not all waste can be recycled. It is just one component of a fully integrated approach to solid waste management. Using the fully integrated approach to waste management means combining waste reduction and disposal practices to maximize the benefits and minimize the costs of each method.

The fully integrated approach implies that a master plan exists that coordinates the types of services being offered in a community to attain a set of goals. One goal might be related to costs. Another might be related to reducing solid waste by 50 percent or some other figure. Balancing these factors requires a complete set of tools. The fully integrated approach is what is inside the solid waste professional's tool box. The tools of the trade include:

1. Education—from elementary schools to high schools, from public meetings to creating booklets, and from advertising to public relations.
2. Curbside recycling programs.
3. Drop-off centers.
4. Buy-back centers and scrap dealers/processors.
5. Commercial collection programs for businesses and others.
6. Special collection days or "events"—Christmas tree day, leaf day, recycling drive day, tire collection day, household hazardous waste day.
7. Composting on a small scale in backyards.
8. Composting on a community-wide scale.
9. Capital intensive solutions, such as resource recovery facilities, materials recovery facilities, transfer stations, waste-to-energy plants, incinerators, and landfill salvage operations.
10. Attracting a secondary material end user to locate in or near the community.

GETTING STARTED

It is not as important where you start in developing a community solution to solid waste and recycling as it is to get started. Many pioneers have already blazed a trail, and their early experiences through trial and error have led to many worthy conclusions. Their experiences are reflected in the following methodology for getting recycling programs off the ground. When the methodology and tools come together, the result can be a fully integrated solid waste plan that is tailored to the community.

PRELIMINARY GOALS

One of the first steps in developing a recycling program is determining the preliminary goals and objectives of the program. Initially, discussions with community leaders, waste haulers, local recyclers, scrap dealers, waste management departments, and departments of public works can begin to build a consensus for shared goals or for areas of potential conflict. It also makes everyone part of the solution and part of a professional problem-solving project for the community.

It only takes a moment to begin compiling an initial list of opinion leaders. In a 10- to 15-minute interview with city council members or a solid waste manager, one question to ask is "Do you know of anyone else who would have an interest in recycling?" Initial interviews can begin with questions such as "Ms. Jones, could I have 10 or 15 minutes of your time to get your ideas about what what our community should be doing about recycling?"

After enough interviews have been conducted to document that recycling is an idea that will be supported by community leaders, chances are that going through with the rest of the process will yield positive results. If the idea is met with opposition at every level in the community, starting a recycling program will take a massive educational effort. Another alternative would be to begin with a very modest program to demonstrate recycling's feasibility to others.

SURVEYING COMMUNITY ATTITUDES

Building community consensus toward developing a recycling program will require more than support from opinion leaders. Surveying the attitudes and perceptions of the entire community can indicate the extent of grass roots support. If it is not practical to survey the entire community, a statistically valid sample can be used. In general, if the sample is chosen randomly, a small percentage of the entire community can be used. If done correctly, the results will be a reliable indicator for the general population.

However, it serves no professional purpose to obtain a biased sample. For example, it would be foolish to ask the recycling club if they would like to see a community-wide program. In later months, it may be extremely important to demonstrate that the information gathering process was credible. In fact, if a third party can be hired, then the data becomes even more acceptable. Firms specializing in market research and analysis can be found in most communities. In an ideal situation the survey might reveal that 95 percent of the community would support a recycling program, and 80 percent would be willing to have their taxes raised to support it.

For government programs, obtaining community approval is a crucial element in gaining political support. Since the public drives this process, an attitude survey should be designed in such a way that politicians will know the sentiment of the general population.

Sample of an Attitude Survey

Please write "1" for top priority, "2" for second priority, "3" for third priority, etc. How would you rank some of the problems facing our community?

Public Education _______
Drug and Alcohol Abuse _______
Economy, Unemployment _______

Environmental Quality ______
Health Care ______

Please indicate whether you strongly agree, agree, disagree, or strongly disagree with the following statements:

Solid waste is *not* a problem in our community.

strongly agree ______
agree ______
disagree ______
strongly disagree ______
no opinion ______

Recycling is a good strategy for managing solid waste.

strongly agree ______
agree ______
disagree ______
strongly disagree ______
no opinion ______

The environment is already permanently damaged.

strongly agree ______
agree ______
disagree ______
strongly disagree ______
no opinion ______

Please check appropriate box(es).

Do you recycle?
- ☐ No
- ☐ Yes. If yes, please indicate frequency
- ☐ about once per year
- ☐ twice per year
- ☐ 3 to 6 times per year
- ☐ once per month
- ☐ once per week

What do you recycle?

☐ aluminum cans ☐ glass ☐ plastic
☐ newspaper ☐ tin cans ☐ shopping bags
☐ cardboard ☐ yard waste
☐ other items ☐ clothing

How do you recycle? Please check appropriate box(es).
☐ curbside
☐ buy-back center
☐ drop-off center
☐ other, specify ______________

Are you satisfied with the recycling programs available to you?

☐ Yes ☐ No If no, please answer the question that follows.

Would you like to see
☐ more drop-off locations
☐ more items recycled
☐ curbside service
☐ other, specify ______________

If additional costs are involved in expanding recycling, are you willing to pay for the expansion?
☐ Yes
☐ No

Do you want to become personally involved in the new recycling project?

☐ Yes. If yes, please include name, address, and phone number.
☐ No

Name: ________________________________
Street: ________________________________
City, State, Zip Code: ______________________
Phone Number: __________________________

UNDERSTANDING THE EXISTING WASTE AND RECYCLING STREAM

"If you've seen one community's trash, you've seen them all" is not a true statement. Every community is comprised of different percentages of business, industry, residential, and multi-family dwellings. For these reasons, each community must tailor its own recycling program.

In all communities, however, there are three basic questions that need to be answered. First, it is important to know where the trash comes from in the community. Second, it is important to determine how much of the waste stream is recyclable. And third, it is important to document the trends. Factual answers to these questions will help determine future programs for managing solid waste that include recycling. Also, from these facts, it is possible to derive information about the potential for new recycling programs. When the data are compiled, one of the key schedules should look like Table 25-1.

TABLE 25-1. Any Community

Results of Solid Waste and Recycling Survey

For the period ________ to _________
________ ___, 199_
By _______________,

Type of Unit	Number of Units	Total Tons Landfilled	Percent of Total	Existing Tons Recycled	Potential Additional Tons Recycled
Residential					
Single-family dwellings					
Multi-family dwellings					
Rural area dwellings					
Subtotal					
Businesses					
Auto and body repair*					
Business parks*					
Demolition firms*					
Gas stations*					
Grocery stores*					
Hospitals*					
Hotels/motels*					
Industrial firms*					
Office buildings*					
Manufacturers*					
Restaurants*					
Shopping malls*					
Small businesses*					
Other					
Subtotal					
Government					
Schools and colleges*					
Office buildings*					
Prisons*					
Civic centers*					
Stadiums*					
Parks*					
Other					
Subtotal					
Miscellaneous					
Grand Total					

*Recycling programs for these specific types of community units are described in this book. A more traditional way of classifying this would be to use the standard industry classification codes.

Compiling data that analyze solid waste composition can be expensive. If you choose to compile the data yourself, rather than hiring a consultant, the place to begin is with the trash haulers who serve the community. Area scrap dealers and processors can also help with the compilation. If you build up good rapport with both the existing scrap dealers/processors and trash haulers during the initial compilation, you can often get the parties interested in recycling together. This can lead to starting up some recycling programs—even during this early stage.

One inexpensive enhancement to the solid waste composition study would be to use a local college as a resource. An environmentally-oriented class or organization might be willing to do an in-depth three-month study for a statistically valid sample of waste-generating households. Once the class or group selects the appropriate households, they would be instructed to sort their trash into three categories: dry trash, compostable material (including yard waste), and wet trash. Either the households or students would weigh the three components for the duration of the experiment. At a central sorting area the dry trash would be sorted by the students into different recyclable materials—newspaper, aluminum cans, mixed paper, and so forth, and the weight of these items would be recorded.

The media could be invited to visually record the growing piles of recyclable materials and to keep the community informed about the progress. At the end of a three-month-long project, the piles of recyclable materials from the selected families would visually demonstrate the amount of waste households accumulate. This pile could be displayed where the public would have access to it, and would function as a pungent reminder about the impact of recycling. In addition to a visual record, valuable data will also have been collected. Some students and teachers would become local authorities about the composition of household trash. These new "authorities" can be used, for example, during public meetings as the community openly discusses the next steps.

If government has set aside a big enough budget for waste study, it would help to interview major businesses and industry in the area. This is because, on a national basis, 50 percent of solid waste is generated by businesses. Diverting business waste is key to helping solve the community's landfill problems.

Clearly, one advantage of having someone in the community doing the study is that the knowledge gained will stay in the community. But consultants who specialize in composition studies are probably more reliable and efficient. Either way, the data will not be 100-percent perfect, but it can be objective and unbiased.

SELECTING THE APPROPRIATE RECYCLING PROGRAMS

It is crucial to be in the right frame of mind in the early stages of developing a recycling program. Initially, the community should develop the attitude that their community's objective is to divert 100 percent of the recyclable waste stream. In the final analysis, every community must face up to some constraints. These may be financial constraints, political constraints, economic constraints, or market constraints. Despite the fact that these constraints must be faced, for this stage recycling should be aggresively pursued.

Single-family Household Recycling

The household is a basic building block for any community and also for any community recycling program. As a result, it is important to understand household recycling and its potential. There are several basic steps in establishing a household program.

Each household must decide what to recycle, what to compost, and what to reuse based on the amount of material presently thrown away as trash. Basic decisions on how solid waste can be avoided can also be made. Each household can support waste reduction and recycling by "voting" with their consumer purchasing habits to change the way items are merchandized and sold. Each household can become vocal at the stores where they shop and can write letters whenever they see opportunities for environmental improvement.

But before each household can take action, it must be decided what commodities will be recycled in the community program. Many programs collect newspaper, aluminum cans, steel cans, glass, mixed paper, magazines, scrap metals, computer printout, plastic bottles, phone books, and cardboard. Next, what waste should be composted and where this will take place must be decided. Compost piles include everything from grass clippings, leaves, and weeds to wood chips and food scraps. Reusing items will also be a critical part of the program's design. Showing the community that it should reuse glass jars, shopping bags, appliances, and so forth, will help reduce solid waste. Finally, the program can help determine what practices should be implemented to avoid excess waste altogether. For example, a mulching lawn mower can cut the lawn faster while negating the need to compost grass clippings. Buying food in bulk will save on unnecessary packaging, as will buying economy size packages when it is appropriate. If households are informed of easy ways to reduce waste, most likely they will implement some of the changes.

Another program development decision is how to collect the materials. There are a multitude of options for residential recycling programs. These range from capital-intensive programs, such as curbside collection, to a simple educational blitz that advises people to bring recyclables to a local collection center. We will discuss a variety of programs to serve this data at length.

Even these simple, common sense changes can have dramatic effects on a community's solid waste disposal problem, as Table 25-2 shows below.

Recycling for Multi-family Dwellings

Recycling programs for multi-family dwellings are differentiated from single-family dwellings in many ways. Storage space for recyclable materials tends to be more

TABLE 25-2. Possible Trash Reduction from Single-family Recycling

Reduce trash by backyard composting	10–18%
Recycle newspaper	8–10%
Recycle glass containers	6–7%
Recycle plastic bottles	2–5%
Recycle steel cans	1%
Recycle phone books	1%
Precycle	1–4%
Total reduction from household recycling	29–46%

limited, the population is more transient, and, for many, multi-family dwellings have a lower income than single-family residents. The collection system for recyclables for this type of dwelling is usually a drop-off center near where the trash is collected. Education and signage is particularly important in these types of dwellings.

Programs may start due to legislation or from the grass roots level. At the grass roots level it is first and foremost important to determine if the residents will support the concept. A survey will help in this process. Next, gaining support from the building management is critical. Without management support, the program has little hope of succeeding. Lastly, it is important to select a person or an organization to provide service to the drop-off center.

After determining that a recycling program may succeed, the next decision is what to collect. This decision will impact the design of the program and the equipment needed for its success. Determining the location for the drop-off center is also a key step. The more convenient the drop-off location, the greater the participation. Since the population usually turns over frequently in multi-family dwellings, there is a greater need than usual for continuing education.

This places great importance on clear signage. In some areas signs should be printed in languages other than English. A simple letter should be handed out by the apartment office. It can simply say:

1. We require tenants to recycle as part of the rules.
2. Recycling also helps the environment.
3. Please separate the following materials and put them in the recycling containers located ____________.
   - ☐ Aluminum cans
   - ☐ Glass containers (rinse, no caps)
   - ☐ Plastic bottles (no caps)
   - ☐ Steel cans (rinse)
   - ☐ Newspapers (no bags, magazines, or phone books)
4. Thank you for supporting recycling.

Convenient drop-off centers are the most effective way of reaching this sector of the community.

RURAL AND SMALL COMMUNITY RECYCLING

Rural areas are characterized by low population densities and are usually at least 50 miles from major metropolitan areas. Transportation costs are a major impediment to recycling because transportation costs typically cost more per ton than can be received per ton for the major bulk of recyclable materials—newspaper, glass, and plastic. What usually makes the difference between having a recycling program or not is the personal characteristics of the people who choose to live in rural areas. Rural populations can generate surprising numbers of energetic volunteers who are willing to work hard to overcome their unique obstacles to recycling. They also appear to be extremely flexible and persistent.

If the population density of the small community allows for individual trash service, then curbside collection is a realistic option. But in some rural areas, each resident must take trash and recyclable materials to a central location. This location may be as near as the mail box, where a curbside-style program then takes over. In other areas a drop-off center for trash and recyclable materials may describe the existing system. And in others, the trash and recyclable materials may be collected at the local landfill.

CURBSIDE RECYCLING

Curbside recycling involves collecting specified recycled materials at each household in a community on a routine schedule. As a service it is similar to getting the mail delivered or getting the trash picked up weekly in the front of each house. Each household usually sorts and stores material as part of their daily routine and places the material in containers at the curb for collection, to be picked up for recycling on the designated day. Because curbside recycling is so convenient, more than 3,000 communities have adopted this method of collection.

Basic Choices

Some basic choices must be made as part of any decision to utilize a curbside collection system. First, you need to determine when the materials will be collected. Pickup service can be on the same day and with the same frequency as waste collection, or it can be with a different frequency or on a different day. Participation is greatest when the recyclable materials are picked up on the same day as the trash. Self-preservation helps most of us remember "trash day," and the tie-in to recycling is logical. Pickup service that uses a different frequency or day tends to do so in order to save money. Pickup service every other week or once a month sacrifices some participation in return for lower operating cost.

Another decision relates to what organization will collect the recyclable materials left at curbside. Pickup service can be performed by a volunteer organization, a private or public trash hauler, or a recycling company. The economies of scale favor a trash hauling company because the trash hauler reaps an immediate benefit—there is less trash to haul to the landfill. The collection costs for the recyclable materials are approximately the same for everyone, but existing trash haulers often have the inside track because a business relationship has already been established.

When areas are served by a number of private trash haulers, curbside recycling erupts into an issue of how many trash and recycling trucks are wanted in residential communities during the week. When each trash hauler adds a recycling truck to his or her route, traffic increases. For example, if there are three routes through a neighborhood, after curbside recycling arrives there will be six. The issue of safety and children playing in the streets is usually raised. The remedy usually is a reduction in the number of trash and recycling haulers serving an area. This occurs through competitive pressures, with the financially strongest usually surviving or by government creating a franchise system whereby haulers bid for each service area.

Special-purpose trucks have been designed to service curbside programs. Communities such as San Jose found that when they added six special recycling trucks, one trash vehicle was eliminated. These trucks have in common that they are compartmentalized to hold different recyclable materials. However, a decision needs to be made as to whether the expense of a special-purpose truck can be justified in improved efficiency. Other methods include building racks to hold recyclable materials as an accessory to existing garbage trucks or using a "blue bag" system, where recyclables are stored in a blue bag and sorted out later at a landfill or transfer station.

If special collection vehicles are required, the selection of the correct vehicle will require a comparison from a wide selection of manufacturers. Factors such as initial cost, number of operators, capacity for collected materials, reliability, frequency of repair and where the vehicle will be maintained, efficiency in loading and unloading, fuel consumption, and vehicle weight need to be considered.

Limitations such as local load limits on roads, height restrictions on bridges, and tight turning radius problems on cul de sacs all must be considered. Like all other recycling programs, curbside recycling faces a decision on what materials to recycle. This decision is often determined by how the material is collected and how it is to be sorted. One method is to use multiple containers for each different material. The other method is to comingle the materials by placing them in the one container. Still another method is to use a hybrid of both systems. Multiple containers are used, but steel cans and aluminum cans can be in one bin, and paper products of all types can be in one bin. No clear superior method has emerged as the way to make this decision. However, the decision made regarding the method of collection clearly influences the next curbside recycling decision: container selection.

Some people argue that a container is not necessary for a curbside recycling program to work. They point out that it takes 15 seconds per stop to place the empty container at the curb and that it is easy to see what is recyclable and what is not. There is probably sufficient evidence that this point of view is wrong.

Containers help the household a great deal in organizing the task of sorting trash and recyclables. On recycling day containers appear like billboards in a neighborhood and serve as reminders that "Today is Recycling Day." In fact, peer pressure can be sufficient to cause some people to put an empty or near-empty recycling containers at the curb just to avoid the appearance of *not* recycling. In any case, the container decision represents a choice regarding number of containers, size of containers, color of containers, and the material from which they are made. Containers can be stackable or non-stackable. Containers may have labels or messages. To complicate things further, containers can be transparent plastic bags or rigid. Solid-colored bags are a problem because it is not immediately obvious what is in them. In either case a continuous supply must be available.

The size of the container is an issue of greater complexity than it first appears. The size of the local paper may have an influence on the size of the container. Also, the bigger the container, the more it holds and the lower the set-out rate. This implies fewer stops and is therefore considered more efficient. However, if the containers get too heavy, the frequency of lifting injuries will increase. Whatever container is chosen, it must be designed to last five to ten years.

Another container issue is "Who pays for them?" Containers are an expense. The options are for the government to pay for them, for participants to pay a deposit on the containers, or for participants to purchase the containers. Finally, there is the issue of who pays the ongoing costs of the curbside service. Some communities have passed regulations mandating that trash haulers provide this service, knowing that in the long run the added costs will be spread among the participants. Others pass along the costs in the form a bill or a line item on a trash bill. Still others charge for special plastic bags as a way to support the recycling program. They cost more than regular garbage bags, which is designed to encourage people to fill them up before they place them outside. Some curbside programs require trash haulers to leave garbage that contain recyclables at the curb. Other programs require haulers to leave all garbage or assess fines as a penalty for non-compliance. Trash haulers know that heavy bags or bags that "clink" contain recyclables, and refuse to collect these bags, forcing people to recycle.

Keys To a Successful Curbside Program

The most important ingredient in making curbside recycling effective is education. Communication at the grass roots level, through block leaders and multi-layered messages, makes the difference between successful programs and poor programs. It is almost impossible to overcommunicate because the objective is to change trash habits formed throughout most people's lifetimes. Meetings, posters, signs, color-coded containers, printed instructions, refrigerator magnets, advertisements, video tapes, and TV messages are all part of the process.

The items to communicate include the program startup and regular pickup dates, materials to be recycled and how to prepare them, and a reminder system to correct problems before they get out of control. Two examples are shown in Figure 25-1 and Table 25-3.

In addition to communication, there are other important variables that help shape a specific curbside recycling program. One of the first things to consider is the area you are serving. Curbside programs work well in urban and suburban locations, but not in rural areas. This is obviously because of the proximity of residences. Understanding demographics is also an important factor with regard to curbside collection. Knowledge of education and income levels will help determine your community's participation levels and how to improve it. If the residents have an understanding of America's solid waste problems, they are more likely to commit

RECYCLING REMINDER

XXX Community
YYYY Street
City, State

(Recycling hotline #)

Just a friendly reminder. . .

that the material deposited in your bin

(Circle appropriate materials)

1. Cans
2. Glass
3. Plastic
4. Newspaper
5. Mixed Paper

____ was not properly rinsed. ____ was in the wrong container.

____ did not have the lids removed.

____ cannot be recycled through this program.

FIGURE 25-1.

TABLE 25-3. Recyclable Materials and How To Prepare Them

Recyclable Material	Preparation Required	Cannot be Included
Newspaper		
Anything included with the newspaper.	Keep dry and away from sunlight.	Exclude plastic and paper bags, phone books, magazines, paperback books.
Plastic		
#1s and #2s (symbol on container)	Rinse clean. Throw away caps and neck rings, and crush when possible.	Plastic bags, plastic wrap, oil cans or plastics that have 3 4 5 6 7
Glass		
Amber (brown), green, and clear glass containers (without lids).	Handle carefully to avoid breakage. Empty contents and rinse clean. Throw away lids, and crush when possible. Labels may be left on.	Light bulbs, plate glass, mirrors, pyrex, ceramics, drinking glasses and ovenware, or other non-container glass.
Beverage Cans And Metal Food Cans		
Aluminum and tin cans.	Rinse clean. It is not necessary to crush or remove labels.	Aluminum foil, cans made of cardboard, aerosol cans, paint cans, oil cans, or other hazardous materials.

to sorting recyclables each week. Lower-income curbside participants will often keep the higher-value materials, to recycle at buy-back centers. Without materials like aluminum and glass, curbside programs face economic problems.

Another crucial factor is whether recycling is a mandatory or voluntary activity. If people are required to recycle, curbside programs are probably the most convenient way to collect materials from residential areas. It is also one of the only ways to regulate the activity. When recycling is voluntary, curbside programs often encourage participation because of peer pressure.

Whether your program is mandated or voluntary, one thing that will help ensure curbside success is the presence of voluntary block leaders. On each block a recycling enthusiast is responsible for reminding others to participate each collection period. Block leaders are wonderful motivators in recycling programs.

Potential Problems

As soon as residents hear about a curbside collection program in their neighborhood, they may immediately begin saving their recyclables. Beginning publicity too soon can result in more materials placed at the curbside on initial collection days than can easily be collected. It is important to carefully time promotional campaigns to avoid being overwhelmed with newspapers, plastic containers, and glass.

When a program is implemented, it is important to carefully decide what materials to collect and how they should be prepared. The public is often slow to respond to requested changes in materials preparation. Do not pick up more types of materials than are marketable and do not pick up comingled materials unless the sorting program can be sustained over the long term.

Another possible obstacle is that curbside recycling is an expensive service. This is complicated by the fact that the revenue earned through recycling does not cover the full cost of the program. The program will suffer a substantial loss of credibility if it is "sold" to the community on any other basis. When implementing a curbside program, it is important to be up front with the costs involved for start up and monthly charges.

Finally, curbside recycling often attracts scavengers. Since recyclables are set out on the curb each week, it is easy to pirate the valuable items left on the curb if they are left unchecked. Anti-scavenging ordinances must accompany the introduction of curbside recycling. One mechanism for enforcing the law is prosecuting at the early stages. This will generally set the correct tone for the future.

DROP-OFF CENTERS

Drop-off centers are the most cost-effective method for recycling residential wastes. Citizens collect separated recyclable materials in their homes and deliver them to a central location. Drop-off centers have the potential advantage of always being available, so residents can recycle as part of their general household or shopping routine. This practice is preferable to curbside collection for some recyclers, but participation depends a great deal on the convenience of the locations. However, no system can compete successfully with the convenience or participation levels of curbside recycling.

While drop-off centers provide collection sites where residents can drop off recyclables, no payment is made for the materials brought in for recycling. These centers can be locations where both the public and businesses can drop off their recyclables. This gives a drop-off center the ability to serve small businesses in a shopping mall setting or in a business park. Drop-off programs can range from seven-day-a-week operations to those that operate once a week. They fill an important role for multi-family dwellings and low-density single-family areas. For many communities, drop-off programs can be looked upon as a start up phase of what can become a comprehensive, community-wide program.

Basic Choices

In designing any drop-off system, the first decision relates to determining which parts of the community are best served by this method. The method works best for multi-family housing, for small businesses, and for low-density residential areas.

The decision regarding who to serve leads directly into choosing how many drop-off centers are needed in a community. Each drop-off center requires some level of service, needs equipment for support, and requires that an educational program be in place. For these reasons, maximizing the number of drop-off sites makes sense. Balancing this factor is the fact that the more convenient the drop-off sites are to users, the greater the participation.

Another decision relates to staffing the drop-off sites. An unsupervised site obviously costs less to operate than a supervised site. A supervised site provides interaction with the public and can be looked at as an extension of the educational program. Especially in the beginning of a program, the public has more questions than can be answered in preprinted handouts. A supervised site also reduces problems concerning litter, the dumping of unwanted materials, and contaminated recyclable materials. As a minimum, some staffing during the start up period should be considered. Since no drop-off center truly "runs itself," some staff will be required to physically inspect each site, maintain good housekeeping, and oversee shipping the materials.

Determining the hours of operation is linked to the decisions regarding staffing levels. Drop-off centers offer the potential of being open 24 hours per day, seven days per week, or they can be open one day per month. In making this decision a great deal depends on the character of the community. If vandalism is a major problem, 24 hour access could prove to be disastrous. Valuable materials could be stolen, or worse, the paper products could be set on fire. On the other hand, some communities welcome a drop-off center and treat the facility with pride and respect.

Naturally, what materials will be recycled must be decided. Newspapers are the most prominent items collected in drop-off programs. Glass, aluminum, and plastic are also collected at many multi-material drop-off centers, even though these materials require more processing to prepare for markets. Cardboard, waste oil, mixed paper, aluminum and steel scrap, and other materials may also be collected. As discussed elsewhere, the availability of markets will influence not only what is collected, but also how it is collected and if further processing is required. The services for removing the recyclable materials can be subcontracted, or equipment can be purchased to haul the containers on a direct basis. Since materials must be shipped when the containers are full, whichever alternative is chosen, the service must be reliable.

When the decision regarding materials has been made, the physical size of the facility can be determined. Space is needed for parking, for delivery and pickup of materials, for containers to hold the material, and for an orderly traffic flow. If the facility is staffed, a building with a restroom may be required. Fencing the facility offers advantages in restricting access and in housekeeping, but fencing also has implications for traffic flow. As a final consideration, zoning restrictions, the availability of space, the cost of space, and the desire to provide for future expansion will influence the physical facility.

Keys to a Successful Drop-off Center

Some of the key elements affecting participation rates are the convenience of the drop-off location and the degree of commitment by community leaders. The quality of communications and the signs at the drop-off site are especially important if the facility is not staffed or is staffed on a part-time basis.

Potential Problem Areas

Some of the problems associated with drop-off programs include difficulty in finding easily accessible drop-off sites. These problems are often complicated by local zoning ordinances. Property owners who donate space for a drop-off center can quickly withdraw their support if the center is not kept clean and attractive or if the property ownership changes hands.

Another difficulty for drop-off centers is that many sites are unstaffed. These sites become targets for vandals, become littered, and experience a high level of contamination of recyclables by unwanted and unmarketable items. In rural areas the drop-off centers are sometimes overwhelmed by trash because of the lack of local landfills. To overcome these problems many communities locate collection sites next to businesses, community service organizations, or city or county government facilities that are willing to provide site security. The theft of recyclable materials that sell for high prices, such as aluminum, is predictable. Safeguards need to be built to minimize the problem.

Sites can overflow quickly. Recycling is very popular during spring cleaning and in the winter, when people are trying to find room to put the car in the garage. It is a good idea to maintain extra capacity at all drop-off sites.

BUY-BACK PROGRAMS

A recycling buy-back program offers the public the opportunity to get paid for their recyclable materials. By offering a financial incentive, those recycling materials that have a high economic value are attracted to the program. Aluminum cans, nonferrous metal, bond quality computer printout, and other high-grade recyclable materials flow towards buy-back centers. Low-valued material, such as newspaper, glass, and plastic, accumulate in higher volumes in curbside and drop-off programs.

Buy-back programs are inherently flexible. Some operations purchase only high-grade metals and aluminum cans. Some purchase various grades of paper. Others offer opportunities to sell just about anything that has an economic value. By adjusting the prices paid for materials, the buy-back center is able to either attract or discourage the recycling of a particular item.

Recyclable materials that are brought in by customers must be weighed, inspected, and graded. Customers are responsible for adequately preparing recyclables for purchase. This preliminary sorting of recyclables greatly improves the quality of materials sent to market. The buy-back center has the right to refuse unacceptable materials for purchase. Purchases are usually paid for by cash, but large purchases should be paid for by check.

Buy-back programs are organized in a variety of ways. They can be a private recycling center, a scrap yard, an operation of a non-profit corporation, or run directly by the community. They can purchase and process the materials, or they can be a simple collection facility. A buy-back program may consist of a reverse vending machine, which accepts aluminum cans and returns cash. In a recent innovation in reverse vending machines by Esmark Manufacturing Company in Denver, Colorado, the "retail robot" machine dispenses both cash and valuable coupons. This innovation may make it attractive for retail businesses to merchandise products through a recycling buy-back program.

Basic Choices

The location of the buy-back center is a critical decision. Customers will come from both small businesses and from the community at large. Usually, these participants recycle in order to supplement their income. Significant numbers of people come from lower-income communities, from the ranks of retired people, and from people who have blue collar jobs. Fewer customers come from high-income occupations and high-income families. Young children from all income levels are attracted to the buy-back centers because parents often let them keep whatever profits are made from the venture. The customer profile helps determine the choice of location. Other factors include the location of competitors, convenience, availability and cost of space, and zoning regulations.

While most buy-back centers operate at a fixed location, some are operated as mobile buy-back units. These are often truck trailers equipped with scales that travel to various locations. Like the central facility, mobile buy-back units weigh materials, purchase them, and transport the recyclables for further processing. Mobile buy-back centers work well in rural or economically depressed areas, where residents would not otherwise travel to the main buy-back center.

Since the objective of a buy-back center relates to economic factors, such as "making a profit," the decisions about which recyclable materials to handle depends *not* just on the existence of markets, but on "good prices." In addition, flexibility must be built into a buy-back center's purchasing program because commodity prices are changing continuously. These decisions determine the size of the facility.

Similar to a drop-off center, space is needed for parking, for delivery and pickup of materials, for containers, and for equipment. Factors such as an orderly traffic flow and room for expansion need to be weighed. Fencing, a building with a restroom, and zoning restrictions will also play a role in determining the size of the facility.

Marketing decisions such as advertising, signs, hours of operation, prices to be paid for materials, positioning of the new buy-back center in relationship to competitors, point-of-purchase posters and handouts, Yellow Page advertising, the name of the business, decisions regarding the "corporate image" of the business, and so forth, reflect the fact that a buy-back center is a business enterprise.

Keys to a Successful Buy-back Program

Successful recycling programs depend on a number of factors. First, they must have a large customer base to provide recyclable materials. Second, buy-back programs need a convenient location for their customers. Without a central location, customers will not likely make the trip to the buy-back center. A third characteristic of a good buy-back center is that it collects a variety of recyclable materials and pays a competitive price for them. Friendly operators and good advertising campaigns also help buy-back programs prevail.

Potential Problem Areas

Significant financial risks are present at a buy-back center because cash is used to make purchases, and the recyclable materials that are handled tend to have a high value. Financial controls should be appropriate for handling cash, and inventory controls must also be effective. Security systems to protect the physical inventory are required, reflecting the fact that risks of theft and misappropriation are significant.

Markets tend to be unpredictable, making it necessary that constant adjustments be required. Management must be flexible because buy-back centers can be costly to operate and the margin of profit can disappear in a recession, during prolonged poor markets, or if buying prices are not kept sufficiently high to allow a profit.

A buy-back center requires substantial capital for start-up costs to establish a facility and to purchase equipment. A buy-back center operates as a business with regular hours and paid staff. It also needs to have funding for advertising and publicity. Buy-back programs must be able to pay customers cash and sell materials on terms as long as 30 or 60 days. For these reasons it is important for the facility to have ongoing cash reserves.

COMMERCIAL PICKUP SERVICE

Scrap dealers/processors exist in every city and almost every community. Almost all offer commercial customers pickup service. Generally, these dealers/processors will provide containers for storing recyclable materials and will pick up these containers on either a "call-in" or scheduled basis. In Chapter 24 "Markets," there is a discussion about how scrap dealers/processors provide markets for recyclable materials.

Most scrap dealers/processors buy and sell millions of dollars of recyclable materials annually and are operated by professional management. A few are "mom-and-pop" size. Some are divisions of major corporations. Depending on the specific company, they can help install office recycling programs, cardboard recycling programs, and curbside programs; often, they will help market material from drop-off programs.

Basic Choices

The business of scrap dealers/processors is very competitive, especially in large market areas, but in more remote parts of the United States there may be less competition. If a pickup program's needs are clearly defined, a scrap dealer/processor can help. If there are many companies to choose from, putting your critical needs in writing may be helpful in the decision-making process.

Keys to a Successful Commercial Pickup Program

A successful relationship comes when both parties recognize that they each have responsibilities for making the recycling program work. High expectations for performance on both sides will ultimately make the recycling program a good one. If clear communications are maintained, a major source of problems will be eliminated.

Potential Problem Areas

Occasionally, scrap dealers/processors will be excluded by community leaders when a community-wide solution to recycling is being discussed. At least part of the problem originates when the proponents of new recycling solutions identify existing scrap dealers as "the old" way recycling was done. It can help the community a great deal if scrap dealers/processors are invited to help solve the community's problems. For example, a duplication of facilities can be avoided, market knowledge can be assembled quickly, and the community may save a great deal of money by subcontracting the processing and hauling functions associated with many recycling programs.

SPECIAL COLLECTION PROGRAMS

Special recycling events have a place in every community. The annual collection of leaves, Christmas trees, tires, oil, white goods, and household hazardous wastes has positive implications for the entire program. An annual spring cleanup of litter can be combined with a special recycling program. For example, it can be combined with a tire collection program or a household hazardous waste program. Leaves can be composted and turned into a topsoil additive. Christmas trees can be shredded and turned into mulch. Worn out tires can be collected, with the good ones sold as used tires, or a tire retreader might be interested in good casings. Oil can be sent to a re-refiner or used in some heating systems. White goods can be restored or sent to an automobile shredder. Household hazardous wastes, like insecticides, paints, solvents, and cleaning agents, can be disposed of properly.

The benefits of these programs seem self-evident, but one that is easily overlooked is that each "event" provides a public relations opportunity to promote and educate regarding the community-wide recycling program.

Basic Choices

One basic decision is to determine how many special events should be scheduled for any one community. A community that encourages backyard composting probably does not warrant a leaf cleanup. There is evidence that an annual household hazardous waste cleanup is insufficient. People who miss the "Special Day" get discouraged that they have to hold onto material for a whole year and end up throwing the hazardous material in the regular trash. More than one household hazardous waste day per year seems to be indicated.

Another unnecessary choice relates to the commitment to have a special collection day: Is the commitment for one year only, or is it for a longer term? The answer to this question determines how the event should be promoted. Another decision relates to services. Items such as Christmas trees and leaves can be collected at the curb or at a central location. Obviously, curbside collection is more costly, but it is also a way to increase participation. Collection at a central location works best if the time period for collecting the material lasts longer than a single day.

Keys to Successful Special Collection Programs

The key to a successful special collection event is promotion. Poor participation almost always means that people were not aware of the special event. Often, more than one date for special collections is necessary to guarantee that people still have time to participate in the event after they hear about it.

Potential Problem Areas

Sometimes a community is surprised by the amount of old household hazardous waste that is collected. Success becomes bittersweet when the community discovers how much money it will cost to properly dispose of the material.

BACKYARD COMPOSTING

Yard waste is seasonal, creates stresses on waste management systems, and amounts to an average of 18 percent of the municipal solid waste stream. Backyard composting eliminates most of this waste and results in leveling the waste stream load. If backyard composting is not part of a community's plan, then remaining systems must be designed to handle this volume with all of the costs associated with the alternative solution. This explains why growing numbers of communities are banning yard waste from residential trash. Backyard composting has the advantage that it is inexpensive and efficient. Finally, yard waste is essentially organic matter that does not provoke groundwater or air quality problems.

The open composting procedure is relatively simple, yet it takes work to compost successfully. The process is not automatic. First, a holding bin or as many as three holding bins are constructed. Ready-made holding bins are available at lawn and garden shops. Otherwise, bins are constructed from snow fencing, from concrete blocks, or from wood. Space to let air into the compost pile must be provided so that the circulated air can help in the decaying process. Water is added to the pile occasionally, and the pile must also be turned occasionally. Gradually, the organic yard waste is turned into a soil additive through composting.

An ordinance prohibiting yard waste from residential trash, a booklet showing how compost bins should be constructed, how the process works, and a promotional program seem to be a very small price to pay if yard waste is a significant component of trash in a specific community.

Basic Choices

Composting can be urged on a voluntary basis or mandated by regulations. If mandated, an enforcement procedure is required. It can be as simple as a reminder left with the trash, a notice explaining why the trash was not picked up, or imposing a small penalty for repeated violations.

Compost bins can be provided by the community, or made available to residents at cost, or the construction of bins can simply be made the residents' responsibility. Books on backyard composting exist and can be made available, or the community can write its own instructional booklet. There are a number of choices about how to get the information into the hands of residents, including direct mail, door-to-door distribution, and handouts at community meetings.

A hotline or some other way of getting help and answers to questions should be available. Some composting piles do not work properly, and although the reason may be simple—not enough water, too much water, not turning the pile, and so on—a resource or reference should be made available to citizens.

Keys to Successful Backyard Composting

A good communication program is the key to getting people to change how they dispose of yard waste. If people understand how much they are contributing to solid waste problems by bagging their yard waste, perhaps they would consider an alternative. Education programs can also emphasize the fact that the composted material would function as a good fertilizer the following spring.

Potential Problem Areas

Probably the biggest problem from backyard composting is odor. Odor occasionally comes from a compost pile if it is overwatered or contains meat. Providing proper instructions to residents can help avoid this problem.

LARGE-SCALE COMPOSTING

Composting facilities can be designed on a large scale to serve a larger community, neighborhood, city, or county. The method can be as simple as turning piles of leaves, or it can be complex, involving shredding to reduce the size of the garbage so that microorganisms can rapidly decompose the organic materials. Large-scale composting can involve mixing shredded garbage with moisture to speed up the decomposition process. There are six basic steps in the high-technology process:

1. Shred materials to increase the exposure to air and microbes.
2. Mix to introduce air and water throughout the pile.
3. Compost by introducing air, which allows the mixture to heat up to a temperature of 130 degrees Fahrenheit. It takes 20 to 30 days.
4. Cure the compost by allowing the pile to cool down, which completes the decaying process. It takes four to six months.
5. Screen pile to remove items that have not decayed, such as glass, metal, and plastic.
6. Sell and distribute the compost.

Large-scale composting uses one of three common methods: Closed vessel method, the aerated pile method, or the windrow method. The closed vessel method puts the composted waste into an enclosed structure with highly controlled amounts of water and air. Often, a rotating drum or an auger mixes the waste as it decomposes. The aerated pile method pumps air through perforated pipes to force air into the compost pile. This means that the piles do not have to be turned.

The windrow method piles material to be composted into long rows of a specific width and height on level, well-drained ground. The leaves and grass clippings are allowed to decompose naturally for 18 to 24 months. The piles are aerated during this time to keep the composting process going and to prevent odors. This is usually accomplished through specialized windrow machinery that turns the compost rows, thereby adding air to speed the decomposition of the materials. At the end of the two-year period the compost may be further ground, shredded, or screened to improve its physical appearance.

Large-scale composting cannot be considered lightly. It is a very capital intensive method of reducing waste. It requires a reliable and proven process and requires an experienced, well-financed organization with a proven track record to install and perhaps to manage the project. Large-scale composting can be combined with a landfill operation, with sewage sludge removal activities, or with a materials recovery facility.

Basic Choices

The materials to be composted will determine the size and scope of the facility. The choices range from composting unsorted trash to composting just leaves and grass clippings.

How the materials are collected is another choice. Compostable materials can be delivered to a site, or they can be picked up at curbside. Large-scale composting requires a reliable technology—including odor control. A thorough selection process involving substantial companies specializing in this area is required. Visits to similar communities with the top systems that appear effective should be arranged. Selecting the right technology and the right company to do the job are important decisions.

The location of the facility is also an involved choice. Zoning regulations, site availability, acquisition cost, and community approval are factors involved in the site selection process.

Keys to Successful Large-Scale Composting

Large-scale composting will succeed if it is properly funded and maintained. The compost keeper must be well educated on how to rotate and water the piles to produce a good product and manage odor. The compost can then be sold to residents and businesses or utilized with the cooperation of the highway or parks department.

Potential Problem Areas

Finding a suitable site that meets with community approval can be a problem. Odors and leachate from compost piles can occur if the site is poorly managed. Other difficulties include logistical problems with yard waste collection.

CAPITAL-INTENSIVE, MACHINERY-INTENSIVE ALTERNATIVES

There are two terms used to describe the methods of recycling—source segregation and resource recovery. Source segregation means recyclable materials are removed *prior* to being thrown out as garbage, and resource recovery refers to removing recyclable materials *after* they are mixed with other types of garbage. As this section will explain, resource recovery also means complex and expensive.

Before we explore the various capital-intensive alternatives designed to handle garbage, consider for a moment the nature of garbage. Most trash is generated in the kitchen. Usually, a bag is inserted into a trash container to help contain liquids. Then, as trash is generated, it is thrown into the kitchen garbage can in sequence—egg shells, coffee grounds, orange juice container, morning newspaper, leftovers from the kitchen sink, milk containers, bread wrappers, glass bottles, chicken parts, grease, empty cans, vegetable peelings, leftovers, and so on, and so forth.

When the bag is full, it is taken outside to be dumped into a much bigger trash receptacle, where it will cook in the heat of the summer days and freeze solid in many climates during the winter. Once a week this bigger container is hauled out to the street for trash pickup. The trash is dumped into a truck that has two massive hydraulic cylinders that will effortlessly compact the trash under thousands of pounds of pressure—enough pressure to crush glass bottles.

To complicate things, assume that a neighbor threw out half a can of paint (not an approved practice—at a minimum the lid should be taken off so that the paint turns into a solid) and that another neighbor threw out a milk jug of oil from his or her recent do-it-yourself oil change. When the garbage truck dumps its load at the landfill, paint and oil will ooze over bags of garbage that have burst open under the pressure of the compaction. The nature of garbage should be kept in mind while looking at capital-intensive solutions to solve landfill problems.

If your community faces severe landfill problems, such that you must look at capital-intensive solutions, the various choices among resource recovery solutions are mind boggling. They include resource recovery facilities, materials recovery facilities, intermediate processing facilities, transfer stations with and without recycling capabilities, waste-to-energy facilities, incinerators, and landfill salvage operations. In examining the alternatives, a community should carefully evaluate sales claims, technology, and equipment. Readers should be aware that no widely accepted definitions exist for these facilities. Great care should be taken to define terms with outside parties to avoid misunderstanding.

Resource Recovery Facilities

A resource recovery facility proposes to do the complete job of maximizing recovery of recyclable materials, obtaining energy value from the balance of the waste stream, and reducing solid waste volumes in the process. The facility has conveyors, hammer mills to reduce the size of materials, provisions for manual sorting, trommel screens for sorting items by size, air classifiers for separating light components, magnetic separators, a waste-to-energy plant, and a minimum production capacity of several hundred tons of garbage per day.

The problem with these facilities is the gooey garbage that results from household disposal.

Material Recovery Facility (MRF)

A MRF generally accepts only selected loads of garbage or mixed recyclables for sorting. In Europe, wet trash and dry trash are collected separately. The dry trash goes to a MRF. In the United States the loads may be from selected businesses, or the material might come from a "blue bag" residential program. The key is that MRF is selective about the material it receives.

Intermediate Processing Facility (IPC)

An intermediate processing facility is for the purpose of preparing recyclable materials by sorting, grading, and packaging material to market to end users. The input material is usually source segregated. The facility may be designed to serve the curbside recycling program or the drop-off program or both. It may be sized to handle other business as well.

Transfer Station Facility

A transfer station is a facility in which small loads of trash are consolidated into larger loads that are placed in larger vehicles, such as trailers, railroad cars, or barges, for transportation to a landfill. The objectives of a transfer station are to reduce the number of trips to the landfill a hauler must make and to save the smaller trucks time to make more stops each day. What makes this system work is that the transfer station is usually located within the city limits, while the landfills are located a great distance away. Tipping fees are often reasonable because the economic factors are easy to understand. Large loads are charged the same tipping fee as small loads, so it makes economic sense to consolidate trash into fewer large loads.

Some transfer stations have a capacity for recycling and by recovering material reduce the volume of material that has to be transported to the landfill. Corrugated cardboard is the most prevalent material recovered from trash; however, recyclables such as glass, aluminum, and plastic may also be recovered. Front-end loaders can move entire loads of material to a sorting area if they are rich in recyclable materials. Other materials can be sorted manually or on conveyers.

Waste-to-Energy Plant

A waste-to-energy plant incinerates waste materials to produce energy in the form of steam or electricity. Some waste-to-energy plants burn unprocessed garbage, a technique known as mass burning. Others use refuse-derived fuel (RDF), which can be obtained by mechanically sorting and removing glass, metals, and other unburnable materials from the waste stream. The RDF is either burned immediately or compressed into pellets for use at a later time. Ideally, waste-to-energy plants do not compete with recycling or composting programs, but in many cases they do.

Typically, revenue is earned from the steam or electricity, and the balance of the cost of operating the waste-to-energy plant is made up by tipping fees. Legislation involving the ban of certain items from the waste stream, such as tires, automobile batteries, motor oil, and batteries, helps reduce the potential for an emissions problem. The keys to limiting emissions problems are: 1) removal of items that contain heavy metals, 2) a reliable system that insures complete combustion, and 3) effective pollution control equipment. Permitting procedures are usually onerous.

The big advantage of waste-to-energy plants is that the volume of garbage can be reduced by 90 percent, thereby saving limited landfill space. Incineration also destroys the liquid components of solid waste, which reduces potential problems of leachate in landfills. The big disadvantages are that emission problems can jeopardize the entire investment and that ash must be disposed of properly. Since many toxic substances are concentrated in the ash, its proper disposal requires careful analysis.

Incinerator

An incinerator burns trash under controlled conditions and thereby reduces its volume. At one time in the United States everybody burned garbage. The open burning of garbage stopped abruptly with the Clean Air Act, but incineration should be looked at as a technological alternative.

In modern day incinerators the temperatures are very high and odor and air pollution are controlled. Incineration is used extensively in Europe and Japan. Unlike waste-to-energy plants, the heat generated is not used except to burn more garbage.

Like the waste-to-energy plant, the big disadvantages are that emissions problems can jeopardize the entire investment and that ash must be disposed of properly.

Landfill Salvage

Landfill salvage operations allow for the immediate recovery of large quantities of recyclable materials before they are dumped into the landfill. These operations are the only ones that do not require a significant public education effort. Many commercial and industrial generators mostly dispose of nearly homogeneous recyclable materials.

The problem with operations located at landfills is that they are usually far removed from where the trash is generated; therefore, all the transportation costs have already been incurred and the landfill disposal fee has been paid. Recycling is twofold: It saves cost and saves landfill space. Here the costs have already been paid, so the savings is not as evident. Another difficulty is that many loads entering the landfill may have a high percentage of recyclable materials, but these materials may be so compacted with other wastes as to make their removal impractical.

Keys to Success in High-capital Solutions

An assured supply of solid waste and income must be available to support these facilities. Capital costs range generally from several million dollars to over $100 million. This assurance is attainable through flow control legislation, which clearly identifies solid waste as a regulated commodity and gives the governmental unit the right to direct what happens to the material. The government then directs the material to its capital-intensive facility and establishes rates that will pay interest expenses, retire debt, and pay for the costs of operation.

One big disadvantage of post collection separation is the high costs for separating and upgrading materials. Another is that the recyclable materials are often contaminated by other wastes, and they may lose their marketability. As a result, the combination of flow control and having the right to charge tipping fees are a key to success.

Other key success strategies include having long-term customers for recyclable materials or energy in the case of waste-to-energy facilities, a time-tested technology, a location that is convenient and meets with zoning and community approval, and a place to dispose of the residual trash or ash.

Potential Problem Areas

Because the operating costs are high and largely fixed, any period of low volume, including a low volume of recyclable materials, can impact the viability of the project.

Waste-to-energy and incineration plants have the potential to generate ill will and to violate the Clean Air Act if emissions are not controlled. Failure to comply with emissions standards or dispose of ash properly can create public pressures to scrap the facility as a poorly conceived idea.

Spending millions creates a financial risk to most communities. These risks can be reduced by taking a regional approach to the problem to spread the risks or by creating an authority with a charter authorized by vote or through state legislation. A special tax district might be created to support the facility with a special tax.

ATTRACTING A SECONDARY MATERIAL END USER

In this new era of minimizing solid waste, a user of secondary materials will be an extremely valuable addition to any community. Normally, business development people associated with state government or chambers of commerce are excited about jobs. With solid waste costs soaring and with markets for secondary materials, there are few additions more valuable to a community than an end user with a voracious appetite for the right materials. Plus they provide jobs.

DESIGN OPTIONS THAT CAN BE CONSIDERED

One way to design a recycling program for the whole community is by using a matrix. The matrix in Table 25-4 will help to cover all the bases. Place an X in each grid to indicate that a plan exists.

TABLE 25-4. Any Community Solid Waste Reduction and Recycling Plan

Approach To Be Used	Single family	Multi-family	Rural Areas	Business	Government
Percentage of waste	*18%*	*20%*	*2%*	*50%*	*5%*
Education and support	X	X	X	X	X
Curbside program	X				
Drop-off program	X	X	X	X	X
Buy-back centers	X	X	X	X	X
Commercial collection		X	X	X	X
Special collections	X	X	X	X	X
Composting, backyard	X		X		
Composting, large scale	X	X	X	X	X
Resource recovery facility	X	X	X	X	X
Materials recovery facility	X	X	X	X	X
Intermediate processing facility	X	X	X	X	X
Transfer station	X	X	X	X	X
Waste-to-energy facility	X	X	X	X	X
Incinerator	X	X	X	X	X
Landfill salvage facility	X	X	X	X	X
Business development plan	X	X	X	X	X

Mandatory or Voluntary

Recycling programs should be designed based on the specific goals and criteria of the community. They will be voluntary or mandatory, depending on the current legislation and landfill problems. Evidence indicates that mandatory programs produce better results, even though they cost more and raise issues like enforcement and penalties for non-compliance or poor compliance.

How Trash Services are Billed

Charging for trash by the container reduces solid waste when recycling alternatives are accessible and convenient. It is a concept that can be sold to the community when they are informed and aware of solid waste issues. Under this variable container concept, households with one container are charged lower disposal costs than those with two or three containers.

Another concept is to charge rates based on the weight of trash in each container. In this system containers are weighed as they are dumped into a trash truck. A computerized code keeps track of each weight per house. This system requires specialized equipment and retrofitted trucks, but early indications show that it will also save landfill space.

Public or Private Haulers

In some communities the choice between public and private trash haulers is obvious. In others, emotions can become involved on both sides of the issue. Probably, the issue should simply be reduced to a cost issue, but it never is, and it is often difficult to understand the costs associated with public hauling. The full ramifications of this decision process require thorough research.

The Future Costs of Recycling and Disposal

The program cost should be forecasted for five years, with appropriate assumptions for growth in the solid waste stream, the trends in the community, the forecasted costs of landfilling, inflation, and the new programs that will be required.

Educational Programs

Recycling education should begin well before any program starts—at least two to three months in advance. It should use a variety of methods to get the information out. People do not catch on if they are exposed to new information only once. During the start up is a good time for an intensive mass media blitz. It is easier to start out correctly than to fix a program once it has been in operation.

Education must also continue during the life of the program. Every community has turnover in its population. Information should be handed out when people sign up for trash service. Follow-up messages should be publicized about the progress of the program. Information about participation rates, volume of materials collected, number of trees saved, energy saved, and cubic yards of landfill space saved is of general community interest.

Information regarding recycling can be compiled from this book to help in the educational process of recycling education for various groups listed in the table:

1. A recycling directory can include a map showing all recycling opportunities, a description of the materials that each facility recycles, and an outline of what each program accepts. It should include hours of operation and emphasize the collection dates for curbside service or for special collection programs.
2. Recycling can be integrated with school curriculums.
3. Posters can be designed for display in stores and schools.
4. Stick-ons can be designed to show that businesses recycle.
5. Advertisements can announce a new program.
6. A recycling hotline can be connected to the recycling manager's office so that questions can be answered on a timely basis.
7. Grocery sack stuffers can announce a new program.
8. Newspaper supplements can discuss recycling in detail.
9. Billboards can create awareness.
10. Refrigerator magnets can serve as reminders.
11. Direct mail can support the program.
12. Pamphlets can be designed in two or three languages if appropriate.
13. Public service announcements can create awareness.
14. Public meetings can be used to discuss recycling in depth.
15. Video tapes can explain recycling.
16. Information for businesses—specific help for specific types of business.
17. Collection bins (residential) can display a number to call for information.

One way to inform travelers about the community's efforts and to help spread recycling outside the community is to construct a large sign or billboard announcing a

This sign will indicate the community's unique spirit and commitment.

MONITOR PROGRESS AND FINE TUNE THE PROGRAM

Once the program is implemented, it will be extremely important to monitor and fine tune the program. This will include documenting participation rates, determining the amount of material collected, monitoring financial results, making comparisons to budgets and long-term plans, and updating collection techniques.

26

Government Cost

Many communities are being called on to perform expensive recycling services, either due to legislation, citizenry, or the landfill crisis. Understanding the high costs involved and developing the funding sources for recycling programs will help recycling coordinators have a realistic grasp of what they can accomplish with limited budgets. However, at the same time the community comes to grip with the high cost of recycling, it might also examine the higher costs of alternatives such as landfills, waste-to-energy plants, and so on.

Starting a recycling program without a basic understanding of the economics of the industry is one of the greatest pitfalls. Even a program that "sounds right" can fail if actual costs become greater than the anticipated costs and if funds are inadequate to support the program. No one wants to start a new program only to have it axed in a budget cutting process.

There are six economic concepts to be considered before discussing the economics of any specific recycling program. These six concepts include actual operating costs, capital requirements, avoided costs, incremental costs and incremental recycling volume, present value costs, and social costs.

Actual operating costs—Actual operating costs are the costs in terms of the cash required to provide services under the recycling program. These include start up fees related to consultants, waste stream audits, programming planning, and costs of obtaining input through surveys of the general public. Operating costs also include the cost of recruiting people for the recycling program; the costs of collecting, sorting, grading, and processing materials; and, finally, obtaining revenue for the recyclable materials or collecting user fees to offset the costs of the program. An operating deficit indicates that supplementary funds must come from other sources, such as grants, tax revenue, or the general budget.

Capital investment—A program's capital is either working capital, required to run the recycling program, or funding for a nonrecurring start up cost, required to purchase the program's tangible assets: equipment, land, and buildings. Depending on the size of the program, funding can range from almost nothing to very substantial commitments requiring the issuance of bonds and the paying of capital costs over a number of years.

Avoided costs—Avoided costs reflect the fact that recycling can save money in three possible areas. Recycling can reduce transportation costs of collecting trash by reducing the volume of trash that needs to be picked up and by reducing the number of trash loads hauled from the community to a distant landfill. Recycling also can reduce the cost of landfill fees or tipping fees required at transfer stations by reducing the volume of material that must be disposed of. Lastly, recycling can possibly extend the life of a landfill, thereby saving the community the cost of building a new one.

Fewer trash trucks serving the community may save money, but will require rerouting trash trucks or some other reorganization, to effectuate a true savings. Some communities served by private haulers may not see a direct savings, as far as a local government budget is concerned. For others, the reduction in the number of trash trucks may be offset with the expense of purchasing recycling trucks. However, if avoided costs can be documented, the savings can be used to support the recycling program.

Incremental costs—Incremental costs represent the added costs that are attributable to recycling. For example, if recycling duties are assigned to an existing department, such as the department of public works, employees might assume new recycling program tasks without a noticeable change in effectiveness... up to a point. Thereafter, new personnel must be added, or the efficiency in executing both the original duties and the new recycling tasks will be impacted. This creates a source of incremental costs that can be documented. Other incremental costs include money spent on educational programs, collecting recyclable materials, and publicity.

Incremental volume—Incremental volume refers to the fact that most communities can document that some recycling activity is going on prior to the involvement of government. This recycling is usually done by a tax-paying private sector at no cost to the government. This existing recycling volume should be a part of each community's analysis.

Another approach to make the program appear less expensive is to utilize the capacity to recycle that already exists in the community. A straightforward analysis should reveal the expected incremental volume of recyclable materials. The new recycling program's true benefit is only for the added volume; therefore, the incremental cost should be related only to the change in volume that will be realized.

Realistically, new recycling programs do add new material, but most programs also acquire volume from existing programs. The usual approach is to design the new recycling program to displace the private sector volume in whole or in part and to show costs in relation to the total volume collected, not the incremental volume. Using the incremental approach gives the community a truer economic picture, relating costs to expected or realized benefits and does not give the new program credit for replacing the volume that was being collected before the program started. As a result, many recycling programs that predate a comprehensive government-sponsored program fail. But this creates a dilemma for the community—whether to design the new recycling program for the incremental volume or the total volume.

Present value—Present value is a financial concept that recognizes that the value of money changes over time: A dollar in today's terms has more value than a dollar received next year. By discounting all dollars in a futuristic model to present value, we have a method of comparing different scenarios by reducing them both to a common denominator. The relevance to recycling is that many communities are spending present dollars in the expectation that trash costs will go up dramatically in the future. The present costs are looked at as an "investment" for the future. Present value methods can help in the evaluation process.

Social costs—Social costs are difficult to document, but are nonetheless "real." Disposal has many social costs. When groundwater is contaminated, people can get ill or die. By recycling materials and not disposing of them in landfills, society is offered the prospect of a lower social cost. Recycling should also be encouraged because it reduces energy consumption and pollution. Using recycled materials in manufacturing should also be encouraged because it can counter our vast consumption of virgin resources that add to, rather than reduce, the volume of material that must be disposed of.

Acid rain is one example of environmental damage created by using fossil fuels. Energy consumption would be less with more recycling. Many people who resist recycling in favor of the status quo with respect to trash disposal are failing to look into the distant future. To a large extent, social costs come to be recognized only over time. Unfortunately, opportunities to reduce social costs have often been recognized mostly by looking into the rear view mirror of history. We should, at a minimum, give social costs some weight in making recycling decisions.

SPECIFIC COSTS OF PROGRAMS

Since citizen interest in recycling programs is currently very high, enlisting their help in the early stages may avoid a program that sounds good but that the community cannot afford. The approach taken in this chapter is to develop a general framework to understand programs first and then to discuss the economics of the following programs:

1. Special collection programs

2. Curbside programs
3. Drop-off centers
4. Buy-back centers
5. Recyclable materials processing facility
6. Major projects (MRFs and waste-to-energy plants)

There are six basic financial elements to each of these types of recycling programs. These include revenue from the sale of recyclable materials, the program's operating costs, operating surplus or deficit, the recruitment of additional income, and net surplus or deficit.

REVENUE

Revenue from the recycling program includes the sale of recyclable materials or compost, the sale of bags for curbside recycling programs, the sale of services such as tipping fees, or special fees billed to households for curbside recycling. In making revenue projections, there should be subcategories for each major grade of recyclable material sold or purchased by the processing center, to help analyze the recycling program's performance.

OPERATING COSTS

Operating costs represent the amount of money consumed in an effort to generate recycling revenue and provide the required recycling services. This includes direct material costs. If the operation purchases recyclable materials, each major grade of material should have a subcategory that corresponds to each subheading in the revenue category. The word direct means that the material is directly related to the material sold. Spending money to collect aluminum cans that are sold later qualifies "aluminum cans" as a subcategory for direct costs and for revenue. The following are various operating costs:

Wages—Wages are also included in operating costs. Wages refer to the direct payments, including overtime pay, made to employees who work on a hourly basis. Subcategories are used to indicate the functional areas in which these people spend the majority of their time. These categories can include receiving material, operating forklifts, sorting scrap material, operating baling equipment, operating front-end loaders, shipping material, maintaining equipment, driving a truck, helping on a truck, or doing clerical work. In some accounting classification systems, vacation, holiday pay, and sick pay are separate expense categories, and in other systems they are included with wages.

Salaries—Salary expenses are also included in operating costs. Salaries refer to the direct payments made to the recycling coordinator or director, supervisors, managers, and other professionals who are employed in the recycling program. Because of their status they are normally exempt from the federal wage and hour regulations. Individuals who are employed by other departments but who spend significant time on recycling might be charged to the recycling program for the pro rata share of their salary.

Payroll taxes—The head taxes related to payroll and the employer portion of social security taxes or the equivalent, as well as federal and state unemployment taxes are categorized as payroll taxe's.

Health insurance—Health insurance is necessary for attracting and keeping productive people. Often, the cost is shared with employees.

Worker's compensation insurance—Workers compensation insurance is related to payroll and the type of work performed. Maintaining this insurance is required by law and provides protection for the employee and employer for on-the-job accidents and injuries. The recycling industry is regarded as fairly hazardous because of the high number of lifting injuries and of abrasions due to sharp objects, such as broken glass and metal edges.

Casualty insurance—Casualty insurance includes fire insurance, general liability insurance, vehicle liability insurance, umbrella liability insurance, employee bonding insurance, and theft insurance. Some categories of insurance are required by law.

Diesel fuel, gas, and oil—Trucks, forklifts, and front-end loaders require refueling on a daily basis to operate. The commuting costs of driving for supervisors, managers, and other professionals are usually covered as travel expenses under a separate expense category. Controlling the expenditures for these items requires establishing clear rules and guidelines.

Truck repair—Truck repair includes the cost of repairing and maintaining trucks. Repair costs can be routine as part of a preventive maintenance program or of an emergency nature.

Equipment repair—The cost of repairing forklifts, front-end loaders, baling equipment, conveyers, glass crushers, trailers, and containers, is considerable. This equipment operates in a dirty environment, requires a good preventive maintenance program, and also frequently needs to be rebuilt due to wear.

Equipment rent—During periods of downtime for existing equipment or during periods of peak demand, it is necessary to rent on a short-term basis different types of equipment. Recycling is a service, and people expect it to be reliable. If the recycling program involves processing, material should not be allowed to pile up because storage becomes a problem and there is an increased risk of fire and litter hazards. During breakdowns or peaks, equipment should be rented to keep up with demand.

Supplies—Operating costs also include specific supplies. There are a number of different types of supplies requiring subcategories. Plant supplies include gaylord boxes, barrels, banding materials, tape, stretch wrap, and miscellaneous supplies. Office supplies includes computer printout, stationery, copy paper, pencils, pens, preprinted forms for purchase orders, invoices, and receiving checks for regular payments and for payroll, and so forth.

Another major supply item is bale ties. When recyclable materials are processed they are often baled in large, specialized machines that compact the materials under hydraulic pressure into bales resembling hay bales, weighing between 300 to 2,000 pounds. Baling wire is used to hold the bales together so that they can be transported. Banding wire may also be used, but if a minor item, it is included under the heading "supplies."

Postage—Funds for sending mail can be substantial if direct mail is used, unless the mailings can be included as inserts with utility bills or other mail.

Dues and subscriptions—Recycling publications are a necessity needed to attain market information and to keep informed about new developments. Some publications cost $400 annually, and it is easy to spend the better part of $1,000 annually. It is harder to find the time to read them.

Outside services—Outside services range over many activities; therefore, subcategories are useful. The types of services include temporary labor, local hauling services, subcontracting the processing of recyclable materials, recycling and solid waste consultants, computer programmers, public relations consultants, legal services, and accounting and auditing services.

Freight costs—Freight costs may be incurred for inbound and outbound shipments.

Taxes and licenses—This includes everything from the cost of license plates for vehicles, to permits for recycling facilities, to sales taxes on equipment.

Trash—Trash is collected along with recyclables and must be disposed of. If market problems become severe it is also possible that collected recyclable materials can become trash despite well-planned efforts to avoid this situation.

Rent—Land and building might be rented if they are not owned.

Property tax—Property tax or renter's taxes relate to buildings and land. Personal property taxes relate to equipment and other capital items.

Depreciation—It is usually appropriate to depreciate capital items by expensing as depreciation the pro rata share of the original cost over the life of the equipment.

Telephone—If recycling hotlines and long distance phone usage is high, the telephone expenses can be significant. To help control costs, especially if there are multiple locations, it is a good idea to ask the phone company to restrict long-distance availability and to block out the access to 900 numbers.

Utilities—Utilities include electricity, gas, and water bills.

Security—If the recycling program occupies a building, an alarm for fire is a minimum requirement, and often a burglar alarm system is included in this expense category. The theft of aluminum cans, copper, and brass is commonplace.

Promotion and education—An extensive recycling program may include newspaper advertising; direct mail; radio and TV advertisements or public service announcements; video tape presentations; and extensive printed material in the form of handouts, notices about how to improve materials left at the curb, brochures or pamphlets, and posters. Signage also is required at most recycling centers and at drop-off locations, to indicate the location and to educate people about what to do. The process should be continuous, but it is especially intensive during the start up phase.

Bad debt and sales adjustment expense—Most scrap sales are exposed to credit risk. Even large companies can adjust invoices and pay less than what has been billed for backcharges for quality problems that may be real or imagined. For some large end users, backcharges increase as recycling markets get weaker and decrease as markets get stronger. Some write-offs are inevitable if for no other reason than that scrap is an imperfect product.

Travel and entertainment expenses—Meeting with brokers, end users, and other clients is a necessity to properly manage any recycling program. Recycling conferences provide worthwhile educational opportunities. Guidelines for business lunches and other forms of entertainment should be written to avoid expense account abuse or friction with management.

Interest expenses and bank charge—Most banks charge to maintain checking accounts and, if the recycling program has leased equipment or borrowed funds, interest expenses will be incurred.

INCOME SUPPLIED FROM OUTSIDE THE RECYCLING PROGRAM

Other income is generated from funds supplied to the recycling program from federal, state, or local government; outright grants; funds from taxing sales; property and trash; advance disposal fees on items such as tires; and annual fees for businesses. Although these funds offset the cost of recycling, they are not a part of the direct operating results of the recycling program.

With an understanding of the various categories, it is possible to use a form to describe the phase of each program, such as planning, decision making, organizing, implementing, and so on, or in comparing types of programs such as curbside, drop-off, and so on, or to show the evolution of any aspect by month or by year. Table 26-1 helps programs keep track of revenue, expense, and operations.

CAPITAL REQUIREMENTS

Capital requirements exist to acquire assets that last for many years. Capital may also be required to establish cash reserves to cover startup costs, the costs of operating the program on a year-to-year basis, and the working capital to be consumed in accumulating inventories and accounts receivable.

A separate category of capital spending includes expenditures for land, build-

TABLE 26-1. Revenue, Expense, Operations costs

Revenue or Expense Description	Phase of Program	Type of Program	Month	Year
Revenue				
Aluminum cans				
Newspaper				
Glass				
Plastic				
Subtotal				
Operating Costs				
Direct material				
Aluminum cans				
Newspaper				
Glass				
Plastic				
Subtotal				
Other operating costs				
Bale ties				
Wages				
Salaries				
Payroll taxes				
Health insurance				
Worker's compensation				
Fuel, gas, and oil				
Truck repair				
Equipment repair				
Supplies				
Postage				
Dues/subscriptions				
Outside service				
Freight costs				
Taxes and licenses				
Trash				
Casualty insurance				
Rent				
Property taxes				
Depreciation				
Telephone				
Utilities				
Security				
Promotion				
Bad debt and adjustment				
Travel and entertainment				
Interest				
Subtotal				
Operating surplus or (deficit)				
Other income and expenses				
Net surplus or (deficit)				

ings, processing equipment, transportation equipment, computers, programming, curbside collection containers, drop-off containers, and other items that have long economic lives, usually of three years or more.

Table 26-2 shows what kind of costs will be associated with different recycling programs.

FINANCIAL CONTROLS

A recycling program can represent a major financial investment for a community. Unless a commensurate commitment is made to financial control, expenses can quickly reach beyond acceptable limits. One of the controls that should be in place is an extensive budget. The budget should be prepared and later can be compared to actual expenses. Financial reports should be completed on a timely basis and circulated to the appropriate people.

Inventory should also be controlled. Incoming material should be weighed, especially valuable commodities, such as aluminum and other nonferrous metals. Shipments should be weighed. A monthly physical inventory should be taken, and shrinkage should be identified by commodity in pounds and in dollars. The monetary consequence of shrinkage can easily be calculated based on selling prices for each respective commodity.

For buy-back programs, an area where shrinkage commonly originates is in the purchase of the recycled materials. It is possible for dishonest people to write extra purchasing tickets and/or to record higher than actual weights for certain customers. It is only through carefully weighing inventory and comparing the figures with reported purchases that these practices can be brought under control.

Recycling programs should be reviewed each year by an independent organization. This is especially true for buy-back programs, where control of cash accounts is normally given to the recycling program staff. Cash reconciliations should be done by a trained accountant.

Another helpful financial control is to limit the amount of credit extended. Credit is usually extended when recyclable materials are sold. Credit limits should be set and payments should be monitored to assure that they are received within agreed upon terms. On the same line, purchases should be controlled through a purchase order system and individuals should be assigned specific limits on the amount that can be spent on an individual transaction and during a monthly or weekly period. When bills are paid, a corresponding purchase order authorizing the purchase and a receiving report should be stapled to the paid invoice.

It also helps to have established freight rates. Freight rates should be agreed to in advance, and each bill should be individually approved and attached to the shipping invoice so that duplicate payments are eliminated.

Expense account guidelines should also be instituted. This can include an

TABLE 26-2. Capital Assets for Various Collection Programs

Type of Capital Asset	Curbside Program	Drop-off Program	Buy-back Center	Material Recovery Facility	Waste-to-Energy Plant
Working capital	Yes	Yes	Yes	Yes	Yes
Collection equipment:					
Curbside containers	Yes	No	No	No	No
Collection trucks	Yes	Yes	Yes	No	No
Roll-off trucks	No	Maybe	Maybe	No	No
Roll-off containers	No	Maybe	Maybe	No	No
Trailers	No	Maybe	Maybe	No	No
Tractors	No	Maybe	Maybe	No	No
Drop-off containers	No	Yes	Maybe	Maybe	Maybe
Processing equipment:					
Specialized equipment	No	No	No	No	Yes
Baler(s)	No	No	Maybe	Maybe	No
Conveyor(s)	No	No	Maybe	Yes	Yes
Can flattener or briquetter	No	No	Maybe	Maybe	No
Glass crusher	No	No	Maybe	Maybe	No
Forklift(s)	No	No	Maybe	Maybe	Maybe
Front-end loader	No	No	Maybe	Yes	Yes
Dock plates	No	No	Maybe	Yes	Maybe
Utility improvements	No	No	Maybe	Yes	Yes
Building improvements	No	No	Maybe	Yes	Yes
Pallet jacks	No	No	Maybe	Yes	Maybe
Crates/storage bins	No	Yes	Yes	Yes	Maybe
Miscellaneous:					
Desks and office equipment	Yes	Yes	Yes	Yes	Yes
Computer	Yes	Yes	Yes	Yes	Yes
Computer programs	Yes	Yes	Yes	Yes	Yes
Signage	No	Yes	Yes	Yes	Yes
Business forms	Yes	Yes	Yes	Yes	Yes
Stationery	Yes	Yes	Yes	Yes	Yes
Brochures	Yes	Yes	Yes	Yes	Yes
Printed materials	Yes	Yes	Yes	Yes	Yes
Obtaining permits	No	Yes	Yes	Yes	Yes
Zoning approval	No	Yes	Yes	Yes	Yes
Program design	Yes	Yes	Yes	Yes	Yes
Funding acquisition	Yes	Yes	Yes	Yes	Yes
Design of facility	No	Yes	Yes	Yes	Yes
Site selection	No	Yes	Yes	Yes	Yes
Consulting costs	Maybe	Maybe	Maybe	Likely	Yes
Recruiting costs	Maybe	Maybe	Maybe	Likely	Likely
Accounting system	Yes	Yes	Yes	Yes	Yes

approval process. Fuel and vehicles should also be controlled so that they are used only for authorized purposes.

Accident reports must be filed promptly after an accident occurs. Worker's compensation claims and insurance claims should be reviewed on a monthly or quarterly basis.

Hiring should be done on a professional basis, and individuals without experience should be trained regarding all of the responsibilities that employees have. Training is a very important function, and it is an area that occasionally is treated in a far too casual manner. References should be checked. Appropriate forms should be filled out completely, including the I-9 form regarding immigration status. Once hired, the punching of time cards should be restricted to the individual involved. Overtime should be authorized by supervisors and time cards should be signed by the appropriate supervisor.

Finally, physical security, particularly with respect to safeguards for valuable equipment, valuable inventory, and important office records should be reviewed at least semiannually.

SUMMARY

Clearly, developing a recycling program requires a great deal of financial planning. With the current recession and unstable market prices, it could easily be argued that recycling costs too much. Capital costs for curbside collection and buy-back centers can be outrageous. But long-term social costs must also be calculated into the equation. Our poor disposal habits have already led to contaminated groundwater supplies throughout the country. With the nation's health at stake, perhaps it is worth investing our money toward a better, more sanitary future.

27

Fund-raising

When civic organizations and charitable groups consider fund-raising, they often try to connect their worthwhile objective with another social good: recycling. Years ago the primary way to raise money by recycling was through a newspaper drive. In today's saturated market, the value of newspaper has declined and barely pays for the gas used to collect it. A newspaper drive now represents a good way to get exercise—and plenty of it. Nevertheless, civic and charitable groups continue to raise money through recycling, and a number of creative strategies meet with success.

NEWSPAPER DRIVES

Newspaper drives continue to enjoy a role in fund-raising. Newspaper drives can be one-time events or can be repeated with varying frequency. Obviously, newspaper drives do not work well in areas where there is competition from curbside collection programs. Also, newspaper markets need to be lined up before a paper drive is started because these markets cannot be taken for granted. In the recent past, many civic and charitable groups have been disappointed that collected newspaper had to be thrown in the trash because of the collapse of formerly reliable markets.

A key to success is an arrangement with a newspaper buyer. This buyer might be a local scrap dealer/processor, or it might be a recycling center in a neighboring city. A letter indicating the commitment to buy a specified quantity of newspaper should be received from the buyer before the paper drive is actually launched. Since some buyers will supply equipment such as roll-off containers or trailers, this also should be stated in the letter.

A key to collecting high volumes of newspaper is advance notice. When awareness is developed three months before the drive, people can begin saving. Usually, the notice of an upcoming paper drive is delivered on a door-to-door basis in the form of flyers or handouts, in addition to a local newspaper article. Included in the notice should be information about what is and what is not to be collected. For example, newspapers and aluminum cans might be collected in bags, and magazines, phone books, and junk mail might be excluded. Another subject covered by the flyer or handout is the collection day and an alternate collection day, in the event of rain or snow.

Another key is to have an ample supply of volunteers for the collection day and ample volunteers with trucks to take the newspaper to the buyer or to the central collection area. It pays to remember that tons of material will be picked up and handled several times and that as part of the arrangement the buyer expects high-quality material. A disposal container for magazines, yellowed newspaper, or wet newspaper should be available. Too few volunteers can make for a very, very tiring collection day.

But to make a newspaper drive a financial success will require an added dimension. Because the value of newspaper is low, consideration should be given to collecting pledges that relate to the tonnage of newspaper that is collected. In a small community, a newspaper drive is a valuable service and might produce 10 to 15 tons of material. A pledge of $1 per ton from 100 businesses and individuals can produce $1,000 to $1,500 from a newspaper drive, even if the newspaper is "sold" for nothing.

ALUMINUM CAN DRIVES

The concept of aluminum can drives came about when newspaper markets were waning. Aluminum cans are worth many times what newspapers are worth per pound. Therefore, less weight of material collected equates to more dollars. Otherwise, can drives work the same way that newspaper drives do. Instead of sorting out unacceptable newspapers, in a can drive the troubleshooting takes the form of sorting steel cans and aluminum foil.

One obstacle in making an aluminum can recycling fund-raiser successful is that a majority of people already collect them and look at them as a cash generator of their own. Donating cans, for these people, is the equivalent of donating cash. Because people do not donate cash readily, a successful can drive depends on people relating closely to the fund-raising objective or to the civic and charitable group doing the collecting.

Another version of the can drive is to require a bag of cans as admission to one of the group's social events, in addition to whatever else is typically required—a type of scavenger's ball.

DROP-OFF CENTERS

Another fund-raising opportunity is to establish a recycling drop-off center. A recognized community group could use its name and subcontract with a recycling business to locate bins around town for the collection of recyclable material. The arrangement can include having the group's name identified on the drop-off container, in exchange for receiving some agreed upon fee for the weight of material that is collected.

Other fund-raising approaches include the group operating the drop-off center(s) and selling the materials collected to a recycling company. Yet another approach is for the group to agree to service the drop-off center(s) for the community for an agreed upon fee.

Basic decisions include what is to be recycled, where the collection centers are to be located, frequency of pickup, monitoring of the sites, and vandalism. Additional information is contained about drop-off centers in Chapter 25.

LOCAL GOVERNMENT RECYCLING

Small towns and rural communities may want a recycling program, but may not be able to afford the high cost of labor to operate the program. In some cases, hiring a civic or charitable group to do the work can be a win-win proposition. The community benefits because it gets a recycling program, and the civic or charitable group benefits because it has a new source of funding. This could be a long-term agreement, or the agreement could rotate among charities.

RECYCLING AT SPECIAL EVENTS

Recycling at special events is another opportunity for fund-raising. This can be profitable under two possible conditions: first, that the group is paid to collect the recyclable materials, and second, that the group negotiates for the exclusive right to pick up large quantities of valuable scrap. An example of the second type of program might be to give a volunteer group the exclusive right to collect aluminum cans at a week-long rodeo. The collection could conceivably earn several thousand dollars.

SCRAP FROM BUSINESSES

Businesses who choose not to give money to charities might consider donating scrap materials, in order to avoid disposal fees. If the business already sells the scrap directly, it must recognize the income and pay taxes on the amount of the sale. But if the business donates scrap, it will in turn recognize a cost for the charitable donation and may pay less taxes. Without examining a particular business, it is difficult to discern how cost-effective these donations would be, but this might be another win-win situation.

For example, if a business pays taxes at a rate of 35 percent of income, the outright sale of one dollar of scrap allows the business to pocket 65 cents on an "after tax" basis. If the same material is donated, the business records an expense of one dollar as a donation, and the impact is that the business pays 35 cents less in taxes because earnings were reduced by the amount of the donation. On the one hand, the business is ahead 65 cents after taxes. On the other hand, the business is ahead only 35 cents. The business lost 30 cents by donating the scrap, but the civic or charitable group made one dollar.

Usually, fund-raising of this type is arranged through a highly placed executive who identifies with the fund-raising objective for the group needing the money.

SELLING RECYCLED PRODUCTS ON A DOOR-TO-DOOR BASIS

Products made from recycled materials, such as greeting cards, door mats, and stationery, are available to be sold on a door-to-door basis.

SHELTERED WORKSHOPS

Many recyclable materials are donated to organizations that provide employment opportunities to handicapped and homeless individuals. Sometimes, as in the case of the Disabled American Veterans, Goodwill Industries, Salvation Army, and Volunteers of America, they are nationally recognized organizations. In other cases, they may be local organizations.

These organizations can be employed to rebuild equipment, give scrap materials a second life through their second-hand retail stores, or disassemble products into their recyclable components. Some organizations operate full-scale recycling operations.

CONCLUSION

Even with the record-setting pace of new recycling programs, a tie-in between fund-raising and recycling can be effective. Success seems limited only by the creativity of fund-raisers and the willingness to do a bit of hard work.

28

Business Programs

Businesses generate approximately half of the solid waste in the United States. Reducing this percentage through recycling plays a critical role in preserving landfill space. Businesses must become active in all aspects of the recycling process, including becoming major consumers of the new supply of recycled materials. Installing a recycling program need not cost a business its competitive edge or affect its ability to meet the bottom line. In fact, when it comes to adjusting to new requirements, recycling is one of the strategies that can become a true winner for business.

Business recycling programs work best when the environmental benefits are obtained along with sound economic objectives. Since the support of all levels of management in the organization are required for a successful recycling program, it is best to keep the bottom line clearly in focus at all times. The recycling program can become a method of enhancing the company's image, an exercise building cooperation throughout the company, and evidence of environmental responsibility. To stay competitive, each business must reduce its waste disposal as much as possible, and recycling will provide the best way to achieve this goal.

Specific goals for the recycling program will vary from business to business based on the type of waste stream generated, the available markets, the profit improvement opportunity, the quality of management, and the regulatory climate. This chapter will lead the reader through the steps required to maximize the economic gain from recycling. The steps apply equally to both small and large businesses, but small businesses may have to network with others to achieve some of the alternatives available to large businesses.

Reduce the cost of trash—Business should develop a recycling program that reduces the projected cost of waste disposal by 50 percent. Reducing the escalating costs of waste disposal can be accomplished by recycling at least half of the waste stream. In order to reduce the amount of trash disposed, it is vital for old habits of disposing waste materials to be willingly replaced by new habits of separating recyclable items from the trash stream. This goal can be accomplished by designing an efficient flow of recyclable materials from their point of generation to the recycling markets. Trash costs can be further deferred by negotiating the best prices for recyclable materials. If capital expenditures are involved to install a recycling program, they may have to meet or exceed corporate guidelines—often a return on investment of 25 percent after taxes is required before spending is approved.

Records destruction—One of the most common arguments against recycling office waste is the danger of leaving confidential papers unprotected in open containers for days at a time before they are removed. Shredding records generated in executive offices, accounting departments, research and development areas, and personnel departments before placing them in recycling bins will assure confidentiality. In some recycling programs, information from an entire high-rise office complex can be stored unprotected in the basement for the period between pickups. Using a records destruction company is another alternative. For more information on this subject, see the section on "Office Recycling" in Chapter 29.

Other programs for reducing waste—If the business has industrial engineers, product design engineers, and purchasing agents, these people need to mobilize to attack waste at the source. Strategies for reducing the waste materials coming into the business, strategies that force vendors to take back the scrap that their products generate, and strategies to make sure that the business sends out products that are designed for recyclability can all become winners.

Improving the quality of products consumed, manufactured, and sent into the world also reduces waste. So does reducing excessive packaging.

Procurement policy—Even before an organized system is in place to collect office waste, businesses can begin purchasing recycled materials and products. Offices should use recycled materials when they can be purchased at the same or lower price. Many office products can be of recycled material with no negative effect on the business: Corrugated boxes, telephone message pads, interoffice mail envelopes, paper towels, and toilet tissue, for example. There may even be marketing advantages to using recycled materials and products. A small footnote "Printed on Recycled Paper" is an inexpensive way for a business to enhance its image on letterhead, envelopes, and business cards. Purchasing recycled materials can also qualify the company for bid preferences on government contracts.

Recycling education and promotion—New recycling programs need all the reinforcement available, especially until they become a part of the corporate culture of the business organization. To install the program, information can be provided to higher management, public relations, and managers at the same time it is presented at employee meetings. Participation at all levels will help ensure the program's success. Training the staff to separate recyclables from trash at the program's onset is important, but flagging enthusiasm must be periodically bolstered. Progress reports detailing pounds recycled by type of material, number of trees saved, amount of energy saved, and dollars saved by purchasing recycled products can be posted to announce the program's success and to encourage continued participation. Charting the response by department might encourage friendly competitions.

Long-term objectives—The long-term objectives for a corporate recycling program should include redesigning processes and products to reduce waste, and replacing raw materials with less expensive recycled materials now becoming available in increasing quantities.

Develop an environmental policy—Every business needs an environmental policy to answer recurring questions and to indicate that disposal is the least desirable alternative of handling waste materials. The policy statement should provide guidance on how to support the concepts of waste reduction, reuse, and recycling, and should be aimed at sales, purchasing, manufacturing, and accounting departments. Enlisting the support of the CEO will give weight to recycling and waste reduction goals.

ANALYZE THE CURRENT SITUATION AND MAKE A PRELIMINARY PROJECTION

A careful analysis of a business' current garbage situation will lead to more accurate projections for a recycling program. The logical starting place is to find out what resources are currently being used to dispose of and to recycle the company's waste materials. Disposal costs are higher than one might think because they include many invisible costs in addition to the more obvious expenses.

Trash costs are the visible aspect of disposal costs, and they are rapidly escalating across the nation. Wide discrepancies in landfill costs exist between different areas of the country. For example, in some areas fees are $15 per ton and in others they are substantially over $100 per ton. This differential makes it attractive to transport trash long distances to save money. Trash is destined to be a significant interstate commodity, and as its volume increases it will become a hot political topic. If a business is a large trash generator, baling trash for interstate shipment bears looking into.

Material handling costs can be very substantial just for the disposal of waste materials, especially in a manufacturing environment or wholesale/distributor-type business. If waste cardboard is generated in large volumes, it may make economic sense to locate a baler at the point of generation to reduce the number of trips to distant locations.

Janitorial costs include a cost component for collecting garbage throughout a building on at least a daily basis. Recycling containers usually don't require daily handling, and some recycling contracts include picking up the containers at each location within a building.

Management and supervision costs may be incurred in large businesses, and these should be added to the cost of waste disposal and recycling.

Fringe benefits and worker's compensation costs are associated with all wage and salary costs and are part of the cost of disposal and recycling.

Supply costs often consist of packaging materials, such as polystyrene peanuts and corrugated boxes. Saving polystyrene peanuts from inbound shipments or using shredded paper can produce a savings. Reusing certain sizes of cardboard boxes or buying misprinted and surplus boxes from outside vendors can produce a substantial savings. Intercompany shipments and interdepartmental shipments often can be in reused boxes. Pallets can be reconditioned or purchased from used pallet vendors. It is even possible to have these vendors stencil your business name on the pallets so that they can be returned. A charge for each pallet might be assigned, with a refund being generated when the pallet is returned in good condition.

Scrap costs are captured by a cost accounting system and, in a manufacturing environment, are looked at as a cost of doing business. A fresh look at these costs may be warranted.

Cost of rework and warranty costs are indicators that waste can be reduced and may become a part of an overall waste reduction plan.

HISTORY OF TRASH COSTS

It is important to assemble historical cost data for the business' trash disposal, to get a picture of the dynamics of what is happening to the specific costs. One objective of collecting three years of history on trash costs is to construct a graph such as the one shown in Figure 28-1.

A trend line can be used to project the costs of trash disposal into the future (Trend line A). A better way would be to ask your waste hauler or landfill what rate increases they are projecting for the future and to project the sales volume for your business.

Current situation:	
Trash costs during base period	$_______
Future costs:	
Percent business volume will increase or decrease	×_______%
Percent of annual trash cost increase	×_______%
Next years estimate of trash disposal costs	$_______

These projections should be continued for three to four years into the future. On the chart the projections will become Trend line B. With these projections in mind, an aggressive approach to recycling can be shown to yield excellent economic results.

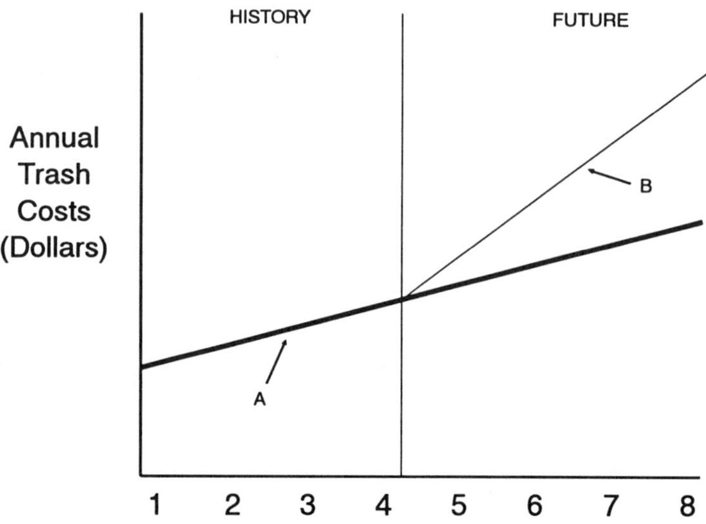

FIGURE 28-1. Trash History. *Source:* Year 1,2,3—Actual trash costs. Trend line A—Extending actual trash costs. Trend line B—Adjusted actual cost to company's volume projections and estimate of ABC Trash Hauler for future disposal costs.

PLANNING FOR IMPROVEMENTS

Additional Fact Finding—Understanding Historical Disposal Costs

In addition to cost information, past trash bills can be used to obtain the cubic yards of trash that has been hauled. The trash bills will provide information about the types of containers being furnished and their frequency of pickup. From this can be derived the total number of cubic yards hauled per month and per year. It is a good idea to determine this data for several years because it will show patterns such as seasonality or it may reflect the businesses' unique garbage cycle. Ultimately, this information is useful in determining a plan for each month because these figures can be used as benchmarks to provide feedback on the effectiveness or lack of effectiveness of the recycling program. For example, if analysis shows that it is possible to reduce volume 50 percent, then future cost estimates for trash disposal must reflect this assumption.

It should be noted that there can be a significant difference between the actual yards of trash and the yards hauled. Trash pickup for large generators can be made on a scheduled basis or on an "on demand" basis, such as within a few hours of a phone call when the container is becoming full. It is almost always the case if trash service is on a scheduled basis that the actual cubic yards generated will be less than the cubic yards hauled. Normally, the schedule is established to avoid overflowing the container, and this simply means that the container is rarely full. It is easy to determine if there's a big difference in any specific case by investigating if the trash containers are full or partially full when they are hauled. If they are less than full, the data needs to be adjusted to an estimate of the yards of trash actually generated.

After collecting specific information about the composition of the waste stream and gathering a general idea about future direction, the next step is to explore how to further reduce trash costs with a meeting or series of meetings with the trash hauler, or possibly separate meetings with a number of trash haulers. Many trash haulers have an expertise in recycling and may be willing to help develop a dual container system that puts trash in one container and recyclable materials in another. When the potential to recycle is known, the subject should be discussed with local scrap dealers and processors. Table 28-1 illustrates one way to track historical disposal fees.

TABLE 28-1. Historical Garbage Analysis

Disposal Costs	Jan	Feb	Mar	Apr	May	Jun	Jul	Aug	Sep	Oct	Nov	Dec	Total
Historical data—cubic yards hauled													
Year 1													
Year 2													
Year 3													
Adjusted (if appropriate to yards generated)													
Year 1													
Year 2													
Year 3													
Cost of disposal													
Year 1													
Year 2													
Year 3													
Cost per yard													
Year 1													
Year 2													
Year 3													

ANALYZING WASTE AND RECYCLING STREAMS

The volume and cost of disposal have been determined from the above data, but where trash is generated in the facility and what types of material account for the volume of trash is still unknown. The waste stream must be broken down into its components. For every business there is not just one waste stream. Like a great river is made from rivulets, creeks, streams, and smaller rivers, a waste stream consists of a number of recycling streams and a number of waste streams. These must be identified, and ultimately the object will be to separate the recyclable materials from the true garbage. In this manner we can understand the potential to recycle for a specific business.

This process of identifying where the waste is generated can represent a significant obstacle because this analysis requires a large time commitment and is reasonably involved. It is not as easy as it sounds to analyze the waste stream for a business, but the payoff in terms of results is much higher with hard data than with a series of uninformed guesses. It is conceivable that even a small business may have a dozen potential recycling streams and one trash stream when the analysis is completed.

For businesses with locations throughout town, the best place to begin is in the location with the highest costs of disposal and to prioritize the rest of the locations in order of trash disposal costs. After selecting a location, a building plan or map of the facility should be obtained, and who has the responsibility for each area should be determined. The lawn and area surrounding the building should be included. A thorough survey will include an interview with each department and area as well as a list of who to contact in advance, if the organization is large. The map or building plan can be used to organize the data, as outlined on Table 28-2, and subdivide the map into the appropriate areas of responsibility.

A walk through the building and grounds with a map is a good strategy. Begin immediately by identifying where the trash containers are located and learn about every existing recycling bin and container. It helps to color code recycling bins and trash containers differently on the map. Look into each container and make brief notes concerning the materials in the containers. A simple prenumbered log for

TABLE 28-2. Waste Stream Analysis

Company Name ______________________ Location ______________________________

Waste and Recycling Stream Analysis—Initial Walkthrough

Date ____________ Analyst Name ______________________

Department or Area	Contact	Phone No.	Equipment	Contents

trash and for recyclable materials can be coordinated with the map. If possible, learn where the different materials are generated. Also learn how these materials get from where they are generated to the container. Use abbreviations for different types of materials and different styles of containers; otherwise, the information will not fit on a spread sheet. A log would have the headings shown on Table 28-3.

TABLE 28-3. Log Headings

Company Name ______________________ Location ______________________

Log of Trash Locations ☐ Blue Pencil

Log of Recycling Locations ☐ Red Pencil

Container Number	Type of Container	Contents Type of Material	Where Generated	How Transported
1				
2				
Etc.				

Record the appropriate container number on the map. Optimizing the solution to reducing disposal costs actually requires that three problems be addressed. Diverting recyclable materials from the waste stream must be maximized. The flow of materials from their point of generation to the recycling system or trash containers must be efficient. This can be achieved by minimizing the number of times material is handled and by minimizing the distances traveled. Recyclable materials must be prepared in a manner that generates the best revenue in relationship to the cost of processing.

When the walkthrough is completed the participants should have a preliminary understanding of how trash flows, what materials have been identified so far, and the status of an existing recycling program. The map helps a great deal on the walkthrough because there is nothing worse than getting far into the waste analysis only to learn at a later time that an entire area has been missed.

The next step after a walkthrough is conducting interviews. Consultants over and over are accused of telling people what they already know and for good reason. The people who operate the business always know more about it than anybody else. Operators are the most valuable sources of information. By treating them accordingly, the agency installing the program will gain new insights and improve the credibility of the final results. It is important to think out interview questions in advance.

The goal is to continue identifying as many recycling streams as possible and to determine the volume of material coming from each area. Even small recycling streams should not be missed because they may consist of electronic parts or precious metals. Identifying where in the facility the bulk materials are coming from is also important. It is very likely that a few areas will generate the highest percentage of the trash. Since the number of cubic yards of trash has already been calculated, the goal is to find out the details that make this the total.

The Initial Department or Area Interview

In attempting to find out about the details making up the total amount of trash, the interviewer will need to keep notes of the conversations with the people who were identified as the appropriate contact people for each area. No two people conduct interviews in the same way. Interviewers do not need to know what they already know. They need fresh information. They need to know what the interviewee knows. For this reason, asking questions is much more important than imparting information. Listening is much more important than talking. A good opening question often is "I'm here to discuss recycling. This interview will take less than a half an hour. *You start*!" It's hard to know where this question will lead. I have used it hundreds of times after learning it from D.A. Benton, a management consultant in Fort Collins, Colorado, and it has produced some of the most unexpected and useful information.

Each interviewer needs to develop his or her own personal interviewing approach. For me, open ended questions have proved extremely fruitful. I enjoy learning from questions such as "Why do you think we generate so much trash around here? What do you think we should do about it? What do you think a recycling program should do for your department?" Sooner or later in the interview, routine subjects must be covered. These are described on the following worksheet, Table 28-4.

A tape measure to obtain dimensions of various containers is a useful thing to

TABLE 28-4

Waste and Recycling Stream Analysis—Initial Interview

Company Name ______________________ Department or Area ____________

Interviewee Name ________________ Date ________ Interviewer ____________

Location Where Wasted Is Generated	Type of Materials	Estimated Volume and Frequency	Cubic Yards Per Month	Recyclable % Volume
Total for Department				

bring to interviews. In the final analysis the locations where the total cubic yards of trash are generated and how much can be recycled need to be pinpointed.

Summarizing the data

When each interview is completed and the total cubic yards are added, it is important to determine whether the total cubic yards has been accounted for. A summary such as the one outlined in Table 28-5 can be used.

TABLE 28-5. Volume of Waste

Company Name ____________________ Location ____________________

Waste Generation by Department

Department	Trash Volume	Recyclable Volume	Percent Recyclable	Potential Savings*
Department A				
Department B				
Etc.				
Facility Total				
Volume Hauled**				
(Over)/Under				

*Use current or projected disposal cost per cubic yard.

**If trash is compacted, it must be converted to its uncompacted volume. Compaction reduces volume to one-half to one-third of its previous, uncompacted volume.

If the volume of trash is approximately accounted for, no other steps are required, but if there is a significant over- or undercounting for volume, additional procedures are required. It is possible to trace materials backward from the trash containers to their departments and to the locations where the material is generated. Additional time may be spent to discover the source of significant discrepancies and to correct the data that has been collected.

Another method for detecting the source of the discrepancy is a physical analysis of a trash load. A scrap dealer/processor or a trash hauler might be willing to perform this service for a fee. The trash load is dumped on the ground and manually sorted by type of material. Then the different materials are weighed. The new data can be compared to the composition of waste derived from the earlier study. The comparison may show more or less of one type of material and point to the cause and location of the discrepancy.

Unusual situations may falsify or mislead the data. For example, a contractor may be involved in a major renovation project, and a great deal of extra debris may have been generated. Not considering that the trash may actually be compacted before being hauled might also affect trash volume data.

When the volume is accounted for, it is possible to complete the above worksheet and determine the potential savings in trash disposal costs by maximizing recycling. It remains at this point an open subject if collecting the recyclable materials that have been identified is affordable. This question cannot be answered until markets are researched.

Can the Recyclable Materials be Marketed?

It is important to understand about the potential revenue that can be earned through recycling. Since recycling markets purchase materials by weight, the data that has been collected on volume in cubic yards must be converted into pounds of available material.

Type of Recyclable Materials	Volume	Lbs/Cubic Yard	Total Pounds

From this data an evaluation of recycling markets can begin. Materials can be marketed in a variety of forms. Materials can be sold in an "as collected" state, it can be processed to improve the purity of the grades of recyclable materials, or it can be packaged to make material suitable for end users or for transportation over long distances. The alternatives that are correct for any particular business depend on the availability of local markets. For simplicity it is desirable to sell materials without an intensive investment in man-hours or equipment. Regrettably, this is not always possible.

Local scrap dealers/processors are a logical place to begin the search for markets. They can help to evaluate options, such as whether compaction of recyclable materials in roll-off containers makes economic sense, if using a downstroke baler is worthwhile, and the extent to which sorting and grading materials might make sense. They probably know more about local markets than anyone. However, a recent trend is that trash haulers are becoming knowledgeable about recycling, so they should also be given an opportunity to address the recycling potential of the business. Both scrap dealers/processors and trash haulers can recommend and supply the types of containers needed. They may do this as part of a contractual agreement, and under some conditions it may make sense for the business to purchase its own containers. A worksheet similar to Table 28-6 may help in deciding how next to proceed.

In evaluating recycling options, there are several points to keep in mind:

- The initial price often changes soon after the contract is signed. Some very large national companies adopt this practice as well as others in the marketplace. Instead of relying on price alone, when choosing a scrap dealer/processor, check references of all companies and ask about the others at the same time. To reduce surprise price increases, consider tying prices to a published benchmark. On the other hand, there are other methods to reduce price from what appears to be a

TABLE 28-6. Contractual Agreement

Company Name ______________________ Location ______________________

Name of Scrap Dealer/Processor or Trash Hauler ______________________

Date __________ Contact ______________ Phone ______________

Services provided:
Equipment:

Pickup Service:
On demand?
Scheduled? Frequency?
Minimum Quantities?
Cost, if any?

Length of contract:
References:

How prices change? ☐ fixed amount ☐ with market ☐ with published market
Current price

	Condition of Material—Price per Pound or Ton			
Type of Recyclable Material	Unit	As Collected	Sorted	Baled
Corrugated	Ton	$	$	$
Aluminum cans				
Computer printout (bond)				
Etc.				

firm bid. For example, some companies aggressively downgrade materials. A business should shop for integrity and reasonable quality standards as well as price, and not necessarily consider company size a substitute for integrity.

- Different companies have different strengths. A paper dealer, a metal scrap yard, and a trash hauler may all play a role in the business' final recycling solution.
- Options such as baling should be evaluated only if the price differential is substantial. Space, baling wire, electricity, worker's compensation exposure, and storage are all costs to be considered, since they are components for baling. The processing of recyclable materials is expensive, and the expense becomes difficult to control in sideline activities.
- To evaluate proposals, a business can multiply the weight of each grade by the price, to determine the value of the total package. This will offset the tendency to overweight a high price on an item with little volume.
- Lastly, if local markets appear inadequate to the needs of the business, the search should be widened to include distant markets but prioritize which materials to focus on.

Knowing what will sell makes deciding what can be collected on an economic basis easy to decide. Revise the amount of recyclable materials that you can divert based on this information. You can also update the chart showing what recycling can save the business. There is little point for a business to collect a recyclable item for which there is no market. This is not to indicate that the business should not continue its search for a market, but until one exists the recycling program runs the risk of incurring trash costs to dispose of unmarketable materials.

Local regulations should be consulted because in some jurisdictions recyclable materials are, or will be, banned from landfills. Recyclable materials that have no market may have to be stored until a disposal alternative exists or until a market is found—very similar to the way some toxic or hazardous materials are being handled today.

Designing an Efficient Internal Flow of Materials

The impact of disposal and recycling on the organization should be reduced to its lowest possible net cost. Unlike trash containers, containers holding recyclable materials do not have to be emptied every day. This should produce a savings in janitorial costs. To avoid confusion on the part of employees and the janitorial staff, recycling containers should have a different color than trash containers. In designing for efficient material handling, both the distance and frequency of hauling should be considered in determining the size of the containers. Obviously, large containers need to be moved less frequently than small ones. However, safety concerns, such as ease of dumping the containers and potential fire hazards in the case of paper, also need to be weighed.

Using the map it should be straightforward to design an efficient material flow. Most older buildings were designed to accommodate a single trash container. One common problem is finding a location for the recyclable materials. If the business has extra truck docks, a 45-foot trailer can be used for inexpensive storage for recyclable materials. The trailer system also avoids extra handling. Another way to handle the problem of limited space is to contract with a scrap dealer/processor to pick up materials from locations within the business. The business can avoid altogether the internal cost of handling by having the material picked up at the point of its generation. Rather obviously, the cost for this service means getting less revenue for the recyclable materials than would otherwise be received, but it is a good solution for businesses that possess limited space. Still another solution is to store recyclables outside in covered containers.

Making the Final Decisions on a System

Businesses are always changing, so recycling programs should be designed for flexibility. This includes flexibility with decisions on equipment and markets, informing those who are new to servicing the business about the hours of operation, elevator restrictions if applicable, and holiday schedules. Inform the trash hauler about the new requirements. Presumably, his or her schedule will be cut in half unless the hauler is involved in your recycling program.

Determine the startup schedule and incorporate many different methods of communication. Employee meetings, handouts, posters, and articles in company publications should be a part of the effort in a large organization. At this stage, monitor progress very carefully, since most problems occur during startup and the quicker they are handled, the better for all concerned. Be on hand to answer questions and to be responsive so that everything gets started professionally. Another common pitfall is to fail to educate new employees. A simple handout given to the personnel department can easily acquaint the new employee with the recycling program.

Lastly, determine a trash disposal budget based on the volume expected after the recycling program is in place, as well as the estimated cost per cubic yard. Compare actual and estimated costs, and investigate variances if they occur. If trash volume is excessive, investigate to see what is not working.

ECONOMICS

Calculating the economic impact of a recycling program involves four types of calculations. First, it is important to evaluate the capital equipment required for the program. Capital requirements can range from a minimal investment in recycling containers to as much as $500,000 for a high-capacity baling system. In the case of the high-volume baling system, it might be justified for a major manufacturing plant that bales recyclables to also save by baling trash, so that it can be shipped out of an area with high disposal costs.

Another cost associated with re-educating an organization about disposal and recycling is training. Company meetings are usually required to explain the objectives of a new recycling program, to "sell" the importance of separating a recycling stream from the waste stream, and to teach the organization that the quality of the recyclable materials will reflect their diligence. These meeting take time, and time costs money. Printed material may be handed out and is part of the training costs.

The third economic set of calculations relates to the revenue that will be earned through recycling. The grades of materials, the volume expected of each material, and the market price will be used to calculate the expected revenue. This revenue will fluctuate over time because the sale of recyclable materials puts the company in a commodities business and prices fluctuate as a matter of course.

The fourth set of calculations relate to the disposal costs that are saved. Based on the volume of material taken out of the waste stream by recycling and the volume saved through the reuse of other items, and the current and expected future cost of disposal, the value of the current disposal savings and the expected future savings can be calculated.

Lastly, any increases in continued operating costs of the program need to be considered. Perhaps a recycling manager has been added to the headcount, or perhaps a baler operator and baling wire are required. Whatever the continuing costs are, they are relevant to the economic performance of the organization's recycling program.

Once this data has been assembled, it can be displayed as shown in Table 28-7.

The bottom line in business is the bottom line. If a recycling program has a high gain after taxes and a high return on investment, it is an excellent program.

TABLE 28-7. Financial Analysis of the Recycling Program

Organization Name

For the period ________ to ________

Startup Costs				
Capital required:	$ ______			
Training required	______			
Total	$ ======			
	Year 1	Year 2	Year 3	Year 4
Continuing Operations				
Revenue	$ ______	$ ______	$ ______	$ ______
Savings in disposal	$ ______	$ ______	$ ______	$ ______
Gains from recycling	$ ______	$ ______	$ ______	$ ______
Less:				
Continuing costs	$ ______	$ ______	$ ______	$ ______
Startup training	$ ______			
Net gain	$ ______	$ ______	$ ______	$ ______
Less: income taxes	$ ______	$ ______	$ ______ $	$ ______
Gain after taxes	======	======	======	======
After tax return on capital Investment	______ %	______ %	______ %	______ %

Gain/Capital = ROI.

29

Office Recycling Programs

An office recycling program is not only appropriate for business and government and for small and large organizations, but it is also a major feature in demonstrating the commitment of the organization to environmental improvement. A maximum office effort will include collecting recyclable materials, using products made of recyclable materials, using two-sided copies when appropriate, and using reusable coffee mugs instead of disposable cups. Clearly, successful office recycling is also a group endeavor requiring the cooperation of everyone, and a well-organized program reflects the overall effectiveness of the organization.

When planning a new program, a business should research organization options, communication methods to increase participation, ways to collect recyclable materials, and strategies to use more products made from recyclable materials.

ORGANIZATION

In a large organization it is extremely helpful to organize a recycling committee, with a member from each department. Normally, these people are very committed, have genuine concerns about the environment, and are respected group leaders. These individuals will help develop the program, and along the way they will become well educated about how the program should work. Later, this knowledge will prove very helpful in answering the many questions that will arise. Since all successful programs also must be monitored, the recycling committee has a useful role that goes well beyond the program startup phase.

The goals of the recycling program should be agreed upon by the committee. In a typical office recycling program, these goals are generally:

1. *To maximize the environmental benefit from the recycling program.* Over the course of the program it is fun and exciting to document the number of trees

saved, energy saved in Btus, cubic yards of landfill space saved, and tons of paper recycled.

2. *To reduce the waste generated from 50 to 75 percent.* This goal is attainable with the cooperation of everyone. Normally, a baseline can be generated by analyzing two years of trash bills, but estimates from the janitorial crew in terms of the number of bins hauled to the dumpster can also serve the purpose.
3. *To reinforce the company's commitment and image to reducing cost and helping the environment.* Costs of disposal vary by region, but when trash hauling, equipment rental, and landfill costs are added together, it can cost from $80 to $200 to dispose of one ton of trash. In the future, costs are expected to rise. For this reason, now is an opportune time to ask people to change their behavior so that these costs are controlled.
4. *To purchase as many products made from recyclable materials as possible.* Provided the cost is not greater than for like quantities of the same item made from primary materials, recycled products should be substituted. Although production costs in making products from secondary materials are generally lower than from primary materials, the pricing of products made from recyclable materials are sometimes higher. Often, this is because purchasing agents do not use the same approach in buying these materials. For example, a decision to use recycled materials is made, and a rush order is placed for relatively small quantities. In other cases the manufacturer, distributor, or retailer might be using an opportunistic approach to pricing. Persistence, however, will ultimately be rewarded because it will not always be necessary to pay more for products made from recycled materials.

THE WASTE STREAM AUDIT

Waste in a typical office environment consists of the following items:

- Computer printout (groundwood free, groundwood, laser).
- Business forms, including NCR paper (white or colored ledger).
- Copy paper (white ledger, usually).
- Newspaper.
- Magazines (magazines or mixed paper).
- Letterhead (white or colored ledger).
- Files and records (sorted files are considered ledger, unsorted are file stock or mixed paper).
- Envelopes (white or colored ledger; kraft envelopes and those with pressure sensitive adhesives are considered mixed paper; plastic window envelopes may be separate or considered mixed paper).
- Writing pads (white or colored ledger).
- Books (mixed paper).

- Carbon paper (trash).
- Coated advertising literature (coated sulfate).
- Junk mail (mixed paper).
- Cardboard boxes (old corrugated containers—OCC).
- Glass containers.
- Aluminum cans.
- Plastic bottles (plastic is usually PET).
- Restroom trash (trash).
- Cafeteria waste (mostly trash).

The type of office recycling program that is right for one company may not be right for another. In a study done for the National Office Recycling Project by Franklin Associates (July 1991), the composite for a number of different office studies resulted in the following breakdown, illustrated in Table 29-1.

TABLE 29-1. National Office Recycling Project

Ledger, computer printout	29%
Mixed paper	23%
Old corrugated	8%
Old newspaper	10%
Subtotal—Paper	70%
Plastic	3%
Glass	5%
Aluminum	1%
Other	21%
Total	100%

Source: Franklin Associates (July 1991).

In many office environments a waste analysis is not necessary, and the process can be reduced to relying on the judgement of an experienced office manager. Each office worker generates between one-half pound to two pounds of waste per day. However, a sampling approach also works.

Using a sample of 5 percent to 10 percent of the work force, selected at random, it is possible to develop a reliable estimate of the total waste generation for a specific office. This estimate would need to be adjusted upward to include waste generation in the copy area, waste generated in the supply receiving area, where presumably a great deal of corrugated is discarded, and waste generated in the annual cleanup of archive records, obsolete forms, and surplus or obsolete sales materials. A reasonable upgrade would be to add 25 percent to the original estimate.

At the same time the data is collected for waste generation, it is possible to collect an estimate of the amount that is recyclable. This will help establish a recovery goal. Unfortunately, human nature being what it is, not everyone will participate. Extraordinary programs might have a 90-percent participation rate, but a good program might be closer to 70 percent.

All of this waste stream analysis can be shortcutted by using an average of one pound per day per worker of recyclable waste generation for a standard organization. It is then easy to reduce the waste stream. An organization with 120 employees is generating 30,000 pounds of recyclable materials annually (120 people × 1 pound × 240 work days = 29,520 pounds). After an office recycling program is in place, a 50-percent reduction of waste would yield only 15,000 pounds annually.

Another approach to estimating the amount of material is to estimate the weight based on the number of cardboard boxes that are filled over a specified period of time. A box of 14 ½-inch × 11-inch computer printout weighs about 40 pounds when received with new paper. It weighs approximately 33 pounds when it is refilled with used paper. A small box can weigh 25 pounds, and a banker's box, which will hold an entire file drawer of paper, weighs approximately 50 pounds. A *full* plastic bag of uncrushed aluminum cans weighs approximately 7 pounds. A stack of newspapers 3 feet high weighs approximately 100 pounds.

SOURCE REDUCTION

Offices can begin recycling efforts well before collection programs are in place. Much of the materials tossed into the trash every day need not go there. For example, offices could encourage employees to use coffee mugs instead of throw-away paper and polystyrene coffee cups. Some companies go so far as to have the cup designed with the company logo and the words "recycle." Another strategy to reduce trash is using double-sided copies whenever possible.

When communicating between offices, employees should consider using electronic mail rather than interoffice memos. Boxes and large envelopes can also be reused, especially for interoffice purposes. It is also possible to reuse file boxes by scheduling the annual disposal of old records prior to having to box the files for the most recent previous year.

Finally, don't automatically buy note pads. Instead, consider using paper scraps. Paper clips, rubber bands, binders and loose-leaf notebooks, and file storage boxes are all items that can be easily reused.

Offices can also request to be removed from junk mail lists by writing to:

Direct Marketing Association
6 East 43rd St.
New York, NY 10017

This can prevent your name from being sold by most large mailing list companies.

WHAT WILL YOUR OFFICE RECYCLE?

The waste stream audit should provide some clues, but most offices review the following list for items to recycle. Look at purchase orders to find out what recyclable items are frequently purchased.

- Aluminum cans
- Corrugated
- Colored office paper*
- Coated stock (i.e., glossy sales materials)
- Computer printout (bond quality)*
- Computer printout (groundwood)*
- Files and records*
- Glass (breakage problems might make this unpractical)
- Newspaper*
- Magazines*
- Obsolete forms*
- White office paper*
- Reuse of laser cartridges
- Reuse of printer ribbons
- Mixed office waste (includes all items with asterisk)
- Telephone books (not possible in many market areas)

One common type of office paper recycling program is called a "white paper recycling program." This type of program is common because white paper is easy to market. Table 29-2 shows what can be included and what cannot be included.

Increasingly, paper mills are able to handle mixed office waste paper, and some office recycling programs are taking advantage of this increased capability by tossing all kinds of paper into bins. The trade-off with not separating white from mixed paper is that the higher grades of paper, such as computer printout, have value, but when thrown into the mixed office waste grade, the value of the computer printout is lost to offset the poor quality of the newspaper and magazine fiber. Some companies make a conscious effort to only recycle the highest grades. In these cases, computer printout (bond quality), aluminum cans, and obsolete forms and sales materials are usually all that can be recycled.

Once a decision is made about what to collect, the next step is to consider how to design the collection of that material at individual work areas.

---

*Indicates mixed office waste.

TABLE 29-2. Types of Paper in *White* Office Programs

Acceptable	Not Acceptable
Letter head (white)	Newspapers
Typing or copy paper	Envelopes (most envelopes)
Interoffice memos (white)	Colored paper
Word processing paper (white)	Carbon paper
Notepad paper (white)	Plastic or paper cups
Green bar computer paper (bond quality)	Manila folders, file folders
Bound reports (if glued bindings are cut off or removed)	Glossy, shiny paper (i.e., fax paper)
	Magazines
Adding machine tape	Wrappers (most wrappers)
Business forms (white or little ink)	Self-stick labels, rubber bands
SEC reports (white with black ink)	Paper with insoluble glue
	Napkins, paper towels, tissues
	Film and photographs, tape
	Styrofoam cups
	Blueprint paper
	Food wrappings
	Binders

SUCCESSFUL PROGRAMS START IN THE EMPLOYEE'S WORK AREA

Either a desk top letter tray, stacking tray, file folder, or specialized recycling container should be stationed at each desk. Some people may prefer to use a spare drawer. At some locations where unusually high volumes of recyclable materials are generated, a specially marked trash container is more appropriate.

Specialized containers with the recycling emblem also work well, especially if your company desires a high-profile program. In employee cafeterias or in areas with vending machines, specialized aluminum can receptacles with a round hole cut in the top, are particularly useful as well as attractive.

Communication is the key to getting employees to modify the old practice of disposing of everything into one container. The key is to make it simple for the employees to make the decision to throw waste into the trash and recyclable material into the recycling container. Often, companies decide to do this in a number of different ways. It is most effective to use a wide variety of methods to maintain high participation levels.

Special recycling meetings will help educate employees about the program. This will, however, cost money. In each meeting, assume that groups will be approximately 30 people, and take an hour for the presentation and questioning period. Assuming that the business has 300 employees, the cost to the business would be 300 work hours. If the company could not afford this type of meeting, a specialized recycling letter or announcements in the company newsletter is another approach to communication.

Some companies purchase desktop file folders or containers with specialized printing for recycling. Information about the organization's name, a message about the recycling, items that are acceptable and unacceptable, and where to call with questions all can be included on file folders. Most of the information that will fit onto a file folder will also fit onto other types of desktop containers.

DESIGNING THE COLLECTION SYSTEM

Almost everyone knows how trash is collected in an office building. Individual trash containers are emptied into bigger containers, and the bigger containers are taken to the basement where they are thrown into the main trash container for the building. This main trash container is then hauled by a trash hauler to a landfill, transfer station, or materials recovery facility (MRF), either on a scheduled basis or on a call-in basis.

Designing a collection system for recyclable materials should be no mystery. Individual employees are usually encouraged to bring the recyclable materials to a conveniently located bigger container. Then, when full, this container is taken to a central pickup area by the janitorial staff or is picked up on a scheduled basis at the location by a recycling company. In this later instance, the workload for the janitorial staff is clearly reduced, but this cost savings is usually made up in some way by the recycling company.

It is a good idea for someone in the recycling committee to occasionally look at the condition of the material in the central areas. A good time is when they are doing their own recycling. Corrective action is necessary if someone's lunch bag is found in the recycling container because even the slightest contamination devalues the material.

Good locations for a recycling bin include near copy machines, alongside computer-driven printers, and in mail rooms.

BUYING PRODUCTS MADE FROM RECYCLABLE MATERIALS

Because the recycling process is not complete until consumers purchase goods made from recycled materials, an office recycling program should include a procurement policy. The following list of products are made from recyclable materials. These products rarely cost more than products made from virgin materials.

- Adding machine tape
- Computer printout
- Copy paper

- Envelopes, letter type
- Envelopes, clasp type large envelopes
- Fax paper
- File folders
- Message pads
- Napkins
- Paper towels, all types
- Post-it notes
- Shredded paper for packing
- Tissue paper
- Toilet paper, all sizes
- Trash can liners
- Writing pads, legal or letter size, white or canary yellow

THE DESTRUCTION OF OFFICE RECORDS

Some records by their nature should be destroyed and handled with greater security than recycling. In a hierarchy of security, records should be destroyed as the top priority, recycled as the second, and disposed of as trash as the third. It is well documented that five types of people go through trash:

1. *Criminals* looking for information that can be used to make money dishonestly. Credit card data and bank account data head their list.
2. *Investigators* looking for incriminating information.
3. *Competitors* looking for the unfair advantage, such as customer lists or information regarding profitability.
4. *Scavengers* looking for scrap to sell.
5. *People at materials recovery facilities and transfer stations,* where trash is dumped to sort out recyclable material.

The law may require the destruction of certain records. The 1974 Federal Privacy Act requires government agencies to destroy records that have information about individuals. This information includes files containing social security numbers, financial data, educational data, and health data.

The law does not apply if the business is not a government agency, but the guidelines have generally been adopted by the private sector. Various specific businesses, such as banks, have specific legal requirements to meet.

Shredding office records does not impact their recyclability unless the records have contaminants in them that are unacceptable. If carbon paper, for example, is shredded along with printout it is impossible to use the material for recycling. The carbon paper simply cannot be economically removed from the printout once the shredded material is mixed together.

Alternatives

Shredding can be done on the premises by an organization, through a full service records destruction company, or by many scrap dealers/processors.

The advantage in dealing with an outside company is that it is usually less expensive. Most shredders have a very limited capacity and jam with great frequency when too much material is fed into them. Also, the volume of paper coming out of a shredder balloons, which creates a dirty, messy job to bag all that fluffy paper, in order for it to be recycled or thrown out. In most organizations, backlogs of paper for shredding are common because operating the shredder is regarded as a demeaning job in many office environments. The result is that records are often thrown out when they accumulate sufficiently to be a fire hazard.

When using a full service records destruction company, normally the destruction of items that are negotiable for cash must be witnessed by a responsible person in the organization. One procedure is that the records destruction company will pick the material up at the customer's facility. With the designated witness, the units of material (such as the number of boxes) to be destroyed will be counted as they are loaded onto the truck. The truck will be followed by the witness to the records destruction plant, where the material will be unloaded. During this unloading process the number of units can be counted again as they are unloaded from the truck, and they can be counted one last time by the witness as they are shredded.

There are two major shredding alternatives. Security shredding implies that the material will be shredded into ¼-inch strips, baled, and promptly sent to a paper mill, where the bales will be reduced to pulp. Industrial shredding implies that the material will be put into a hammermill, where the material is ripped apart by 24 ten-pound swinging hammers that are strategically placed along a shaft that spins at 2,000 RPM. Not all material entering the hammermill is shredded, particularly when large volumes are thrown into the hammermill, but the material is randomized and is baled as part of the process. The bales are sent to a paper mill, where they are reduced to pulp. This method is the least expensive and complies with the requirements of the 1974 Federal Privacy Act. It is used for most commercial purposes.

NEGOTIATING WITH A SCRAP DEALER/PROCESSOR

Negotiating with a scrap dealer/processor is extremely simple. Dealers need to know what grades of material a program will recycle, how many crates with wheels are initially required, and whether the pickup service will be scheduled or will be on a call-in basis when the crates are full.

For records destruction, scrap dealers/processors need to know the approximate volume of material to be picked up and the type of destruction required. It also helps to know if crates with lockable tops should be provided.

Most scrap dealers/processors will work with recycling programs to design a customized collection service. However, based on the services and market conditions, there may be a service charge for the program or the program may produce revenue. Some scrap dealers/processors will suggest that the program keep all of the recyclable materials together at a loading dock. It is possible to arrange to have the dealer pick up recyclables at multiple locations, but the service might cost extra.

EVALUATION

Choosing a scrap dealer/processor is an important process because it will directly impact the effectiveness of the program. Calling the dealer/processor's current accounts is probably the best way to ascertain whether pickup service is reliable.

WHAT IF THE OFFICE IS TOO SMALL?

Small offices may not generate enough office paper for a scrap dealer/processor to pick up on an ongoing basis. Scrap dealers/processors may, however, pick up large quantities of stored material. Another option is that material can be collected and dropped off at a recycling center personally. Another option is finding someone else in the same building with a recycling program and arranging to have your material picked up at the same time. Yet another option is to create a building-wide or community-wide recycling program that will provide service for a host of small businesses.

30

Cardboard Recycling

Why a special section about cardboard? Just about every product imaginable is packaged in a cardboard box, and cardboard boxes appear everywhere. Cardboard is not only abundant in terms of supply, but it also has a very low density; it is both strong and light, which accounts for why it is so plentiful. It is precisely because cardboard is such a common packaging material and has a low density that it presents unique problems and opportunities.

The terms *cardboard* and *corrugated* mean the same thing and are therefore interchangeable. They are not to be confused with boxboard, chipboard, or paperboard, which is the type of material used in making cereal boxes, or the material used for backing pads of paper. The term *old* corrugated containers (OCC) has a more specific meaning than cardboard; it refers to a specific marketable grade of waste paper. OCC, for example, does not include waxed or plastic-coated cardboard commonly used for packaging meat. OCC implies that contamination does not exceed specific limits. Table 30-1 lists some of OCC quality standards.

REUSE OPTIONS

Cardboard boxes are in general highly reusable, but this reusability is mostly a product of supply and demand conditions in a given market. There are six major places to look for demand for reusable boxes:

1. A business can reuse its own cardboard boxes instead of purchasing all new ones. Recycled boxes can be used internally or externally—if the company is concerned that reusing old boxes looks "cheap," it can purchase a big stamp that indicates "recycled" and convert a possible negative impression into a positive impression.
2. Employees can reuse a business box for storage, moving, and shipping.
3. Suppliers send businesses the boxes; perhaps they would like them back. If

TABLE 30-1. Quality Standards of Old Corrugated Containers

Acceptable	Not Acceptable
Cardboard boxes	Waxed cardboard
	Plastic-coated cardboard
	Plastic bags
	Polystyrene (Styrofoam)
	Wood
	Metal
	Rice paper (some exported boxes)
	Excessive tape

suppliers can be encouraged to backhaul OCC, the business is spared the hassle of disposing of them.

4. Neighboring organizations might appreciate buying OCC as an alternative to purchasing new boxes.
5. Companies that specialize in buying and selling reusable boxes can be found in the local Yellow Page listings under "boxes."
6. Recycling firms and scrap dealers/processors often know what sizes of OCC are reused in your local area, and, if not, they can probably recycle the boxes.

Reusability is also a function of the size of the boxes and the quantity available in one specific size. Boxes that are misprinted, obsolete, or a product of freight claims are great candidates for a reuse market. The two most popular "reuse" sizes are "book" boxes and "gaylord" boxes. A book box is a small and sturdy box of a convenient size to handle when moving and looking for the ideal box for packing books. Its dimensions are approximately as follows:

Length = 15 inches
Width = 11 to 12 inches
Height = 10 inches

Gaylord boxes are designed to fit on a 4-foot × 4-foot pallet, and normally contain plastic granules or another type of product loaded in bulk form. The box walls are extremely thick and are industrial strength, and the dimensions are approximately as follows:

Length = 42″
Width = 42″
Height = 36″

RECYCLING OPTIONS

Compared to many other materials, cardboard is not an easy item to prepare for marketing because of its bulky nature. The most expensive way to dispose of cardboard is to simply throw a box away in its assembled, bulky form. Table 30-2 shows how to prepare cardboard for recycling.

TABLE 30-2. Preparing Cardboard for Recycling

Preparation	How Recycled
Flattened and stacked	Drop-off center, possible curbside program, delivered to scrap dealer
Flattened and banded to pallet	Picked up with other recycled material or loaded onto truck
Compacted into roll-off container	Delivered to processing facility or scrap dealer
Baled in downstroke baler	Can be picked up economically or loaded and/or stored in trailer
Baled in horizontal baler	Loaded into trailers for shipment through broker or direct sale

To determine the best method of recycling depends entirely on the economics of disposal and recycling in the specific market area. The following framework outlined in Table 30-3 will help in evaluating the alternatives.

Table 30-4 shows a comparison among three alternatives—disposal, compaction, and baling.

TABLE 30-3. Variables Required to Evaluate Preparation Alternatives

Key Variable	Example	Your Data
Disposal cost—uncompacted	$400 per ton	
Compactor rental	$350 per month	
Hauling and disposal charge for one load compacted material	$300 per haul	
Weight of cardboard per compacted load	7,500 pounds	
Hauling charge to recycling center	$100 per haul	
Price paid for OCC loose, delivered	$15 per ton	
Rental cost—downstroke baler	$290 per month	
Baling wire cost per bale, 5 wires per bale	$1.35 per bale	

TABLE 30-3. *(Continued)*

Key Variable	Example	Your Data
Price paid for OCC, picked up	$35 per ton	
Labor cost	$6.00 per hour	
Fringe benefit cost	25%—$1.50/hour	
Worker's compensation cost	15%—$ .90/hour	
Tons of cardboard per month	20 tons, or 40,000 pounds	

TABLE 30-4. Disposal, Compaction, Baling fees

Method	Calculations+m	Cost per Month	Total Cost
Disposal—Whole boxes	20 tons × $400 per ton	$8,000	$8,000
Compaction and disposal	• Rental cost for compactor	$ 350	
	• Hauls/ Mo. 40,000 pounds/7,500 per haul =5.33 hauls		
	• Hauling cost= 5.33 × $300	$1,599	$1,949
Compaction and recycling	• Rental cost for compactor	$ 350	
	• Hauls/month 40,000 pounds/7,500 pounds = 5.33 hauls		
	• Hauling cost = 5.33 × $100	$ 533	
	• Revenue = 20 tons × $15	$(300)	$ 588
Baling	• Lease cost for baler	$ 290	
	• Number of bales 40,000 pounds/800 per bale = 50 bales		
	• Baling wire cost = 50 × $1.35	$ 68	
	• Labor cost = $6.00 + $1.50 + $.90 = $8.40/hour. It takes 1.3 hours to make a bale × 50 bales = 65 hrs × $8.40 =	$ 546	
	• Revenue = 20 tons × $35 =	$ (700)	$ 204

31

Specialized Programs

Elsewhere in this book there are chapters on business recycling, government recycling, office recycling, and cardboard recycling. However, similar business types frequently have the same recycling opportunities. This chapter contains brief narrative descriptions concerning recycling programs and checklists for some specific business types, organizations, or events.

The central process in all cases is to identify the different waste streams and then determine what materials can be recycled. It is also important to learn about the regulations in any specific geographical area. Recycling programs may be mandatory or voluntary. Certain materials may be banned from disposal in ordinary garbage.

AUTO REPAIR AND BODY SHOPS

An auto repair or body shop has many unique recycling opportunities. Most of these relate to replacing parts, fixing damage, and performing preventive maintenance on vehicles. The basic function of these businesses is extending the life of automobiles—a valuable service in saving resources and energy itself. Use of reconditioned parts in lieu of new parts can achieve a cost savings for customers and conserve resources in the process. Auto repair shops are also in the business of making vehicles operate efficiently. An efficient automobile consumes less gas and pollutes less air.

Some of the recycling opportunities for auto repair and auto body shops include:

Automobile fluids—Antifreeze, crankcase oil, differential oil, brake fluid, and power steering fluid are all automobile fluids that can be recycled. The fluids are not usually economically recyclable because there often is a substantial cost to getting these items recycled. However, many of these fluids are prohibited from landfills, and recycling can be a cheaper alternative than disposal in a hazardous waste facility. The key to recycling is the use of clearly marked storage tanks. But first it is essential to find a recycling company who will provide reliable service. The best source of information for companies who recycle these materials is through the specific product's supplier.

Freon in air conditioners—Freon, a gas used in automobile air conditioning systems, is particularly damaging to the earth's ozone layer. Recycling systems are available to collect the freon gas from auto air conditioning systems during their repair. The gas can be recycled instead of being released into the atmosphere. The air conditioning system can be recharged with the recycled freon when the repair is completed. This recycling equipment is expensive and is not a common piece of equipment in auto repair shops, but soon consumers may take the extra trouble to find shops capable of recycling freon in order to protect the environment. It might be important for a repair shop to be a community leader, rather than watch business go elsewhere when air conditioning repairs are necessary.

Office recycling—Since most of the activity involved in auto repair takes place outside the office, providing a collection container for aluminum cans might be the only collection system warranted for smaller repair operations. For larger service stations, a paper collection program can be considered.

Scrap materials—Parts that cannot be repaired have value as scrap because they are made of steel, zinc, aluminum, and copper. In addition, auto battery manufacturers usually offer a rebate for used batteries, or, if this value is not higher than the scrap market, auto batteries can be sold as scrap. Scrap dealers/processors are typically buyers of these materials, and they can be found in the Yellow Pages.

Solvents and cleaning fluids—Paint thinner and cleaning solution can be recycled after their useful life is consumed. Chemical or solvent recyclers can be found in the Yellow Pages.

Used parts—Parts can purchased from modern automotive "junk" yards or can be purchased from parts rebuilders. Items such as motors, transmissions, alternators, and fuel pumps are readily available in most areas. Automotive radiators can be sent out for repair or can be purchased in a reconditioned state. Tires that have a significant tread life remaining can also be purchased.

Buying recycled products—Items such as business cards and business forms, hand towels, stationery, rags, re-refined oil, recapped tires, solvents, toilet paper, and tissues represent opportunities to buy recycled goods. In addition, in some market areas it is possible to buy paper for masking cars prior to painting from a scrap dealer/processor far cheaper than buying this paper from a paint supplier.

SMALL BUSINESSES

Small businesses have all of the solid waste problems of big businesses, except that they usually do not generate sufficient volumes of recyclable material to make economic sense out of recycling or to attract the attention of scrap dealers/processors. There are many notable exceptions to be found among plumbers, electricians, aluminum siding companies, radiator shops, and so forth, but for the business that does not produce high-grade materials, the recycling alternatives are few and far between.

The recycling strategies that work for small businesses include:

1. Taking material to a recycling center or a drop-off center.
2. Using the recycling program of a neighboring larger company to "piggyback" the small business program onto the larger business's program.
3. Joining together with others in an office building or business park to create a recycling program for the larger community with a central location for consolidating material.

Typically, a small business would have the following recycling opportunities:

Office recycling—Aluminum cans, bond quality computer printout, copy paper, and business forms can be collected. Recycled products, such as business cards and business forms, computer ribbons, laser cartridges, hand towels, stationery, toilet paper, and tissues represent opportunities to buy recycled goods. When recycled paper is used it will enhance the image of the business to indicate "Printed on recycled paper" in small letters on the bottom of stationery items and business cards.

Cardboard recycling—Cardboard boxes can be reused and as a minimum should be broken down and flattened before collection.

High-grade scrap—Some small businesses produce high-grade scrap and, despite the amount of recycling education that exists, are missing a profitable opportunity. One need only see "dumpster divers" in the neighborhood to know that someone nearby is missing an opportunity. For example, even a small frame shop can produce several barrels of aluminum scrap per year from the scrap ends of extruded aluminum material. A small lock and key shop can produce 25 to 100 pounds annually of scrap brass keys, and a retail store may throw out clothing and products that are obsolete but that may have value to a charity that has a secondhand store. To the credit of the retail food industry, some food products that are safe to eat are donated to food banks.

CONSTRUCTION SITES

When projects are under construction, waste materials accumulate rapidly, and frequently only one 30- or 40-cubic yard container is provided for the waste materials. As a result, everything is landfilled. Recycling opportunities exist, but are ignored due to the urgency of getting the project completed on schedule. In addition, gaining cooperation among a number of subcontractors is sometimes more difficult than it should be. Another obstacle to recycling at construction sites can be a prevailing belief that the valuable scrap will mysteriously disappear from the job site with or without a recycling program.

Just like the construction project itself, the key to a successful recycling program is in organizing the project on the front end. In the bidding process, if all organizations involved in the project are made aware that an area exists for recycling and for disposal, it establishes a better basis for cooperation. The recycling and disposal area needs to have signs indicating where waste materials are expected to be discarded. Signs that indicate cardboard, steel, copper, aluminum, and trash should identify separate containers large enough for the project.

Two major possibilities in seeking bids for the services are needed. Either agreements can be reached with recyclers in the community to haul cardboard or steel separately from the trash disposal service, or the trash hauler may be asked to supply containers for the different recyclable materials as well as the trash. In either case, avoiding landfill costs for at least part of the normal quantity of trash can produce a substantial cost savings. Contributing to this savings is an opportunity to earn revenue on at least a part of what is recycled.

Obviously, construction sites vary based on the structure, but the following recyclable items are frequently present:

Cardboard—Few items are more expensive to dispose of than cardboard boxes that are not broken down. All cardboard should be flattened. A 40-cubic yard, open top, roll-off container holds between 2,500 and 4,000 pounds of flattened boxes. Trailers that are 45 feet in length hold 4,500 to 6,500 pounds of flattened cardboard boxes. Savings can be considerable based on transportation distances to a recycler versus transportation distances to a landfill. Disposal savings depend on the landfill rate and whether or not the charge is based on the number of cubic yards or on the actual weight of material. Revenue can depend on the competitiveness of the local scrap market and the overall level of prices in the area.

Another technique for reducing wastc is to require that suppliers remove their own packaging.

Scrap metal—The amount of scrap steel, copper wire, copper pipe, and aluminum that is expected will help to determine a direction for negotiating with local scrap dealers/processors. One container for all metals may be appropriate, or one container for each type of material may be indicated.

FAIRS, PARADES, PARKS, AND SPECIAL EVENTS

Wherever people gather in large numbers for the purpose of entertainment or for special events, there are opportunities for recycling. At state and county fairs, during visits to the local park or national parks, or at special events, there is a great deal competing for attention. Recycling could hardly be described as a "front-of-the-mind" activity. For this reason, recycling programs need highly visible signs, posters, and clear explanations about how materials are to be separated. Even with an extraordinary effort to create this visibility, contamination is a problem.

Contamination is a problem even if the special event is a recycling convention; therefore, you can imagine the problem at a championship sports event, a folk festival, a rodeo, or during the town or city parade. However, to shy away from a recycling program just because of contamination problems misses the point that events of this nature present unique opportunities to create awareness about recycling. Recycling programs also gain recognition for their sponsors and help sponsors associate with helping the environment.

In addition to posters and education, basic decisions are required regarding what materials to recycle and what types of containers to use. Items that are often recycled include aluminum cans, glass, office paper, cardboard, pallets, plastic eating utensils, and steel cans.

Recycling programs of this nature are not profitable. They cost money. As a result, an essential component is in finding sponsors to fund the cost of planning, awareness, containers, and collection. In return for the funding, it is usually critical that the sponsor receive recognition on all signage, containers, and literature.

GROCERY STORES AND HIGH-VOLUME RETAIL STORES

Most products shipped to grocery stores and high-volume retail stores come packaged in cardboard boxes. Rather than disposing of these materials as trash, these stores either use downstroke balers to compact cardboard or use roll-off containers with compaction units. In all cases, some method of compaction is used for the cardboard to minimize material handling costs, and a separate system is used for trash.

Some stores contract separately to have cardboard removed, and others use the trucks that deliver fresh goods to the store to backhaul baled cardboard to a central distribution facility. Ordinarily, when large volumes of cardboard are concentrated in one location, it improves the bargaining power of the scrap generator and saves in overall transportation costs.

There are other elements of recycling that may be shared by grocery stores and high-volume retail stores, including:

Green marketing—Increasingly, consumers are looking for recycled products and environmentally friendly products, and entire sections in retail stores are being devoted to merchandizing these products. When stores sell recycled goods, they are making a significant contribution to recycling.

Pallets—Pallets made of wood or plastic are used by these stores to reduce material handling costs. These pallets can be repaired when they are broken and put back into service. Some companies do their own repair work, but others contract the service to pallet companies. Used pallets can be purchased at significant savings.

Becoming a recycling center—Becoming a recycling center is one way that these stores attract traffic and demonstrate a degree of environmental concern to its customers. A basic decision is what materials to recycle and how to collect them. Some stores recycle glass, plastic, newspapers, and aluminum cans. Others simply recycle aluminum cans. If the program is comprehensive, the space costs and labor costs can be quite significant. If reverse vending machines are used, the cost of doing business is reduced.

HOSPITAL RECYCLING

Developing hospital recycling programs is particularly challenging. Health issues understandably dominate all programs that include recycling, and infectious waste must be rigorously kept separate from regular trash. But, beyond that, hospitals are similar to hotels, restaurants, and offices because a hospital is all of these businesses at the same time.

The Joint Commission on Accreditation of Healthcare Organizations (JCAHO) has indicated that seven criteria must be met in order for recycling containers to be approved by their organization (Thorek, 1991):

1. The hospital must have a recycling program that is described in a written manual. The recycling manual should indicate the programs goals and objectives, policies and procedures, as well as the specific duties and responsibilities of the staff.
2. Recycling containers must be clearly labeled with a recycling logo and describe what materials are to be collected in the recycling container.
3. The recycling container should be of a color not normally purchased for use as a wastebasket.
4. Recycling containers should not be stored in utility rooms, soiled linen rooms, or other such rooms that are protected as hazardous areas, unless adequately safeguarded.
5. All hospital personnel that might come into contact with a recycling container should receive in-service education specific to the proper use of the container and the hospital's recycling program.
6. Removal schedules for the recycling container should be established to maintain the flammable and combustible fire load to the lowest level necessary for daily operations.
7. Recycling containers should never be placed in patient rooms, patient treatment rooms, corridors, or other spaces open to the corridor. Since these criteria are subject to change, it is important to obtain the latest information from the JCAHO.

To complete a comprehensive hospital recycling program, valuable information can be found in this book under the following subjects: office recycling, cardboard recycling, hotel recycling, restaurant recycling, and records destruction. In addition, a hospital can recover silver from fixer solution and from X-ray negatives.

HOTELS

Hotels produce a large volume of recyclable materials because they represent a gathering of a large number of people. It is probably stretching the point to say that these people are a community, but hotels certainly generate scrap like a community—one that eats out a great deal.

Hotels are good candidates for an office recycling program and, since hotels usually contain at least one restaurant, all of the recycling options that exist for restaurants apply. In addition, hotels generate large volumes of newspapers, aluminum cans, and magazines. When hotels serve as convention centers, large volumes of surplus literature can be left for disposal. For the most part, this literature is recyclable.

In some geographical areas telephone books are recyclable. Telephone pads and stationery can be printed on recycled paper, and the commitment to recycling will be noticed by a large share of guests if "Printed on Recycled Paper" appears in small letters. Obviously, hotels have a substantial opportunity to purchase toilet paper and boxes of tissue made from recycled paper.

RESTAURANTS

Restaurants often are small businesses and cannot attract recycling services to come to them due to low volumes of recyclable materials, but there are many recycling opportunities for the average restaurant:

Cans—Aluminum cans, bi-metal cans, and food cans are recyclable. Food cans must be cleaned, and it helps save space if they are flattened. They can be opened on both ends with a can opener and are easily flattened once this is done.

Cardboard—Cardboard is recyclable and is a large part of what most restaurants discard as trash. Flattening the cardboard boxes helps to reduce storage space and makes it easier to take the cardboard to a recycling center or drop-off area.

Aluminum foil—Aluminum foil, aluminum pie plates, and aluminum baking pans are recyclable as "aluminum foil." Aluminum foil is a low grade of aluminum, but in some areas foil can be recycled along with aluminum cans.

Glass—Glass is recyclable and usually must be rinsed and sorted by color. The lead seal from wine bottles must be removed and, if there is porcelain or metal attached into the glass, it cannot be recycled.

Grease—Grease containers are most often stored outside and are provided by some rendering firms. When the grease container is full, a specialized truck will come and pick up the grease.

Plastic milk jugs—A plastic milk jug is usually made from high-density polyethylene (HDPE) and is recyclable.

Other options for reducing solid waste—In an effort to reduce waste, a restaurant should consider the following:

1. Replacing bottles and cans with soft drinks and beer served on tap.
2. Replacing disposable cups, utensils, dishes, napkins, tablecloths, and placemats with reusable ones.
3. Buying in bulk to save on packaging.
4. Providing a small discount if customers bring their own coffee mug.
5. Printing the menu on recycled paper and buying toilet paper made from recycled paper. Also, if paper napkins are used they can be made from recycled paper.

INDUSTRY AND MANUFACTURERS

Major industrial facilities and manufacturers have an opportunity to launch far-reaching programs emphasizing waste reduction and recycling. Because these industrial facilities and manufacturers produce the nation's raw materials, durable goods, automobiles, and other products, they are in a unique position to make recycling more prominent as a way of life in the United States. Frankly, they are also in a position to do absolutely nothing or to make token changes. Their decisions shape the choices that are available to consumers.

Here are some exciting industry options:

Cogeneration opportunities—The conversion of waste products to energy can be achieved economically when an industry or manufacturer uses a great deal of steam or electrical power and also generates a waste by-product that can serve as a low-cost fuel. Often, the disposal cost that is avoided can make a cogeneration project economically feasible. With trash costs increasing rapidly, more and more cogeneration projects will become necessary.

Equipment—Industry and manufacturing is equipment-intensive. Extending the life of this equipment through preventive maintenance reduces potential waste. Equipment and products can be rebuilt, remanufactured, reconditioned, and restored, often at an economically attractive cost. Also, less solid waste results.

Pallets and containers—Pallets and containers can be designed as throwaways or as reusable items. Often, it is less expensive to buy reused pallets than to purchase new ones. For more details, see the discussion of pallets under "Grocery Stores and High-volume Retail Stores" in this chapter.

Policy regarding buying recycled products—It is the responsibility of top management and the board of directors to adopt socially responsible policies, but when it comes to the subject of recycling, because recycling is new, there may be no stated policy. A policy that deals with recycled materials and the conditions for their purchase should be considered. For example:

1. Should the organization encourage the purchase and use of recycled materials and products? If the answer is yes, under what conditions?
2. Must recycled products be cheaper or the same price, or can they be even a little higher priced than the same materials made from primary materials? Over the next few years this question will be asked within organizations with increasing frequency and at all levels. A policy will provide some needed direction.

Product design—Through product design emphasis, packaging can be reduced, products can last longer, products can be made easier to repair, and products can be more recyclable at the end of their product life. Product design activities can dramatically reduce waste, and it is conceivable that less packaging and more recycling will also improve profits. Certainly in the regulatory climate where state and local laws must deal with solid waste issues, there will be less likelihood that commerce will be disrupted in the future by new regulations if products are voluntarily designed with recycling and waste issues in view today.

Quality control—Quality control implies less waste in producing products and products that last longer when they reach the consumer. A strong emphasis on quality will help reduce solid waste, rework, and product warranty claims and will usually result in higher earnings.

Sales of obsolete or surplus equipment, furniture, and products—Some organizations have areas where obsolete or surplus equipment, furniture, and products are made available to employees for their purchase. Periodically, outside buyers are invited to bid on items to clear out unsold merchandise. While this is not exactly recycling, the items may serve a few extra years of use before becoming waste. Besides, the disposal costs will be incurred by someone else.

Recovering oils and solvents and reducing waste—Within each industrial facility the recycling of oil and solvents should be investigated using equipment designed for the specific materials. Reducing waste in the handling of liquids requires that container lids be fastened securely and that pumps be used to transfer materials to prevent spilling.

Scrap materials—Each industry generates its own specific list of recyclable materials. A comprehensive recycling program should be designed to deal with all of them. Some scrap dealers/processors will handle trailer loads containing many different types of recyclable materials. This can be especially useful if space is a consideration or if the facility is in a remote location.

Waste exchanges—A waste exchange is an information source where buyers and sellers provide data that serves to match both parties. For difficult-to-move materials, a waste exchange may help locate possible buyers. Since many industries and manufacturers generate some materials that are difficult to market or that are possibly hazardous, a waste exchange can provide some very valuable information. On the other hand, materials that are needed in a specific industry may be by-products from some other process, and through a waste exchange an inexpensive new source of needed materials may be developed. Graphite, acetone, sulfuric acid, textiles, plastics, and scrap metals are usually among the items that are listed. Waste exchanges are listed in the Appendix.

PRINTERS

Approximately 15 percent of the paper that a printer purchases goes out the door as waste paper. This waste paper accumulates due to the overruns from each project, the trim associated with each job, and rejects generated by quality standards. Controlling overruns saves paper and ink, but there are many additional materials that can be recycled by printers:

Cardboard—Cardboard packaging is used for new paper and to contain many of the materials purchased by a printer. When the boxes are flattened, the cardboard can usually be recycled along with the other grades of waste paper that the printer recycles.

Lithoplate—Lithoplates are used to apply ink to paper. Lithoplate material is generally made of aluminum, and it is a grade of scrap known as "lithoplate." It is recognizable to scrap metal dealers, and quotations can be obtained by using the telephone.

Miscellaneous scrap materials—Plastic strapping, metal strapping, metal end caps from rolls of paper, and wood pallets can be recycled. The plastic strapping is frequently sold back to the supplier; metal end caps and strapping are sold as steel scrap. Pallets can be repaired and reused. Used pallets can be purchased at a fraction of the cost of new pallets.

Office recycling program—A printer's office generates computer printout scrap, copy paper, and aluminum cans just like any typical office. Aluminum cans should also be collected in the plant area.

Silver—Silver can be recovered from fixer and from film. The silver from fixer can be recovered in the form of silver flake through units that remove the silver electrostatically. The film negatives can be sold as scrap due to their high concentration of valuable silver. Since the blacker the negative, the higher the silver content, clear negatives have no silver content and are worthless.

Solvents—Cleaning materials, such as toluene, can be recovered from cleaning rags in a centrifuge and then reused.

Using recycled paper—A printer has the opportunity to offer many grades of recycled paper to its clients.

SHOPPING MALLS

Shopping malls are often a collection of many small businesses and a few large ones. For the most part the large tenants have their own recycling programs and the small tenants have none. Common areas usually exist for disposing of garbage. To make recycling practical these areas need to be expanded to accommodate recycling for, at a minimum, cardboard. It is only through the property management that this type of change can be accomplished, but in many geographical areas disposal fees are already high enough to justify significant alterations in the way waste materials are handled.

Additional materials that can be recycled include glass, wood pallets, and office papers.

SCHOOLS

Elementary schools, high schools, and colleges present opportunities to recycle and to introduce recycling into the educational process. In elementary schools and high schools, recycling programs can also be directed into the community in the form of can drives or newspaper drives.

As with all other recyclable materials, it makes sense to be certain that a market exists for any materials being considered for collection. It can take three months to put a recycling drive together, and there are few nightmares worse than collecting 40,000 pounds of newspaper and having no place to go with the material.

Cafeteria—The cafeteria may present an opportunity to recycle steel cans, aluminum foil, and Styrofoam.

Office recycling—The office may present an opportunity to recycle copy paper, white bond quality paper, and aluminum cans.

Student population—The student population may present opportunities to recycle aluminum cans, white paper, books, and unclaimed clothing from the lost and found department. They may also create community recycling drives for aluminum cans and newspaper. As mentioned, markets should be checked out thoroughly, perhaps by an adult, prior to starting recycling drives, especially for newspapers, in view of possible weak markets for that commodity.

V

Completing the Cycle

32

Completing the Cycle

INTRODUCTION

The future growth of recycling depends on consumers purchasing recycled products. Without the consumption of recycled materials/products the cycle is incomplete. Every individual who makes purchasing decisions—from the household to the corporate level—is responsible for closing the recycling loop. If consumers do not vote with their dollars and choose products with recycled content over ones that are made from virgin goods, then manufacturers will have little incentive to use recycled materials.

As a result, curbside programs across the country will serve little function beyond collecting plastic bottles, newspapers, and glass. Eventually, government will choose not to foot the bill. For this reason the real future of recycling is in the hands of individuals who make the buying decisions.

Procurement Regulations

To some degree, regulations at the federal and state level have already attempted to influence purchasing decisions. The EPA has recommended that most government organizations give bid preferences for recycled products. Almost uniformly there is little to no enforcement of these regulations. In the final analysis the action steps required to purchase recycled goods depends on the responsiveness of specific individuals and organizations to the regulations.

Labeling

To the delight of everyone supporting recycling, grass roots purchasing decisions are being made in favor of recycled products. The three rotating arrows that symbolize recycling are influencing buying decisions. Hence, its use will be subject to labeling regulations. Organizations such as Green Cross independently certify specific product claims about a product. Their criteria include recycled content, biodegradability, and energy efficiency. This Green Cross certification lends the credibility of third party evaluation to specific products, and is presently used for 1,000 items. In addition to certifying specific product claims, Green Cross also offers a broader evaluation service of a product's environmental claims. Information for manufacturers or consumers can be obtained from:

Green Cross Certification Company
1611 Telegraph Ave., Suite 1111
Oakland, CA 94612-2113
Phone: 510-832-1415

Another organization, Green Seal, develops criteria for product categories based on an evaluation of all aspects of the product category. Green Seal then informs manufacturers about the criteria and, if the manufacturer has its products tested against the criteria and they meet or exceed the standards, the product is awarded a Green Seal. Information can be obtained from:

Green Seal
1733 Connecticut Ave., N.W.
Washington, D.C. 20009
Phone: 202-328-8095

Organizational Policies

Another method for encouraging the purchase of recycled products is through a formal statement of policy. Every business and government organization should have a formal policy encouraging the purchase of recycled materials and products. A policy statement can be as simple as, "It is the policy of this organization to aggressively reduce material waste and purchase goods made from recycled materials in all areas of the organization and to suggest that our suppliers do the same." It is helpful to go further, if possible, to suggest specific goals, such as:

1. 50 percent of office supplies will be made from recycled materials.
2. Packaging will be reduced 20 percent without adversely impacting sales.
3. Packaging and products will be made of recycled materials so that they can carry the recycled symbol.
4. Bidding preferences of 10 percent will be allowed for recycled goods.
5. Purchasing specifications shall be reviewed annually to remove biases for primary materials and to encourage recycled goods as much as possible.

Awareness

Andy Mckean, the executive director of the Complete the Cycle Center in Denver, CO (303-333-3434), indicates that the number 1 problem of a new recycled product is getting it to the shelves of retail stores and distributors. The Complete the Cycle Center is a non-profit organization that exists for the purpose of helping establish markets for recycled products. McKean's experience suggests that, after a few people have tried most recycled products, word of mouth generates future sales.

Education

Individuals and managers involved in recycling need to adopt the "complete the cycle" theme in all educational programs. Significant education has been required to get the collection effort started. The manufacturing wave is now underway. It will take a consumer effort to close the circle.

SPECIFIC COMPLETE-THE-CYCLE PRODUCTS

Everyone knows how to spend money. This chapter does not address making purchasing decisions. It merely serves as a reminder of how important your own purchasing decisions are to the future of recycling. No amount of regulation can take the place of a marketplace that absorbs recycled products like a sponge and thirsts for more.

Easy reminders like the recycling logo, Green Cross, and Green Seal will take time to become established. The role of recycling managers and dedicated recyclers is to get the ball rolling and create greater awareness about the need to buy recycled products. This begins by publicizing the types of products that can be purchased. A society changes one person at a time until a wave is created that sweeps many along the same direction. For the time being, recycling could use a few hundred thousand wave makers—recruited one at a time.

In creating awareness, the following lists include some of the products now made from recycled products and the areas where they can be used:

Office areas:

- Entrance mats
- Phone message pads
- Copy paper (legal and standard sizes, available in different paper weights)
- Computer paper (bond quality and groundwood quality)
- Word processing paper (9½ inches × 11 inches)
- Note pads (yellow and white, legal and standard size)
- Adding machine tape
- Fax paper
- Columnar pads
- Envelopes (from conventional legal and standard envelopes to clasp type)
- Stationery

Calendars
Self-stick notes
File folders, all types
Trash cans
Trash can liners
Desk top recycling bins
Laser cartridges

Households:

See "Office areas," above, for some ideas
Loose-leaf note paper
Fireplace logs
Garbage cans
Curbside recycling containers
Compost bins
Mulch
Tissue, toilet
Tissue, facial
Paper towels
Plastic scrubbing pads
Lawn furniture
Railroad ties
Coloring books
Greeting cards

Restrooms:

Toilet paper (all types of rolls, from jumbo to regular and folded types)
Hand towels (rolled and folded in all sizes)
Tissue, facial
Garbage can liners

Retail stores:

See "Office areas," and "Restrooms," above
Cash register tapes
Bags (all sizes in paper and plastic)
Wrapping paper
Print advertisements on recycled paper

Cafeteria and restaurant:

See "Office areas" and "Restrooms," above
Napkins (from cocktail size to dinner napkins)
Menus
Cash register tape
Guest receipts
Food service trays

Construction:
- Asphalt
- Aggregate
- Plastic lumber
- Ceiling tiles
- Rugs
- Undercarpeting
- Gypsum board
- Insulation (fiberglass and cellulose)
- Parking lot stops
- Speed bumps
- Traffic barricades
- Traffic cones
- Decking
- Plastic posts
- Plastic fences
- Plastic pilings for docks
- Wall panels
- Plastic pipe
- Benches and picnic tables
- Specify that printers use recycled paper
- Specify that subcontractors use recycled products

Manufacturing:
- See "Office areas", "Restrooms", and "Construction," above
- Raw materials (metal, paper, plastic, etc.)
- Cardboard boxes
- Pallets
- Fuel for cogeneration facility
- Re-refined lubricating and hydraulic oil
- Rags (wipers)
- Solvents
- Tubestock
- Paper for masking prior to painting
- Packing materials (peanuts, shredded paper, cellulose)
- Molded paper corners (for protecting corners in shipment)
- Specify that printers use recycled paper
- Specify that subcontractors use recycled products

A resource that is perfectly suited for helping locate products and sources is *The Recycled Products Guide.* The publication is revised yearly and includes over 2,900 listings. At last printing, the listings were free for manufacturers and distributors who certify the recycled content of the products listed. The address/phone number is:

American Recycling Market Inc.
P.O. Box 577
Ogdensburg, NY 13669
Phone: 1-800-471-3258

The best thing about completing the cycle is that it then can start all over again.

VI

Technical Assistance

Appendix Disclaimer

These lists do not constitute an endorsement of any company or business. Although an effort was made to make these lists complete, we regret that there are probably many omissions and some incorrect information. Please verify the data yourself.

We strongly advocate using Yellow Page information because it tends to be current. If you note corrections or omissions, please send a note to: David Powelson, 13881 W. Alaska Place, Lakewood, Co. 80228.

Appendix A

End Users

Automobile Shredders

See Yellow Pages for local area and nearby metropolitan areas under the listings "Automobile Shredders" or "Scrap Metals."

Building Materials

See Yellow pages for local area and nearby metropolitan areas under the listing "Building Materials."

Cement Kilns

See Yellow Pages for local area and nearby metropolitan areas under the listing "Cement."

Chemical and Solvent Reprocessors

Alabama

M & M Chemical & Equipment Co.
(Oldover, a subsidiary of Solite Corp.)
1229 Valley Drive
Attalla, AL 35954
tel: (205) 538-3800
fax: (205) 538-1836
contacts: Vicki Leeth; Don Burris

Allworth, Incorporated
(A Southdown Environmental Systems Company)
500 Medco Road
Birmingham, AL 35217
tel: (205) 841-1707
fax: (205) 841-1744
contact: Ronald Entrup

Systech Environmental Corp.
P.O. Box 1097
Arcola Road
Demopolis, AL 36732
tel: (205) 289-3222
fax: (205) 289-3104
contact: Fred Perry

Chemical Waste Management (CAM), Inc.
EMELLE
Highway 17 North
Emelle, AL 35459
tel: (205) 652-9721
fax: (205) 652-9721
contact: John Hanley

Arizona

Romic Chemical Company, Southwest
(A subsidiary of Romic Chemical Corporation)
6760 West Allison Road
Chandler, AZ 85226
tel: (602) 961-1040
fax: (602) 961-7944
contact: Jack R. McClary

California

Oil and Solvent Process Company
(A subsidiary of Chemical Waste Management)

P.O. Box 907
Azusa, CA 91702
tel: (818) 334-5117
fax: (818) 334-4563
contact: William J. Mitzel

Romic Chemical Corporation
2081 Bay Road
East Palo Alto, CA 94303
tel: (510) 324-1638
fax: (510) 324-2965
contacts: Pete Schneider; Mike Schneider

Rho-Chem Corporation
(A Southdown Environmental Systems Company)
425 Isis Avenue
Inglewood, CA 90301
tel: (213) 776-6233
fax: (213) 645-6379
contact: Shankar Sarkar

Systech Environmental Corp.
P.O. Box 837
State Route 138
Lebec, CA 93243
tel: (805) 248-6749
fax: (805) 248-6052
contact: Greg Cape

Detrex
3027 Fruitland Avenue
Los Angeles, CA 90058
tel: (213) 583-8736
fax: (213) 588-9216
contact: Darrel Craft

Solvent Service
Subsidiary of USPCI
660 Lenfest Road
San Jose, CA 95133
tel: (408) 259-9910
fax: (408) 251-7554
contact: Customer service

Colorado

O.S.C.O.—Colorado (CWM)
P.O. Box 360
Commerce City, CO 80037
tel: (303) 289-4827
fax: (303) 289-3520
contact: William Shortreed

Connecticut

North East Chemical Corp.
North East Regional Sales Office
550 N. Main Street
Southington, CT 06489
tel: (203) 621-8383
fax: (203) 621-0810
contact: Environmental Manager

Florida

Laidlaw Environmental Services, Inc.
170 Bartow Municipal Airport
Bartow, FL 33830-9504
tel: (813) 533-6111
fax: (813) 533-5152
contact: Paul Manak

Oldover
P.O. Box 297
Green Cove Springs, FL 32043
tel: (904) 269-6206
fax: (904) 284-6925
contacts: Al Galliano; Tony Saunders

Georgia

M & J Solvents Company
1577 Marietta Road, N.W.
P.O. Box 19703
Station N
Atlanta, GA 30325
tel: (404) 355-8240
fax: (404) 355-3629
contact: Donald McQueen

Illinois

Industrial Fuels and Resources, Inc.
13701 South Kostner Avenue
Crestwood, IL 60445
tel: (708) 597-3380
fax: (708) 389-3741
contact: Environmental Manager

Safety Kleen Corporation
777 Big Timber Road
Elgin, IL 60120
tel: (708) 697-8460
fax: (708) 697-4295
contact: Richard J. Lavoie

Detrex
2537 LeMayne Avenue
Melrose Park, IL 60160
tel: (708) 345-3806
fax: (708) 345-3903
contact: Dan Anderson

Clayton Chemical Company
1 Mobile Street
Sauget, IL 62201
tel: (618) 271-0467
fax: (618) 271-9521
contact: Edward J. Reidy, Jr.

Indiana

Safety-Kleen
4921 Oak Creek Court
Fort Wayne, IN 46835
tel: (219) 485-1264
fax: (219) 485-6157

Systech Environmental Corp.
P.O. Box 485
Limedale Road
Greencastle, IN 46135
tel: (317) 653-2606
fax: (317) 653-7141
contact: Jerry Forgey

Detrex
2263 Distributors Drive
Indianapolis, IN 46241
tel: (317) 241-9379
fax: (317) 241-1060

Reclaimed Energy Company, Inc.
P.O. Box 1111
Indianapolis, IN 46206
tel: (317) 781-4440
fax: (317) 781-4401
contacts: Robert Wakefield; Robert W. Anderson

Cemtech
P.O. Box 825 (Rt. 2)
Logasport, IN 46947
tel: (219) 772-1108
fax: (219) 772-6823
contact: Mike Shaw

Cadence Chemical Resources, Inc.
P.O. Box 770
One Marine Drive
Michigan City, IN 46360
tel: (219) 879-0371
fax: (219) 879-0390
contacts: Theodore J. Reese; Michael R. Benoit; Scott Ellis

Industrial Fuels & Resources, Inc.
604 S. Scott Street
South Bend, IN 46625
tel: (219) 234-0441
fax: (219) 234-0336

Avganic Industries
1330 Lockport Road
Terre Haute, IN 47802
tel: (812) 232-5411
fax: (812) 232-1148
contact: Curt Carey

Kansas

Systech Environmental Corp.
P.O. Box 111
South Cement Road
Franconia, KS 66736
tel: (316) 378-4451
fax: (316) 378-4453
contact: Paul Peters

Cemtech
P.O. Box 428
Independence, KS 67301
tel: (316) 331-0200
fax: (316) 331-3890
contact: Steve Aemisegger

USPCI—Hydrocarbon Recycling Services
2549 N. New York Avenue
Wichita, KS 67219
tel: (316) 268-9490
fax: (316) 268-9418
contact: David Trombold

Kentucky

Kentucky Solite Corporation
P.O. Box 39 / 1797 Coral Ridge Road
Brooks, KY 40109
tel: (502) 957-2105
fax: (502) 957-4333
contacts: Bud White; John Kulken

Louisiana

Laidlaw Environmental Services, Inc.
P.O. Box 283
Crowley, LA 70527-0283
tel: (318) 783-2624
fax: (318) 783-2651
contact: Mike Sanderock

CWM, Inc.
Rt. 2 Box 1955
Sulphur, LA 70663
tel: (318) 583-2169
fax: (318) 583-4615
contact: Bill Kitto

Maryland

Cemtech
P.O. Box 592
117 S. Main Street
Union Bridge, MD 21791
tel: (301) 775-0110
fax: (301) 775-7169

Michigan

Systech Environmental Corp.
P.O. Box 588
1480 Ford Avenue
Alpena, MI 49707
tel: (517) 354-3122
fax: (517) 356-4592
contact: Gil Petersen

Detrex Corporation
Solvents and Environmental Services Division
999 Haynes, Suite 305
Birmingham, MI 48008
tel: (313) 645-0890
fax: (313) 645-1094
contact: Michael J. Tepatti

Detrex
12886 Eaton Avenue
Detroit, MI 48227
tel: (313) 491-4550
fax: (313) 491-8044
contact: Rob Swan

Nortru, Inc.
515 Lycaste
Detroit, MI 48214
tel: (313) 824-5850
fax: (313) 824-5436

Detrex
312 Ellsworth Avenue, S.W.
Grand Rapids, MI 49503
tel: (616) 454-9269
fax: (616) 454-9529
contact: Sharon Burns

Michigan Recovery Systems, Inc.
36345 Van Born Road
Romulus, MI 48174
tel: (313) 326-3100
fax: (313) 326-5670
contact: Christopher Kolb

City Environmental, Inc.
Calahan Facility
29163 Calahan
Roseville, MI 48066
tel: (313) 778-1414
fax: (313) 778-7027
contacts: Thomas Zaracki; Tony Coraci

Missouri

Cemtech (Selma Plant)
P.O. Box 338
Festus, MO 63028
tel: (314) 933-3963
fax: (314) 933-4010
contact: Van Rogers

Industrial Fuels & Resources, Inc.
3100 Industrial Fuels Drive
Scott City, MO 63780
tel: (314) 651-3444
fax: (314) 651-3821
contact: Environmental Manager

New Jersey

Pride Solvents & Chemicals Co. of New Jersey, Inc.
211 Randolph Avenue
Avenel, NJ 07001
tel: (908) 499-0123
fax: (908) 381-3614
contact: Rob Dohm

Detrex
835 Industrial Highway, Unit 1
Cinnamonson, NJ 08077

tel: (609) 786-8686
fax: (609) 692-0080
contact: Malcolm Weckerly

Cemtech, L.P.
Suite 12
1273 Bound Brook Road
Middlesex, NJ 08846
tel: (908) 805-9595
fax: (908) 469-6709
contacts: Herbert Case; Carl Ling; Brian Dawson

Marisol, Inc.
125 Factory Lane
Middlesex, NJ 08846
tel: (908) 469-5100
fax: (908) 469-1957
contacts: H. Peter Nerger; John P. Nerger

New York

Model City Facility (CWM)
1135 Balmer Road
Model City, NY 14107
tel: (716) 754-8231
fax: (716) 754-8231 ext. 211
contact: Dr. John Stanulonis

Pride Solvents & Chemical Company
88 Lamar Street
West Babylon, NY 11704
tel: (516) 643-4800
fax: (516) 643-4813
contact: Art W. Dohm, Jr.

North Carolina

Oldover (A subsidiary of Solite Corp.)
P.O. Box 987
Albemarle, NC 28001
tel: (704) 474-3165
fax: (704) 474-4071
contacts: John Burgess; James Colburn

Detrex
3114 Cullman Avenue
Charlotte, NC 28206
tel: (704) 372-9280
fax: (704) 376-0732
contact: Mark Teal

Ohio

Hukill Chemical Corporation
7013 Krick Road
Bedford, OH 44146
tel: (216) 232-9400
fax: (216) 232-9477
contacts: Robert Hukill; James Hukill

North East Chemical Corporation
3301 Monroe Avenue
Cleveland, OH 44113
tel: (216) 961-8618
fax: (216) 961-7812
contacts: Ernest Petrey; F. Philip Stapf

Systech Environmental Corp.
P.O. Box 266
County Road 176
Paulding, OH 45879
tel: (419) 399-4835
fax: (419) 399-4876
contact: Terri Kanouse

CWM Resource Recovery, Inc.
(Subsidiary of Chemical Waste Management)
P.O. Box 453
West Carrollton, OH 45449
tel: (513) 859-6101
fax: (513) 859-6282

Systech Corporation
245 North Valley Road
Xenia, OH 45385
tel: (513) 372-8077
fax: (513) 372-8099
contacts: Mel Eifert; Joe Durczynski; Jerry Trumpey

Oklahoma

USPCI—Hydrocarbon Recycling Services
5354 West 46th Street, S.
P.O. Box 9557
Tulsa, OK 74157
tel: (918) 446-7434
fax: (918) 445-1640
contact: Jim Gibson

Pennsylvania

Cemtech
P.O. Box 153 (Rt. 18)
Wampum, PA 16157

tel: (412) 535-4361
fax: (412) 535-2065
contact: Don Harper

Rhode Island

Chem Pak Corporation
Plant Site
167 Mill Street
Cranston, RI 02920
tel: (401) 738-2200
fax: (401) 461-7767

Chem Pak Corporation
P.O. Box 7151
Warwick, RI 02887
tel: (401) 738-2200
fax: (401) 461-7767

South Carolina

Giant Resource Recovery Co., Inc.
P.O. Box 352 / Highway 453 North at 1-26
Harleyville, SC 29448
tel: (803) 496-7676
fax: (803) 496-5380
contacts: Gerald Breininger; Steadman Matthews

Southeastern Chemical and Solvent
P.O. Box 1755
755 Industrial Road
Sumter, SC 29150
tel: (803) 773-7387
fax: (803) 775-7016
contact: Harold Talbert

Texas

Detrex
322 International Parkway
Arlington, TX 76011
tel: (817) 640-6017
fax: (817) 633-6034
contact: Brad Marks

Chemical Reclamation Services, Inc.
(A Southdown Environmental Systems Company)
P.O. Box 69
Avalon, TX 76623
tel: (214) 229-5043
fax: (214) 627-3415

Gibraltar Chemical Resources, Inc.
P.O. Box 1640
Kilgore, TX 75663
tel: (903) 984-0270
fax: (903) 983-1227
contact: Tom Mobley

USPCI—Hydrocarbon Recycling Services
4303 Profit Drive
San Antonio, TX 78219
tel: (512) 333-4011
fax: (512) 333-2041
contact: Dave Petersen

Virginia

Oldover Corporation (A Subsidiary of Solite Corp.)
P.O. Box 228
Ashland, VA 23005
tel: (804) 798-7981
fax: (804) 752-6310
(804) 798-3422
contact: Susan Hillsman

Oldover (A subsidiary of Solite Corp.)
Rt. 1, State Route 652
Arvonia, VA 23004
tel: (804) 581-3226
fax: (804) 581-1106
contacts: Richard Dunkum; L.K. Childress

Oldover (A subsidiary of Solite Corp.)
Rt. 1, Box 101
Cascade, VA 24069
tel: (804) 685-3564
fax: (804) 685-1523
contacts: Betty Talley; C.II. Gover

Washington

Burlington Environmental, Inc. (BEI)
Chempro Division
2203 Airport Way, S. S/B 1 Suite 400
Seattle, WA 98134
tel: (206) 223-0500
fax: (206) 223-7791
contact: Michael Keller

BEI—Chempro Division
Washougal Facility
625 S. 32nd Street
Washougal, WA 98671

tel: (206) 835-8743
fax: (206) 835-8872
contact: Al Kakovich

Wisconsin

Milsolv Companies
14765 West Bobolink Avenue
Menomonee Falls, WI 53501
tel: (414) 252-3550
fax: (414) 252-3961
contacts: C.A. Douthitt; Bob Heitzer

Waste Research & Reclamation
Route No. 7
Eau Claire, WI 54701
tel: (715) 834-9624
fax: (715) 836-8785
contacts: James Hager; George Anderson

C.A. Douthitt
ZECOL, Inc.
3270 S. Third Street
P.O. Box 1100
Milwaukee, WI 53207
tel: (414) 483-6400
fax: (414) 483-6826

Avganic Industries, Inc.
114 North Main Street
P.O. Box 276
Cottage Grove, WI 53527
tel: (608) 257-1414
fax: (608) 839-4293
contacts: Jim Gourley; Tom Miazga

Canada

Allied Environmental
4623 Byrne Road
Burnaby, British Columbia, Canada V5J 3H
tel: (604) 431-8780
fax: (604) 888-3916
contact: Peter Henricsson

Anachemia Solvents, Ltd.
3549 Mavis Road
Mississauga, Ontario, Canada L5C 1T7
tel: (416) 279-5122
fax: (416) 279-4130
contacts: Jack McGregor; G.J. Wentlandt

Systech Environmental Corp.
3 Chemin Lafarge
P.O. Box 218
St. Constant, Quebec, Canada, J5A 2G3
tel: (514) 635-1275
fax: (514) 635-1277
contact: Bruno Pelletier

Europe

De Neff Chemrec
Industrie Park 8
2220 Heist-op-Den Berg
Belgium
tel: 32 15-246231
fax: 32 15-248072
contact: Pol Kriekemans

Bitolea S.P.A. Chimica Ecologica
Centro Commerciale Via Gandhi nr. 15/21
I 20017 RHO-MILANO
Italy
contact: D. Intini

Valls Quimica, S.A.
Poligone Industrial
Valls c/h, s/n
43800 Valls (Tarragona)
Spain
Contact: J. Campama Cusoo

Cobalt

African Metals Corporation
1212 Avenue of the Americas
New York, NY 10036
tel: (212) 764-0880

The Shepherd Chemical Co.
4900 Beech Street
Cincinnati, OH 45212
tel: (513) 731-1110

Mooney Chemicals Inc.
2301 Scranton Road
Cleveland, OH 44113-9988
tel: (216) 781-8383

Glass Manufacturers

Arkansas

Arkansas Glass Container Corp.
516 W. Johnson Avenue
P.O. Box 1717

Jonesboro, AR 72403
tel: (501) 932-4564

California

Anchor Glass Container Corp.
1400 W. 4th Street
P.O. Box 656
Antioch, CA 94509
tel: (510) 757-0500

Ball-InCon Glass Packaging Co.
P.O. Box 5238
4000 N. Arden Drive
El Monte, CA 91735
tel: (818) 448-9831

Anchor Glass Container Corp.
22302 Hathaway Avenue
P.O. Box 3427
Hayward, CA 94541
tel: (510) 581-5025

Anchor-Latchford Glass
Container Corp.
7507 Roseberry Avenue
Huntington Park, CA 90255
tel: (213) 587-7721

Foster-Forbes Glass Container
Division
American National Can
4855 E. 52nd Place
Los Angeles, CA 90040
tel: (213) 562-0580

Madera Glass Co.
Ball-InCon Glass Packaging
Corporation
24441 Avenue 12
Madera, CA 93637
tel: (209) 674-8861 ext. 44
contact: Fred Spicer (Purchasing)
mat'l handled: container (sort by color)

Gallo Glass Co.
Oregon Drive
P.O. Box 1230
Modesto, CA 95353
tel: (209) 579-3126
(209) 579-3411
contact: Al Menshew (Purchasing)
mat'l handled: container; mixed color

Owens-Brockway
3600 Alameda Avenue
P.O. Box 1019
Oakland, CA 94604
tel: (510) 436-2000

Owens-Brockway
1331 E. Philadelphia Street
P.O. Box 2389
Pomona, CA 91769
tel: (714) 628-6081

Anchor-Latchford Glass Container Corp.
1940 Fairway Drive
San Leandro, CA 94577
tel: (510) 357-6060

Kerr
1221 E. St. Andrews Place
Santa Ana, CA 92707
tel: (714) 557-3770
contact: Pete Dargi (Purchasing
Agent—authorized recyclers only)
mat'l handled: container (sort by color)

Owens-Brockway
14700 W. Schulte Road
P.O. Box 30
Tracy, CA 95376
tel: (209) 835-5701

Owens-Brockway
2901 Fruitland Avenue
P.O. Box 3818, Term. Annex
Vernon, CA 90051
tel: (213) 586-4200

Colorado

Coors Brewing Co.
Glass Manufacturing Division
10619 W. 50th Avenue
Wheat Ridge, CO 80033
tel: (303) 425-7842
contact: Randy Cook (Purchasing Manager)
mat'l handled: container

Connecticut

Anchor Glass Container Corp.
Route 101
Dayville, CT 06241
tel: (203) 774-9636

Florida

Tropicana Products
P.O. Box 338
Bradenton, FL 34206
tel: (813) 747-4461

Anchor Glass Container Corp.
2121 Huron Street
P.O. Box 6932
Jacksonville, FL 32236
tel: (904) 786-1010

Owens-Brockway
2222 W. Bella Vista Street
Lakeland, FL 33809
tel: (813) 680-4800

Georgia

Owens-Brockway
3107 Sylvan Rd., East
Atlanta, GA 30354
tel: (404) 765-8600

Anchor Glass Container Corp.
Booth Road
Warner-Robins, GA 31088
tel: (912) 922-4271

Illinois

Owens-Brockway
1131 Arnold Street
Chicago Heights, IL 60411
tel: (708) 757-5555

Ball-InCon Glass Packaging Corporation
13850 Cottage Grove Avenue
Dolton, IL 60419
tel: (708) 849-1500
mat'l handled: container

Anchor Glass Container Corp.
1955 Delaney Road
Gurnee, IL 60031
tel: (708) 244-1000
mat'l handled: container

Hillsboro Glass Co.
Hiram Walker, Inc.
20th & Schram Avenue
P.O. Box 430
Hillsboro, IL 62049
tel: (217) 532-3976
mat'l handled: container

Ball-InCon Glass Packaging Corporation
1200 N. Logan Street
Lincoln, IL 62656
tel: (217) 735-1511
mat'l handled: container

Kerr Glass Manufacturing Corporation
1500 North Route 59
Plainfield, IL 60544
tel: (815) 436-5651
mat'l handled: container

Anchor Glass Container Corp.
End of Walnut Street
P.O. Box 490
Streator, IL 61364
tel: (815) 672-2951
contact: Robert Wright (Purchasing)
mat'l handled: container (sort by color); plate glass

Owens-Brockway
901 N. Shabbona Street
Streator, IL 61364
tel: (815) 672-3141

Indiana

Kerr Glass Manufacturing Corporation
524 E. Center Street
Dunkirk, IN 47336
tel: (317) 768-7891

Owens-Brockway
Brookside Road
P.O. Box 368
Lapel, IN 46051
tel: (317) 534-3121

Anchor Glass Container Corp.
200 W. Belview Drive
Lawrenceburg, IN 47025
tel: (812) 537-1655

Foster-Forbes Glass Division
American National Can
E. Charles Street
P.O. Box 249
Marion, IN 46952
tel: (317) 668-1200

Anchor Glass Container Corp.
603 E. North Street

Winchester, IN 47394
tel: (317) 584-6101
contact: L. Hollowell
mat'l handled: flint only

Louisiana

Ball-InCon Glass Packaging Corporation
U.S. Highway 20
P.O. Box 789
Ruston, LA 71270
tel: (318) 247-8041

Maryland

Carr-Lowrey Glass Co.
2201 Kloman Street
P.O. Box 356
Baltimore, MD 21203
tel: (301) 347-8800

Massachusetts

Foster-Forbes Glass Division
American National Can
1 National Street
P.O. Box 398
Milford, MA 01757
tel: (508) 478-2500, ext. 215
mat'l handled: container (sorted by color)

Michigan

Owens-Brockway
500 Packard Highway
Charlotte, MI 48813
tel: (517) 543-1400

Minnesota

Anchor Glass Container Corp.
4108 Valley Industrial Boulevard, N.
P.O. Box 69
Shakopee, MN 55379
tel: (612) 445-5000
mat'l handled: container (crushed)

Missouri

Wheaton Glass
Division of Wheaton Industries
1000 Taylor Avenue
Flat River, MO 63601
tel: (314) 431-5743
mat'l handled: container; flint

Foster-Forbes Glass Division
American National Can
1500 Foster-Forbes Drive
P.O. Box 729
Pevely, MO 63070
tel: (314) 479-4421
mat'l handled: container (crushed)

New Jersey

Leone Industries
443 Southeast Avenue
P.O. Box 400
Bridgeton, NJ 08302
tel: (609) 455-2000

Ball-InCon Glass Packaging Corporation
1 Minue Street
Carteret, NJ 07008
tel: (201) 969-1400 (plant)
(317) 741-7137 (purchasing)
contact: Paul A. Hummel (Purchasing Manager—Recycling)
mat'l handled: container; flint; sort by color, furnace-ready quality

Anchor Glass Container Corp.
Cliffwood Avenue
P.O. Box 557
Cliffwood, NJ 07721
tel: (201) 566-4000

Foster-Forbes Glass Division
American National Can
328 S. Second Street
Millville, NJ 08332
tel: (609) 825-5000

Wheaton Industries
1101 Wheaton Avenue
Millville, NJ 08332
tel: (609) 825-1400

Anchor Glass Container Corp.
83 Griffith Street
Salem, NJ 08079
tel: (609) 935-4000

New York

Miller Brewing Co.
Central New York Bottling Co.
R.D. #6, County House Road
Auburn, NY 13021
tel: (315) 255-5201

Anchor Glass Container Corp.
1901 Grand Central Avenue
P.O. Box 849
Elmira, NY 14902
tel: (607) 737-1933
contact: Dowain Nielsen (Purchasing)
mat'l handled: container; flint; sort by color

Owens-Brockway
Great Bear Road, R.D. #5
P.O. Box 125
Fulton, NY 13069
tel: (315) 598-0931
contact: Brian Houger (Purchasing)
mat'l handled: Container; flint; amber; sort by color

North Carolina

Ball-InCon Glass Packaging Corporation
1856 Hendersonville Road
Asheville, NC 28803
tel: (704) 274-2255
contact: E.V. Gouge (Purchasing)
mat'l handled: container (sort by color only)

Ball-InCon Glass Packaging Corporation
U.S. Highway #1 Bypass
P.O. Box 887
Henderson, NC 27536
tel: (919) 492-1131 (plant)
(317) 741-7137 (purchasing)
contact: Paul Hummel (Purchasing Manager—Recycling)
mat'l handled: container; flint (some green, locally only); sort by color, furnace-ready quality

American National Can
Foster-Forbes Glass Division
2200 Firestone Parkway
P.O. Box 1757
Wilson, NC 27893
tel: (919) 291-1500
contact: Carol Whitehead (Purchasing)
mat'l handled: container (sort by color only)

Owens-Brockway
Highway 52-S at Midway
P.O. Box AE, Salem Station
Winston-Salem, NC 27108
tel: (919) 764-2900

Ohio

Owens-Brockway
1700 State Street
P.O. Box 2488
Zanesville, OH 43701
tel: (614) 455-4500

Oklahoma

Owens-Brockway
300 E. Arlington Street
P.O. Box 249
Ada, OK 74820
tel: (405) 332-0415
mat'l handled: container

Anchor Glass Container Corp.
McLaughlin Road
Route 3, P.O. Box 908
Henryetta, OK 74437
tel: (918) 652-9631
mat'l handled: container

Owens-Brockway
York & Shawnee Streets
P.O. Box 8
Muskogee, OK 74402-0008
tel: (918) 682-6621
mat'l handled: container; flint (clear and green)

Ball-InCon Glass Packaging Corporation
800 S. Madison
P.O. Drawer 1217
Okmulgee, OK 74447
tel: (918) 756-5990 (plant)
tel: (317) 741-7137 (purchasing)
Contact: Paul A. Hummel (Purchasing Manager—Recycling)
mat'l handled: container; flint; sorted by color, furnace-ready quality

Kerr
S. Main Street & Morrow Road
P.O. Box 97

Sand Springs, OK 74063
tel: (918) 245-1313
mat'l handled: container

Liberty Glass Company
1000 N. Mission
Sapulpa, OK 74066
tel: (918) 224-1440
contacts: Mr. Terry Kelley (Management);
Donna Wilson (Scrap broker)
mat'l handled: container; flint; green and amber, sort by color

Oregon

Owens-Brockway Glass Container Inc.
A Unit of Owens—Illinois, Inc.
5850 N.E. 92nd Drive
P.O. Box 20067
Portland, OR 97220
tel: (503) 251-9432
(503) 251-9402
contact: Bob Dolphin or Carol Rissell (Purchasing)
mat'l handled: container (sort by color)

Pennsylvania

Owens-Brockway
Plant #18
McCullough Avenue
Brockway, PA 15824
tel: (814) 261-6200

Owens-Brockway
Plant #19
R.D. #2
Crenshaw, PA 15824
tel: (814) 261-5389

Owens-Brockway
151 Grand Avenue
P.O. Box 150
Clarion, PA 16214
tel: (814) 226-0500

Glenshaw Glass Co.
1101 William Flinn Highway
Glenshaw, PA 15116
tel: (412) 486-9100

Ball-InCon Glass Packaging Corporation
One Glass Place
Port Allegany, PA 16743
tel: (814) 642-2521

Anchor Glass Container Corp.
1926 Baldridge Street
S. Connellsville, PA 15425
tel: (412) 628-4000

South Carolina

Ball-InCon Glass Packaging Corporation
One Catherine Street
P.O. Drawer 9
Laurens, SC 29360
tel: (803) 984-2541

Texas

Anchor Glass Container Corp.
4202 Fidelity Street
P.O. Box 24218
Houston, TX 77229
tel: (713) 672-0591

Owens-Brockway
5200 Beverly Drive
P.O. Box 20728
Waco, TX 76702
tel: (817) 754-9500

Foster-Forbes Glass Division
American National Can
2400 Interstate 35 East
Waxahachie, TX 75165
tel: (214) 937-3430

Virginia

Owens-Brockway
Route 3
P.O. Box 190
Danville (Ringgold), VA 24586
tel: (804) 799-5880

Owens-Brockway
150 Industrial Boulevard
P.O. Box 400
Toano, VA 23168
tel: (804) 566-1200

Washington

Ball-InCon Glass Packaging Corporation

5801 E. Marginal Way, S.
Seattle, WA 98134
tel: (206) 762-0660

West Virginia

Owens-Brockway Glass Containers
8th Avenue & 5th Street, W.
P.O. Box 640
Huntington, WV 25701
tel: (304) 528-6730—Gary Booth (Purchasing)
(419) 247-1199 (Patti Hansen, Purchasing, Toledo, Ohio)

Anchor Glass Container Corp.
Waxler Road Industrial Park
P.O. Box 968
Keyser, WV 26726
tel: (304) 788-4055
mat'l handled: container; flint; amber and green, locally only, all glass must be sorted by color

Wisconsin

Foster-Forbes Glass Division
American National Can
815 S. McHenry Street
P.O. Box 128
Burlington, WI 53105
tel: (414) 763-9161

Lead Smelters

Alabama

Interstate Lead
1247 Borden Avenue
Leeds, AL 35094
tel: (205) 699-6171
contact: Roy Bray (Purchasing Agent)
mat'l handled: secondary lead smelter

Sanders Lead
P.O. Box 707
Troy, AL 36081
tel: (205) 566-1563
fax: (205) 566-0107
contact: Jim DeBray, (Purchasing Agent)
mat'l handled: secondary lead smelter

California

GNB, Inc.
2700 S. Indiana Street
P.O. Box 23957
Los Angeles, CA
tel: (213) 262-1101
mat'l handled: secondary lead smelter

Georgia

GNB, Inc.
Resource Recycling Division
P.O. Box 2165
Columbus, GA 31902
tel: (404) 689-0761
mat'l handled: secondary lead smelter

Indiana

R S R Corp.
7870 W. Morris Street
Indianapolis, IN 46231
tel: (317) 247-1303
fax: (317) 244-4653
mat'l handled: secondary lead smelter

Exide Corp.
2601 W. Mount Pleasant Boulevard
P.O. Box 2098
Muncie, IN 47302
(home office: Reading, PA)
tel: (317) 747-9980
contact: Lou Madgits (Purchasing Agent)
mat'l handled: lead and lead alloys

Louisiana

Schuylkill Metals Corp.
P.O. Box 74040
Baton Rouge, LA 70874
tel: (504) 775-3040
fax: (504) 775-3057
mat'l handled: secondary lead smelter

Missouri

Schuylkill Metals Corp.
P.O. Box 156
Forest City, MO 64451-0156
(home office: Baton Rouge, LA)
tel: (816) 446-3321

fax: (816) 446-3324
contact: Dick Mongold (Office and Purchasing Manager)
mat'l handled: Auto batteries (truck load quantity); secondary lead smelting

New York

RSR Corp.
Ballard Road
Middletown, NY 10940-9775
tel: (914) 692-4414
contact: C. Moccia (Purchasing Agent)

Ohio

Master Metals
2850 W. Third Street
Cleveland, OH 44113-2516
tel: (216) 621-2361
fax: (216) 621-7475
contact: Jerry Moody (VP—Marketing)
mat'l handled: secondary lead smelting

Pennsylvania

East Penn Manufacturing Co., Inc.
Deka Road
Lyon Station, PA 19536-9998
tel: (215) 682-6361
fax: (215) 682-4781
contact: James Sikora (VP—Marketing)

Exide Corp.
645 Penn Street
P.O. Box 1262
Reading, PA 19603-1262
tel: (215) 378-0500
contact: Gary Hackenberg (Purchasing Agent)

Tennessee

General Smelting & Refining
Highway 31A
P.O. Box 37
College Grove, TN 37046
tel: (615) 368-7125
fax: (615) 368-7714
contact: Billy Cole (Purchasing Agent)

Ross Metals, Inc.
100 N. Railroad Street
P.O. Box 57
Rossville, TN 38066
tel: (901) 853-7701
fax: (901) 853-3551
contact: Larry Scheuer (Purchasing Agent)

Texas

Dixie Metals Co.
Division of Exide
3030 McGowan
P.O. Box 8625
Dallas, TX 75216-0625
tel: (214) 946-2132
fax: (214) 946-9349
contact: Don Francis (General Manager)
mat'l handled: lead smelting

G N B, Inc.
7471 S. 5th Street
P.O. Box 250
Frisco, TX 75034-0250
tel: (214) 377-2121
fax: (214) 377-2707
contacts: Doris Davis (Sales and Marketing Manager)
mat'l handled: lead smelting

Standard Industries, Inc.
Nelson Road & Reliable Drive
P.O. Box 27500
San Antonio, TX 78227-0500
tel: (512) 623-3131
fax: (512) 623-4461
contacts: Al Koppen (Purchasing Agent); Elvin Schofield (Sales and Marketing Manager)

Mercury

New York

Mercury Refining Co., Inc.
790 Waterville-Shaker Road
Latham, NY 12110
tel: (518) 785-1703
contact: Barbara Sauer

Nickel-Cadmium

Arizona

Cyprus Miami Mining Corp.
P.O. Box 4444

Claypool, AZ 85532
tel: (602) 473-7080

California

Kinsbursky Brothers, Inc.
1314 N. Lemon Street
Anaheim, CA 92801
tel: (714) 738-8516
(800) 548-8797
fax: (714) 441-0857

Idaho

Excess Recycling
600 Baldy Mountain Road
Sandpoint, ID 83864
tel: (208) 263-7259

Oregon

Environmental Pacific Co.
P.O. Box 2116
Lake Oswego, OR 97035
tel: (503) 226-7331
fax: (503) 636-3912

Washington

Chemical Processors
625 S. 32nd Street
Washougal, WA 98671
tel: (206) 853-8743

Non-ferrous Metals

Alaska

Engelhard Industries Inc.
301 West Northern Lights #101
Anchorage, AK 99503
tel: (907) 274-2211

Engelhard Industries West Inc.
NBA Building
613 Cushman Avenue Suite 206
Fairbanks, AK 99701
tel: (907) 452-5395
mat'l handled: precious metals

Arizona

Copperstate Metals Inc.
3720 W. Lower Buckeye Road
P.O. Box 18787
Phoenix, AZ 85009
tel: (602) 272-6434
fax: (602) 272-8063
contact: David M. Zack (President)
mat'l handled: ferrous and nonferrous metals, precious metals, and special metals

Southwest Refining Corp.
1201 W. Hilton Street
Phoenix, AZ 85007
tel: (602) 258-0657
contact: Allyn Kluger (President)
mat'l handled: nonferrous (all grades)

Arkansas

Wabash Alloys, Div. Connell Limited
Off Hwy 229
P.O. Box 909
Benton, AR 72015
tel: (501) 776-0621
(800) 255-9081
fax: (501) 776-0621
contacts: Al Hall (Scrap Purchaser); Anita Ward (Scrap Purchaser)
mat'l handled: aluminum

California

Liston Aluminum Brick Co.
P.O. Box 1869
Corona, CA 91718-1869
tel: (714) 277-4221
fax: (714) 272-8382
contact: Jack Hall (President)

Grande Vista Steel/Metal
8221 S. Atlantic Avenue
Cudahy, CA 90201
tel: (213) 773-8032
fax: (213) 771-1182
contact: Abe Schulman (President)
mat'l handled: ferrous & nonferrous metals

Handy & Harmon
1849 Business Center Drive
P.O. Box B
Duarte, CA 91010-0256
tel: (818) 358-5854

fax: (818) 357-5056
contact: Jules J. Nissim (District Sales Manager)
mat'l handled: precious metals

Triangle Used Equipment
198 E. Evan Hewes Highway
El Centro, CA 92243
tel: (619) 353-4409
contact: David L. Lara, Jr. (Owner)
mat'l handled: nonferrous and ferrous metals

CMX
366 E. 58th Street
Los Angeles, CA 90023-4268
tel: (213) 234-9281
fax: (213) 234-0814
contact: Timothy Strelitz
mat'l handled: nonferrous metals (all grades)

Metal Briquetting Company
1960 E. 48th Street
Los Angeles, CA 90058
tel: (213) 582-5347
contacts: Timothy F. Strelitz (President); Keith Beaumont (Purchasing Manager)

United Surplus
18333 Eddy Street
Northridge, CA 91325
tel: (818) 701-0590
contact: John E. Curry (Owner)

Armor Equipment Sales Corp.
1137 57th Avenue
Oakland, CA 94621
tel: (510) 532-0688
contacts: R.G. Knox; Richard Young
mat'l handled: nonferrous metal—zinc

ECS Refining
705 Reed Street
Santa Clara, CA 95050
tel: (408) 988-4386
contacts: Jim Taggart (President); Jerry Winsted (Buyer); John Lerohl (Buyer)
mat'l handled: electronic scrap, silver bearing negatives

Colorado

Cyprus Copper Minerals Corp.
9100 E. Mineral Circle
Englewood, CO 80155
tel: (303) 643-5306
fax: (303) 643-5960
contact: Michael Jaap
mat'l handled: copper scrap

Golden Aluminum Co.
1600 Jackson Street
Golden, CO 80401
tel: (303) 277-7500
fax: (303) 277-7584
contact: Linda Wesely
mat'l handled: aluminum cans

Florida

Resources, Alloys & Metals
250 Business Park Way, Suite 1
Royal Palm Beach, FL 33411
tel: (407) 790-7200
fax: (407) 790-6950
contact: Richard C. Roles
mat'l handled: lead, zinc, copper, aluminium, cobalt

Georgia

Taracorp, Inc.
3490 Piedmont Road Suite 1311
Atlanta, GA 30305
tel: (404) 233-1971
fax: (404) 233-4536
contacts: Stan Sobel (President), Mark Taylor (Senior VP Buyer)
mat'l handled: nonferrous metals; purchase in large quantities; make lead products and solder

Alcan Ingot & Recycling
Div. of Alcan Aluminum Corp.
Willowrun Road
P.O. Box 837
Greensboro, GA 30642-0837
tel: (404) 453-2244
fax: (404) 453-2695
contacts: Jane Waldermar (Purchasing), Robert Harris (Plant Manager)
mat'l handled: used beverage cans, consumer-smelter; purchase in rail car size or 18-wheelers

Illinois

Baker Film Salvage Inc.
3918 S. Wallace Avenue

Chicago, IL 60609
tel: (312) 254-9271
mat'l handled: precious metals
contact: Sherwin Baker

Clearing Alloys Corporation
5811 W. 66th Street
Chicago, IL 60638
tel: (312) 581-3500
fax: (312) 581-7604
contacts: Ed Cohen (Purchasing)
mat'l handled: zinc alloyer

Kramer, H & Co.
1339–1345 W. 21st Street
Chicago, IL 60608
tel: (312) 226-6600
fax: (312) 226-4713
contacts: P. Boyle; Steve Buchweitz
mat'l handled: brass, bronze, copper, tin, zinc, nickel; purchase in large quantities; make ingots

R. Lavin & Sons Inc.
3426 S. Kedzie Avenue
Chicago, IL 60623
tel: (312) 847-1800
contacts: Hal Lennon; Martin Blinn; David Lennon
mat'l handled: aluminum

Midwest Zinc
1001 W. Weed Street
Chicago, IL 60622
tel: (312) 944-1505
fax: (312) 944-5915
contact: Tom Perry (Purchasing Agent)
mat'l handled: zinc foundry

Sipi Metals Corp.
1720 N. Elston Avenue
Chicago, IL 60622
tel: (312) 276-0070
fax: (312) 276-7014
contact: Len Stack
mat'l handled: bronze, copper, precious metals, tin, zinc, nickel; secondary smelter; makes ingots

Handy & Harman
1900 Estes Avenue
Elk Grove Village, IL 60007
tel: (708) 437-3883
fax: (708) 437-0029
contact: Gil
mat'l handled: precious metals

Mastco Co.
1596 Old Skokie Road
Highland Park, IL 60035
tel: (708) 251-8835
fax: (708) 831-0790
contacts: Ed Alpert (President); Louis O. Alpert (Secretary)
mat'l handled: lead, precious metals, tin

Heraeus Inc.
466 Central Avenue
Northfield, IL 60093
tel: (708) 446-0380
mat'l handled: precious metals

Alumax Extrusions Inc.
1 Foxfield Square
Saint Charles, IL 60174
tel: (708) 584-1000
fax: (708) 584-1243
contacts: Don L. Barber (Manager/Raw Material Purchaser); Greg Newlijn (Raw Material Buyer)
mat'l handled: aluminum, magnesium

American Chemical & Refining Co.
1179 N. Ellsworth Avenue
Villa Park, IL 60181
tel: (708) 530-7950
fax: (708) 530-4651
contact: Donald E. Walsh (Director of Sales and Marketing)
mat'l handled: reprocessor, precious metals

Indiana

Refined Metals
3700 S. Arlington Street
P.O. Box 188
Beech Grove, IN 46107-0188
tel: (317) 787-6364
contact: R. Widner (Plant Manager)
mat'l handled: secondary nonferrous smelting

Aluminum Conversion Inc.
Kreager Industrial Park
P.O. Box 137
Cromwell, IN 46732-0137
tel: (219) 856-2180
contact: Mike Smith

mat'l handled: aluminum (smelting)

U.S. Reduction Co.
4610 Kennedy Avenue
East Chicago, IN 46312
tel: (219) 392-8028
(219) 392-8035
contacts: David Neufeld; Maurice Berglund
mat'l handled: nonferrous metals (all grades)

Advanced Aluminum Products Inc.
6527 Columbia Avenue
Hammond, IN 46320
tel: (219) 932-2717
(800) 458-7757
fax: (219) 933-2728
contacts: Alan Sallee (VP Sales); William D. Cherny (Purchasing Agent)
mat'l handled: aluminum

Wabash Alloys
Div. of Connell Ltd. Partnership
Old U.S. 24 W.
P.O. Box 466
Wabash, IN 46992-0466
tel: (219) 563-7461
(800) 348-0571
In Indiana (800) 552-0502
fax: (219) 563-5997
contacts: Gary W. Griffith (VP Metal Purchasing); Mike Rubin (Purchasing Agent)
mat'l handled: aluminum, used beverage containers, copper, magnesium, zinc, nickel

American Solder Corporation
2230 Indianapolis Blvd.
Whiting, IN 46394
tel: (219) 659-0600
(312) 375-4573
fax: (312) 221-2292
contact: Otto Jefimenko (President and Sales Manager)
mat'l handled: lead, tin

Iowa

M. Feder & Sons
600 4th St., N.E.
P.O. Box 1473
Cedar Rapids, IA 52406
contacts: I. Mervin Feder; Theodore F. Feder
mat'l handled: nonferrous metals, ferrous metals

Massachussets

Consolidated Smelting & Refining Corporation
9 Harback Road, RFD4
Sutton, MA 01527
tel: (508) 865-9201
(508) 865-1120
fax: (508) 865-1659
contact: Lowell Fiengold (President)
mat'l handled: aluminum, lead, brass, copper, tin, zinc; smelter

New England Smelting Works, Inc.
502 Union Street
P.O. Box 29
West Springfield, MA 01090
tel: (413) 734-6491
contacts: David Saffer; Sandy Saffer; Doug Saffer
mat'l handled: nonferrous metals, special metals

Michigan

Arco Alloys Corp.
1891 Trombly Street
Detroit, MI 48211
tel: (313) 871-2680
fax: (313) 871-9145
mat'l handled: zinc

Peninsula Copper Industries Inc.
1700 Duncan Avenue
P.O. Box 509
Hubbell, MI 49934
tel: (906) 296-9918
fax: (906) 296-9484
contact: Ken Cygan (Manager—Raw Materials)
mat'l handled: copper-clad metals

Bohn Eng. & Foundry
220 Aylworth Avenue
South Haven, MI 49090
tel: (616) 637-5161
contact: Roy Anger (Buyer—Nonferrous Metal)
mat'l handled: nonferrous metals

Missouri

Consolidated Aluminum Corp.
11960 Westline Industrial Drive
P.O. Box 14448
Saint Louis, MO 63141
tel: (314) 878-6950

fax: (314) 851-2444
contact: James P. Kelemetc (Manager—Metal Supply)
mat'l handled: all types of aluminum, including used beverage cans, aluminum smelter

Montana

Allied Manufacturing Corporation
P.O. Box 794
Bozeman, MT 59715
tel: (406) 586-6630
contact: W.J. Sullivan
mat'l handled: nonferrous metals (secondary smelting)

Chovanak, Inc.
675 Myles Road
Helena, MT 59601
tel: (406) 442-6317
contact: Mike Chovanak
mat'l handled: nonferrous metals (secondary smelting)

Nebraska

Mid America Refining Co.
22222 Fishery Road
Gretna, NE 68028
tel: (402) 332-3828
contact: Roger Weblemore (Owner)
mat'l handled: precious metals (refine silver)

Northwestern Metal Co.
3900 Industrial Avenue
P.O. Box 81826
Lincoln, NE 68501
tel: (402) 464-6341
contact: Dave Hedges (President)
mat'l handled: scrap metal and scrap iron (secondary smelting)

Norfolk Iron & Metal Company
300 Braasch Avenue
P.O. Box 1129
Norfolk, NE 68701
tel: (402) 464-6341
contact: Richard A. Robinson (President)
mat'l handled: aluminum (secondary smelting)

Magnolia Metal
6161 Abott Drive
Omaha, NE 68119
tel: (402) 455-8760
contact: Mark Stevens
mat'l handled: copper, brass

New Hampshire

N. Kamenske & Co. Inc.
5 Otterson Court
P.O. Box 724
Nashua, NH 03061
tel: (603) 882-5113
contacts: Max Silber (President); Mrs. Marvis Mellen (General Manager); Allan Silber (VP)
mat'l handled: brass and bronze (secondary smelting)

New Jersey

Aluminum Smelters of N.J., Inc.
9000 River Road
Delair, NJ 08110
tel: (609) 662-5500
fax: (609) 662-5605
contact: Don Ottenger (x210) (Scrap Purchasing Manager)
mat'l handled: aluminum, magnesium

Pashelinsky Smelting & Refining Corp.
20 Carbon Place
Jersey City, NJ 07305
tel: (201) 333-6606
fax: (201) 333-2536
contacts: Martin Pashelinsky; Bernard Pashelinsky
mat'l handled: nonferrous metals, precious metals; smelter; ferrous metals; handles large and small quantities; smelts nickel alloys

RFE Industries Inc.
Foot of Jersey Avenue
Jersey City, NJ 07302
tel: (201) 451-1593
(201) 451-0229
contact: Jack Leiner (President)
mat'l handled: precious metals, tin

Madison Industries, Inc.—Old Bridge Chemicals
Old Waterworks Road
P.O. Box 194
Old Bridge, NJ 08857
tel: (908) 727-2225

fax: (908) 727-2653
contacts: H. Bzura (President); B. Bzura (VP—Brass); Joel Goldschmidt (Copper); Joel Bzura (Zinc)
mat'l handled: brass, copper, zinc

Possehl, Inc. (Sole agent for Huettenwerke Kayser)
1 Maynard Drive
Park Ridge, NJ 07656
tel: (201) 307-1500
fax: (201) 307-0540
contacts: Ral Astermann (Buyer, Seller); Sidney Silver (Buyer, Seller)
mat'l handled: nonferrous metals

Engelhard Corp.
2655 U.S. Highway 22
Union, NJ 07083
tel: (908) 964-2700
mat'l handled: precious metals

Essex Metal Alloy Co., Inc.
1000 Brighton Street
P.O. Box 558
Union, N.J. 07083
tel: (908) 688-9010
fax: (908) 688-6438
contacts: Steven Salomon (President); Phil Arnela (Buyer)
mat'l handled: nonferrous metals

Johnson Matthey, Inc.
2001 Nolte Drive
West Deptford, NJ 08066
tel: (609) 853-8000
contact: Martin Durney (Marketing Manager)
mat'l handled: precious metals, consumer; refiner, consumer; smelter

New Mexico

Academy Corporation
6905 Washington, N.E. #A
Albuquerque, NM 87109
tel: (505) 345-1805
contact: Keith Phillipi (President)
mat'l handled: precious metal refining

New York

Manitoba Corporation
69 Vandalia Street
P.O. Box 1125, Ellicott Square
Buffalo, NY 14205
tel: (716) 854-7000
fax: (716) 842-0785
contacts: Joseph Baker; Joe Sliwinski; Richard Shine; Brian Shine
mat'l handled: nonferrous metals

Roth Bros. Smelting Corp.
6223 Thompson Road
P.O. Box 639
East Syracuse, NY 13057
tel: (315) 463-9500
fax: (315) 433-9069
contacts: Laurence Roth (President); Paul Roth (VP); Lee Raymond; Eric Rochelson
mat'l handled: nonferrous metals, used beverage containers

Monarch Brass & Copper Corp.
75 Beechwood Avenue
P.O. Box 500
New Rochelle, NY 10802
tel: (914) 235-3000
contacts: Malcolm Mogol (CEO and President); Endecott Perry (Executive VP); Dennis Mullin (Purchasing Agent)
mat'l handled: nonferrous metals, mill

Unique Precious Metal Refining Co., Inc.
385 Wyandanch Road
Sayville, NY 11782
tel: (516) 567-4671
contacts: T. Richard Stablein
mat'l handled: precious metals

Sabin Metal Corp.
1647 Wheatland Center Road
Scottsville, NY 14546
tel: (716) 538-2194
mat'l handled: precious metals

North Carolina

Biltmore Iron and Metal Co.
P.O. Box 5616
Asheville, NC 28803
tel: (704) 253-9317
mat'l handled: nonferrous metals (secondary smelting)

Shulimson Brothers Co. Inc.
100 Meadow Road
Asheville, NC 28803
tel: (704) 253-2771
mat'l handled: segregated nonferrous scrap metal (secondary smelting)

SCM Metal Products, Inc.
2601 Weck Drive
Research Triangle Park, NC 27709
tel: (919) 544-8090
fax: (919) 544-7996
contact: Jerry R. Johnson (Directer/Purchasing and Quantity)
mat'l handled: copper, tin, nickel

Ohio

Barmet Aluminum Corp.
753 W. Waterloo Road
P.O. Box 26010
Akron, OH 44319-6010
tel: (216) 753-7701
contacts: Richard D. Pollock (President); Ralph Hartman (Buyer)
mat'l handled: nonferrous metals; mill; consumer; smelter

Maxwell Recycling
480 5th Street N.E.
Barberton, OH 44203
tel: (216) 848-1815
contact: Howard Maxwell
mat'l handled: nonferrous metals, used beverage containers, steel cans, paper, polyethylene terephthalate, high-density polyethylene

Colonial Metals
2797 Belgrave Road
Cleveland, OH 44124
tel: (216) 464-1940
mat'l handled: precious metals

Lamotite, Inc.
Division of Bonwater Industries
2909 E. 79th Street
Cleveland, OH 44104
tel: (216) 883-8484
contact: Al Soltis (VP/Operations)
mat'l handled: nonferrous metals

I. Schumann & Company
22500 Alexander Road
P.O. Box 46271
Cleveland, OH 44146
tel: (216) 439-2300
fax: (216) 439-0317
contacts: David M. Schumann (Sales Manager); David Lloyd (Purchasing Agent)
mat'l handled: brass, bronze, copper, tin, zinc, nickel

Easco Aluminum Co.
706 S. State Street
P.O. Box 60
Girard, OH 44420-0060
tel: (216) 545-4311
fax: (216) 545-3302
contacts: Robert Cleary (Sales Manager)
mat'l handled: aluminum, copper, magnesium

Ohio Precious Metals, Inc.
305 Water Street
P.O. Box 605
Jackson, OH 45640
tel: (614) 286-6457
contacts: Walter Luhrman; Miriam Rader (Buyer)
mat'l handled: precious metals

J. M. Cousins, Inc.
Crawford Avenue
P.O. Box 787
Mansfield, OH 44901-9998
tel: (419) 525-0011
fax: (419) 525-4961
contacts: Steven Senser (President); Tom Skidmore (VP)
mat'l handled: aluminum (smelter)

Aluminum Smelting & Refining Co., Inc.
Div. of Delaware North Co.
5463 Dunham Road
Maple Heights, OH 44137
tel: (216) 662-3100
(800) 522-8525
contact: Terrence Szarka
mat'l handled: Aluminum (smelter)

The Federal Metal Co.
7250 Division Street
Oakwood Village, OH 44146-5406
tel: (216) 232-8700
fax: (216) 232-8726

contact: Rik Kohn (VP—Purchasing)
mat'l handled: brass, bronze

Doehler-Jarvis
Div. of Icm Industries Inc.
5400 N. Detroit Avenue
P.O. Box 902
Toldeo, OH 43612
tel: (419) 470-8020
fax: (419) 470-8185
contacts: Tom Tozzini (VP), David W. Adkins (Purchasing Agent)
mat'l handled: aluminum, copper, zinc

Metallic Resources, Inc.
2116 Enterprise Parkway
P.O. Box 177
Twinsburg, OH 44087
tel: (216) 425-3155
fax: (216) 425-2180
contacts: Robert Apple (Director of Marketing); Eric Ozan (Purchasing Agent)
mat'l handled: electronic solders and precious metal refining

Oklahoma

U.S. Reduction Aluminum Serv.
100 E. Apex Road
P.O. Box 409
Checotah, OK 74426
tel: (918) 473-2321
contact: Ronald L. Abernathy
mat'l handled: aluminum

T & T Pipe and Steel
506 S. 6th
Duncan, OK 73533
tel: (405) 255-4114
contacts: Terry Trent (President); Pete Trent (VP)
mat'l handled: nonferrous metals, used beverage containers, steel cans

Pennsylvania

Cressona Aluminum Company
55 Pottsville Street
Cressona, PA 17929-0129
tel: (717) 385-8705
(800) 233-3165
fax: (800) 252-4646
contact: Robert J. McHale (Metal Manager)
mat'l handled: aluminum

Gettysburg Foundry & Specialty Co.
2664 Emmitsburg Road
P.O. Box 3785
Gettysburg, PA 17325-3785
tel: (717) 334-7661
fax: (717) 334-8941
contact: Roger Melton
mat'l handled: aluminum (smelting)

Alcoa Recycling Co., Inc.
Alcoa Bldg. Rm 2820
Pittsburgh, PA 15219
tel: (412) 553-4645
contact: George L. Cobb (President)
mat'l handled: nonferrous metals, consumer (mill), consumer (smelter)

Keystone Resources
330 Grant Street, Suite 1700
Pittsburgh, PA 15219
tel: (412) 288-2200
contact: Robert Rese (President)
mat'l handled: base metals and aluminum

Rhode Island

Boliden Metech, Inc.
1 Main Street
P.O. Box 500
Mapleville, RI 02839
tel: (401) 568-0711
(401) 431-1300
fax: (401) 438-6931
contact: James K. Gardner
mat'l handled: catalytic converters, copper, precious metals, special metals

South Carolina

Allied Steel
Meeting & Mt. Pleasant
P.O. Box 814
Charleston Heights, SC 29400
tel: (803) 552-6300
mat'l handled: secondary smelting (nonferrous metals)

K & W Alloys Inc.
Torrington Road
P.O. Box 240

Clinton, SC 29325-0240
tel: (803) 833-3444
mat'l handled: secondary smelting (nonferrous metals)

AT & T Nassau Metals
AT & T Technologies
Box 218
Gaston, SC 29053-0218
tel: (803) 796-4720
mat'l handled: secondary smelting (nonferrous metals)

Industrial Scrap Inc.
P.O. Box 1861
Pinsly Circle
Berea Industrial Park
Greenville, SC 29602-1861
tel: (803) 246-1431

Batchedler-Blasius Inc.
P.O. Box 5503
Fairmont Street
Spartanburg, SC 29304-5503
tel: (803) 439-6321
mat'l handled: secondary smelting (nonferrous metals)

Ackerman Metals Inc.
P.O. Box 1916
Sumter, SC 29151-1916
tel: (803) 775-8383
mat'l handled: secondary smelting (nonferrous metals)

Tennessee

Wabash Alloys, Div. Connell Ltd.
Printwood Drive
P.O. Box 341
Dickson, TN 37055
tel: (615) 446-0600
(800) 922-9961
fax: (615) 446-5354
contacts: Dennis Luma (Plant Manager); Steve Veverka (Metal Purchasing Manager); Paul Gamary (Receiving Manager)
mat'l handled: nonferrous metals, consumer (smelter)

American Silver Co.
6167 S. Mt. Juliet Road
Hermitage, TN 37076
tel: (615) 871-4301
contact: Walter B. McDade (President)
mat'l handled: precious metals

IMCO Recycling Inc.
U.S. Highway 27
P.O. Box 268
Rockwood, TN 37854
tel: (615) 354-3626
contact: Richard Kerr
mat'l handled: nonferrous metals

Texas

Alumax Recycling Group
104 Japhet, Bldg A
Houston, TX 77020
tel: (713) 671-2561
fax: (713) 671-2967
contacts: Robert Bullard (Regional Manager); Eddie Garner (Plant Superintendent); Mark Manning (Buyer)
mat'l handled: aluminum, used beverage containers, steel cans

Engelhard Corporation
1800 St. James
Houston, TX 77056
tel: (713) 627-2160
contact: Vince Brogan
mat'l handled: precious metals

Kocide Chemical Corp.
12701 Almeda Road 77045
P.O. Box 450529
Houston, TX 77245-0529
tel: (713) 433-6404
fax: (713) 433-0898
contacts: J.F. Strand (Manager—Sourcing & Traffic); Glen E. Fess Butch Frazee (General Manager)
mat'l handled: Copper

Aluminum Co. of America
Market Road
P.O. Box 472
Rockdale, TX 76567-0472
tel: (512) 446-8346
fax: (512) 446-8447
contact: W.J. Drake (General Manager)
mat'l handled: aluminum (secondary smelter)

Virginia

Bellwood Reclamation Plant
1711 Reymet Road
Richmond, VA 23234
tel: (804) 743-6578
mat'l handled: secondary smelting (nonferrous metals)

Hoover & Strong Inc.
10700 Trade Road
Richmond, VA 23236-3039
tel: (804) 794-3700
mat'l handled: secondary smelting (nonferrous metals)

Washington

Goldmark Jewelry/Metals
10325 Aurora N.
Seattle, WA 98133
tel: (206) 527-4646
contact: Gerald Olson (Owner)
mat'l handled: precious metals

Wisconsin

Hy-Lo Silver
6411 Windsor Prairie Road
De Forest, WI 53532
tel: (608) 221-1375
contact: Joe Weiss (Owner)
mat'l handled: precious metals

KSG Industries Inc.
1731 Industrial Parkway
Marinette, WI 54143
tel: (715) 732-0181
contact: Kim Kehoe (Purchasing Manager)
mat'l handled: ferrous metals, nonferrous metals

Oil Re-refiners

Arkansas

Mid America Distillations Inc.
P.O. Box 2880
Hot Springs, AR 71914
tel: (501) 767-7776
fax: (501) 767-6672

California

Dremenno/Kerdoon
2000 N. Alameda Street
Compton, CA 90222
tel: (213) 537-7100
fax: (213) 639-2946

Evergreen Holdings
18001 Cowan Suites C&D
Irvine, CA 92714
tel: (714) 757-7770
fax: (714) 474-9149

Evergreen Oil
6880 Smith Avenue
Newark, CA 94560
tel: (510) 795-4400
fax: (510) 791-0126

Illinois

Motor Oils Refining Company
7601 W. 47th Street
McCook, IL 60525
tel: (708) 442-6000
fax: (708) 442-6027

Indiana

BresLube USA Safety-Kleen Corp.
601 Riley Road
East Chicago, IN 46312-1698
tel: (219) 397-1131
fax: (219) 398-3412

Consolidated Recycling
8 Commerce Drive
P.O. Box 55
Troy, IN 47588
tel: (812) 547-7951
fax: (812) 547-7954

Kentucky

Ecogard (Consolidated Recycling)
P.O. Box 14047
Lexington, KY 40512-4047
tel: (606) 264-7304
fax: (606) 264-7012

Canada

Mohawk Lubricants Ltd.
170 Harbor Avenue
N. Vancouver, BC, Canada V7J 2E6

tel: (604) 929-1285
fax: (604) 929-8371

BresLube Div Safety-Kleen Canada
300 Woolwich Street S.
P.O. Box 130
Breslau, Ontario, Canada NOB 1MO
tel: (519) 648-2291
fax: (519) 348-3488

Paper Mills

Alabama

Keyes Fibre Co.
Mathis Hill Road
Albertville, AL 35950
tel: (205) 878-8900
contact: Newell N. Smith (Plant Manager)
mat'l handled: corrugated

National Gypsum Co.
P.O. Box 1380
Anniston, AL 36201
tel: (205) 831-6900
contact: Bill Chappell
mat'l handled: corrugated

Alabama River Newsprint Co.
(Abitibi-Price/Parsons & Whittemore Inc.)
Claiborne, AL
tel: (205) 575-2800
contact: Steve Hughes
planned new mill: planned de-inking line—will accept newspaper and coated groundwood

Kimberly-Clark Corp.
Cocoa Pines, AL
planned new mill: considering de-inking plant
mat'l to be handled: newsprint

Champion International
County Line Rd. 29
P.O. Box 189
Courtland, AL 35618
tel: (205) 637-2741
fax: (205) 637-6706
contact: R.L. Marlewski (VP, Operations Manager)
mat'l handled: pulp substitutes

Gulf States Paper Corp.
Hwy. 80 West
Demopolis, AL 36732
tel: (205) 289-1242
contact: Pete Tucker (Manager—Secondary Fiber)
mat'l handled: high-grade de-inking

Armstrong World Industries Inc.
P.O. Box 2088
Mobile, AL 36652
tel: (205) 433-3971
fax: (205) 432-1127
contact: Brad Sterling (Purchasing Agent)
mat'l handled: corrugated, newspapers

GAF Building Materials Corp.
2400 Emogene Street
P.O. Box 6377
Mobile, AL 36660
tel: (205) 478-6311
contact: E.J. Flood, Plant Manager
mat'l handled: corrugated

International Paper Co.
P.O. Box 2448
Mobile, AL 36652
tel: (205) 470-4000
mat'l handled: pulp substitutes

Newark Box Board Co.
701 Mobile St.
P.O. Box 7395
Mobile, AL 36607
tel: (205) 478-6391
contact: Bob Mitchell
mat'l handled: mixed papers, newspapers, corrugated, pulp substitutes

Scott Paper Co.
P.O. Box 2447
Mobile, AL 36601
tel: (205) 456-9060
contact: J.H. Speier, Plant Manager
mat'l handled: pulp substitutes

James River Corp.
Towel & Tissue Business
Naheola Mill
Pennington, AL 36916
tel: (205) 459-1900
fax: (205) 459-1303
contact: George E. Rogers
mat'l handled: pulp substitutes

Mead Coated Board, Inc.
Mahrt Division

P.O. Box 940
Phenix City, AL 36868-0940
tel: (205) 855-4711
contact: Dennis Dawson (Purchasing Agent)
mat'l handled: coated board

MacMillan Bloedel, Inc.
P.O. Box 366
Pine Hill, AL 36769
tel: (205) 963-4391
fax: (205) 963-4850
contact: Edward Harvey
mat'l handled: corrugated

Union Camp Corp.
100 Jensen Road
Prattville, AL 36067
tel: (205) 361-2100
fax: (205) 361-2390
contact: Mike Petrunic (Purchasing Agent)
mat'l handled: corrugated

Mead Corp
P.O. Box H
Stevenson, AL 35772
tel: (205) 437-2161
mat'l handled: corrugated

Arizona

Pondersosa Paper Products, Inc.
P.O. Box JJ
Flagstaff, AZ 86001
tel: (602) 774-7375
mat'l handled: pulp substitutes, high-grade de-inking

Stone Container Corp., Inc.
P.O. Box 128
Snowflake, AZ 85937
tel: (602) 536-4314
mat'l handled: newspapers, corrugated

Arkansas

Georgia-Pacific Corp.
P.O. Box 496
Ashdown, AR 71822
mat'l handled: pulp substitutes

International Paper Co.
P.O. Box 2045
Camden, AR 71701
tel: (501) 231-4321
mat'l handled: pulp substitutes

Georgia-Pacific Corp.
P.O. Box 520
Crossett, AR 71635
tel: (501) 567-8111
mat'l handled: pulp substitutes

Green Bay Packaging
P.O. Box 711
Highway 113S
Morrilton, AR 72110
tel: (501) 354-4521
contact: Dave Cowein
mat'l handled: corrugated, pulp substitutes, high-grade de-inking

Gaylord Container Corp.
500 McFadden Road
P.O. Box 7857
Pine Bluff, AR 71611
tel: (501) 541-5000
contact: Glen Hendricks
mat'l handled: pulp substitutes

California

Simpson Paper Co.
Shasta Division
P.O. Box 637
Anderson, CA 96007
tel: (916) 365-2711
fax: (916) 365-2642
contact: Ted E. Reinhardt (Operations Manager)
mat'l handled: pulp substitutes

Gaylord Container Corp.
Antioch Mills
1779 Wilbur Avenue
P.O. Box 10
Antioch, CA 94509-0901
tel: (415) 779-3200
fax: (415) 779-3298
contact: R.V. Christensen (VP, General Manager)
mat'l handled: corrugated

Louisiana-Pacific Corp.
Wilbur Avenue
P.O. Box 190
Antioch, CA 94509
tel: (415) 757-4000

Packaging Co. of California
18752 San Jose Avenue
City of Industry, CA 91748
tel: (818) 912-2531
fax: (818) 912-9248
contact: Rob Jennett (Plant Manager)
mat'l handled: newspapers

Sonoco Products Company
166 North Baldwin Park Boulevard
City of Industry, CA 91749
tel: (818) 369-6927
fax: (818) 369-1688
contact: Elaine Corboy (Manager—Consumer)
mat'l handled: corrugated news, tube scrap

Tzeng Long U.S.A. Inc.
2801 Vail Avenue
Commerce, CA 90040
tel: (213) 722-5353
fax: (213) 722-5311
contacts: John Su (President); Jack Fong (Manager)
mat'l handled: OCC, ONP, DLK, grader, packer, broker

Owens-Corning Fiberglas Corp.
1501 N. Tamarind Street
Compton, CA 90223
tel: (213) 631-5131

America Chung Nam, Inc.
10301 E. Garvey Avenue #204
El Monte, CA 91733
tel: (818) 443-6613
fax: (818) 443-7192
contacts: Cheung Yan, (President); Liu Ming Chung (VP)
mat'l handled: newspaper, corrugated, high grades, magazine

Fontana Paper Mills, Inc.
13733 E. Valley Boulevard
Fontana, CA 92335
tel: (714) 823-4100
contact: Jim Nugent
mat'l handled: mixed papers, newspapers, corrugated

Kimberly-Clark Corp.
Consumer Products
2001 E. Orangethorpe Avenue
Fullerton, CA 92634-5396
tel: (714) 773-7500
contact: Charles A. Lynch (Mill Manager)
mat'l handled: pulp substitutes

Leatherback Industries Inc.
901 Prospect Avenue
Hollister, CA 95023
tel: (408) 637-5841
fax: (408) 636-9669
contact: R.J. Ableidinger (President)
mat'l handled: roofing felt paper

Orchid Paper Products
5911 Fresca Drive
La Palma, CA 90623
tel: (714) 523-7881
contact: Bob Everett

Paper-Pak Products, Inc.
1941 White Avenue
La Verne, CA 91750
tel: (714) 392-1200
fax: (714) 392-1204
contacts: Lee Larsonneur (President); Jan Baldwin (VP Sales—East); Jim Gillispie (VP Sales—West)
mat'l handled: high-grade de-inking

Cal-Fiber Co.
625 S. Anderson Street
Los Angeles, CA 90023
tel: (213) 268-0191
fax: (213) 268-1511
contact: Peter Kahn III (Owner)
mat'l handled: overissue and mixed news, foam rubber

Federal Paper Board Co., Inc.
6001 S. Eastern Avenue
Los Angeles, CA 90040
tel: (213) 685-5180
mat'l handled: mixed papers, newspapers, corrugated, pulp substitutes

Los Angeles Paper Box & Board Mills
5959 E. Randolph Street
P.O. Box 60830
Los Angeles, CA 90060-0830
tel: (213) 685-8900
contact: Ted Thiel
mat'l handled: newspapers, corrugated

Inland Container Corporation
37333 Cedar Boulevard
Newark, CA 94560

tel: (714) 983-8111
contact: Ken Enderle (Manager of Recycled Materials)
mat'l handled: corrugated

Cascade Fibers International, Inc.
tel: (714) 944-2599
Sales Office: (714) 944-2539
Main Office: Portland, OR (503)231-1166
mat'l handled: secondary fiber (all grades)

Temple-Inland Container Corporation
5100 Jurupa Street
Ontario, CA 91761
tel: (714) 983-8111
contact: Ken Enderle (Manager of Recycled Materials)
mat'l handled: corrugated
Planned expansion capacity 1991/92 to increase corrugated consumption.

Procter & Gamble Paper Products Co.
800 N. Rice Avenue
Oxnar, CA 93030
tel: (805) 485-8871
contact: J.C. Crouse (Plant Manager)
mat'l handled: pulp substitutes

Smurfit Newsprint Co., Inc.
Mill and Corporate Office
2205 W. Mt. Vernon Avenue
Pomona, CA 91768
tel: (714) 623-6601
fax: (714) 623-7607
contact: David C. Hendrickson (President)
mat'l handled: mixed papers

Sierra Tissue Co.
560 East Commercial Street
Pomona, CA 91767
tel: (714) 623-8101
mat'l handled: mixed papers, corrugated

Simpson Paper Co.
San Gabriel Mill
100 Erie Street
P.O. Box 2648
Pomona, CA 91769
tel: (714) 622-1321
contact: David J. De Young (Operations Manager)
mat'l handled: pulp substitutes

Willamette Industries, Inc.
Perkins Road
P.O. Box 519
Port Hueneme, CA 93041
tel: (805) 986-3881
mat'l handled: corrugated

Packaging Co. of California
Molded Fibre Product Group
Diamond Avenue
P.O. Box 1500
Red Bluff, CA 96080
tel: (916) 529-3340
fax: (916) 527-8036
contact: H.W. Haser (Plant Manager)
mat'l handled: mixed papers, newspapers

Simpson Paper Co.
942 S. Stockton Avenue
P.O. Box 757
Ripon, CA 95366
tel: (209) 599-4241
fax: (209) 599-7301
contacts: Roger Huckendubler (Operations Manager), Pat Mickelson, (plant manager)
mat'l handled: pulp substitutes

Cascade Fibers International, Inc.
Sales Office: (916) 361-0128; Main Office: Portland, OR (503) 231-1166
tel: (916) 361-9037
mat'l handled: secondary fiber (all grades)

Keyes Fibre Co.
8450 Gerber Road
Sacramento, CA 95828
tel: (916) 689-2020
(916) 423-2086
mat'l handled: newspapers, corrugated, pulp substitutes

Domtar Gypsum America, Inc.
1988 Marina Boulevard
P.O. Box 2018
San Leandro, CA 94577
tel: (415) 483-7580
contact: John Schaeffer
mat'l handled: mixed papers, newspapers, corrugated, high-grade de-inking

B.J. Fibers, Inc.
2701 Birch Street
Santa Ana, CA 92707
tel: (714) 540-0650

California Paperboard Corp.
525 Mathew Street
P.O. Box 58044
Santa Clara, CA 95052
tel: (408) 727-7377
contact: Judy Banks
mat'l handled: mixed papers, newpapers, corrugated

Jefferson Smurfit Corp.
2600 De La Cruz Boulevard
Santa Clara, CA 95050
tel: (408) 496-5118
contact: Owen T. Reeves (General Manager)
mat'l handled: mixed papers, newspapers, corrugated, pulp substitutes

Specialty Paper Mills, Inc.
8834 S. Millergrove Drive
P.O. Box 3188
Santa Fe Springs, CA 90670
tel: (213) 723-1034
mat'l handled: mixed papers, newspapers, corrugated

Anchor Paper Mills, Inc.
9301 Garfield Avenue S.
South Gate, CA 90280
tel: (213) 927-6551
(213) 773-4244
contact: Harry Mantooth

Lunday-Thagard Roofing Co.
9302 Garfield Avenue
P.O. Box 1519
South Gate, CA 90280
tel: (213) 773-4244
fax: (213) 928-5623
contact: J.W. Ricketts (President)
mat'l handled: newspapers, corrugated

United States Gypsum Co.
4500 Ardine Street
South Gate, CA 90280
tel: (213) 582-5911
contact: A. Chavez
mat'l handled: mixed papers, newspapers, corrugated, pulp substitutes

Daishowa America Co.
Stockton, CA
Planned new mill to handle linerboard (1993-1994).

Newark Sierra Paperboard Corp.
800 W. Church Street
Stockton, CA 95203
tel: (209) 466-5251
fax: (209) 942-1214
contact: Donald Gagnon (Purchasing Agent)
mat'l handled: mixed papers, newspapers, corrugated, pulp substitutes

Reprocell
9189 De Garmo Avenue
P.O. Box 1063
Sun Valley, CA 91352
tel: (213) 875-0587
contact: Tom Fry (President)

Domtar Gypsum
2116 E. 55th Street
Vernon, CA 90058
tel: (213) 583-0094
fax: (213) 585-7409
contact: Roland A. Johnson (Plant Manager)
mat'l handled: mixed papers, newspapers, corrugated, pulp substitutes

Jefferson Smurfit Corp.
2001 E. 57th Street
Vernon, CA 90058
tel: (213) 583-3421
mat'l handled: mixed papers, newspapers, corrugated, pulp substitutes

Pabco Paper
4460 Pacific Boulevard
P.O. Box 58367
Vernon, CA 90058
tel: (213) 581-6113
fax: (213) 581-0125
mat'l handled: mixed papers, newspapers, corrugated, high-grade de-inking

Colorado

Colorado Fiber Products, Inc.
5701 Dexter Street
Commerce City, CO 80022
tel: (303) 289-5803
contact: Steve Staley (Plant Manager)
mat'l handled: newspaper

Republic Paperboard Co.
5501 Brighton Boulevard
P.O. Box 1268

Denver, CO 80022
tel: (303) 287-7456
mat'l handled: mixed papers, corrugated

Connecticut

Lydall, Inc.
One Colonial Road
P.O. Box 871
Manchester, CT 06040
tel: (203) 646-1233
mat'l handled: mixed paper, newspaper, corrugated

Rand-Whitney Paperboard Corp.
Rt. 163
Montville, CT 06353
tel: (203) 848-9231
contact: Charles Whitney
mat'l handled: mixed papers, newspapers, corrugated, pulp substitutes, high-grade de-inking

Simkins Industries, Inc.
259 East Street
P.O. Box 1870
New Haven, CT 06508
tel: (203) 787-7171
contact: F.P. Camera (General Manager)
mat'l handled: mixed papers, newspapers, corrugated, pulp substitutes

Kimberly-Clark Corp.
Consumer Products
58 Pickett District Road
New Milford, CT 06776-4493
tel: (203) 354-4481
contact: T.J. Davis (Mill Manager)
mat'l handled: pulp substitutes

Rogers Corp.
One Technology Drive
Rogers, CT 06263
tel: (203) 774-9605
contact: Gary Abell

Champion International Corp.
1 Champion Plaza
Stamford, CT 06291
tel: (203) 358-7000

Uncasville
Stone Container Corp.
125 Depot Road
P.O. Box 1500
Uncasville, CT 06382
tel: (203) 848-1500
contact: Jim Oettinger
mat'l handled: corrugated

Versailles
Federal Paper Board Co. Inc.
Sprague Board Mill
Inland Road
Versailles, CT 06383
tel: (203) 823-3650
fax: (203) 822-8257
contact: Debbie Zajac
mat'l handled: mainly corrugated; some box board cuttings, SBS Improved machinery for increased capacity completed 1991.

Delaware

Curtis Paper
Div. James River Corp.
225 Paper Mill Road
P.O. Box 8567
Newark, DE 19714-8567
tel: (302) 738-7851
contact: Edward G. Gremban (VP, General Manager)
mat'l handled: pulp substitutes

Florida

Jefferson Smurfit Corp.
N. Eighth Street
Fernandina Beach, FL 32034
tel: (904) 261-5551
mat'l handled: corrugated
Considering expanding OCC recycling facility.

Atlas Tissue Mills
3725 E. 10th Court
Hialeah, FL 33013
tel: (305) 835-8046
contact: Remberto Bastanzuri (President)
mat'l handled: pulp substitutes, high-grade deinking

Jefferson Smurfit Corporation
4300 Talleyrand Avenue
Jacksonville, FL 32201
tel: (904) 353-3611
fax: (904) 355-1923
contact: George W. Russell

mat'l handled: corrugated

Jefferson Smurfit Corporation
124 Watts Street
Jacksonville, FL 32204
tel: (904) 356-7122
fax: (904) 356-7266
contact: Terry R. Cowgill (General Manager)
mat'l handled: corrugated

Seminole Kraft Corp.
P.O. Box 26998
Jacksonville, FL 32218
tel: (904) 751-6400
contacts: James B. Heider, (VP); T. Frank Lee (General Manager)
mat'l handled: corrugated

U.S.A. Paper, Inc.
3722 Bright Avenue
Jacksonville, FL 32205
tel: (904) 358-2404
fax: (904) 358-2602
contact: John Clews (President)
mat'l handled: waste paper (white ledger, color ledger, laeser free CPO)

United States Gypsum Co.
6825 Evergreen Avenue
Jacksonville, FL 32208
tel: (904) 768-2501
contact: Edward Gerny (Plant Manager)
mat'l handled: mixed papers, newspapers, corrugated, pulp substitutes

Maypan, Inc.
1150 N.W. 72nd Avenue #360
Miami, FL 33126-1920
tel: (305) 592-1321
fax: (305) 592-7704
contact: Manuel Delfino (President)

Georgia-Pacific Corp.
John Campbell Highway 216
P.O. Box 919
Palatka, FL 32077
tel: (904) 325-2001
mat'l handled: pulp substitutes

Stone Container Corp.
P.O. Box 2560
Panama City, FL 32402
tel: (904) 785-4311
mat'l handled: corrugated

St. Joe Forest Products Co.
P.O. Box 190
Port St. Joe, FL 32456-0190
tel: (904) 227-1171
contact: Harold R. Quackenbush (VP)
mat'l handled: corrugated

Georgia

Procter & Gamble Paper Products Co.
P.O. Box 1747
Albany, GA 31702
tel: (912) 883-2000
contact: R.L. Taff (Plant Manager)
mat'l handled: pulp substitutes

Sonoco Products Co.
2490 Marietta Rd., N.W.
P.O. Box 39098
Atlanta, GA 30318
tel: (404) 799-6821
(404) 799-3814
fax: (404) 794-2582
contact: Jim McKellar
mat'l handled: mixed papers, newspapers, corrugated

Augusta Newsprint Co.
P.O. Box 1647
Augusta, GA 30913
tel: (404) 798-3440
fax: (404) 793-4149
contact: Richard Sundberg (General Manager)
mat'l handled: newspapers

Federal Paper Board Co., Inc.
Augusta Operations Route 56
P.O. Box 1425
Augusta, GA 30913-1699
tel: (404) 798-5711
fax: (404) 796-5599
contact: Mark Massey (VP, Resource Manager)
mat'l handled: pulp substitutes

Ponderosa Georgia Corp.
P.O. Box 6428
Augusta, GA 30916
tel: (404) 793-5447
fax: (404) 793-6120
contact: Robert E. Smith (Regional Manager)

Westfield River Paper Co.
Deerfield Specialty Papers

Old Savannah Road
P.O. Box 5437
Augusta, GA 30916-5437
mat'l handled: pulp substitutes

Caraustar Industries
3100 Washington Street
Austell, GA 30001
tel: (404) 948-3100
contact: Bob Prillaman (VP)
mat'l handled: mixed papers, newspapers, corrugated

Sweetwater Paper Board Co., Inc.
5700 Paper Mill Road
Austell, GA 30001
tel: (404) 944-9350
contact: Lee Hammonds (Purchasing Agent)
mat'l handled: CBD, CPO

Brunswick Pulp & Paper Co.
West 9th Street
P.O. Box 1438
Brunswick, GA 31521
tel: (912) 265-5780
contact: H.D. Dowdy

Georgia Pacific
Container Board Operation
P.O. Box 44
Cedar Springs, GA 31732
tel: (912) 372-5541
fax: (912) 372-5369
contact: Charlie Grantland (Manager—Purchasing Recycled Materials)
mat'l handled: old corrugated containers, double-lined kraft

Jefferson Smurfit Corp.
101 Pine Street
P.O. Box 900
Cedartown, GA 30125
tel: (404) 748-0085
(404) 748-1370
mat'l handled: mixed papers, newspapers, corrugated

Universal Paper Corp.
4130 Clairmont Road
Chamblee, GA 30341
tel: (404) 458-2859

Southeast Paper Mfg. Co.
P.O. Box 1169
Dublin, GA 31040
tel: (912) 272-1600
fax: (912) 275-6301
contact: Ronald F. Wilson (President and General Manager)
mat'l handled: newspapers

Armstrong World Industries, Inc.
4520 Broadway
P.O. Box 4288
Macon, GA 31213
tel: (912) 788-4811
contact: Bruce Hettel
mat'l handled: mixed papers, newspapers

Macon Kraft Co.
P.O. Box 3215
Macon, GA 31205
tel: (912) 788-6160
contact: Virginia Wind
mat'l handled: corrugated

Packaging Corp. of America
7670 Airport Drive
LB Wilson Airport
Macon, GA 31297
tel: (912) 781-1474
mat'l handled: newspapers

Rock-Tenn Co.
Recycled Fiber
504 Thrasher Street
P.O. Box 4098
Norcross, GA 30091
tel: (404) 448-2193

Stone Container Corp.
1 Bonnybridge Road
Port Wentworth, GA 31407
tel: (912) 964-1271
contact: James H. Lewis (General Manager)
mat'l handled: corrugated

Interstate Paper Corporation
1 Interstate Road
Riceboro, GA 31323
tel: (912) 884-3371
fax: (912) 884-7255
contact: T.L. Owens (Purchasing)
mat'l handled: OCC, DLK, corrugated

Fort Howard Corp.
Route 1, Bakerhill Road
Rincon, GA 31326-0828

tel: (912) 826-5216
mat'l handled: mixed papers, newspapers, corrugated, pulp substitutes, high-grade de-inking

Neenah Paper
1400 Holcomb Bridge Road
Roswell, GA 30076
tel: (800) 241-3405

Gilman Paper Company
1000 Osborne Street
P.O. Box 878
Saint Marys, GA 31558
tel: (912) 882-4241
contact: Alan Harrelson
mat'l handled: pulp substitutes

Union Camp Corp.
P.O. Box 570
Savannah, GA 31402
tel: (912) 238-6000
mat'l handled: corrugated

Paper-Pak Products, Inc.
One Paper-Pak Parkway
Washington, GA 30673
mat'l handled: pulp substitutes, high-grade de-inking

Idaho

Potlatch Corp.
Pulp, Paperboard & Packaging Group
P.O. Box 1016
Lewiston, ID 83501
tel: (208) 799-0123
contacts: Charles R. Pottenger (VP); G.D. Cran (Mill Manager)
mat'l handled: newspapers

Illinois

FSC Paper Company
13101 S. Pulaski Road
Alsip, IL 60658
tel: (708) 389-8520
fax: (708) 389-8237
mat'l handled: mixed papers, newspapers, pulp substitutes, high-grade de-inking

Jefferson Smurfit Corp.
10 Cut Street
P.O. Box 9021
Alton, IL 62002
tel: (618) 463-6212
mat'l handled: mixed papers, corrugated

Aurora Paperboard Div.
The Davey Co.
705 N. Fransworth Avenue
Aurora, IL 60507
tel: (708) 898-4231
fax: (708) 898-5763
contact: John C. Dodd (President)
mat'l handled: mixed paper

Jefferson-Smurfit Corporation
450 East North Avenue
Carol Stream, IL 60188
tel: (708) 260-3600
contact: Phil Ohst
mat'l handled: all grades paper

Chicago Paperboard Corp.
900 N. Ogden Avenue
Chicago, IL 60622
tel: (312) 997-3131
mat'l handled: mixed papers, newspapers, corrugated

Packaging Corp. of America
1603 Orrington Avenue
Evanston, IL 60204
tel: (708) 492-5713
(708) 492-4458
contacts: Mark Smith; Warren Hazelton

Moore Business Forms & Systems Division
1205 North Milwaukee Avenue
Glenview, IL 60025-2496
tel: (708) 480-3000
contacts: Gorlyn H. Bronstad; Robert C. Sweeney
mat'l handled: secondary fiber, wood chips, wood pulp

Ivex Corp.
292 Logan Avenue
Joliet, IL 60433
tel: (815) 740-3838
fax: (815) 740-6481
contacts: Lew Brown (VP—Mill Division); Ken Meyer (Sales Manager)
mat'l handled: mixed papers, corrugated, pulp substitutes

Manville Sales Corp.
P.O. Box 3429

Joliet, IL 60434
tel: (815) 744-1545
mat'l handled: newspapers

The Quaker Oats Co.
1650 S. 2nd Street
P.O. Box 520
Pekin, IL 61554
tel: (309) 346-4118
fax: (309) 346-2150
contacts: Warren Feerer (Plant Manager); Lonnie Gossage (Production Manager)
mat'l handled: newspapers, corrugated

Ivex Corporation
Paper Mill Div.
Foot of Sloan Street
P.O. Box 1820
Peoria, IL 61656
tel: (309) 686-3830
fax: (309) 686-0324
contact: Dennis Potts (Plant Manager)
mat'l handled: corrugated, pulp substitutes

The Celotex Corporation
901 South Front
Quincy, IL 62301
tel: (217) 224-3800
fax: (217) 224-9057
contact: J.T. McCluskey (Plant Manager)
mat'l handled: newspapers, corrugated

Sonoco Products Co.
Hawick at Prairie Avenue
P.O. Box 327
Rockton, IL 61072
tel: (815) 624-8891
fax: (815) 624-7921
mat'l handled: mixed paper, newspapers, corrugated

Georgia-Pacific Corp.
Hopper Paper Div.
Elm Street and Hopper Drive
P.O. Box 369
Taylorville, IL 62568
tel: (217) 824-9611
contact: Thomas J. Clark (General Manager)
mat'l handled: pulp substitutes

Indiana

Kieffer Paper Mills, Inc.
1220 W. Spring Street
Brownstown, IN 47220
tel: (812) 358-4150
contact: Tom Haas
mat'l handled: mixed papers, newspapers, corrugated, high-grade de-inking

Container Corp. of America
S. Main Street
P.O. Box 278
Carthage, IN 46115
tel: (317) 565-6111
fax: (317) 565-6225
contacts: John Fay (General Manager); Sam Gray (Product Manager)
mat'l handled: corrugated

Regal Industries, Route 1
P.O. Box 46
Crothersville, IN 47229
tel: (812) 793-2214
contact: Chuck Rose
mat'l handled: mixed papers

Rock-Tenn Co.
Route 1
P.O. Box 1A
Eaton, IN 47338
tel: (317) 396-3317
contact: Stan Collins (VP)
mat'l handled: mixed papers, newspapers, corrugated

Georgia-Pacific Corp.
2nd Place and Waite Street
Gary, IN 46404
tel: (219) 882-1640
mat'l handled: corrugated, pulp substitutes, high-grade de-inking

Packaging Corp. of America
300 W. Main Street
Griffith, IN 46319
tel: (219) 924-4105
fax: (219) 924-1234
contact: Ron Bullock (Plant Manager)
mat'l handled: newspapers

Keyes Fibre Co.
6629 Indianapolis Boulevard
Hammond, IN 46320
tel: (219) 844-8950
contact: Kenneth Orze (Plant Manager)
mat'l handled: newspapers, corrugated

VISY Board Packaging Co.
Subs. of Pratt Group Co.
P.O. Box 366
Hartford City, IN 47348
tel: (317) 348-5440
mat'l handled: mixed papers, newspapers, corrugated

Beveridge Paper Co., Inc.
717 W. Washington Street
Indianapolis, IN 46204
tel: (317) 635-4391
contact: Carl Lalioff
mat'l handled: pulp substitutes, newspapers, corrugated

Jefferson Smurfit Corp.
40 Chestnut Street
P.O. Box 5149
Lafayette, IN 47903
tel: (317) 423-5631
contact: David Mosher (General Manager)
mat'l handled: mixed papers, newspapers, corrugated

Inland Container Corporation
Cayuga Road
P.O. Box 428
Newport, IN 47966
tel: (317) 492-3341
contact: Dave Fox (Purchasing Agent)
mat'l handled: old corrugated containers

Energy Control Inc.
804 W. Mill Street
Ossian, IN 46777
tel: (219) 622-7614
fax: (219) 622-7604
contact: Kent Ringger (President)
mat'l handled: newspaper

Weston Paper & Mfg. Co.
2001 N. 19th Street
P.O. Box 238
Terre Haute, IN 47808
tel: (812) 234-6688
contact: Gene Rohrback
mat'l handled: corrugated
Planned expansion and upgrade of OCC recycling plant for 1991-1992.

Jefferson Smurfit Corp.
455 W. Factory Street
Wabash, IN 46992
tel: (219) 563-3102
mat'l handled: mixed papers, newspapers, corrugated, pulp substitutes

Iowa

Consolidated Packaging Corp.
P.O. Box 250
Fort Madison, IA 52627
tel: (319) 372-3152
contact: John Huprich
mat'l handled: corrugated

Jefferson-Smurfit Corporation
1601 Tri-View Avenue
Sioux City, IA 51103
tel: (712) 252-3861
mat'l handled: corrugated

Packaging Corp. of America
South Siegel Street
P.O. Box 117
Tama, IA 52339
tel: (515) 484-2884
fax: (515) 484-4234
contacts: J. Pogue (General Manager); Cecil Bearden (Superintendent); Allan Atchison (Waste Procurement)
mat'l handled: mixed papers, newspapers, corrugated, high-grade de-inking

Kansas

Republic Paperboard Co.
1st & Halstead Streets
P.O. Box 1267
Hutchinson, KS 67504
tel: (316) 662-2331
contact: Dale Wilson (Purchasing Manager—Waste Paper)
mat'l handled: mixed papers, newspapers, corrugated, pulp substitutes, high-grade de-inking

Tamko Asphalt Products of Kansas, Inc.
P.O. Box 326
Phillipsburg, KS 67661
tel: (913) 543-2156
contact: Dale Streit
mat'l handled: mixed papers, corrugated

Kentucky

Willamette Industries, Inc.
P.O. Box 130
Hawesville, KY 42348
tel: (502) 927-6961
contact: Arnie Elliott
mat'l handled: corrugated

Temple-Insland Inc.
Maysville, KY
Considering planned new mill and recycling plant—1993.

Scott Paper Co.
Owensboro, KY
Planned new mill; possibly will include de-inking plant.

Louisiana

Gaylord Container Ltd.
P.O. Box 1060
Bogalusa, LA 70427
tel: (504) 732-8001
mat'l handled: corrugated

Willamette Industries, Inc.
P.O. Box 377
Campti, LA 71411
tel: (318) 476-3392
mat'l handled: corrugated

Boise Cascade Corp.
Taylor Rd.
P.O. Box 1060
Deridder, LA 70634
tel: (318) 463-4461
contact: N. David Spence (VP—Southern Operations)
mat'l handled: corrugated

Stone Container Corp.
Mill Street
Hodge, LA 71247
tel: (318) 259-4421
contact: M.L. Burn (General Manager)
mat'l handled: corrugated, pulp substitutes

Southeast Recycling Corp.
246 St. George
P.O. Box 10557
Jefferson, LA 70181
tel: (504) 733-1954
fax: (504) 734-9248
matl handled: news, CPO, white, color

Valentine Paper Co.
P.O. Box 280
Lockport, LA 70374-0280
tel: (504) 532-3313
contact: George Dillon (President)
mat'l handled: pulp substitutes

Celotex Corp.
P.O. Box 26
Marrero, LA 70073
tel: (504) 341-5671
contact: V. Puls (Product Supervisor)
mat'l handled: newspapers

Georgia-Pacific Corp.
Port Hudson Div.
P.O. Box 430
Zachary, LA 70791
tel: (504) 654-2761
contact: Jerry Kincaid (General Manager)
mat'l handled: pulp substitutes

G.S. Roofing Products Co.
620 Aero Drive
Shreveport, LA 71102
tel: (318) 677-2701
contact: W.E. McClung (Plant Manager)
mat'l handled: mixed papers, corrugated

Manville Forest Products Corp.
1000 Jonesboro Road
P.O. Box 35800
West Monroe, LA 71294-5800
tel: (318) 362-2000
contact: Grant Webb
mat'l handled: mixed papers, corrugated

Maine

Statler Tissue Co.
Maple St.
P.O. Box 587
Augusta, ME 04330
tel: (207) 623-4731
mat'l handled: corrugated, pulp substitutes

Eastern Fine Paper, Inc.
P.O. Box 129
Brewer, ME 04412
tel: (207) 989-7070
contact: Rob Brooks

mat'l handled: pulp substitutes

Yorktowne Paper Mills of Maine, Inc.
721 Water Street
P.O. Box 420
Gardiner, ME 04345
tel: (207) 582-3230
mat'l handled: mixed papers, newspapers, corrugated, pulp substitutes

Lincoln Pulp & Paper Co., Inc.
Subsidiary of Preco Corp.
Lincoln, ME 04457
tel: (207) 794-6721
contact: Robert W. Ackerman, President
mat'l handled: pulp substitutes

James River Corp.
Old Town Mill
Old Town, ME 04468
tel: (207) 827-7711
contact: J.W. Griffith (Director Mill Operations)
mat'l handled: pulp substitutes

Caithness King Inc.
Pejepscot, ME
Planned new mill with flotation deinking; projected 50% each, newspaper and magazines.

Scott Paper Co.
Somerset Mill
RFD 3
Skowhegan, ME 04976
mat'l handled: pulp substitutes

Keyes Fibre Co.
Upper College Ave.
Waterville, ME 04901
tel: (207) 873-3351
mat'l handled: newspapers, corrugated, pulp substitutes

S.D. Warren Co.
Div. of Scott Paper Co.
89 Cumberland Street
Westbrook, ME 04092
tel: (207) 856-6911
contact: Charles S. Rose (VP, Resource Manager)
mat'l handled: pulp substitutes

Scott Paper Co.
14 Benton Avenue
Winslow, ME 04901
tel: (207) 872-2751
contact: Daniel Veilleux
mat'l handled: high-grade de-inking

Georgia-Pacific Corp.
Northeast Div.
Mill Street
Woodland, ME 04694
tel: (207) 427-3111
contact: Jerry L. Robinson (Resource Manager)
mat'l handled: pulp substitutes

Maryland

The Cheasapeake Paperboard Co.
Fort Avenue & Woodall Street
Baltimore, MD 21230
tel: (301) 752-1842
fax: (301) 837-5526
contact: C.J. Smith (President)
mat'l handled: mixed papers, newspapers, pulp substitutes

TRI-State Envelope Corporation
6900 Faigle Road
Beltsville, MD 20705
tel: (301) 953-3570
contact: David Zukerberg

Simkins Industries, Inc.—Maryland Board Div.
P.O. Box 3249
Cantonsville, MD 21228
tel: (301) 747-5100
contact: Vernon Russell (Purchasing Agent/Administrative Manager)
mat'l handled: mixed papers, newspapers, corrugated, pulp substitutes

Weyerhaeuser Paper Co.
Weyerhaeuser Recycling Div.
7270 Park Circle Drive
Dorsey, MD 21076
tel: (301) 796-7000
fax: (301) 796-0234
contacts: Keith McKale (Plant Manager); Sharon Sands (East Coast Sales Manager); Alda Little and Jamie Waldren (Service Representatives)
mat'l handled: high-grades, OCC, paper only

Southeast Recycling Corp.
Silver Spring Division

9001 Brookville Road
Silver Spring, MD 20910
tel: (301) 589-4002
fax: (301) 588-8436
contacts: Rob Barnwell (Area Manager); Tony Greene (Collection Programs Manager; Dan Kaplan (Division Manager Grader)
mat'l handled: newspaper, OCC, CPO, aluminum and glass

Massachusetts

Baldwinville Products, Inc.
Mill Street
Baldwinville, MA 01436
tel: (508) 939-5359
contact: Lawrence Zanga

National Fiber Insulation
3 Depot Street
Belchertown, MA 01007
tel: (413) 283-8747
contact: Mr. Fusco (President)
mat'l handled: newspaper

Hyde Park Paper, Inc.
892 River Street
Hyde Park, MA 02136
tel: (617) 361-3500
fax: (617) 361-5077
contact: David Weinstein (President)

Perkit Folding Box Corp.
36 Poydras Street
Mattapan, MA 02126
tel: (617) 361-1057
contact: Mr. Plummer
mat'l handled: mixed papers, newspapers, corrugated, pulp substitutes

Crane & Co., Inc.
30 South Street
Boston, MA 01226
tel: (413) 684-2600
mat'l handled: pulp substitutes, high-grade deinking

James River Corp.
Main Street
P.O. Box 1370
Boston, MA 01463
mat'l handled: mixed papers

Baldwinville Products, Inc., Subsidiary of Erving Paper Mills
P.O. Box 158
Erving, MA 01344-0158
mat'l handled: mixed papers, newspapers, corrugated, pulp substitutes, high-grade de-inking

Erving Paper Mills
47 E. Main Street
P.O. Box 158
Erving, MA 01344
tel: (508) 544-2711
contact: Larry Zanga
mat'l handled: pulp substitutes, high-grade de-inking

James River-Fitchburg Div.
Old Princeton Road
Fitchburg, MA 01420
tel: (508) 345-2161
contact: Henry Finnegan
mat'l handled: pulp substitutes

Haverhill Paperboard Corp.
100 S. Kimball Street, N.E.
P.O. Box 31
Haverhill, MA 01830
tel: (617) 289-9400
contact: D. Stewart (Purchasing Manager)
mat'l handled: mixed papers, newspapers, corrugated, pulp substitutes

Sonoco Products Co.
2 Sargeant Street
Holyoke, MA 01040
tel: (413) 536-9077
(413) 536-4546
fax: (413) 536-0165
contacts: Tom Fournier; Cas Biela
mat'l handled: mixed papers, newspapers, corrugated, pulp substitutes

Patriot Paper Co.
Hyde Park, MA
Planned mill opening with flotation de-inking system—approximately 1991.

Merrimac Paper Co., Inc.
9 S. Canal Street
Lawrence, MA 01842
tel: (508) 683-2754
fax: (508) 975-2708
contact: Albert Evans (President, CEO)

mat'l handled: newspapers, pulp substitutes

Newark Atlantic Paperboard Corp.
250 Canal Street
Lawrence, MA 01842
tel: (508) 687-7100
fax: (508) 682-4306
contact: Robert Quinlan (VP and General Manager)
mat'l handled: mixed papers, newspapers, corrugated, pulp substitutes

Kimberly-Clark Corp., Specialty Products
Lee, MA 01238
tel: (413) 243-1000
fax: (413) 243-4255
contact: W. Larmon (Mills Manager)
mat'l handled: pulp substitutes

American Paper Recycling Corp.
87 Central Street
P.O. Box 258
Mansfield, MA 02048
tel: (508) 339-5551
fax: (508) 339-6346
contacts: Helena Fisher (Sales Manager); Robert J. Castelli (Plant Manager)
mat'l handled: high-grades, pulp substitutes

Natick Paperboard Corp.
N. Main Street
P.O. Box 89
Natick, MA 01760
tel: (508) 653-9100
contact: Ed Melton
mat'l handled: mixed papers, newspapers, corrugated

Seaman Paper Co. of Mass., Inc.
Main Street
Otter River, MA 01436
tel: (508) 939-2146
fax: (508) 939-2359
contacts: George Jones (President); Charles Smith (VP—Purchasing)
mat'l handled: high-grade pulp substitutes

James River-Pepperell, Inc.
Main Street
P.O. Box 1370
Pepperell, MA 01463
tel: (508) 433-6951
contact: Paul Roussel

Westfield River Paper Co., Inc.
Station Road
Russell, MA 01071
tel: (413) 862-3636
fax: (413) 862-4538
contact: John Conner (Mill Manager)
mat'l handled: pulp substitutes

Cascades Diamond, Inc.
Church Street
P.O. Box 627
Thorndike, MA 01079
tel: (413) 283-8301
fax: (413) 283-4756
contact: Ron Beaumont (Mill Manager)
mat'l handled: mixed papers, pulp substitutes

Strathmore Paper Co.
S. Broad Street
Westfield, MA 01085
tel: (413) 568-9111
contact: Stuart Miller (Plant Superintendent)
mat'l handled: pulp substitutes

James River Corp.
Front Street
P.O. Box 6001
West Springfield, MA 01090-6001
tel: (413) 736-4554
fax: (413) 736-6630
contacts: William S. Linnell (VP, General Manager)
mat'l handled: pulp substitutes

Michigan

Fletcher Paper Co.
318 W. Fletcher Street
Alpena, MI 49707
tel: (517) 354-2131
fax: (517) 356-6327
contact: Paul Hoelderle (President)
mat'l handled: pulp substitutes

Michigan Paperboard Corp.
79 E. Fountain Street
Battle Creek, MI 49016
tel: (616) 963-4004
mat'l handled: mixed papers, newspapers, corrugated, high-grade deinking

Waldorf Corp.
177 Angell Street

Battle Creek, MI 49016-3433
tel: (616) 963-5511
mat'l handled: mixed papers, newspapers, corrugated, pulp substitutes, high-grade de-inking

Procter & Gamble Paper Products
547 S. Main Street
Cheboygan, MI 49721
mat'l handled: pulp substitutes

Simplex Industries Inc.
E. 3rd Street
Constantine, MI 49042
tel: (616) 435-2425
mat'l handled: mixed papers, corrugated, pulp substitutes

Detroit River Paper Co.
9125 W. Jefferson Avenue
Detroit, MI 48209
tel: (313) 842-0042
contact: William P. Roschek (VP and General Manager)
mat'l handled: pulp substitutes

Packaging Corp. of America
P.O. Box 316
Manistee
Filer City, MI 49660
tel: (616) 723-9951
fax: (616) 723-9951
contact: Fred J. Fragomeli (VP, Manager)
mat'l handled: corrugated

Georgia-Pacific Corp.
2425 King Highway
Kalamazoo, MI 49003
tel: (616) 382-2890
mat'l handled: pulp substitutes, high-grade de-inking

James River Corp.
Paperboard Pkg. Group
243 E. Patersen Street
Kalamazoo, MI 49007
tel: (616) 383-5000
mat'l handled: mixed papers, newpapers, corrugated, pulp substitutes

Packaging Corp. of America
P.O. Box 316
Mainstee, MI 49660
tel: (616) 723-9951

Manistique Papers Inc.
453 South Mackinac
Manistique, MI 49854
tel: (906) 341-2175
fax: (906) 341-5635
contacts: Leif Christensen (President and General Manager); Eric Bourdo (Manager—Recycling Operations); Ed Leonard (Wastepaper Buyer); Larry Kiski (General Sales Manager)
mat'l handled: coated magazines, coated sections

Menominee Paper Co., Inc.
144 First Street
P.O. Box 300
Menominee, MI 49858
tel: (906) 863-5595
contact: Don Beason
mat'l handled: corrugated, pulp substitutes

Jefferson Smurfit Corp.
Industrial Packaging Div.
1151 W. Elm Avenue
Monroe, MI 48161
tel: (313) 241-7776
contact: Robert H. Degraer (General Manager)
mat'l handled: mixed papers, corrugated

Monroe Paper Co.
1220 E. Elm Avenue
Monroe, MI 48161
tel: (313) 241-7700
contact: Nathan Lee
mat'l handled: mixed papers, newspapers, corrugated, high-grade de-inking

S.D. Warren Co.
Div. Scott Paper Co.
2400 Lakeshore Drive
Muskegon, MI 49443
tel: (616) 755-3761
contact: Norman A. Russell (Mill Superintendent)
mat'l handled: pulp substitutes

French Paper Company
100 French Street
Niles, MI 49120
tel: (616) 683-1100
contact: J.E. French (CEO)
mat'l handled: paper manufacturer

Simplicity Pattern Co., Inc.
901 Wayne Street
Niles, MI 49121
tel: (616) 683-4100
contact: Mr. Stewart (Purchasing)
mat'l handled: mixed papers, pulp substitutes

Stone Container Corp
One Superior Way
Ontonagon, MI 49953
tel: (906) 884-2021
contact: Ron Howard (General Manager)
mat'l handled: corrugated

Mead Corp.
P.O. Box 187
Otsego, MI 49078
tel: (616) 692-6211
contact: Howard Klein

Menasha Corp.
N. Farmer Street
P.O. Box 155
Otsego, MI 49078
tel: (616) 692-6141
contact: Jeff Burleigh (Purchasing Manager); Jim Porter (General Manager)
mat'l handled: corrugated

Rock-Tenn. Co.
Paperboard Products Div.
431 Helen Avenue
Otsego, MI 49078
tel: (616) 692-6211
fax: (616) 692-6581
contacts: Walter K. Lancaster (Mill Manager)
mat'l handled: mixed papers, corrugated

Big M Paperboard, Inc.
6240 E. US-223
P.O. Box 135
Palmyra, MI 49268
tel: (515) 263-5160
contact: Kathleen Sorensen
mat'l handled: mixed papers, newspapers, corrugated, pulp substitutes

James River Corp
KVP Group
100 Island Avenue
Parchment, MI 49004
tel: (616) 383-5000
mat'l handled: pulp substitutes

Simpson Plainwell Paper Co.
200 Allegan Street
Plainwell, MI 49080
tel: (616) 685-6504
contact: Bryce Seidi (Operations Manager)
mat'l handled: pulp substitutes

Dunn Paper Div. James River Corp.
KVP Group
218 Riverview Street
P.O. Box 227
Port Huron, MI 48061-0227
tel: (313) 984-5523
contacts: James R. Scohy (VP and Resource Manager)
mat'l handled: pulp substitutes

James River-Rochester, Inc.
340 Mill Street
Rochester, MI 48063
tel: (313) 651-8121
contact: Stanley S. Luczycki (Resource Manager)
mat'l handled: corrugated

Converters Paperboard
7734 Childsdale Road
Rockford, MI 49341
tel: (616) 866-3421
mat'l handled: newspapers, corrugated, pulp substitutes, high-grade de-inking

Simpson Paper Co.
Washington Street
Vicksburg, MI 49097
tel: (616) 649-0510
mat'l handled: pulp substitutes

White Pigeon Paper Co.
P.O. Box 277
White Pigeon, MI 49099
tel: (616) 483-7601
contact: James V. LaMarre (President)
mat'l handled: mixed papers, newspapers, corrugated, pulp substitutes

Peninsular Paper Co.
1000 N. Huron Street
Ypsilanti, MI 48917
tel: (313) 482-2600
mat'l handled: pulp substitutes

Minnesota

Grand Rapids
Blandin Paper Co.
115 First Street
S.W. Grand Rapids, MN 55744-3699
tel: (218) 327-6200
fax: (218) 327-6212
mat'l handled: pulp substitutes

Hennepin Paper Co
100 S.W. 5th Avenue
P.O. Box 90
Little Falls, MN 58343
tel: (612) 632-3684
contact: Alan Loken
mat'l handled: pulp substitutes

Waldorf Corp.
2250 Wabash Avenue
St. Paul, MN 55114
tel: (612) 641-4874
fax: (612) 641-4791
mat'l handled: mixed papers, newspapers, corrugated, pulp substitutes

CertainTeed Corp
3303 4th Avenue
E. P.O. Box 177
Shakopee, MN 55379
tel: (612) 445-6450
contact: Roland Doerr
mat'l handled: mixed papers, newspapers

Mississippi

Atlas Roofing Corp.
Route #5
Valley Road
P.O. Box 5777
Meridian, MS 39301
tel: (601) 483-7111
contact: Jim Wilhelm (Purchasing Agent)
mat'l handled: mixed papers, newspaper, corrugated

Georgia-Pacific Corp.
P.O. Box 608
Monticello, MS 39654
tel: (601) 587-7711
contact: David Bouin
mat'l handled: corrugated

Manville Building Materials Corp.
Liberty Road
P.O. Box 1288
Natchez, MS 39120
tel: (601) 445-4641
mat'l handled: newspapers

Natchez Paper Mill
Cargill and Majorca Roads
Natchez, MS 39120
tel: (601) 442-1621

Burrows Paper Corp.
Pickens, MS 39146
tel: (601) 468-2172
fax: (601) 468-2860
contact: Charles Simpson (Plant Manager)
mat'l handled: pulp substitutes

International Paper Co.
P.O. Box 950
Vicksburg. MS 39180
tel: (601) 638-3665
contact: Gary Hemphill
mat'l handled: corrugated

Missouri

Huebert Fibreboard, Inc.
East Morgan Street
P.O. Box 167
Boonville, Missouri 65223
tel: (816)882-2704
contact: Gerald Heubert
mat'l handled: mixed papers

Tamko Asphalt Products Inc.
Rangeline and Newman Road
P.O. Box 1404
Joplin, Missouri 64802
tel: (417) 624-7410
contact: Walt Conard
mat'l handled: mixed papers, corrugated

United States Gypsum Co.
1115 Armour Road
North Kansas City, Missouri 64116
tel: (816) 471-4298
mat'l handled: mixed papers, newspapers, corrugated, pulp substitutes

Montana

Stone Container Corp.
P.O. Drawer D
Missoula, MO 59806
tel: (406) 626-4451
contact: L. Clayton Smith (General Manager)
mat'l handled: corrugated

New Hampshire

James River Corp.
650 Main Street
Berlin, New Hampshire 03570
tel: (603) 752-4600
contact: Mark C. Tasso (Manager)
mat'l handled: pulp operations, mixed papers, pulp substitutes

CPM Inc.
P.O. Box 1280
131 Sullivan Street
Claremont, NH 03743
tel: (603) 542-2592
fax: (603) 542-4974
contact: Harvey D. Hill (CEO)
mat'l handled: pulp substitutes

Groveton Paper Board, Inc.
Mechanic Street
Groveton, NH 03582
tel: (603) 636-1154
contact: Joe Lacroix
mat'l handled: corrugated, pulp substitutes

Ashuelot Paper Co.
P.O. Box 26
Hinsdale, NH 03451
tel: (603) 336-5961
contact: Brad Silver
mat'l handled: pulp substitutes

Paper Services Ltd.
P.O. Box 45
Hinsdale, NH 03451
tel: (603) 336-5311
fax: (603) 239-8861
contact: Russell O'Neal (President and Treasurer)
mat'l handled: pulp substitutes

Penacook Fibre Co.
12 N. Main Street
Penacook, NH 03301
tel: (603) 753-6521
contact: Bud Collins
mat'l handled: newspapers, corrugated

Papertech Corp.—Boxboard Div.
P.O. Box 247
Contoocook, NH 03229
tel: (603) 746-3500
fax: (603) 746-3505
contact: Joseph L. Artiga (President)
mat'l handled: mixed papers, newspapers, corrugated

New Jersey

Camden Paper Board
267 Jefferson Street
Camden, NJ 08104
tel: (609) 963-5900
mat'l handled: mixed papers, newspapers, corrugated

United States Gypsum Co.
1255 Raritan Road
P.O. Box 978
Clark, NJ 07066
tel: (908) 388-9100
contact: Bob Helminski
mat'l handled: mixed papers, newspapers, corrugated, pulp substitutes

Recycled Paperboard, Inc. of Clifton
One Ackerman Avenue
Clifton, NJ 07011
tel: (201) 546-0030
fax: (201) 546-1349
contact: Frank Costa
mat'l handled: CBO Mix

Georgia-Pacific Corp.
P.O. Box 338
Delair, NJ 08110
tel: (609) 663-6015
mat'l handled: corrugated, pulp substitutes, high-grade de-inking

Garden State Paper Company, Inc.
River Drive Center 2
Elmwood Park, NJ 07407
tel: (201) 796-0600
fax: (201) 796-8470
contact: Dr. James L. Burke (President and COO)

mat'l handled: newsprint

Marcal Paper Mills, Inc.
1 Market Street
Elmwood Park, NJ 07407
tel: (201) 796-4000
contact: E. Trovato
mat'l handled: pulp substitutes, high-grade de-inking

Garden State Paper Co., Inc.
950 River Drive
Garfield, NJ 07026
tel: (201) 772-8700
(201) 796-0600
fax: (201) 772-9232
contact: Ernie Roseowian
mat'l handled: newspapers

Millen Industries, Inc.
93 North Avenue
P.O. Box 257
Garwood, NJ 07027
tel: (908) 789-2424
fax: (908) 789-9461
contact: A.Polo
mat'l handled: mixed papers, newspapers, corrugated

Riegel-Fitchburg
Div. James River Corp.
Hughesville, NJ 08848
tel: (908) 995-2411
contact: Kenneth P. Blessing (Operations Manager)
mat'l handled: pulp substitutes

The Davey Co.
164 Laidlaw Avenue
P.O. Box 8128
Five Corners Stn.
Jersey City, NJ 07308
tel: (201) 653-0606
fax: (201) 653-0872
contacts: Tom Morrow (Plant Engineer); Jim Bottoriff (Mill Manager)
mat'l handled: mixed papers

James River Corp., Riegel Div.
Route 619, P.O. Box R
Milford, NJ 08848
tel: (908) 995-2411
contact: Bill Turner
mat'l handled: pulp substitutes

Celotex Corp.
Herbert and Market Streets
Perth Amboy, NJ 08862
tel: (201) 826-6881
mat'l handled: mixed papers

Lowe Paper Co.
River Street
P.O. Box 239
Ridgefield, NJ 07657
tel: (201) 945-4900
contacts: George Clark, Mike Dalton, Anna Western, P.A.
mat'l handled: newspapers, corrugated, pulp substitutes, white ledger, double lined kraft, corrugated clippings

Riegel-Fitchburg
Div. James River Corp.
Warren Glen, NJ 08848
tel: (201) 995-2411
contact: L.E. Carlson (Operations Manager)
mat'l handled: pulp substitutes

Homasote Company
Lower Ferry Road
West Trenton, NJ 08628
tel: (609) 883-3300
fax: (609) 530-1584
contact: Shanley E. Flicker (President)
mat'l handled: #6 regular news, newspapers

New Mexico

Leatherback Industries
1621 Williams Street, S.E.
Albuquerque, NM 87102
tel: (505) 242-5246
mat'l handled: mixed papers, corrugated

New York

Tagsons Paper, Inc.
P.O. Box 1888
Albany, NY 12201-1999
tel: (518) 462-0200
fax: (518) 462-9717
contact: Eugene J. Galante (President)

Sonoco Products Co.
58-61 Forest Avenue
Amsterdam, NY 12010
tel: (518) 842-1010

mat'l handled: mixed papers, newspapers, corrugated

Specialty Paperboard, Inc.
Latex Fiber Products, Latex Mill
P.O. Box 130
Beaver Falls, NY 13305
tel: (315) 346-1111
mat'l handled: corrugated, high-grade deinking

Brownville Specialty Paper Products, Inc.
Bridge Street
Brownville, NY 13615
tel: (315) 782-4500
fax: (315) 782-3964
contact: Gene Rood (President)
mat'l handled: recycled paper boards

Climax Mfg. Co.
Paperboard Div.
30 Champion Street
Carthage, NY 13619
tel: (315) 493-2120
fax: (315) 493-0812
contact: Gerald Slote (General Manager)
mat'l handled: mixed papers, newspapers, corrugated, pulp substitutes

James River Corp.
695 West End Avenue
Carthage, NY 13619
tel: (315) 493-3010
contact: Ray Wheeler (Resource Manager)
mat'l handled: mixed papers, corrugated, pulp substitutes

Fort Orange Paper Co., Inc.
1900 River Road
Castleton-on-Hudson, NY 12033
tel: (518) 732-7722
contact: Dan Luizzi
mat'l handled: mixed papers, newspapers, corrugated, high-grade de- inking

The Columbia Corp.
P.O. Box 330
Chatham, NY 12037
tel: (518) 392-4000
contact: William G. Ryan (Superintendent—Mixed Papers)
mat'l handled: newspapers, corrugated, pulp substitutes

International Paper Co.
Pine Street
Corinth, NY 12822
tel: (518) 654-9031
Cornwall Paper Mills Co.
Forge Hill Road
Cornwall, NY 12518
tel: (914) 534-2525
contact: Grace San Giacomo
mat'l handled: newspapers, corrugated

McIntyre Paper Co., Inc.
131 Mill Street
Fayetteville, NY 13066
tel: (315) 637-3166
contact: F.D. Fournier
mat'l handled: mixed papers, pulp substitutes

Scott Paper Co.
Packaged Products Div.
Fort Edward, NY 12828
tel: (518) 747-4151
mat'l handled: pulp substitutes

Armstrong World Industries, Inc.
RD 2, Box 184
Fulton, NY 13069
tel: (315) 598-4271
contact: Edward Kronenberg (Plant Manager)
mat'l handled: mixed papers, newspapers, corrugated, pulp substitutes

Finch, Pruyn & Co., Inc.
1 Glen Street
Glens Falls, NY 12801-0396
tel: (518) 793-2541
fax: (518) 793-7364
contact: Richard J. Carota (Chairman, President, and CEO)
mat'l handled: pulp substitutes

Bio-Tech Mills, Inc.
RD #2
Greenwich, NY 12834
tel: (518) 692-7957
fax: (518) 692-7095
contact: Mr. Ferris
mat'l handled: all grades of secondary fiber

Stevens & Thompson Paper Co., Inc.
P.O. Box 206
Greenwich, NY 12834-0206
tel: (518) 692-2211
fax: (518) 692-9720

contacts: Lawrence Myers (V.P.—Operations); Emory Waldrip (President); Ray Stocker (V.P.—Finance); William Gnater (V.P.—Sales); Lawrence Reddon (Manager—Materials)
mat'l handled: coated book, black and white ledger, laser free C.P.O., high-grade de-inking

Lydall, Inc.
12 Davis Street
P.O. Box 400
Hoosick Falls, NY 12090
tel: (518) 686-7313
contact: Woodrow R. McKay (Plant Manager)
mat'l handled: pulp substitutes

Burrows Paper Corp.
501 W. Main Street
Little Falls, NY 13365
tel: (315) 823-2300
fax: (315) 823-2417
contact: Fred G. Scarano (Superintendent)
mat'l handled: pulp substitutes

Mohawk Valley Paper Co., Inc.
501 E. Main Street
Little Falls, NY 13365
tel: (315) 823-2300
contact: John Hart
mat'l handled: pulp substitutes

Domtar Gypsum
Stevens Street
P.O. Box 508
Lockport, NY 14094
tel: (716) 434-8881
contact: James Ganina
mat'l handled: newspapers, corrugated, pulp substitutes

Burrows Paper Corp.
Lyonsdale, NY 13368
tel: (315) 348-8491
fax: (315) 348-8002
contacts: John Hart; Rob Renzulli

The Martisco Paper Co., Inc.
4747 Route 174
P.O. Box 198
Marcellus, NY 13108
tel: (315) 673-2071
fax: (315) 673-4963
contact: Howard H. Spencer (General Manager)
mat'l handled: old newspaper, chip board, double lined kraft, corrugated

Tagsons Papers, Inc.
2 Waterford Road
Mechanicville, NY 12118
tel: (518) 462-0200
fax: (518) 664-9808
contact: Gary Boyea (VP—Manufacturing)
mat'l handled: mixed papers, newspapers, corrugated, pulp substitutes, high-grade de-inking

Repap Sales Corp.
99 Park Avenue
New York, NY 10018
tel: (212) 687-7111
contact: Eric Christensen

Westvaco Corp.
299 Park Avenue
New York, NY 10171
tel: (212) 688-5000
contact: John Luppino

Papyrus Newton Falls, Inc.
P.O. Box 253
Newton Falls, NY 13666
tel: (315) 848-3321
fax: (315) 848-2081
contacts: Leif Smedman (President); Dennis Bunnell (VP—Sales and Marketing)

Cascades Niagara Falls, Inc.
4001 Packard Road
P.O. Box 1830
Niagara Falls, NY 14302
tel: (716) 285-3681
contact: Suzanne Blanchet (General Manager)
mat'l handled: corrugated

Columbia Corp.
Route 67
North Hoosick, NY 12133
mat'l handled: mixed papers, newspapers, corrugated, pulp substitutes

Hammermill Papers Business
Oswego Mill
Mitchell Street
P.O. Box 238
Oswego, NY 13126-0238
tel: (315) 343-1581
contact: David E. Herlt, Mill Manager

mat'l handled: high-grade de-inking

Georgia-Pacific Corp.
327 Margaret Street
P.O. Box 789
Plattsburgh, NY 12901
tel: (518) 561-3500
mat'l handled: high-grade de-inking

Packaging Corp. of America
Molded Fibre Products Group
98 Weed Street Extension
Plattsburgh, NY 12901
tel: (518) 561-4880
fax: (518) 561-6968
contact: Stephen J. Cernak, Plant Manager
mat'l handled: pulp substitutes

Potsdam Paper Mills, Div. Little Rapids Corp.
Route #4
Potsdam, NY 13676
tel: (315) 265-4000
fax: (315) 265-4005
mat'l handled: pulp substitutes

Schoeller Technical Papers, Inc.
Centerville Rd.
P.O. Box 250
Pulaski, NY 13142-0250
tel: (315) 298-5133
fax: (315) 298-4337
contact: R.O. Gall (President and General Manager)
mat'l handled: pulp substitutes

Red Hook Paper, Inc.
24 Linden Ave.
Red Hook, NY 12571
tel: (914) 758-9200
fax: (914) 758-9200
contact: Barry A. Hull (President)
mat'l handled: newspaper and cardboard chipboard

Certified Document
1 Curlew
Rochester, NY 14606
tel: (718) 458-9873
mat'l handled: newspaper

Flower City Tissue Mills Co.
700 Driving Park Avenue
P.O. Box 13497
Rochester, NY 14613-0497
tel: (716) 458-9200
fax: (716) 458-3812
contacts: William F. Shafer III (President); William F. Shafer IV (Mill Manager)
mat'l handled: pulp substitutes

Spector Waste Paper Corp.
1436 Scottsville Road
Rochester, NY 14624
tel: (716) 235-8856
fax: (716) 235-0948
contacts: Morris Spector, Sidney Spector, David Greenfield
mat'l handled: CPO

Crown Zellerbach Corp.
1 River Street
South Glens Falls, NY 12801
tel: (518) 793-5684
mat'l handled: high-grade de-inking

James River Corp.
1 River Street
South Glens Falls, NY 12803
tel: (518) 793-5684
fax: (518) 793-2650

Harmon & Associates Corp.
86 Garden Street
Westbury, NY 11590
tel: (516) 997-3400
fax: (516) 997-3409
mat'l handled: broker, exporter, all grades (high and low)

North Carolina

Champion International
Park Street
P.O. Box C-10
Canton, NC 28716
tel: (704) 646-2000
contact: J. Oliver Blackwell (VP and Manager)
mat'l handled: pulp substitutes

Carolina Paper Board Corp.
443 Gardner Ave.
P.O. Box 668305
Charlotte, NC 28266
tel: (704) 376-7474
contact: William Wood
mat'l handled: mixed papers, newspapers, corrugated, pulp substitutes

Laurel Hill Paper Co.
P.O. Box 159
Cordova, NC 28330
tel: (919) 997-4526
contacts: L.V. Hogan (President)
mat'l handled: high-grade de-inking

Celotex Corp.
Old Mt. Olive Road
Goldsboro, NC 27530
tel: (919) 736-7520
mat'l handled: mixed papers, corrugated

U.S. Packaging, Inc.
P.O. Box 415
Maxton, NC 28364
tel: (919) 844-5293
contact: Ray Walden
mat'l handled: scrap label, envelope stock, no types of film

Cellu Products Div.
River Road
Patterson, NC 28661
tel: (704) 758-5151
fax: (704) 754-8567
contact: Garrett Manass
mat'l handled: pulp substitutes

Ecusta Corp., Div. P.H. Glatfelter Co.
P.O. Box 200
Pisgah Forest, NC 28768-0200
tel: (704) 877-2211
contact: W.F. Boswell (President)
mat'l handled: pulp substitutes

Weyerhaeuser Paper Co.
P.O. Box 787
Plymouth, NC 27962
tel: (919) 793-8111
fax: (919) 793-8154
contact: Lewis Tuttle
mat'l handled: corrugated

Champion International
Roanoke Avenue
P.O. Box 580
Roanoke Rapids, NC 27870
tel: (919) 537-6011
contact: Kevin Smith
mat'l handled: pulp substitutes

Halifax Paper Board Co., Inc.
Roanoke Avenue
P.O. Box 368
Roanoke Rapids, NC 27870
tel: (919) 537-4127
contacts: mixed papers, newspapers, corrugated, pulp substitutes

Canusa Corporation
P.O. Box 578
805 Midway Road
Rockingham, NC 28379
tel: (919) 895-7731
fax: (919) 895-9887
contact: Karen Smith (Broker)

Jackson Paper Mfg. Co.
Highways 19A and 23
P.O. Box 667
Sylva, NC 28779
tel: (704) 586-5534
contact: Johnny Extine
mat'l handled: corrugated

Ohio

Certain Teed Corp.
P.O. Box 600
Milan, OH 44846
tel: (419) 499-2581
contact: Cindy Rentz
mat'l handled: mixed papers, newspapers

Gaylord Container Ltd.
210 Water Street
Baltimore, OH 43105
tel: (614) 862-4161
contact: Joy Schwamberger
mat'l handled: corrugated

Ivex Corporation
Mill and Cleveland Streets
Chagrin Falls, OH 44022
tel: (216) 247-5530
contact: B. Glover
mat'l handled: pulp substitutes

Mead Corp.
Chillicothe Operations, Fine Paper Div.
401 S. Paint Street
Chillicothe, OH 45601
tel: (614) 772-3111
fax: (614) 772-3200
contact: Donald A. Russell (VP—Operations)
mat'l handled: pulp substitutes

Celotex Corp.
320 S. Wayne Avenue
Lockland, OH 45220
tel: (513) 792-8210

Cincinnati Paperboard Corp.
5500 Wooster Road
Cincinnati, OH 45226
tel: (513) 871-7112
contact: Charlie Brook (Buyer)
mat'l handled: mixed papers, newspapers, corrugated

Ohio Pulp Mills, Inc.
2100 Losantiville Road
Cincinnati, OH 45237
tel: (513) 631-7400
fax: (513) 351-2129
contact: Robert Mendelson (President)

PM Company
24 Triangle Park Drive
Cincinnati, OH 45246
tel: (800) 327-4359
contact: Jody Winters

Rock-Tenn Co.
Paperboard Products Div.
3347 Madison Road
Cincinnati, OH 45209
tel: (513) 871-5000
fax: (513) 533-2154
contact: J.B. Harvey (General Manager)
mat'l handled: mixed papers, corrugated, high-grade de-inking

Container Corp. of America
401 W. Mill Street
Circleville, OH 43113
tel: (614) 474-2146
mat'l handled: corrugated

Stone Container Corp.
500 N. 4th Street
Coshocton, OH 43812
tel: (614) 622-6543
mat'l handled: corrugated

Ampad
Courthouse Plaza Northeast
Dayton, OH 45463
tel: (800) 426-1368

Howard Paper Mills
354 S. Edwin C. Moses Boulevard
Box 982
Dayton, OH 45401-0982
tel: (800) 543-5010
(513) 224-1211
contacts: Jim Sherman or Nelson Boyer

Franklin Boxboard Corp.
50 E. 6th Street
P.O. Box 427
Franklin, OH 45005-0427
tel: (513) 746-6493
contact: Don Macspere
mat'l handled: mixed papers, newspapers, corrugated, high-grade de-inking

Georgia-Pacific Corp.
125 N. River Street
Franklin, OH 45005
tel: (513) 746-9941
mat'l handled: mixed papers, corrugated

United States Gypsum Co.
Gypsum, OH 43433
tel: (419) 734-3161
contact: Jim Wadsworth
mat'l handled: mixed papers, newspapers, corrugated, pulp substitutes

Beckett Paper Co.
Div. Hammermill Paper Co.
400 Dayton Street
Hamilton, OH 45011
tel: (513) 863-5641
fax: (513) 863-7782
contact: James E. Reid (VP—Marketing)
mat'l handled: pulp substitutes

Champion International
601 North B. Street
Hamilton, OH 45013
tel: (513) 868-6660
contact: J.D. Banks (VP—Operations Manager)
mat'l handled: pulp substitutes

Sonoco Products Company
831 South Memorial Drive
Lancater, OH 43130
tel: (614) 687-8875
fax: (614) 653-2924
contact: Rick Schein
mat'l handled: corrugated, news, DLK, mixed papers, newspapers

Erving Paper Mills

P.O. Box 15099
Lockland, OH 45215
tel: (513) 761-9500
contact: Don Kolda

Jefferson Smurfit Corp.
S. Cooper Avenue
Lockland, OH 45215
tel: (513) 821-2090
mat'l handled: mixed papers, newspapers, corrugated, pulp substitues

Cleaners Hanger Co.
670 17th Street, N.W.
P.O. Box 453
Massillon, OH 44646
tel: (216) 837-5151
mat'l handled: corrugated

Greif Board Corp.
9420 Warmington Street
P.O. Box 553
Massillon, OH 44648
tel: (216) 879-2101
mat'l handled: mixed papers, corrugated, pulp substitutes

Bay West
700 Columbia Avenue
P.O. Box 810
Middletown, OH 45042
tel: (513) 424-2999
fax: (513) 424-4999
contact: Bruce Hynes (VP and General Manager—Towel and Tissue Division)

Crystal Tissue Co.
3120 S. Verity Parkway
P.O. Box 449
Middletown, OH 45052
tel: (513) 423-0731
contact: Dan Price
mat'l handled: pulp substitues

Jefferson Smurfit Corp.
407 Charles Street
Middletown, OH 45042
tel: (513) 422-2772
mat'l handled: mixed papers, newspaper, corrugated, pulp substitutes

Middletown Paperboard Co.
427 Vanderveer Street
P.O. Box 29
Middletown, OH 45042
tel: (513) 422-6641
contact: Marvin Havens

Newark Boxboard Co.
427 Vanderveer Street
P.O. Box 914
Middletown, OH 45042-0914
mat'l handled: mixed papers, newspapers, corrugated

Simpson Paper Co.
Harding-Jones Mill
S. Main Street
P.O. Box 40
Middletown, OH 45042
mat'l handled: pulp substitutes

Sorg Paper Co.
Subsidiary of Moseinee Paper Corp.
901 Manchester Avenue
Middletown, OH 45042-0628
tel: (513) 420-5300
fax: (513) 420-5324
contact: Don Martin (VP and General Manager)
mat'l handled: mixed papers, corrugated, pulp substitutes, high-grade de-inking

Sonoco Products Co.
59 N. Main Street
P.O. Box 217
Munroe Falls, OH 44262
tel: (216) 688-6460
fax: (216) 688-6434
contacts: C.R. Hemphill (Plant Manager); A. Wiggins (Buyer/Office Manager)

Packaging Corp. of America
Industrial Street
Rittman, OH 44270
tel: (216) 925-0222
mat'l handled: mixed papers, newspapers, corrugated

Mactac
Printing Products Division
4560 Darrow Road
Stow, OH 44224
tel: (216) 688-1111
contact: Barry Madel

Valley Converting Co.
Loretta Avenue
P.O. Box 279

Toronto, OH 43964
tel: (614) 537-2152
mat'l handled: mixed papers, newspapers, coruugated, pulp substitutes

Howard Paper Mills, Inc.
W. Church Street
Urbana, OH 43078
tel: (513) 653-7151
fax: (513) 652-1722
contacts: D.L. Sprague (Manufacturing Superintendent)
mat'l handled: pulp substitutes

Appleton Paper, Inc.
1030 W. Alex.-Bellbrook Road
P.O. Box 68
West Carrollton, OH 45449
tel: (513) 859-8261
mat'l handled: pulp substitutes, high-grade de-inking

Cross Pointe Paper
Miami Mill
P.O. Box 66
West Carrollton, OH 45449
tel: (513) 859-5101
fax: (513) 865-6099
contact: Jobe Morrison (President)
mat'l handled: pulp substitutes, high-grade de-inking

Miami Paper Corp.
South Smith Street
P.O. Box 66
West Carrollton, OH 45449
tel: (513) 859-5101
contact: Barney Johnson

Oklahoma

Georgia-Pacific Corp.
2300 P St. N.E.
P.O. Box 908
Ardmore, OK 73401
tel: (405) 223-3760
contact: Neva Lindreth
mat'l handled: mixed papers, corrugated

Fort Howard Paper Co.
5600 Chandler Road
P.O. Box 1888
Muskogee, OK 74402-1888
tel: (918) 683-7671
mat'l handled: mixed papers, newspapers, corrugated, pulp substitutes, high-grade de-inking

Georgia-Pacific Corp.
P.O. Box 578
Pryor, OK 74361
tel: (918) 825-4100
mat'l handled: mixed papers, newspapers, corrugated, pulp substitutes

National Gypsum Co.
P.O. Box 428
Pryor, OK 74361
tel: (918) 825-0142
contact: John Cartwright

Robel Tissue Mills, Inc.
Route 3, P.O. Box 70
Pryor, OK 74361
tel: (918) 825-0616
contact: Michael Sage (VP)
mat'l handled: pulp substitutes, high-grade de-inking

Weyerhaeuser Co.
P.O. Drawer C
Valliant, OK 74764
tel: (405) 933-7211
mat'l handled: corrugated

Oregon

Willamette Industries Inc.
Albany Paper Mill
P.O. Box 339
Albany, OR 97321
tel: (503) 926-2281
fax: (503) 967-2343
contact: W.B. Hammond (Regional Manager)
mat'l handled: mixed papers

James River Corp.
Route 2, P.O. Box 2185
Clatskanie, OR 97016
tel: (503) 455-2221
contact: A.M. Neeley (VP)
mat'l handled: pulp substitutes

International Paper Co.
P.O. Box 854
Gardiner, OR 97441
tel: (503) 271-2184
mat'l handled: corrugated

James River Corp.
P.O. Box 215
Halsey, OR 97348
tel: (503) 369-2293
fax: (503) 369-1221
contact: Charles Warren (VP)
mat'l handled: pulp substitutes

Smurfit Newspaper Corp.
P.O. Box 70
Newberg, OR 97132
tel: (503) 538-2151
(503) 650-4211
contact: Truman L. Sturdevant (VP)
mat'l handled: newspapers

Weyerhaeuser West Coast, Inc.
P.O. Box 329
North Bend, OR 97459
tel: (503) 756-5171
contact: Connie Boddie
mat'l handled: corrugated

Smurfit Newsprint Corp
419 Main Street
Oregon City, OR 97045
tel: (503) 656-5211
(503) 650-4211
fax: (503) 656-5211
mat'l handled: newspaper

Smurfit Recycling Corp.
427 Main Street
Oregon City, OR 97045
tel: (503) 650-4282
fax: (503) 655-0288
mat'l handled: all grades of secondary fibers

Cascade Fibers International
1505 S.E. Gideon Street
P.O. Box 3915
Portland, OR 97202
tel: (503) 230-1359
fax: (503) 230-2290
contact: Rick Meyers, Sales Manager
mat'l handled: all grades of secondary fiber, wood chips, wood pulp

Willamett Industries, Inc.
3800 1st Interstate Tower
Portland, OR 97201
tel: (503) 227-5581

Weyerhaeuser Co.
P.O. Box 275
Springfield, OR 97477
tel: (503) 726-2670
mat'l handled: corrugated, pulp substitutes

Georgia-Pacific Corp.
P.O. Box 580
Toledo, OR 97391
tel: (503) 336-2211
fax: (503) 336-3019
contact: Bill Parsons (Secondary Fiber Buyer)
mat'l handled: corrugated, pulp substitutes

Pennsylvania

Chanbersburg Waste Paper Co, Inc.
Box 720
Chambersburg, PA 17201
tel: (717) 264-4890
fax: (717) 264-6393
contact: Larry Freedman (President)
mat'l handled: all grades; also handle glass, aluminum, copper, brass and nonferrous metals

Scott Paper Co.
Front and Market Streets
Chester, PA 19013
tel: (215) 874-4331
contact: David C. Bernhard (Pulp Division Manager)
mat'l handled: newspapers, pulp substitutes

Rock-Tenn Co.
Paper Mill Road
Delaware, PA 18327
tel: (717) 476-0120

Brandywine Paperboard Mills, Inc.
131 Wallace Avenue
P.O. Box 161
Downingtown, PA 19335
tel: (215) 269-1400
mat'l handled: mixed papers

The Davey Co.
Drawer H
Downingtown, PA 19335
tel: (215) 269-2030
contact: Stephen C. Dodd (Managing Director)
mat'l handled: mixed papers

Shryock Brothers
P.O. Box 157
Downingtown, PA 19335
tel: (215) 269-0155
contact: Charles Barber

Sonoco Products Co.
300 S. Brandywine Avenue
Downingtown, PA 19335
tel: (215) 269-3300
contact: Edward DuLuigi
mat'l handled: mixed papers, newspapers, corrugated

Hammermill Papers, Inc.
Erie Plant
1540 E. Lake Road
P.O. Box 1440
Erie, PA 16533
tel: (814) 456-8811
contact: J.J. Jacobson (Plant Manager)
mat'l handled: pulp substitutes

American Paper Products Co.
New Holland Pike and Landis Valley Road
Lancaster, PA 17601
tel: (717) 397-2789
contact: Eldon Tottel
mat'l handled: pulp substitutes

Henry Molded Products, Inc.
71 N. 16th Street
P.O. Box 75
Lebanon, PA 17042
tel: (717) 273-3714
contact: Brad Arnold

Hammermill Papers Business
Lock Haven Mill
P.O. Box 268
Lock Haven, PA 17745
tel: (717) 748-4045
contact: J. Ralph Lovette (Mill Manager)
mat'l handled: mixed papers, newspapers, corrugated

Procter & Gamble Paper Products Co.
P.O. Box 32, Route 87
Mehoopany, PA 18629
tel: (717) 833-5141
contact: L.D. Ketchum (Division Manager)

National Gypsum Co.
P.O. Box 338
Milton, PA 17847
tel: (717) 538-2531
mat'l handled: pulp substitutes

Simpson Paper Co., Valley Forge Mill
Manor Road
Miquon, PA 19452
tel: (215) 828-5800
fax: (215) 828-5940
contact: W.A. Schul (Operations Manager)
mat'l handled: mixed papers, newspapers, corrugated

Exton Paper Manufacturers
500 E. Lincoln Highway
P.O. Box 158
Modena, PA 19358
tel: (215) 384-2650
contact: Robert E. Davis (Manager—Paper Mill Operations)
mat'l handled: corrugated, pulp substitutes

Valley Paper Mill
Meredith Road
Modena, PA 19358
tel: (215) 384-2650
contact: Henry Tober

A.J. Catagnus, Inc.
1299 W. James Street
Norristown, PA 19491
tel: (215) 277-2727
fax: (215) 277-4272
contact: A.J. Catagnus (VP)
mat'l handled: high-grade waste paper; also handle metals, ferrous and nonferrous

Connelly Containers, Inc. of Philadelphia
4368 Main Street
Philadelphia, PA 19127
tel: (215) 839-6400
contact: Charlotte Bernstein
mat'l handled: corrugated

Newman & Co., Inc.
6101 Tacony Street
Philadelphia, PA 19135
tel: (215) 333-8700
contact: Mr. Myatt
mat'l handled: mixed papers, newspapers, corrugated, pulp substitutes

Pope & Talbot, Inc.
Main Street

Ransom, PA 18653
tel: (717) 388-6161
fax: (717) 388-4125
contact: L.J. Peterson (Resource Manager)
mat'l handled: pulp substitutes, high-grade de-inking

Georgia-Pacific Corp., Inc.
450 River Front Drive
P.O. Box 1536
Reading, PA 19603
tel: (215) 375-4281
mat'l handled: mixed paper, newspapers, corrugated, pulp substitutes

Rock-Tenn Co.
Paper Mill Road
Delaware Water Gap
Stroudsburg, PA 18327
mat'l handled: mixed papers, newspapers, corrugated, pulp substitutes

Tarkett, Inc.
1139 Lehigh Avenue
Whitehall, PA 18052
tel: (215) 266-5500

Stone Container Corp.
423 Kings Mill Road
P.O. Box 1429
York, PA 17405
tel: (717) 843-8901
contact: Paul Slonaker
mat'l handled: mixed papers, newspapers, corrugated

Yorktowne Paper Mills, Inc.
Loucks Mill Road
York, PA 17405
tel: (717) 843-8061
contact: Russ Yoras
mat'l handled: mixed papers, newspapers, corrugated, pulp substitutes

South Carolina

Kimberly-Clark Corp.
P.O. Box 112
Beech Island, SC 29841
tel: (803) 827-1100
contact: J.A. Van Steenberg (Mill Manager)
mat'l handled: pulp substitutes

Union Camp Corp., Fine Paper Div.
Fine Paper Div.
Eastover, SC 29044
contact: R.E. Simmons (Resource Manager)
mat'l handled: pulp substitutes

Stone Container Corp.
P.O. Box 4000
Florence, SC 29501
tel: (803) 662-0313
contact: Baker Jones
mat'l handled: corrugated

Sonoco Products Company
N. 2nd Street
Hartsville, SC 29550
tel: (803) 383-7665
fax: (803) 383-3445
contact: Ronnie Grant
mat'l handled: consumer. corrugated, news, tube scrap, CPO, tabs

Carotell Paper Board Corp.
Alexander Drive
P.O. Box 655
Taylors, SC 29687
tel: (803) 244-6221
contact: Ms. Bitten Bortone, purchasing agent
mat'l handled: mixed papers, newspapers, corrugated, pulp substitutes

Tennessee

Bowater Inc./Advance Publications
Calhoun, TN
tel: (803) 271-7733
contact: Larry Green
new planned mill: planned de-inking line; will take newspaper and coated groundwood

Chattanooga Paperboard Corp.
P.O. Box 431
2100 Rossville Avenue
Chattanooga, TN 37401
tel: (615) 267-3801
contact: W.S. Schillhahn (President)
mat'l handled: OCC, mixed paper, news, HWE, unprinted and printed bleached sulfate, newspapers, corrugated, pulp substitutes, high-grade de-inking

Rock-Tenn Co.
Mill Div. Manufactureres Road

P.O. Box 4068
Chattanooga, TN 37405
tel: (615) 266-7381
mat'l handled: mixed papers, newspapers, corrugated, pulp substitutes

Tennessee River Pulp & Paper Co.
Box 33
Counce, TN 38326
tel: (901) 689-3111
contact: R.F. Frey
mat'l handled: corrugated

Lydall, Inc.
P.O. Drawer 1
Covington, TN 38019
tel: (901) 476-7174
mat'l handled: corrugated, pulp substitutes

Clinch River Corp.
728 Emory Street
P.O. Box 909
Harriman, TN 37748
tel: (615) 882-1494
fax: (615) 882-7444
contact: William Donohoo (President)
mat'l handled: corrugated

Mead Corp
P.O. Box 1964
Kingsport, TN 37662
tel: (615) 247-7111
contact: W.H. Kirk (VP—Operations)
mat'l handled: pulp substitutes

Tamko Asphalt Products of Tennessee, Inc.
2506 Johnston Street, N.W.
P.O. Box 4409
Knoxville, TN 37921
tel: (615) 637-0145
contact: Gary Neely
mat'l handled: mixed papers, corrugated.

International Paper
6400 Poplar Avenue
Memphis, TN 38197
tel: (800) 223-1268

Kimberly-Clark Corp.
400 Mahannah Avenue
P.O. Box 7066
Memphis, TN 38107
tel: (901) 529-3800
contact: C.J. Jacoby (Mill Manager)
mat'l handled: pulp substitutes

Ponderosa Fibres
1531 N. Thomas Street
P.O. Box 7395
Memphis, TN 38107
tel: (901) 525-0404
contact: Kenneth W. Freeman (Mill Manager)

Packaging Corp. of America
100 Riverhills Drive
Nashville, TN 37210
tel: (615) 889-0605
fax: (615) 889-0610
contact: Martin T. Rusk (Plant Manager)

Inland Container Corporation
Conalco Road
P.O. Box 299
New Johnsonville, TN 37134
tel: (615) 535-2161
contact: Jim Shupe (Recycle Material)
mat'l handled: corrugated

Sonoco Products Company
Rankin Road
Newport, TN 37821
tel: (615) 623-8611
fax: (615) 625-1482
contact: Dennis Newsome
mat'l handled: consumer, corrugated, news, mixed, tube scrap

Texas

Pronapade Fibre, Inc.
1720 Regal Row
Suite 235
Dallas, TX 75235
tel: (214) 637-5003
fax: (214) 637-5011
contact: Gustavo De Gortari (VP)
mat'l handled: de-ink news, overissue news and white newsblanks

Rock-Tenn Co
1120 E. Clarendon Drive
P.O. Box 1291
Dallas, TX 75221
tel: (214) 941-3400
contact: James Nealy
mat'l handled: mixed papers, newspapers,

corrugated, pulp substitutes, high-grade de-inking

Georgia-Pacific Corp.
130 E. Farm Market
P.O. Box 700
Daingerfield, TX 75638
mat'l handled: mixed papers, corrugated

Corrugated Services Inc.
P.O. Box 847
Forney, TX 75126
tel: (214) 552-2267
fax: (214) 564-4014
contact: Jones Felvey II (President)
mat'l handled: corrugated

United States Gypsum Co.
1201 Mayo Shell Road
P.O. Box 525
Galena Park, TX 77547
tel: (713) 672-8261
contact: Dan Smith (Paper Buyer)
mat'l handled: mixed papers, newspapers, corrugated, pulp substitutes

Willamette Ind.
1200 W.N. Carrier Parkway
Grand Prairie, TX 75050
tel: (214) 647-8522
fax: (214) 641-7113
contact: Roger Young (Secondary Fiber Manager)
mat'l handled: OCC

Smurfit Recycling Company
14950 Heathrow Forest Parkway
Houston, TX 77032
tel: (713) 449-8971
fax: (713) 449-5123
contact: Tim Haugh (Sales Manager)

Uni-Trade International, Inc.
5050 Campbell Road
Suite E
Houston, TX 77041
tel: (713) 690-7595
fax: (713) 690-7596
contact: Kip Dornhorst (President)
mat'l handled: newsprint, kraft, chip

Equitable Bag Co., Inc.
P.O. Box 991
Orange, TX 77631
tel: (713) 883-4305
mat'l handled: pulp substitutes

Inland-Orange, Inc.
Old Highway 87 North
P.O. Box 2500
Orange, TX 77630
tel: (409) 746-2441
contact: John Carroll (Production Superintendent)
mat'l handled: corrugated

Simpson Pasadena Paper Co.
San Jacinto Mill
P.O. Box 872
Pasadena, TX 77501
tel: (713) 475-6200
contact: E.G. Lalouche (Operations Manager)
mat'l handled: pulp substitutes

Butts Recycling, Inc.
502 Wool St.
San Angelo, TX 76903
tel: (915) 653-8957
contact: Charles C. Butts
mat'l handled: CPO, OCC, de-ink news

Celotex Corp.
2943 W. Southcross Avenue
San Antonio, TX 78211
tel: (512) 924-4301
contact: Arnie DelaRosa
mat'l handled: mixed papers, corrugated

Champion International Corp.
Sheldon, TX
tel: (713) 456-8780
contact: Mike Sullivan
Planned new mill: planned de-inking line; will take newspaper and coated groundwood

Vermont

Specialty Paperboard, Inc.
Box 498
Brattleboro, VT 05302
tel: (802) 257-0365
fax: (802) 257-5973
contact: Alex Kwader (General Manager)
mat'l handled: mixed papers, pulp substitutes

CPM, Inc.
P.O. Box 95
East Ryegate, VT 05042

tel: (802) 757-3353
mat'l handled: mixed papers, newspapers, pulp substitutes, high-grade deinking

Georgia-Pacific Corp.
Riveside Avenue
Gilman, VT 05904
tel: (802) 892-5515
mat'l handled: pulp substitutes

Putney Paper Co., Inc.
P.O. Box 226
Old Depot Road
Putney, VT 03546
tel: (802) 387-5571
fax: (802) 387-5297
contact: Buddy J. Edwards (Executive VP and General Manager)
mat'l handled: coated book, white ledger, IGS hot melt

Boise Cascade Corp.
Sheldon Springs, VT 05485
tel: (802) 933-7733
contact: Mary Lou Belanger (Materials Manager)

Specialty Paperboard, Inc.
Mill Street
Sheldon Springs, VT 05485
mat'l handled: newspapers, pulp substitutes

Virginia

Virginia Fibre Corp.
P.O. Box 339
Amherst, VA 24521
tel: (804) 933-4100
fax: (804) 933-4107
mat'l handled: corrugated

Bear Island Paper Co.
P.O. Box 2119
Ashland, VA 23005
tel: (804) 227-3394
contact: E. Gary Graham (VP and General Manager)
mat'l handled: newspapers

Owens-Brockway Glass Containers
P.O. Box 40
Big Island, VA 24526
tel: (804) 299-5911
contact: L.D. Garner
mat'l handled: corrugated

Georgia Bonded Fibers, Inc.
1040 W. 29th Street
Buena Vista, VA 24416-0751
tel: (703) 261-2181
fax: (703) 261-3784
contact: James C. Kosteini (President)
mat'l handled: high-grade de-inking

Westvaco Corp.
Bleached Board Div.
Covington, VA 24426
tel: (703) 969-5000
contact: W.R. Small (Mill Manager)
mat'l handled: corrugated

Stone Container Corp.
910 Industrial Street
P.O. Box 201
Hopewell, VA 23860
tel: (804) 541-9600
contact: Milton I. Hargrave (General Manager)
mat'l handled: corrugated

Mead Corp.
P.O. Box 980
Lynchburg, VA 24505
tel: (804) 847-5521
mat'l handled: mixed papers, corrugated

James River Corp.
P.O. Box 2218
Richmond, VA 23217
tel: (804) 649-4213
fax: (804) 649-4402
contact: J.J. Lacina (Resource Manager)
mat'l handled: pulp substitutes

Manchester Board and Paper Co., Inc.
P.O. Box 38129
Richmond, VA 23231
tel: (804) 232-7867
contact: Tom Harris
mat'l handled: mixes papers, newspapers, corrugated, pulp substitutes

Sonoco Products Company
1850 Commerce Road
P.O. Box 1155
Richmond, VA 23209
tel: (804) 233-5411
contact: Harris J. Bacon (Mill Manager)

mat'l handled: mixed papers, newspapers, corrugated, pulp substitutes

Virginia Fibre Corp.
P.O. Box 7
Riverville, VA 24553
tel: (804) 933-8643
contact: Douglas Dray
mat'l handled: corrugated

Richmond Recycling, Div. Chesapeake Corp.
5600 Lewis Road
Sandston, VA 23150
tel: (804) 226-0383
contact: Tom Stecher
mat'l handled: corrugated, ledger, computer forms, file stock, aluminum cans and glass

Chesapeake Corp.
19th and Main Street
P.O. Box 311
West Point, VA 23181
tel: (804) 843-5423
fax: (804) 843-5690
contact: Chuck Murray (Materials Manager)
mat'l handled: corrugated

Washington

Georgia-Pacific Corp.
300 Laurel Street
P.O. Box 1236
Bellingham, WA 98225
tel: (206) 733-4410

James River Corp.
4th and Adams Streets
Camas, WA 98607
tel: (206) 834-3021
fax: (206) 834-8176
contact: A.G. Elsbree (VP)
mat'l handled: pulp substitutes

Scott Paper Co.
Northwest Operations
2600 Federal Way
P.O. Box 925
Everett, WA 98206
tel: (206) 259-7333
contact: Gerald Willis (Division VP)
mat'l handled: mixed papers, pulp substitutes

Weyerhaeuser Paper Co.
Pulp Div.
101 E. Marine View Drive
Everett, WA 98201
tel: (206) 339-2800
fax: (206) 339-2844
contact: Carl W. Geist (VP and General Manager)
mat'l handled: pulp and secondary fiber

Longview Fibre Co.
P.O. Box 639
Longview, WA 98632
tel: (206) 425-1550
contact: Jerry Calbaum (Supply Manager)
mat'l handled: corrugated

North Pacific Paper Company
Longview, WA
tel: (503) 223-3692
contact: John Herpers
New planned mill: planned deinking line; will accept newspaper

Weyerhaeuser Paper Company
P.O. Box 188
Longview, WA 98632
tel: (206) 425-2150
fax: (206) 636-6333
contact: Frank Guthrie (VP)
mat'l handled: Corrugated

Inland Empire Paper Co.
N. 3320 Argonne Road (Spokane)
Millwood, WA 99212-2099
tel: (509) 924-1911
contact: Jim Glift; for information on planned de-inking line call Dan Stryker
mat'l handled: newspaper

Port Townsend Paper Corp.
P.O. Box 3170
Port Townsend, WA 98368
tel: (206) 385-3170
contact: Richard D'Agostino (Mill Manager)
mat'l handled: mixed papers, newspapers

Boise Cascade Corp.
Steilacoom, WA 98388
tel: (208) 384-6471
contact: Lance Richardson
New planned de-inking line; will accept newspaper and coated groundwood

Sonoco Products Co.
P.O. Box 3170

Sumner, WA 98390
tel: (206) 863-6366
fax: (206) 863-0223
contact: K.B. Jhala (Plant Manager); A.L King (Superintendent)
mat'l handled: consumer, corrugated, news, DKL

Container Corp. of America
817 E. 27th Street
Tacoma, WA 98421
tel: (206) 627-1197
mat'l handled: mixed papers, corrugated

Simpson Tacoma Kraft Co.
801 Portland Avenue
P.O. Box 2133
Tacoma, WA 98401
tel: (206) 572-2150
fax: (206) 596-0156
contact: Richard P. Gallagher (General Sales Manager)
mat'l handled: pulp substitutes

Weyerhaeuser Company
Tacoma, WA 98477
tel: (206) 924-2905
fax: (206) 924-3670
contact: George Weyerhaeuser (Chairman of Board)

Boise Cascade Corp.
907 W. 7th Street
P.O. Box 690
Vancouver, WA 98666
tel: (206) 693-2567
mat'l handled: high-grade de-inking

Boise Cascade Corp.
P.O. Box 500
Wallula, WA 99363
tel: (509) 547-2411
contact: James T. Williams (Resource Manager)
mat'l handled: corrugated

Keyes Fibre Co.
3715 Chelan Highway
P.O. Box 460
Wenatchee, WA 98801
tel: (509) 663-8537
mat'l handled: newspapers, corrugated

Weyerhauser Co.
24100 Woodinville Snohomish Road
Woodinville, WA 98072
tel: (206) 485-0955

West Virginia

Halltown Paperboard Co.
P.O. Box 10
Halltown, WV 25423
tel: (304) 725-2076
fax: (304) 725-2076
contact: C.C. Hammann (President)
mat'l handled: folding grades, colors, mixed papers, newspapers, corrugated, pulp substitutes, high-grade de-inking

Banner Fibreboard Co.
P.O. Box 390
Wellsburg, WV 26070
tel: (304) 737-3711
contact: D.L. Laughlin (Executive VP)
mat'l handled: newspapers, corrugated, pulp substitutes

Wisconsin

Fox River Paper Co.
200 E. Washington Street, Suite 300
P.O. Box 2215
Appleton, WI 54913
tel: (414) 733-7341
fax: (800) 942-3350
contact: William G. Fineran (Mill Manager)

Kerwin Paper Co.
800 S. Lawe Street
Appleton, WI 54911
tel: (414) 733-5546
contact: Dick Austin

Riverside Paper Co.
110 N. Kensington Drive
P.O. Box 179
Appleton, WI 54912
mat'l handled: pulp substitutes

James River Corp.
23rd Avenue
East and Front Street
P.O. Box 353
Ashland, WI 54806
tel: (715) 682-4561
fax: (715) 682-9284
contact: John F. Morgan (Mill Manager)

mat'l handled: high-grade de-inking

Beloit Box Board Co., Inc.
801 2nd Street
P.O. Box 386
Beloit, WI 53512
tel: (608) 365-6671
contacts: Everette Lange (Sales Manager)
mat'l handled: mixed papers, newspapers, corrugated

Wausau Paper Mills Co.
P.O. Box 305
Brokaw, WI 54417
tel: (715) 675-3361

Genstar Building Materials Co.
50 Bridge Street
P.O. Box 707
Cornell, WI 54732
tel: (715) 239-6424
mat'l handled: newspapers, corrugated

U.S. Paper Mills Corp.
824 Fort Howard Avenue
P.O. Box 3309
De Pere, WI 54115
tel: (414) 336-4229
contact: Larry Van Vonderen
mat'l handled: mixed papers, corrugated, pulp substitutes

Pope & Talbot, Inc.
1200 Forest Street
Eau Claire, WI 54703
tel: (514) 834-3461
mat'l handled: high-grade de-inking

Fort Howard Paper Co.
1919 S. Broadway
P.O. Box 19130
Green Bay, WI 54307-9130
fax: (414) 435-8821
mat'l handled: mixed papers, newspapers, corrugated, pulp substitutes, high-grade de-inking

Fox River Mill
P.O. Box 8020
Green Bay, WI 54308
mat'l handled: pulp substitutes

Green Bay Packaging, Inc.
P.O. Box 19017
Green Bay, WI 54307
tel: (414) 433-5027
fax: (414) 433-5105
contacts: Russ Oettel (Manager)
mat'l handled: corrugated

James River Corp.
Day Street
P.O. Box 790
Green Bay, WI 54305-5790
tel: (414) 433-6200
fax: (414) 433-6352
contact: James G. Fox (Directer—Mill Operations)
mat'l handled: mixed papers, high-grade de-inking

Procter & Gamble Paper Products Co.
East River Mill
800 University Avenue
P.O. Box 8010
Green Bay, WI 54308-8010
contacts: B.A. Boor (Division Manager)
mat'l handled: pulp substitutes

Thilmany Pulp & Paper Co.
Thilmany Road
P.O. Box 600
Kaukauna, WI 54130
tel: (414) 766-4611
contact: Donald Brown
mat'l handled: pulp substitutes

Midtec Paper Corp.
N. Main Street
Kimberly, WI 54136-1490
tel: (414) 788-3511
fax: (414) 788-5368
contacts: Gary B. Fenton (VP and General Manager); David R. Vanderhei (Mill Manager)
mat'l handled: pulp substitutes

Pope & Talbot, Inc.
P.O. Box 129
Ladysmith, WI 54848
tel: (715) 532-5541
contact: Gerald D. Miller (Production Manager)
mat'l handled: paper, pulp substitutes, high-grade de-inking

Scott Paper Co.
3120 Riverside Avenue
Marinette, WI 54143
tel: (715) 735-6644

contact: Philip Monroe (General Manager)
mat'l handled: pulp substitutes

Gilbert Paper
430 Ahnaip Street
P.O. Box 260
Mensasha, WI 54952-0260
tel: (414) 729-7744
contact: Mark Manske
mat'l handled: pulp substitutes

U.S. Paper Mills Corp.
Menasha Div.
60 Washington Street
P.O. Box 568
Menasha, WI 54952-0568
tel: (414) 725-7115
fax: (414) 725-4869
contact: Keith D. Mutchler (Division Manager)
mat'l handled: mixed papers, corrugated

Geo. A. Whiting Paper Co.
100 River Street
Menasha, Wi 54952
tel: (414) 722-3351
fax: (414) 722-9553
contact: Frank Whiting (CEO)
mat'l handled: pulp substitutes

Wisconsin Tissue Mills, Inc.
P.O. Box 489
Menasha, WI 54952
tel: (414) 725-7031
contact: James Rausch
mat'l handled: corrugated

Ward Paper Co.
N. Mill Street
P.O. Box 587
Merrill, WI 54452
tel: (715) 536-5591
contact: Bruce Skofronick
mat'l handled: pulp substitutes

Wisconsin Paperboard Corp.
1514 E. Thomas Avenue
Milwaukee, WI 53211-4397
tel: (414) 271-9000
fax: (414) 271-1001
contact: James B. Hoover (President)
mat'l handled: mixed papers, newspapers, corrugated

P.H. Glatfelter Co., Bergstrom Div.
225 Wisconsin Avenue
Neenah, WI 54956
tel: (414) 727-2200
contact: L.K. Wilhelm (Mill Manager)
mat'l handled: pulp substitutes, high-grade de-inking

Kimberly-Clark Corp.
Lakeview Mill
249 N. Lake Street
Neenah, WI 54956
tel: (414) 729-1212
contact: D.L. Rothwell (Operations Manager)
mat'l handled: pulp substitutes

Niagara of Wisconsin Paper Corp.
1101 Mill Street
Niagara, WI 54151
tel: (715) 251-3151
fax: (715) 251-1730
contact: Mike Warner

Ponderosa Pulp Products Corp.
2800 N. Main Street
Oshkosh, WI 54901
tel: (414) 233-6739
contact: Dave Young

Nekoosa Papers, Inc.
100 Wisconsin River Drive
Port Edwards, WI 54469-1496
tel: (715) 887-5111
fax: (715) 887-5555
contacts: Roger H. Brear (Mill Manager)
mat'l handled: pulp substitutes

Rhinelander Paper Co., Inc.
515 W. Davenport Street
Rhinelander, WI 54501
tel: (715) 369-4100
fax: (715) 369-4141
contact: M.L. Davidson (VP and General Manager)
mat'l handled: pulp substitutes

Shawano Paper Mills, Div. Little Rapids Corp.
P.O. Box 437
Shawano, WI 54166-0437
tel: (715) 526-2181
fax: (715) 524-3149
contact: Donald W. Childs (VP—Sales)
mat'l handled: pulp substitutes

Nekoosa Packaging
N. 9090 Highway E.
Tomahawk, WI 54487
tel: (715) 453-7049
contact: William M. Buedingen (VP)
mat'l handled: corrugated

Tomahawk Tissue Corp.
858 W. Leather Avenue
P.O. Box 266
Tomahawk, WI 54487
tel: (715) 453-2139
fax: (715) 453-5818
contact: Paul Mikunda

Wisconsin Pulp, Inc.
N. 10099 Kings Road
Tomahawk, WI 54487
tel: (715) 453-5376
mat'l handled: high-grade de-inking

Consolidated Papers Inc.
231 1st Avenue North
P.O. Box 50
Wisconsin Rapids, WI 54494
tel: (715) 422-3111
contact: Peter Thomas

Consolidated Papers, Inc.
P.O. Box 8050
Wisconsin Rapids, WI 54495-8050
mat'l handled: mixed papers, newspapers, corrugated

Canada

Alberta

IKO Industries, Ltd.
1600 42nd Avenue S.E.
Calgary, Alberta, Canada T2P 2L2
tel: (403) 265-6022
fax: (403) 266-2644

IKO Industries, Ltd., Softboard Mill
15th Street and 42nd Avenue
Calgary, Alberta, Canada T2G 1Z8
tel: (403) 265-6022
fax: (403) 266-2644
contact: A.D. McIntosh (General Manager)

BPCO, Inc., Roofing Div.
3703 101st Ave. N.E.
Edmonton, Alberta, Canada T5J 2K8
tel: (403) 466-1135
fax: (403) 465-0897
contact: C.G. Meimar (VP—Western Manufacturing)

British Columbia

Fletcher Challenge Canada Ltd.
Crofton, British Columbia, Canada
tel: (604) 654-4301
contact: Tom Torrence
New planned mill: planned deinked pulp; will accept newspaper and coated groundwood

Fletcher Challenge Canada Ltd.
Elk Falls Mill, Campbell River
British Columbia, Canada
tel: (604) 654-4301
contact: Tom Torrence
New planned mill: planned de-inked pulp; will accept newspaper and coated groundwood

Island Paper Mills, Ltd.
1010 Derwent Way
Annacis Island, New Westminster, British Columbia, Canada V3L 5A5
tel: (604) 526-5521
fax: (604) 526-2356
contacts: C. Lance Skerratt (President and CEO); Carmel Cosgrove (VP Operations); Bruce Fowler (Director—Marketing and Sales)

MacMillan Bloedel Ltd.
Port Alberni, British Columbia, Canada
tel: (604) 661-8602
contact: Jim Kirkland
New planned mill: planned de-inked pulp; will accept newspaper and coated groundwood

MacMillan Bloedel Ltd.
Powell River, British Columbia, Canada
tel: (604) 661-8602
contact: Jim Kirkland
New planned mill: planned de-inked pulp; will accept newspaper and coated goundwood

Manitoba

Gateway Packer, Ltd.
782 Main Street
Winnipeg, Manitoba, Canada R2W 3N4
tel: (204) 589-5311

fax: (204) 956-5273
contacts: Sheldon Balnk (VP); Mrev Chochinov (General Manager)
mat'l handled: all grades paper stock

New Brunswick

Consolidated-Bathurst, Inc.
891 Main Street
P.O. Box B
Bathurst, New Brunswick, Canada E2A 4A3
tel: (506) 546-3361

Fraser, Inc.
27 Rice Street
Edmundston, New Brunswick, Canada E3V 1S9
tel: (506) 735-5551
contact: Roger Michaud

Nova Scotia

Minas Basin Pulp & Power Co., Ltd.
Prince Street
Hantsport, Nova Scotia, Canada BOP 1PO
tel: (902) 684-3236
contact: Don Rockwell

Ontario

IKO Industries, Ltd.
710 Orenda Road
Brampton, Ontario, Canada L6W 1V8
tel: (416) 457-4321

Reid Dominion Packaging, Ltd.
81 Elgin Street
P.O. Box 1360
Brantford, Ontario, Canada N3T 5T6
tel: (519) 753-8427
contact: Jim LeClair

Sonoco Ltd.
33 Park Avenue E
P.O. Box 1208
Brantford, Ontario, Canada N3T 5T5
tel: (519) 752-6591
contact: Donna Slack

Domtar, Inc.
P.O. Box 40
Cornwall, Ontario, Canada K6H 5S3
tel: (613) 932-6620

Domtar Packaging Recycling
66 Shorncliffe Road
Etobicoke, Ontario, Canada M8Z 5K1
tel: (416) 231-2525
fax: (416) 232-8825
contacts: Jeff Remouche (Paperstock); Geoff Rathbone (Plastics)

Trent Valley Paperboard Mills
P.O. Box 821
Trenton, Glen Miller, Ontario, Canada K8V 5R8
tel: (613) 392-1231

Spruce Falls Power
Kapuskasing, Ontario, Canada
contact: Bruce Bud
New planned mill: will accept newspapers

Domtar Packaging
Containerboard Div.
7447 Bramalea Road
Mississauga, Ontario, Canada L5S 1C4
tel: (416) 671-2940
fax: (416) 671-2448
contact: Tom Swider (Mill Manager)

Domtar, Inc.
343 Glendale Avenue
Saint Cahtarines, Ontario, Canada L2T 2L9
tel: (416) 227-3721
contact: Marlene Watson

Atlantic Packaging Products Ltd.
111 Progress Avenue
Scarborough, Ontario, M1P 2Y9
tel: (416) 298-5307
fax: (416) 298-5352
contact: Donna O'Neill

Beaver Wood Fibre Co.
319 Allanburg Road
Thorold, Ontario, Canada L2V 3Z8
tel: (416) 227-6651
contact: Howard Bradley; Harry Fox

Domtar Construction Materials
Allanburg Road
P.O. Box 10
Thorold, Ontario, Canada L2V 3Y7
tel: (416) 227-3714
contact: L. Panunto

Fraser, Inc.
John Street
P.O. Box 1046

Thorold, Ontario, Canada L2V 3Z7
tel: (416) 227-5271

Quebec & Ontario Paper Co.
Allanburg Road
P.O. Box 1040
Thorold, Ontario, Canada L2V 3Z5
tel: (416) 227-1121
contacts: Colin Johnston (Manager—Paper Recycling)

Abitibi-Price Inc., Ft. William Division
Thunder Bay, Ontario, Canada
tel: (416) 369-6700
contact: Ed Sparks
New planned mill: planned de-inking line; will accept newspaper and coated groundwood

Canadian Pacific Forest Products Ltd.
Thunder Bay, Ontario, Canada
tel: (803) 271-7733
contact: Larry Green
New planned mill: planned de-inking line; will accept newspaper and coated groundwood

Domtar Packaging—Recycling Division
66 Shorncliffe Road
Toronto, Ontario, M8Z 5K1
tel: (416) 231-2525
fax: (416) 232-8825
contact: Jeff Remouche (Manager of Corrugated Recycling/Business Development Program)
mat'l handled: OCC

Paperboard Industries Corp.
495 Commissioners Street
Toronto, Ontario, M4M 1A5
tel: (416) 461-8261

Domtar Packaging
P.O. Box 807
Trenton, Ontario, Canada K8V 5R8
tel: (613) 392-6505
fax: (613) 392-3026

Quebec

Desencrage Cascades, Inc.
739 St. Augustin Avenue
Breakeyville, Quebec, Canada GOS 1EO
tel: (418) 832-6115
fax: (418) 832-5598
contact: Jim Scott

Kruger Inc.
Bromptonville, Quebec, Canada
tel: (514) 737-1131
contact: Richard Loyst
New planned mill: planned de-inking line; will accept newspaper and coated groundwood

Papier Cascades (Cabano) Inc.
P.O. Box 190
Cabano, Quebec, Canada GOL 1EO
tel: (418) 854-2803

Perkins Papers Ltd.
75 Marie Victorin Boulevard
Candiac, Quebec, Canada J5R 1C2
tel: (514) 659-6541
contact: Jean Gervais

Bennett Fleet, Inc.
2700 Bourgogne Street
Chambly, Quebec, Canada J3L 4B6
tel: (514) 658-1771
contact: Jacques Burelle

Donohue Inc.
Clermont, Quebec, Canada
tel: (418) 684-7700
contact: Jerry Arseneault
New planned mill: planned de-inked pulp; will accept newspaper and coated groundwood

Scott Paper Ltd.
P.O. Box 500
Crabtree, Quebec, Canada JOK 1BO
tel: (514) 754-2855

Canadian Pacific Forest Products Ltd.
Gatineau, Quebec, Canada
tel: (514) 878-6012
contact: Reid Murphy
New planned mill: planned de-inking line; will accept newspaper and coated groundwood

Consolidated-Bathurst, Inc.
225 First Street
Grand'Mere, Quebec Canada G9T 5L2
tel: (819) 538-3341

Kingsey Falls Paper, Inc.
P.O. Box 150
Kingsey Falls, Quebec, Canada JOA 1BO
tel: (819) 363-2702
fax: (819) 363-2570
contact: Carleton Morill (General Manager)

Les Industries Cascades Ltd.
P.O. Box 210
Kingsey Falls, Quebec, Canada JOA 1BO
tel: (819) 363-2704

Building Products of Canada, Ltd.
240 St. Patrick Street
LaSalle, Quebec, Canada H8R 1R9
tel: (514) 364-0161
contact: Aurele Bourbonnais

Price Wilson, Inc.
115 Princess Street
Lachute, Quebec, Canada J8H 3X5
tel: (514) 562-8585
contact: Brent Laurin

Scott Paper Ltd.
8 College Road
Lennoxville, Quebec, Canada J1M 1Z4
tel: (819) 565-8220

Orford Recycling, Inc.
416 Rue Street
Luc, Magog, Quebec, J1X 2X1
tel: (819) 843-1323
contacts: Jeanne D'Arc Ouellet (President); R. Bob Parenteau (VP);
mat'l handled: all grades; specialize in high grades; export, import, grader, packer, broker, importer, exporter, waste hauler

James Maclaren Industries Inc.
Masson, Quebec, Canada
tel: (819) 986-3345
contact: William Benn
New planned mill: planned de-inked pulp; will accept newspaper and coated groundwood

CIP, Inc.
90 Industrial Park
Matane, Quebec, G4W 3M9
tel: (418) 566-2266

Kruger Inc.
5845 Turcot Place
Montreal, Quebec, Canada H4C 3J7
tel: (514) 934-0845
mat'l handled: secondary fibers, linerboard mill

Kruger, Inc.
3285 Bedford Road
P.O. Box 769
Montreal, Quebec, Canada H3C 2V2
tel: (514) 737-1131
contacts: Pierre Hamelin; Serge Castonquay

BPCO, Inc.
420 DuPont Street W.
Pont-Rouge, Quebec, GOA 2XO
tel: (418) 873-2521
fax: (418) 873-2340
contact: Andre Desroches (VP—Manufacturing)
mat'l handled: manufacture fiberboard products

Daishowa Forest Products Ltd.
Quebec, Quebec, Canada
tel: (418) 525-2939
contact: Barry Hutchison
New planned mill: planned de-inking line; will accept newspaper and coated groundwood

Papeterie Reed Ltd.
10-16 Blvd. Des Capucins
P.O. Box 1487
Quebec City, Quebec, Canada G1K 7H9
tel: (418) 525-2500

St. Raymond Paper Ltd.
P.O. Box 609
St. Raymond, Quebec, GOA 4GO
tel: (418) 337-2261
contact: Guy Tremblay

Sonoco Ltd.
25 Rue Langlois
Terrebonne, Quebec, J6W 4H4
tel: (514) 471-4153
fax: (514) 471-4777
contacts: Daniel Thorpe (Mill Manager)

Consolidated-Bathurst, Inc.
P.O. Box 128
Trois Rivieres, Quebec, Canada G9A 5E9
tel: (819) 373-9230

Kruger Inc.
Trois-Rivieres, Quebec, Canada
tel: (514) 737-1131
contact: Richard Loyst
New planned mill: planned de-inked pulp

India

Bombay

Amar Paper and Board Mills
Charai Gaon
Chembur Naka, Bombay 400071 India
tel: (022) 520330 and 520339

contacts: Mr. M.B. Kanchwala; Mr. W.M. Kanchwala
mat'l handled: all types of waste paper; commercial solid waste
operation: manufacturers kraft paper, importer and indenting agency for all types of waste paper

B.K. Paper Mills Ltd.
1301/1318 Dalamal Tower
211 Nariman Point
Bombay-400 021 Maharashtra India
tel: 234908/234995
contact: Mr. Bhagwati Saraf, Sr. Ex.
mat'l handled: commercial solid waste operation

Plastic Manufacturers

Alabama

Plastic Services of America/ Subsidiary of Sabel Industries
650 Fountain Street
P.O. Box 964
Montgomery, AL 36101
tel: (205) 264-9578
fax: (205) 262-5067
mat'l handled: post-industrial scrap, PET, HDPE, LDPE, PP, polycarbonate

Tulip Corporation
197 Main Street
Springville, AL 35146
tel: (205) 467-6181 (plant)
tel: (414) 963-3120 (purchasing)
fax: (414) 962-1825 (purchasing)
contact: Michael Machalk (Purchasing—Wisconsin)
mat'l handled: HDPE, polypropylene, ABS

Webster Industries
2705 Gunter Park W.
Montgomery, AL 36109
tel: (508) 532-2000 ext. 372 (main hdqt. Peabody, MA)
mat'l handled: Clean LDPE film; post-industrial and post-consumer

KW Plastics
Henderson Road
P.O. Box 707
Troy, AL 36081
tel: (205) 566-5184
contact: Wiley C. Sanders, Jr. (CEO)
mat'l handled: polypropylene

California

International Chemco Inc.
2717 Tanager Avenue
City of Commerce, CA 90040
tel: (213) 888-6100
fax: (213) 888-1300
mat'l handled: HDPE, LDPE, LLDPE, polypropylene (prefer film grades), Nylon PA 6; prefer natural color for all above; truck load quantities only

National Polystyrene Recycling Co. Inc.
Corona, CA
tel: (708) 945-2139
contact: Ellen Kosty
mat'l handled: polystyrene food service products and protective foam packaging

Bay Polymer Corporation
44530 Grimmer Boulevard
Fremont, CA 94538
tel: (415) 490-1791
fax: (415)490-5914
mat'l handled: HDPE, LDPE, LLDPE, polypropylene, polystyrene

National Polystyrene Recycling Co. Inc.
Hayward, CA
tel: (708) 945-2139
contact: Ellen Kosty
mat'l handled: polystyrene food service products and protective foam packaging

Dawson Industrial Group
2623 Medford Street
Los Angeles, CA 90033
tel: (213) 227-4244
fax: (213) 227-1422
contact: Scott Jennings
mat'l handled: HDPE, LDPE, flexible PVC, polystyrene, polypropolyne

Western Gold Thermoplastics
815 E. 61 Street
Los Angeles, CA 90001-1024
tel: (213) 235-3387
fax: (213) 233-8640
contact: Daniel Hoyer (President)
mat'l handled: HDPE, LDPE, PP, PS

Joe's Plastics
7065 Paramount Boulevard
Pico Rivera, CA 90660
tel: (213) 777-6622
fax: (213) 949-8677
contact: Joe LaFountain
mat'l handled: HDPE, LDPE, PP, ABS

Plastics Pilings, Inc.
8560 Vineyard Avenue, Suite 510
Rancho Cucamonga, CA 91730
tel: (714) 989-7685
mat'l handled: mixed plastics

N & N Industry
75 S. Ritchey Street
Santa Ana, CA 92705
tel: (714) 259-7575
mat'l handled: HDPE, PET

RPX Resins, Inc.
1300 So. El Camino Real, #300
San Mateo, CA 94402
tel: (415) 571-5511
fax: (415) 574-8607
mat'l handled: HDPE, LDPE, LLDPE, MDPE

Container Corp. of America
Subsidiary of Jefferson Smurfit Corp.
20502 S. Denker Street
Torrance, CA 90501
tel: (213) 533-0333
contact: Vincent Christakos
mat'l handled: PET, HDPE, LDPE, other plastic

Talco Plastics Inc.
11650 Burke Street
Whittier, CA 90606
tel: (310) 699-0550
fax: (310) 692-6008
contact: Dean Rogers, Purchasing Agent
mat'l handled: Post consumer plastics; Post industrial plastic scrap and regrind (3000 pound minimum preferred) Call for more information.

Colorado

Manley Plastics
3360 Denargo Street
Denver, CO 80216
tel: (303) 295-7775
contact: Gene Dilger
mat'l handled: plastics, all types

Reprocessing Plastic Co.
2950 Arkins Court
Denver, CO 80216
tel: (303) 294-0364
fax: (303) 292-6657
contact: Mark Hopkins
mat'l handled: LDPE, HDPE, PVC

Connecticut

Plastics Recovery Corporation
P.O. Box 7080
New Haven, CT 06519
tel: (203) 785-0458
fax: (203) 624-3377
mat'l handled: 38 plastics, including engineering resins

Florida

Kwiat Trading Corp.
10155 Collins Avenue, #403
Bal Harbour, FL 33154
tel: (305) 868-4819
mat'l handled: HD, LD, PVC, polypropylene, PC, polystyrene, ABS, SAN, and other engineering resins in a full 40-ft. container (exporter)

Micronized Fluoropolymer Products, Inc.
1055 SW 15th Avenue
Delray Beach, FL 33444-1256
tel: (407) 265-1800
fax: (407) 265-1876
contact: Dietmar Reichenbacher (VP—Marketing and Purchasing)
mat'l handled: reprocessed plastic resins

Convert/EDA
6212 Highway 98 North
Lakeland, Fl 33809
tel: (813) 859-1414
fax: (813) 859-3532
mat'l handled: HDPE

Alaric Inc.
2110 N. 71st Street
Tampa, FL 33619-2938
tel: (813) 626-0458

fax: (813) 620-1653
contact: Peter C. Blyth (President, Sales Manager)
mat'l handled: Acrylic

Georgia

Image Carpets, Inc.
P.O. Box 5555
Armuchee, GA 30105
tel: (404) 235-8444
(800) 722-2504
contact: Pat Evans
mat'l handled: PET

Cairo Manufacturing Inc.
147 3rd Street S.E.
Cairo, GA 31728-2741
tel: (912) 377-3738
fax: (912) 377-9010
contact: Ronald Whitfield (President)

Cycle-tec
111 West Westcott
Dalton, GA 30727
tel: (800) 356-0216
contact: Phil Neff (President)
mat'l handled: plastics

Innovative Plastic Products Inc.
109 Stewart Parkway
P.O. Box 898
Greensboro, GA 30642
tel: (404) 453-7552
mat'l handled: PET, polypropylene, high and low density

Professional Packaging Products
1660 Waterville Road
Macon, GA 31206
tel: (912) 743-7240
fax: (912) 743-7255
contact: Phillip Davis
mat'l handled: all types of PET and HDPE

Able Plastics
4500 Ashburn Walk
Marietta, GA 30068
tel: (404) 565-1522
mat'l handled: LDPE film and white PVC in truckload quantities; post-consumer and post-industrial plastics

M.A. Industries
Polymers Division
Kelley and Dividend Drive
P.O. Box 2322
Peachtree City, GA 30269-2322
tel: (404) 487-7761
(800) 241-8250
fax: (404) 631-4679
contact: C. McInvale (Purchasing); Roger Geyer (Sales)
mat'l handled: PET, HDPE, polypropylene

Image Carpets
Box 193-B
Summerville, GA 30747
tel: (404) 857-6481
fax: (404) 857-7618
mat'l handled: PET, polyester, bottle regrind, preforms, post-consumer, packaging scrap, clear and green, full truck loads, also baled PET bottles

Illinois

Eaglebrook Plastics, Inc.
2600 W. Roosevelt Road
Chicago, IL 60608
tel: (312) 638-0006
fax: (312) 638-2567
contact: Andrew Stephens
mat'l handled: HDPE, PET, polypropylene, PVC

MRC Polymers, Inc.
1716 West Webster
Chicago, IL 60614
tel: (312) 276-6345
fax: (312) 276-4431
mat'l used: 100% recovered nylon, PC

Plastics Recycling Alliance
11600 Marshfield Road
Chicago, IL 60643
tel: (312) 928-8788
contact: Mike Crucello
mat'l handled: PET, HDPE

National Polystyrene Recycling Company
25 Tri State International
Lincolnshire, IL 60069
tel: (708) 945-2139
contact: Ellen Kosty
mat'l handled: polystyrene food service products and protective foam packaging

Webster Industries
Route 2
Macomb, IL 61455
tel: (508) 532-2000 ext. 372 (headquarters in Peabody, MA)
mat'l handled: clean LDPE film; post-industrial and post-consumer

Maine Plastics, Inc.
1550 W. 24th Street
North Chicago, IL 60064
tel: (800) 338-7728
(708) 473-3553
fax: (708) 473-3611
contact: Ron Stoller (Purchasing Agent)
mat'l handled: PBS, polyethylene, polypropylene, ABS, polystyrene, engineering grades; broker

Stericycle, Inc.
3501 Algonquin Road, Suite 220
Rolling Meadows, IL 60008
tel: (708) 398-3100
fax: (708) 398-3296
mat'l handled: polypropylene

Poly Pro Products Inc.
P.O. Box 69
Thornton, IL 60476
tel: (815) 727-3739
mat'l handled: MDPE, LDPE, HDPE

Iowa

Hammer Plastics Recycling Corp.
R.R. 3 Box 182
Highways 20 and 65 North
Iowa Falls, IA 50126
tel: (515) 648-5073
(800) 338-1438
fax: (512) 648-5074
contacts: Tammy Dunbar (Sales Manager); JoAnn Schnebly (Purchasing Agent)
mat'l handled: PET, miscellaneous

Maryland

Polysource Polymer Resource Group, Inc.
P.O. Box 20191
Baltimore, MD 21284-0191
tel: (301) 337-9525
fax: (301) 321-1268
mat'l handled: HDPE, PET, LDPE

Massachusetts

Atlantic Poly Inc.
Envirotech Division
670 Canton Street
Norwood, MA 02062
tel: (617) 769-6420
fax: (617) 769-5722
mat'l handled: LDPE film scrap, bags, stretch, shrink, roll stock, post-industrial and post-consumer

Webster Industries
58 Pulaski Street
Peabody, MA 01960
tel: (508) 532-2000 ext. 372
mat'l handled: Clean LDPE film; post-industrial and post-consumer

Michigan

Intermet, Ltd.
6000 Buchanan Street
Detroit, MI 48210
tel: (313) 894-0545
fax: (313) 334-5111
contact: Julius J. Rim (President)
mat'l handled: mixed plastics, HDPE, LDPE, LLDPE; purchased in 10-ton quantity or more

Processed Plastics Company
P.O. Box 68
Ionia, MI 48846
tel: (616) 527-6677
mat'l handled: mixed plastics

Minnesota

Master Mark Plastic Products
Division of Avon Plastics Inc.
30 East Railroad Avenue
Albany, MN 56307
tel: (612) 845-2111
fax: (612) 845-7093
mat'l handled: HDPE

Poly Plastics Inc.
3280 Park Drive

Owatonna, MN 55060
tel: (507) 451-8650
fax: (507) 451-0638
mat'l handled: HDPE, PVC, polypropylene, polyethylene

New Jersey

National Polystyrene Recycling Co.
Bridgeport, N.J.
tel: (708) 945-2139
contact: Ellen Kosty
mat'l handled: polystyrene, food service product, and protective foam packaging

New York

Clearvue Resource Management Ltd.
P.O. Box 8
Amsterdam, NY 12010-0008
tel: (518) 842-7134
fax: (518) 786-6210
mat'l handled: HDPE, PVC

Unicorn
8900 Old Lake Shore Road
Angola, NY 14006
tel: (716) 549-6078
mat'l handled: mixed plastics

DEBCO Plastics, Inc.
14 Maple Place
Freeport, NY 11520
tel: (516) 379-2470
fax: (516) 279-9127
mat'l handled: post-industrial/post-commercial/post-consumer plastics; truckloads and L.T.L.

North American Plastics Recycling Corp.
Towpath Road
Fort Edward, NY 12828
tel: (518) 747-4195
fax: (518) 747-7167
contact: Susan Roberts
mat'l handled: HDPE, LDPE, LLDPE, rigid containers 1–7

NICON Plastics, Inc.
4–11 47th Avenue
Long Island City, NY 11101
tel: (718) 392-1177
fax: (718) 392-0162
mat'l handled: PET/HDPE, polypropylene

National Waste Technologies, Inc.
67 Wall Street, Suite 2411
New York, NY 10005
tel: (212) 323-8045
mat'l handled: mixed plastics

Tulip Corporation
3125 Highland Avenue
Niagara Falls, NY 14305
tel: plant (716) 282-1261
tel: purchasing (414) 963-3120
fax: purchasing (414) 962-1825
contact: Michael Machalk (Wisconsin)
mat'l handled: HDPE, polypropylene, ABS

Ontario Recycling
12 Cairn Street
Rochester, NY 14611
tel: (716) 328-4253
fax: (716) 328-4256
mat'l handled: HDPE, LDPE

Enstar Corporation
777 Hoosick Road
Troy, NY 12180
tel: (518) 279-4311
fax: (518) 279-9127
mat'l handled: post-industrial thermoplastics, all surplus scrap, clean or contaminated

North Carolina

Plastic Materials Group
P.O. Box 2345
Fayetteville, NC 28302
tel: (800) 752-5237
contact: Ken Poole
mat'l handled: HDPE fractional melt, industrial or post-consumer scrap, mixed colors okay; large or small volumes acceptable

Mountain Polymers Inc.
5426 Garden Lake Drive
Greensboro, NC 27410
tel: (919) 294-1248
fax: (919) 855-6879
mat'l handled: HDPE, PET, polypropylene

Environmental Recycling Inc.
6212 Westgate Road
Raleigh, NC 27613
tel: (919) 881-4163
fax: (919) 881-4156

mat'l handled: HDPE, PET, polypropylene, polystyrene

Southeastern Industries
P.O. Box 809
Reidsville, NC 27320
tel: (919) 349-6243
fax: (919) 342-4101
mat'l handled: HDPE

Plastic Recy-colors Inc.
P.O. Box 11288
Winston-Salem, NC 27106
tel: (919) 744-0313
fax: (919) 744-1838
mat'l handled: ABS, LDPE, PC

Ohio

Cleveland Reclaim Inc.
2366 Woodhill Road
Cleveland, OH 44106
tel: (216) 791-2100
fax: (216) 791-7117
mat'l handled: HDPE

Plastic Lumber
209 South Maine Street
P.O. Box 80075
Akron, OH 44308
tel: (216) 762-8989
fax: (216) 434-7905
mat'l handled: mixed plastics

Quantum Chemical Corp.
Div. of USI Chemicals Co.
1855 James Parkway
Heath, OH 43056-9998
tel: (614) 929-5521
fax: (614) 928-2077
contact: G. Diederen (Plant Manager)
mat'l handled: PET/HDPE

United Resource Recovery, Inc.
Div. of Hancor Corp.
600 Kohler Street
Kenton, OH 43326
tel: (419) 424-8327
contact: C.H. Traweek; Steve Hagerty (Plant Manager)
mat'l handled: HDPE, PP

United Resource Recovery, Inc.
411 Olive Street
Findlay, OH 45840
tel: (419) 424-8327
fax: (419) 424-8300
mat'l handled: HDPE

Oregon

Denton Plastics Inc.
4427 NE 158th
Portland, OR 97230
tel: (503) 257-9945
fax: (503) 252-5319
mat'l handled: ABS, PE, polypropylene, polystyrene

Pennsylvania

Municipal Waste Recycling, Inc.
110 Chaucer Court
Coraopolis, PA 15108
tel: (412) 264-7999
fax: (412) 264-8070
mat'l handled: post-household and post-industrial plastic

St. Jude Polymer
400 S. Broad Mountain Avenue
Frackville, PA 17931-2402
tel: (717) 874-1220
contact: John Guers (Plant Manager)
mat'l handled: PET

Dart Container Corp. of Pennsylvania
60 E. Main Street
P.O. Box 546
Leola, PA 17540
tel: (717) 656-2236
contact: John Murray (Plant Manager)
mat'l handled: polystyrene

Graham Recycling Company
505 Windsor Street
P.O. Box 2618
York, PA 17405-2618
tel: (717) 852-7744
contact: Kim Watkins (Purchasing Agent)
mat'l handled: baled HDPE plastic bottles

South Carolina

Wellman Industries, Inc.
Highway 41–51
P.O. Box 188

Johnsonville, SC 29555-1088
tel: (803) 386-2011
contact: Bob Daston
mat'l handled: PET, HDPE

Unifibres, Inc.
P.O. Box 3145 CRS
Rock Hill, SC 29731
tel: (803) 328-1836
contact: Susan Newman (Georgia Office) (404) 442-1379
mat'l handled: truckloads only

Texas

Poly-America
2000 W. Marshall Drive
Grand Prairie, TX 75051
tel: (800) 527-3322 ext. 288
contact: Don Perry, materials manager
mat'l handled: LDPE/HDPE

Vermont

Casella Waste Management
P.O. Box 866
Ruthland, VT 05702
tel: (802) 775-9908
mat'l handled: PETE, HDPE

Vermont Rural Recyclers
P.O. Box 5
Marshfield, VT 05658
tel: (802) 426-3793
mat'l handled: HDPE

Washington

Partek
3209 N.W. Lower River Road
P.O. Box 1387
Vancouver, WA 98666
tel: (206) 695-1777
(800) 326-1777
fax: (206) 695-8994
mat'l handled: HDPE

Wisconsin

Riverside Materials
800 South Lane
P.O. Box 815
Appleton, WI 54912
tel: (414) 749-2237
fax: (414) 749-2354
mat'l handled: HDPE, LDPE, polypropylene, HIPS, etc.

REC Systems of WI, Inc.
2600 Energy Drive
East Troy, WI 53120
tel: (414) 642-3363
fax: (414) 642-9734
mat'l handled: HDPE

Midwest Plastics
580 Albion Road
P.O. Box 332
Edgertown, WI 53534
tel: (608) 884-3433
fax: (608) 884-6306
contact: Gary Fish
mat'l handled: HDPE

Poly-Anna Plastics
6960 N. Teutonia Avenue
Milwaukee, WI 53209
tel: (414) 351-5990
fax: (414) 351-3443
contact: Don Menefee
mat'l handled: high-impact polystyrene; ABS; polycarbonate; acrylic; PVC rigid white; HDPE (low melt)

Tulip Corporation
714 Keefe Avenue
Milwaukee, WI 53212
tel: (414) 963-3120
fax: (414) 962-1825
contact: Michael Machalk (Purchasing Agent)
mat'l handled: polypropolyne, ABS, HDPE

Canada

Resource Plastics Corp.
P.O. Box 3688
Brantford, ONT N3T 6HZ
tel: (519) 754-1754
fax: (519) 754-1742
mat'l handled: HDPE, LDPE, LLDPE, polypropylene

Plastigrind Inc.
15 Biggar Avenue
Hamilton, Ontario, Canada L8L 3Z3

tel: (416) 549-5272
fax: (416) 549-2119
mat'l handled: PVC, HDPE, LDPE

Steel End Users

See Yellow Pages for local area and nearby metropolitan areas under the listings "Foundry" and "Steel." There are approximately 5,000 steel foundries in the United States.

Alabama

Southern United Steel
300 Riverchase Galleria
P.O. Box 1208
Birmingham, AL 35244
tel: (205) 985-9290
contact: Jim C. Nuckels (Purchasing)
mat'l handled: steel can scrap buyer (truck or railcar loads)

Structural Metals, Inc.
Birmingham, AL
tel: (205) 592-8981
contact: Bishop Reeves (Purchasing)
mat'l handled: steel can scrap buyer (truck or railcar loads)

American Alloy Products Inc.
1725 Orphans Home Road NE
P.O. Box 1247
Cullman, AL 35056
tel: (205) 739-3560
mat'l handled: stainless steel

U.S. Steel
Fairfield, AL
tel: (412) 433-3926
contact: John Risser (Purchasing)
mat'l handled: steel can scrap buyer (truck or railcar loads)

Gulf States Steel
Gadsden, AL
tel: (205) 543-6166
contact: Chuck Durham (Purchasing)
mat'l handled: steel can scrap buyer (truck or railcar loads)

Proler International Corporation
Guntersville, AL
tel: (800) 347-2281
contact: Jerry Bailey (Purchasing)
mat'l handled: steel can scrap buyer (truck or railcar load)

Arizona

MRI/Proler
Randloph, AZ
tel: (800) 347-4337
contact: Jack Force (Purchasing)
mat'l handled: steel cans (truck and railcar loads)

Arkansas

Nucor Steel
Blytheville, AR
tel: (513) 621-8770
contact: Richard Jordan (David J. Joseph Co.) (Purchasing)
mat'l handled: steel can scrap buyer (truck and railcar loads)

California

Barbary Coast Steel
Emeryville, CA
tel: (205) 985-9290
contact: Jim C. Nuckels (Purchasing)
mat'l handled: steel can scrap buyer (truck and railcar loads)

MRI/Proler
Lathrop, CA
tel: (800) 347-4337
contacts: Jack Force (Purchasing)
mat'l handled: steel can scrap buyers (truck and railcar loads)

MRI/Proler
Los Angeles, CA
tel: (800) 347-4337
contact: Jack Force (Purchasing)
mat'l handled: steel can scrap buyers (truck and railcar loads)

Schnitzer Steel
Foot of Adeline Street

P.O. Box 747
Oakland, CA 94604
tel: (916) 985-4810
contacts: Steve Blackman (Ferrous Buyer); Steve Carney (Nonferrous Buyer)
mat'l handled: nonferrous and ferrous metals, used beverage containers, steel cans

MacLeod Metals
South Gate, CA
tel: (213) 567-7767
contact: Bill Lambert (Purchasing)
mat'l handled: steel can scrap buyer (truck and railcar loads)

Colorado

Pueblo Metals
A Division of C F & I Steel
728 Harlem
P.O. Box 2007
Pueblo, CO 81005
tel: (719) 545-0265
contact: Gus Turri (Purchasing)
mat'l handled: steel scrap

Florida

Florida Steel
Jacksonville, FL
tel: (513) 621-8770
contact: Richard Jordan (David J. Joseph Co.) (Purchasing)
mat'l handled: steel can scrap buyer (truck and railcar loads)

Florida Steel
Tampa, FL
tel: (513) 621-8770
contact: Richard Jordan (David J. Joseph Co.) (Purchasing)
mat'l handled: steel can scrap buyer (truck and railcar loads)

Magnimet Corporation
Tampa, FL
tel: (813) 677-4471
contact: Mike McVey (Purchasing)
mat'l handled: steel can scrap buyer (truck and railcar loads)

Georgia

Atlantic Steel
Cartersville, GA
tel: (404) 897-4622
contact: Rudy Garcia (Purchasing)
mat'l handled: steel can scrap buyer (truck and railcar loads)

Illinois

Illinois Steel
Bourbonnais, IL
tel: (205) 985-9290
contact: Jim C. Nuckels (Purchasing)
mat'l handled: steel can scrap buyer (truck and railcar loads)

Proler International Corporation
Chicago, IL
tel: (312) 768-9199
contact: Phillip Greenberg (Purchasing)
mat'l handled: steel can scrap buyer (truck and railcar loads)

U.S. Steel
Chicago, IL
tel: (412) 433-3926
contact: John Risser (Purchasing)
mat'l handled: steel can scrap buyer (truck and railcar loads)

Granite City Steel
20th and State Street
Granite City, IL 62040
tel: (618) 451-3251
contacts: Mike Rowda (Purchasing), Barbara Rieder (Raw Material Manager)
mat'l handled: ferrous metals, steel cans

Riverside Products
Division of Sivyer Steel
400 21st Street
P.O. Box 884
Moline, IL 61265
tel: (309) 764-2020
fax: (309) 764-9953
contact: Kris Brotherton (Purchasing Agent)
mat'l handled: mananese, low-alloy steel (8600 series steel), "1010" plate carbon steel

Acme Steel
13500 S Perry Avenue

Riverdale, IL 60627-1182
tel: (312) 849-2500 ext. 2350
contacts: Dick Small (Purchasing)
mat'l handled: steel can scrap buyer (truck and railcar loads)

Indiana

Bethlehem Steel
Highway 12
P.O. Box 248
Burns Harbor, IN 46304-0248
tel: (215) 694-6232
contact: Gus Perfetti (Purchasing)
mat'l handled: steel can scrap buyer (truck and railcar loads)

Nucor Steel Corporation
R.R. 2 P.O. Box 311
Crawfordsville, IN 47933
tel: (513) 621-8770
contact: Richard Jordan (David J. Joseph Co.) (Purchasing)
mat'l handled: steel can scrap buyer (truck and railcar loads)

AMG Resources Corp.
459 N. Cline Avenue
Gary, IN 46406-1049
tel: (412) 777-7312
contacts: Bob Chevalier and James Orendorff (Purchasing Agents)
mat'l handled: steel can scrap buyer (truck and railcar loads)

U.S. Steel
Gary, IN
tel: (412) 433-3926
contact: John Risser (Purchasing)
mat'l handled: steel can scrap buyer (truck and railcar loads)

LTV Steel
Indiana Harbor, IN
tel: (216) 622-4822
contact: Bob Muhlhan (Purchasing)
mat'l handled: steel can scrap buyer (truck and railcar loads)

Iowa

Sivyer Steel
225 S. 33rd Street
Bettendorf, IA
tel: (319) 355-1811
fax: (319) 355-3946
contact: John Wood (Purchasing Agent)
mat'l handled: magnesium, low-alloy steel (8600 series) carbon steel ("1010" plate)

North Star Steel
Wilton, IA
tel: (612) 688-1243
contact: Jim Schultz (Purchasing)
mat'l handled: steel can scrap buyer (truck and railcar loads)

Kansas

Prolerized Steel Corporation
Kansas City, KS
tel: (800) 347-2281
contact: Jerry W. Bailey (Purchasing)
mat'l handled: steel can scrap buyer (truck and railcar loads)

Kentucky

Newport Steel
Newport, KY
tel: (513) 621-8770
contact: Richard Jordan (David J. Joseph Co.) (Purchasing)
mat'l handled: steel can scrap buyer (truck and railcar loads)

Louisiana

Moresia Foundry Inc.
P.O. Box 512
Jeanerette, LA 70544
tel: (318) 276-4533
contact: Charlene Meeks (Sales Manager)
mat'l handled: cast iron

Bayou Steel
LaPlace, LA
tel: (504) 652-0338
contact: C. Frank Cambron (Purchasing)
mat'l handled: steel can scrap buyer (truck and railcar loads)

Maryland

AMG Resources Corp.
2415 Grays Road

P.O. Box 6501
Baltimore, MD 21219
tel: (412) 777-7312
contacts: Bob Chevalier and James Orendorff (Purchasing)
mat'l handled: steel can scrap buyer

Bethlehem Steel
Sparrows Point, MD
tel: (215) 694-6232
contact: Gus Perfetti (Purchasing)
mat'l handled: steel can scrap buyer (truck and railcar loads)

Michigan

National Steel
Detroit, MI
tel: (313) 297-2145
contact: Tom Trupkovich (Purchasing)
mat'l handled: steel can scrap buyer (truck and railcar loads)

North Star Steel
Monroe, MI
tel: (612) 688-1243
contact: Jim Schultz (Purchasing)
mat'l handled: steel can scrap buyer (truck and railcar loads)

Minnesota

AMG Resources Corp.
1303 Red Rock Road
Saint Paul, MN 55119
tel: (800) 633-3606 (Purchasing)
contacts: Bob Chevalier (Purchasing)
mat'l handled: steel can scrap buyer (truck and railcar loads)

North Star Steel
St. Paul, MN
tel: (612) 688-1243
contact: Jim Schultz (Purchasing)
mat'l handled: steel can scrap buyer (truck and railcar loads)

Mississippi

Mississippi Steel
Jackson, MS
tel: (205) 985-9290
contact: Jim C. Nuckels (Purchasing)
mat'l handled: steel can scrap buyer (truck and railcar loads)

Nebraska

Nucor Steel Corporation
Norfolk, NE
tel: (513) 621-8770
contact: Richard Jordan (David J. Joseph Co.), Purchasing
mat'l handled: steel can scrap buyer (truck and railcar loads)

New Jersey

Electrum Recovery Works, Inc.
827 Martin Street
Rahway, NJ 07065
tel: (908) 396-1616
fax: (908) 396-9390
contacts: Jack Douglas, John Silva
mat'l handled: Electronic residues, metal solder scrap, printed circuit boards with precious metal content, base metals; truck load quantity or less accepted.

AMG Resources Corporation
Roseland, NJ
tel: (201) 228-6604
contact: Roger Levine, Purchasing
mat'l handled: steel can scrap buyer (truck and railcar loads)

New York

Auburn Steel Company, Inc.
Quarry Road
P.O. Box 2008
Auburn, NY 13021
tel: (315) 253-4561
contacts: Gary Caldwell, Purchasing
mat'l handled: steel can scrap buyer (truck and railcar loads)

North Carolina

Florida Steel
Charlotte, NC
tel: (513) 621-8770
contact: Richard Jordan (David J. Joseph Co.), Purchasing
mat'l handled: steel can scrap buyer (truck and railcar loads)

Ohio

The Timken Company
1835 Dueber Avenue
Canton, OH 44706
tel: (216) 430-7036
contacts: Richard Menster, Purchasing
mat'l handled: steel can scrap buyer (truck and railcar loads)

Republic Engineered Steels
2633 8th Street, NE
P.O. Box 700
Canton, OH 44701-0700
tel: (216) 837-7032
contact: Ron Ebner, Purchasing
mat'l handled: steel can scrap buyer (truck and railcar loads)

Proler International Corp.
Cincinnati, OH
tel: (312) 819-0070
contact: Phillip Greenberg (Purchasing)
mat'l handled: steel can scrap buyer (truck and railcar loads)

LTV Steel
Cleveland, OH
tel: (216) 622-4822
contact: Bob Muhlhan (Purchasing)
mat'l handled: steel can scrap buyer (truck and railcar loads)

Proler International Corporation
East Liverpool, OH
tel: (800) 347-2281
contact: Jerry W. Bailey (Purchasing)
mat'l handled: steel can scrap buyer (truck and railcar loads)

U.S. Steel (Kobe Steel Co.)
1807 E. 28th Street
Lorain, OH 44055-1803
tel: (412) 433-3926
contact: John Risser (Purchasing)
mat'l handled: steel can scrap buyer (truck and railcar loads)

Wheeling-Pittsburgh Steel
Steubenville, OH
tel: (304) 234-2820
contact: Paul Schiffer (Purchasing)
mat'l handled: steel can scrap buyer (truck and railcar loads)

Magnimet Corporation
Toledo, OH
tel: (419) 697-2604
contact: Marie Clark (Purchasing)
mat'l handled: steel can scrap buyer (truck and railcar loads)

North Star Steel
Div. of Cargill, Inc.
2669 Martin Luther King Drive
Youngstown, OH 44510-1033
tel: (612) 688-1243
contact: Jim Schultz (Purchasing)
mat'l handled: steel can scrap buyer (truck and railcar loads)

Pennsylvania

Bethlehem Steel Corp.
Bethlehem, PA 18017
tel: (215) 694-6232
contacts: Gus Perfetti (Purchasing)
mat'l handled: steel can scrap buyer (truck and railcar loads)

Lukens Steel
50 S. First Avenue
Coatesville, PA 19320-3418
tel: (215) 383-2000
contact: Don Markward (Purchasing)
mat'l handled: steel can scrap buyer (truck and railcar loads)

U.S. Steel
Fairless Hills, PA
tel: (412) 433-3926
contact: John Risser (Purchasing)
mat'l handled: steel can scrap buyer (truck and railcar loads)

North Star Steel
230 Lower Market Street
P.O. Box 337
Milton, PA 17847
tel: (612) 688-1243
contact: Jim Schultz (Purchasing)
mat'l handled: steel can scrap buyer (truck and railcar loads)

AMG Resources Corp.
4100 Grand Avenue
Pittsburgh, PA 15225
tel: (412) 777-7312

contacts: Bob Chevalier and James Orendorff (Purchasing)
mat'l handled: steel can scrap buyer (truck and railcar loads)

U.S. Steel
600 Grant Street
Pittsburgh, PA 15219-4776
tel: (412) 433-3926
contact: John Risser (Purchasing)
mat'l handled: steel can scrap buyer (truck and railcar loads)

Bethlehem Steel
Steelton, PA
tel: (215) 694-6232
contact: Gus Perfetti (Purchasing)
mat'l handled: steel can scrap buyer (truck and railcar loads)

South Carolina

Nucor Steel Corporation
Dovesville Highway
P.O. Box 525
Darlington, SC 29532-9301
tel: (513) 621-8770
contact: Richard Jordan (David J. Joseph Co.) (Purchasing)
mat'l handled: steel can scrap buyer (truck and railcar loads)

Tennessee

Proler International Corporation
Chattanooga, TN
tel: (800) 347-2281
contact: Jerry Bailey (Purchasing)
mat'l handled: steel can scrap buyer (truck and railcar loads)

Florida Steel
Jackson, TN
tel: (513) 621-8770
contact: Richard Jordan (David J. Joseph Co.) (Purchasing)
mat'l handled: steel can scrap buyer (truck and railcar loads)

Florida Steel
Knoxville, TN
tel: (513) 621-8770
contact: Richard Jordan (David J. Joseph Co.) (Purchasing)
mat'l handled: steel can scrap buyer (truck and railcar loads)

Texas

Proler International Corporation
Canutillo, TX
tel: (800) 347-2281
contacts: J.W. Bailey (Purchasing)
mat'l handled: steel can scrap buyer (truck and railcar loads)

Proler International Corporation
7501 Wallisville
P.O. Box 286
Houston, TX 77001-0286
tel: (800) 347-2281
contact: Jerry W. Bailey (Purchasing Agent)
mat'l handled: steel can scrap buyer (truck and railcar loads)

Nucor Steel Corporation
Jewett, TX
tel: (513) 621-8770
contact: Richard Jordan (David J. Joseph Co.) (Purchasing)
mat'l handled: steel can scrap buyer (truck and railcar loads)

Chaparral Steel
Div. of Texas Industries, Inc.
300 Ward Road
Midlothian, TX 76065-9646
tel: (214) 775-8241
contact: Richard T. Jaffre (Purchasing)
mat'l handled: steel can scrap buyer (truck and railcar loads)

Structural Metals, Inc.
Div. of Commercial Metals Inc.
Mill Rd. P.O. Box 911
Seguin, TX 78156-0911
tel: (512) 379-7520
contact: Monty Parker (Purchasing)
mat'l handled: steel can scrap buyer (truck and railcar loads)

Utah

Nucor Steel Corporation
Plymouth, UT

tel: (513) 621-8770
contact: Richard Jordan (David J. Joseph Co.) (Purchasing)
mat'l handled: steel can scrap buyer (truck and railcar loads)

Virginia

Roanoke Electric Steel
102 Miller Street, N.W.
P.O. Box 13948
Roanoke, VA 24038
tel: (513) 621-8770
contact: Richard Jordan (David J. Joseph Co.) (Purchasing Agent)
mat'l handled: steel can scrap buyer (truck and railcar loads)

Washington

MRI/Proler
Seattle, WA
tel: (800) 347-4337
contact: Jack Force (Purchasing)
mat'l handled: steel can scrap buyer (truck and railcar loads)

Salmon Bay Steel
Seattle, WA
tel: (205) 985-9290
contact: Jim C. Nuckels (Purchasing)
mat'l handled: steel can scrap buyer (truck and railcar loads)

West Virginia

Weirton Steel
Weirton, WV
tel: (304) 797-2257
contact: John T. Turner (Purchasing)
mat'l handled: steel can scrap buyer (truck and railcar loads)

Canada

Metal Recovery Industries
Hamilton, Ontario, Canada
tel: (416) 549-9894
contact: Bill Wittig (Purchasing)
mat'l handled: steel can scrap buyer (truck and railcar loads)

Dofasco, Inc.
Hamilton, Ontario, Canada
tel: (416) 544-3761 ext. 4048
contact: Marty Harris (Purchasing)
mat'l handled: steel can scrap buyer (truck and railcar loads)

Stelco Steel
Hamilton, Ontario, Canada
tel: (416) 528-2511 ext. 4097
contact: Ross Morrell (Purchasing)
mat'l handled: steel can scrap buyer (truck and railcar loads)

Textiles Markets

There are approximately 350 firms that recycle textiles in the United States. See Yellow Pages for local area and nearby metropolitan areas under the headings "Wiping Cloths" or "Textiles."

Tire Markets

California

Coast Rubber Products
P.O. Box 1509
Bellflower, CA 90706
tel: (619) 246-7171
fax: (619) 246-7150
contact: Bruce Wills
mat'l handled: scrap tires

Atlas Rubber Inc.
1522 Fishburn Avenue
Los Angeles, CA 90063-2504
tel: (213) 266-4570
fax: (213) 267-4312
contacts: Robert E. Winters (President and General Manager); Ken Winters (Executive VP and Production Manager); Roger Rogers, Plant Engineer)
mat'l handled: scrap tires

Oxford Tire Recycling, Inc.
c/o Oxford Energy Group
3510 Unocal Place
Santa Rosa, CA 95403
tel: (707) 575-3939
(916) 487-8991
contact: James Sabraw (VP—Marketing)

Connecticut

Oxford Energy
1414 Norwich Road
Plainsfield, CT 06374
tel: (800) USE-TIRE
contact: Bill Delaney
mat'l handled: scrap tires

Florida

Rubber Products, Inc.
4521 W. Crest Avenue
Tampa, FL 33614
tel: (813) 870-0390
fax: (813) 875-2312
contact: Dave Truelove
mat'l handled: rubber buffing dust from tire recapping: high-percentage natural color rubber scrap

Georgia

Georgia Tire Dealers & Retreaders Assoc.
300 West Wieuca Road, N.E., Suite 115
Atlanta, GA
tel: (404) 252-6282
contact: Susan Saleska
mat'l handled: scrap tires

Indiana

Baker Rubber, Inc.
700 W. Chippewa Avenue
P.O. Box 2438
South Bend, IN 46680-2438
tel: (219) 291-5101
fax: (219) 291-5192
contact: William E. Stoler (Sales and Marketing Manager)
mat'l handled: scrap tires

R M H Resources
4407 Railroad Avenue
East Chicago, IN 46312
tel: (219) 397-8309
contact: Jack Filler
mat'l handled: scrap tires

Kansas

Tire Town, Inc.
401 South 2nd Street
Levinworth, KS 66048
tel: (913) 682-3201
contact: Duane Becker
mat'l handled: scrap tires

Minnesota

Whirl Air Rubber Products Inc.
1515 Central Avenue, N.E.
Minneapolis, MN 55413
Plant: Babbitt, MN
tel: (612) 781-3461
contact: Rick Johnson
mat'l handled: shredded tires 3-inch pieces or smaller

New York

Coletta Recycling Corp.
1629 Redfern Avenue
Far Rockaway, NY 11691
tel: (718) 327-4740
fax: (718) 868-0615
mat'l handled: scrap tires

North American Tire Recycling
Towpath Road
Fort Edward, NY 12828
tel: (518) 747-4195
contact: Carol Walkup
mat'l handled: scrap tires

Ohio

Mid West Elastomers
700 Industrial Drive
P.O. Box 1997
Wapakoneta, Ohio 45895-1997
tel: (419) 738-9634
fax: (419) 738-4504
contacts: Jerry J. Leyden (VP—Sales and Marketing); Ken Hirsch (Purchasing Agent)
mat'l handled: truck tires

Pennsylvania

J.H. Beers Inc.
Male Street
P.O. Box 669
Wind Gap, PA 18091
tel: (215) 759-7628
contact: Blaine Masemore

mat'l handled: scrap tires

Texas

Gibson Recycling
P.O. Box 1208
Atlanta, TX 75551
tel: (800) 245-2171
fax: (903) 796-9335
contact: Gerald Rich
mat'l handled: scrap tires

Canada

Dura Undercushions Ltd.
8525 Delmeade Street
Montreal, PQ Canada H4T 1M1
tel: (514) 737-6561
fax: (514) 342-7940
mat'l handled: scrap tires

Tungsten

Amax, Inc.
Highway 61 South, P.O. Box 220
Fort Madison, IA 52627
tel: (319) 463-7151
contact: Tom Anderson
mat'l handled: tungsten

Wood Pallets

See Yellow Pages for local area and near by metropolitan areas under the listing "Pallets."

Appendix B

Marketing Service Organizations

Industry Associations

Aluminum Association
900 19th Street, N.W.
Washington, D.C. 20006
tel: (202) 862-5100

Aluminum Recycling Association
1000 16th Street, N.W., Suite 603
Washington, D.C. 20036
tel: (202) 785-0951

American Forest Council
1250 Connecticut Avenue, N.W., Suite 320
Washington, D.C. 20036
tel: (202) 463-2455
President: Laurence D. Wiseman

American Foundrymen's Society
Golf and Wolf Roads
Des Plaines, IL 60016
tel: (312) 824-0181

American Institute of Chemical Engineers
345 E. 47th Street
New York, NY 10017
tel: (212) 705-7338
Executive Director: Dr. Richard E. Emmert

American Institute of Chemical Engineers
Forest Products Div.
Oregon State University
Chemical Engineering Dept.
Corvallis, OR 97331
tel: (503) 754-3155
Chairman: W. James Frederick, Jr.

American Institute of Mining, Metallurgical and Petroleum Engineers
345 E. 47th Street
New York, NY 10017
tel: (212) 705-7679
Executive Director: Robert H. Marcrum

American Institute of Steel Construction, Inc.
400 N. Michigan Avenue
Chicago, IL 60611-4185
tel: (312) 670-2400
President: Neil W. Zundel

American Iron & Steel Institute
1101 17th Street, N.W., 13th Floor
Washington, D.C. 20036
tel: (202) 452-7100
President: Milton Deaner

American Mining Congress
1920 N. Street, N.W., Suite 300
Washington, D.C. 20036
tel: (202) 861-2800

American Newspaper Publishers Association
The Newspaper Center
P.O. Box 17407
Dulles International Airport
Washington, D.C. 20041
tel: (703) 648-1000
President: Jerry W. Friedheim

American Paper Institute Inc.
260 Madison Avenue, 10th Floor
New York, NY 10016
tel: (212) 340-0600 or (800) 878-8878
President: Red Cavaney

American Pulpwood Association Inc.
1025 Vermont Avenue, N.W., Suite 1020
Washington, D.C. 20005
tel: (202) 347-2900
Chairman: C.F. Glatfelder, Jr.

American Retreaders' Association, Inc.
P.O. Box 17203
Louisville, KY 40217
tel: (800) 426-8835
(502) 367-9133
Executive Director: Marvin Bozarth

Asphalt Rubber Producers Group
3336 N. 32nd Street, Suite 106
Phoenix, AZ 85018
tel: (602) 955-1141
contact: Al France

American Tin Trade Association
P.O. Box 1347
New York, NY 10150
tel: (212) 715-5266
President: Rosemary Worns
Secretary: Terry Ford

Association of Independent Corrugated Converters
801 N. Fairfax Street, Suite 211
Alexandria, VA 22314
tel: (703) 836-2422
Executive VP: J. Richard Troll

Association of Iron and Steel Engineers
Three Gateway Center, Suite 2350
Pittsburgh, PA 15222
tel: (412) 281-6323
Managing Director: Herschel B. Poole

Association of Petroleum Re-Refiners
P.O. Box 605
Ellicott Station
Buffalo, NY 14205-0605
tel: (716) 855-2757
fax: (716) 855-0339
Public Relations: Mary Brandys

Association of Steel Distributors
111 East Wacker Drive, Suite 600
Chicago, IL 60601
tel: (312) 644-6610
Executive Director: Edward M. Craft

Association of Western Pulp and Paper Workers (AWPPW)
P.O. Box 4566
1430 S.W. Clay
Portland, OR 97208-4566
General VP: James A. Thompson

Automotive Dismantlers & Recyclers Association
10400 Eaton Place, Suite 203
Fairfax, VA 22030
tel: (703) 385-1001
Executive VP: William P. Steinkuller

Battery Council International
111 East Wacker Drive
Chicago, IL 60601
tel: (312) 644-6610
Executive Secretary: Edward Craft

The Beer Institute
1225 Eye Street, N.W., Suite 825
Washington, D.C. 20005
tel: (202) 737-2337

Brass and Bronze Ingot Manufacturers
300 W. Washington, Suite 1500
Chicago, IL 60606
tel: (312) 236-2715
fax: (312) 236-8772

Cadmium Association
34 Berkeley Square
London WIX 6AJ, England
tel: 01-499-8422
telex: 261286
Chief Executive: F. David Ward

Cadmium Council Inc.
292 Madison Avenue
New York, NY 10017
tel: (212) 578-4750
Executive Director: Hugh Morrow

Can Manufacturers Institute, Inc.
1625 Massachusetts Avenue, N.W.
Washington, D.C. 20036
tel: (202) 232-4677
Manager, Public Affairs: Jenny L. Day

Canadian Association of
Recycling Industries
415 rue Yonge Street, Suite 1620
Toronto, Ontario M5B 2E7, Canada
tel: (416) 595-5552
Executive Director: Stan Parker

Cast Metals Federation
(Iron Castings Society)
(National Foundry Association)
(Steel Founder's Society of America)
(Non-Ferrous Founders Society)
20611 Center Ridge Road
Rocky River, OH 44116
tel: (216) 333-9600

Center for Plastics Recycling Research
Rutgers, The State University of New Jersey
Busch Campus, Building 3529
P.O. Box 1179
Piscataway, NJ 08855
tel: (201) 932-3683

Cobalt Development Institute
95 High Street
Slough SL11DH, England
tel: 0753-38735
telex: 847466 Gobal G
contact: J.M. Johnston

Construction Industry Manufacturers
Association
111 E. Wisconsin Avenue, Suite 1700
Milwaukee, WI 53202
tel: (414) 272-0943
President: Fred J. Broad

Copper & Brass Servicenter Association
Adams Building, Suite 109
251 West DeKalb Pike
King of Prussia, PA 19406
tel: (215) 265-6658
Executive VP: R. Franklin Brown, Jr.

Copper Development Association, Inc.
Greenwich Office Park 2
Box 1840
Greenwich, CT 06836-1840
tel: (203) 625-8210

Copper Smelters and Refiners Association
10 Greenfield Crescent
Edgbaston, Birmingham B15 3AU, England
tel: 021-456-3322
telex: 339161 NOASER G
fax: 021-456-1394

Council for Solid Waste Solutions
1275 K Street, N.W., Suite 400
Washington, D.C. 20005
tel: (800) 243-5790
(202) 371-5319

Council on Plastic and Packaging in the
Environment
1275 K Street, N.W., Suite 900
Washington, D.C. 20005
tel: (202) 789-1310

Diamond Wheel Manufacturers Institute
712 Lakewood Center N.
14600 Detroit Avenue
Cleveland, OH 44107
tel: (216) 226-7700
Manager: A.P. Wherry & Assoc., Inc.

Ductile Iron Society
615 Sherwood Parkway
Mountainside, NJ 07092
tel: (201) 232-3080

Envelope Manufacturers Association
1600 Duke Street
Alexandria, VA 22314
tel: (703) 739-2200
Executive VP: Maynard H. Benjamin

European Zinc Institute
P.O. Box 2126
5600 CC Eindhoven, The Netherlands
tel: (40) 122497
telex: 51860 EZINC NL
fax: 31-40-122585
Chairman: T.J.C. Smid

Fibre Box Association
10 Gould Center 412
Rolling Meadows, IL 60008
tel: (312) 364-9600
President: Bruce Benson

Foodservice and Packaging Institute
1025 Connecticut Avenue, N.W., Suite 513
Washington, D.C. 20036
tel: (202) 822-6420
President: Joseph W. Bow

Glass Packaging Institute
1801 K Street, N.W., Suite 1105L

Washington, D.C. 20006
tel: (202) 887-4850
fax: (202) 785-5377

The Gold Institute
1026 16th Street, N.W., Suite 101
Washington, D.C. 20036
tel: (202) 783-0500
Managing Director: John H. Lutley

Independent Zinc Alloyers Association
1000 16th Street, N.W., Suite 603
Washington, D.C. 20036
tel: (202) 785-0558
Executive Director: R.M. Cooperman

INDA, Association of the Nonwoven Fabrics Industry
1001 Winstead Drive, Suite 460
Cary, NC 27513
tel: (919) 467-4632
President: John J. Mead

Industrial Diamond Association of America
3008 Millwood Avenue
Columbia, SC 29205
tel: (803) 252-5646

Institute of Scrap Recycling Industries, Inc.
1627 K Street, N.W., Suite 700
Washington, D.C. 20006-1704
tel: (202) 466-4050
fax: (202) 775-9109
Executive Director: Herschel Cutler
President: David Seris

International Association of Wiping Cloth Manufacturers
7910 Woodmont, Suite 1212
Bethesda, MD 20814
tel: (301) 656-1077
Executive Director: Bernie Brill

International Business Forms Industries Inc.
1730 N. Lynn Street, Suite 501
Arlington, VA 22209
tel: (703) 841-9191
Chairman: Jack Kennedy

International Copper Research Association, Inc.
708 Third Avenue
New York, NY 10017
tel: (212) 697-9355
President: Lennart Gustaffson

International Iron and Steel Institute
Rue Col. Bourg, 120
B-1140 Brussels, Belgium
tel: 735.90.75
telex: 22639
fax: 735-80-12

International Lead Zinc Research Organization, Inc.
2525 Meridan Parkway
P.O. Box 12036
Research Triangle Park, NC 22709-2036
tel: (919) 361-4647
fax: (919) 361-1957

International Magnesium Association
7927 Jones Branch Drive
Lancaster Building, Suite 400
McLean, VA 22102
tel: (703) 442-8888

International Precious Metals Institute
Government Building, ABE Airport
Allentown, PA 18103
tel: (215) 266-1570
fax: (215) 266-1008
Executive Director: David E. Lundy

International Primary Aluminum Institute (PAI)
New Zealand House, 9th Floor
Haymarket
London SW1Y 4TE, England
tel: 01-930-0528
telex: 917837 IPAI London
fax: 01-321-0183

International Tungsten Industry Association
280 Earls Court Road
London SW5, England
tel: 01-373-7413
Secretary General: Michale Maby

Iron and Steel Society of AIME
410 Commonwealth Drive
Warrendale, PA 15086
tel: (412) 776-1535
Executive Director: Lawrence G. Kuhn

Lead Development Association
34 Berkeley Square
London W1X 6AJ, England
tel: 01-499-8422

telex: 261286
Chief Executive: F. David Ward

Lead Industries Association, Inc.
292 Madison Avenue
New York, NY 10017
tel: (212) 578-4750
Executive Director: Jerome F. Smith

Midwest Paper Association
2510 Dempster, Suite 109
Des Plaines, IL 60016
tel: (312) 296-7788
Executive Director: Warren W. Finding

NATAS
National Appropriate Technology Assistance Service
U.S. Department of Energy
P.O. Box 2525
Butte, MT 59702-2525
tel: (800) 428-2525
in Montana: (800) 428-1718

National Association of Aluminum Distributors
1900 Arch Street
Philadelphia, PA 19103
tel: (215) 564-3484
Executive VP: Kenneth R. Hutton
Consulting Director: R. Bruce Wall

National Association of Chemical Recyclers
1333 New Hampshire Avenue, N.W., Suite 1100
Washington, D.C. 20036
tel: (202) 463-6956
Executive Director: Brenda Pulley

National Association for Plastic Container Recovery
4828 Parkway Plaza Boulevard
Charlotte, NC 28217
tel: (704) 357-3250
(800) 7NAPCOR

National Association of Recycling Industries, Inc.
330 Madison Avenue
New York, NY 10017
tel: (212) 867-7330

National Business Forms Association
433 E. Monroe Avenue
Alexandria, VA 22301
tel: (703) 836-6225
Executive Director: Peter Colaianni

National Oil Recyclers Association
2777 Broadway Avenue
Cleveland, OH 44106
tel: (216) 623-8383
fax: (216) 623-8393
Public Relations: Kitty McWilliams

National Paper Trade Association, Inc.
111 Great Neck Road
Great Neck, NY 11021
tel: (516) 829-3070
President: John J. Buckley, Jr.

National Polystyrene Recycling Company
P.O. Box 66495
Washington, D.C. 20035
tel: (202) 296-1954

National Recycling Coalition
1101 30th Street, N.W., Suite 305
Washington, D.C. 20007
tel: (202) 625-6406
fax: (202) 625-6409

National Resource Recovery Association
1620 I Street, N.W.
Washington, D.C. 20006
tel: (202) 293-7330
Executive Secretary: Ron Musselwhite

National Soft Drink Association
Solid Waste Management Dept.
1101 16th Street, N.W.
Washington, D.C. 20036
tel: (202) 463-6700

National Solid Waste Institute
10928 North 56th Street
Tampa, FL 33617
tel: (813) 985-3208

National Solid Wastes Management Association
1730 Rhode Island Avenue, N.W., Suite 1000
Washington, D.C. 20036
tel: (202) 659-4613

National Textile Processors Guild, Inc.
75 Livingston Street
Brooklyn, NY 11201
tel: (718) 875-2300

National Tire Dealers and Retreaders Association
1250 I Street, N.W., Suite 400
Washington, D.C. 20005

tel: (202) 789-2300

New York Association of Dealers in Paper Mills' Supplies Inc.
35 W. 45th Street
New York, NY 10036
tel: (212) 966-9710

Nickel Development Institute
15 Toronto Street, Suite 402
Toronto, Ontario M5C 2E7, Canada
tel: (416) 362-8850
fax: (416) 362-3346
President: J.P. Schade
Executive Director: Michael O. Pearce

Non-Ferrous Founders' Society, Inc.
455 State Street, Suite 100
Des Plaines, IL 60016
tel: (312) 299-0950
Executive Director: James L. Mallory, CAE

Non-Ferrous Metals Producers Committee
1225 19th Street, N.W., Suite 210
Washington, D.C. 20036
tel: (202) 466-7720
contact: Dr. Kenneth R. Button

Northwest Pulp and Paper Association
1300 114th Avenue, S.E., Suite 110
Bellevue, WA 98004
tel: (206) 455-1323
Executive Director: Liewellyn Matthews

Pacific Coast Association of Pulp and Paper Manufacturers
1225 American Bank Building
Portland, OR 97205
Managing Director: R.W. Hess

Pacific Coast Paper Box Manufacturers' Association
2301 E. Vernon Avenue
P.O. Box 60957
Los Angeles, CA 90060
tel: (213) 581-1183
President: John T. Fredrick Jr.

The Paper Bag Institute Inc.
505 White Plains Road
Tarrytown, NY 10594
tel: (914) 631-0696
Executive VP: B.C. Dixon

Paperboard Packaging Council
1101 Vermont Avenue, N.W., Suite 411
Washington, D.C. 20005
tel: (202) 289-4100
contact: S. Edward Iciek

Penton Directory
Foundry Marketing Services Department
Penton Plaza
Cleveland, OH 44114

The Plastic Bottle Information Bureau
1275 K Street, N.W.
Washington, D.C. 20005
tel: (202) 371-5244

Plastic Recycling Corp. of California
3345 Wilshire Boulevard, Suite 1105
Los Angeles, CA 90010
tel: (213) 487-1544

Plastic Recycling Corp. of New Jersey
P.O. Box 6316
North Brunswick, NJ 08902
tel: (201) 821-0254

Plastics Recycling Foundation
1275 K Street, N.W.
Washington, D.C. 20005
tel: (202) 371-5337

Platinum Guild International (USA) Inc.
1212 Avenue of the Americas, 11th Floor
New York, NY 10036
tel: (212) 827-0510
fax: (212) 827-0518

Polystyrene Packaging Council Inc.
1025 Connecticut Avenue, N.W.
Washington, D.C. 20036
tel: (202) 822-6424

Pulp & Paper Manufacturers Association (Lake States)
2000 S. Memorial Drive
Appleton, WI 54915
tel: (414) 734-5778
Executive Director: Bradford K. Libby

Rubber Manufacturers Association
1400 K Street, N.W.
Washington, D.C. 20005
tel: (202) 682-4800

Scrap Tire Management Council
1400 K Street, N.W.
Washington, D.C. 20005

tel: (202) 408-7781
fax: (202) 682-4854
Executive Director:
Michael H. Blumenthal

The Silver Institute
1026 16th Street, N.W., Suite 101
Washington, D.C. 20036
tel: (202) 783-0500

Silver International
292 Madison Avenue
New York, NY 10017
tel: (212) 689-4737
Director: Linda Meeham

Silver Users Association
1717 K Street, N.W. Suite 1206
Washington, D.C. 20006
tel: (202) 785-3050
Executive VP: Walter L. Frankland

Society of Mining Engineers, Inc.
P.O. Box 625002
Littleton, CO 80162-5002
tel: (303) 973-9550
fax: (303) 973-3845

Society of Plastics Engineers
14 Fairfield Drive
Brookfield Center, CT 06804-0403
tel: (203) 775-0471
Executive Director: Robert D. Forger

Society of the Plastics Industry, Inc.
1275 K Street, N.W., Suite 400
Washington, D.C. 20005
Tel: (202) 371-5200
President: Larry L. Thomas

South East Asia Iron & Steel Institute
Room 507 Ortigas Building
Ortigas Avenue, Pasig 1600
Metro Manila, Philippines
tel: 673-216/2069/1456
telex: 66396 SEASI PN
29084 SEAISI PH
fax: 632-673-3290

Southern Forest Products Association
2900 Indiana Avenue
Kenner, LA 70065
tel: (504) 443-4464
President: Karl Lindberg

Steel Bar Mills Association
25 N. Brentwood Boulevard
Clayton, MO 63105
tel: (314) 862-0034
fax: (314) 721-5083

Steel Can Recycling Association
2 Gateway Center
Pittsburgh, PA 15222
tel: (412) 456-3864
President: Kurt Smalberg

Steel Can Recycling Institute
Foster Plaza 10
680 Andersen Drive
Pittsburgh, PA 15220
tel: (800) 876-SCRI

Steel Manufacturers Association
815 Connecticut Avenue, N.W., Suite 304
Washington, D.C. 20006
tel: (202) 331-7027
fax: (202) 331-7675
President: James F. Collins

Steel Plate Fabricators Association, Inc.
2400 S. Downing Avenue
West Chester, IL 60154
tel: (312) 562-8750
Executive Director: Ward A. Gill

Steel Service Center Institute
1600 Terminal Tower
Cleveland, OH 44113
tel: (216) 694-3630
President: Andrew G. Sharkey

Steel Shipping Container
Institute, Inc.
2204 Morris Avenue
Union, NJ 07083
tel: (201) 688-8750
President: Arthur J. Schutz, Jr.

Steel Structures Painting Council
4400 Fifth Avenue
Pittsburgh, PA 15213
tel: (412) 268-3327
Publication Orders: (412) 268-3455
Director: Bernard R. Appleman

Steel Tank Institute
728 Anthony Trail
Northbrook, IL 60062
tel: (312) 498-1980

Executive VP: Brian C. Donovan

Steel Tube Institute of North America
522 Westgate Tower
Cleveland, OH 44116
tel: (216) 333-4550
Executive Director: Robert Boeddener

Tantalum-Niobium International
Study Center
Rue Washington 40
1050 Brussels, Belgium
tel: 322-649.51.58
fax: 322-649.32.69
President: Dr. Harry Stuart

Tantalum Producers Association
1230 Keith Building
Cleveland, OH 44115
tel: (216) 241-7333
Executive Director:
Charles M. Stockinger

TAPPI (Technical Association of the Pulp and Paper Industry)
Technology Park
P.O. Box 105113
Atlanta, GA 30348
tel: (404) 446-1400
Executive Director: William L. Cullison

Technical Association of the Pulp & Paper Industry
P.O. Box 105113
GA 30348-5113

Texas Association of Steel Importers, Inc.
P.O. Box 920919
Houston, TX 77292-0919
tel: (713) 681-5461
President: Mike Evans

Textile Fibers & By-Products Association
4108 Park Road, Suite 202
P.O. Box 11065
Charlotte, NC 28220
tel: (704) 527-5593

Tin Research Institute, Inc.
1353 Perry Street
Columbus, OH 43201
tel: (614) 424-6200
Manager: Daniel J. Maykuth

Tire Retread Information Bureau
900 Weldon Grove
Pacific Grove, CA 93950
tel: (408) 372-1917
fax: (408) 372-9210
Managing Director: Harvey Brodsky

Titanium Development Association
11 W. Monument Avenue, Suite 510
P.O. Box 2307
Dayton, OH 45401
tel: (513) 223-8432
President: Frederick Gieg

The Vinyl Institute
155 Route 46 West
Wayne, NJ 07470
tel: (201) 890-9299

The Wire Association
International, Inc.
P.O. Box H
1570 Boston Post Road
Guilford, CT 06437
tel: (203) 453-2777
Member Services: S.M. Pascarelle

Trees for Tomorrow Inc.
P.O. Box 609
Eagle River, WI 54521
tel: (715) 479-6456
Executive Director: Henry H. Haskell

Wire Industry Suppliers Association
7297 Lee Highway, Suite N
Falls Church, VA 22042
tel: (703) 533-9530
faz: (703) 241-5306
Executive Director:
Harry W. Buzzerd, Jr.

Wire Reinforcement Institute
8361 A Greensboro Drive
McLean, VA 22102
tel: (703) 790-9790
President: Milton R. Sees

Wisconsin Paper Council
111 E. Wisconsin Avenue
P.O. Box 718
Neenah, WI 54957-0718
tel: (414) 722-1500
President: Thomas H. Schmidt

Wisconsin Paper Group Inc.
P.O. Box 746

Neenah, WI 54956
tel: (414) 722-2863
General Manager: James W. Vander Hyden

World Bureau of Metal Statistics
27a High Street
Ware, Herts, SG12 9BA, England
tel: 0920 61274
telex: 817746 wbms
fax: 0920-4258

Zinc Development Association
34 Berkeley Square
London W1X 6AJ, England
tel: 01-499-6636
telex: 261286
Chief Executive: F. David Ward

Commodity Exchanges

Illinois

Chicago Board of Trade
141 West Jackson Boulevard
Chicago, IL 60604
tel: (312) 435-3500
Chairman: Karsten Mahlmann
President: Thomas R. Donovan

International Monetary Market
(Chicago Mercantile Exchange)
30 South Wacker Drive
Chicago, IL 60606
tel: (312) 930-1000

Mid America Commodity Exchange
141 West Jackson
Chicago, IL 60604
tel: (312) 435-3500

New York

Commodity Exchange, Inc.
4 World Trade Center
New York, NY 10048
tel: (212) 938-2900
Chairman: John Hanemann

New York Mercantile Exchange
4 World Trade Center
New York, NY 10048
tel: (212) 938-2242
Chairman: Lou Guttman

Canada

The Winnipeg Commodity Exchange
500-360 Main Street
Winnipeg, Manitoba, Canada R3C 3Z4
tel: (204) 949-0495
fax: (204) 943-5448
Secretary: M. Perring
Treasurer and Compliance Manager:
R. Bouchard
Information Services Manager:
K. Emmond

England

London Metal Exchange
Plantation House, Fenchurch Street
London EC3M 3AP, England
tel: 01-626-3311
telex: 8951367

Waste Exchanges

Alabama

Alabama Waste Exchange
The University of Alabama
Bill Herz
P.O. Box 870203
Tuscaloosa, AL 35487-0203
tel: (205) 348-8401

California

California Waste Exchange
Department of Health Services
Robert McCormick
P.O. Box 942732
Sacramento, CA 94234-7320
tel: (916) 324-1807

San Francisco Waste Exchange
Portia Sinnott
2524 Benvenue, #35
Berkeley, CA 94704
tel: (415) 548-6659

Florida

Southern Waste Information Exchange Service
Eugene B. Jones

P.O. Box 960
Tallahassee, FL 32302
tel: (800) 441-7949
fax: (904) 574-6704

Illinois

Hazardous Waste Research and Information Center
320 William Pett Way
Pittsburgh, PA 15238
tel: (412) 826-5320

Industrial Materials Exchange Service
Diane Shockey
2200 Churchill Road, Suite 24
P.O. Box 19276
Springfield, IL 62794-9276
tel: (217) 782-0450
fax: (217) 524-4193

Indiana

Indiana Waste Exchange
Purdue University
Lynn A. Corson
2129 Civil Engineering Building
West Lafayette, IN 47907
tel: (317) 494-5036
fax: (317) 494-6422

Michigan

Great Lakes/Midwest Waste Exchange
Kay Ostrowski
400 Ann Street, N.W., Suite 201A
Grand Rapids, MI 49504-2054
tel: (616) 363-3262

Montana

Montana Industrial Waste Exchange
Montana Chamber of Commerce
Don Ingles
2030 11th Avenue
P.O. Box 1730
Helena, MT 59624
tel: (406) 442-2405

New Hampshire

New Hampshire Waste Exchange
Gary J. Olson
c/o NHRRA
P.O. Box 721
Concord, NH 03301
tel: (603) 224-6996

New Jersey

Industrial Waste Information Exchange
New Jersey Chamber of Commerce
William E. Payne
5 Commerce Street
Newark, NJ 07102
tel: (201) 623-7070

New York

Enstar Corporation
John T. Engster
P.O. Box 189
Latham, NY 12110
tel: (518) 785-0470

Northeast Industrial Waste Exchange, Inc.
Lewis Cutler, Manager
90 Presidential Plaza, Suite 122
Syracuse, NY 13202
tel: (315) 422-6572
fax: (315) 422-9051

North Carolina

Southeast Waste Exchange
Ms. Maxie L. May
Urban Institute
University of North Carolina at Charlotte
Charlotte, NC 28223
tel: (704) 547-2307

Ohio

Investment Recovery Association
712 Lakewood Center North
14600 Detroit Avenue
Cleveland, OH 44107
tel: (216) 226-7700

Industrial Association of Central Ohio
Douglas R. Palmer
1646 W. Lane Avenue Suite 7
Columbus, OH 43221
tel: (614) 486-6741

Wastelink, Div. of Tencon Inc.
Mary E. Malotke
140 Wooster Pike
Milford, OH 45150
tel: (513) 248-0012

Pennsylvania

Center for Hazardous Materials Research
320 William Pett Way
Pittsburgh, PA 15238
tel: (412) 826-5320

Tennessee

Tennessee Waste Exchange
Patti Christian
226 Capitol Boulevard, Suite 800
Nashville, TN 37202
tel: (615) 256-5141

Texas

RENEW
Texas Water Commission
Hope Castillo
P.O. Box 13087
Austin, TX 78711-3087
tel: (512) 463-7773

Washington

Industrial Materials Exchange
Jerry Henderson
172 20th Avenue
Seattle, WA 98122
tel: (206) 296-4633

Pacific Materials Exchange
Bob Smee
South 3707 Godfrey Boulevard
Spokane, WA 99204
tel: (509) 623-4244

Washington, D.C.

Pollution Prevention Information Clearinghouse
EPA
401 M Street, S.W.
Washington, D.C. 20460
tel: (202) 475-7161
RCRA/Superfund Hotline: (800) 424-9346

Canada

Alberta

Alberta Waste Material Exchange
Alberta Research Council
William C. Kay
250 Karl Clark Road
P.O. Box 8330, Postal Station F
Edmonton, Alberta, Canada T6H 5X2
tel: (403) 450-5408

British Columbia

British Columbia Waste Exchange
Judy Toth
2150 Maple Street
Vancouver, B.C. Canada V6J 3T3
tel: (604) 731-7222

Manitoba

Manitoba Waste Exchange
c/o Biomass Energy Institute
James Ferguson
1329 Niakwa Road
Winnipeg, Manitoba, Canada R2J 3T4
tel: (204) 257-3891

Ontario

Canadian Waste Materials Exchange
ORTECH International
Sheridan Park Research Community
Dr. Robert Laughlin
2395 Speakman Drive
Mississauga, Ontario, Canada L5K 1B3
tel: (416) 822-4111 (ext. 265)

Peel Regional Waste Exchange
Regional Municipality of Peel
Glen Milbury
10 Peel Center Drive
Brampton, Ontario, Canada L 6T 4B9
tel: (416) 791-9400

Quebec

Canadian Chemical Exchange
Philippe LaRoche
P.O. Box 1135
Ste-Adele, Quebec, Canada J0R 1L0
tel: (514) 229-6511

Appendix C

Periodicals Concerned with Recycling

Metals and Metalworking Periodicals

Metal Producing
Penton Publishing Co.
600 Sumner Street
Stamford, CT 06904
tel: (216) 696-7000
fax: (216) 696-8765

Alloys Index
A/S/M Intl.
Route 87 Materials Park
Materials Park, OH 44073
tel: (216) 338-5151
fax: (216) 338-4634

Aluminum Developments Digest
Aluminum Association
900 19th Street, N.W.
Washington, D.C. 20006
tel: (202) 862-5100

Aluminum Ingot and Mill Products
U.S. Bureau of the Census
U.S. Dept. of Commerce
Washington, D.C. 20233
tel: (301) 763-4100

Aluminum Situation
Aluminum Association
900 19th Street, N.W.
Washington, D.C. 20006
tel: (202) 862-5100

Aluminum Statistical Review
Aluminum Association
900 19th Street, N.W.
Washington, D.C. 20006
tel: (202) 862-5100

American Iron and Steel Institute, Annual Statistical Report
American Iron & Steel Institute
1133 15th Street, N.W., #300
Washington, D.C. 20005-2701
tel: (202) 452-7100

Buyers Guide
International Magnesium Association
2010 Corporate Ridge, #700
McLean, VA 22102-7838
tel: (703) 442-8888
fax: (703) 821-1824

Canadian Metallurgical Quarterly
Pergamon Press, Inc., Maxwell House
Fairview Park
Elmsford, NY 10523
tel: (914) 592-7700
fax: (914) 592-3625

Directory of Iron and Steel Plants
Association of Iron
3 Gateway Center, Suite 2350
Pittsburgh, PA 15222
tel: (412) 281-6323

Ductile Iron News
Charnas, Inc.
76 Eastern Boulevard
Glastonbury, CT 06033-1201
tel: (201) 232-3080

Forging Industry Association Member Companies
Forging Industry Assn.
25 Prospect Avenue West
#300-LTV
Cleveland, OH 44115
tel: (216) 781-6260
fax: (216) 781-0102

International Journal of Powder Metallurgy
American Powder Metallurgy Institute
105 College Road E.
Princeton, NJ 08540
tel: (609) 452-7700
fax: (609) 987-8523

Iron Age Scrap Price Bulletin
Fairchild Publications
201 King of Prussia Rd.
Radnor, PA 19089
tel: (215) 964-4307

Iron and Steel Engineer
Association of Iron
3 Gateway Center, Suite 2350
Pittsburgh, PA 15222
tel: (412) 281-6323

JOM (Journal of Metals)
Minerals, Metals & Materials Society
420 Commonwealth Drive
Warrendale, PA 15086
tel: (412) 776-9070
fax: (412) 776-3770

Lead
Lead Industries Association, Inc.
292 Madison Avenue
New York, NY 10017
tel: (212) 578-4750

Light Metal Age
Fellom Publishing Co.
693 Mission Street
San Francisco, CA 94105
tel: (415) 781-1431

Magnesium
International Magnesium Association
2010 Corporate Ridge, #700
McLean, VA 22102-7838
tel: (703) 442-8888
fax: (703) 821-1824

Magnesium Monthly Review
Magnesium Monthly Review
106 Spring Forest Road
Greenville, SC 29615
tel: (803) 244-5718

Metal Can Shipments Report
Manfacturers Institute
1625 Massachussetts Avenue, N.W.
Washington, D.C. 20036
tel: (202) 232-4677

Metal Center News
Fairchild Publications
7 E. 12th Street
New York, NY 10003
tel: (212) 741-6483

Metal Fabricating News
Metal Fabricating Institute
Box 1178
Rockford, IL 61105
tel: (815) 965-4031

Modern Metals
Delta Communications, Inc.
400 N. Michigan Avenue
Chicago, IL 60611
tel: (312) 222-2000
fax: (312) 222-2026

Nonferrous Edition of 33 Metals
Penton Publishing
1100 Superior Avenue
Cleveland, OH 44114
tel: (216) 696-7700
fax: (216) 696-7658

Recycling Today—Scrap Market Edition
(Secondary Raw Materials)
GIE, Inc.
4012 Bridge Avenue
Cleveland, OH 44113
tel: (216) 961-4130
fax: (216) 961-0364

Silver Institute Letter
Silver Institute
1026 16th Street, N.W., Suite 101
Washington, D.C. 20036

tel: (202) 783-0500

Silver Market
Handy
850 Third Avenue
New York, NY 10022
tel: (212) 752-3400

Silver Refiners of the World
Silver Institute
1026 16th Street, N.W., Suite 101
Washington, D.C. 20036
tel: (202) 783-0500

Stainless Steels Digest
A/S/M International
Route 87, Materials Park
Materials Park, OH 44073
tel: (216) 338-5151

Steel Industry Review
Data Resources Inc.
24 Hartwell Avenue
Lexington, MA 02173
tel: (617) 863-5100

Steel Mill Products
U.S. Bureau of the Census
U.S. Department of Commerce
Washington, D.C. 20233
tel: (301) 763-4100

Tin and Its Uses
Tin Information Center of North America
1353 Perry Street
Columbus, OH 43201
tel: (614) 424-6200

Titanium Digest
A/S/M International
Route 87 Materials Park
Materials Park, OH 44073
tel: (216) 338-5151

Titanium Mill Products, Ingot and Castings
U.S. Bureau of the Census
U.S. Department of Commerce
Washington, D.C. 20233
tel: (301) 763-4100

Treasure Hunter's News
Treasure Trove Archives
210 N. Main Street
Ames, NE 68621
tel: (402) 721-8588

World Aluminum Abstracts
Aluminum Association
900 19th Street, N.W.
Washington, D.C. 20006
tel: (202) 862-5100

Sanitation Periodicals

BioCycle-Journal of Waste Recycling
J.G. Press, Inc.
419 State Avenue
Emmaus, PA 18049
tel: (215) 967-4135

Solid Waste Management; Available Information Materials
U.S. Environmental Protection Agency
401 M Street, S.W., A-107
Washington, D.C. 20460
tel: (202) 382-4522

Solid Waste Management Newsletter
Cooperative Extension Service
Cook College, Rutgers University
New Brunswick, NJ 08903
tel: (908) 932-9443

Solid Waste Report
Business Publishers, Inc.
951 Pershing Drive
Silver Spring, MD 20910-4464
tel: (301) 587-6300
fax: (301) 587-1081

Waste Age
National Solid Wastes Management Association
1730 Rhode Island Avenue, N.W., Suite 1000
Washington, D.C. 20036
tel: (202) 861-0708
fax: (202) 659-0925

Environmental and Ecology Periodicals

Amicus Journal
Natural Resources Defense Council
40 W. 20th Street, 11th Floor
New York, NY 10011
tel: (212) 727-2700
fax: (212) 727-1773

Audubon
National Audubon Society
950 Third Avenue
New York, NY 10022
tel: (212) 832-3200

Beyond Waste
Oregon Department of Environmental Quality
811 SW 6th Avenue
Portland, OR 97204
tel: (503) 229-6044

Bottle/Can Recycling Update
Resource Recycling, Inc.
Box 10540
Portland, OR 97210
tel: (503) 227-1319
fax: (503) 227-6135

Buzzworm: The Environmental Journal
Buzzworm, Inc.
1818 16th Street
Boulder, CO 80302
tel: (303) 442-1969

CAW Waste Watch
Californians Against Waste
Box 289
Sacramento, CA 95802
tel: (916) 443-5422

Canadian Association of Recycling Industries, Newsletter
Canadian Association of Recycling Industries
415 Yonge Street, #1620
Toronto, Ontario, M5B 2E7 Canada

Conservation Commission News
New Hampshire Association of Conservation Commissions
54 Portsmouth Street
Concord, NH 03301
tel: (603) 224-7867

Conservationist
New York State Department of Environmental Conservation
50 Wolf Road
Albany, NY 12233
tel: (518) 457-6668
fax: (518) 457-1088

Cycle
Environmental Action Coalition
625 Broadway, 2nd Floor
New York, NY 10012
tel: (212) 677-1601

Directory of Environmental Organizations
Educational Communications
Box 35473
Los Angeles, CA 90035
tel: (213) 559-9160

Directory of National Environmental Organizations
U.S. Environmental Directories
Box 65156
St. Paul, MN 55165

EDF Letter
Environmental Defense Fund
257 Park Avenue S., 16th Fl.
New York, NY 10010-7304
tel: (212) 505-2100

EPA Bulletin
U.S. Environmental Protection Agency
401 M Street, S.W., A-107
Washington, D.C. 20460
tel: (202) 755-0890

EPA Journal
U.S. Environmental Protection Agency
401 M Street, S.W., A-107
Washington, D.C. 20460
tel: (202) 382-4393

EPA Newsletter
U.S. Environmental Protection Agency
College Station Road
Athens, GA 30605

EPA Policy Alert
Inside Washington Publishers
1235 Jeff Davis Highway, #1206
Arlington, VA 22202
tel: (703) 892-8500

EPA Publications Bibliography Quarterly
NTIS
5285 Port Royal Road
Springfield, VA 22161
tel: (703) 487-4650

Environmental Action
Environmental Action, Inc.
1525 New Hampshire Avenue, N.W.
Washington, D.C. 20036
tel: (202) 745-4870

fax: (202) 745-4880

Environmental Forum
Environmental Law Institute
1616 P Street, N.W., #200
Washington, D.C. 20036
tel: (202) 328-5150
fax: (202) 338-5002

Environmental News (NJ Environmental Times)
New Jersey Department of Environmental Protection
401 E. State Street, CN 402
Trenton, NJ 08625
tel: (609) 984-6773

Forest Notes
Society for the Protection of New Hampshire Forests
54 Portsmouth Street
Concord, NH 03301
tel: (603) 224-9945

Garbage: The Practical Journal for the Environment
Garbage: The Practical Journal for the Environment
Box 56520
Boulder, CO 80321-6520

Greenpeace
Greenpeace
1436 U Street, N.W.
Washington, D.C. 20009
tel: (202) 462-1177
fax: (202) 462-4507

Groundwater Pollution News
Bureau of National Affairs, Inc.
Buraff Publications, Inc.
1350 Connecticut Avenue, N.W. #1000
2445 M Street #275
Washington, D.C. 20036
tel: (202) 862-0990
fax: (202) 862-0999

Hazmat World
Tower-Borner Publishing, Inc.
800 Roosevelt Road Bldg. C Suite 206
Glen Ellyn, IL 60137
tel: (708) 858-1888
fax: (708) 858-1957

J.G. Press, Inc.
419 State Avenue
Emmaus, PA 18049
Tel: (215) 967-4135

Inside EPA
Inside Washington Publishers
1235 Jeff Davis Highway, #1206
Arlington, VA 22202
tel: (703) 892-8500

Inside EPA's Environmental Policy Alert
Inside Washington Publishers
1235 Jeff Davis Highway, #1206
Arlington, VA 22202
tel: (703) 892-8500
fax: (703) 685-2606

Journal of Environmental Education
(Environmental Education)
Heldref Publications, Inc.
4000 Albemarle Street, N.W.
Washington, D.C. 20016
tel: (202) 362-6445
fax: (202) 537-0287

Materials Recycling Markets
Recoup Publishers Ltd.
Box 8465 Main Terminal
Ottawa, ON K1G 3H9 Canada
tel: (613) 448-2383

NYS Environment
New York State Department of Environmental Conservation
50 Wolf Road
Albany, NY 12233
tel: (518) 457-2344

New England Environmental Network News
Lincoln Filene Center for Citizenship
Civic Education Foundation/Tufts
Medford, MA 02155
tel: (617) 381-3451

Ohio Environmental Report
Ohio Environmental Council
22 E. Gay Street, #300
Columbus, OH 43215
tel: (614) 224-4900

Oil & Chemical Pollution
Elsevier Science Publishing Co., Inc.
Journal Information Center
655 Avenue of the Americas
New York, NY 10010
tel: (212) 370-5520

Ontario Recycling Update
Recycling Council of Ontario
489 College Street, #504
Toronto, ON M5S 2S8 Canada

Paper Stock Report
McEntee Media Corp.
13727 Holland Road
Cleveland, OH 44142-3920
tel: (216) 362-7979
fax: (216) 362-4623

Pennsylvania Environmental Law Letter
Andrews Communications, Inc.
1646 Westchester Pike
Westtown, PA 19395
tel: (215) 399-6600

Plastics Recycling Update
Resource Recycling, Inc.
Box 10540
Portland, OR 97210
tel: (503) 227-1319
fax: (503) 227-6135

Ranger Rick
(Ranger Rick's Nature Magazine)
National Wildlife Federation
1400 16th Street, N.W.
Washington, D.C. 20036-2266
tel: (703) 790-4000

Recycling Related Newsletters, Publications, Etc; A Reference
Recycling Consortium
Box 570213
Houston, TX 77257
tel: (713) 866-4027

Recycling World
Environmental Defense Fund
257 Park Avenue, S., 16th Floor
New York, NY 10010-7304
tel: (212) 505-2100

Renewable Resources Journal
(Resources Evaluation Journal)
Renewable Natural Resources Foundation
5430 Grosvenor Lane
Bethesda, MD 20814
tel: (301) 493-9101

Resource Recovery
Resource Recovery Report
5313 38th Street, N.W.
Washington, D.C. 20015
tel: (202) 362-6034
fax: (202) 362-6632

Resource Recycling
Resource Recycling Inc.
Box 10540
Portland, OR 97210
tel: (503) 227-1319
fax: (503) 227-6135

Resources
Resources for the Future, Inc.
1616 P Street, N.W.
Washington, D.C. 20036
tel: (202) 328-5113

Resources, Conservation & Recycling
Pergamon Press, Inc.
Maxwell House, Fairview Park
Elmsford, NY 10523
tel: (914) 592-7700

Reuse/Recycle
Technomic Publishing Co., Inc.
851 New Holland Avenue
Box 3535
Lancaster, PA 17604
tel: (717) 291-5609
fax: (717) 295-4538

Sierra
(Sierra Club Bulletin)
Sierra Club
730 Polk Street
San Francisco, CA 94109
tel: (415) 923-5656
fax: (415) 776-0350

State Solid Waste Report
(Solid Waste Issues)
American Paper Institute—Government Affairs Department
1619 Massachusetts Avenue, N.W.
Washington, D.C. 20032
tel: (202) 332-1050

State of the States
Renew America
1400 16th Street, N.W., #710
Washington, D.C. 20036
tel: (202) 232-2252

Tennessee Conservationist
Tennessee State Department of Conservation

701 Broadway
Nashville, TN 37243-0440
tel: (615) 742-6746
fax: (615) 742-6594

Tennessee Environmental Report
Tennessee Environmental Council
1725 Church Street
Nashville, TN 37203-2921
tel: (615) 321-5075

Texas, Natural Resources Information System, Newsletter
Natural Resources Information System
Box 13231
Austin, TX 78711
tel: (512) 463-8337

U.S. Congress Environmental and Energy Study Conference Weekly Bulletin
U.S. Congress, Environmental, H2-515, House Annex 2
Washington, DC 20515
tel: (202) 226-3300

Utah Environmental News
Utah State Division of Health, Environmental Health Branch
44 Medical Drive
Salt Lake City, UT 84113
tel: (801) 533-6121

Vermont Environmental Report
Vermont Natural Resources Council
9 Bailey Avenue
Montpelier, VT 05602-2152
tel: (802) 223-2328

Vision
Keep America Beautiful, Inc.
9 W. Broad Street
Stamford, CT 06902
tel: (203) 323-8987

Washington Environmental Protection Report
(Federal Programs Report)
Callahan Publications
Box 3751
Washington, D.C. 20007
tel: (202) 356-1925

Waste Business International
Canadian Hazardous Materials Management
12 Salem Avenue
Toronto, ON M6H 3C2 Canada
tel: (416) 536-5974
fax: (416) 588-3422

Waste Disposal
Wakeman/Walworth
300 N. Washington Street
Alexandria, VA 22314
tel: (703) 549-8606

Waste Information Digests
International Academy at Santa Barbara
800 Garden Street, Suite D, Department ADWL-R
Santa Barbara, CA 93101
tel: (805) 965-5010
fax: (805) 965-6071

Waste Watch
California Against Waste
Box 289
Sacramento, CA 95802
tel: (916) 443-5422

Wisconsin Department of Natural Resources, Technical Bulletin
Wisconsin Department of Natural Resources
101 S. Webster
Box 7921
Madison, WI 53707
tel: (608) 266-3369

Wisconsin Natural Resources Magazine
(Wisconsin Conservation Bulletin)
Wisconsin Department of Natural Resources
101 S. Webster
Box 7921
Madison, WI 53707
tel: (608) 266-1510

Wisconsin's Environmental Decade
(Eco-Bulletin)
Wisconsin's Environmental Decade
14 W. Mifflin Street, #5
Madison, WI 53703
tel: (608) 251-7020

World Resource Review
Supcon International
1 Heritage Plaza
Woodridge, IL 60517
tel: (708) 910-1551
fax: (708) 910-1561

World Resources
Basic Books Inc.
10 E. 53rd Street
New York, NY 10022
tel: (212) 207-7000

World Watch
Worldwatch Institute
1776 Massachusetts Avenue, N.W.
Washington, D.C. 20036
tel: (202) 452-1999

Worldwatch Papers
Worldwatch Institute
1776 Massachusetts Avenue, N.W.
Washington, D.C. 20036
tel: (202) 452-1999

Plastics Periodicals

Plastics
D.A.T.A. Business Publishing
8977 Activity Road
San Diego, CA 92126
tel: (619) 578-7600
fax: (619) 530-0637

Plastics
Western Plastics News, Inc.
1704 Colorado Avenue
Santa Monica, CA 90404
tel: (213) 829-4876

Plastics News
Crain Communications Inc.
1725 Merriman Road, #300
Akron, OH 44313-5251
tel: (216) 836-9180
fax: (216) 836-1005

Plastics Technology
Bill Communications, Inc.
341 White Pond Road
Akron, OH 44313
tel: (212) 986-4800

Plastics World
Cahners Publishing Co.
275 Washington Street
Newton, MA 02158-1630
tel: (617) 964-3030

Plastics World Suppliers Reference File
Cahners Publishing Co.
275 Washington Street
Newton, MA 02158-1630
tel: (617) 536-7780

Rauch Guide to the U.S. Plastics Industry
Rauch Associates
Box 6802
Bridgewater, NJ 08807
tel: (908) 231-9548

Trends in End-Use Markets for Plastics
Springborn Laboratories, Inc.
10 Springborn Center
Enfield, CT 06082
tel: (203) 749-8371
fax: (203) 749-7533

Rubber Periodicals

Rubber Chermistry & Technology
American Chemical Society
1155 16th Street, N.W.
Washington, D.C. 20036
tel: (216) 375-7814

Rubber & Plastics
American Chemical Society
1155 16th Street, N.W.
Washington, D.C. 20036
tel: (216) 375-7814

Rubber & Plastics News
Crain Communications Inc.
1725 Merriman Road #300
Akron, OH 44313-5251
tel: (216) 836-9180
fax: (216) 836-1005

Rubber World
Lippincott
1867 W. Market Street
Box 5485
Akron, OH 44313
tel: (216) 864-2122

Scrap Tire News
c/o Recycling Research, Inc.
133 Mountain Road
Suffield, CT 06078

Appendix D

Governmental Contacts

Government Recycling Resources

Association of State and Territorial
Solid Waste Management Officials
444 North Capitol Street, N.W., Suite 388
Washington, D.C. 20001
tel: (202) 624-5828

Coalition of Northeastern Governors
400 North Capitol Street, N.W.
Washington, D.C. 20001
tel: (202) 783-6674

EPA Office of Solid Waste
401 M Street, S.W.
Washington, D.C. 20460
tel: (202) 260-2090
(800) 424-9346 for pamphlet

Governmental Refuse Collection and Disposal Association
8750 Georgia Avenue, Suite 123
P.O. Box 7219
Silver Spring, MD
tel: (301) 585-2898

Local Government Commission
909 12th Street, Suite 205
Sacramento, CA 95814
tel: (916) 448-1198

National Association of Counties
440 First Street, N.W.
Washington, D.C. 20001
tel: (202) 393-6226

National Association of Towns and Townships
1522 K Street, N.W., Suite 730
Washington, D.C. 20005
tel: (202) 737-5200

National League of Cities
1301 Pennsylvania Avenue, N.W.
Washington, D.C. 20004
tel: (202) 626-3000

U.S. Conference of Mayors
1620 I Street, N.W. 4tn Floor
Washington, D.C. 20006
tel: (202) 293-7330
affiliate: National Resource Recovery Association

U.S. Bureau of Mines
810 7th Street, N.W.
P.O. Box 2150
Washington, D.C. 20241
tel: (202) 501-9770

U.S. Department of Commerce
14th & Constitution Avenue, N.W.
Washington, D.C. 20230
tel: (202) 377-2000

U.S. Department of Energy
1000 Independence, S.W.
Washington, D.C. 20585
tel: (202) 586-5000

EPA Regional Offices

Region 1
Environmental Protection Agency
Office of Public Affairs

JFK Federal Building
Boston, MA 02203
tel: (617) 565-3715

Region 2
Environmental Protection Agency
Office of External Programs
26 Federal Plaza
New York, NY 10278
tel: (212) 264-2515

Region 3
Environmental Protection Agency
Office of Public Affairs
841 Chestnut Street
Philadelphia, PA 19107
tel: (215) 597-9370

Region 4
Environmental Protection Agency
Public Affairs Branch
345 Courtland Street, N.E.
Atlanta, GA 30365
tel: (404) 347-3004

Region 5
Environmental Protection Agency
Office of Public Affairs
230 South Dearborn
Chicago, IL 60604
tel: (312) 353-2072

Region 6
Environmental Protection Agency
Office of Public Affairs
1445 Ross Avenue
Dallas, TX 75202
tel: (214) 655-2200

Region 7
Environmental Protection Agency
Office of Public Affairs
726 Minnesota Avenue
Kansas City, KS 66101
tel: (913) 236-2803

Region 8
Environmental Protection Agency
Office of External Affairs
999 18th Street, Suite 500
Denver, CO 80202-2402
tel: (303) 293-1603

Region 9
Environmental Protection Agency
Office of External Affairs E-1
1235 Mission Street
San Francisco, CA 94103
tel: (415) 556-6387

Region 10
Environmental Protection Agency
1200 Sixth Avenue
Seattle, WA 98101
tel: (206) 442-1220

State Environmental Protection Offices and State Energy Resource Offices

Alabama

Bureau of Environmental and Health Service Standards
434 Monroe Street, Room 247
Montgomery, AL 36130
tel: (205) 261-5004

Alabama Department of Economic and Community Affairs
Science, Technology & Energy Division
3465 Norman Bridge Road
P.O. Box 205347
Montgomery, AL 36125-0347
tel: (205) 284-8952

Alaska

Department of Environmental Conservation
P.O. Box O
Juneau, AK 99811
tel: (907) 465-2600

Arizona

Office of Environmental Quality
2005 N. Central Avenue, 7th Floor
Phoenix, AZ 85004
tel: (602) 257-2300

Arizona Energy Office
Department of Commerce
3800 N. Central Avenue, 12th Floor
Phoenix, AZ 85012
tel: (602) 280-1401

Arkansas

Pollution Control & Ecology
8001 National Drive

P.O. Box 9583
Little Rock, AR 72219
tel: (501) 562-7444

Arkansas Industrial Dev. Comm.
Established Industries Division
1 State Capitol Mall
Little Rock, AR 72201
tel: (501) 682-7315

California

Environmental Affairs
1102 Q Street
Sacramento, CA 95814
tel: (916) 322-5840

Conservation & Development Commission
Energy Resources
1516 9th Street
Sacramento, CA 95814
tel: (916) 324-3326

Colorado

Health & Environmental Protection
Department of Health
4210 E. 11th Avenue
Denver, CO 80220
tel: (303) 331-4510

Office of Energy Conservation
112 East 14th Avenue
Denver, CO 80203
tel: (303) 894-2144

Connecticut

Department of Environmental Protection
165 Capitol Avenue
Hartford, CT 06106
tel: (203) 566-2110

Office of Policy & Management
Energy Division
80 Washington Street
Hartford, CT 06106
tel: (203) 566-2800

Delaware

Dept. of Natural Resources & Environmental Control
89 Kings Highway
P.O. Box 1401
Dover, DE 19903
tel: (302) 736-4403

Florida

Department of Environmental Regulation
2600 Blair Stone Road
Twin Towers
Tallahassee, FL 32399-2400
tel: (904) 488-4805

Governor's Energy Office
The Capitol
214 South Bronough Street
Tallahassee, FL 32399-0001
tel: (904) 488-6764

Georgia

Department of Natural Resources
205 Butler Street, Suite 1252
Atlanta, GA 30334
tel: (404) 656-3500

Office of Energy Resources
270 Washington Street, S.W.
Suite 615
Atlanta, GA 30334

Hawaii

Hawaii Department of Health
P.O. Box 3378
Honolulu, HI 96801
tel: (808) 548-4139

State Energy Division
Department of Business & Economic Development
335 Merchant Street, Room 110
Honolulu, HI 96813
tel: (808) 548-4150

Idaho

Division of Environmental Quality
Department of Health & Welfare
450 W. State Street
Boise, ID 83720
tel: (208) 334-5840

Department of Water Resources
Statehouse Mail, 1301 N. Orchard
Boise, ID 83720
tel: (208) 327-7910

Illinois

Environmental Protection Agency
900 Churchill Road
Springfield, IL 62706
tel: (217) 782-3397

Department of Energy & Natural Resources
325 W. Adams Street
Springfield, IL 62704
tel: (217) 785-2002

Indiana

Environmental Management Board
105 South Meridien
P.O. Box 6015
Indianapolis, IN 46206-6015
tel: (317) 232-8603

Office of Energy Policy
Indiana Department of Commerce
Indiana Commerce Center
One North Capitol, Suite 700
Indianapolis, IN 46202-2288
tel: (317) 232-8946

Iowa

Department of Natural Resources
Wallace State Office Building
Des Moines, IA 50319-0034
tel: (515) 281-5385

Iowa Department of Natural Resources
Waste Management Authority Division
Wallace State Office Building
E. 9th and Grand
Des Moines, IA 50319
tel: (515) 281-8975

Kansas

Division of Environment
Department of Health & Environment
Forbes Field—Building 740
Topeka, KS 66620
tel: (913) 296-1535

Energy Program Division
Docking Office Building, 4th Floor
Topeka, KS 66612-1571
tel: (913) 296-5460

Kentucky

Natural Resources & Environmental Protection
Capital Plaza Tower
Frankfort, KY 40601
tel: (502) 564-3350

Governor's Office for Coal and Energy Policy
3572 Iron Works Road
P.O. Box 11888
Lexington, KY 40578
tel: (606) 252-5535

Louisiana

Office of Environmental Quality
P.O. Box 44066
Baton Rouge, LA 70804
tel: (504) 342-9103

Office of Conservation
Department of Natural Resources
P.O. Box 94275, Capitol Station
Baton Rouge, LA 70804-9275
tel: (504) 342-5500

Maine

Department of Environmental Protection
State House, Station 17
Augusta, ME 04333
tel: (207) 289-2811

Energy Conservation Division
Department of Economic and Community
Development
State House, Station 53
Augusta, ME 04333
tel: (207) 289-6000

Maryland

Maryland Environmental Services
2020 Industrial Drive
Annapolis, MD 21401
tel: (301) 974-7281

Massachusetts

Office of Environmental Affairs
100 Cambridge Street, 20th Floor
Boston, MA 02202
tel: (617) 727-9800

Division of Energy Resources
100 Cambridge Street, Room 1500
Boston, MA 02202
tel: (617) 727-4731

Michigan

Office of Energy Programs
Michigan Public Service Commission
6545 Mercantile Way/P.O. Box 30221
Lansing, MI 48909
tel: (517) 334-6272

Minnesota

Pollution Control Agency
520 Lafayette Road
St. Paul, MN 55155
tel: (612) 296-6300

Environmental Quality Board
300 Centennial Building
658 Cedar Street
St. Paul, MN 55155
tel: (612) 296-9027

Minnesota Department of Trade & Economic Development
900 American Center Building
150 E. Kellogg Boulevard
St. Paul, MN 55101
tel: (612) 296-4039

Mississippi

Bureau of Pollution Control
Department of Environmental Quality
P.O. Box 10385
Jackson, MS 39289-0385
tel: (601) 961-5171

Department of Economic and Community Development
Division of Energy & Transportaion
510 George Street, Suite 400
Dickson Building
Jackson, MS 39202-3096
tel: (601) 961-4733

Missouri

Division of Environmental Quality
Department of Natural Resources
P.O. Box 176
205 Jefferson Street
Jefferson City, MO 65102
tel: (314) 751-4810

Montana

DHES—Department of Health & Environmental Sciences
Cogswell Building
Capitol Station
Helena, MT 59620
tel: (406) 444-3948

Department of Natural Resources & Conservation
1520 E. 6th Avenue
Helena, MT 59620-2301
tel: (406) 444-6699

Nebraska

Department of Environmental Control
P.O. Box 98922
301 Centennial Mall South
Lincoln, NE 68509
tel: (402) 471-2186

Energy Office
P.O. Box 95085
State Capitol, 9th Floor
Lincoln, NE 68509-5085
tel: (402) 471-2867

Nevada

Division of Environmental Protection
Department of Conservation & Natural Resources
123 West Nye Lane
Carson City, NV 89710
tel: (702) 885-4670

Governor's Office of Community Services
Capitol Complex

Carson City, NV 89710
tel: (702) 687-4990

New Hampshire

Governor's Energy Office
2½ Beacon Street
Concord, NH 03301
tel: (603) 271-2711

New Jersey

Department of Environmental Protection
401 East State Street
Trenton, NJ 08625-0402
tel: (609) 292-2885

Division of Energy Planning & Conservation
2 Gateway Center
Newark, NJ 07102
tel: (201) 648-6289

New Mexico

Environmental Improvement Division
Health & Environmental Department
1190 St. Francis Drive
Santa Fe, NM 87503
tel: (505) 827-2850

Energy, Minerals and Natural Resources
2040 South Pacheco
Santa Fe, NM 87505
tel: (505) 827-5950

New York

Division of Solid Waste
Department of Environmental Conservation
50 Wolf Road, Room 212
Albany, NY 12233-4010
tel: (518) 457-6603

New York State Energy Office
Empire State Plaza
Agency Building 2
Albany, NY 12223
tel: (518) 473-4376

North Carolina

Environment, Health and Natural Resources
P.O. Box 27687
Raleigh, NC 27611
tel: (919) 733-4984

Department of Economic and Community Development
Division of Energy
430 N. Salisbury Street
Raleigh, NC 27611
tel: (919) 733-2230

North Dakota

Environmental Health Section
State Department of Health
1200 Missouri Avenue
P.O. Box 5520
Bismarck, ND 58502-5520
tel: (701) 224-2374

Office of Intergovernmental Assistance
Office of Management and Budget
State Capitol
600 East Boulevard, 14th Floor
Bismarck, ND 58505
tel: (701) 224-2094

Ohio

Environmental Protection Agency
1800 Watermark Drive
P.O. Box 1049
Columbus, OH 43266-0149
tel: (614) 644-3020

Department of Development
77 South High Street, 29th Floor
P.O. Box 1001
Columbus, OH 43266-0101
tel: (614) 466-3379

Oklahama

Department of Pollution Control
P.O. Box 53504
Oklahoma City, OK 73152
tel: (405) 271-4468

Department of Commerce
Energy Conservation Programs
6601 Broadway Extension
Oklahoma City, OK 73116-8214
tel: (405) 521-3941

Oregon

Department of Environmental Quality
811 S.W. Sixth Avenue
Portland, OR 97204
tel: (503) 229-5300

Department of Energy
625 Marion Street, N.E.
Salem, OR 97310
tel: (503) 378-4128

Pennsylvania

Department of Environmental Resources
P.O. Box 2063
Fulton Building, 9th Floor
Harrisburg, PA 17120
tel: (717) 787-2814

Pennsylvania Energy Office
116 Pine Street
Harrisburg, PA 17101
tel: (717) 783-9981

Rhode Island

Department of Environmental
Management
9 Hayes Street
Providence, RI 02908
tel: (401) 277-2771

Public Utilities Commission
100 Orange Street
Providence, RI 02903
tel: (401) 277-3500

South Carolina

Environmental Quality Control
Health & Environmental Control
2600 Bull Street
Columbia, SC 29201
tel: (803) 734-4880

Governor's Office of Energy, Agriculture and
Natural Resources
1205 Pendleton Street, 3rd Floor
Suite 333
Columbia, SC 29201
tel: (803) 734-0445

South Dakota

Division of Land and Water Quality
Department of Water & Natural Resources
Foss Building
Pierre, SD 57501
tel: (605) 773-3151

Tennessee

Bureau of Environment
Health & Environment Department
150 Ninth Avenue, N.
Nashville, TN 37247-3001
tel: (615) 741-3657

Energy Division
320 6th Avenue, N.
Rachel Jackson Building, 6th Floor
Nashville, TN 37243-0405
tel: (615) 741-2994

Utah

Division of Environmental Health
P.O. Box 16690
Salt Lake City, UT 84116-0690
tel: (801) 538-6421

Energy Office
Department of Natural Resources
3 Triad Center, Suite 450
Salt Lake City, UT 84180-1204
tel: (801) 538-5428

Vermont

Agency of Natural Resources
103 S. Main Street, Center Building
Waterbury, VT 05676
tel: (802) 244-7347

Virginia

Council on the Environment
903 Ninth Street Office Building
Richmond, VA 23219
tel: (804) 786-4500

Washington

Waste Reduction, Recycling & Litter Control
Program
Department of Ecology

Mail/Stop PV-11
Olympia, WA 98504
tel: (206) 438-7145

Washington State Energy Office
809 Legion Way, S.E.
Mail Stop FA-11
Olympia, WA 98504
tel: (206) 586-5000

West Virginia

Department of Natural Resources
1900 Kansas Boulevard, East
Building #3, Room 669
Charleston, WV 25305
tel: (304) 348-2754

Fuel & Energy Office
Office of Community & Industrial Development
1204 Kanawha Boulevard, E., 2nd Floor
Charleston, WV 25301
tel: (304) 736-4403

Wisconsin

Division for Environmental Quality
Department of Natural Resources
P.O. Box 7921
Madison, WE 53707
tel: (608) 266-1099

Division of Energy & Intergovernmental Relations
P.O. Box 7868
Madison, WI 53707
tel: (608) 266-8234

Wyoming

Environmental Quality Department
Herschler Building
122 W. 25th Street
Cheyenne, WY 82002
tel: (307) 777-7938

Wyoming Economics Development & Stabilization Department
Energy Division
Herschler Building, 2nd Floor
Cheyenne, WY 82002
tel: (307) 777-7284

Puerto Rico

Environmental Quality Board
P.O. Box 11488
Santurce, PR 00910
tel: (809) 725-5140

Energy Office
P.O. Box 41089, Minillas Station
Santurce, PR 00940
tel: (809) 726-4740

State Contacts on Used Oil Recycling

Alabama

Ms. Christina Shirley
Pollution Control Specialist
Hazardous Waste Branch
Department of Environmental Management
1751 Congressman W.L. Dickinson Drive
Montgomery, AL 36130
tel: (205) 271-7746

Ms. Janet Graham
Project ROSE Coordinator
P.O. Box 870203
Tuscaloosa, AL 35487-0203
tel: (205) 348-1735

Alaska

Mr. Jeff Ingells
Mr. Dave Wigglesworth
Department of Environmental Conservation
Hazardous and Solid Waste Management Division
P.O. Box O
Juneau, AK 99811
tel: (907) 465-2671

Arizona

Ms. Michelle Diaz
Administrative Assistant
Department of Environmental Quality
Solid Waste Unit
2005 North Central Avenue G-200
Phoenix, AZ 85004
tel: (602) 257-2349

Arkansas

Ms. Jane Schwartz
Department of Pollution Control & Ecology
Solid Waste Division
8001 National Drive
Little Rock, AR 72219
tel: (501) 562-6633

California

Mr. Ken Hughes
Integrated Waste Management Board
8800 Cal Center Drive
Sacramento, CA 95826
tel: (916) 255-2347

Mr. Lief Peterson
Department of Toxic Substances Control
Alternative Technology Section
P.O. Box 94732
Sacramento, CA 94234-7320
tel: (916) 324-1807

Colorado

Department of Health
Public Assistance
Hazardous Materials and Waste Management Division
4210 East 11th Ave.
Denver, CO 80220
tel: (303) 331-4400

Connecticut

Mr. Charles Zieminski
Department of Environmental Protection
State Office Building
165 Capitol Avenue
Hartford, CT 06106
tel: (203) 566-4633
(800) 842-2220

Delaware

Mr. John Posdon
Division of Facilities Management
Energy Office P.O. Box 1401
Dover, DE 19903
tel: (302) 739-5644
(800) 282-8616

District of Columbia

Ms. Michelle Fowler
D.C. Department of Energy
Office of Recycling
65 K Street, N.E.
Washington, D.C. 20002
tel: (202) 727-5856

Florida

Ms. Betsy Galocy
Department of Environmental Regulation
Solid & Hazardous Waste Section
Twin Towers Office Building
2600 Blair Store Road, Room 479
Tallahassee, FL 32399-2400
tel: (904) 488-0300

Georgia

Ms. Pam Thomas
Environmental Protection Division
Department of Natural Resources
Floyd Towers East Room 1154
205 Butler Street, S.E.
Atlanta, GA 30334
tel: (404) 656-0772

Hawaii

Ms. Arlene Kabei
Branch Chief Solid & Hazardous Waste
Department of Health
500 Ala Moana Boulevard, Suite 250
Honolulu, HI 96813
tel: (808) 548-6455

Idaho

Mr. Jerome Jankowski
Dept. of Health & Welfare
450 West State Street
3rd Floor
Boise, ID 83720
tel: (208) 334-5855

Illinois

Mr. James Mergen
Environmental Protection Agency

2200 Churchill Road
P.O. Box 19276
Springfield, IL 62794-9276
tel: (217) 782-8700

Indiana

Mr. James Hunt
Department of Environmental Management
105 South Meridian Street
Indianapolis, IN 46206
tel: (317) 232-4535

Iowa

Mr. Scott Cahail
Department of Natural Resources
900 East Grand
Des Moines, IA 50319
tel: (515) 281-8263

Kansas

Mr. Sam Sunderraj
Department of Health & Environment
Solid Waste Division
Building 740, Forbes Field
Topeka, KS 66520
tel: (913) 296-1609

Kentucky

Mr. Charles Peters
Department of Environmental Protection
Natural Resources & Environmental Protection Cabinet
18 Reilly Road
Frankfort, KY 40601
tel: (502) 564-6716

Louisiana

Mr. Tom Patterson
Department of Environmental Quality
Hazardous Waste Division
P.O. Box 82178
Baton Rouge, LA 70884-2178
tel: (504) 765-0246

Maine

Mr. Richard Kasalis
Department of Environmental Protection
State House Station #17
Augusta, ME 04333
tel: (207) 289-2651

Maryland

Ms. Debbie Wagner
Maryland Environmental Services
2020 Industrial Drive
Annapolis, MD 21401
tel: (301) 974-7254
(800) 482-9188

Massachusetts

Ms. Cynthia Bellamy
Division of Solid & Hazardous Waste
Department of Environmental Quality Engineering
One Winter Street, 5th Floor
Boston, MA 02108
tel: (617) 292-5848

Michigan

Ms. Mindy Koch
Department of Natural Resources
Waste Management Division
Resource Recovery Section
P.O. Box 30241
Lansing, MI 48909
tel: (517) 335-4090

Minnesota

Mr. LaAllan Estrem
Office of Waste Management
1350 Energy Lane, Suite 201
St. Paul, MN 55108
tel: (612) 649-5750

Mr. Patrick Carey
Minnesota Pollution Control Agency
520 Lafayette Road
St. Paul, MN 55155-3898
tel: (612) 297-8320
(800) 652-9747

Mississippi

Mr. David Lee
Office of Pollution Control
Department of Environmental Quality

P.O. Box 10385
Jackson, MS 39289-0385
tel: (601) 961-5377

Missouri

Ms. June Sullens
Hazardous Waste Section
Waste Management Program
Department of Natural Resources
P.O. Box 176
Jefferson City, MO 65102
tel: (314) 751-3176
(800) 334-6946

Montana

Mr. Bill Portts
Solid Waste Management Bureau
Department of Health & Environmental Sciences
Cogswell Building, Room B-201
Helena, MT 59620
tel: (406) 444-1430

Nebraska

Mr. Gene Hanlon
Department of Economic Development
County-City Building
555 South 10th Street
Lincoln, NB 68508
tel: (402) 471-7043

Nevada

Mr. Curtis Framel
Ms. Harriet Schaller
Office of Community Service
Capital Complex
Carson City, NV 89710
tel: (702) 687-4908

New Hampshire

Mr. Michael Wimsatt
Waste Management Division
Department of Environmental Services
Health & Welfare Building
6 Hazen Drive
Concord, NH 03301
tel: (603) 271-2942

New Jersey

Ms. Ellen Bourton
Office of Recycling
Department of Environmental Protection
CN-414
850 Bear Tavern Road
Trenton, NJ 08625-0414
tel: (609) 530-4001

New Mexico

Mr. George Beaumont
Solid Waste Bureau
Environmental Department
P.O. Box 26110
Santa Fe, NM 87502
tel: (505) 827-2775

New York

Mr. Kenneth Brezner
Department of Environmental Conservation
Hunters Point Plaza
4740 21st Street
Long Island, NY 11101
tel: (718) 482-4996

North Carolina

Mr. Paul Crissman
Department of Environment, Health & Natural Resources
Hazardous Waste Section
P.O. Box 27587
Raleigh, NC 27611
tel: (919) 733-0692

Ms. Maxi May
Southeast Waste Exchange
University of North Carolina at Charlotte
Charlotte, NC 28223
tel: (704) 547-2307

North Dakota

Mr. Curtis Erickson
Division of Waste Management
Department of Health
1200 Missouri Avenue
P.O. Box 5520
Bismarck, ND 58502-5520
tel: (701) 221-5166

Ohio

Mr. Art Coleman
Environmental Protection Agency
1800 Water Mark Drive
Columbus, OH 43266-0149
tel: (614) 644-2956

Oklahoma

Mr. Bryce Hulsuy
Solid Waste Management Service
Department of Health
P.O. Box 53551
Oklahoma City, OK 73152
tel: (405) 271-7193

Oregon

Mr. Peter Spendeour
Department of Environmental Quality
811 SW 6th Avenue
Portland, OR 97204
tel: (503) 229-5253
(800) 452-4011 (In-state only)

Pennsylvania

Mr. Bill LaCour
Department of Environmental Resources
Box 2063
Harrisburg, PA 17105-2063
tel: (717) 787-7382

Rhode Island

Mr. Eugene Pepper
Department of Environmental Management
83 Park Street
Providence, RI 02903
tel: (803) 734-5915

South Carolina

Mr. Robert Fairy
Department of Health & Environmental Control
2600 Bull Street
Columbia, SC 29201
tel: (803) 734-5915

South Dakota

Ms. Kerry Jacobson
Department of Water & Natural Resources
Office of Waste Management Programs
319 S. Coteau
c/o 500 East Capital
Pierre, SD 57501
tel: (605) 773-3153

Tennessee

Mr. Mike Apple
State of Tennessee
Department of Health & Environment
Division of Solid Waste Management
701 Broadway, 4th Floor
Nashville, TN 37247-3530
tel: (615) 741-3424

Texas

Mr. Ken Zarker
Texas Water Commission
Hazardous & Solid Waste Division
P.O. Box 13087, Capitol Station
Austin, TX 78711
tel: (512) 463-7751
(512) 463-7761

Utah

Ms. Sandy Hunt
Division of Oil, Gas and Mining
355 West North Temple
3 Triad Center, Suite 350
Salt Lake City, UT 84180-1203
tel: (801) 538-5340

Vermont

Mr. Gary Gulka
Agency of Environmental Conservation
103 South Main Street
Waterbury, VT 05671-0404
tel: (802) 244-8702

Virginia

Ms. Susan Thomas
Division of Energy
2201 West Broad Street
Richmond, VA 23220

tel: (804) 367-0928
(800) 552-3831

Washington

Mr. Steve Barrett
Department of Ecology
Mail Stop PV-11
Olympia, WA 98504-8711
tel: (206) 459-6286

West Virginia

Mr. Dale Moncer
Community Development Office
Department of Natural Resources
Fuels & Energy Office
1204 Kanawhas Boulevard, 2nd Floor
Charleston, WV 25301
tel: (304) 348-6350

Wisconsin

Mr. Paul Koziar
Department of Natural Resources
Bureau of Solid & Hazardous Waste Management
P.O. Box 7921 SW-3
Madison, WI 53707-7921
tel: (608) 266-5741
(608) 267-9388 (Direct)

Wyoming

Mr. Carl Anderson
Solid Waste Management Program
Department of Environmental Quality
Henschler Building
122 West 25th Street
Cheyenne, WY 82002
tel: (307) 777-7752

State Recycling Agencies

Alabama

Department of Environmental Management
Solid Waste Branch, Land Division
1751 Congressman Dickinson Drive
Montgomery, AL 36130
tel: (205) 271-7700
Hazardous waste office (205) 271-7726
Director: Leigh Pegues

Alaska

Department of Environmental Conservation
Solid Waste Program
P.O. Box O
Juneau, AK 99811-1800
tel: (907) 465-2671

Arizona

Department of Environmental Quality
Waste Planning Section, 4th Floor
2005 N. Central Avenue
Phoenix, AZ 85004
tel: (602) 257-2372
Director: Andy Soesilo

Department of Commerce, Energy Office
3800 N. Central, Suite 1200
Phoenix, AZ 85012
tel: (800) 352-5499

Arkansas

State of Arkansas
Department of Pollution Control & Ecology
Solid Waste Management Division
8001 National Drive
P.O. Box 8913
Little Rock, AR 72219-8913
tel: (501) 562-6533
fax: (501) 562-2541
contact: Donna H. Etchieson, Recycling Coordinator

California

Department of Conservation
Division of Recycling
1025 P Street, Room 401
Sacramento, CA 95814
tel: (800) 642-5669 (Consumer Information Hotline)
tel: (800) 332-SAVE (Redemption Recycling Center Hotline)
Contact: Jane Irwin (Acting Chief—Division of Recycling)

Integrated Waste Management
1020 Ninth Street, Suite 300
Sacramento, CA 95814
tel: (916) 322-3330

Colorado

Department of Health
Hazardous Materials & Waste Management Division
4210 E. 11th Avenue, Room 351
Denver, CO 80220
tel: (303) 331-4830

Connecticut

Waste Management Bureau
Planning and Standards Division
Department of Environmental Protection
165 Capitol Avenue
Hartford, CT 06106
tel: (203) 566-8722
contact: Kim M. Trella, (Recycling Education Coordinator)

Delaware

Department of Natural Resources & Environmental Control
Division of Air & Waste Management
P.O. Box 1401
89 Kings Highway
Dover, DE 19903
tel: (302) 739-3820 (Solid Waste Off.)
Director: Phillip Retallick

District of Columbia

Office of Recycling
65 K Street, Lower Level
Washington D.C. 20002
tel: (202) 939-7116

Florida

Clean Florida Commission
605 Suwannee Street, MS-2
Tallahassee, FL 32399-0450
tel: (904) 488-2756
(800) BAN-TRASH
fax: (904) 488-8404
contact: Barbara Mason (Director)

Florida Department of Environmental Regulation
Division of Waste Management
Bureau of Waste Planning and Regulation
2600 Blairstone Road
Tallahassee, FL 32399-2400
tel: (904) 922-6104
fax: (904) 922-4939
contact: Bill Hinkley (Section Administrator)
contact: Ron Henricks (Environmental Supervisor)

Georgia

Georgia Department of Community Affairs
1200 Equitable Building
100 Peachtree Street
Atlanta, GA 30303
tel: (404) 656-3836
fax: (404) 656-9792

Georgia Department of Natural Resources
205 Butler Street, S.E., Suite 1258
Atlanta, GA 30334

Department of Natural Resources
Environmental Protection Division
3420 Norman Berry Drive, 7th Floor
Hapeville, GA 30354
tel: (404) 656-2836

Hawaii

Department of Health
Solid & Hazardous Waste Division
5 Waterfront Plaza, Suite 250
500 Ala-Moana Boulevard
Honolulu, HI 96813
tel: (808) 543-8227

Idaho

Idaho Department of Health and Welfare
Division of Environmental Quality
1410 N. Hilton Statehouse Mail
Boise, ID 83706-9000
tel: (208) 334-0502
contact: Jaime Z. Fuhrman (Technical Information Specialist)

Illinois

Illinois Department of Energy and Natural Resources
325 W. Adams Street, Room 300
Springfield, IL 62704-1892
tel: (217) 524-5454
fax: (217) 785-2618
contact: David E. Smith (Program Management Section); Tracy Garner (Public Information Officer—Office of Recycling and Waste Reduction)

Indiana

State of Indiana
Department of Environmental Management
Office of Pollution Prevention and Technical Assistance
105 S. Meridian Street
P.O. Box 6015
Indianapolis, IN 46206-6015
tel: (317) 232-8883
(800) 451-6027

Iowa

Iowa Department of Natural Resources
Waste Management Division
Wallace State Office Building
900 E. Grand Avenue
Des Moines, IA 50319-0034
tel: (515) 281-8941
fax: (515) 281-8895
contact: Julie Kjolhede (Waste Management Division); Larry J. Wilson (Director)

Kentucky

Division of Waste Management
Resources Recovery Branch
18 Reilly Road
Frankfort, KY 40601
tel: (502) 564-6716

Lexington-Fayette Urban County Government
Department of Public Works
Division of Sanitation
2181 Old Frankfort Pike
Lexington, KY 40510

Louisiana

Department of Environmental Quality
Division of Solid Waste
P.O. Box 82178
Baton Rouge, LA 70884-2178
tel: (504) 765-0645
Director: Bill Mollere

Maine

Maine Waste Management Agency
Executive Department
State House Station, #154
Key Plaza, 286 Water Street
Augusta, ME 04333-0154
tel: (207) 289-5300
(800) 662-4545
fax: (207) 289-5425
contact: Jody Harris (Director—Office of Waste Reduction & Recycling)

Maryland

Maryland Department of the Environment
Office of Waste Minimization and Recycling
2500 Broening Highway
Baltimore, MD 21224
tel: (301) 631-3315
contact: Lori Scozzafava (Chief Office of Waste Minimization & Recycling)

Massachusetts

Department of Environmental Protection
Division of Solid Waste Management
1 Winter Street, 4th Floor
Boston, MA 02108
tel: (617) 292-5960
Director: Willa Kuh (Recycling Director)

Michigan

State of Michigan
Department of Natural Resources
Stevens T. Mason Building
P.O. Box 30241
Lansing, MI 48909
tel: (517) 373-2730
contact: Delbert Rector (Director)

Minnesota

Minnesota Pollution Control Agency
520 Lafayette Road
St. Paul, MN 55155
tel: (612) 296-6300
contact: Chuck W. Williams (Commissioner)

Mississippi

State of Mississippi
Department of Environmental Quality
Office of Pollution Control
P.O. Box 10385
Jackson, MS 39289-0385
tel: (601) 961-5171
contact: Larry Estes (Solid Waste Coordinator)

Missouri

Department of Natural Resources
P.O. Box 176
Jefferson City, MO 65102
tel: (314) 751-3176

Montana

Department of Health & Environmental Science
Solid & Hazardous Waste Bureau, Cogswell Building
Helena, MT 59620
tel: (406) 444-2821
contact: Lara M. Dando (Solid Waste Program)

Nebraska

Nebraska Department of Environmental Control
State Office Building, Fourth Floor
301 Centennial Mall South
Lincoln, NE 68509-8922
tel: (402) 471-2186
Director: Randolf Wood

Nevada

State of Nevada
Office of Community Services
400 W. King Street, Suite 400
Capitol Complex
Carson City, NV 89710
tel: (702) 687-4908
fax: (702) 687-4914
contact: Harriet Schaller (Manager Institutional Conservation Program)

New Hampshire

Environmental Services Department
Waste Management Division
6 Hazen Drive
Concord, NH 03301-6509
tel: (603) 271-2926
Director: Philip J. O'Brien, Ph.D.

New Jersey

Department of Environmental Protection
Office of Recycling
850 Bear Tavern Road
Trenton, NJ 08625-0414
tel: (609) 530-4001

New Mexico

State of New Mexico
State Recycling Coordinator
Solid Waste Bureau
Environment Department
P.O. Box 26110
Santa Fe, NM 87502
tel: (505) 827-2892
contact: Marilyn G. Brown

New York

New York Department of Environmental Conservation
Waste Reduction & Recycling
50 Wolf Road
Albany, NY 12233-4015
tel: (518) 457-7337

North Carolina

Solid Waste Section
P.O. Box 27687
Raleigh, NC 27611-7687
tel: (919) 733-0692

North Dakota

North Dakota State Department of Health and Consolidated Laboratories
1200 Missouri Avenue Room 302
P.O. Box 5520
Bismark, ND 58502-5520
tel: (701) 221-5166
fax: (701) 221-5200
contact: Catherine A. Berg (Environmental Scientist—Solid Waste Program, Division of Waste Management)

Ohio

Ohio Department of Natural Resources
Division of Litter Prevention & Recycling
1889 Fountain Square Ct.—F-2
Columbus, OH 43224
tel: (614) 265-6376
fax: (614) 262-9387
contact: Frances S. Buchholzer (Director)

Oklahoma

Department of Health
Solid Waste Services
1000 N.E. Tents
Oklahoma City, OK 73117-1299
tel: (405) 271-7169
contact: Fenton Rood (Director)

Oregon

Department of Environmental Quality
Waste Reduction Section
811 S.W. Sixth Avenue, 8th Floor
Portland, OR 97204
tel: (503) 229-6165
contact: Pat Vernon (Manager—Solid Waste Division)

Pennsylvania

Department of Environmental Resources
Bureau of Waste Management
Division of Waste Minimization & Planning
P.O. Box 2063
Harrisburg, PA 17105-2063
tel: (717) 787-7382

Rhode Island

Department of Environmental Management
O.S.C.A.R.
83 Park Street, 5th Floor
Providence, RI 02903-1037
tel: (401) 277-3434
contact: Terri Bisson or Mara Cherkasky (Municipal recycling program); Carole Bell or Susan Cabeceiras (Commercial recycling)

South Carolina

Bureau of Solid & Hazardous Waste
2600 Bull Street
Columbia, SC 29201
tel: (803) 734-5200

South Dakota

Department of Water & Natural Resources
Waste Management Program
319 S. Coteau
Pierre, SD 57501
tel: (605) 773-3153
Director: Dave Templeton

Tennessee

Department of Health & Environment
Solid Waste Management Division
701 Broadway, 4th Floor, Customs House
Nashville, TN 37247-3530
tel: (615) 741-3424

Texas

Department of Health
Bureau of Solid Waste Management
1100 W. 49th Street
Austin, TX 78756
tel: (512) 458-7271

Utah

State of Utah
Department of Environmental Health
Solid and Hazardous Waste
288 North 1460 West
P.O. Box 16690
Salt Lake City, UT 84116-0690
tel: (801) 538-6170

Vermont

Department of Environmental Conservation
Solid Waste Division
103 S. Main Street, West Building
Waterbury, VT 05676
tel: (802) 244-7831

Virginia

Virginia Department of Waste Management
Division of Litter Control & Recycling
11th Floor, The Monroe Building
101 N. 14th Street
Richmond, VA 23219
tel: (804) 371-0044
contact: R. Allan Lassiter, Jr. (Director)

Washington

Washington State Department
of Ecology
Office of Waste Reduction
Recycling and Litter Control
P.O. Box 47600
Olympia, WA 98504-7600
tel: (206) 459-6000
(206) 438-7472
(800) RECYCLE
contact: Joy St. Germain

West Virginia

Division of Natural Resources
Solid Waste Section
1356 Hansford Street
Charleston, WV 25301
tel: (304) 348-5993
Director: Dick Cook

Wisconsin

Wisconsin Department of Natural Resources
Bureau of Solid & Hazardous Waste
Management
P.O. Box 7921
101 S. Webster
Madison, WI 53707-7921
tel: (608) 267-7566

Wyoming

Department of Environmental Quality
Solid Waste Management
122 W. 25th Street
Herschler Building, 4th Floor West
Cheyenne, WY 82002
tel: (307) 777-7752

Appendix E

State Recycling Associations

Alabama

Southeast Glass Recycling Program
(Alabama, Florida, Georgia, Mississippi)
P.O. Box 5951
Clearwater, FL 34618
tel: (813) 799-4917

Steel Can Recycling Institute
Southeastern Region (Alabama, Arkansas, Florida, Georgia, Louisiana, Mississippi)
4900 Bayou Boulevard, Suite 110C
Pensacola, FL 32503
contact: Suzette Miller (Recycling Representative)
tel: (904) 479-7208

Arizona

California Glass Recycling Corporation
(Arizona, California, Idaho, Montana, Nevada, Utah, Washington)
5709 Marconi Avenue, Suite C
Carmichael, CA 95608
tel: (916) 483-8585

Steel Can Recycling Institute
Southwestern Region (Arizona, Colorado, Kansas, Nebraska, New Mexico, Oklahoma, Texas, Utah)
363 North Sam Houston Parkway, Suite 1100
Houston, TX 77060
contact: Gary Gallo (Recycling Representative)
tel: (713) 820-7837

Arkansas

Mid-America Glass Recycling Program
(Arkansas, Colorado, Kansas, Louisiana, Missouri, New Mexico, Oklahoma, Texas)
824 N. Mission
Sapulpa, OK 74066
tel: (918) 227-3889
fax: (918) 227-3958
contact: Gail Ederer, (Executive Director)

Steel Can Recycling Institute
Southeastern Region (Alabama, Arkansas, Florida, Georgia, Louisiana, Mississippi)
4900 Bayou Boulevard, Suite 110C
Pensacola, FL 32503
contact: Suzette Miller (Recycling Representative)
tel: (904) 479-7208

California

Californians Against Waste Foundation
909 12th Street, Suite 201
P.O. Box 289
Sacramento, CA 95814
tel: (916) 443-8317
contact: Sandra E. Jerabek (Executive Director)

California Glass Recycling Corporation
(Arizona, California, Idaho, Montana, Nevada, Utah, Washington)
5709 Marconi Avenue, Suite C
Carmichael, CA 95608
tel: (916) 483-8585

California Resource Recovery Association
13223 Black Mountain Road I-300
San Diego, CA 92129

Northern California Recycling Association
P.O. Box 5581
Berkeley, CA 94705

Steel Can Recycling Institute
Western Region (California, Idaho, Montana, Nevada, Oregon, Washington, Wyoming)
5150 E. Pacific Coast Highway, Suite 200
Long Beach, CA 90804
tel: (213) 597-1545
contact: Betsey Meyer (Recycling Representative)

Colorado

Mid-America Glass Recycling Program
(Arkansas, Colorado, Kansas, Louisiana, Missouri, New Mexico, Oklahoma, Texas)
824 N. Mission
Sapulpa, OK 74066
tel: (918) 227-3889
fax: (918) 227-3958
contact: Gail Ederer (Executive Director)

Steel Can Recycling Institute
Southwestern Region (Arizona, Colorado, Kansas, Nebraska, New
Mexico, Oklahoma, Texas, Utah)
363 North Sam Houston Parkway, Suite 1100
Houston, TX 77060
contact: Gary Gallo (Recycling Representative)
tel: (713) 820-7837

Connecticut

Connecticut Recyclers Coalition
P.O. Box 445
Stonington, CT 06378

Steel Can Recycling Institute
Northeastern Region (Connecticut, Maine, Massachusetts, New Hampshire, New York, Rhode Island, Vermont)
97 Lowell Road, Suite 1000
Concord, MA 01742
contact: Paula Thompson (Recycling Representative)

Delaware

Pennsylvania Glass Recycling Corporation
(Delaware, Pennsylvania)
509 North Second Street
Harrisburg, PA 17101
tel: (717) 234-8091

Steel Can Recycling Institute
Mid-Atlantic Region (Delaware, District of Columbia, Maryland, New Jersey, North Carolina, South Carolina, Tennessee, Virginia)
One Park West Circle, Suite 101
Midlothian, VA 23113
tel: (804) 378-2302
contact: Chuck Nettleship (Recycling Representative)

Florida

Keep Florida Beautiful, Inc.
402 W. College Avenue
Tallahassee, FL 32301
tel: (904) 561-0700
fax: (904) 561-6558
Frank Walper (Executive Director)

Recycle Florida
c/o Department of Environmental Regulation
Solid Waste Division
2600 Blairstone Road
Tallahassee, FL 32301

Southeast Glass Recycling Program
(Alabama, Florida, Georgia, Mississippi)
P.O. Box 5951
Clearwater, FL 34618
tel: (813) 799-4917

Steel Can Recycling Institute
Southeastern Region (Alabama, Arkansas, Florida, Georgia, Louisiana, Mississippi)
4900 Bayou Boulevard, Suite 110C
Pensacola, FL 32503
contact: Suzette Miller (Recycling Representative)
tel: (904) 479-7208

Georgia

Southeast Glass Recycling Program
(Alabama, Florida, Georgia, Mississippi)

P.O. Box 5951
Clearwater, FL 34618
tel: (813) 799-4917

Steel Can Recycling Institute
Southeastern Region (Alabama, Arkansas, Florida, Georgia, Louisiana, Mississippi)
4900 Bayou Boulevard, Suite 110C
Pensacola, FL 32503
contact: Suzette Miller (Recycling Representative)
tel: (904) 479-7208

Hawaii

Recycling Association of Hawaii
162-B North King Street
Honolulu, HI 96817
tel: (808) 939-2985

Idaho

California Glass Recycling Corporation
(Arizona, California, Idaho, Montana, Nevada, Utah, Washington)
5709 Marconi Avenue, Suite C
Carmichael, CA 95608
tel: (916) 483-8585

Steel Can Recycling Institute
Western Region (California, Idaho, Montana, Nevada, Oregon, Washington, Wyoming)
5150 E. Pacific Coast Highway, Suite 200
Long Beach, CA 90804
tel: (213) 597-1545
contact: Betsey Meyer (Recycling Representative)

Illinois

Central States Glass Recycling Program
(Kentucky, Indiana, Illinois, Ohio, Wisconsin, Tennessee)
770 East 73rd Street
Indianapolis, IN 46240
tel: (317) 251-0131

Illinois Recycling Association
407 S. Dearborn, #1775
Chicago, IL 60605
tel: (312) 939-2985
fax: (312) 939-2536
contact: Jay Sherwood (President)

Steel Can Recycling Institute
Central Northern Region (Illinois, Iowa, Michigan, Minnesota, Missouri, North Dakota, South Dakota, Wisconsin)
3800 N. Wilke Road, Suite 379
Arlington Heights, IL 60004
tel: (708) 818-1755
contact: Dave Keeling (Recycling Representative)

Indiana

Central States Glass Recycling Program
(Kentucky, Indiana, Illinois, Ohio, Wisconsin, Tennessee)
770 East 73rd Street
Indianapolis, IN 46240
tel: (317) 251-0131

Indiana Recycling Coalition
P.O. Box 2044
Indianapolis, IN 46220-0444
tel: (317) 283-6226
contact: Janet F. Neltner (Administrative Coordinator)

Steel Can Recycling Institute
Central Eastern Region (Indiana, Kentucky, Ohio, Pennsylvania, West Virginia)
680 Andersen Drive
Pittsburgh, PA 15220
contact: Jeff Langford (Recycling Representative)
tel: (800) 876-SCRI

Iowa

Iowa Recycling Association
P.O. Box 3184
Des Moines, IA 50316

Steel Can Recycling Institute
Central Northern Region (Illinois, Iowa, Michigan, Minnesota, Missouri, North Dakota, South Dakota, Wisconsin)
3800 N. Wilke Road, Suite 379
Arlington Heights, IL 60004
tel: (708) 818-1755
contact: Dave Keeling (Recycling Representative)

Kansas

Mid-America Glass Recycling Program
(Arkansas, Colorado, Kansas, Louisiana, Missouri, New Mexico, Oklahoma, Texas)
824 N. Mission
Sapulpa, OK 74066
tel: (918) 227-3889
fax: (918) 227-3958
contact: Gail Ederer, Executive Director

Steel Can Recycling Institute
Southwestern Region (Arizona, Colorado, Kansas, Nebraska, New Mexico, Oklahoma, Texas, Utah)
363 North Sam Houston Parkway, Suite 1100
Houston, TX 77060
contact: Gary Gallo (Recycling Representative)
tel: (713) 820-7837

Kentucky

Central States Glass Recycling Program
(Kentucky, Indiana, Illinois, Ohio, Wisconsin, Tennessee)
770 East 73rd Street
Indianapolis, IN 46240
tel: (317) 251-0131

Bluegrass Regional Recycling Corporation
P.O. Box 796
Frankfort, KY 40602
contact: Mr. Mickey Mills (Executive Director)

Kentucky Recycling Association
c/o Lexington Fayette Urban County Government
2181 Old Frankfort Pike
Lexington, KY 40510
tel: (606) 258-3470
contact: Mr. Steve Feese (Recycling Coordinator)
contact: Mr. Tony Knoll (President)

Steel Can Recycling Institute
Central Eastern Region (Indiana, Kentucky, Ohio, Pennsylvania, West Virginia)
680 Andersen Drive
Pittsburgh, PA 15220
contact: Jeff Langford (Recycling Representative)
tel: (800) 876-SCRI

Louisiana

Mid-America Glass Recycling Program
(Arkansas, Colorado, Kansas, Louisiana, Missouri, New Mexico, Oklahoma, Texas)
824 N. Mission
Sapulpa, OK 74066
tel: (918) 227-3889
fax: (918) 227-3958
contact: Gail Ederer, Executive Director

Steel Can Recycling Institute
Southeastern Region (Alabama, Arkansas, Florida, Georgia, Louisiana, Mississippi)
4900 Bayou Boulevard, Suite 110C
Pensacola, FL 32503
contact: Suzette Miller (Recycling Representative)
tel: (904) 479-7208

Maine

Maine Resource & Recovery Association
c/o Maine Municipal Association
Community Drive
Augusta, ME 04330

Steel Can Recycling Institute
Northeastern Region (Connecticut, Maine, Massachusetts, New Hampshire, New York, Rhode Island, Vermont)
97 Lowell Road, Suite 1000
Concord, MA 01742
contact: Paula Thompson (Recycling Representative)

Maryland

Maryland Recycling Coalition
101 Monroe, 6th Floor
Rockville, MD 20850

Mid-Atlantic Glass Recycling Program
(District of Columbia, Maryland, Virginia, West Virginia)
1800 Diagonal Road, Suite 600
Alexandria, VA 22314
tel: (703) 836-4655

Steel Can Recycling Institute
Mid-Atlantic Region (Delaware, District of Columbia, Maryland, New Jersey, North

Carolina, South Carolina, Tennessee, Virginia)
One Park West Circle, Suite 101
Midlothian, VA 23113
tel: (804) 378-2302
contact: Chuck Nettleship (Recycling Representative)

Massachusetts

MassRecycle
P.O. Box 3111
Worcester, MA 01613

Steel Can Recycling Institute
Northeastern Region (Connecticut, Maine, Massachusetts, New Hampshire, New York, Rhode Island, Vermont)
97 Lowell Road, Suite 1000
Concord, MA 01742
contact: Paula Thompson (Recycling Representative)

Michigan

Michigan Recycling Coalition
P.O. Box 10240
Lansing, MI 48901

Steel Can Recycling Institute
Central Northern Region (Illinois, Iowa, Michigan, Minnesota, Missouri, North Dakota, South Dakota, Wisconsin)
3800 N. Wilke Road, Suite 379
Arlington Heights, IL 60004
tel: (708) 818-1755
contact: Dave Keeling (Recycling Representative)

Minnesota

Recycling Association of Minnesota
c/o The Minnesota Project
2222 Elm Street, S.E.
Minneapolis, MN 55414

Steel Can Recycling Institute
Central Northern Region (Illinois, Iowa, Michigan, Minnesota, Missouri, North Dakota, South Dakota, Wisconsin)
3800 N. Wilke Road, Suite 379
Arlington Heights, IL 60004
tel: (708) 818-1755
contact: Dave Keeling (Recycling Representative)

Mississippi

Southeast Glass Recycling Program
(Alabama, Florida, Georgia, Mississippi)
P.O. Box 5951
Clearwater, FL 34618
tel: (813) 799-4917

Steel Can Recycling Institute
Southeastern Region (Alabama, Arkansas, Florida, Georgia, Louisiana, Mississippi)
4900 Bayou Boulevard, Suite 110C
Pensacola, FL 32503
contact: Suzette Miller (Recycling Representative)
tel: (904) 479-7208

Missouri

Mid-America Glass Recycling Program
(Arkansas, Colorado, Kansas, Louisiana, Missouri, New Mexico, Oklahoma, Texas)
824 N. Mission
Sapulpa, OK 74066
tel: (918) 227-3889
fax: (918) 227-3958
contact: Gail Ederer, Executive Director

Missouri State Recycling Association
P.O. Box 331
St. Charles, MO 63301

Steel Can Recycling Institute
Central Northern Region (Illinois, Iowa, Michigan, Minnesota, Missouri, North Dakota, South Dakota, Wisconsin)
3800 N. Wilke Road, Suite 379
Arlington Heights, IL 60004
tel: (708) 818-1755
contact: Dave Keeling (Recycling Representative)

Montana

Associated Recyclers of Montana
458 Charles Street
Billings, MT 59601

California Glass Recycling Corporation

(Arizona, California, Idaho, Montana, Nevada, Utah, Washington)
5709 Marconi Avenue, Suite C
Carmichael, CA 95608
tel: (916) 483-8585

Keep Montana Clean and Beautiful
P.O. Box 5925
2021 11th Avenue
Helena, MT 59601
tel: (406) 443-6242
contact: Peggy Mathews

Montana Environmental Information Coalition (M.E.I.C.)
P.O. Box 1184
Helena, MT 59604
contact: Brian McNitt

Steel Can Recycling Institute
Western Region (California, Idaho, Montana, Nevada, Oregon, Washington, Wyoming)
5150 E. Pacific Coast Highway, Suite 200
Long Beach, CA 90804
tel: (213) 597-1545
contact: Betsey Meyer (Recycling Representative)

Nebraska

Nebraska State Recycling Association
P.O. Box 80729
Lincoln, NE 68501
tel: (402) 475-3637

Steel Can Recycling Institute
Southwestern Region (Arizona, Colorado, Kansas, Nebraska, New Mexico, Oklahoma, Texas, Utah)
363 North Sam Houston Parkway, Suite 1100
Houston, TX 77060
contact: Gary Gallo (Recycling Representative)
tel: (713) 820-7837

Nevada

California Glass Recycling Corporation
(Arizona, California, Idaho, Montana, Nevada, Utah, Washington)
5709 Marconi Avenue, Suite C
Carmichael, CA 95608
tel: (916) 483-8585

Nevada Recycling Coalition
2550 Thomas Jefferson
Reno, NV 89509

Steel Can Recycling Institute
Western Region (California, Idaho, Montana, Nevada, Oregon, Washington, Wyoming)
5150 E. Pacific Coast Highway, Suite 200
Long Beach, CA 90804
tel: (213) 597-1545
contact: Betsey Meyer (Recycling Representative)

New Hampshire

New Hampshire Resource Recovery Association
P.O. Box 721
Concord, NH 03301
tel: (603) 224-6996

Steel Can Recycling Institute
Northeastern Region (Connecticut, Maine, Massachusetts, New Hampshire, New York, Rhode Island, Vermont)
97 Lowell Road, Suite 1000
Concord, MA 01742
contact: Paula Thompson (Recycling Representative)

New Jersey

ANJEC
Association of New Jersey Environmental Commissions
300 Mendham Road
Route 24, Box 157
Mendham, New Jersey 07945
tel: (201) 539-7547
fax: (201) 539-7713

Association of New Jersey Environmental Commissions
P.O. Box 157
Mendham, NJ 07945

Association of New Jersey Recyclers
120 Finderne
Bridgewater, NJ 08807
tel: (201) 722-7575

New Jersey Glass Recycling Association
P.O. Box 8169
Glen Ridge, NJ 07028
tel: (201) 748-4855

Steel Can Recycling Institute
Mid-Atlantic Region (Delaware, District of Columbia, Maryland, New Jersey, North Carolina, South Carolina, Tennessee, Virginia)
One Park West Circle, Suite 101
Midlothian, VA 23113
tel: (804) 378-2302
contact: Chuck Nettleship (Recycling Representative)

New Mexico

Mid-America Glass Recycling Program (Arkansas, Colorado, Kansas, Louisiana, Missouri, New Mexico, Oklahoma, Texas)
824 N. Mission
Sapulpa, OK 74066
tel: (918) 227-3889
fax: (918) 227-3958
contact: Gail Ederer, Executive Director

Recycle New Mexico
c/o Office of Recycling
City of Albuquerque
P.O. Box 1293
Albuquerque, NM 87103
tel: (505) 761-8176

Steel Can Recycling Institute
Southwestern Region (Arizona, Colorado, Kansas, Nebraska, New Mexico, Oklahoma, Texas, Utah)
363 North Sam Houston Parkway, Suite 1100
Houston, TX 77060
contact: Gary Gallo (Recycling Representative)
tel: (713) 820-7837

New York

New York State Association for Recycling
1152 County Road, #8
Farmington, NY 14425

Steel Can Recycling Institute
Northeastern Region (Connecticut, Maine, Massachusetts, New Hampshire, New York, Rhode Island, Vermont)
97 Lowell Road, Suite 1000
Concord, MA 01742
contact: Paula Thompson (Recycling Representative)

North Carolina

Carolinas Glass Recycling Program (North Carolina, South Carolina)
908 South Tryon Street, Suite 2200
Charlotte, NC 28202
tel: (704) 332-2030

North Carolina Recycling Association
P.O. Box 25368
Raleigh, NC 27611-5368
tel: (919) 782-8933

Steel Can Recycling Institute
Mid-Atlantic Region (Delaware, District of Columbia, Maryland, New Jersey, North Carolina, South Carolina, Tennessee, Virginia)
One Park West Circle, Suite 101
Midlothian, VA 23113
tel: (804) 378-2302
contact: Chuck Nettleship (Recycling Representative)

North Dakota

North Dakota Recyclers Association
c/o Sam McQuade
P.O. Box 1196
Bismarck, ND 58502-1196

Steel Can Recycling Institute
Central Northern Region (Illinois, Iowa, Michigan, Minnesota, Missouri, North Dakota, South Dakota, Wisconsin)
3800 N. Wilke Road, Suite 379
Arlington Heights, IL 60004
tel: (708) 818-1755
contact: Dave Keeling (Recycling Representative)

Ohio

Adams Brown Clermont Recycling
9620 Mt. Orab Pike
Georgetown, Ohio 45121
tel: (513) 378-3431
contact: Daniel Wickerham (Environmental Education Coordinator)

Association of Ohio Recyclers
200 South Green Street
Georgetown, Ohio 45121
tel: (513) 378-3431

Central States Glass Recycling Program
(Kentucky, Indiana, Illinois, Ohio, Wisconsin, Tennessee)
770 East 73rd Street
Indianapolis, IN 46240
tel: (317) 251-0131

Steel Can Recycling Institute
Central Eastern Region (Indiana, Kentucky, Ohio, Pennsylvania, West Virginia)
680 Andersen Drive
Pittsburgh, PA 15220
contact: Jeff Langford (Recycling Representative)
tel: (800) 876-SCRI

Oklahoma

Mid-America Glass Recycling Program
(Arkansas, Colorado, Kansas, Louisiana, Missouri, New Mexico, Oklahoma, Texas)
824 N. Mission
Sapulpa, OK 74066
tel: (918) 227-3889
fax: (918) 227-3958
contact: Gail Ederer, Executive Director

Steel Can Recycling Institute
Southwestern Region (Arizona, Colorado, Kansas, Nebraska, New Mexico, Oklahoma, Texas, Utah)
363 North Sam Houston Parkway, Suite 1100
Houston, TX 77060
contact: Gary Gallo (Recycling Representative)
tel: (713) 820-7837

Oregon

Association of Oregon Recyclers
P.O. Box 15279
Portland, OR 97215
tel: (503) 255-5087
contact: Charlotte Becker (Resource Coordinator)

Steel Can Recycling Institute
Western Region (California, Idaho, Montana, Nevada, Oregon, Washington, Wyoming)
5150 E. Pacific Coast Highway, Suite 200
Long Beach, CA 90804
tel: (213) 597-1545
contact: Betsey Meyer (Recycling Representative)

Pennsylvania

Pennsylvania Glass Recycling Corporation
(Delaware, Pennsylvania)
509 North Second Street
Harrisburg, PA 17101
tel: (717) 234-8091

Pennsylvania Resources Council
25 W. Third Street
P.O. Box 88
Media, PA 19063
tel: (215) 565-9131
fax: (215) 892-0504
contact: Kevin McCollister (Director—Education & Research)

Steel Can Recycling Institute
Central Eastern Region (Indiana, Kentucky, Ohio, Pennsylvania, West Virginia)
680 Andersen Drive
Pittsburgh, PA 15220
contact: Jeff Langford (Recycling Representative)
tel: (800) 876-SCRI

Rhode Island

Steel Can Recycling Institute
Northeastern Region (Connecticut, Maine, Massachusetts, New Hampshire, New York, Rhode Island, Vermont)
97 Lowell Road, Suite 1000
Concord, MA 01742
contact: Paula Thompson (Recycling Representative)

South Carolina

Carolinas Glass Recycling Program
(North Carolina, South Carolina)
908 South Tryon Street, Suite 2200
Charlotte, NC 28202
tel: (704) 332-2030

Recycling Association
c/o S.C. Clean & Beautiful
1205 Pendleton Street, Room 203
Columbia, SC 29201
tel: (803) 734-0143

Steel Can Recycling Institute
Mid-Atlantic Region (Delaware, District of Columbia, Maryland, New Jersey, North Carolina, South Carolina, Tennessee, Virginia)
One Park West Circle, Suite 101
Midlothian, VA 23113
tel: (804) 378-2302
contact: Chuck Nettleship (Recycling Representative)

South Dakota

Recycling Coalition of South Dakota
1800 Otonka Ridge
Sioux Falls, SD 57069

Steel Can Recycling Institute
Central Northern Region (Illinois, Iowa, Michigan, Minnesota, Missouri, North Dakota, South Dakota, Wisconsin)
3800 N. Wilke Road, Suite 379
Arlington Heights, IL 60004
tel: (708) 818-1755
contact: Dave Keeling (Recycling Representative)

Tennessee

Central States Glass Recycling Program
(Kentucky, Indiana, Illinois, Ohio, Wisconsin, Tennessee)
770 East 73rd Street
Indianapolis, IN 46240
tel: (317) 251-0131

Steel Can Recycling Institute
Mid-Atlantic Region (Delaware, District of Columbia, Maryland, New Jersey, North Carolina, South Carolina, Tennessee, Virginia)
One Park West Circle, Suite 101
Midlothian, VA 23113
tel: (804) 378-2302
contact: Chuck Nettleship (Recycling Representative)

Tennessee Recycling Coalition
1725 Church Street
Nashville, TN 37203

Texas

Mid-America Glass Recycling Program
(Arkansas, Colorado, Kansas, Louisiana, Missouri, New Mexico, Oklahoma, Texas)
824 N. Mission
Sapulpa, OK 74066
tel: (918) 227-3889
fax: (918) 227-3958
contact: Gail Ederer, Executive Director

Recycling Coalition of Texas
P.O. Box 2359
Austin, TX 78768

Steel Can Recycling Institute
Southwestern Region (Arizona, Colorado, Kansas, Nebraska, New Mexico, Oklahoma, Texas, Utah)
363 North Sam Houston Parkway, Suite 1100
Houston, TX 77060
contact: Gary Gallo (Recycling Representative)
tel: (713) 820-7837

Utah

California Glass Recycling Corporation
(Arizona, California, Idaho, Montana, Nevada, Utah, Washington)
5709 Marconi Avenue, Suite C
Carmichael, CA 95608
tel: (916) 483-8585

Steel Can Recycling Institute
Southwestern Region (Arizona, Colorado, Kansas, Nebraska, New Mexico, Oklahoma, Texas, Utah)
363 North Sam Houston Parkway, Suite 1100
Houston, TX 77060
contact: Gary Gallo (Recycling Representative)
tel: (713) 820-7837

Vermont

Association of Vermont Recyclers
P.O. Box 1244
Montpelier, VT 05601
tel: (802) 229-1833

Steel Can Recycling Institute
Northeastern Region (Connecticut, Maine, Massachusetts, New Hampshire, New York, Rhode Island, Vermont)

97 Lowell Road, Suite 1000
Concord, MA 01742
contact: Paula Thompson (Recycling Representative)

Virginia

Mid-Atlantic Glass Recycling Program
(District of Columbia, Maryland, Virginia, West Virginia)
1800 Diagonal Road, Suite 600
Alexandria, VA 22314
tel: (703) 836-4655

Steel Can Recycling Institute
Mid-Atlantic Region (Delaware, District of Columbia, Maryland, New Jersey, North Carolina, South Carolina, Tennessee, Virginia)
One Park West Circle, Suite 101
Midlothian, VA 23113
tel: (804) 378-2302
contact: Chuck Nettleship (Recycling Representative)

Washington

California Glass Recycling Corporation
(Arizona, California, Idaho, Montana, Nevada, Utah, Washington)
5709 Marconi Avenue, Suite C
Carmichael, CA 95608
tel: (916) 483-8585

Washington State Recycling Association
203 E. Fourth Avenue, #307
Olympia, WA 98501
tel: (206) 352-8737

Steel Can Recycling Institute
Western Region (California, Idaho, Montana, Nevada, Oregon, Washington, Wyoming)
5150 E. Pacific Coast Highway, Suite 200
Long Beach, CA 90804
tel: (213) 597-1545
contact: Betsey Meyer (Recycling Representative)

Washington, D.C.

Mid-Atlantic Glass Recycling Program
(District of Columbia, Maryland, Virginia, West Virginia)
1800 Diagonal Road, Suite 600
Alexandria, VA 22314
tel: (703) 836-4655

Steel Can Recycling Institute
Mid-Atlantic Region (Delaware, District of Columbia, Maryland, New Jersey, North Carolina, South Carolina, Tennessee, Virginia)
One Park West Circle, Suite 101
Midlothian, VA 23113
tel: (804) 378-2302
contact: Chuck Nettleship (Recycling Representative)

West Virginia

Mid-Atlantic Glass Recycling Program
(District of Columbia, Maryland, Virginia, West Virginia)
1800 Diagonal Road, Suite 600
Alexandria, VA 22314
tel: (703) 836-4655

Steel Can Recycling Institute
Central Eastern Region (Indiana, Kentucky, Ohio, Pennsylvania, West Virginia)
680 Andersen Drive
Pittsburgh, PA 15220
contact: Jeff Langford (Recycling Representative)
tel: (800) 876-SCRI

Wisconsin

Associated Recyclers of Wisconsin
16940 W. Shadow Drive
New Berlin, WI 53151
tel: (414) 679-2132

Central States Glass Recycling Program
(Kentucky, Indiana, Illinois, Ohio, Wisconsin, Tennessee)
770 East 73rd Street
Indianapolis, IN 46240
tel: (317) 251-0131

Steel Can Recycling Institute
Central Northern Region (Illinois, Iowa, Michigan, Minnesota, Missouri, North Dakota, South Dakota, Wisconsin)
3800 N. Wilke Road, Suite 379
Arlington Heights, IL 60004

tel: (708) 818-1755
contact: Dave Keeling (Recycling Representative)

Wyoming

Wyoming Citizens for Recycling
P.O. Box 2393
Casper, WY 82602-2393

Steel Can Recycling Institute
Western Region (California, Idaho, Montana, Nevada, Oregon, Washington, Wyoming)
5150 E. Pacific Coast Highway, Suite 200
Long Beach, CA 90804
tel: (213) 597-1545
contact: Betsey Meyer (Recycling Representative)

Appendix F

National Environmental Groups

America the Beautiful Fund
219 Shoreham Building
Washington, D.C. 20005
tel: (202) 638-1649
Executive Director: Paul B. Dowing

Citizens Clearinghouse for Hazardous Wastes
P.O. Box 926
Arlington, VA 22216
tel: (703) 276-7070

The Conservation Foundation
1250 24th Street, N.W.
Washington, D.C. 20037
tel: (202) 293-4800
President: Kathryn Fuller

Earthworm, Inc.
186 South Street
Boston, MA 02111
tel: (617) 426-7344

Environmental Action Coalition
625 Broadway
New York, NY 10012
tel: (212) 677-1601
Executive Director: Nancy A. Wolf

Environmental Action Foundation
1525 New Hampshire Avenue, N.W.
Washington, D.C. 20036
tel: (202) 745-4879
contact: Jeanne Wirka

Environmental Defense Fund
257 Park Avenue, S.
New York, NY 10010
tel: (212) 505-2100
Executive Director: Frederic D. Krupp

Environmental Law Institute
1616 P Street
Washington, D.C. 20036
tel: (202) 328-5150
President: J. William Futrell

EPA Office of Solid Waste
401 M Street, S.W.
Washington, D.C. 20460
tel: (202) 260-4610
(800) 424-9346 Hotline for brochures

Friends of the Earth
218 D Street, S.E.
Washington, D.C. 20003
tel: (202) 544-2600
President: Michael S. Clark

Greenpeace USA
4649 Sunnyside Avenue, N.
Seattle, WA 98103
tel: (206) 632-4326
fax: (206) 632-6122

Inform, Inc.
381 Park Avenue, S., Suite 1201
New York, NY 10016-8806
tel: (212) 689-4040

fax: (212) 447-0689
Can provide publication lists giving names of research reports
President: Joanna D. Underwood

Institute for Local Self-Reliance
2425 18th Street, N.W.
Washington, D.C. 20009
tel: (202) 232-4108

Keep America Beautiful, Inc.
Mill River Plaza
9 West Broad Street
Stamford, CT 06902
tel: (203) 323-8987
fax: (203) 325-9199
President: Roger W. Powers

League of Women Voters of the United States
1730 M Street, N.W.
Washington, D.C. 20036
tel: (202) 429-1965
Director—Membership Development: Sandra Gillis

Local Solutions to Global Pollution
2121 Bonar Street, Studio A
Berkeley, CA 94702
tel: (415) 540-8843

National Association of Counties
440 1st Street, N.W., 8th Floor
Washington, D.C. 20001
tel: (202) 393-6226
Executive Director: John P. Thomas

National Audubon Society, Inc.
950 Third Avenue
New York, NY 10022
tel: (212) 832-3200
President: Peter A. Berle

National Consumers League
815 15th Street, N.W., Suite 928-N
Washington, D.C. 20005
tel: (202) 639-8140
Executive Director: Linda F. Golodner

National Council of the Paper Industry for Air and Stream Improvement
260 Madison Avenue
New York, NY 10016
tel: (212) 532-9000
President: Dr. Isaiah Gellman

National Parks and Conservation Association
1015 31st Street, N.W.
Washington, D.C. 20007
tel: (202) 944-8530
President: Paul C. Pritchard

National Recreation and Park Association
3101 Park Center Drive
Alexandria, VA 22302
tel: (703) 820-4940
Executive Director: Dean Tice

National Recycling Coalition, Inc.
1101 30th Street, N.W., Suite 305
Washington, D.C. 20007
tel: (202) 625-6406
fax: (202) 625-6409
President: Mary Wiard
Executive Director: David Loveland

The National Urban Coalition
8601 Georgia Avenue, Suite 500
Silver Spring, MD 20910
tel: (301) 495-4999
President: Ramona H. Edelin, Ph.D.

National Wildlife Federation
1400 16th Street, N.W.
Washington, D.C. 20036
tel: (202) 797-6800
President: Jay D. Hair

Natural Resources Defense Council, Inc.
40 West 20th Street
New York, NY 10011
tel: (212) 727-2700
Executive Director: John Adams

Plastics Recycling Foundation
1275 K Street, N.W., Suite 400
Washington D.C. 20005
tel: (202) 371-5212

Renew America
1400 16th Street, N.W., #700
Washington, D.C. 20036
tel: (202) 232-2252

Resources for the Future
1616 P Street, N.W.
Washington, D.C. 20036
tel: (202) 328-5000
President: Robert W. Fri

Division of Publications and Communication: (202) 328-5009

Sierra Club
730 Polk Street
San Francisco, CA 94109
tel: (415) 776-2211
President: Susan Merrow

SWICH
P.O. Box 7219
Silver Spring, MD 20901
tel: (202) 638-6300

Urban Initiatives
530 W. 25th Street
New York, NY 10001
tel: (212) 620-9773
President: Gianni Longo

Urban Land Institute
625 Indiana Avenue, N.W., Suite 400
Washington, D.C. 20004
tel: (202) 624-7000
Executive VP: David E. Stahl

Izaak Walton League of America
1401 Wilson Boulevard, Level B
Arlington, VA 22209
tel: (703) 528-1818
Executive Director: Jack Lorenz

Water Pollution Control Federation
601 Wythe Street
Alexandria, VA 22314-1994
tel: (202) 684-2400
Executive Director: Dr. Quincalee Brown

World Environment Center
419 Park Avenue, S., Suite 1404
New York, NY 10016
tel: (212) 683-4700
President and CEO: Anthony G. Marcil

World Wildlife Fund
1250 24th Street, N.W., Suite 500
Washington D.C. 20037
tel: (202) 293-4800
President: Kathryn Fuller

Worldwatch Institute
1776 Massachusetts Avenue, N.W.
Washington, D.C. 20036-1904
tel: (202) 452-1999
President: Lester R. Brown

Appendix G

Chemical Testing Supplies

Recycling Options
13881 West Alaska Place
Lakewood, CO 80228
tel: (303) 987-3132

Bibliography

GENERAL

Abrahamson, Peggy. "U.S. Urged to Set Up Separate Recycling Rules." *American Metal Market* (June 10, 1991).

"All that glitters Is Not Gold." *The Denver Business Journal* (January 1991) p. 17–22.

American Forest Council. "Stewardship and Environmental Responsibility: Answers to Some Frequently Asked Questions About America's Forest Products Industry," pp. 1–23.

American Recycling Market Inc. *1991 Directory/Reference Manual* (1991).

American Recycling Market Inc. *The Official Recycled Products Guide: The Official Purchasing Guide and News Source on Recycled Products Since 1989 3, 1*. New York: American Recycling Market Inc (1991).

Arkansas Solid Waste Fact Finding Task Force. "Solid Waste Strategies." Little Rock, AR: Department of Pollution Control and Ecology (October 1990).

Armbrister, Senator. "Texas Senate Bill 444." Austin, TX (April 1989).

"Ask Garbage." *Garbage* (November/December 1990), p. 72.

Association of New Jersey Environmental Commissions. "List of Publications." Mendham, NJ.

Aware Diaper Inc. "100% cotton flannel diaper." Greely, CO.

Bartlett, Albert A. "Forgotten Fundamentals of the Energy Crisis." *Am. J. Phys.* (September 1978) pp. 876–888.

Batty, Sandy. "Spreading the Word: A Publicity Handbook for Recycling." Association of New Jersey Environmental Commissions (1986).

Beck, R. W. and Associates. *Denver/Aurora Waste-To-Energy Feasibility Study—Volume 1*, Executive Summary. Denver, CO (1989).

Belaval, Judy. "Connecticut Recycles Office Paper" (January 1990).

Bell, Ruth P. and Robertson, Robin L.M. "Commercial Waste Audits." *BioCycle* (December 1989).

Bennett, Steven J. *Ecopreneuring*. New York: John Wiley & Sons, Inc. (1991).

Binder, James A. "Getting to 'Yes' on Waste-to-Energy." *Waste Age* (April 1990), pp. 148–152.

"Biomass Energy Program Report." *Biologue* (1988): 12–14.
Board of Supervisors Township of Middletown. "Ordinance No. 90–11." Middletown, PA (June 1991).
Breen, Bill. "Landfills Are #1." *Garbage* (September/October 1990): 42–47.
Breen, Bill. "Truckin' Trash." *Garbage* (January/February 1991), pp.48–51.
Brown County Solid Waste District. *A Guide to Safe Management of Household Hazardous Waste*. OH.
Brown, Mary Daniels. "The Act of Making a Molehill Out of a Mountain: Recycling and Reusing." *Current Health* Vol. 2 (1991), pp. 25–27.
Bureau of Waste Reduction and Recycling. "Change Your Own Oil?"
Bureau of Waste Management, Division of Waste Minimization & Planning. "Fact Sheet #1 Act 101." Harrisburg, PA.
The Bureau of National Affairs, Inc. "U.S. Environmental Laws."
Byron, Christopher. "The Bottom Line, Trash Fiction." *New York* (May 6, 1991).
Calandra, Thom. "Environmental Investment Fund Weighs in as Top U.S. Performer." *San Francisco Examiner* (July 6, 1990).
Californians Against Waste. "Issue Alert." California: 1991.
California Resource Recovery Association. "A Recycling Agenda for the 1990s." San Diego, CA: California Resource Recovery Association (August 1991).
California Resource Recovery Association. "Reduce Reuse Recycle."
Californians Against Waste Foundation. "Reducing the Plague of Packaging: An Integrated Solution." Sacramento, CA: Californians Against Waste Foundation (September 1990).
Californians Against Waste. "Summary of 1991 Solid Waste Legislation." Sacramento, CA (September 26, 1991).
Californians Against Waste. "Waste Watch." Sacramento, CA (1990).
Californians Against Waste. "Waste Watch." Sacramento, California (Fall 1990).
Californians Against Waste. "Waste Watch." Sacramento, CA (1991).
Californians Against Waste. "Waste Watch." Sacramento, CA (Summer 1991).
Camp Dresser & McKee Inc. "Office and Commercial Waste Reduction." IL (1991).
Cassel, Thomas A.V., Ph.D.,P.E. "The Integrated Approach to Solid Waste Disposal." *Independent Energy* (November 1990), pp. 76–78.
Center for ecological technology. "Commercial Recycling and Waste Reduction." (June 1990).
Cerrato, David S. "Estimating Recyclables." *Resource Recovery* (August 1989), pp. 19–21.
Chandler, William U. "Materials Recycling: The Virtue of Necessity." *Worldwatch Paper 56* (October 1983).
Chen, Edward T. "Houston Recycles with Foresight." *Waste Age* (February 1991).
Christensen, Karen. *Home Ecology: Simple and Practical Ways to Green Your Home*. Golden, CO: Fulcrum Publishing (1990).
Citizen's Clearinghouse for Hazardous Wastes, Inc. "Recycling, The Answer to Our Garbage Problem" (May 1987).
City of Allentown, Bureau of Health. "Curbside Recycling in Allentown." Allentown, PA.
City of Allentown, Bureau of Health. "Guide to Apartment Recycling." Allentown, PA.
City of Allentown, Bureau of Health. "Recycling... Make It Your Business." Allentown, PA (September 1990).
City of Allentown, Department of Health. " "Recyclar" en Allentown." Allentown, PA.

Clarke, Marjorie J. "A Solid Waste Research Agenda." *Waste Age* (April 1990), pp. 233–238.

Combs, Susan. " 'Chipping' to Recycle Wood Waste." *Waste Age* (May 1990).

Combs, Susan. "The Cost of Free Recycling." *Waste Age* (July 1991), pp. 89–90.

Combs, Susan. "MRFing Las Vegas Style." *Waste Age* (July 1991).

Connecticut Department of Environmental Protection. "How to Bring Home Less Trash."

Connecticut Department of Environmental Protection. "How to Save the Planet in 2 Minutes."

Connecticut Department of Environmental Protection. "How to Turn Cans into Cars."

Connecticut Department of Environmental Protection. "Mandatory Recycling Regulation" (February 28, 1989).

Connell, Jeffrey J. "Minnesota's Public-Private Partnership." *Waste Age* (October 1990).

Cooper, Charles B. "The Changing Permitting Picture." *Independent Energy* (May/June 1991), pp. 68–70.

Cooper, Victoria. "Ecoteams Make Clean Sweep." *Rocky Mountain News* (April 22, 1991).

Council Member Potter. "Bill 32-90." Montgomery County, MD: County Council (November 13, 1990).

Councilmember Potter. *Procurement—Recycled Materials and Supplies.* Montgomery County, MD (February 1991).

Council on Plastics and Packaging in the Environment. "The COPPE Environmental Report." *COPPE Quarterly* Vol. 5, No. 3 (1991), pp. 1–6.

Council President at the Request of the County Executive. "Bill No. 54–88." Montgomery County, MD: County Council for Montgomery County, MD (August 1, 1989).

Council President. "Solid Waste—Recycling." Montgomery County, MD: City Council for Montgomery County, MD (1989).

Culviner, Prall. "Paper Chase in the '90s." *Waste Age* (February 1991).

Dane, Sally. *The National Buyer's Guide to Recycled Paper.* Washington, D.C.: Environmental Educators, Inc. (1973).

Darcey, Susan. "Recycling Resurges as Viable Option to Disposal." *World Wastes* (July 1987).

David, Alan and Kinsella, Susan. "Recycled Paper Exploding the Myths." *Garbage* (May/June 1990), pp. 48–55.

Decker, Caroline. "Household Recyclables Piling Up." Little Rock, AR: *Little Rock Arkansas Gazette* (February 10, 1991).

DeGrane, Susan. "XL Disposal's Automated Recycling." *Waste Age* (July 1990).

Department of Environmental Quality. "Oregon's Recycling Education and Promotion Activities" (August 1991).

Department of Environmental Resources. "Recycling Works. Here's How." Harrisburg, PA.

Diaz, Luis F. and Golueke, Clarence G. "Status of Composting in the United States." *Resource Recycling* (February 1990).

DiChristina, Mariette. "How We Can Win the War Against Garbage." *Popular Science* (October 1990).

Division of Waste Management. "Summary of Senate Bill 2." KY.

Earth Coalition of Charlotte-Mecklenburg. "Earth Days." Charlotte, NC (July/August 1991).

The Earthworks Group. *The Recycler's Handbook: Simple Things You Can Do.* Berkelely, CA: EarthWorks Press (1990).

Environmental Defense Fund. *Coming Full Circle: Successful Recycling Today.* New York: Environmental Defense Fund (1988).

Environment Protection Service. "Office Paper Recovery: Role of the Sheltered Workshop" (October 1980).

Environmental Protection Division of Georgia. "Recycling in Georgia—What's Going on Here?" (June 1991).

"Facts on Municipal Solid Waste." *Focus* No.3 (May 1990).

Federal Register. "Environmental Protection Agency" Vol. 56, No. 191 (Wednesday, October 2, 1991).

Fehling, Kenneth. "Recycled Products at New York's State University." *Waste Age* (April 1990), pp. 52–54.

Fibre Market News. *1991 Paper Recycling Markets*. OH: GIE Inc., 1991.

Fierman, Jaclyn. "The Big Muddle in Green Marketing." *Fortune* (June 3, 1991).

Fong, Tillie. "Ken Caryl to Begin Recycling." *Rocky Mountain News* (January 4, 1990).

"Free Speech in the Woods." *Garbage* (July/August 1991), pp. 16–19.

Freeman, Stan. "Recycling Comes of Age in WMass." Springfield, MA: *Sunday Republican* (January 14, 1990).

Garbage Recarnation, Inc. "The Sometimes Monthly Recycle Rag." Santa Rosa, CA (September, 1991).

Gazella, Kim. "Recycling Project Picks Up in Schools." *York Observer* (September 17, 1989).

Gelgen-Miller, Peter. "Global Action Plan." *The London Free Press* (December 15, 1990).

Geller, Peter. "Conference Paints Recyclables as Pot of Gold." *Plain Dealer* (January 31, 1991).

Georgia Department of Natural Resources. "Air in Georgia." Atlanta, GA.

Georgia Department of Natural Resources. "Composting in Your Own Back Yard." Atlanta, GA.

Georgia Power Company. "A Guide to Recycling." Atlanta. GA (1989).

Georgia Power Company. "A Guide to Solid Waste Disposal Options." Atlanta, GA.

Georgia Department of Natural Resources. "Help Protect the Environment—Recycle Used Oil." Atlanta, GA.

Georgia Department of Natural Resources. "Household Hazardous Waste." Atlanta, GA.

Georgia Department of Natural Resources. "Recycling in Georgia—Why." Atlanta, GA.

Georgia Department of Community Affairs. "Solid Waste: Management Alternatives" (December 1990).

Georgia Department of Community Affairs. "Solid Waste: Management Alternatives" (December 1990).

"Getting Rid of Garbage." *Garbage* (September/October 1991), pp. 30–33.

Glenn, Jim. "Containers at Curbside." *BioCycle* (March 1988).

Glenn, Jim. "Recycling Hits the Workplace." *BioCycle* (February 1990).

Glenn, Jim. "The State of Garbage in America." *BioCycle* (March 1990).

Goldberg, Dan. "Growing 'Backward' with Milliron." *Waste Age* (July 1990).

Goldberg, Dan. "It's a Small, Small World." *Waste Age* (April 1990), pp. 158–160.

Goldberg, Dan. "Teaching the Roots About Grass." *Waste Age* (April 1990).

Goldman, Matthew. "What Do Those Numbers Mean?" *Waste Age* (February 1991), pp. 53–58.

Golueke, Clarence G. and Diaz, Luis F. "Quality Control and Waste Management." *BioCycle* (July 1989).

Goodwin, Goodwin E. "Study Finds California Bottle Law Highly Effective." *American Metal Market* (June 17, 1991).

Goodwin, Morgan. "In California Recycling Flood Yields Dry Hole." *American Metal Market* (August 29, 1991).

Gould, Robert N. "MRFs, Past and Future." *Waste Age* (July 1990).

Governor's Select Committee on Packaging and the Environment. "Final Report" (December 18, 1990).

Governor's Task Force on Integrated Solid Waste Management. "Interim Report of the Governor's Task Force on Integrated Solid Waste Management" (January 1990).

Grady, Julie C. "Thrifty Yankees Recycle and Save." *Waste Age* (December 1987), pp. 39–42.

Gross, Don. "Cost of Recycling Trash More than City Expected." New York: *Staten Island Advance* (February 25, 1991).

Gross, Don. "Officials Say Recycling Isn't Garbage Cure-all." New York: *Staten Island Advance* (February 10, 1991).

Grossman, John. "Resurrecting Auto Graveyards." *Inc.* (March 1983), pp. 71–80.

Hedzik, Kimberly. "Networking, Education, and Common Sense." *Waste Age* (August 1990).

Hemenway, Caroline G. "Asphalt Recycler Saves Cities $$, Landfill Space." *Environment Today* (June 1990).

Hertzberg, Richard. "Old News Is Good News at Garden State Paper." *Resource Recycling* (July/August 1985).

Idaho Waste Reduction Assistance Program. "Batteries—Friends or Foes?" Boise, ID.

Idaho Waste Reduction Assistance Program. "Lead-acid Battery Storage." Boise, ID (May 1990).

Idaho Waste Reduction Assistance Program. "Office Paper Recycling." Boise, ID (June 1990).

Idaho Waste Reduction Assistance Program. "Recycling Awareness Program." Boise, ID (June 1990).

Idaho Waste Reduction Assistance Program. "Recycling Has Come of Age!" Boise, ID.

Illinois Department of Energy and Natural Resources. "Clip Art—A Collection Waste Reduction Graphics." IL (June 1991).

Illinois Department of Natural Resources. "Consumer Tips for Reducing Waste."

Illinois Cooperative Extention Service. "A Homeowner's Guide to Recycling Yard Wastes." Urbana-Champaign, IL: University of Illinois (May 1990).

Illinois Department of Energy and Natural Resources. "Illinois' Solid Waste Legislation 1991." Springfield, IL (October 23, 1991).

Illinois Recycling Association. "Newletter." Chicago, IL (July 1991).

Illinois Recycling Association. "Newsletter." Chicago, IL (October 1991).

Illinois Department of Energy and Natural Resources. "Office and Commercial Waste Reduction" (1991).

Illinois Hazardous Waste Research and Information Center. "Paint Disposal the Right Way."

Illinois Department of Energy and Natural Resources. "Program Services and Funding Summary for Solid Waste Management." Springfield, IL (Spring 1991).

Illinois Department of Energy and Natural Resources. "Publications and Videos on Recycling, Composting and Solid Waste Management." Springfield, IL.

Illinois Department of Energy and Natural Resources. "Recycle: Be Part of the Solution, Not Part of the Problem." Springfield, IL.

Illinois Department of Energy and Natural Resources. "Recycling Update." Springfield, IL (Summer 1991).

Illinois Department of Energy and Natural Resources. "The Three R's—Reduce. Reuse. Recycle." Springfield, IL (Fall 1991).

Illinois Department of Energy Conservation Center. "Your Recycled Paper Procurement Guide."

Indiana Institute on Recycling. *Special Report No. 1 to the Indiana General Assembly: A Legislative Proposal to Improve Recycling Through Better Public Disclosure of the Cost of Municipal Waste Management.* Terre Haute, IN (December 1990).

Iowa Department of Natural Resources. "Iowa's Solid Waste Stream: Characterization and Management Strategy" (July 1990).

Iowa Department of Natural Resources. "Local Government Recycling Guide for Iowa Communities" (December 1990).

Iowa Department of Natural Resources. "Waste Management in Iowa." DesMoines, IA (April 1991).

Iowa Department of Natural Resources. "Waste Reduction Assistance Program." Des Moines, IA.

Kane County Board, Solid Waste Program. "Kane County Recycles." IL (Spring 1991).

Keep America Beautiful, Inc. "Marketing Recyclables." *Focus: Facts on Municipal Solid Waste* Vol. 3 (1990).

Keep America Beautiful, Inc. "Overview: Solid Waste Disposal Alternatives." Stamford, CT (1990).

Keep America Beautiful, Inc. "Recycling." *Focus: Facts on Municipal Solid Waste* Vol. 2 (1990).

Keep America Beautiful, Inc. "Recycling." *Focus: Facts on Municipal Solid Waste* Vol. 1 (1991).

Keep America Beautiful, Inc. "Recycling and Waste-to-Energy Work Together." *Focus: Facts on municipal solid waste* Vol. 6 (1991).

Keep Montana Clean & Beautiful, Inc. "Montana Recycling Directory."

"Keeping the Customer Satisfied." *Waste Age* (August 1991), pp. 97–98.

Keller, Richard. "A History of the 'Buy Recycled' Movement—Where Do We Go From Here?" Atlanta, GA: Northeast Maryland Waste Disposal Authority (1991).

King, Michael. "Ecology Is Serious Business." Appleton, WI: *Post-Crescent,* June 3, 1990.

Kiste, Stan. "Collecting and Processing Plastic Dairy Containers." *Resource Recycling* (July 1988).

Kleiner, Art. "Brundtland's Legacy." *Garbage* (September/October 1990), pp. 58–62.

Kleiner, Art. "The Greening of Jay Hair." *Garbage* (January/February 1991), pp. 54–57.

Kleiner, Art. "Theatre of the McServed." *Garbage* (September/October 1991), pp. 52–57.

Kourik, Robert. "Burying the Myths of Tree Planting." *Garbage* (January/February 1991), pp. 43–47.

Kourik, Robert. "What's So Great About Seattle." *Garbage* (November/December 1990).

Kovacs, Williams L. "The Coming Era of Conservation and Industrial Utilization of Recyclable." *Ecology Law Quarterly* (1988).

Kovacs, William L. "Dark Clouds." *Resource Recovery* (August 1989).

Kraybill, Daniel D. and Wickliff, Alisa. "Used Lead-acid Batteries: Management Tips." Champaign, IL: Illinois Department of Energy and Natural Resources (May 1991).

Krigman, Alan Editor. "Waste Recovery Report." Philadelphia, PA ICON/Information Concepts, Inc. (November 1991).

Kvaal, Greg. "Don't Throw This Away!" *Minnesota Real Estate Journal* (August 5, 1991).

Lackawanna County Recycling Center. "You Are Now in a Recycling Zone" (Scranton, PA).

Lexington-Fayette Urban County Government. "Corporate Commitment Program."

Lin, Harry. "This County is a Marketer." *Waste Age* (April 1990).

Lindqvist, Thomas. "Deposit Systems and Materials Recycling." *BioCycle* (July 1989), pp. 48–52.

Little, Arthur D., Inc. "The Life Cycle Energy Content of Containers: 1984 Up." *Final Report to American Iron and Steel Institute* (April 1984).

Local Emergency Planning Committees. "It's Not Over in October!" Washington, D.C. (September 1988).

Lodge, George C. and Rayport, Jeffrey F. "Knee-deep and Rising: America's Recycling Crisis." *Harvard Business Review* (1991), pp. 128–139

Louisiana Department of Environmental Quality. "The Louisiana Recycling Awareness Program" (October 1991).

Lueck, Guada Woodring. "Pieces to the Puzzle." *Waste Age* (July 1991).

Lueck, Guada Woodring. "Elementary Lessons in Garbage Appreciation." *Waste Age* (September 1990).

Lueck, Guada Woodring. "A Simple Way to Track and Reward Recyclers." *Waste Age* (July 1991), pp. 59–64.

Lueck, P. Anthony. "Is Landfill Hauling's Future on Track?" *Waste Age* (April 1990), Chapter 6, pp. 114–116.

Maine Waste Management Agency. "Recycling Market and Resource Directory" (January 1991).

Mansur, Michael. "Government Slow to Join Recycling Push." Kansas City, MO: *Kansas City Star* (March 26, 1990).

Marier, Donald. "No Silver Bullet." *Independent Energy* (July/August 1990).

Marinelli, Janet. "Packaging." *Garbage* (May/June 1990), pp. 28–33.

Maryland Environmental Service. "1991 Maryland Recycling Directory." MD (1991).

Maryland Department of the Environment. "The Maryland Recycling Act Fact Sheet."

Maryland Department of the Environment. "Reduce—Reuse Recycle."

MassRecycle. "The Massachusetts Recycling Coalition Newsletter." Worcester, MA (Spring 1991).

MassRecycle. "The Massachusetts Recycling Coalition Newsletter." Worcester, MA (Summer 1991).

McCarty, Patrick and Jorgenson, Thair. "Fluidized Bed for Resource Recovery." *Independent Energy* (October 1990).

McLaurin, Wayne J. and Wade, Gary L. "Composting and Mulching." University of Georgia (January 1991).

Meade, Kathleen. "Food Composting: No Small Potatoes." *Waste Age* (April 1990), pp. 203–206.

Meade, Kathleen. "Recycling 50%: It's How You Count It." *Waste Age* (October 1990).

Mendieta, P. E. "State Implementation of Subtitle D Regulations." Texas Department of Health.

Merry, William. "Taking a Profitable Approach to Recycling." *World Wastes* (July 1990).
Michigan Department of Natural Resources. "Buy Recycled Products."
Michigan Department of Natural Resources. "Composting at a Glance."
Michigan Department of Natural Resources. "A Guide to Recycling in Your Community."
Michigan Department of Natural Resources. "Have Fun with Recycling." Lansing, MI.
Michigan Department of Natural Resources. "Help Stop this Growing Garbage Crisis."
Michigan Department of Natural Resources. "Michigan Solid Waste Policy." (June 1988).
Michigan Department of Natural Resources, the McNelly Group. "Mulching and Backyard Composting."
Middletown Township Board of Supervisors. "Middletown Township Newsletter." Levittown, PA (May 1988).
Middletown Township. "Recycling Mix Glass & Cans in '89'." Levittown, PA (1989).
Middletown Township. "Recycling in Middletown Township, Proud to Be a Leader." Levittown, PA.
Middletown Township Board of Supervisors. "Resolution No. 84-3or." Levittown, PA.
Mielke, Gary and Walters, David. "A Planning Guide for Residential Recycling Programs in Illinois." Springfield, IL (May 1988).
"Mining Recyclables from our Garbage." *Garbage* (September/October 1990), pp. 16–21.
Minnesota Pollution Control Agency. "Breaking the Landfill Habit #1" (May 1991).
Minnesota Pollution Control Agency. "Breaking the Landfill Habit #3."
Minnesota Pollution Control Agency. "Breaking the Landfill Habit #1, #2, #3, #4, #5" (May 1991).
Minnesota Pollution Control Agency. "Guidance Manual for Solid Waste Recycling Facilities." St. Paul, MI (March 1989).
Minnesota Office of Waste Management. "Major Appliances" (April 1991).
Minnesota Pollution Control Agency. "Minnesota Solid Waste Management." St. Paul, MN (July 1, 1991).
Minnesota Office of Waste Management. "October 1991 Program Update" (October 1991).
Minnesota Office of Waste Management. "Old Newsprint Recycling Markets" (November 1990).
Minnesota Office of Waste Management. "Recycling" (October 1990).
Minnesota Office of Waste Management. "SCORE Waste Reduction and Recyling Legislation Impact on Counties" (October 1989).
Minnesota Office of Waste Management. "Solid Waste Composting" (July 1990).
Minnesota Pollution Control Agency. "Solid Waste Briefing" St. Paul, MI (May/June 1991).
Minnesota Office of Waste Management. "Spent Lead-acid Batteries" (September 1989).
Minnesota Office of Waste Management and Minnesota Pollution Control Agency. "State Solid Waste Policy Report" (November 28, 1990).
Minnesota Office of Waste Management. "Used Motor Oil" (May 1991).
Minnesota Office of Waste Management. "Waste Source Reduction."
Misner, Michael. "Debating Recycling Markets Incentives." *Waste Age* (October 1990), pp. 68–70.
Misner, Michael. "Finland's Thirst for Recycling." *Waste Age* (April 1990).
Missouri Department of Natural Resources. "Buying Recycled Products: Consuming Wisely."
Missouri Environmental Improvement and Energy Resources Authority. "Homeowners' Composting Guide."

Missouri Department of Natural Resources. "Recycling Economics: Higher Costs Are an Illusion."

Mitlo, Cindy. "The Business of Recycling." *Building Economic Alternatives* (1989), pp. 10–12.

Montana Department of Health and Environmental Sciences. "Motor Vehicle Recycling and Disposal Act." (1989).

Montgomery County Government. "A New Arrival." MD.

Montgomery County Government. "A New Arrival." MD.

Montgomery County Government Department of Environmental Protection. "Recycling in Montgomery County: It's Something You Can Do!" MD (1991).

Montgomery County Government. "Recycling in Montgomery County: It's Something You Can Do!" MD (July 1, 1991).

Montgomery County Government Department of Environmental Protection. "Recycling Centers in Montgomery County." MD.

Montgomery County Government. "Recycling—The More You Do, the More It Matters..." Maryland.

Montgomery County Government. "Recycling—The More You Do, the More It Matters." MD.

Moore, Dennis. "Recycling: Where Are We Now?" *Rodale's New Shelter* (February 1982) pp. 56–69.

Mulford, Jon K. "Federal Land Sales and Exchanges." Boulder, CO: Natural Resources Law Center (1984).

Naber, Thomas. "Today's Landfill Is Tomorrow's Playground." *Waste Age* (September 1987).

National Association of Towns and Townships. "Why Waste a Second Chance?: A Small Town Guide to Recycling." Washington, D.C.: National Association of Towns and Townships (1989).

National Business Forms Association. "Guide to Recycled Paper." *Form* (August 1990).

National Recycling Coalition. "Federal Legislation in the 102nd Congress" (September 1991).

National Recycling Coalition. "The National Policy on Recycling." Washington, D.C.

National Recycling Coalition. "The NRC Connection." Washington, D.C. (1991).

Natural Resources Defense Council. *The Amicus Journal* Vol. 13, No. 4 (1991).

National Solid Wastes Management Association. "Privatizing Municipal Waste Services: Saving Dollars and Making Sense" (1991).

National Solid Wastes Management Association. "Public Attitudes Toward Garbage Disposal" (May 3, 1990).

National Solid Wastes Management Association. "Recycling in the States" (Mid-Year Update, 1990).

Nebraska Department of Environmental Control. "Litter Reduction and Recycling Program" (February 15, 1991).

Nebraska Legislature. "Nebraska Litter Reduction and Recycling Act" (1987).

Nevada Legislature. "AB-320: Omnibus Recycling Bill."

New Hampshire Resource Recovery Association. "Cooperative Marketing of Recyclables." Concord, NH (September 3, 1991).

New Jersey Department of Environmental Protection. "Steps in Organizing a Municipal Recycling Program" (1986).

New Mexico Health and Environment Department. "Focus on Solid Waste." Santa Fe, NM (Fall 1990).
New Mexico Legislature. "Solid Waste Act Article 9."
New York State Department of Environmental Conservation. "6 NYCRR Part 368 Recycling Emblems" (December 14, 1990).
New York State Department of Environmental Conservation. "Householder's Recycling Guide" (April 1990).
New York State Department of Environmental Conservation. "It's the Law in 1992" (February 1991).
New York State Department of Environmental Conservation. "Lead-acid Battery Recycling" (March 1991).
New York State Department of Environmental Conservation. "The Recycling Bulletin" (June 1990).
New York State Department of Environmental Conservation. "Reduce, Reuse, Separate and Recycle!" (November 1989).
New York State Department of Environmental Conservation. "Reuse It or Lose It!" Albany, New York (January 1991).
New York State Department of Environmental Conservation. "Save that Office Paper."
New York State Department of Environmental Conservation. "Solid Waste Management Act of 1988."
New York State Department of Environmental Conservation. "Sorry, Full" (May 1990).
North Carolina Department of Natural Resources. "Comprehensive Municipal Recycling Implementation Plan" (October 15, 1987).
North Carolina Recycling Association. "The R-Word." Raleigh, NC (Summer 1991).
North Carolina Recycling Association. "The R-Word." Raleigh, NC (Fall 1991).
North Dakota State Department of Health and Consoliated Laboratories. "Composting for the North Dakota Citizen" (September 1991).
North Dakota State Department of Health. "Let's Dump the Dump." Greenfield, MA: Channing L. Bete Co.
North Dakota State Department of Health and Consolidated Laboratories. "Solid Waste Management in North Dakota."
Northeast Industrial Waste Exchange, Inc. "Listings Catalog." Vol. 41 (1991).
O'Leary, Philip R., Walsh, Patrick W., and Ham, Robert K. "Managing Solid Waste." *Scientific American* (December 1988), pp. 36–42.
Office of Recycling and Waste Reduction, Illinois Department of Energy and Natural Resources. "Recycling Update." Springfield, IL (Summer 1991).
Office of Recycling, Solid Waste Authority of Palm Beach County. "Multi-family Recycling Guide."
Ohio Department of Natural Resources. "Recycling Basics: A Positive Waste Management Alternative for Ohio" (1989).
Ohio Department of Natural Resources. "Reduce Reuse Recycle" (March 1991).
Ohio Department of Natural Resources. "Waste Reduction Guide for Ohio's Business and Industry" (1991).
Oregon Department of Environmental Quality. "The Garbage Glossary" (1980).
Overview: Solid Waste Disposal Alternatives. "Recycling—An Overview." *Public Works* (August 1990).

Pennsylvania Department of Environmental Resources. "Recycling Lesson Plans Pennsylvania Recycling Month." Harrisburg, PA.

Palm Beach County. "Office Paper Recycling Program." (1990).

Paper Stock Institute. "Scrap Specifications Circular 1990."

Parker, Carl et al. "Senate Bill 1340." Austin, TX (May 1991).

Parker, Legislative Senator. "Senate Bill 1340." Austin, TX (1991).

Parker, Legislative Senator and Saunders, Legislative Representative. "Senate Bill 1340 by Parker & House Bill 1986 and 1763 by Saunders." Austin, TX (1991).

Parker, Legislative Senator. "State Bill 1340 (Used Oil)." Austin, TX (1991).

Paul, Bill. "Even the Kitchen Sink Will Be Collected in New Recycling Program in Colorado." *The Wall Street Journal* (April 2, 1990).

Pear, Robert. "U.S. Sets Rules to Cut Landfill Pollution." *The New York Times* (September 12, 1991): A18.

Pennsylvania Resources Council. "All About Recycling." Media, PA: Pennsylvania Resources Council (September/October 1991).

Pennsylvania Resources Council. "Pencycle, Pennsylvania's Resource and Information Exchange." Media, PA.

Pennsylvania Resources Council. "Publications Materials for Schools, Businesses, Consumers and Municipalities." Media, PA.

The Pennsylvania Resources Council, Inc. "Become an Environmental Shopper." Media, PA.

Perkins, Ronald A. "Curbside Collection of Recyclables." *National Recycling Coalition.* (October 24, 1991).

Peterson, Todd. "Educating for Moment of Decision." *Waste Age* (September 1990).

Platt, Brenda *Beyond 40 Percent: Record-setting Recycling and Composting Programs* Island Press (1991).

Poley, Larry. "Big Profits in Recycling." (1983), pp. 1–22.

Pollock, Cynthia. "Mining Urban Wastes: The Potential for Recycling." *Worldwatch Paper 76* (April 1987).

Post, James E. "The Greening of Management." *Issues In Science and Technology* (Summer 1990).

Powell, Jerry. "All Plastics Are Not Created Equal." *Resource Recycling* (May 1990).

Powell, Jerry. "Keeping It Separate or Commingling It: The Latest Numbers." *Resource Recycling* (March 1991).

Powell, Jerry. "Recycle or Die: The Latest in Packaging Initiatives." *Resource Recycling* (February 1990).

Rathje, William L. "Archaeologists Bust Myths About Solid Waste and Society." *Garbage* (September/October 1990).

Rautenber, Carla. "Glass Markets Improve with Solid Waste Concerns." *Recycling Today* (December 1987).

Recycle New Mexico. "State Directory of Recyclers." Albuquerque, NM: pp. 1990–1991.

Recycling & Waste Reduction Division. "How to Recycle in L.A." Los Angeles, CA (June 30, 1991).

Recycling Association of Minnesota. "Newsletter" (October 1991).

Recycling Coalition of Texas. "Resource Manager." Austin, TX (3rd and 4th quarters of 1991).

"Recycling." *Waste Solutions* (April 1990), pp. 32–53.

"Recycling Manager: The Independent Weekly Guide to Marketing Secondary Materials." New York: Capital Cities/ABC Inc., Diversified Publishing Group (1991).
Recycling Today. Cleveland, OH: GIE Inc. (1991).
Remondini, David J. "State Recycling Effort Down in the Dumps." *Indianapolis Star* (August 23, 1990).
Repa, Edward Ph.D. "The Changing Regulatory Climate." *Waste Age* (August 1990).
Representative Gibson. "House Bill 1489." State of Arkansas (1991).
Representative Gibson. "House Bill 1488." State of Arkansas (1991).
Representative Gibson. "House Bill 1447." State of Arkansas (1991).
Representative Gibson. "House Bill 1172." State of Arkansas (1991).
Representative Gibson. "House Bill 1171." State of Arkansas (1991).
Representative Gibson. "House Bill 1170." State of Arkansas (1991).
Representative Gibson. "House Bill 1168." State of Arkansas (1991).
Representative Gibson. Representatives Hawkins, Miller, Cunningham, and Arnold. "House bill 1168." State of Arkansas (1991).
Rhode Island Solid Waste Management Corp. "The Rhode Island Recycling Act and the Rhode Island Municipal Recycling Program." Providence, RI (April 1, 1991).
Richman, Tom. "The Language of Business." *Inc.* (February 1990), pp. 40-50.
Riggle, David. "Recycling Plastic Grocery Bags." *BioCycle* (June 1990).
Rogers, Diana. "Recycling at National Events/Facilities." *Solid Waste Insight.*
Roy, Natalie and Laster, Tyrone. "Mandatory Recycling Works!" *Public Works* (April 1991).
Salimando, Joe. "The 'Allied' Lomanginos Are 'Star' Recyclers." *Waste Age* (July 1990).
Salimando, Joe. "Recycling's Future Is Now." *Waste Age* (October 1987), pp. 75-78.
Salimando, Joe. "Winzinger Women—Dedicated Recyclers."
San Francisco Recycling Program, adapted in Colorado by the Office of Energy Conservation. "Recycling Office Waste Paper: A Step By Step Guide," pp. 1-21.
Sarasota County Government Environmental Services Department. "Our Commitment to the Environment." FL: (January 1991).
Sarasota County Government Environmental Services Department. "Our Commitment to the Environment" (January, 1991).
Schauer, Dawn. "Coordinators of Recycling." *BioCycle* (March 1987).
Scheinberg, Anne and Cotherman, Dee. "Westchester County Business Recycling Manual" (1989).
Scrap Tire Management Council. "Questions and Answers About Scrap Tire Management." Washington, D.C.
Sedlock, Jospeh T. "Curbside Sorting or Source Separation?" *Waste Age* (October 1990).
Senators Hall, Bilbo Bond, Keeton, Renick, and Stogner. "Mississippi Senate Bill No. 2568" (1990).
Senators Hall, Bilbo, Bond, Keeton, Renick, Stogner, and Morgan. "Mississippi Senate Bill No. 2984" (1991).
Senators Hall, Bilbo Bond, Keeton, Renick, Stogner, and Dearing. "Mississippi Senate Bill No. 2985" (1991).
Senators Hall, Bond, Renick, Keeton, Stogner. "Mississippi Senate Bill No. 3009" (1991).
Senators Bean and Tate. "Mississippi Senate Bill No. 2989" (1991).
Sherrod, Pamela. "Environmental Fund Does Well By Investing." *Chicago Tribune* (July 8, 1990).

Shotwell, Robert E. "Brentano's Family Plan Is Working." *Waste Age* (April 1990), pp. 90–99.
"Sludge Composting Facilities." *Resource Recycling* (1990), pp. 41–42.
Smith, Paul I. "Recycling Waste." *Scientific Publications* (1976).
Solid Waste Alternatives Project. "Small Town and Rural Recycling." *Resource Recycling* (March/April 1988).
Solid Waste Composting Council. "Solid Waste Composting Council."
Solid Waste Management Authority of Lackawanna County, PA. "Composition of Recyclables, Lackawanna County Recycling Center." Scranton, PA (September 26, 1991).
Solid Waste Management Authority of Lackawanna County, PA. "Important Issues." Scranton, PA.
Solid Waste Management Authority of Lackawanna County, PA. "Lackawanna County Recycles." Scranton, PA.
Solid Waste Management Authority of Lackawanna County, PA. "Recycling Guidelines." Scranton, PA.
State of Wisconsin. "1989 Wisconsin Act 335." (1989).
State of New York. "In Assembly" (February 21, 1989).
State of New York. "Senate—Assembly" (February 26, 1990).
State of New York. "Senate—Assembly" (March 5, 1991).
State of New York. "Senate—Assembly" (March 26, 1991).
State of Ohio Environmental Protection Agency. "State Solid Waste Management Plan" (1989).
State of Nebraska, Department of Environmental Control. "Litter Reduction and Recycling Program."
Stauffer, Roberta Forsell. "Energy Savings from Recycling." *Resource Recycling* (January/February 1989).
Strathmann, David C. and Drake, Barbara. "How Your Business Can Profit from a Recycling Program" (1990).
Strauss, Gary. "Investors Find Gold in Landfill Stocks." *USA Today* (July 12, 1990). p. 3B.
Stroessner, Wayne. "Small Town Recycling." *Resource Recycling* (March/April 1988).
SunShares staff. "SunShares Newsletter" (Summer 1991).
Swanson, Stevenson. "Miracle Cure for Garbage Glut." *The Denver Post* p. 13A.
Texas Department of Health. "Helping Texas Shrink Its Waste." Austin, TX.
Texas Department of Health. "Municipal Waste Matters." Austin, TX: *Newsletter of the Bureau of Solid Waste Management* (August 1991).
Texas Department of Health. "Municipal Solid Waste Grants Program." Austin, TX.
Texas Department of Health. "Recycling Plastic...It's Becoming So Easy a Child Can Do It." Austin, TX.
Thurner, Christian and Ashley, Dayna. "Developing Recycling Markets and Industries." (July 1990).
"Total Quality System: An Overview of....the Window of Opportunity" (1991).
Town of Bloomsburg, Recycling Center. "Recycle with Us." Bloomsburg, PA.
Township of Middletown. "Middletown Township Newsletter." (Fall 1990).
U.S. Department of the Interior Bureau of Mines. "Mineral Commodity Summaries 1991." 1–196. Washington, D.C.: U.S. Government Printing Office (1991).
U.S. Environmental Protection Agency. "What You Can Do To Recycle More Paper" (1975).

United States Environmental Protection Agency. "Characterization of Municipal Solid Water in the United States" (June 1990).
United States Environmental Protection Agency. "Characterization of Municipal Solid Waste in the United States" (June 13, 1990).
United States Environmental Protection Agency. "Decision-makers Guide to Solid Waste Management" (November 1989).
United States Environmental Protection Agency. "Environmental Fact Sheet" (September 1991).
United States Environmental Protection Agency. "Marketing Waste Paper: A Recycling Coordinator's Handbook." *Great Lakes Region Waste Paper Work Group* (May 1991).
United States Environmental Protection Agency. "Office Recycling Handbook, Recycle Today for Tomorrow" (February 1991).
United States Environmental Protection Agency. "Operating a Recycling Program: A Citizen's Guide" (1979).
United States Environmental Protection Agency. "Procurement Guidelines for Government Agencies" (December 1990).
United States Environmental Protection Agency. "School Recycling Programs" (August 1990).
United States Environmental Protection Agency. "The Solid Waste Dilemma: An Agenda for Action" (February 1989).
United States Environmental Protection Agency. "State and Local Solution to Solid Waste Management Problems" (January 1989).
United States Environmental Protection Agency. "State and Local Solutions to Solid Waste Management Problems" (January 1989).
United States Environmental Protection Agency. "State and Local Solutions to Solid Waste Management Problems" (January 1989).
The University of Georgia. "Composting, Feed Your Landscape." Athens, GA.
The University of Georgia. "Mulching—Feed Your Landscape, Not the Landfill." Athens, GA.
University of Idaho. "University of Idaho Recycling." Boise, ID.
University of Kentucky. "Grass roots recycling." April, 1991.
University of New Mexico Institute for Public Policy. "Executive Summary."
Utah Bureau of Solid & Hazardous Waste. "Administrative Rules."
Van Sant, Kathryn. "Too Much of a Good Thing." Burlington, VT: *Burlington Free Press* (April 22, 1990).
Vessell, Nancy. "Newspapers Pile Up as Recycling Market Dwindles." *Jefferson City News and Tribune* (November 18, 1990).
Virginia Department of Waste Management. "1991 Summary of Legislation." Richmond, VA.
Virginia Department of Waste Management. "House Bills." Richmond, VA (1990).
Vogler, Jon. "Scrap Lead Refining in Jamaica." *Resource Recycling* (1984), pp. 24-26.
Voigt, T. B. and Fermanian, T.W. "Controlling Thatch in Turfgrass." Urbana-Champaign, IL University of Illinois (1990).
Voigt, T. B. and Fermanian, T.W. "Turfgrass Management Strategies for Reducing Landscape Waste." Urbana-Champaign, IL: University of Illinois (1990).
The Warmer Campaign. "Warmer Bulletin," No. 30 (August 1991).

Washington State Department of Ecology. "Best Management Practices Study Highlights." *Focus* (August 1989).

Washington State Department of Ecology. "Fact Sheet: Used Oil Recycling Program" (April 1988).

Washington State Department of Ecology. "Hazardous Waste Reduction Act." *Focus* (April 1991).

Washington State Department of Ecology. "The Model Litter Control and Recycling Act." *Focus* (February 1991).

Washington State Department of Ecology. "Packaging Action Plan." *Focus* (January 1991).

Washington State Recycling Association. "US West Direct Begins Telephone Book Recycling Project" (May 1991).

Washington State Department of Ecology. "Washington's G.O.L.D. Plan." *Focus.*

Washington State Department of Ecology. "The Waste Not Washington Act." *Focus* (August 1989).

Washington State Department of Ecology. "Waste Reduction in Your Business" (February 1991).

Washington State Department of Ecology Waste Reduction, Recycling and Litter Control Program. "Fact Sheet 1." Olympia, WA (June 1990).

Washington State Department of Ecology Waste Reduction, Recycling and Litter Control Program. "Fact Sheet 2." Olympia, WA (June 1990).

Wislocki, John. "Market for Recycled Newsprint Inadequate." *Tribune Review* (December 24, 1990).

Woods, Randy. "Send It to the Slammer!" *Waste Age* (April 1990).

WPCF Government Affairs Committee. "Waste Minimization and Waste Reduction." *Journal WPCF* Vol. 61, No. 2 (1989), p. 184.

ALUMINUM

Abbate, S.T. "Use of Aluminum Recovered from Municipal Solid Waste," *Resource Recovery and Utilization, ASTM STP 592.* American Society for Testing Materials (1975), pp. 106–113.

Blayden, Lee C. "The Chemistry of Recycling Aluminum," *Energy and Resource Recovery from Waste AIChE Symposium* Vol. 73, No. 162 (1975), pp. 86–90.

"Bottle/Can Recycling Update." Resource Recycling Inc. (September 1991).

Cooperman, R.M. "Aluminum Recycling Industry—A U.S. Viewpoint." *Aluminum World,* pp. 37–39.

Furukawa, Tsukasa. "Japan Acts to Spur Aluminum, Steel Can Recycling." *American Metals Market* (September 6, 1991).

Goodwin, Morgan. "Bottle Makers Lose Round in Processing-fee Suit." *American Metals Market* (September 23, 1991).

Kuster, Ted. "Aluminum Scrap Picture Hazy." American Metals Market (June 24, 1991).

Regan, Bob. "Aluminum Profile." *Metal Statistics 1989,* pp. 16–27.

Regan, Bob. "Aluminum Scrap Big in Business." American Metals Market (September 24, 1991).

Rich, Patrick, Jean Jaques. "World Trends in the Primary Aluminum Industry." *Aluminum World,* p. 29.

ANTIMONY

The Economics of Antimony, 4th Ed. Roskill Information Services LTD. (1980). 2 Clapham Road. London Square.

Worden, Edward. "Antimony Profile." *Metal Statistics 1989,* American Metals Market, pp. 29-33.

AUTOMOBILES

Automotive Dismantlers & Recyclers Association. "Recycled Auto & Truck Parts."

"Automobile Recycling Offers Renewable But Changing Resource." *Automotive Engineering* (May 1979) pp. 56-58.

Dean, K.C., Sterner, J.W., Shirts, M.B., and Froisland, L.J. "Bureau of Mines Research on Recycling Scrapped Automobiles." *Bulletin 684* (1985), 45 pp.

Scrap Age. "Exclusive Updated Survey of Automobile Shredding." *Scrap Age* (October 1980), pp. 91-98.

Fowler, James E. "Processing Automobile Hulks." Resource Recycling. (March/April 1984), pp. 14-18.

Grossman, John. "Resurrecting Auto Graveyards." *INC.* (March 1983), pp. 71-79.

Hardin, Charles. "Scrap Metals & Auto Recycling Industries." *Automotive Recycling,* pp. 14-15.

Miller, Bernie. "Auto Giant BMW Set to Recycle Scrapped Cars." *Plastics World* (October 1990), pp. 12-13.

Nussbaum, Howard. "Automotive Recycling: The State of Our Industry." *Automotive Recycling,* pp. 10-13.

"Peugeot Set on Recycling." *American Metals Market* (June 28, 1991).

"Recycling of Automobiles Containing Unspent Air Bags." Institute of Scrap Recycling Industries, Inc.

Regan, James G. "Target: All-Recyclable Auto." *American Metals Market* (September 6, 1991).

Wrigley, Al. "Automakers Honk for Stainless." American Metals Market, (August 12, 1991).

BATTERIES

Goodwin, Morgan. "Battery Recycling Laws Enacted by 37 States." American Metals Market (August 19,1991).

Telzrow, T.N. "Battery Industry Initiative." Paper presented at the National Recycling Coalition Conference, Oct. 22-24, 1991.

COPPER

Schmitt, William. "Copper Profile." *Metal Statistics 1989.* American Metals Market, pp. 51-63.

CADMIUM

Worden, Edward. "Cadmium Prices Are in a Run-up." American Metals Market (September 2, 1991).

Worden, Edward. "Cadmium Profile." *Metal Statistics 1989.* American Metals Market, pp. 38-41.

CHROMIUM

Gerety, Justine. "Chromium Profile." *Metal Statistics 1989.* American Metals Market, pp. 42-43.

The Economics of Chromium, 3rd. Ed. 1978. Roskill Information Services, Ltd. London SW IP 3rd.

COBALT

"Cobalt." *Metal Statistics 1989.* American Metals Market, pp. 47-49.

Munford, Christopher. "Price Rise Predicted for Cobalt." American Metals Market (August 13, 1991).

GLASS

Bartlett, Albert A. "Forgotten Fundamentals of the Energy Crisis." *American Journal of Physics* Vol. 46, No. 9. (September 1978), pp. 876-890.

Besso, Robert A. "Commercial Glass Recycling in San Francisco." *Resource Recycling* (November/December 1987), pp. 22-24.

Cummings, John P. "Recovery and Reuse of Waste Glass." Forest Products and the Environment. AIChE Symposium No. 133. Vol. 69. pp. 34-46.

Duckett, Joseph. "Glass Recovery and Reuse." *NCRR Bulletin* (Fall 1978), pp. 87-94.

Gibboney, Douglas L. "Closing the Loop with Glass Recycling." *Biocycle* (April 1990).

"Glass Recycling: Making it Work in Your Community." Glass Recycles. Central States Glass Recycling Program (1991).

"Glass Recycling in MidAmerica." MidAmerica Glass Recycling Program (January 1991).

"Glassified News." Owens-Brockway Awareness Committee (1991).

Hecht, Roger. "Speech by Roger Hecht, The Bassichis Company." First National Symposium on Recycled Glass (June 25, 1991) Los Angeles, CA.

Howard, Stephen E. "Glass Recycling: State of the Art Overview, 1980s Outlook." Resource Recovery Consultant, Glass Packaging Institute.

Peters, Dean. "Growth Ahead for Glass Recycling." *Recycling Today* (July 1987), pp. 62-65.

"Questions and Answers about the Reclamation and Recycling of Glass Containers." Glass Packaging Institute.

Rosenberg, Arnie. "Glass Makers are Perfectly Clear on Cullets Rise to Prominence." *Recycling Today* Vol. 27, No. 2 (December 1989).

Sedlock, Joseph T. "Bottle Bills—Recyclings Boon... or Doom." *Waste Age* (October 1990), pp. 58-59.

Seeley, C.E. "Glass in Solid Waste Recovery Systems." *Resource Recovery and Utilization,* ASTM STP 592, American Society for Testing and Materials (1975), pp. 114-121.
"The Status of Glass Recycling: An Interview with Gifford Stack." *Resource Recycling* (July/August 1982), pp. 13-15.

GOLD

"How to Refine Scrap Gold & Silver" (1979).
Kaufmann, Thomas D. "The Witchcraft and Logic of Gold Pricing—Politics, Inflation, Speculation, and the Value of the Dollar Are All Contributing Factors." *Mining Engineering* (September 1987), pp. 857-858.
Meredith, Lawrence Charles. "How to Buy Scrap Gold and Silver" (1987).
Trunick, Perry A. "Global Nature Affects Golds Market." *Recycling Today* (September 1987), pp. 46-49.
Werber, Marilyn. "Gold Profile." *Metals Statistics 1989,* pp. 76-79.

MAGNESIUM

Regan, Bob. "Dow Magnesium Eyeing Automotive Markets." American Metals Market (June 24, 1991).
Regan, Bob. "Magnesium Profile." *Metals Statistics 1989,* pp. 92-93.
The Economics of Magnesium Metal, 2nd. Ed. (1978). Roskill Information Services, Ltd. London SW IP 3rd.

MANGANESE

Munford, Christopher. "Output Rates Raise for Ferromanganese." American Metals Market (August 12, 1991).
Scolieri, Peter. "Manganese Profile." *Metal Statistics 1989,* pp. 98-100.

NICKEL

Gerety, Justine. "Nickel Profile." *Metal Statistics 1989,* pp.108-110.
McDermott, Michael. "Nickel Outlook Strong, Challenging." *American Metals Market.*
Munford, Christopher. "Sluggish Stainless Steel Demand Hits Nickel." *American Metals Market* (August 19, 1991).

OIL

Elliott, Cindy. "Canada's Oil Re-refining Industry." *Resource Recycling* (May/June 1987), pp. 26-28.
Emond, Mark. "Is the Used Oil Recycling Program in Jeopardy?" *National Petroleum News* (February 1991), pp. 35-38.
Grassy, John. "The Waste Oil Monster." *Garbage* (July/August 1991), pp. 34-47.

Lowrance, Sylvia. "Regulatory Determination on Used Oil Filters." Memo. United States Environmental Protection Agency (October 30, 1990).

MacKenzie, R.C. "Lube Oil Recycling: Alberta Sets the Pace." *Resource Recycling* (January/February 1984).

Papke, Chuck. "Oil Recycling's Burning Issues." *Resource Recycling* (November/December 1983). pp. 26-27.

U.S. Department of Energy. "Waste Oil: Technology, Economics, and Environmental Health and Safety Considerations." Prepared by Mueller Associates, Inc., DOE/EV/10450-H2, Washington D.C. (January 1987).

United States Environmental Protection Agency. "How to Set up a Local Program to Recycle Used Oil." Solid Waste and Emergency Response. 32 pp.

U.S. Environmental Protection Agency. "Environmental Consequences of Waste Oil Disposal in POTWs." Prepared by Pope/Reid Associates, Inc, Washington D.C. (July 21, 1987).

PAPER

American Paper Institute. "1990 Annual Statistical Summary Waste Paper Utilization" (June 1991), 89 pp.

American Paper Institute. "Key Questions and Answers on Paper Recycling" (1991).

American Paper Institute and the National Forest Products Association. "The American Forest: Facts and Figures 1991."

Campbell, Dr. John R. "Feed Grade Corrugated Paper for Feeding Ruminant Animals." Flett Development Company. Chicago, IL (1975).

Case, Clifford and Keller, Richard. "Buying Recycled Paper: The Story Continues." *Resource Recycling* (July/August 1985), pp. 22-23.

Garbutt, Tom. "Advances in Deinking Technology." *Wastepaper I: Demand in the 90's.* Chicago, IL (May 14-15, 1990).

Hertzberg, Richard. "Old News Is Good News at Garden State Paper." *Resource Recycling* (July/August 1985), pp.14-17.

Hintz, Dr. Harold F. "Feed Grade Corrugated Paper for Feeding Horses." Flett Development Co., Chicago, IL (1976).

Johnson, Spencer A. Personal correspondence. Paperboard Packaging Council (August 26, 1991).

Kovacs, William L. "Mandating Markets for Recycled Grades." Conference on Waste Paper Demand in the 90's (May, 14, 1990).

Locke, Ralph E. "Can 100% Recycled Containerboard Compete?"

Lyden, John Kevin. "Recycled Newsprint Mills to the Rescue." Managing Director, Shotton Paper Company.

Nielsen & Nielsen, Inc. "U.S. Exports of Waste Paper in 1983." Pomona, CA (1983).

Sisler, Gordon. "Opportunities for Fine Paper Producers." Manager—Product Development, Noranda Forest Recycled Papers.

Sproule, Kimberly A. "Animal Bedding Operations in Wisconsin." *Resource Recycling* (September/October 1987), pp. 24-25.

United States Department of Agriculture Forest Service RPA Assessment. "An Analysis of the Timber Situation in the United States 1989-2040" (December 1990). Richard W. Haynes, coordinator. 269 pp.

Usherson, Judy. "End Users Speak Out." *Wastepaper I: Demand in the 90's.* Chicago, IL (May 14-15, 1990).
Veverka, Arthur C. "Cost Competitive Aspects of Recycled Fibre Usage." Jaakko Poyry Consulting Inc. President.
"Waldens Fiber & Board Report." Walden-Mott Corp., 475 Kinderkamack Road, Oradell, N.J.
Wiseman, Clark. "Will Recycling Save the Forests?" Resources for the Future, Washington D.C.

PLASTIC

Abrahamson, Peggy. "Plastic Pipes Growth Cuts into Copper Usage." *American Metal Market* (September 4, 1991).
Center for Plastics Recycling Research. "Market Research on Plastic Recycling."
Holmes, Hannah. "Recycling Plastics." *Garbage.* (January/February 1991), pp. 33-39.
Keep America Beautiful. "Plastic Recycling by the Number." Undated.
Mack W.A. "Recycling Plastics: The Problems and Potential Solutions," Disposal of Plastics with Minimum Environmental Impact, ASTM STP 533. American Society for Testing and Materials (1973), pp.3-16.
Moskowitz, Marcie. "Solid Waste Council Targets 25%—Bottle Recycle Rate." *Plastics World* (April 1991). pp.58-60.
"Post Consumer PP Mixes with Recycled HDPE." *Plastics World* (March 1991), pp. 120-121.
Smith, Randolph B. "Pressure for Plastic Recycling Prompts a Mix of Tough Laws and Cooperation." *The Wall Street Journal.*
The Council for Solid Waste Solutions. "The Blueprint for Plastics Recycling" (1991).
The Council for Solid Waste Solutions "Recycling Mixed Plastics: New Markets" (1991).
The Plastics Recycling Foundation. "Plastics Recycling: An Overview" (1991).
The Plastics Recycling Foundation. "Plastic Recycling: From Vision to Reality" (1991).
United States Environmental Protection Agency. "Methods to Manage and Control Plastic Wastes." EPA/530-SW-89-051 A. (February 1990).

SILVER

Werber, Marilyn. "Silver Profile." *Metals Statistics 1991,* pp. 125-134.

STEEL

Apotheker, Steve and Marksthaler, Elizabeth. "Tin Cans: History and Outlook." *Resource Recycling* (January/February 1986), pp. 12-15.
American Iron & Steel Institute. "America Grows with Iron and Steel." Undated.
Forcinio, Hallie. "Steel, Wheres it Headed." *Food & Drug Packaging* Vol., No. 53, Issue No. 8 (August 1989), pp. 1-8.
Institute of Iron and Steel. "Metallic Scrap—The Manufactured Resource."
Institute for Iron and Steel. "Steel Making Flow Lines." Undated.
Institute of Iron and Steel. "Steel Processing Flow Lines."
Institute of Iron and Steel. "The Cradle of an American Industry."

Institute of Scrap Iron and Steel, Inc. "Can Steel Stem the Rising Tide of Adversity?" *Phoenix Quarterly*. Steel Advisory Committee.

Institute of Scrap Recycling Industries, Inc. "Recycling Scrap Iron and Steel" (1990).

Kaplan, R.S. "Deterrents to the Recycling of Ferrous Scrap from Urban Refuse." Resource Recovery and Utilization, ASTM STP 592, American Society for Testing Materials (1975), pp. 91–105.

Misner, Michael. "The Steel Can's Push for Recycling Respect." *Waste Age* (February 1991), pp. 69–71.

Ostrowski, Edward J. "The Bright Outlook for Recycling Ferrous Scrap from Solid Waste." AIchE Symposium Series No. 162, Vol. 73 (1974), pp. 93–96.

Ostrowski, Edward J. "Recycling of Ferrous Scrap from Solid Waste." Forest Products and the Environment. AIChE Symposium Series, pp. 37–43.

Peters, Dean M. "Minimills Nurtured by Ferrous Scrap." *Recycling Today* (December 1987), pp. 95–100.

Powell, Jerry. "Can Steel Can Recycling Catch Up?" *Resource Recycling* (November/December 1987), p. 12.

Steel Can Recycling Institute. "The Recycling Magnet" (Fall 1990).

"The Steel Import Issue." *Resource Recycling* (November/December 1982), pp. 11–13.

Trunick, Perry A. "Stainless Steel Shows Strong Growth Potential." *Recycling Today* (September 1987), pp. 42–44.

TEXTILES

Vogler, Jon. "The Rag Trade." *Resource Recycling* (January/February 1987), pp. 26–27.

TIN

King, Angela. "Tin Profile." *Metals Statistics 1989*, pp. 171–181.

Regan, James. "Oversupplies Still Haunt Tin Producers." American Metals Market (June 24, 1991).

TIRES

Aguirre, R.G. "Cut Your Tire Problems—Now!" *Waste Age* (September 1987), p. 60.

Apotheker, Steve and Markstahler, Elizabeth. "Scrap Tires Fuel Cement Kilns." *Resource Recycling* (November/December 1984), pp. 20–22.

Blumenthal, Michael. "Scrap Tire Markets: A Status Report." *Resource Recycling* (December 1991), pp. 60–65.

Blumenthal, Michael. "Using Scrap Tire Rubber in Asphalt." *Biocycle* (October 1991), p. 47.

Carpenter, Joseph R. and Hemphill, Thomas A. "New Jersey Tire Recycling: The Public Policy Report." *Resource Recycling* (February 1990), pp. 43–44.

Culviner, Prall. "From Energy to Roads: New Uses for Old Tires." *World Wastes* (October 1990), p. 50.

Gallon, Gary. "Mammoth Fire Sparks Canadian Recycling." *Resource Recycling* (December 1991), p. 51.

Goldstein, Jerome. "Different Approaches to Using Discarded Tires." *Biocycle* (March 1988).

Hershey, Robert, et al. "Waste Tire Utilization." For the U.S. D.O.E. (April 1987).

Kearney, A.T. "Scrap Tire Management Council / Scrap Tire Use and Disposal Study" (September 11, 1990).

Koziar, Paul J. "Overview of Regional Waste Tire Management Opportunities for Electric Utilities." Wisconsin Department of Natural Resources, Bureau of Solid and Hazardous Waste Management (1991).

Martin, Amy. "The Bumpy Road to Tire Recycling in America." *Garbage Magazine* (May/June 1990), pp. 28-37.

Matthis, Ann H. "How to Make 40 Million Tires Disappear." *Waste Age* (January 1988), p. 46.

McGowin, C.R. "Tire-Derived Fuel Quality Requirements For Electric Power Generation" Presented at the 1991 Scrap Tire Trade Show and Conference, American Retreaders Association.

Powell, Jerry. "Tire Recycling: Proven Solutions and New Ideas." *Resource Recycling* (January/February 1987), pp. 12-14.

Powell, Jerry. "Tire Recycling Bounces Along." *Resource Recycling* (July 1988), p. 22.

Riggle, David. "Recycled Rubber Roads." *Biocycle* (February 1989).

Schnormeier, Russel. "Recycling Tires into Pavement." *Resource Recycling* (January/February 1988), pp.18-21.

SCS Engineers. "Feasiblity Study to Site and Operate a Tire Recycling Facility in Washington State." Washington State Department of Trade and Economic Development Business Trade Center and the Washington State Department of Ecology (January 1989).

SCS Engineers. "Market Assessment for Use of Recycled Tires." Washington Committee for Recycling Markets and The Department of Trade and Economic Development (October 1990).

SCS Engineers. "Survey of Potential Demonstration Projects Utilizing Waste Tires." Oregon Department of Environmental Quality (March 1990).

"Scrap Tires in the 90's, Recycling Recovery Disposal." *Scrap Tire News.* Special Report from Scrap Tire News.

Sikora, Mary. "Beyond Bouncing Rubber Baby Buggy Bumpers." *Waste Age Magazine* (April 1990), p. 242-248.

Spencer, Robert. "New Approaches to Recycling Tires." *Biocycle* (March 1991), pp. 32-35.

Tongo, Peter. "Old Tires Bounce Back as New Rubber Products." *Christian Science Monitor* (August 9, 1988).

Trojak, Larry. "Scrap Tires: Six Years Later and Counting." *Waste Age* (August 1991), pp. 46-52.

Vogler, Jon. "Rubber Recyclers Show the West the Way." *Resource Recycling* (May/June 1984), pp. 20-22.

Wiekierak, Gaye A. "Waste Tire Abatement in Iowa—A Study to the General Assembly." Waste Management Authority Division. Iowa Department of Natural Resources (January 1991).

TUNGSTEN

Munford, Christopher. "Delayed Reaction to China's Withdrawal from the U.S. Market." American Metals Market (August 26, 1991).

Paprock, Judy. "Tungsten Profile." Metals Statistics (1989), pp.188–189.

Poley, Larry G. "Tungsten Carbide and Other Exotic Metals Handbook." Poley's Industrial Salvage Co. (1980).

Roskill Information Services. *The Economics of Tungsten,* 3rd. Ed. London, England.

Index